THE OFFICIAL® PRICE GUIDE TO

COLLECTOR KNIVES

FOURTEENTH EDITION

C. HOUSTON PRICE

HOUSE OF COLLECTIBLES

RANDOM HOUSE REFERENCE

NEW YORK TORONTO LONDON SYDNEY AUCKLAND

Important Notice. All of the information, including valuations, in this book has been compiled from the most reliable sources, and every effort has been made to eliminate errors and questionable data. Nevertheless, the possibility of error in a work of such immense scope always exists. The publisher will not be held responsible for losses that may occur in the purchase, sale, or other transaction of items because of information contained herein. Readers who feel they have discovered errors are invited to *write* and inform us, so they may be corrected in subsequent editions. Those seeking further information on the topics covered in this book are advised to refer to the complete line of *Official Price Guides* published by the House of Collectibles.

Published by Random House Reference, an imprint of the Random House Information Group, 1745 Broadway, New York, NY 10019, and simultaneously in Canada by Random House of Canada Limited, Toronto.

www.houseofcollectibles.com

Manufactured in the United States of America

ISSN: 0747-5357

ISBN: 1-4000-4834-6

10 9 8 7 6 5 4 3 2 1

Fourteenth Edition

ACKNOWLEDGMENTS

Earlier research and published works encourage as well as inform one undertaking a task such as this. John Goins, Bernard Levine, Dewey Ferguson, Jim Parker, Bruce Voyles, Jim Sargent, Howard Cole, W. C. Karsten, Dennis Ellingsen, Michael Silvey, Frank Trzaska, Gary Boyd, Allen Swayne and Geoffrey Tweedale are but a few of the many whose efforts I salute. Without them and many others who share their knowledge, knife collecting would have many more tribulations and significantly fewer pleasures.

Mark D. Zalesky not only continues to share his friendship and knowledge on a regular basis, but manages as well to be my "sounding board" on many occasions. My wife, Carolyn, has read and scanned through several hundred pages of manuscript; it seems she always finds those carefully hidden "oops." My thanks to both of them.

A considerable number of fellow collectors and close friends continue to share their knowledge and offer encouragement. So many names and faces come to mind as I write this that I don't dare list them, but I do offer sincere appreciation.

And there are others. Since publication of this book's earlier editions, numerous inquiries and tidbits of information have come from knife collectors in most parts of the country. To those that I know personally as well as those who I know only through their voice on the phone or signature on a letter, I offer my thanks as well.

This book is dedicated to all who pursue the hobby of knives. Whether they have recently joined our ranks, have the experiences of many seasons, or will catch the enthusiasm at some future date, I trust the rewards they find will be enhanced by the information it contains.

CONTENTS

OVERVIEW OF KNIFE COLLECTING

KNIVES AND MAN

Wherever on this planet archaeologists find evidence of man's existence, there will also be found knives in some form. Knives represent one of man's first and most useful tools of survival because, without the knife and its development over the ages, there would be no civilization today.

The precursor of the knife was a flake of broken stone, created by nature and used by man. So far back as a million years, its utility of adding a cutting edge to the hand would be recognized and the edged tool would help assure man's dominance over lower animals. Some fifty thousand years ago, man learned to improve upon nature by flaking both sides of the stone into beveled edges. In this manner, the first knife was created. The stone age gave us cutting, scraping and stabbing tools. They were made of flint, obsidian, slate or other stones such as quartz or hard limestone. Although stone was most often used for early mans' knives, it was sometimes supplemented by bone, teeth, stag horn or other animal origin materials. As we view these cutlery artifacts today, they may seem crude but our very existence should be a reminder that they served man and they served them well.

The cave dwellers who used these crude cutlery tools understood their importance for survival. One has only to closely examine a stone-age flint knife to gain respect for the attention paid to the quality of raw materials (stone) and the care dedicated to shaping it into a tool designed for a specific purpose. Wherever it was available, flint stone was recognized as the desirable cutlery material and it was often used in preference to most other minerals. There is even evidence that flint stone was traded and transported from areas of abundance to other areas lacking in the desirable stone. As a tool, as a weapon, and as the working implement most personal to man, knives meant survival. Nothing else could have been so important to those who carved the beginnings of our modern civilization.

With the passage of thousands of years, knives made from stones such as flint, obsidian or slate were replaced with knives and other cutting instruments made of metals. Man had already learned that chipping these stones into certain shapes made them more useful for specific purposes. Stone knives for defense against predators and for taking game as food were usually shaped differently from those that were used in other ways. The discovery and development of bronze and iron, copper and tin, and eventually steel allowed man greater freedom to shape and design cutting or stabbing instruments. The knife was made much longer and became a sword. It was shaped into a long curved knife and became a scythe. It could be given greater weight and a special new shape to become an axe. Whatever shape it took, the knife as a tool was becoming more and more useful.

The making of edged tools became so important that an industry of sorts began to develop. Man had learned not only how to best shape metals for knives of their purpose, but, as early as 1000 B.C., they learned to harden metals to make knives of better quality. The cutlers trade, as we would understand it today, began to take shape in the Middle Ages. Production of steel had started to develop in England and Germany during the 10th and 11th centuries. It was only natural that cutlery crafting would follow.

Cutlery centers developed in several parts of the world so that, when we think of swords, the names Samurai (Japan) or Toledo (Spain) or Damascus (Syria) come to mind. Likewise, when we think of pocketknives, the names Sheffield and Solingen remind us that England and Germany have had the greatest influence upon America's cutlery industry. Not only did a large percentage of our earlier knives come from those countries, but our own manufacturing processes most closely followed theirs. Many of the founders of and workers in our early cutlery industry had emigrated from England and Germany. The knowledge and skills brought with them helped ensure the success of an infant industry in a young country; an industry that would produce the knives we so highly value today.

For all those thousands of years, the knife has remained the tool which has been most personal to man. Whether it's of flint or steel, an old knife is a material piece of history. It is a personal tool that has survived its maker and original owner. It is our connection to the past—our tangible proof that the old times did exist. Therein lies its romance as a collectible.

HISTORY OF KNIFE COLLECTING

Welcome to a knife renaissance. Although not exactly new, the interest in knives as collectibles is still in its infancy throughout the United States and in an increasing number in other countries. The late 1900s represented an era of growing interest in knives as history, knives as examples of hand craftsmanship, and knives as art objects. Whatever the specialized cutlery interest, knives are now recognized as items to be accumulated and passed on to succeeding generations. They are also recognized as collectibles of real and increasing value.

Each year, knife shows held throughout the nation attract more and more collectors, dealers and custom knife makers. Knife clubs, both national and local in scope, continue to add new collectors to their membership rolls. Publishers have printed scores of books and a growing number of magazines regularly publish information about knives. As with most aspects of life in the 21st century, the internet has made a major impact upon the collecting of knives and information about them. It's only natural that we wonder where, when and how it all began.

Because it is impossible to separate knife collecting from knife trading, the genesis of our hobby is likely in our country's earliest days. The knife was a very personal tool and one that was often the object of personal pride. Man has always been persuaded to continually seek something perceived as better. "Trading up" to a knife, a gun or a horse of better quality was a normal event during the pioneering days. It will likely prevail during this 21st century.

Knife trading has often been attributed to the "court house whittlers," who whittled and whiled the time away as they praised the virtues of their pocketknives. Before long, that special knife was traded and would become the pride and joy of another whittler; that is, until it was traded again, often within hours of the earlier trade.

"First Monday Trade Days" were monthly highlights in the lives of many rural folk during much of the last century. That day, especially for the men, was not for work—unless farm-raised products were to be taken for sale or trade. Instead, it was a day to take horses and mules, guns and knives, and whatever else one may want to "swap on" to town to the "bone yard." It was not unusual for a man to spend the entire day "horse trading" on dozens of objects only to trade again for whatever he had brought that morning. After all, that item was too popular as a trade item to let it go! The spirit of "trade days" still lives today, although much more modernized in garage sales and flea markets.

Some say that knife trading began in the southeast and many collectors refer to that part of the country as "the knife collecting capital of the world." Knife trading and, as a consequence, knife accumulating has been a part of our nation's history from its earliest days. Regardless of whether we hail from north, south, east, west or somewhere in between, most of us can recall swapping knives. Knife trading, knife accumulating and, ultimately, knife collecting has always been and will continue to be a national avocation.

So, the evolution of knife collecting and trading may have taken centuries or even millenniums—perhaps even the cavemen swapped their flint stone knives and spears. But, the revolution began only four decades ago and continues today.

There have been several factors contributing to the growing interest in knives as collectibles and as investment pieces. One catalyst was the Gun Control Act of 1968 which made selling and trading guns much more difficult. Since gun shows were already quite popular, the transfer of interest and trading activities from guns to knives was a rather natural course. Through the gun show circuits, antique bowie knives and military cutlery items had already found their fanciers; antique pocketknives and modern custom knives would soon follow.

A little earlier, in 1965, new government regulations had required every piece of cutlery sold in the U.S. to be stamped with the country of its origin. W. R. Case & Sons Cutlery, one of the nation's leading knife manufacturers, revamped its marking system. The trademark Case XX was changed to Case XX USA. That change had drawn very little attention until the 1968 Act curtailed the gun collectors' interstate trading and many of them decided to switch to knives.

Because Case already enjoyed an excellent reputation for quality and their system made it easy to understand dates of manufacture, Case knives quickly captured the lead in the demand for older knives. Before long, growing numbers of bargain hunters and knife traders made their rounds to practically every country store, buying complete dealer displays of Case knives. Other recognized brands such as Winchester and Remington could often be found in the dealer's stock purchased years earlier. As these back-road-riding entrepreneurs began gathering for their own buy, swap, and sell events, the knife show came into its own.

Several of these knife traders and seekers of opportunity began to make collectible knives their business. They had the foresight to expand their activities into areas that were nearly impossible to reach by personal travel. The answer was advertisements seeking knives to buy and offering knives for sale in the gun traders' standby, *Shotgun News*, and other magazines such as *Antique Trader*. And, before long they began to mail lists of old knives for sale or trade to collectors or other dealers who would subscribe.

With the arrival of the 1970s, collectors and dealers saw Case again change its tang stamping, this time adding 10 dots under the Case XX USA marking. The announced intent was to remove a dot each year until 1980, at which time the marking would again change. The dealers and collectors who had chased after the Case XX dealer display boards were now joined by newcomers as they competed in the search for those containing knives stamped USA. Even as they searched, these knife enthusiasts were aided by a new reference book, *Romance of Collecting Case Knives,* written by Dewey Ferguson.

The only exclusively knife publication at that time was *The Blue Mill Blade*, edited by Roy Scott of Del Rio, Tennessee. At Scott's suggestion, a small group of dealers and collectors met on June 9, 1972, and formed the National Knife Collectors and Dealers Association (NKC&DA). This organization, whose members were primarily concerned with antique factory-made knives, would be a positive force in the growing interest of collecting. Meanwhile, another organization, the Knife Collectors Club, was founded by A. G. Russell of Springdale, Arkansas. His primary emphasis was in custom knives.

The NKC&DA began to sponsor knife shows in a number of cities promoting trading, buying and selling of pocketknives. Promotion of custom knives was spearheaded by a new magazine, *The American Blade,* whose premier issue was published in Atlanta in 1973—just as the new knife shows were becoming a reality. Other publications soon followed. In 1975, a classified trade paper named *Knife World* was first published in St. Louis. Two years later, under new ownership, it was relocated to Knoxville, Tennessee, and the format changed to include editorial coverage of collectible knives. The NKC&DA introduced its newsletter in 1976 and built it into the *National Knife Collector* magazine in 1977. Reference books and regularly published resource materials were sorely needed by collectors during these early years. Those published during the 1970s can be credited with not only providing information, but also with increasing public awareness of a new hobby.

Another major undertaking was begun in 1978, when the National Knife Collectors Association vowed to build a knife museum. Three years later, the National Knife Collectors Museum's grand opening was held.

Continued growth in numbers of collectors went hand-in-hand during the past quarter-century, with a substantial increase in published works relating to knives. The cause and effect relationship was good for the hobby. Knife collecting interest grew at a rather rapid pace as more and more collectors came to recognize the fascination of old knives as pieces of Americana to which most of them could personally relate. And, they came to recognize their increasing value. Coincidentally, this period also saw the number of established custom knife makers increase from a few dozen to several hundred. Their customers were people with the desire to own a very special knife and willing to pay a relatively high price for it. The common denominator was recognition of the value of knives, whether antique or newly made one-of-a-kind pieces.

Collectors are still learning that there is something in the knife collecting field for every budget and with their investment, regardless of whether it is in knives valued a few dollars each or that cost several hundred dollars, comes the satisfaction of building a meaningful collection—one that should pay dividends if and when the decision is made to sell.

If you have been a part of the hobby during these years, you should be proud for the part you've played in its growth. If you're a newcomer, welcome—and enjoy!

KNIFE COLLECTING—FOR PLEASURE, FOR PROFIT

Every collector, regardless of the collecting field, has decided to become involved for specific and personal reasons. They may be many or few and the incentives for one may not necessarily be so important to another; they are often very different. The two primary inducements for most collectors, however, are pleasure and profit. The differences usually come in the emphasis one places on each of these motivating factors. Knife collecting can and will fulfill either or both of these goals; the degree of gratification depends upon the goals set and steps taken to achieve those goals.

Whether or not pleasure is the primary motivating factor, no one should be involved in knife collecting unless some degree of personal pleasure is derived from the hobby. Regardless of the priority, pleasure in collecting must have its place on the bottom line. To the person who likes knives, collecting them will reap rewards and bring few disappointments. On the other hand, the person who has little fondness or appreciation for knives and is simply seeking profit may do just as well—perhaps even better—in a different field.

But make no mistake, there is definitely the potential for profit to the knife collector who defines his or her goals and invests wisely. Knives, both new and old, have an excellent track record for value increase. As with other types of collectibles, the rate of increase will vary with overall economic conditions. Recession and boom periods, times of varying consumer confidence, job layoffs, and a host of other factors definitely bring changes to spending priorities. Discretionary spending for collectibles is usually one of the first categories affected. Inflation rates and, particularly in recent years, monetary exchange rates have a definite influence in the collectibles market. During periods of low to moderate inflation rates, the value increase tends to be substantially less than in higher inflationary periods. At these times, overall value gains of 10% per annum are generally considered good. But, when inflation rate is high, as it was during the early part of the 1980s, collectibles tend to outpace many other investments in their value increase. For instance, near the turn into the 1980s knives joined other collectibles in value gains of up to three times the inflation rate. Even with the relatively low rate of inflation during the past several years, collector values for desirable knives have been much more attractive than other investments.

One may wonder why inflation has such an effect on the prices of knives and other collectibles. Since they are basically resale items, the cost of manufacturing, advertising and marketing has been borne years ago. While some people consider collectibles as secondhand junk, the collector knows that they are in demand—demand which affects selling price and selling price establishes value. Collectible knives are certainly valuable, but they are also tangible items which can be held, admired and put away as hedges against inflation. Whenever traditional investments in stocks, bonds and securities disappoint investors as in very recent times, they look for so-called hard assets. Precious gems and metals are joined by collectibles and, in the realm of collectibles, knives have performed extremely well.

A great number of knives purchased a few short years ago are now selling for considerably more than their purchase prices. Although potential profit is recognized by their owners, it may not be realized for a long while because many of these knives are owned by collectors and knife enthusiasts who refuse to sell. And one must always remember that profit or loss does not occur without a sales transaction. So long as demand exceeds supply, prices will continue to rise. For years, comments have been made that the older and more respectable collector knives were getting very hard to find. These comments were often interpreted as a sales pitch to the novice collector. But, the time has arrived when practically every collector recognizes the continually increasing demand for those choice collectibles that can be found in the marketplace.

The prices paid for more desirable antique knives continue to rise and one can only guess when and at what level the peak will come. Record prices, some almost beyond belief, raise eyebrows each month as choice antique pieces change ownership.

But there is one foreseeable aspect to the inflation of knife values and that is the increasing demand for collectible knives in less than mint condition. Although there was a time when the collector was advised to only purchase mint-condition knives, that advice is less sound with passing years. Today's astute collector may well be found purchasing knives that, a few years ago, would have been passed by in the search for a mint specimen. There are now a number of collectors who will reconcile themselves to adding these "good" condition knives to their collections, hoping to use them as hedges to increasing knife values and waiting for the opportunity to trade up to an ever better specimen. Meanwhile, the pleasure of the search, the gratification of the find and the pride of owning the new addition to the collection is there.

No one can tell you when to buy—for, whenever that is, it will have been too late. No one can tell you when to sell—for, whenever that is, it will have been too early. Will Rogers has been credited with advising a prospective investor, "If it goes up, sell; if it don't go up, don't buy." The decision to buy or to sell must be a personal one but should always be made based upon the best information at hand. A major factor in the decision should always be one's personal feelings about the knife being bought or sold—keep pleasure and profit in their proper perspective. The "what ifs," the "I wish I hads" and the "I shouldn't haves" will haunt every stock investor, every land speculator and—yes—every knife collector who has profit as the primary inducement. If pleasure has played its role, the profits will be sweet; if there are losses, they will not be nearly so bitter.

It is not the purpose of this book to tell one when to buy or when to sell or at what price. Its purpose is to offer information and resources that will help in making these decisions. Only through learning more about knives can the serious collector reap the harvests of pleasure and profit. Assimilation of information should go hand-in-hand with the acquisition of knives. For collectors who know knives and know the market, profits can be earned on any given day. But, those who combine their knowledge with a fondness for knives will profit every day in the pleasure derived from their hobby.

SPECIALIZATION

The majority of knife collectors began their involvement in the hobby as accumulators and there is nothing at all wrong with this approach. It is, after all, a normal occurrence for the person who likes knives to like them well enough to buy more than can be carried or used at any one time. The foundation for many of today's highly regarded collections was laid by the purchase of knives that especially appealed to the budding collector. They were carried, used, and eventually put alongside others in a dresser drawer or box where they became part of the accumulation. Usually, the growth in interest goes hand-in-hand with the increase in number of knives, and a decision is made to specialize.

Specialization in knife collecting is heartily recommended for several reasons. It makes a collection even more meaningful when specific goals are pursued. A sense of rhyme, reason and direction adds to the pleasure of acquiring more knives. With a goal comes challenge and, with challenge, comes the satisfaction of achieving those goals. Specialization allows one to tailor his or her collecting to best suit the budget while conscientiously building a collection that is likely to appreciate in value.

Further, specialization allows for a high level of expertise in the chosen area. With the thousands of different knives available to collectors, it is practically impossible to learn a great deal about the majority of them. On the other hand, it is not only possible but entirely feasible for a collector to become an expert in one or a few knife collecting specialties.

Knife collecting is certainly one of today's most versatile hobbies and there is a special area suited for almost everyone. Choosing a specialty is in no way making a permanent commitment and one should recognize that a change or further refinement is often in store at some future date whenever the collection becomes more "mature." The search for a greater challenge most always reveals another specialty—another opportunity—just around the corner.

Perhaps you have already selected one or a few areas for concentrating your efforts and funds as your collection grows, or you may have specialized in an area and determined that further refinement is in order. If a newcomer to the hobby, you may be now at the point of refining an accumulation of knives into a more meaningful collection. Whatever the situation, one should be aware of the choices available in order to determine which best fits a particular interest, the goals in collecting, and the financial means to pursue these goals. Some general areas to consider in choosing a collecting specialty are factory-made or production knives, custom knives, commemorative or limited edition knives, antique bowie knives, military knives, silver fruit knives and trend knives. Each area has its challenges and rewards; each has its pros and cons. The following discussions may be helpful in determining which is best for you.

Factory or Production Knives

Those who elect to collect factory-made knives represent the majority of knife collectors. But, that is appropriate since the greatest share of knives produced were and still are those made by cutlery manufacturers. The collector who determines that the knives he or she likes best are those made in industrial settings still has a near endless number of choices available. The most distinct line for division of collectible factory knives is that of antique or old knives and those of modern or current manufacture.

To the average factory knife collector, "old knives" is a relative term and one subject to individual interpretation. Old may not necessarily mean antique, although antique always signifies old. Either category most always means collectible and valuable. As a case in point (pun not intended) are those knives made by W. R. Case & Sons Cutlery forty years ago and stamped Case XX USA. They would not yet qualify as antiques but still are highly desirable to collectors. As a consequence, their current market value is several times their retail price when originally marketed. The fact of collector demand for and value of old and antique knives has been well established over a period of several years. Names such as Case, Remington, Winchester, Ka-Bar and Cattaraugus join with a host of others in singing magic to the ears of collectors. Their worth has been proven and their values continue to climb, making them a specialty that generally requires a higher "entry fee." But, the established "market" allows one to determine which brand, pattern, era of manufacture, etc. best suits his or her collecting interest and his or her pocketbook.

Somewhat to the contrary, knives of modern or current manufacture offer greater speculative latitude. This is not to imply that knives in this category are not in demand and valued quite highly by collectors—far from it. Perhaps the area presenting the greatest opportunity to the greatest number of collectors during this decade is new knives. Several brand names, although relatively new, still have a high degree of visibility in the knife collecting world. Rather than being obscure or of little collector interest, knives stamped with names such as Fight'n Rooster, Cripple Creek, Bulldog, Parker-Frost, or several others can be dominant at some knife shows and in other trading circles. These brands, along with current reproductions of some famous old brands, are examples of new knives that are well entrenched within the knife world. Unlike the antique knives that were designed, manufactured and sold to be used, these knives were born of the recent collecting renaissance. Their popularity as collectibles was and is a major purpose of their manufacture. A very respectable number of these knives have proven or are currently proving their worth as collectibles—especially in certain regions of the country. However, their recognition and acceptance on a national basis is yet to come. Therein lies their speculative nature. Building a collection of current knives will require a lower cash outlay, but still will offer rewards such as pride of ownership and potential value appreciation.

Once a collector determines whether to collect old or current knives, he or she still has further opportunities for refinement. It may be specialization by manufacturers' brand, especially if that manufacturer has produced or is producing a rather limited number of patterns or models. Whenever the numbers become too large, further specialization is in order. These specialties may be in the form of patterns and/or in handle materials, or they may relate to knives with a particular tang stamping. For example, it is not unusual to find a Case collector specializing in bone handled muskrat pattern knives made prior to the 1960s or to find a collector of Remington knives specializing in the famed Remington "Bullets." Likewise, a collector of relatively new brands such as Fight'n Rooster may elect to build a collection of pearl handled beauties of varied patterns.

Specialization may take the form of knife types and be totally unrelated to manufacturer or handle material. Examples of this would be collections of plier and wrench knives as made by various manufacturers during the first quarter of the 20th century, picture handle knives made about the same time, or whittler patterns made either a century ago or last month. Tactical knives, many featuring unique locking systems or blade designs, are current high-profile offerings from several young but quite respectable manufacturers.

To see specialization firsthand, one only needs to visit a local knife show and spend an enjoyable hour or so studying the collector displays. Since the major portion of this book features factory-made knives, its listings of notable manufacturers, patterns, handle materials and dates of manufacture will also be of value in selecting a specialty.

Custom Knives

The collector who leans towards those knives made one-at-a-time by individual makers also has several avenues available in choosing a specialty. Similar to the choice in factory knives, one may elect to concentrate on knives made by 20th-century pioneer makers such as Scagel, Richtig, Ruana and Randall—all now deceased. Many collectors of custom knives have an appreciation for the fact that in buying a knife, they are also buying a piece of the maker's life. It is not unusual, therefore, that these people wish to collect the knives of makers they can get to know—either personally, by telephone conversation or through correspondence.

Some elect to collect knives of only one maker. That maker may be one who is well established and whose knives have been proven as desirable. Usually, these knives either require a rather long waiting period or, if found on the secondary market, a higher price. Other more speculative collectors may like the work of one or a few makers and be willing to invest money, hoping that the knives bought at relatively low prices, while the maker and his work are relatively unknown, will someday bring high prices because that maker's knives are in demand.

Custom knife collectors usually concentrate on either fixed blade knives or folders. Similar to factory knives, a host of possibilities lie within either of these areas. The fixed blade fancier may chose further refinement into designs such as bowies, fighters, survival knives, hunters and skinners. One who prefers the handmade folder may also make further choices in design such as locking mechanisms or unique blade design.

Another choice in custom knives is between those made by bladesmiths who forge their blades and those made by makers using the stock removal method. And, as if the above avenues aren't enough, there's the choice between the knife that is without decorations such as engraving, file work and scrimshaw and those embellished with one or more of these art forms. Some art knives seem to practically reach into a knife world of their very own, offering a truly unique specialty for a few collectors. Further comments regarding collecting customs as a specialty and sources of custom knives can be found in chapter 3.

Commemorative or Limited Edition Knives

The rapidly increasing interest in knives as collectibles has led to near countless numbers of commemorative and/or limited edition knives being made and sold within the collector market. Although some of these have been handmade or custom knives, by far the majority have been factory knives. The collector who chooses this type knife as a specialty has fewer alternatives than those described earlier but, still, choices do exist.

One distinct and viable specialty would be those knives that are handmade by custom makers or knives that are factory made but which feature decorative work done one-at-a-time by recognized artists. These knives are most always limited to relatively small quantities and are truly unique. The advantages of this specialty are pride of ownership and potential value appreciation. After all, not many collectors can own one of Randall Knives 50th Anniversary limited edition knives or Gil Hibben's handmade Rambo III. Most collectors would not limit their collecting to this specialty because the total number of knives owned would be quite small while the investment would be quite large.

Club knives are limited editions that have proven to be meaningful as well as valuable collectibles. Clubs such as the National Knife Collectors Association as well as regional clubs usually have limited numbers of knives made each year for their clubs' membership. Not only are these knives in demand by the clubs' members, but several of them are subject to growing demand and value appreciation outside that membership circle. Club knives, if produced for a regional club, are usually limited in number from 50 to 300, rarely more. National club knives have varied from 1,200 to as many as 10,000 pieces in production. A few have been sold out to the membership before production is complete, cultivating demand and resale profit.

Factory-made commemorative knives may be issued by the manufacturer or, as is often the case, by individual entrepreneurs. They may celebrate an event of national importance or they may commemorate something or someone of significance to a very small percentage of our population. Usually, those that are privately issued are based upon a popular pattern knife that is in full-scale production. That rather ordinary knife is made into something not so common by special blade etching, boxing and serial numbering. Collectors to whom these knives appeal will likely decide to collect upon a theme since there are such a large number available that meaningful parameters would need to be defined. An example would be the theme that has become increasingly popular in recent years and in most parts of the nation: NASCAR races and NASCAR theme knives.

Limited edition and commemorative knives are discussed in more detail and listed in chapter 6.

Antique Bowie Knives

Because of the rarity and relative value of most knives in this area, those who collect antique bowie knives may not elect to specialize further. Even a so-called accumulation of antique bowies would be so difficult to garner that further refinement would be pointless. Collectors considering the antique bowie specialty should definitely study any and all reputable reference works on the subject. Prices recently realized for exchange in ownership of choice pieces have been staggering; a specialty not to be taken lightly! Presented in this book, with the cooperation of a recognized and respected authority, is a separate discussion of bowies and a listing of prominent makers of these very old and very desirable pieces. It is likely the most comprehensive overview of the antique bowie market extant.

Military Knives

Collecting of military knives represents a rather dynamic area of cutlery collecting and one that is already quite specialized, much as antique bowie knives. Their range, however, is quite broad—from antique swords to weapons used during recent military excursions. These cutlery items of warfare are collected not only by knife enthusiasts, but by military history buffs and antique collectors as well. Military knives are so closely related to other items of warfare that their collecting theme often follows specific wars and/or the several branches of the military establishments fighting in those wars. Other choices include special fighting or commando knives, bayonets, machetes and bolos, as well as general utility knives used in the military. Further discussion and a listing of the more prominent military knives may be found in chapter 3.

Silver Fruit Knives

Folding fruit knives, many of them made during the 18th and 19th centuries, offer a rewarding specialty. These knives appeal to both men and women alike, but they seem to be special favorites of female collectors. Although they may be found in knife trading circles, they are often encountered at estate sales and in antique shops. Their hallmark stampings allow for accurate cataloging and learning the system can be a hobby in itself. For further information about silver fruit knives, refer to part 3.

Trend Knives

Trends and fads have long been, and will continue to be, an important part of buying, selling and trading of most any product. Knives are no exception. One has only to look back to the mid-1800s to recognize one important trend in knives that was started by Col. James Bowie. Or, within many of our lifetimes, to recall the popularity of a knife pattern named for an English cutler named Barlow and popularized by an American author's stories about two youngsters named Sawyer and Finn.

But, there has probably been no period in cutlery history that has produced so many trendy knives as have the past three decades. Knife designers, custom knife makers and large-scale knife producers alike have created designs that captured the imaginations, the fantasies and the pocketbooks of knife buyers; at least for a while.

There have been "survival knives"—distinctive fixed blade knives that capitalized on saw-teeth backs, compass butt caps and a hollow handle filled with useless gadgets as well as items of practical use for surviving in the wilds. They were popularized by movie makers who introduced us to superheroes wielding super knives. Custom makers made them by the thousands; factories made and sold them by the millions. Now, less than twenty years after their heyday, it is difficult to find collectors with interest in any survival knife except those made by already famous custom makers.

Designs known as "tantos" were also made popular by the silver screen martial artists and, in theory, they were fashioned after some of the blades of the Samurai warriors. During the early 1980s, practically every custom knife maker who wanted to sell knives sold at least one knife designed in accordance with his or her interpretation of the tanto. Several makers of production knives built businesses based on their versions of the tanto. With rare exceptions, neither the customs nor the factory knives are in favor today.

A similar story could be told about the Bali-Song or "butterfly knife" of Philippine origin. The fad came and flourished for a short while before the butterfly knives fluttered into near obscurity.

During the 1990s and continuing today, the trend has been to big knives—bowie and or bowie/machete types. Custom knife makers had continued to make and sell these large utility knives over the years, but the fad swept through much of the factory knife industry—again with much of the credit due to hero images.

As the last century came to its close within the field of custom folders, the liner lock mechanism was very much in favor. The trend continues. In spite of the fact that several custom makers claim credit, the mechanism is near identical to that of utility pocket knives made many years ago by the factory knife producers.

Although most of these examples have originated with custom knives, the rage for specific knife designs is not limited to them. In fact, a significant trend was begun during recent years and continues to expand as this century begins. Led by the visionary leadership of Sal Glesser at Spyderco, production knives designed by custom knife makers have created an exciting niche in the knife collector and knife user market. Several leading manufacturers have teamed up with respected custom makers to create special knives that compare favorably with the true "custom" piece. Factory-made custom design knives are well worth the collector's attention.

The pattern popularly known as a "trapper" has been a standard production knife for practically all knife manufacturers for decades. During the past decade and still today, it could be considered the king of pocketknife collectible patterns. Its popularity is not so much because of the pattern itself as its use for scores of limited editions and commemorative series. In reading and referring to this book's section on those special production knives, you will become increasingly aware of the impact of the trapper pattern upon today's and tomorrow's collectors.

There's little doubt that the trapper pattern will still be popular when most of today's collectors are history. Likewise, the bowie has long been a part of Americana and will undoubtedly remain in favor. Whether the other "hero knives" will someday be valuable collectibles can only be speculated, but there are collectors of Lone Ranger knives and Batman memorabilia. One relatively new and interesting, but low-priced area is modern reproductions of those knives named for stars of the comic books and the silver screen. It's not unreasonable to anticipate a future demand for knives representing heroes of the late 20th century. Most of them were first purchased because of their vogue status and with little concern about their future value. And, anyone who would dare say that short-lived popularity will not create a collectible knife can be brought back to reality when reminded of the unique and valuable collections built around knives such as plier knives, cotton samplers, fleam knives, timber scribes and picture handled knives.

Just as did knife buyers of the earlier times, if you like them, buy and enjoy them.

STARTING AND BUILDING A COLLECTION

Getting started as a knife collector is extremely easy. The chances are good that most people have the beginnings of a collection tucked away in dresser drawers, trunks, closets, attics, basements and even shoe boxes. Those are favorite places for storing items handed down from prior generations or from our own past and, after all, every collection began with a first knife.

A knife collection does not have to be large in numbers to be worthwhile. It is true that some collections contain hundreds or even thousands of knives, but others contain less than a dozen. Each offers rewards to the collector. There are so many opportunities that anyone interested in knives can get involved in the hobby.

Knife collecting doesn't necessarily require one to spend large amounts of money. So, anyone interested in knives should not be deterred by the high prices of rare knives. A collection can be started with a modest budget and built in the same manner. Even if there are no knives stored away at home, there are numerous opportunities for starting a collection at whatever investment level one finds feasible.

Knives Are Where You Find Them

There are a number of places where collectible knives may be found and purchased; most of them represent good market places for selling knives as well. In practically every town and on most weekends, one can find flea markets, garage sales and estate sales to visit. They may be as close as a few blocks away from home or as far away as the other side of town, but they are convenient. Auctions and knife shows are most often less convenient but they are almost always worth the time and expense of travel.Whether buying or selling, the collector should never overlook the market that is as close as the mailbox or telephone. And the relatively new name of "E-Bay" has stirred the whole industry. Quite a large volume of collector knife sales are consummated from the home with professional knife dealers and with other collectors. Very few collectors will pass up the advertisements in the knife publications as they seek new contacts for buying and selling collectible knives.

None of these should be overlooked since each has an important place within the boundaries of the knife world. There are still excellent bargains to be found and choice pieces traded at reasonable prices. Knife collecting is no different than other endeavors in that the harder and smarter one works at the hobby, the luckier he or she becomes. And, yes, luck still plays its important part, especially when it is supported by knowledge. The following discussion about these various sources for knives may help to determine areas to use your own expertise and to try your own luck in making that rare find. Good hunting!

GARAGE AND ESTATE SALES

Garage and estate sales can offer opportunities for buying knives, especially to collectors who already enjoy chasing after bargains at these weekend affairs. With the minimal amount of travel and time required, they should never be overlooked. One very important thing to remember is to ask about knives. Since they usually find their way into dresser drawers, trunks and boxes, knives may have been forgotten or assumed by the seller to be of little interest and value.

Expect to sift through a lot of junk and expect to find many sales with no collectible knives, but expect also that persistence can pay off. After all, at some point in time, a large number of the knives found at knife shows and through dealers entered the collector market by way of a well-informed and fortunate sale shopper.

FLEA MARKETS

Although many good knives exchange owners through flea markets, their percentage is small when compared to the practically worthless ones to be found on these trading grounds. Their abundance and close proximity are the greatest advantages of flea markets. There are disadvantages to be considered also, especially by the novice collector. The average flea market is usually lacking knowledgeable fellow collectors or dealers, leaving the untrained collector much on his or her own. Knowing knives and their values is essential to successful flea market buying. Most flea market dealers acknowledge that some knives are valuable. Recognizing this fact but often knowing little else about collectible knives, these dealers are usually inclined to overprice their knives for fear of selling them for too little.

Because a large portion of the knives found at flea markets have come out of attics, garages and basements, their appearance is likely to be less impressive than those found at shows or on the professional dealers' tables. But ordinary dirt and grime can be cleaned off and should be no deterrent to buying a knife that is considered a bargain. And, their source often means that the flea market dealer has very little investment in the knife; his or her interest in it could be even less. The collector who looks earnestly and evaluates wisely may find him- or herself a genuine bargain.

AUCTIONS

Concurrent with the growing interest in knives as collectibles, there has been an increasing number of auctions specializing in them. These auctions have become one of the best places to buy knives. If the sale is from a well-established collection, the knives offered may be quite rare and difficult to find elsewhere. If the knives are from an estate, a quick sale may take priority over selling price. Even though some prices paid at auctions offer surprises on both extremes—unquestionable bargains to ridiculously high—most are good indications of the true collector values of the knives represented.

Some auctions are highly publicized, draw collectors from distant areas and often welcome absentee bids. Others may only be publicized by direct mail notification or local newspaper advertising. They can offer opportunities to purchase desirable knives at very reasonable prices or they may also be routes used for disposing of junk. If the auction is well publicized, if the knives are listed well in advance of the sale and if they are available for inspection prior to the actual sale, these sales are an excellent means for learning the real value of knives.

In addition to the more commonly recognized type of auction, informal and sometimes spontaneous auctions are held at knife show locations. These auctions are often lighthearted gatherings that offer collectors and dealers the opportunity to bid on one another's knives and to swap stories as well. Sitting in on one of these informal affairs of the knife collecting hobby can often be a special treat.

CLUB SWAP MEETS

Most knife clubs meet on a regular basis and the major portion of the time spent is in buying, selling and trading knives. Some meetings are followed by a minishow with dealers and collectors spreading out their wares on tables and welcoming offers to buy, sell or trade. Newcomers to these events not only bring new faces and personalities, but they also bring "new" (different) knives into the relatively small circle; visitors and new members are usually very much welcomed.

MAIL ORDER

An avenue for buying and selling knives that is available to most everyone is personal contact with other collectors and dealers via mail and telephone. In most instances, the initial contact between buyer and seller will have been made as the result of an advertisement in a regular knife publication. Shopping the "for sale" and "wanted" columns of classified ad pages is a high priority activity for many knife collectors.

There are numerous dealers who conduct a large share of their business in this manner. Most of them regularly distribute lists of knives they have for sale and knives which they seek, either for their personal collection or for those of regular customers. Collectors wishing to either sell or buy a number of knives may be well advised to compile a similar listing to be sent to other collectors or to dealers.

Newcomers to the hobby may be surprised to learn that a lot of knife trading is conducted in this manner and with relatively few problems. So long as both the prospective buyer and seller accurately represent the knives to be traded and agree to reasonable return privileges, there will be few grievous mail order transactions.

DEALERS

Knife dealers are businesspeople much like those in other fields. Their goal is to purchase and to market their goods at a price which allows sufficient margin to pay operating expenses plus a reasonable profit. As in any business, there are a few dealers who may seek excessive profits or conduct their business dealings unfairly. The vast majority of knife dealers deal very fairly with their customers. They are well aware that their own business health is based upon good customer relations and most knife dealers recognize that the same collector who buys knives from him on one occasion may be selling him knives on another. Since knife dealers are both buyers and sellers, their service can usually be beneficial to collectors at most any time.

The professional dealer is most often an expert in a wide variety of collectible knives and usually has a large number of contacts who may be helpful. Through these contacts, the dealer is often able to sift through the national knife market, rather than just the local area. The knowledgeable dealer usually has the expertise to detect and reject counterfeits so that his or her customers can buy with a greater degree of confidence. He or she offers convenience and often saves the knife buyer or seller money in travel and other expenses required to buy or sell a knife. There are no special secrets to the dealer's supply source; it's the same knife market that the individual collector works within. The primary difference is in the volume of knives and the size of the investment. Although many dealers are also collectors, their primary goal in buying and selling knives is turning their inventory as quickly and as profitably as possible. While the primary goal of most collectors is building a respectable collection, profit—usually long term—also plays a role in their activities. It is not unusual that many collectors become dealers since they buy, trade and sell while seeking to collect.

KNIFE SHOWS

Knife shows have, or at least should have, an entirely different atmosphere from that of flea markets. This does not mean one cannot find bargains at a show. To the contrary, the knife show is perhaps the best single source of good knives at fair prices. Shows are gathering places for the leading dealers and active collectors and, as such, they are ideal forums for building a collection (buying) or refining one (selling).

Table renters at a knife show are not always full-time dealers. Oftentimes they are collectors who are refining their collection by selling duplicates or knives that are less desirable to them because their collecting interest has changed. These collectors are usually excellent sources for good knives, often at prices below their current value. In addition, they can often offer the bonus of rather extensive information about the specific knife being transferred from one collection to another.

Knife shows offer collectors an opportunity to get personally acquainted with dealers, often the beginning of a long-term relationship. Visiting at a dealer's table offers firsthand information about the type and quality of the knives he or she sells.

Expect a large percentage of knife show visitors to be reasonably well informed and experienced. This means tough competition for the best bargains and the astute collector seeking knives will arrive as early as possible to survey the offerings. But it also means that knife shows can offer a wealth of firsthand information. To be a good show, in my opinion, it will feature a number of "exhibit only" tables, used by collectors who proudly display their knives for the education of others. These displays offer opportunities for collectors to see many rare and valuable knives, often accumulated through years of searching and substantial financial investment. One can most always expect these collectors to freely share the benefit of their hard-earned wisdom.

Knife shows can be impressionable events, especially to the novice collector. Just as they can leave the visitor with good or bad impressions, shows also offer the foundation upon which the visitor can build a reputation—good or not so good. Although there are no posted rules of etiquette, there are rules of courtesy that one should keep in mind. Doing so will make the experience more enjoyable for everyone concerned. Here are several suggestions.

Ask permission before handling a knife. This courtesy is especially important if the knife is for display only and not for sale. The collector who is displaying his or her collection is usually doing so without compensation. These collectors have invested considerable expense and effort to show their knives and to share their knowledge with other collectors and show visitors. Cleaning fingerprints off knives after they have been handled by visitors is certainly no reward for their selfless efforts.

Do not handle the blade or its edge. If invited to examine a knife, open it carefully by the nail nick and avoid touching the blade itself. Not only could you leave it with a blemish, but a sharp blade carelessly handled can return the insult with injury.

Do not open more than one blade of a folding knife at any one time. Doing so can weaken the springs and will not be appreciated by the dealer or collector who has both pride and money invested in the knife. Once you've opened a blade, resist the temptation to hear the resounding snap of its closing. If the knife "walks and talks," your sense of touch will find its quality as evident as will your sense of hearing.

Do not participate uninvited or interfere with other persons' knife trading business. Whatever transpires is their personal affair and, even though you may be very interested in the knife being discussed, wait your turn. If their transaction is not completed, then and only then feel free to enter into your own transaction.

Do not block a dealer's table from his prospective customers if you are just browsing his wares. Most dealers invite casual lookers, but they have traveled to the show and paid their table fees in order to sell knives. Preventing them from doing so is unfair to both the dealer and the prospective buyer.

Unless invited to do so, do not use the table of another collector or dealer to sell or trade knives you may have brought to the show. The effect of this discourteous act should require no explanation.

Attendance and participation in a knife show can and should be a very rewarding experience, an experience that the serious collector can ill afford to miss. Listings of show dates and locations for most shows can be found in the regular knife publications such as *Knife World*, *Knives Illustrated* and *Blade Magazine*.

INTERNET

The most recent of venues for buying, selling and trading of knives has rapidly become a major influence in collector markets. Thousands of knives are sold each day on Internet auction sites by faceless and pseudonamed cyberspace creatures. Whether they truly are reputable dealers and collectors or are masquerading as such may only be known after the deal has been comsumated. In many instances, the visitors to knife-oriented auction sites are prospective buyers and sellers testing the waters, looking for that illusive treasure for sale at a pittance.

Internet knife "trading" has the potential for being, at any one time, the best and the worst of both worlds. A visit there can be made without leaving home; it can last for a few moments or for several hours. It can introduce the beginning collector to more knives than would otherwise be possible in any other venue. It can present opportunities for an education in cutlery collecting and it can indeed be the avenue for making the purchase of a lifetime. To the contrary, life's hard knocks and memorable lessons can be experienced and learned in short order. How Internet knife trading affects you and your collection depends upon you and the degree that you have armed yourself with knowledge.

LEARNING MORE ABOUT KNIVES

KNIFE NOMENCLATURE

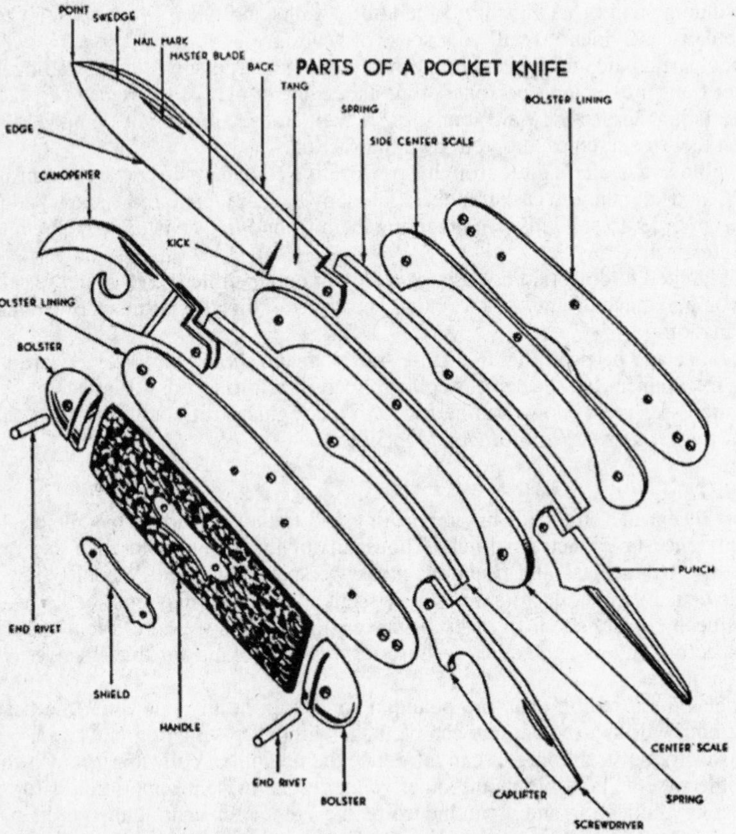

Blades, Patterns and Handles

Blade patterns—their shape and size—are influenced by their intended use. Blade names are usually derived from the tasks they were designed to perform or, occasionally, from their shapes. Some blades are quite commonly used in numerous styles of knives and have been for centuries. The pen blade was originally used for trimming quill pens for office work and has been a very popular blade that has found many other uses in modern times. The spear and sheepfoot blades, named for their shapes, are joined by the clip and spey blades as blade types most used and widely recognized. The function of several other blade types such as nail file, leather punch, screwdriver, cap lifter, spatula, cotton sampler and timber scribe offered obvious names for them.

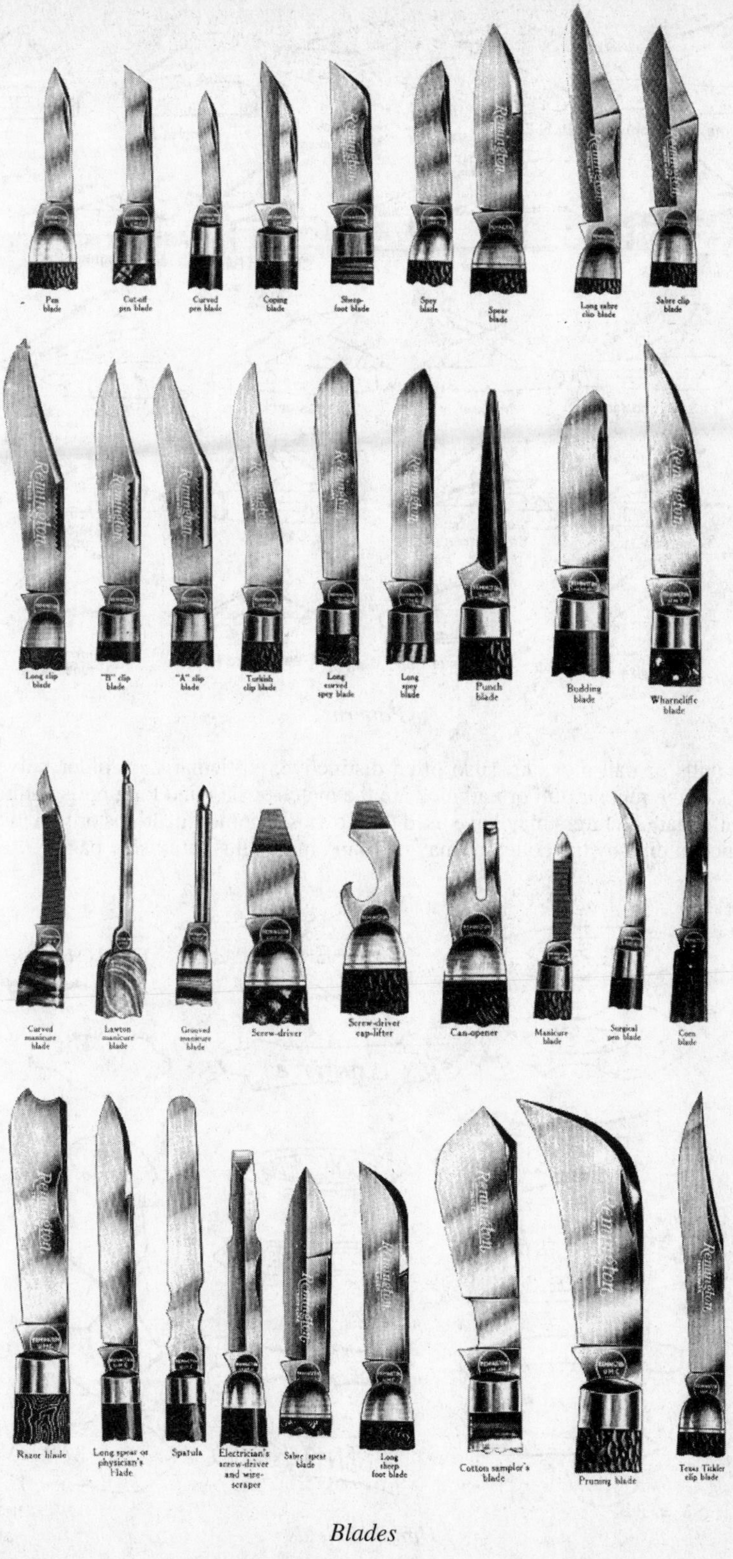
Pen blade
Cut-off pen blade
Curved pen blade
Coping blade
Sheep-foot blade
Spey blade
Spear blade
Long sabre clip blade
Sabre clip blade
Long clip blade
"B" clip blade
"A" clip blade
Turkish clip blade
Long curved spey blade
Long spey blade
Punch blade
Budding blade
Wharncliffe blade
Curved manicure blade
Lawton manicure blade
Grooved manicure blade
Screw-driver
Screw-driver cap-lifter
Can-opener
Manicure blade
Surgical pen blade
Corn blade
Razor blade
Long spear or physician's blade
Spatula
Electrician's screw-driver and wire-scraper
Sabre spear blade
Long sheep foot blade
Cotton sampler's blade
Pruning blade
Texas Tickler clip blade

Blades

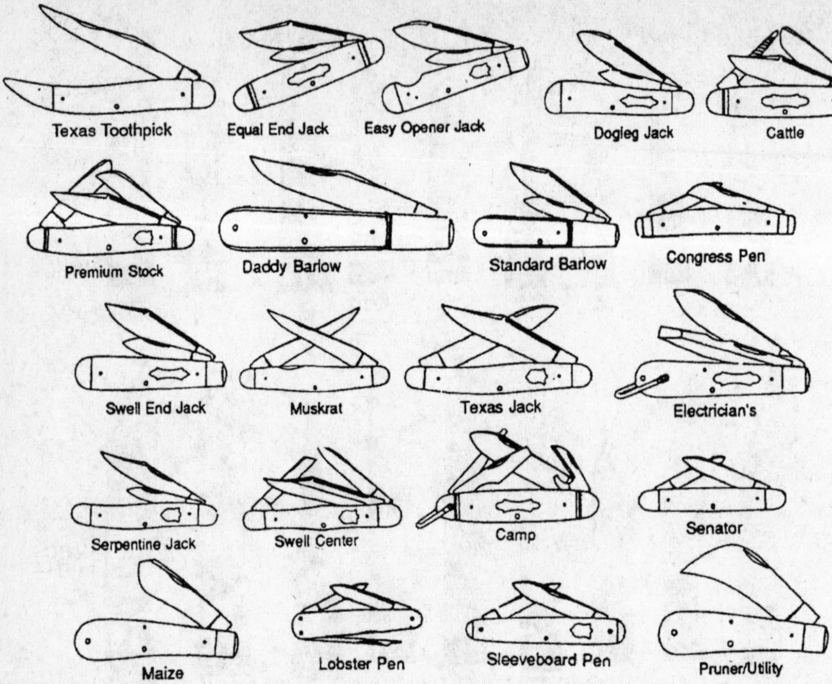

Patterns

Blade pulls or nail nicks are also often distinctive, particularly on older knives. Some variations of the regular pull or nail nick are the match-striker and long pulls. Although different knife manufacturers may have used their own slight modifications or variations, most blades encountered by the collector may be found in the illustrations on page 15.

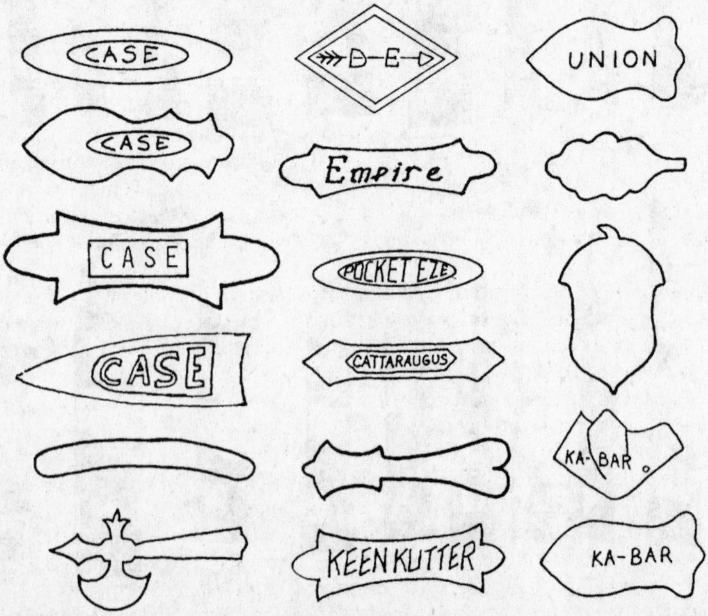

Handle Shields

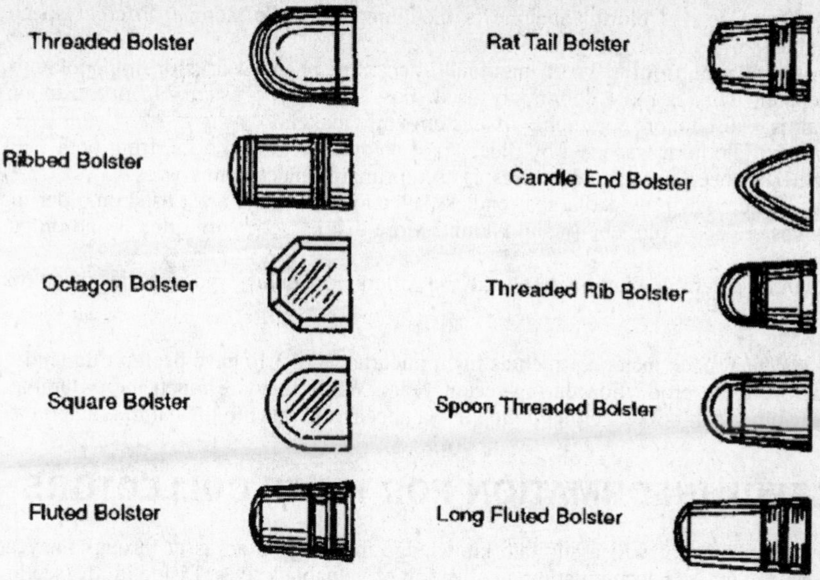

Bolsters

Pocketknife styles or shapes are derived from handle frame patterns. Their names have most often been derived from overall appearance or their similarity with another object. Whether or not their name is one that would immediately come to mind, most knife enthusiasts find that names are fitting with the patterns they represent. Names such as equal end, swell center, serpentine, teardrop and dog leg are as appropriate today as when they were first used many decades ago. The illustration that follows will help to identify some of the more common patterns.

In studying the illustrations, keep in mind that several handle dies have been used to make a variety of styles. For instance, equal end jacks and cattle knives are often the same shape and size, their difference being primarily in selection of blade types. Likewise, swell center or balloon knives have been used for whittlers, jacks, folding hunters and a number of other knife types.

Pocketknife names are usually derived from the combination of handle frame pattern and the blades used within that frame. Pen knives may take the shapes known as lobster, senator, or sleeveboard but their primary blade type is pen. An equal end pattern may be called a jack or, with blades of use to farmers or ranchers, it may be called a cattle knife. Serpentine patterns may have long skinning blades and be called a muskrat or may have different blades such as spey, sheepfoot and clip and be called a stock knife or stockman pattern. Numerous variations will be noted in illustrations contained throughout this book's listings.

Handle shields may be considered primarily decorative but they were often used as a trademark, by their shape alone or as the location for stamping a brand or trademark name.

Bolsters have many names, most of which are descriptive of their appearance. Square, crimped, tip, rat tail, threaded or fluted are typical bolster types found on pocketknives.

Both natural and man-made materials are used for knife handles. Those most commonly used for pocketknives are listed below.

Bone—usually from the cow shin bone; most often dyed with various coloring agents; can be smooth, scored or jigged (often referred to as "bone stag").

Stag—genuine stag is the outside layer of antlers from deer and other related species and has a natural rough texture and appearance. A material called second cut stag is the underneath layer. It is usually jigged or textured to simulate stag or bone.

Shell—from the shells of reptiles (tortoise) or mollusks. "Pearl" as used for knife handles, comes from the inner lining of mollusk (oyster) shells and is more accurately called mother-of-pearl. Colorful abalone is the lining of shells from a different species of mollusk.

Ivory—can come from tusks of mammals such as elephant, walrus or hippopotamus, but elephant ivory is more commonly used. Fossilized ivory, usually from mastodon and walrus, is used more commonly by custom knife makers.

Horn—buffalo horn was used by older knife companies. Sheep horn, from both wild and domestic sheep and related species, is used primarily on custom knives.

Wood—nature has provided a near endless selection, but those most used on older factory knives are cocobolo, ebony and walnut. More exotic woods are often found on custom knives.

Celluloid—a durable man-made plastic that offers near endless possibilities of colors and patterns.

Other man-made materials such as linen micarta and delrin have been prominently used in factory knife production during recent years. While they are much more durable than their natural look-a-like, neither compares in appeal nor value to the natural materials.

USEFUL INFORMATION FOR KNIFE COLLECTORS

The astute collector will assimilate knowledge that will be an asset throughout years of buying, trading and accumulating a collection of valuable knives. Listed in this section are tidbits of information which will be of assistance in determining country of origin, probable dates of manufacture, etc.

Some of the terms listed below may occasionally be found as a part of a knife's stamping. While not actually a part of the manufacturer's mark, they can be quite helpful in researching the knife's history. These markings indicate things such as place of manufacture, patent or trademark protection, and rust-free or stainless steel designations.

Place Names—Location of Manufacture

Albacete (Spain)....................Pavlovo (Russia)
Eskilstuna (Sweden)....................Rampur (India)
Frosolone (Italy)....................Seki (Japan)
Kauhava (Finland)....................Sheffield (England)
Maniago (Italy)....................Solingen (Germany)
Nogent (France)....................Thiers (France)
Ohligs (Germany)....................Toledo (Spain)

Patent, Trademarks, Steel Type, Etc.

Arbolito....................“Little Tree” (Tree Brand in Spanish)
Colt Riun....................cutlers union (Italian)
D.R.G.M. ....patented (German)
D.R.P....................patented (German)
D.R.Pat....................patented (German)
Depose....................registered (French)
Fein Stahl....................fine steel (German)
Gebr....................brother (German)
Ges. Gesch....................design patent (German)
Guss Stahl....................cast steel (German)
Hecho en Mexico....................made in Mexico (Spanish)
Inox....................stainless (French)
Nachf....................successor (German)
Nirosta....................no rust (German)
Rostfrei....................stainless (German)
Veritable....................genuine (French)
Weidmannshell....................good hunting (German)

Helpful Dating Information

Cast steel was used from the late 1700s until the first quarter of the 1900s.
Knives marked "Shear Steel" usually date to the 19th century.
Stellite as blade material was first used about 1910.
Stainless steel was first used on knives about 1916.
Chrome plating of knife blades was used from the 1930s to the 1960s.
Sterling silver, a designation after 1860, refers to 92.5% silver content.
Coin silver refers to 90% silver content and usually dates pre-1868.
Sterling silver fruit knives were rarely made after 1925.
Celluloid handles were first used on knives about 1870.
Aluminum handles were first used on knives about 1886.
Hard rubber handles were first used on knives about 1850.
Bakelite material was commonly used for knife handles during the second quarter of the 20th century.
Pick bone (bone stag) handles date from the 19th century.
Etched tang stamps date to approximately 1880.
Prussia stamped as country of origin was used prior to 1915.
Rhineland stamped as country of origin was used from 1920 to 1935.
Occupied Japan stamping as country of origin was used from 1945 to 1952.
Country-of-origin stamp was required on knives imported into U.S. after the 1890 Tariff Act.
Freeze treatment of stainless steel blades was developed about 1950.
Frosted etch on blades was first used about 1940.
Fruit knives were first made in France beginning in the 17th century.
Fork/knife combinations were first made in America in the early 1860s.
Integral iron bolsters and liners date from about 1860.
Iron liners were used on Case knives prior to 1920.
Liner lock mechanism date from the early 1900s.
Nickel silver dates from the early 1800s.
Official Boy Scout knife designation was adopted in 1911.
Switchblade knives made in U.S. date before 1958.
Zip code use in addresses began in 1963.

Patent Numbers and Dates

If a knife bears a patent number, one can determine from this number that the knife cannot have been made earlier than a particular year. The following table shows the beginning invention (not design) patent numbers issued by the U.S. Patent Office for each year from 1836 until 2002.

1836	1
1837	110
1838	546
1839	1,061
1840	1,465
1841	1,923
1842	2,413
1843	2,901
1844	3,395
1845	3,873
1846	4,348
1847	4,914
1848	5,409
1849	5,993
1850	6,981
1851	7,865
1852	8,622
1853	9,512
1854	10,358
1855	12,117
1856	14,009
1857	16,324
1858	19,010
1859	22,477
1860	26,642
1861	31,005
1862	34,045
1863	37,266
1864	41,047
1865	45,685
1866	51,784
1867	60,658
1868	72,959
1869	85,503
1870	98,460
1871	110,617
1872	122,304
1873	134,504
1874	146,120
1875	158,350

1876	171,641
1877	185,813
1878	198,733
1879	211,078
1880	223,211
1881	236,137
1882	251,685
1883	269,820
1884	291,016
1885	310,163
1886	333,494
1887	355,291
1888	275,720
1889	395,305
1890	418,665
1891	443,987
1892	466,315
1893	488,976
1894	511,744
1895	531,619
1896	552,502
1897	574,369
1898	596,467
1899	616,871
1900	640,167
1901	664,827
1902	690,385
1903	717,521
1904	748,567
1905	778,834
1906	808,618
1907	839,799
1908	875,679
1909	908,436
1910	945,010
1911	980,178
1912	1,013,095
1913	1,049,326
1914	1,083,267
1915	1,123,212
1916	1,166,419
1917	1,210,389
1918	1,251,458
1919	1,290,027
1920	1,326,899
1921	1,364,063
1922	1,401,948
1923	1,440,362
1924	1,478,996
1925	1,521,590
1926	1,568,040
1927	1,612,700
1928	1,654,521
1929	1,696,897
1930	1,742,181
1931	1,787,424
1932	1,839,190
1933	1,892,663
1934	1,941,449
1935	1,985,878
1936	2,026,516
1937	2,066,309
1938	2,104,004
1939	2,142,080
1940	2,185,170
1941	2,227,418
1942	2,268,540
1943	2,307,007
1944	2,338,081
1945	2,366,154
1946	2,391,856
1947	2,413,675
1948	2,433,624
1949	2,457,797
1950	2,494,944
1951	2,536,016
1952	2,580,379
1953	2,624,046
1954	2,664,562
1955	2,698,434
1956	2,728,913
1957	2,775,762
1958	2,818,567
1959	2,866,973
1960	2,919,443
1961	2,966,681
1962	3,015,103
1963	3,070,801
1964	3,116,487
1965	3,163,865
1966	3,226,729
1967	3,295,143
1968	3,350,800
1969	3,419,907
1970	3,487,470
1971	3,551,909
1972	3,633,214
1973	3,707,729
1974	3,781,914
1975	3,858,241
1976	3,930,271
1977	4,000,520
1978	4,065,812
1979	4,131,952
1980	4,180,867
1981	4,242,757
1982	4,308,622
1983	4,366,579
1984	4,423,523
1985	4,490,885
1986	4,562,596
1987	4,633,526
1988	4,716,594
1989	4,794,652
1990	4,890,335
1991	4,980,927
1992	5,077,836
1993	5,177,810
1994	5,274,846
1995	5,377,359
1996	5,479,658
1997	5,590,420
1998	5,704,062
1999	5,855,021
2000	6,009,555
2001	6,167,569
2002	6,334,220

COUNTERFEIT KNIVES

Those of us who enjoy the hobby of knife collecting view it, for many good and valid reasons, as a wholesome one. Consequently, it's sometimes uncomfortable to acknowledge that counterfeits are found in the knife marketplace. But, fakes are an unfortunate fact of life and perhaps it is a backhanded compliment about the value of knives as collectibles that we must be concerned with them. Whether the area of collecting is stamps, coins, antique furniture, paintings or an endless list of others, so long as there are objects of value being sold or traded, there will be those who choose to profit by trickery. As such, our refusal to discuss counterfeit knives is certainly not the answer. Hopefully, a general awareness of the practice and the practitioners will make it more difficult for counterfeit knives to be sold and traded.

While no single specialty of knife collecting is immune, primary targets for the counterfeiters' forgeries are antique bowies and medium-priced factory pocketknives. As a rule, pocketknives selling in the $150 to $300 range are most subject to deceptive practices. Knives selling for less would hardly be worth the counterfeiter's time, effort and risk; knives selling for higher amounts would normally be subject to greater scrutiny by the prospective buyer.

Guarding against buying counterfeit knives is not unlike caution used with other collectibles. The best rule is to first know your knives and, whenever possible, know the seller. The collector who has done his or her homework well should be able to spot inconsistencies either in the piece or in the story behind it, perhaps in both. If the knife and/or its bargain price are too good to be true, that's quite often the case.

One should learn as much as possible about the tricks of the counterfeiter as well as the craft of knife restoration. There is a difference in a knife that has been restored and is represented as such and one that has been altered with an intent to deceive. Properly restored knives or knives that have been taken apart for cleaning, although valued at less than a true mint piece, are certainly acceptable in the marketplace. Counterfeits are not.

Restoration

It is not unusual to find knives that have been heavily cleaned, repaired or restored by replacement of a part or parts as originally used in that specific knife at the time of its manufacture. Knife repair and partial restoration are generally viewed as acceptable so long as the knife is represented as such and there is no deception in intent or practice. Still, no matter how it appears, it is not a mint knife; it may, however, be a very valuable one. Restored knives are not only acceptable and in demand but one has to be a little bewildered when advertisements for antique knives are found that state "can be restored to mint." That's a contradiction in and of itself and evidence that many collectors, whether novice or seasoned, need to better understand the real meaning of the words "mint," "original" and "restored."

There are competent knife repairers who disassemble, completely clean and reassemble a knife, maintaining its integrity of original parts throughout the process. That knife should be represented and offered for sale as such and the collector who adds it to his or her collection can usually be proud to own it. Similarly, the competent craftsperson can repair or restore an old knife by interchange of a part such as a handle or blade. So long as the substituted part is original to the pattern and period of the knife to which it has been added, it may correctly be sold or traded as a restored knife and the buyer can have pride in ownership. There are many knives that may be found in excellent and original condition with the exception of a cracked handle. In these and similar cases, the repaired knife will most always be preferred to its unrepaired condition, similar to repairing the dented fender of an antique automobile.

The bottom line is one of semantics and they boil down to honesty. Reworking a knife with the intent to make it appear to be something it is not or misrepresenting it will qualify for *Webster's* definition of "counterfeit." So, when considering an antique knife to purchase, determine if the knife has been taken apart. If it has, ask what work was done to determine if all its parts are original and, if not, which were replaced. Don't be shy about asking the question, because in most cases you will receive an honest answer. But, if in doubt, ask. Don't assume the information will be freely offered.

While restoration is an accepted practice, one should recognize that there are collectors who would prefer that the old piece of history reflect its age and use. While very few would want a rusty piece of junk, the preference often leans toward the finely made piece seasoned with patina, mild pitting or signs of handle wear instead of a shiny piece that has had the flavor buffed away or removed by an overly enthusiastic "cleaner-upper." It becomes a matter of individual and personal taste, but one that deserves consideration before committing a rare old antique for restoration.

Counterfeiting

In one sentence above, a fine-line distinction was made (intent) between a restored knife and a counterfeit. But what about the outright counterfeit, the imitation of an old Remington, Case or Winchester represented as a genuine valuable knife? Fortunately, there are very few counterfeiters who possess sufficient skill and the necessary equipment to make a foolproof counterfeit knife. But there are those who are able to fool the inexperienced or naive collector, and even the expert can be fooled on occasion.

In discussing counterfeit knives, we should recognize that there are three classes, or grades, of counterfeits. The first consists of those that have been so poorly reworked that they would only deceive the most naive or truly neophyte collector. While one would think that such poorly constructed counterfeits would never find their way into the trading circles, that is far from the truth. Their presence is not unusual at flea markets, occasional auctions and—yes—even at knife shows. By reasonably close observation and comparison with other knives, these knives are relatively easy to spot.

The second classification of counterfeits are those that are more difficult to detect. They will usually deceive the novice and occasionally the experienced collector alike. The workmanship used in remaking the knife is of sufficiently high quality that collectors who are considered experts often disagree as to whether the knife is in fact a counterfeit and just what is correct or incorrect about it. Still, the seasoned collectors' evaluation and advice should be sought whenever there is any reason to doubt a knife's authenticity. It is not unusual for the experienced collector to ask for the opinion of his peers and no one should be ashamed to seek help.

While it's possible that the third classification is purely hypothetical, it likely exists in actuality, even if in small numbers. These are the counterfeit knives that are so masterfully done that they can even deceive a group of experts; only the craftsperson who masterminded and created the deception knows for sure.

There are several methods or combinations of methods that an unscrupulous person may use to counterfeit a knife. The more common "tricks" that a counterfeiter is likely to try include, but certainly are not limited to the following:

Grinding off the original tang stamp and restamping the blade tang with one that was used on a knife of much greater value.

Removing the master blade and/or other blades and replacing them with blades from an older, more valuable knife.

Replacing the handles of a knife with a different type as would have been used on more expensive knives of the same frame pattern and blade designs.

Using a knife with blades that are badly worn but with good quality tangs and welding on new blades to replace those that are worn.

Taking old knife parts and making them into a complete knife that has collector appeal and value.

Replacing or adding a shield to the knife handle, thereby making the knife appear to be older or of greater value than it actually is.

Re-etching blades that have been cleaned and/or refinished, thereby making them appear to have had much less use and wear.

Artificially aging a knife to make it appear to be older than it really is.

Taking knives, old or new, that were not stamped and stamping the mark of a rare knife.

In order to guard against the counterfeit, there are several precautions to take or areas to closely watch. A key one is to know your knives. Learn as much as possible about materials used, methods of manufacture, patterns, stampings, dates that particular features were commonly used, etc. Since it's impossible to know everything, don't be too shy or too proud to ask the opinion of a reputable and knowledgeable collector.

Look for signs of work on the knife. A near new blade or handle on a knife that is otherwise well worn should arouse suspicion just as should marks on the inside of the knife, which may indicate it has been taken apart. Do the handles match and are they correct for the knife in question? A large percentage of the old Remington, Winchester, Case, Queen and most other popular brands have their own distinct jigging pattern on their bone or bone stag handles. Check also to see if the handles have been glued onto the liners or if the shield has been glued into the handle rather than pinned or riveted on.

Are blades and backsprings in similar condition and of the same thickness? Does the thickness of the blade tang indicate that it may have been ground down for restamping? Use your magnifying glass to closely examine the stampings and, if suspicious, compare them with those on other knives you know to be correct.

Do the rivets look original in form, color and fit? Do the parts seem to belong together as units of the whole knife? Not only should they physically fit one with the other but they should be in keeping one with another. If the liners are brass, usually the pins and rivets are brass; if one is nickel silver, chances are good that the other should be also.

In short, you must be able to spot inconsistencies, either in the piece or in the story behind it—or in both. Use intelligence and common sense to evaluate what your eyes see, what your hands feel and what your ears hear—above all, listen to your intuition.

There are times when intuition may be the deciding factor and the decision may be to buy the knife. After all, there are knives that are extremely unusual but are not counterfeit. Knives in this category may be salesman or customer samples of knives or prototypes that were never put into production and aren't found listed in catalogs or perhaps any company records. On occasion, knife company executives may have asked for a few special knives to be used as gifts. Since there was no thought at the time they were done—fifty, seventy-five or a hundred years ago—that someday these knives would be prized collectibles, no one gave any thought to cataloging or maintaining records. New finds are not so unusual and one of them might be your own.

Any discussion of counterfeiting is sure to concoct negative thoughts about knives and knife collecting. But, let's finish this chapter by putting things into proper perspective within the overall market. There are thousands of collectible knives bought, sold and traded each month. Although no one knows the percentage that are counterfeit, practically all experienced collectors would agree that it is very, very small. Yes, even one counterfeit is too many, but there are large collections of antique knives that are totally genuine. Yours can be too. At the beginning of this chapter, knife collecting was referred to as a wholesome hobby. It was, it is, and it will continue to be. Enjoy!

FACTORS AFFECTING KNIFE VALUES

The axiom that an item's value is precisely the amount of money or goods that a seller is willing to accept and a buyer is willing to pay is never so true as within the collector market. Value must stand this test and does so numerous times every day and in almost any location. In any situation, the two perceptions of value are that of the prospective seller and the prospective buyer. Whenever the two are compromised and the knife changes ownership, true value for that knife at that time and that place has been established. It may be different at another time, another place and with other prospective trade partners. Still, in spite of the variables, this measurement signifies true value because it directly relates to the willing buyer/seller axiom. Another type of value is mentioned here only because it seems to be so prominent in any collecting field. It is value perceived and that value may or may not pass the market test. This very personal value is one that a collector often places upon knives or other possessions. Knives that are of special significance to their owner may be "valued" at several times the amount that they would bring in the market place. Often, the knife is really not for sale; if that is the case, value is a moot point anyway.

The value estimates presented in this guide are what one can expect to find in a "typical," if there is in fact such a thing, marketplace. There are numerous factors that affect the value of a knife as a collectible. Primary considerations are first with the knife itself and include things such as age, manufacturer, brand stamping, pattern, number of blades, handle material, shield, rarity and condition.

A knife's brand, manufacturer and stamping are fundamental to the collector value of a knife. Although age is usually of importance, it does not always directly relate with value. Just because a knife is 50 or 150 years old doesn't mean that its value is higher than a knife of more recent manufacture. Likewise, relating quality to value can be misleading. Some extremely well-made knives are not so highly valued as those of perhaps lesser quality but greater desirability in the marketplace. The importance of brand stamping can be illustrated by considering two old and near identical knives made by Camillus, their difference being the brand stamping. Ironically, the contract knife is often valued higher than the one marketed with the manufacturer's own brand stamping.

Rarity plays a significant role in establishing the value of any collectible. To a degree, the numbers of knives produced contributes to rarity, but this is not always true. For instance, Remington produced near unbelievable numbers of some knife patterns but, because they were intended for use and they were well used, the relatively few found in mint condition are highly valued. On the other hand, there are knives of relatively recent production that were produced in very limited numbers and were seldom used. Rarity can also relate directly to specific patterns, handle materials, stampings or a variety of other things.

Directly related to rarity (supply and demand) is locality. The collector should be aware that time and place has a significant effect upon the buying and selling price of a knife. We're not speaking of the good fortune known as "being in the right place at the right time" or the distress sale factor but, instead, the direct relationship of supply and demand within varying locations. To recognize and appreciate these geographical area variations, one only needs to visit with a few dealers at knife shows in various parts of the country. A dealer from the southeast may have attended a northwestern show and sold very few knives. Still, because he has been able to purchase knives known to return a profit in other areas, participation in the show may be considered very rewarding.

The universally accepted variable affecting value is condition and it should always be kept in mind when referring to this or other pricing guides. Grading the condition of a knife varies with the individual and is almost always interpreted differently and not impartially by the prospective buyer and the seller. The most widely accepted guidelines, however, are those established by the National Knife Collectors Association and described below. These grading definitions were intended to apply specifically to antique or other collector-grade pocketknives, but the terms may be helpful also in grading other knives such as military knives, modern custom knives or antique bowies.

Mint: A knife that is absolutely original as it came from the manufacturer. Never used, carried, sharpened, or heavily cleaned. An unblemished knife.

Near Mint: A new condition knife that may show very slight signs of carry or shop wear. Blades are not worn and snap perfectly. Handles show no cracks. Most of original finish is obvious.

Excellent: A knife that shows no more than 10% blade wear. Handles are sound with no cracks. Blades snap well. Some discoloration of blades or handles is acceptable. May have been heavily cleaned.

Very Good: A knife with up to 25% blade wear and slight cracks in handles. No blades or other parts have been replaced or repaired. Stamping is clearly visible to the naked eye.

Fair: A knife with up to 50% blade wear and cracks or chips in handles. Blades are "lazy" (lacking snap) and may have been repaired. Stamping is faint but readable with magnifying glass.

Poor: Blades are very worn or may have been replaced with ones of same type. Handles are bad or missing. Reading of stamping is near impossible. A knife valued only for its parts.

Unless otherwise specified, the value guides offered in this book are for knives in mint condition. A knife that has been sharpened after leaving the factory may be near to mint condition but it definitely is not a mint knife and its value is approximately no more than 70% of a true mint knife. As the knife's condition grading further diminishes, so does its value. At or near the bottom of the grading scale (poor to fair), a knife may bring no more than 10% of its mint value.

When using this or any other pricing reference work, one should always be mindful that they are guides and only guides. Used as such, to enhance one's knowledge of specific areas of interest or of knife prices in general, pricing guides are valuable aids to buyer and seller alike. When mistakenly used as "gospel," without consideration of other circumstances, the pricing guide loses much of its potential value to both the buyer and seller. Hopefully, this book will be a guide not only to prices, but also to greater pleasures and profits to be found in the knife collecting hobby.

FUTURE OUTLOOK

One can not review the progress made during recent years or witness the atmosphere of the knife collecting community without a great deal of optimism. The number of collectors continues to grow and their collecting interests are diversifying into fields that lay near dormant a few short years ago. The increasing availability of reference materials has positively affected the popularity of knives as collectibles, and that trend continues. Concurrent with the rise in collector numbers, there are new and near-limitless opportunities for personal involvement and for self-education, both of which are necessary for the health of any hobby. Collecting clubs, shows and swap meets come to mind as active holdovers from our recent past. Most notably, the Internet offers a medium for learning, sharing, buying or selling that is near staggering to the imagination.

The introduction of knife collectors to "Cyberspace" has been a revelation that could tell us that the future is already in the here and now. With access to so much information, today's knife collector has a decided advantage over those of a few short years ago who had less resources available and were necessarily dependent upon the trial and error method. Still, however, experience will remain a great teacher—especially for those who leap first and learn later. The astute collector or investor will utilize the many resources, establish goals and plan collecting activities that will help achieve these goals.

One should anticipate prices of desirable antique knives to rise continually and considerably during coming years. Finding these knives is becoming increasingly difficult and, whenever they can be found, they are already far from inexpensive. Purchasing knives for investment means that one should acquire the very best examples that the budget will allow. Because the pieces in excellent condition are becoming harder to find, expect an increasing demand for and a rather steady rise in value of knives in less than mint or excellent condition. Purchasing a desirable knife rated in good condition is an excellent hedge against future value inflation. If and when a better piece for the collection becomes available, the knife purchased earlier will go far in paying for it.

As talented craftspersons enter the field, custom knives will continue to be an exciting and growing area to watch. This specialty is, however, one that merits a great deal of attention to the information available. Selected handmade knives will represent some of the greatest investment opportunities, but, as a rule, don't expect the aftermarket in the average custom knife to be especially strong. The strength of custom knives will, by and large, remain in their appeal to pride of ownership.

Military knives—especially those used by our own country's armed forces—have become one of the nation's "hottest" cutlery collectibles during the 1990s. A few short years ago and with a few exceptions, they were items that could be bought for a relatively small investment. Already, knives that were selling for $20 in the late 1980s are being resold for ten or more times that amount. One can expect these special knives to continue to attract collectors and increase in demand and value.

Antique bowie knives represent another area that has shown phenomenal growth, in both interest and value, within a short span of time. These special knives have long been considered the preeminent example of knife collecting. They have offered challenges in the search and have been purchased at relatively high prices for several decades. Still, however, no one would have predicted the developments witnessed during the past few years as prized pieces sold for tens of thousands of dollars each time the auctioneer's gavel fell. Just before the end of 2002, one bowie sold at an auction for approximately a quarter-million dollars.

Just as antique bowies offer exciting opportunities and challenges, they offer costly disappointments as well. Counterfeits and misrepresented pieces have been around for several decades and there's now even more cause to be cautious.

During the late 1900s, limited production, commemorative and reproduction knives became specialties of opportunity. That trend continues into the 21st century. These knives had long appealed to the beginning collector but, in many cases, they have not represented significant investment opportunities. While that has not changed to a great degree, some of the greatest value increases can be found in a number of knives in this category. A theme of great interest and one to watch carefully is NASCAR. Race car fans are strongly competing with knife fans when NASCAR-related commemorative and limited edition knives are introduced. Within the constraint of wise choices, collecting special limited edition knives will offer excellent opportunities; just be sure that production is truly limited to relatively small numbers.

Reproduction knives warrant a good degree of attention, even to those who have no desire to collect them. First, they do offer the opportunity to build meaningful collections at moderate entry prices. Second, respectable though not spectacular value appreciation is near certain. Third, some of them could be the makings of tomorrow's counterfeit "antique" and the collector of antique knives surely needs to study the reproductions as a safeguard for the future.

To the majority of pocketknife collectors, Case knives have reigned as king of the collectibles during past decades. Antique knives by Case have continued to be quite desirable and valuable but, steadily increasing interest in other brands is adding diversity to the specialty of antique pocketknives. Names such as Remington, Winchester, Ka-Bar, Western States, Cattaraugus and Marbles have been respected for generations and they have long been sought as collectibles. Not only do these brands compete strongly for the collectors' time and monetary investment, they are joined by others that were recognized for quality but widely overlooked for collectibility. Robeson, Schrade, Queen and a number of other names will continue to gain in popularity and value. Case knives will no doubt hold the leadership position, but their unique position in antique pocketknife specialty has some strong challengers. Even at the premium prices realized for the more desirable patterns, these other respected brands may well be the "sleepers" of this first decade of the 21st century.

Not unlike other areas of collecting, knives have been and will continue to be subject to cyclic changes—some gradual and reasonably predictable and others relatively rapid and often surprising. At times, it appears that the only constant is the variability. But, the collector who looks toward the future with optimism tempered by knowledge will find many rewards in the hobby of collectible knives.

COLLECTING SPECIALTIES

BOWIE KNIVES

There has been no knife style that has been linked with and the subject of so much adventure, fantasy, conjecture and controversy as the one named for James Bowie. There are so many legends about Bowie and his knife that drawing distinct lines between fact and fiction have long been near impossible for historians and collectors alike.

Even his place and year of birth has been in debate for a century or more, but is now known to have been Logan County, Kentucky, in about 1795. We know that Bowie's family moved to Louisiana where he later became a planter, a land speculator and—in the meantime—a legend, even before his unforgettable death at the Alamo in 1836. His stature, in the minds and imaginations of many, became bigger than life and the knife made famous by those legends grew in renown even beyond the man himself. Although he may have had some local reputation, Bowie's fame was set afire on September 19, 1827. That's the date that an "affair of honor" took place on a Mississippi River sandbar near the town of Natchez. The duel that became a near free-for-all for the dozen or so men present came to be called the "Vidalia Sandbar Duel." The knife Bowie carried and used to save his own life, at the expense of Major Norris Wright, carved its image into history.

Through telling and retelling of the story, the excellent qualities of the knife Bowie used became near magical in the minds of those who read and heard it. Even in the absence of television, radio, satellite news transmittal and the wide screen cinema, Bowie was quickly fashioned into an early 19th century "Rambo." It seems that practically everyone wanted a knife "just like Bowie's." This country's knife makers obliged, but their efforts were dwarfed by those of cutlers from other parts of the world, especially the highly regarded Sheffield, England, cutlery center.

Although he is often credited with its invention, Jim Bowie most likely did not design the knife named for him. The knife used at the duel reportedly had been loaned to him by his brother, Rezin. The knife's basic design was by no means new in 1827 and this specific knife had been made for Rezin Bowie by a plantation blacksmith. Even if Jim Bowie did later develop or suggest a knife design, he certainly had no input into the innumerable variations that were made—many of which are still sold today as "the original Bowie knife." Just like the legends about Bowie, the styles of what became known as the bowie knife were created by colorful journalism and vivid imaginations.

But, this is not to say that the knife design was and is without merit. Far from it! It was not unlike an improvement, with specific purposes in mind, upon the butcher knife or chef's knife. The primary purpose for the bowie knife as well as for the variations made before and after 1827 was fighting; whether defensive or offensive mattered not. It was a knife designed to take a life or to save a life by taking one in exchange. The cap and ball pistol had superseded the sword as a primary weapon but it had its shortcomings. Consequently, even if two small pistols were carried, there needed to be a backup weapon. Knives of the dagger type had been used for centuries and, after its ballooning reputation, the bowie knife was envisioned as the ideal compliment to the single shot and not-so-trustworthy pistol.

Students of the bowie knife, along with students of close combat, will verify that "a knife like Bowie's" could often have made the difference in a life and death encounter. The fact that the knives that became so popular after Bowie's well publicized duel may or may not have been just like the one used on the sandbar does not detract from the utility of the knives that would become known as bowies. Regardless of knives marked and/or marketed as a reproduction of the original Bowie knife, there is still an absence of documentation that would tell or show us the exact design of either the knife Jim Bowie used in 1827 or in

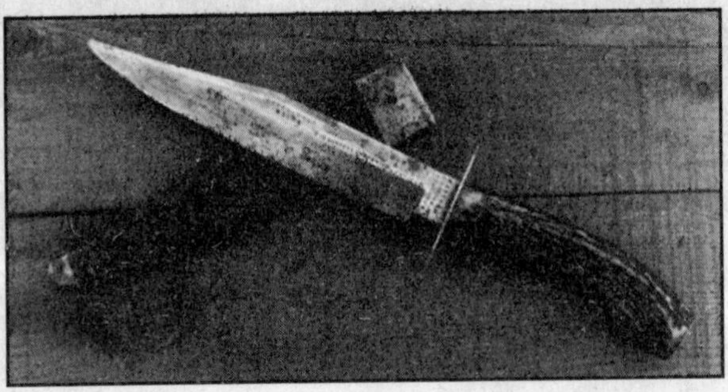

Left:
Edward Barnes & Sons, Sheffield, c.1850s. 6½" clip point bowie, one-piece stag handle, blade stamped with hunting scene, excellent condition. $1000. Without scene on blade, $450. Original sheath adds 10% (missing tip).
(Photo by Mark Zalesky, courtesy of Knife World*)*

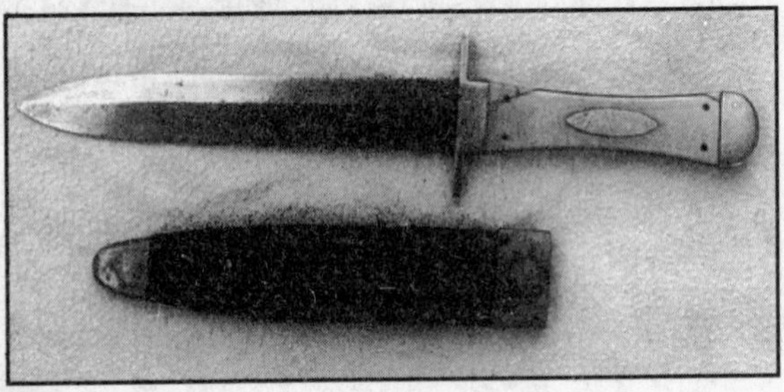

Right:
G. Woodhead, Sheffield, c.1850s. 6⅛" spear point bowie, two-piece ivory handles, excellent condition (minor cracks). $1100. If stag handles, $700. Original sheath adds 10% (replacement tip).
(Photo by Mark Zalesky, courtesy of Knife World*)*

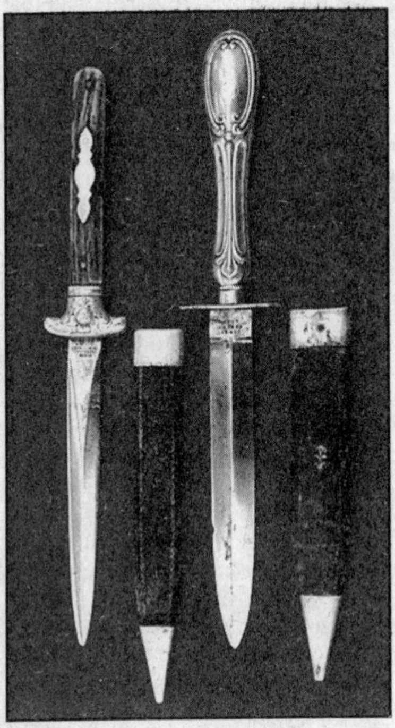

Left: (L to R)
Marsh Bros. & Co., Sheffield, c.1850s–60s. 4½" double edge dirk, two-piece stag handles, ornate shield, floral patterned guard, excellent condition. $375. With plain trim and shield, $250.
and . . .
Henry Hobson, Sheffield, c.1860s–70s. 4⅞" double edge dirk, metal "cutlery" handle, blade etched "Self Protector," excellent condition. $400. Without etch $225 (etches with better themes more). Original sheaths add 15%.
(Photo by Mark Zalesky, courtesy of Knife World*)*

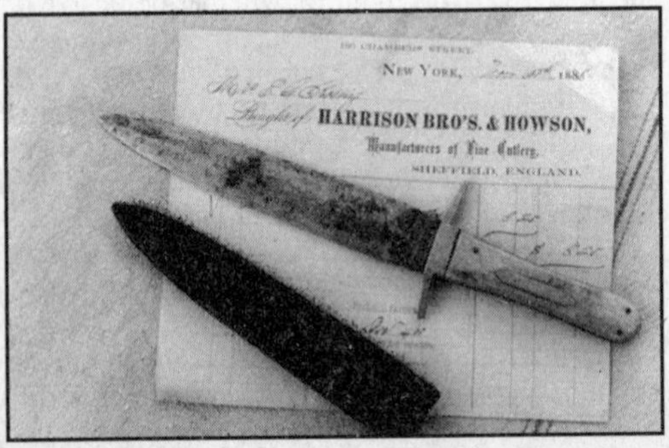

Right:
Harrison Bros. & Howson, Sheffield, c.1860s. 7¼" double edged bowie, two-piece ivory handles, excellent condition. $750. If stag handles, $450. Original sheath adds 15%.
(Photo by Mark Zalesky, courtesy of Knife World*)*

Left:
Jonathan Crookes, Sheffield c.1880s–90s. 6" bowie-hunter. Jigged bone handles. The handle's taper towards the butt, the flat guard, and clip blade clearly identify this as a late bowie-style hunting knife. Jigged bone was never used on pre-1880s bowies. Exc. condition. $130. Sheath a later replacement.
(Photo by Kipp Baker, courtesy of Knife World*)*

Right:
Buck Bros., Worchester, Mass. c.1860s. 7 1/4" double edge bowie. Turned wooden handle, excellent plus condition. $1500. If very good condition, $900. Most true American bowie makers more.
(Photo by Mark Zalesky, courtesy of Knife World*)*

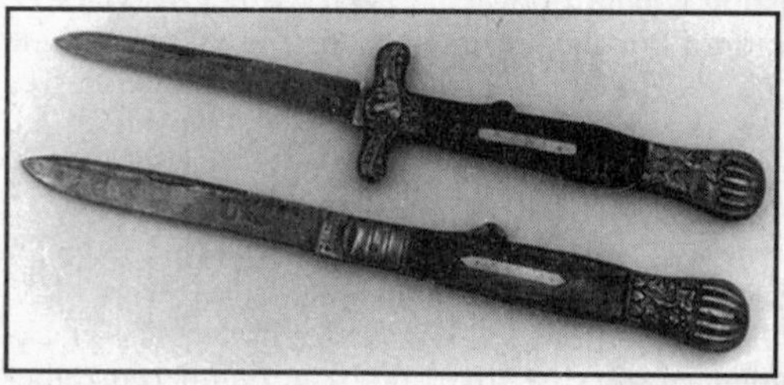

Above (T to B)
R. Bunting and Son, Sheffield c.1860s. 5 1/8" closed folding dirk knife. Horn handle, ornate pommel, "Liberty and Union" guard, lockback feature. Very good condition. $500. If excellent, $1200. and . . .
R. Bunting and Son, Sheffield c.1860s. 5 1/4" closed folding dirk knife. Horn handle, ornate pommel, fileworked front bolster (no guard), lockblade feature. Excellent condition. $550. With floral pattern guard, $900.
(Photo by Mark Zalesky, courtesy of Knife World*)*

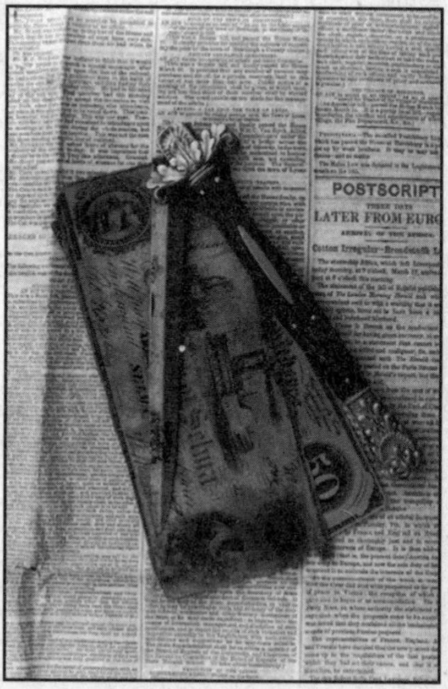

Right:
S. C. Wragg, Sheffield, c.1840s. 7 1/8" closed folding dirk knife. Ornate trim, stag handles, lockback feature, excellent plus condition. $4000. Large, superb example. Smaller knives significantly less.
(Photo by Mark Zalesky, courtesy of Knife World*)*

1836 at the Alamo. Bowie knives of both 19th- and 20th-century origins are variations, limited only by the imagination, of a very sensible piece of combat cutlery. Those that were made and sold in the 1800s as bowies had blades that could be considered as relatively short or long for a fighting knife. The blades were both double and single edged and they had either spear or clip points or variations of the two. The fact that the thousands upon thousands made and sold were not in fact "exactly like Bowie's" made little difference. They were formidable knives; they still are.

As the 19th century drew to a close, there was less need—either imagined or real—for such a weapon. In fact, the knife earned such a reputation that several states had prohibited the wearing, sale or ownership of these knives. Some of these laws are still on the books. The primary factor, however, in the diminishing demand for the bowie knife was developed by a man named Samuel Colt. And, as the revolver became more reliable, the perception of the need for a large backup knife diminished. The "Iron Mistress" was not quite so necessary, but today, it is often considered the king of cutlery collectibles.

The Knives Called Bowies

Preceding editions of this book referred to bowie knife prices by stating, "The quality pieces are held in such high regard that price often takes second place to ownership—whether it's the prospective buyer or seller who wants most to call the piece his own." The truth in this statement was brought home when, in early 1992, an auction of rare and beautiful bowie knives saw prices far above what anyone would have expected. When a large share of the pieces sold brought prices well into five figures and one bowie sold for more than $130,000, high-dollar gamesmanship was surely at play. Whether you intend to actively join the fraternity of bowie collectors in the high-dollar game or to share the excitement from the sidelines, learning more about bowies is in order.

Earlier editions have listed a large number of bowie makers and markings, but have not offered specific value information. The listing which follows has been written by Mark D. Zalesky. As a researcher, writer and collector of knives—one with a "first love" for antique bowie knives—Mark is well qualified to do so. His listing and evaluation guide addresses the majority of bowies that a collector is likely to encounter. It is arguably the most accurate and practical bowie knife maker listing ever published and is likely the most comprehensive bowie value guide extant.

It is impossible to know every maker of bowie knives, but the listing includes the major 19th-century makers whose knives one may encounter. Bear in mind that knives were often made in those days by craftsmen bearing titles other than knife maker or cutler. The blacksmith, the gun maker, the surgical instrument maker, the silversmith, and numerous other tradesmen were called upon to make knives along with the established cutlers. The knives they made during the 1800s are, in the majority, highly desirable as collectibles. It should be no surprise, therefore, that their prices are normally quite high. The majority of bowies a collector will encounter came from Sheffield, England, and only a small percentage were made in this country. Whether of U.S. or other origin, top-grade bowies command prices into the thousands of dollars.

An antique bowie knife must be evaluated upon its own specific merits. Size, period, style, quality, condition, appearance and maker are all determining factors to value. Most antique bowies one will encounter are one-of-a-kind pieces and deserve individual evaluation. Some generalized guidelines are offered, however, so that one may conclude an approximate range of value.

With the exception of the most important American makers, condition, size, style and approximate age are more important factors in determining value than the maker of the knife. The value guide associated with the following list is based on the rarity of and demand for the types of knives usually found with each particular maker's mark. As many makers produced knives over a long period of time and in varying degrees of quality, it is to be stressed that the valuing information provided with the following list is a guide and that determining an accurate value can only be accomplished by careful study of how all factors interrelate with demand on the collector market.

For instance, bowies made in this country during the first quarter to half of the 19th century most always demand prices of $1,000 and up. If made by well-known and respected makers and if their condition is extremely good, prices into the tens of thousands are not uncommon. Don't expect that every bowie made in the early 1800s would be valued at $10,000, but it would not be unusual to learn that quite a few, if in excellent condition, would be worth $5,000 to $15,000. Those made in the later half of the 1800s by individual makers or even some made by cutlery manufacturers could be valued from a couple hundred dollars to over $2,500.

Although not generally valued as highly, bowies imported from other countries during the same periods may range in value from $400 to several thousand dollars, depending again upon the period, maker, materials, decoration and—as always—condition.

Bowie Knives—Makers, Markings and Value Guides

by Mark D. Zalesky

Due to space constraints, it is not possible to list every known bowie knife maker in this book. The following listing has been compiled from published sources and from my research to be an accurate and practical guide of reasonable length and, as such, of benefit to both novice and advanced bowie collectors. Our thanks go out to Bernard Levine, John Goins, Geoffrey Tweedale and countless others for their contributions in this area of study.

Most Confederate bowies are unmarked and relatively crude. Due to these factors and the demand for this type of knife, a majority of the knives of this type offered for sale are fakes, and experience combined with careful study is the only logical way to approach collecting them. A well-read skeptic may gather a small collection, but he or she will avoid a boxful of expensive mistakes.

An approximate value guide to dirk and folding dirk knives is included as well. These knives were the smaller counterparts to the bowie knife, and were produced by the same makers and carried for many of the same reasons that their larger brethren were. In the last several years, collector interest has surged in these types of knives, due in large part to the fact that prices for better-than-average bowies have climbed beyond the realm of the average collector.

Bowie-style hunting knives ("bowie hunters" for short) are a type of knife that came to prominence in the 1870s and 1880s, sufficiently resembling the bowies in profile to attract those who thought that this was what an ideal hunting knife should look like. The vast majority of these knives bear a saber-ground clip point blade, a flat double guard, and two-piece handles of either stag, jigged bone or black imitation stag, tapering slightly towards the butt. While these knives have a place in history, they do not as yet carry the same collector interest as the older knives and should not be confused with them. With the exception of a few American brands, Rodgers, Wostenholms and those of large size, these knives are rarely worth more than $250 each.

In addition to the dates given below, the use or nonuse of a country-of-origin mark can be helpful in determining the age of specific examples. Bear in mind, though, that knives made for sale outside the U.S. were not required to utilize this marking. Also, English knives can often be dated by the use of the reigning monarch's cipher, or the use of "His" or "Her Majesty." The silver fruit knife listings indicate the periods and they are designated as well in the chart located on page 113.

Our suggestion is that the list be used to help identify a bowie's time and place of origin as well as to determine its maker. From that point, a great deal of research into the specific knife may be in order. Whether or not the knife in question has a value into the five figure area, using the bowie as a vehicle for a trip back into history makes the world of antique bowies worthy of considerable collector interest.

Some general characteristics that affect a knife's value are:

Condition: Knives of the bowie era are very rarely found in a condition approaching mint. Those that are demand a significant premium.

Style/appearance: Style can be an overwhelming factor in determining the value of a bowie knife. Those that are highly popular with collectors will demand large sums of money regardless of the marking on the tang. For example, a superbly crafted knife of the early and rare "dog-bone" handle style brought $85,000 at auction in early 1997, despite the fact that the blade was unmarked and bore moderate pitting.

Blade length: Bigger knives are always more desirable than smaller ones. Be aware, however, that a large percentage of fake bowie knives are excessively large and heavy, to the point of being a tip-off to their true age.

Blade shape: Generally speaking, a clip point is more desirable than a spear point, which is more desirable than a double-edged (dagger-style) blade. Overall appearance and personal taste prevail, however.

Age: Early knives are much more desirable than later ones, with the 1860s being the decade of greatest production due in no small part to the Civil War.

<— less desirable . . . . . more desirable —>
<1880+--------1870s--------1860s--------1850s--------1840s--------1830s>

Handle materials: Stag is the most commonly found handle material on both American and foreign knives. All else being equal, the more fragile and expensive materials demand higher collector values.

<— less desirable . . . . . more desirable —>
<Enamel/Metal/Wood---Bone----Horn----Stag----Pearl/Tortoiseshell----Ivory>

Etched or stamped mottoes, scenes or advertising [not including trademarks]: Add to the value of a knife to varying degrees depending on the rarity of and demand for the device in question.

Handles/blades with patriotic or other "interesting" themes: In keeping with the period during which many of these knives were produced, patriotic devices such as eagles and liberty caps, mottoes such as "Liberty and Union," and military figures such as Zachary Taylor were popular with the young men heading off to war. Their popularity remains with the collectors of today.

Original sheath: adds 10–20% to a knife's value. Original all-metal sheaths will bring an additional premium.

For **bowie knives** (6″–8″ blade, without excessive adornment or unusual features)
[*: $100–$300] [**: $300–$700] [***: $700–$1200] [****: $1200–$2500] [*****: $2500+]
For **dirk knives** (4″–6″ blade, without excessive adornment or unusual features)
[*: $70–$200] [**: $200–$350] [***: $350–$550] [****: $550–$1200] [*****: $1200+]
For **folding dirk knives**, one or two blades (ornate mounts with crossguard, lockback feature) 4½″–6″ closed
[*: $75–$350] [**: $500–$750] [***: $750–$1200] [****/*****: $1200+]
Deduct for no crossguard, no pommel, plain mounts or no locking feature.
Add 100% for switchblade mechanism.
For **folding bowies** [extra large and heavy lockbacks with ornate nickel silver mounts, including crossguard], values start at $2000 and go up from there.

Key:
[VALUE]-[**MAKER**]-[LOCATION]-[**TRADEMARK (uppercase-text, lowercase-picture)**]-[DATES]-[INFO]

** **Alexander**, Sheffield. **[N(shield)Y]** c.1850–1876. R. H. Alexander was a New York importer of and dealer in Sheffield-made cutlery. A great many small dirks and bowies are found bearing his mark.

* **Joseph Allen & Sons**, Sheffield. **[NON-XLL]** c.1864–1959. Allen was probably the most prolific maker of dirk knives and bowie-style hunting knives in the late 19th and early 20th centuries.

**** **Nathan Peabody Ames**, Chicopee, Mass. c.1829–47. Maker of some one-of-a-kind bowies.

**** **Ames Mfg. Co.**, Cabotville and Chicopee, Mass. c.1829–1900. America's premier sword makers also produced the 1849 Riflemans knife, 1861 Riflemans knife and Dahlgren bowie-bayonet for the U.S. military, as well as private purchase knives. Their knives tend to show certain sword-like characteristics.

** **Aragon**, 7 Aldama & 44 Rayon, Oaxaca, Mexico. c.1860s–present. One of few known Mexican makers.

** **Arnachellum**, Salem, Madras, India. c.19th c. India-based maker of good quality bowie-style knives.

**** **John Ashmore**, Philadelphia, Penn. c.1832–50. Maker of relatively simple bowies and other knives.

** **Austin**, Trinchopoly, Madras, India. c.19th c. India-based maker of quality bowie-style knives.

** **Edward Barnes & Sons**, Edward and Solly Streets, Sheffield. **[U*S]** c.1833–76. This firm was a prolific maker of bowie and dirk knives, both fixed and folding. Sometimes only their trademark was used.

** **Fred Barnes**, Tower Hill, Sheffield. c.19th c.

** **Isaac Barnes**, 103 Broad Lane and 9 Suffolk St. (1864), Sheffield. c.1837–70

* **J. & J. Beal**, Red Hill Works, 8 Silver St., Sheffield. **[ENDURE/boar]** c.1871–1953. Late bowie maker.

**** **Amos Belknap**, St. Johnsbury, Vt. c.1839–83. Belknap was a blacksmith who made several bowie knives.

**** **John Belknap**, St. Johnsbury, Vt. c.1860s. Son of Amos, John was a gunsmith who made knives as well.

***** **Samuel Bell**, Knoxville, Tenn. c.1819–52, San Antonio, Texas c.1852–82. Knives stamped with the Knoxville mark were Sheffield-made for Bell; most of his own knives were unmarked. Beware of fakes.

** **Best English Cutlery**. Unidentified mark found on mid-19th century Sheffield-made knives.

***** **James Black**, Washington, Ark. c.1826–39. Claimed to have made a knife for James Bowie. There is a great deal of controversy surrounding Black and his claim, and it is doubtful that we will ever know the truth about the "first" bowie knife maker, whoever it may be. No marked knives are known.

* **Edwin Blyde & Co.**, Charleston Works, Sheffield. c.1870–1953. Late maker of bowie-style hunting knives.

* **John Blyde**, Burgess St., Sheffield. **[GENIUS/saturn]** c.1841–1950s. Maker of mainly later knives.

** **Henry Carr Booth & Co.**, Norfolk Works, 20 Norfolk Lane, Sheffield. c.1856–76.

**** **Martin L. Bradford (& Son)**, Boston, Mass. c.1845–65. A dealer in sporting goods, the few Bradford knives known may have been made by the Hassam brothers.

** **Bridgeport Gun Implement (B.G.I.) Co.**, c.1876–1907. This retailer of guns and accessories (including fast-draw rigs) had bowie-style hunters made for them. At least some of their blades were imported.

** **William Broadhurst & Son**, 27 Westfield Tce., Sheffield. **[NON-XLL]** c.1849–70.

** **Brookes & Crookes**, Atlantic Works, 55 St. Phillips Rd., Sheffield. **[bell]** c.1858–1957.

** **Abram Brooksbank**, Malinda St., Sheffield. **[DEFIANCE/cannon]** c.1849–1965. Produced largely folding knives.

***** **Broomhead & Thomas**, Sheffield. c.19th c. Maker of a very few early, top-notch English bowies. Beware of fakes.

*** **John Brown & Co.**, Atlas and Columbia Works, Sheffield. c.?–1839. Bowie/dirk knife and steel maker.

**** **Buck Brothers**, Worchester, Mass. c.1853–64, Millbury, Mass. 1864–1900s. Edged tool makers, made simple wood-handled bowies during the Civil War.

*** **Robert Bunting**, Radford St. and 39 Regent St., Sheffield. c.1825–41.

*** **Robert Bunting & Son**, Columbia Works, 39 Regent, 10 Howard, and West Streets, Sheffield. c.1841–50.

*** **Richard Bunting**, Sheffield. c.1850–83. The Buntings were specialists in folding bowies and dirks, and made some fine nonfolders as well.

**** **Burger & Bros.**, Eighth and Arch Streets, Richmond, Va. c.1860s. This firm made bowies for the CSA.

** **James Burnand & Sons**, Leicaster Works, Sheffield. **[SELF-DEFENCE/indian]** c.1850–1930. Many of this firm's knives are marked only with their trademark.

*** **Samuel Butcher**, Sheffield.

***** **William Butcher**, Sheffield.

***** **W. & S. Butcher**, Eyre Lane, Arundel and Furnival Streets, Sheffield. c.1819–1959. William & Samuel Butcher were makers of some very fine early bowie knives. Later knives are marked Wade and Butcher.

* **George Butler & Co.**, Trinity Works, Sheffield. **[ART]** c.1768–1952. Maker of late bowie-type knives.

* **Cambridge Cutlery Works**, Sheffield. Maker of late 19th-century bowie-type knives.

* **Challenge Cutlery Co.**, Sheffield. c.1877–1914. Mark used by cutlery importing firm Wiebusch and Hilger of New York on late English made bowie-style hunting knives.

***** **John D. Chevalier**, 360 Broadway, New York. c.1835–59.

***** **John D. Chevalier & Sons**, New York. c.1859–66. Chevalier was a dental instrument maker who also produced many fine bowie knives, from plain to ornate.

* **John Clarke & Son**, Harvest Lane and Mowbray St., Sheffield. c.1848–1983.

*** **John Coe**, Albion Works, 23 Burgess St. & 18 Green Lane, Sheffield. c.1849–88. Coe's knives often feature "cyphered" blades.

** **Collins & Co.**, Hartford, Conn. c.1826–1966. Axe and machete maker, some of their production falls into the bowie knife category.

***** **Charles Congreve**, Gell and Arundel Streets, Sheffield. c.1833–41. Perhaps the most desired of all the Sheffield bowie and folding bowie makers, Congreve's knives are often large and ornate. Beware of fakes.

** **Corsan, Denton & Co.**, 105 Eyre St., Sheffield. c.1850–52.

** **Corsan, Denton, Burdekin & Co.**, 105 Eyre St., Sheffield. c.1852–62. This firm made a variety of bowies and dirks for the U.S. market.

**** **Ward M. Cotton**, Leominster, Mass. c.1829–75. Machinery mfr., made some simple bowies in the 1860s.

** **Crookes Brothers**, Sheffield. c.1856–1893. Maker of typical small bowies and dirks in the mid–1800s.

*** **G. Crookes & Co.**, 2 Anson St. & 95 Norfolk St., Sheffield. c.1836–56. Maker of quality folders and fixed blades.

** **Crookes & Co.**, Sheffield. c.1856–67. Successors to the above firm.

**** **Jonathan Crookes**, Rockingham and Baily Lanes, and Eldon St., Sheffield. **[heart & pistol]** c.1827–1914. Crookes made both early bowies and late bowie-hunters. Beware of knives made in the 1970s and 1980s by Sheffield's H. M. Slater.

*** **Abraham Davy**, Springlane, Brookhall St., Sheffield. c. 1836–56.

*** **Abraham Davy & Sons**, Exchange Works, Headford St., Sheffield. c.1856–70. Davy seems to have made a number of folding knives, as well as some fixed-blade bowies and dirks.

* **E. M. Dickinson**, Murray Works, Sheffield. **[INVICTA/wood screw]** c.1880–1940. Maker of late knives; both average and high quality.

** **James Dixon & Son**, Cornish Place, Sheffield. **[trumpet & banner]** c.1805–1990. Primarily a powder flask maker, produced knives as well.

**** **Charles B. Drabble**, Fitzwilliam St., Sheffield. c.1836.

**** **Enoch Drabble**, 28 Bailey St., Sheffield. c.1833–39. Both Drabbles were considered desirable makers of fine, early knives.

***** **Alfred H. Dufilho**, New Orleans. c.1853–78. Maker of Confederate swords, as well as fine bowie knives and push daggers.

*** **Thomas Ellin & Co.**, Sylvester Works, 273 Arundel St., Sheffield. **[vulcan]** c.1797–1933. Few bowie-type knives known.

** **Joseph Elliot & Sons**, Hollis Croft, Sheffield. **[maltese cross surrounded by two *Cs*]** c.1795–1990. Maker of some early knives as well as late bowie-style hunting knives.

***** **J. English**, Philadelphia, Penn. 1819–1828, 1837–40; Newark, N.J. 1830-34, 1842-53.

***** **Joseph English & Henry & F. A. Huber**, Sheffield Works, Philadelphia, Penn. c.1834–37. Maker of some distictive early bowies with studded, waisted handles, as well as a few plainer knives. See Henry Huber.

** **Eyre, Ward & Co.**, Sheaf Works, Sheffield. c.1852–59. Maker of mainly smaller bowies and dirks.

**** **Fenton & Shore**, 46 Division St. and 6 Suffolk St., Sheffield. c.1833–62. Made a few fine horsehead pommel bowie knives.

** **H. M. Finch**. c.19th c. Nothing is known about Finch, but his knives appear to be post–Civil War and of English manufacture.

***** **Rees Fitzpatrick**, Baton Rouge, La. c.1833–39, Natchez, Miss. c.1839–67. Very desirable maker of superb early American bowies.

** **G. Gelston & Son**, New York.

** **G. Gelston Mfg. Co.**, New York. c.1892. This firm may have been an importer of Sheffield-made knives.

** **William Gilchrist**. **[bow]** c.1852–61. An importer of English-made cutlery, located in New York, Jersey City, N.J., and Philadelphia, successively.

***** **F. C. Goergen**, New Orleans. c.1840s–49. Offered distinctive bowies etched with humorous mottoes. It's not known whether these knives were imported or domestic.

**** **W. R. Goulding**, New York. c.1837–53. Goulding was primarily a surgical instrument maker, but made a few bowies as well.

***** **Graveley and Wreaks**, New York. c.1830–37. Importers of and dealers in bowie knives and other items. Several fine, early examples of both English and American manufacture are marked with this firm's name.

** **William Greaves & Sons**, Sheaf Works, Sheffield. c.1724–1877. Not many knives are seen with this famous firm's mark, those that are span the range from very early to relatively late.

** **Hall & Colley**, 32 Arundel St. (to 1856) and 9 Eyre Lane (1856–1876), Sheffield. c.1849–76. Few bowie-style knives known by this maker.

** **George Hancock & Sons**, 15 South St., Sheffield. c.19th c.

** **Samuel Hancock & Son**, Peacroft and Mazeppa Works, Sheffield. **[MAZEPPA/man on horse]** c.1841–1914. Made a variety of knives for the U.S. market, many marked only with the firm's trademark.

** **Hargreaves, Smith & Co.**, 28 Eyre Lane, Sheffield. c.1841–1959.

** **Harrison Bros. & Howson**, 45 Norfolk St., Sheffield. **[ALPHA/crown]** c.1847–1959. This firm manufactured fine quality bowies and dirks as well as fancy tableware and other silver goods.

***** **Frederick F. Hassam**, Boston. c.1853–56.

***** **Hassam Bros.**, 146 Washington St., Boston. c.1860–66. Makers of distinctive stag and carved ivory handled bowies. Beware of fakes, many of which do not even resemble real Hassams.

***** **M. J. Hayes & Son**, San Francisco. c.1887–1901. Maker of superb knives in the California style.

** **Joseph Haywood**, Glamorgan Works, Victoria, Holly, and Garden Streets, Sheffield. **[teapot]** c.1843–1902. Well-made knives both early and late.

**** **Rochus Heinisch**, Newark, N.J. c.1825–1914. This world-famous scissor and shear maker made a handful of unusual bowies with cast iron handles. A few are known in other materials as well.

***** **A. G. Hicks**, Cleveland, Ohio. c.1857–66 (earlier?) This maker of wooden planes has been given credit for making the first knives issued to U.S. troops. Recent research has not been able to back this claim up.

** **Hill & Co.**, 4 Haymarket, London. c.19th c. Maker of London-style hunting knives.

*** **George Willis Hinchliffe**, 87 Eyre St., Sheffield. c.1839–43. Succeeded by his nephew, Joseph Haywood.

*** **John Hinchliffe**, Hermitage St. & 20 Earl St., Sheffield. c.1837–62. Bowies, dirks and daggers, especially folding versions.

** **Henry Hobson & Sons**, 28 Eyre Lane, Sheffield. c.1860s–1920s.

** **John B. Hobson**, Sheffield. c.1855. Maker of folding dirk knives and probably other types as well.

**** **Joseph Holmes**, 5 Cross Smithfield, Sheffield. c.1830s–40s. Maker of distinctive "Arkansaw Toothpicks" and folding dirks.

** **Holtzapffel & Co.**, 64 Charing Cross (to 1901), 13-14 New Bond St (1902–07), 53 Haymarket (1907–30), 79 Wigmore (1930–38), London. c.1828–1938. Maker of London-style hunting knives.

*** **W. & S. Horrabin**, 12 Red Hill, Sheffield. **[phoenix]** c.19th c. Few bowie-type knives known.

***** **H. Huber** Steel, Philadelphia, Penn. c.1832–33.

***** **H. Huber**, C. Steel, Philadelphia, Penn. c.1837–68. Important early American bowie maker. There is some evidence to suggest Huber made a knife for James Bowie. See English and Hubers.

*** **Nehmiah Hunt**, 128 Washington St., Boston, Mass. 1843–51. Hunt's knives are similar in style to those of other Boston makers such as Hassam.

* **W.R. Humphreys & Co.**, Advance Works, Eyre and Denby Streets, Sheffield. **[RADIANT]** c.1880–1970.

***** **Alfred Hunter**, New York. c.1830–35; 145 Quarry St. & 25 Sheffield St., Newark, N.J. c.1835–65. Very desirable American maker of bowies with rosewood or carved ivory handles.

* **Michael Hunter & Son**, Talbot Works, Saville and Reed Streets, Sheffield. **[bugle]** c.1780–1911. Generally late bowie-type knives.

*** **Ibbotson, Peace, & Co.**, Eagle Works, 84 Russell St., Sheffield. c.1845–62. A few very fine bowies are known by this firm.

** **Iver Johnson Sporting Goods Co.**, Adams Square, Boston, Mass. c.1871–1925. Had bowie-style hunting knives made for them by J. Russell & Co.

**** **Samuel Jackson**, Baltimore, Md. c.1833–70. Surgical instrument maker who produced a few bowies.

*** **William F. Jackson & Co.**, Sheaf Island Works, Pond Hill, Sheffield. c.1852–62. Most famous for the "Rio Grande Camp Knives" bearing his mark, Jackson produced a variety of cutlery for the U.S. market.

James & Lowe, Sheffield, c.1971–86??

Fred James, Sheffield. c.1971–86. James assembled bowie knives in the 1970s, using his own marks, George Wostenholm's, or those of other famous 19th-century Sheffield makers. These knives are usually identifiable by their size, weight, finish, etching styles and other distinguishing factors.

** **Christopher Johnson & Co.**, Western Works, 207 Portobello Rd., Sheffield. **[flag with "C.J."]** c.1865–1920. Generally late bowie-type knives. Trademark used by G. Wostenholm into the 1970s. Beware of modern knives made by Fred James.

***** **Frederick Kesmodel**, Baltimore, Md. c.1838–1856, c.1872–1901; 904 Powell St., San Francisco, Calif. c.1856–67. Rare make of high quality knives.

***** **Kingman & Hassam**, Boston. c.1856–60. Cutlers. See Hassam Brothers.

** **S. & J. Kitchin**, Hollis Croft and Summerfield St., Sheffield. **[FAME/snake]** c.1855–1960s. Much of their product was made for South America.

***** **Thomas Lamb**, Washington City (now D.C.) c.1843–55. Maker of surgical instruments, razors and a very few fine early bowies.

*** **Lamson & Co.**, S. Falls Works, Shelburne Falls, Mass. c.1842–44.

** **Lamson & Goodnow Mfg. Co.**, S. Falls Works, Shelbourne Falls, Mass. c.1844–present. Table cutlery manufacturer, made a few rather plain bowies as well.

* **Landers, Frary & Clark**, New Britain, Conn. c.1862–1965 (bowie types after 1890s). Makers of late bowie-style hunters in both stag and imitation stag handles, popular in the first quarter of the 20th century.

***** **J. Lasserre**, New Orleans, La. c.1860.

** **A. Leon**, Solly St., Sheffield. c.mid-19th c. While a fairly common name, little is known about this maker.

*** **Joseph Lingard**, 158 Matilda St., Sheffield. c.1842–1925.

*** **Robert Lingard**, Arundel St., Sheffield. c.1862–1890s.

*** **John Lingard**, Peacroft, Sheffield. c.1852–76.

*** **Lingard**, Peacroft, Sheffield. c.1852–76. The Lingard family tended towards ornate bowies and dirks.

** **Lockwood Bros.**, 74 Arundel St., Sheffield. **[C+X, PAMPA]** c. 1767–1933. Much of their product was made for South America.

** **J. P. Lower**, 1511 Laimer St., Denver, Colo. c.1880s. A dealer in sporting goods, Lower had some late English bowies made for his store.

** **Lund**, Fleet Street, London. c.19th c. Maker of London-style hunting knives.

***** **Hugh McConnell**, 116 Pacific St. & Jackson St., San Francisco, Calif. c.1852–63. Early very desirable maker of California-style knives.

**** **W. J. McElroy**, Macon, Ga. c.1846–88. McElroy made knives and swords for the CSA.

** **Maher & Grosh Cutlery Co.**, Toledo, Ohio. c.1877–1980s. Mail-order retailer, sold some later bowies.

* **Maleham & Yeomans**, 49 Bowdon St., Sheffield. Beware of fakes, most knives with this stamp are suspect.

** **Manhattan Cutlery Co.**, Sheffield. c.1868–1916. This trademark was owned by Boker, and is a relatively common find among bowies. It appears that the knives were made by John Newton & Co.

** **Manson**, Sheffield. c.19th c. It has been speculated that Manson was a yet-unidentified importer here in the U.S. Knives bearing his mark are relatively common and are generally considered to be of Civil War vintage.

*** **Joseph Mappin & Co.**, Sheffield. **[sun]** c.1810–41.

** **Mappin Bros.**, Queens Cutlery Works (1851–?), Sheffield. **[sun]** c.1841–1903.

** **Mappin & Webb**, 76 Eyre St., Sheffield. **[sun]** c.1868–present. Mappin was known for of all types of high-quality cutlery throughout each firm's existence.

***** **Marks & Rees**, Cincinnati, Ohio. c.1833–39. Surgical instrument makers, their mark has been found on a few fine, early coffin-hilt bowies.

*** **Marshes & Shepherd**, Ponds Works (1828–?), Sheffield. **[ROXO]** c.1780–1841. A couple of superb bowies known.

** **Marsh Bros. & Co.**, Ponds Works, Forge Lane, Sheffield. **[ROXO]** c.1841–1960s. Generally average quality dirks and folders.

** **Thomas Marsh**, Cricket Inn Rd., Sheffield. c.1836. The Marshes were a steelmaking family that produced cutlery as well.

* **Needham, Veall & Tyzack**, Eye Witness Works, Milton St., Sheffield. **[eye/WITNESS]** c.1879–1975.

* **Francis Newton & Sons**, 127 Portobello St., Sheffield. **[swan]** c.1838–1920. Generally later bowie-type knives and folders.

* **John Newton**, Manhattan Works, Arundel Lane, Sheffield. **[frog]** c.1861–1926. Maker of late bowie-style hunting knives.

** **William Nicholson**, Sycamore St., Sheffield. c.1846–64. Maker of often plain knives, mainly folders.

** **George Nixon & Co.**, Mount Pisgah, Sheffield. c.1841–64.

** **Nixon & Winterbottom**, Pyramid Works (1876–), Sheffield. **[pyramid]** c.1864–1975.

***** **John C. Nixon & Son**, New York. c. 1830s–64. Cutler, produced a few plain but well-made bowies.

**** **George W. Nixon**, New York. c.1864–70s. Cutler with similar production to his father (above).

** **J. Nowill & Sons**, Meadow St. (to 1856) & Scotland St. (1856–present), Sheffield. **[D*, crossed keys]** c.1836–1960s.

** **Richard Paget**, 185 Piccadilly, London. c.1822–? Maker of London-style hunting knives.

*** **Parker Bros.**, 76 Eyre St., Sheffield. c.1847–60.

*** **Charles Pickslay & Co.**, Royal York Works, 60 Solly St., Sheffield. c.1841. A few fine folding dirks are known.

Poker & Live. This marking was used on some fantasy bowie knives made in England during the late 1960s. Authentic bowie-era examples do not exist.

***** **Blaise Pradel**, St. Charles, Chartres and Poydras Streets, New Orleans, La. c. 1853–95. Knives by this surgical instrument maker are very rare.

***** **Michael Price**, San Francisco, Calif. c. 1859–89. The most revered maker of California-style knives. Price's knives ranged from plain to fancy, but each is a prime example of the cutler's art. Beware of fakes.

**** **Rau & Kohnke**, San Francisco, Calif. c.1871–75.

**** **Rau & Todt**, San Francisco, Calif. c.1875–80. California maker of bowie-style hunting knives.

***** **Charles C. Reinhardt**, 24 Lombard St. (1837–42), 8–9 Light St. (1843–54), 7 N. Gay St. (1855–64), Baltimore, Md. c.1837–64.

***** **Charles C. Reinhardt, & Bro.,** 7 N. Gay St., Baltimore, Md. c.1865–67.

***** **Henry D. Reinhardt**, Meeting & King Streets, Charleston, S.C. 1852–60. A famed family of bowie makers, all Reinhardt knives are rare and many are large.

*** **Samuel Robinson**, Sheffield. c.1840.

***** **Christopher Roby & Co.**, West Chemsford, Mass. c.1861–67. Maker of swords and bowie knives for the Union during the Civil War. Beware of fakes.

** **G. Rodgers & Co.**, 13 Norfolk Lane, Sheffield. c.1840–62.

** **G. Rodgers & Sons**, 5 Silver St., Sheffield. c.1850.

** **Henry Rodgers Sons & Co.**, Eyre St., Sheffield. **[winged horse]** c.1878.

*** **James Rodgers**, Sheffield. Mark used concurrently with Unwin & Rodgers. See Unwin & Rodgers.

** **Joseph Rodgers & Sons**, #6 Norfolk St., Sheffield. c.1724–1975. **[star & maltese cross]** The world's most famous cutlery firm in the 19th century, Rodgers' reputation for top-notch goods caused their very name to be the equivalent of "quality" worldwide. While their bowies are common and most are of relatively late manufacture, they remain popular with collectors today.

**** **J. B. Rogers**, York, Maine. Rogers was an eclectic traveler, prospector and gunsmith. It is not known at what time his knives were made, as early as the 1880s or as late as World War II.

***** **Peter Rose**, New York. c.1828–45. This surgical instrument maker made fine, desirable bowies.

** **John Russell & Co.**, Green River Works, Greenfield (c.1834–70) and Turners Falls (c.1870–1933), Mass. This famous maker of generally late bowie and hunting knives is very popular with collectors. They continued to make knives of bowie type well into the 20th century.

***** **William Sansom & Co.**, 36 Norfolk St., Sheffield. **[ALPHA/crown]** c.1832. Little known but very early, high-quality knives.

***** **Sansom & Harwood**, Sheffield. **[ALPHA/crown]** c.1830s. Very early maker of coffin-hilt knives.

***** **Jacob H. Schintz**, San Francisco, Calif. c.1860–1906. Maker of excellent knives in the California style.

***** **Henry Schively, Jr.**, 75 Chestnut St., Philadelphia. c.1810–49. One of two cutlers to have made knives for Rezin Bowie to present to friends, Schively's work is among the most desired of all American makers. Succeeded in business by sons Charles and George.

**** **John M. Schmid**, 158 Westminster, Providence, R.I. c.1857–71. Cutler and surgical instrument maker. Bowies were of distinctive style.

***** **Daniel Searles**, Baton Rouge, La. c.1828–60. This cutler and gunsmith is one of two to have made presentation knives for Rezin Bowie. There are but a handful of his knives known to exist, and all are top-notch.

** **William Shirley**, Crescent and Boston Works, Sheffield. **[OIO]** c.1860–79. Typical bowie knives and dirks of mid-1800s.

*** **Thomas Short, Jr.**, Sheffield. c.1850. Maker of some fine, ornate bowies.

** **Slack & Grinold**, 53 Bath St., Sheffield. **[ONWARD]** c.1867.

** **H. M. Slater**, 105 Arundel St., Sheffield. c. 1850.

** **Slater Bros.**, Beehive Works, Eyre St., Sheffield. **[VENTURE/beehive/IYNOT]** c.1858–1990.

* **Southern & Richardson**, Wheeldon Works (to 1851), Don Cutlery Works (1851–), Sheffield. **[bird's nest]** c.1847–1975. Maker of mainly late bowie-style hunting knives.

** **Stacey Bros. & Co.**, 17 Orange and 76 Eyre Streets, Sheffield. c.1847–1920.

* **Standard Cutlery Co.**, Sheffield. c.late 19th–early 20th c. Maker of late bowies and bowie-style hunters.

** **William T. Staniforth**, Eldon Works (1876–?), Ascend Works (1884–), Sheffield. **[ASCEND]** c.1849–1914.

*** **Robert S. Stenton**, Sheffield. c.1846–47. Stenton was originally the New York agent for Sheffield's Geo. Wostenholm. In 1846 he started his own importing business in that city.

***** **George Stewart**, Norwich, Conn. c.1857–60. Gunsmith known to have made a few bowies.

**** **Steven Taft**, Millbury, Mass. c.1860s. Taft is thought to have worked for the Buck Brothers.

** **H. H. Taylor and Bro.**, Times Works, Sheffield. c.1862–63.

**** **J. Teufel**, Philadelphia, Pa. Teufel was a surgical instrument maker active in the mid to late 1800s.

** **Walter Thornhill & Co.**, 44 New Bond St., London. c.19th c. Maker of London-style hunting knives.

**** **Tiffany & Co.**, Union Square, New York. Tiffany made a few silver-mounted knives. Beware of fakes. There are no known legitimate Tiffany knives with their name stamped into the blade.

*** **Thomas Tillotson & Co.**, Columbia Place (1852–present), Sheffield. c.1825–62. This well-known maker produced a variety of bowie, dirk and folding knives for the American market.

**** **John Todt**, San Francisco, Calif. c.1880–1915. California maker of bowie-style hunting knives.

* **Edward K. Tryon & Co.**, Philadelphia, Penn. **[3/T]** c.1811–1952. This sporting goods firm had late bowie-style hunting knives made for their store.

** **Thomas Turner & Co.**, Suffolk Works, Sheffield. **[ENCORE]** c.1802–1932. Many folding knives, most bowies are rather plain.

** **Underwood**, 56 Haymarket St., London. c.19th c. Maker of London-style hunting knives.

*** **Unwin & Rodgers**, Rockingham Works, 124 Rockingham St., Sheffield. **[NON*XLL]** c.1833–1910. Made bowies, dirks and knife-pistols for the American trade. See James Rodgers.

** **Wade and Butcher**, Eyre Lane, Furnival St., Sheffield. **[XCD]** c.1819–1918. See W. & S. Butcher. Robert Wade was the Butchers' New York agent. Knives with this mark date later than those with the W. & S. Butcher marking; the majority of W&B's "bowies" are actually late bowie-hunters. Beware of fakes.

** **Wade, Wingfield, and Rowbotham**, 82 Tenter St., Sheffield. c.1825–52. See Wingfield, Rowbotham & Co.

**** **Silas A. Walker**, Bennington, Vt. c.1862. Made a few simple clip point bowies for Civil War use.

**** **John Walters & Co.**, Globe Works, 7 Carver St., Sheffield. c.1841–65. Maker of a wide range of knives, including some large, fancy, pearl handled models that are very much in demand.

* **F. Ward & Co.**, Sheffield. **[B4*ANY]** c.1856–81. Maker of simple bowies and bowie hunters.

** **William Webster**, 55 Hermitage and 14 Sycamore St., Sheffield. c.1852–69.

** **John Weiss & Son**, 62 Strand, London. c.1832–83.

** **John Weiss & Sons**, 17 Wigmore St., London. c.1883–present. Top-quality English-style hunting knives.

*** **James Westa**, Lord St., Sheffield. **[DCL]** c. 19th c. Unidentified maker of mid-19th-century bowies. Probable connection to Wilson Swift, as they utilized the same trademark.

** **W. & H. Whitehead**, Sheffield. Unidentified maker of Civil War–era bowies, some etched "Death to Traitors."

**** **H. Wilkinson**, Hartford, Conn. c.1860. The one known example bears similarities to some Alfred Hunters.

***** **F. Will**, San Francisco, Calif. c.1863.

***** **Will and Finck**, San Francisco, Calif. c.1863–1932. This famed San Francisco firm is well known for their California-style knives. Beware of fakes. If the partners' names are misspelled, the knife is not authenic.

* **Alfred Williams**, Sheffield. **[EBRO]** c.1900–46. A trademark of Adolph Kastor, used on late bowie hunters.

** **Williamson**, Oxford, England. c.19th c. Maker of London-style hunting knives.

*** **Wilson, Hawksworth & Moss**, Sheffield. c.1832–46.

** **Wilson, Hawksworth, Ellison & Co.**, Carlisle Works, Sheffield. c.1846–70. Successors to the above firm.

*** **Wilson Swift**, Broad St., Sheffield. **[DCL]** Unidentified maker of mid-19th century bowies. Probable connection to James Westa, based on the fact that they used the same trademark.

** **Wingfield, Rowbotham & Co.**, 82 Tenter St., Sheffield. c.1852–98. Successors to Wade, Wingfield, and Rowbotham.

***** **Wolfe and Clarke**, New York. c.1830s. Importers of fine, early Sheffield-made knives, likely by J. Crookes.

**** **Woodhead and Hartley**, 7 Lambert St., Sheffield. c.1841–47; 36 Howard St., Sheffield. c.1847–49.

*** **George Woodhead**, 36 Howard St., Sheffield. c.1849–76.

** **G. Woodhead & Son**, Sheffield. c.1876–84. Popular bowie knife makers, these firms probably produced more alligator, horse-alligator, and reclining lion pommel bowies than all other makers combined.

**** **George Wostenholm & Son**, Rockingham Works, Sheffield. **[I*XL]** c.1745–1848. Rare mark.

** **George Wostenholm & Son**, Washington Works, Sheffield. **[I*XL]** c.1848–1983. Wostenholm was undoubably the most prolific manufacturer of bowie knives for the American market. They will be found in a wide variety of patterns and sizes, and cover the price range from the low-end bowie-hunters up to $130,000 for one exhibition knife. Beware of knives made in the 1960s and 1970s by Fred James.

*** **Samuel C. Wragg**, 25 and 38 Furnace Hill, Sheaf Island Works, Sheffield. c.1817–52. A desirable English bowie manufacturer, Wragg made both fixed-blade and folding knives for the American market.

* **W. H. Wragg**, Sheffield. Maker of 20th-century bowies, according to one source the grandson of S. C. Wragg.

(Mark D. Zalesky is not only a collector of knives and other cutlery items, he is a collector of information as well. An avid reader with an energetic drive for learning more, he has become a very competent researcher of cutlery history, and bowies are his specialty. A widely respected authority, Zalesky often shares his knowledge through articles published in cutlery magazines as well as through presentations to collector and historical groups. Since early 1997, Zalesky has been the editor of *Knife World*, the monthly publication for the worldwide knife collecting community.)

CUSTOM KNIVES

Although the major portion of this book is devoted to manufactured or factory-made knives, the field of custom knives shall not be overlooked. Collecting of handmade or custom knives is an exciting and dynamic part of the overall knife collecting hobby.

Collector as well as user interest in these knives, made one-at-a-time by an ever increasing number of knife crafters, has grown at a very rapid pace during the past three decades. Handmade or, as most knife fanciers prefer, custom-made knives are far from a passing fad. Nor is the custom blade merely a status symbol or a statement of affluence. Whether the knife is purchased to use or just to add to a collection, the demand is real and it is here to stay.

Some estimates indicate that close to 200,000 "custom" knives are now being made each year. When compared to the millions of commercial factory knives made annually, those numbers may seem small. But, when one considers the relative infancy of the custom knife industry as compared to the manufactured knife industry, they are impressive indeed.

It was about thirty-five years ago that knife collecting began to attract attention. At that time, one could count the number of nationally known custom makers on two hands. Their numbers steadily grew for a decade or more and then, during the past quarter-century, increased in near geometric proportions. The continual growth in numbers is evidenced by the list of knife makers included in this section.

Many of the finest knives to be found in the world today are coming from the workshops of custom makers. Not only are they excellent examples of quality utilitarian cutlery, but many of them surpass the name, "knife," and are recognized as real works of art. Like fruits of the labors of a fine painter, a sculptor or a composer, these knives are recognized and appreciated as creations of another type artist—the knife maker. One only has to see maker Buster Warinski's "King Tut Dagger," a re-creation (including twenty ounces of gold plus numerous precious stones) of the dagger found in the ancient Egyptian tomb, or Gil Hibben's "Saint George's Axe" to be convinced that knife crafters are indeed artists. Numerous examples are deserving of mention, but no words can compare to pictures. Anyone interested in the art of custom knives would be well advised to obtain a copy of *Points of Interest.* Now available in five editions, these books are a colorful wonderland of custom knife photography by Jim Weyer.

Just as many knife makers are truly artists working in the medium of steel, there are others

Truly in the American spirit, Aubrey G. Barnes forged this large bowie knife in his Hagerstown, Md., bladesmith shop. (Photo by Point Seven)

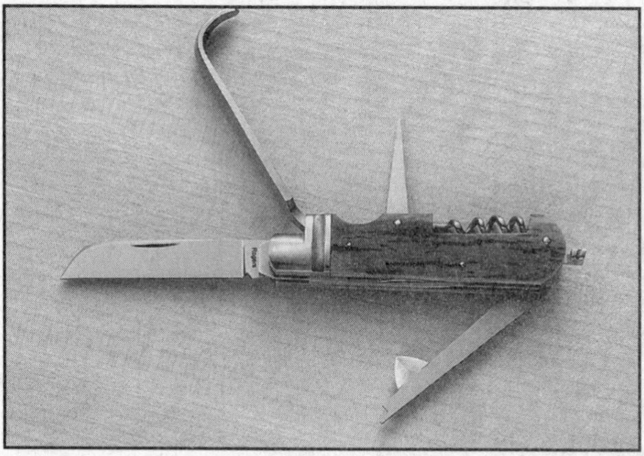

In the style of famed European cutlers, Richard Rogers of Magdalena, N.M., made this Horseman's Knife from ATS-34 steel and handled it in mammoth ivory. (Photo by Point Seven)

ABS master smith, Hanford Miller, hammered out this "Gentleman's Fighter" in his Cowdrey, Colo., shop. It is handled with mastadon ivory scales. (Photo by Point Seven)

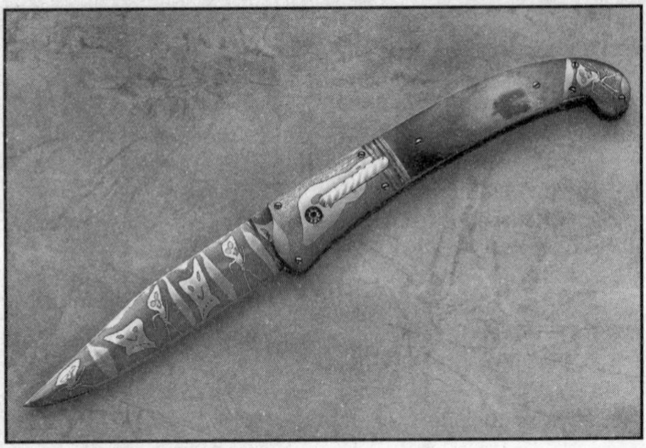

"Thorns and Thistles" is the pattern for Mosaic Damascus on a 52100 center core. Mastadon ivory was selected as handle material. The Smiths Grove, Ky., Master Smith, Steve Dunn, named the exquisite piece "Dancing Ghosts." (Photo by Point Seven)

Steve Fecas of Anderson, S.C., used genuine stag, mother-of-pearl and mammoth ivory to handle these Damascus liner-lock folders. (Photo by Point Seven)

Larry Harley of Bristol, Tenn., used L-6 and O-1 steel as top and bottom bars for this Damascus hunter's blade. The middle bar was from a chainsaw's chain and Rosewood was used for the knife's handle. (Photo by Point Seven)

Larry Fuegen of Prescott, Ariz., carved the mammoth ivory handle and tastefully added ostrich leather to the custom sheath for this Damascus hunter. (Photo by Point Seven)

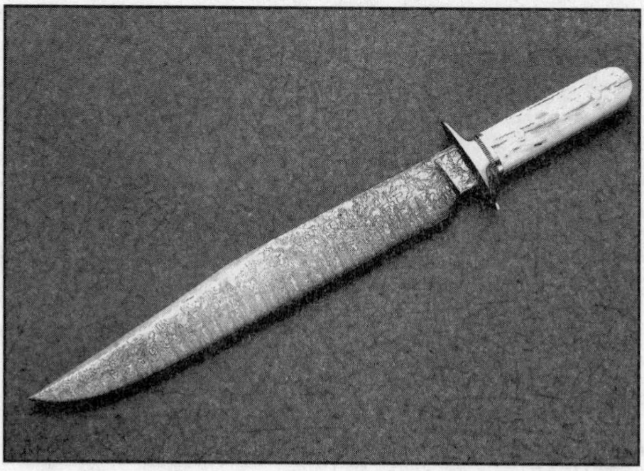

It's big and it's beautiful. The 12 1/4" Damascus bowie blade was made by El Dorado, Ark., bladesmith, Joe Flournoy. The bark ivory handle extends the overall length to 16 7/8". (Photo by Point Seven)

Former ABS chairman and master smith, E. Jay Hendrickson of Frederick, Md., combined 5160 Damascus blade, fine silver-wire inlay, nickle silver, curly maple and detailed carvings of leaves and acorns to create this exceptional bowie. (Photo by Point Seven)

This Damascus hunter was made from 1084, 52100 and L-6 steels. Its maker, Red St. Cyr, of Wilmington, Calif., uniquely finished it off with giraffe bone handle. (Photo by Point Seven)

After Florida knife maker Don Lozier made this exquisite Persian fighter from ATS-34 steel, nickel silver and ivory, he employed the talents of engraver Julie Warenski and scrimshander Sandra Brady. (Photo by Point Seven)

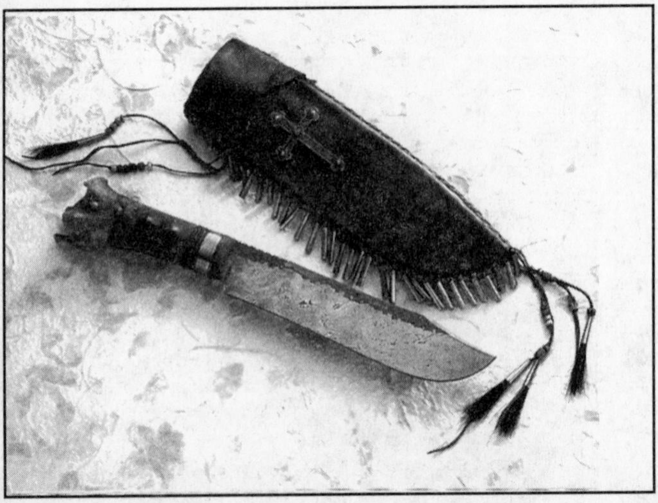

Bladesmith Daniel Winkler of Blowing Rock, N.C., hammered out this primitive Damascus camp knife and handled it in stag. The sheath was made of leather, bone and rawhide by Karen Shook. (Photo by Point Seven)

whose artistic capabilities are evident in their decoration of pieces that may otherwise be only cutting tools. Hand engraving, exquisite file work or scrimshawed handles are a few of the several ways that knife makers have gone beyond the craft to the art. But, whether a specific handmade knife can or should be called a work of art is perhaps secondary to the fact that it most always is a finely crafted piece of cutlery.

The term "custom knife" has become widely accepted as applying to practically all the products of "custom knife makers." Some knife fanciers will differ on terminology as to whether these knives should be referred to as handmade, benchmade or custom made. While it is important for the collector to understand the fine-line difference in the terminology, the net effect on the values of these knives is negligible. Therefore, except for the following brief explanation, the term "custom" will be used in this discussion.

The true custom-made knife is made exclusively for a specific customer and usually to his or her specifications, with slight artistic license offered the maker. In the real world today, however, most knives in this specialty are not truly custom made. Instead, they are variations of fairly standard designs preferred by a particular maker and often combined with the customer's choice of handle material, decoration, etc. So, while it is reasonable to assume that any true custom knife is a handmade knife, the majority of handmade knives one will find on the collector market are not custom knives in the true sense of the word. Whether the knife is a true custom or one of the maker's standard selections with special options, they are one-of-a-kind knives made one-at-a-time usually in a home shop, and they are highly prized throughout most of the modern world.

Today's custom knives indeed take numerous shapes and forms and they deal with the cold hard facts of using fine cutlery or with artistic fantasy. They are made by crafters and artists working with bar-stock steel and skillfully changing that rather ordinary commodity into a special knife. They are also made by bladesmiths who use heat and hammers to alter the steel's nature along the way to making it into that fine piece of cutlery. Fixed blade knives now take many blade forms to become hunters or skinners, fighters or survival knives, camp knifes or bowies, while folding knives now feature unique locking or opening mechanisms that work so smoothly that they could only come from a knife maker's shop. After the revival of the ancient art, hand-forged damascus blades have become quite popular with collectors. Because there is so much available in the custom knife area, the collector who chooses to specialize is making a wise decision.

Custom Knife Maker List

The custom knife collector has several routes to satisfaction in his or her collecting hobby and, hopefully, to profitable investing. One is to buy from a relatively unknown knife maker who produces a superior knife but has not achieved the fame of other better known makers. If his or her knives are truly superior, they will soon be sought by custom knife fanciers and collectors. As demand for this maker's knives rise, so will their prices and knives purchased earlier will have considerably appreciated in value. This method can be a rather speculative route to follow. If the maker loses interest or if his or her sales do not justify his or her staying in business long enough to have established a favorable reputation (read demand), the collector may have knives of excellent quality but of low resale value. Conversely, if the maker and his or her work earn the sought-after fame, the collector will realize considerable appreciation in the value of his or her knives.

One can also buy only knives made by well-known and established makers. An obvious advantage is an easier market, if and when you decide to sell. Remember that each custom knife is unique but the makers' name can open the door for their sale. If one offers for sale a knife made by Moran, Frank, Henry, Lake, Loveless or a few dozen other makers, collectors will recognize it as a desirable piece to own and the only matter to resolve is its price. The disadvantage to this method is that many of these makers are several years behind in fulfilling their orders. A long wait may be in store and, if waiting is a problem, the alternative is to pay an appreciated price to another collector for one of the maker's creations. Either way, owning one of their knives will require a relatively high investment. It can also offer a relatively high financial return and pride of ownership.

Another system is to seek knives of deceased makers; to many collectors, owning a creation of a knife making pioneer has its own special meaning. Oftentimes, when compared to modern-day makers, the knife may be crude and very seldom is it decorated. But, numerous collectors are willing to part with several thousand dollars to own a knife made by William Scagel or Michael Price. Advertising a Moran, a Richtig, a Loveless, a Frank or a McBurnette for several hundred dollars will bring buyers to your doorstep. Most of these knives are far from easy to find and, as should be expected, not inexpensive to buy. Knowledge of the custom market is especially important in this method. One should not assume that the knives made by a deceased maker are valuable; nor should one assume that, just because a maker is still making knives for sale, his or her knives are not highly desirable and quite expensive.

Whichever route one determines to take, the collector should endeavor to buy the very best examples that he or she can afford and ones that he or she will enjoy owning. Whether or not there are financial returns on the investment, an almost certain return in custom knives is pride of ownership.

Prices for custom knives will range from about $80 to several thousand dollars. Their price depends not only upon style, age, quality of workmanship and amount of decoration, but on the maker as well. There have been several hundred thousand knives made by hand and many of these are available to the collector market. Since no two are exactly alike, it would be virtually impossible to offer meaningful pricing within the scope of this book. Instead, we offer suggestions for sources of information on specific knives.

Custom knives have their specialty dealers just as do the collectible factory knives. These purveyors of the knife makers' craft and art have studied their field and have developed a high level of expertise. They are not only excellent sources for knives, but most are quite helpful in providing information. The novice collector of custom knives would be well advised to use them as key contact persons.

Attendance at knife shows will usually be quite helpful in learning more about knives and their makers as well. Unlike factory knives that were produced in large quantities and meet specifications of style, handles, etc., custom knives can best be evaluated when personally examined. The show can offer this opportunity. If your interest is primarily in custom knives, choose your show rather carefully before traveling a great distance to be sure that it is one normally attended by makers, collectors or purveyors of custom knives.

Other marketing channels present opportunities for learning more specifically the value of a custom knife or knives. Advertisements, especially within the classified sections of knife publications, most always reveal contacts for trading of either knives or information.

As with other collecting specialties, your own reading and research will be of key importance. Fortunately, there has been much written about custom knives and the few dollars spent in reference materials can definitely pay dividends when high-dollar knives are involved.

The final and very important suggestion has been made easier for you by this book. If you seek information about a knife that is marked with the maker's last name or initials—and the majority are—the best source is usually the maker. The listing of makers that follows is the most extensive one included in any publication. Although some no longer craft knives, most are known to be currently active. Addresses given are the last known and the majority were current as of this writing. Compare the knife's marking with the knife maker list and you're most likely well on your way to learning more about your knife from the person who knows it best—its maker.

Custom Knifemakers of the United States

Abbott, William M., RR 2 Box 102-A, Chandlerville, IL 62627
Abdulky, Al, 2630 Michaelangelo Dr, Stockton, CA 95207
Abdulky, Jamin, 2630 Michaelangelo Dr, Stockton, CA 95207
Abernathy, Paul J., 3033 Park St, Eureka, CA 95501
Ackerson, Robin E., 119 W Smith St, Buchanan, MI 49107
Adair, Earl, 4714 44th St, Dickinson, TX 77539
Adams, Les, 6413 NW 200th St, Hialeah, FL 33015
Addison, Ed, 325 E Pritchard St, Asheboro, NC 27203
Adkins, Richard L., 138 California Ct, Misson Viejo, CA 92692
Albach, Larry, 7537 Del Mar Ln, La Palma, CA 90623
Alden Jr., Kenneth E., PO Box 1995, Ramona, CA 92065
Alderman, Robert, 2655 Jewel Lake Rd, Sagle, ID 83860

Alexander, Darrel, PO Box 381, Ten Sleep, WY 82442
Alexander, Eugene, PO Box 540, Ganado, TX 77962
Allen, Mike, 12745 Fontenot Acres Rd, Malakoff, TX 75148
Allen, Steve, 200 Forbes St, Riverside, RI 02915
Allen, Joe, RR 3 Box 182, Princeton, IN 47670
Allred, Bruce F., 1764 N Alder, Layton, UT 84041
Allred, Elvan, 2403 Lansing Blvd, Wichita Falls, TX 76309
Alverson, R. V., 215 111 St, Orofino, ID 83544
Amero, Tony, 21920 Piedra Dr, Tehachapi, CA 93561
Ames, Mickey L., 1521 N Central Ave, Monett, MO 65708
Amick, Ron, RR 7 Box 668-B, Sylacauga, AL 35150
Amor Jr., Miguel, 485-H Judie Lane, Lancaster, PA 17603
Amoureux, A. W., PO Box 776, Northport, WA 99157
Amspoker, Kirk, 3161 Claudia Dr, Concord, CA 94519
Anders, David, 157 Barnes Dr, Center Ridge, AR 72027
Anders, Jerome, 157 Barnes Dr, Center Ridge, AR 72027
Anderson, Mel, Rt 1 1718 Lee Lane, Cedaredge, CO 81413
Anderson, Charles, Westshore Dr, Polson, MT 59860
Anderson, Charles B., PO Box 209, Lampe, MO 65681
Anderson, Chuck, PO Box 508, Estes Park, CO 80517
Anderson, Edwin, 189 Forest Ave, Glen Cove, NY 11542
Anderson, Gary D., RR 2 Box 2299-C Spring Grove, PA 17362
Anderson, Marvin, 7745 NW Cardwell Hill Dr, Corvallis, OR 97330
Anderson, Mel, 1718 Lee Ln, Cedaredge, CO 81413
Anderson, Michael., 1741 Weiler Blvd., Ft Worth TX 76112
Anderson, Tom, 955 Canal Rd, Manchester, PA 17345
Anderson, Virgil W., 16318 SE Taggart St, Portland, OR 97236
Andress, Ronnie, 415 Audubon Dr N, Satsuma, AL 36572
Andrews, Don, 5155 N Ezy St, Coeur D Alene, ID 83814
Andrews, Eric, 132 Halbert St, Grand Ledge, MI 48837
Andrews, E. R., 131 Sterling Ave, Sugar Creek, MO 64054
Ankrom, W. E., 14 Marquette Dr, Cody, WY 82414
Anselmo, Victor, 11100 Cumpston St, North Hollywood, CA 91601
Antonio, William Jr., 6 Michigan State Dr, Newark, DE 19713
Aoun, Charles, 69 Nahant St, Wakefield, MA 01880
Appleton, Ray, 244 S Fetzer St, Byers, CO 80103
Arbuckle, James M., 114 Johnathon Jct, Yorktown VA 23693
Archer, Bent E., PO Box 128, Steilacoom, WA 98401
Archer, Ray, PO Box 129, Medicine Bow, WY 82329
Arnett, Todd J., 4191 N Euclid Ave, Bay City, MI 48706
Arrowwood, Dale, 556 Lassetter Road, Sharpsburg, GA 30277
Ashby, Douglas, 10123 Deermont Trl, Dallas, TX 75243
Ashworth, Boyd, 3135 Barrett Ct, Powder Springs, GA 30073
Atkinson, Dick, General Delivery, Wausau, FL 32463
Babcock, Raymond G., Box 328-A, Vincent, OH 45784
Bagley, R. Keith, 4415 Hope Acres Dr, White Plains, MD 20695
Bagwell, Bill, PO Box 265, Marietta, TX 75566
Bailey, Joseph D., 3213 Jonesboro Dr, Nashville, TN 37214
Bailey, Kirby C., 2055 FM 2790 W, Lytle, TX 78052
Bailey, Ryan, 4185 S St Rt 605, Galena, OH 43021
Baker, Herb, 326 S Hamilton St, Eden, NC 27288
Baker, Ray, PO Box 303, Sapulpa, OK 74067
Baker, Vance, 574 Co Rd 675, Riceville, TN 37370
Baker, Wild Bill, Box 361, Boiceville, NY 12412
Baldwin, Phillip, PO Box 563, Snohomish, WA 98290
Ball, Ken, 127 Sundown Manor, Mooresville IN 46158
Ball, Robert, 809 W 7th Ave, Port Angeles, WA 98362
Ballew, Dale, PO Box 1277, Bowling Green, VA 22427

Balzar, John, 925 L St Apt 680, Sacramento, CA 95814
Banks, David L, 99 Blackfoot Ave #3, Riverton, WY 82501
Barbee, Jim, Rt 1 Box B, Ft. Stockton, TX 79735
Barber, Robert E., 1828 Franklin Dr, Charlottesville, VA 22911
Barber, Will, RR 2, Shiloh, OH 44878
Bardsley, Norman P., 197 Cottage St, Pawtucket, RI 02860
Barefoot, Joe W., 117 Oak Brook Dr, Liberty, SC 29657
Barker, Reggie, 603 S Park Dr, Springhill, LA 71075
Barker, Robert G., 2311 Branch Rd, Bishop, GA 30621
Barlow, Ken, 3800 Rohner Dr, Fortuna, CA 95540
Barminski, Tom, 809 S Del Norte Ave, Loveland, CO 80537
Barnes, Aubrey G., 11341 Rock Hill Rd, Hagerstown, MD 21740
Barnes, Gary L., PO Box 138, New Windsor, MD 21776
Barnes, Jack, P.O Box 1315, Whitefish, MT 59937
Barnes, Jim, 2909 Forest Trail, San Angelo, TX 76904
Barnes, Marlen R., 904 Crestwood Dr S, Atlanta, TX 75551
Barnes, Wendell, 2160 Oriole Dr, Missoula, MT 59808
Barnett, Jack, PO Box 1315, Whitefish, MT 59937
Barnett, Van, 1135 Terminal Way, Reno, NV 89502
Barney, Richard, PO Box 375, Mount Shasta, CA 96067
Barngrover, Jerry, RR 4 Box 1230, Afton, OK 74331
Barr, A. T., 153 Madonna Dr, Nicholasville, KY 40356
Barr, Judson C., 1905 Pickwick Cr, Irving, TX 75060
Barret, Cecil T., 2514 Linda Ln, Colorado Springs, CO 80909
Barrett, Jack, 2133 Peach Orchard Rd, Augusta, GA 30906
Barrett, R. W., 3212 Montrose St SW, Huntsville, AL 35805
Barron, Brian, 123 12th Ave, San Mateo, CA 94402
Barron, David, PO Box 133, Etowah, NC 28729
Barron, Jay L., 1910 Jerome Ave SW, Grand Rapids, MI 49507
Barry III, James J., 115 Flagler Promenade N, West Palm Beach, FL 33405
Barry, Scott, PO Box 354, Laramie, WY 82070
Barth, J. D., 101 4th St, Alberton, MT 59820
Bartlow, John, 5078 Coffeen Ave, Sheridan, WY 82801
Barton, Almon T., 802 Crestview Ct, San Marcos, CA 92069
Bartrug, Hugh E., 2701 34th St N St, Pertsburg, FL 33713
Baskett, Lee Gene, 427 Sutzer Creek Rd, Eastview, KY 42732
Bass, Bill, 690 Lincoln Rd E, Vallejo, CA 94591
Bassney, John, RR 3 Box 277-A, Lodi, WI 53555
Bates, Ken, 3051 Henrietta Ave, La Crescenta, CA 91214
Batson, James, 176 Brentwood Ln, Madison, AL 35758
Batson, Richard D., 6591 Waterford Rd, Rixeyville, VA 22737
Batts, Keith, 450 Manning Rd, Hooks, TX 75561
Baylis, Brian R., PO Box 1771, San Marcos, CA 92079
Bear, Charles, 4042 Bones Rd, Sebastopol, CA 95472
Beam, John R., 1310 Foothills Rd, Kalispell, MT 59901
Beaty, Robert B., 1995 Big Flat Rd, Missoula, MT 59804
Beatty, Gordon H., 121 Petty Rd, Seneca, SC 29672
Beauchamp, Dan, 467 8th Ave, Menlo Park, CA 94025
Beaver, Devon (Butch), 48835 N 25th Ave, Phoenix, AZ 85027
Beck, P. F., 1504 Hagood Ave, Barnwell, SC 29812
Beck, Wayne, Route 2 Ridgecrest Dr, High Point, NC 27260
Beckett, Norman L., 1501 N Chaco Ave, Farmington, NM 87401
Beckwith, Michael R., 48282 Donahue St, New Baltimore, MI 48047
Beers, Ray, 8 Manor Brook Rd, Monkton, MD 21111
Behnke, William, 931 W Sanborn Rd, Lake City, MI 49651
Belk, Jack, 5321 County Road 3, Marble, CO 81623
Bell, Frank, 409 Town & Country Dr NW, Huntsville, AL 35806
Bell, Michael, 88321 N Bank Ln, Coquille, OR 97423

Benitez, David, PO Box 584, Guerneville, CA 95446
Benjamin, George Jr., 3001 Foxy Ln, Kissimmee, FL 34746
Benson, Don, 2505 Jackson Ave Trlr, 112, Escalon, CA 95320
Benton, Dale, RR 1 Box 395, Ingleside, TX 78362
Benton, W. F., 104 Lapine Dr, Eufaula, AL 36207
Ber, Dave, 656 Miller Rd, San Juan Island, WA 98250
Berendt, Andrew G., 2803 S 48th St, Milwaukee, WI 53219
Berger, Max A., 35716 John Richard Ct, Carmichael, CA 95608
Berglin, Bruce D., 17441 Lake Terrace Pl, Mt Vernon, WA 98274
Bernhardt, J., PO Box 28066, Dallas, TX 75228
Berryman, Les, 39885 San Moreno Ct, Fremont, CA 94539
Berzas, Larry, 208 W 26th St, Cut Off, LA 70345
Besedick, Frank E., Rt 2 Box 802, Ruffsdale, PA 15679
Besic, Leroy, 40881 Johnston Ave, Hemet, CA 92544
Bethke, Lora Sue, 13420 Lincoln St, Grand Haven, MI 49417
Beubendorf, Bobby, 221 Summit St, Bridgeport, CT 06606
Beverly II, Larry H., PO Box 741, Spotsylvania, VA 22553
Biggs, H. I., 3816 Via Selva, Palo Verde, CA 92266
Biggers, Gary, 1278 Colina Vista, Venrtura, CA 93003
Birch, Robert F., PO Box 1901, Huntsville, TX 77342
Birt, Sid, RR 1 Box 352, Nashville, IN 47448
Bizal, Paul W., PO Box 19834, Raytown, MO 64133
Bizzell, Robert, 145 Missoula Ave, Butte, MT 59701
Black, Earl, 3466 S 700 E, Salt Lake City, UT 84106
Black, J. C., 3218 Castle Rock Ln, Garland, TX 75044
Black, Robert, 3688 Quaker Ln, North Kingstown, RI 02852
Black, Scott, 27100 Leetown Rd, Picayune, MS 39466
Black, Tom, 921 Grecian Dr NW, Albuquerque, NM 87107
Black, T. J., 1507 Wayne St, Alexandria, LA 71301
Blackton, Andrew E., 12521 5th Isle, Bayonet Point, FL 34667
Blackwood, Edward W., 235 Montgomery St, San Francisco, CA 94104
Blade, Joe, PO Box 526, Port Townsend, WA 98368
Blakley, William E., Rt 4 Box 106b, Fredericksburg, VA 22405
Blalock, Keith W. Jr., 1611 The Lane St, Pleasanton, TX 78064
Blanchard, Gary, 5917 Negril Ave, Las Vegas, NV 89130
Blasingame, Robert, 2906 Swanson Ln, Kilgore, TX 75662
Blaum, Roy, 319 N Columbia St, Covington, LA 70433
Bledsoe, Orville, RR 3 Box 280, Dobson, NC 27017
Blomberg, Gregg, RR 1 Box 1762, Lopez, WA 98261
Bloomer, Alan T., 116 E 6th St, Maquon, IL 61458
Bloomfield, L. H., PO Box 3588, Kingman, AZ 86402
Blum, Chuck, 743 S Brea Blvd Ste 10, Brea, CA 92621
Blum, Kenneth, 1729 Burleson, Brenham, TX 77833
Blum, Ronald A., 201 Masters Ct #4, Walnut Creek, CA 94598
Boatright, Basel, 11 Timber Point, New Braunfels, TX 78132
Bochman, Bruce, 183 Howard Pl, Grants Pass, OR 97526
Bocco, Gordon, 175 Ash St, Hayden, CO 81639
Bodewitz, Dennis, PO Box 77, Davenport, CA 95017
Bodner, Jerry, 4102 Spyglass Ct, Louisville, KY 40229
Boeckman, R. Von, PO Box 40506, Memphis, TN 38174
Boguszewski, Phil, PO Box 99329, Tacoma, WA 98499
Bohannon, Mike, 19755 SW Marlin Ave, Beaverton, OR 97007
Bohrmann, Bruce, 29 Portland St, Yarmouth, ME 04096
Boleware, David, PO Box 96, Carson, MS 39427
Bolton, Charles B., PO Box 6, Jonesburg, MO 63351
Bone, Knife Company, 4009 Avenue A, Lubbock, TX 79404
Bonner, Jeremy, RR 5 Box 427-A, Asheville, NC 28803
Booco, Gordon, 175 Ash St, Hayden, CO 81639

Booth, Lew, 16 Cypress Ter, Boonton, NJ 07005
Booth, Phillip, 301 S Jeffrey Ave, Ithaca, MI 48847
Bose, Reese, 9014 S Co. Rd 550 W, Lewis, IN 47858
Bose, Tony, 7252 N Co. Rd 300 E, Shelburn, IN 47879
Bosworth, Dean, 329 Mahogany Dr, Key Largo, FL 33037
Boultinghouse, David, RR 6 Box 265, Leander, TX 78641
Bouse, D. Michael, 1010 Victoria Pl, Waldorf, MD 20602
Bowen, Tilton, RR 1 Box 225-A, Baker, WV 26801
Bowles, Chris, PO Box 985, Reform, AL 35481
Boxer, Rex, 965 N River Rd, Sylva, NC 28779
Boyd, Francis, 1811 Prince St, Berkeley, CA 94703
Boye, David, PO Box 1238, Dolan Springs, AZ 86441
Boyer, Mark, 10515 Woodinville Dr #17, Bothell, WA 98011
Boyes, Tom, W16140 Robin Hood Dr, Menomonee Falls, WI 53051
Brack, Douglas D., 119 Camino Ruiz #71, Camirillo, CA 93012
Bradburn, Gary, 1714 Park Place, Wichita, KS 67203
Bradley, Dennis, 2410 Bradley Acres Rd, Blairsville, GA 30512
Bradley, Gayle, 205 Oak Forest Trl, Euless, TX 76039
Bradley, John, PO Box 37, Ponomo Park, FL 32081
Bradshaw, Bailey, 17800 Dickerson St, Dallas, TX 75252
Bragg, Jerry, PO Box 4289, Visalia, CA 93278
Brandon, Matthew, 4435 Meade St, Denver CO 80211
Brandsey, Edward P., 335 Forest Lake Dr, Milton, WI 53563
Brandstetter, Larry, 827 N 25th St, Paducah, KY 42001
Brandt, J. H., PO Box 5493, Irving, TX 75062
Brannan, Ralph, RR 1 Box 342, West Frankfort, IL 62896
Branton, Robert, 4976 Seewee Rd, Awendaw, SC 29429
Bray Jr., Lowell W., 6931 Manor Beach Rd, New Port Rickey, FL 34652
Brayton, Jim, 713 Park St, Burkburnett, TX 76354
Brdlik, Dan, 166 Campbell St S, Prescott, WI 54021
Breed, Kim, 733 Jace Dr, Clarksville, TN 37040
Breeze, Oran E., Hc 1 Box 266-C, Blue Eye, MO 65611
Breiter, Thomas, Rose Ln, 1-B, Topanga, CA 90290
Brend, Walter J., 309 S Forest Cir, Walterboro, SC 29488
Brennan, Judson, PO Box 1165, Delta Junction, AK 99737
Breshears, Clint, 1261 Keats St, Manhattan Beach, CA 90266
Breuer, Lonnie, PO Box 877384, Wasilla, AK 99687
Brewer, Jack, 2202 Beck Ln, Lafayette, IN 47905
Bridges, Justin W., Fish Hatchery Rd, Dubois, WY 82513
Bridwell, Richard A., Route 2 Milford Church Rd, Taylors, SC 29687
Brightwell, Mark, 21104 Creekside Dr, Leander, TX 78641
Brignardello, Ed, 71 Village Woods Dr, Crete, IL 60401
Britton, Tim, 5645 Murray Rd, Winston-Salem, NC 27106
Broadwell, David, PO Box 4314, Wichita Falls, TX 76308
Brock, Kenneth L., PO Box 375, Allenspark, CO 80510
Bromley, Peter, 1408 S Beltman, Spokane, WA 99212
Brooker, Dennis, RR 1 Box 12-A, Derby, IA 50068
Brooks, Michael, 4625 52nd St, Lubbock, TX 79414
Brooks, Steve R., 1610 Dunn Ave, Walkerville, MT 59701
Broome, Thomas A., 1212 E Aliak Ave, Kenai, AK 99611
Brothers, Robert L., 989 Philpott Rd, Colville, WA 99114
Broughton, Don R., 4690 Edwardsville Galena Rd, Floyds Knobs, IN 47119
Brower, Max, 2016 Story St, Boone, IA 50036
Brown, Bud, 306 W Rialto Ave, Clovis, CA 93612
Brown, D. L., 1803 Birdie Dr, Toledo, OH 43615
Brown, David B., 500 E. Main St, Steele City, NE 68440
Brown, Floyd E., 1940 SW 83rd Ave, Miami, FL 33155
Brown, Harold E., 3654 NW Hwy 72, Arcadia, FL 33821

Brown, Jim, 1097 Fernleigh Cove, Little Rock, AR 72210
Brown, L. E., 9533 Cedar St, Bellflower, CA 90706
Brown, Ted, 7621 Firestone Blvd, Downey, CA 90241
Brown, Tom, Suite 106 5710-K High Point Rd, Greensboro, NC 27407
Brown, Troy, 22945 W867 Rd, Park Hill, OK 74451
Brown, William Faye, RR 1 Box 295, Hope Hull, AL 36043
Browne, Rick, 980 W 13th St, Upland, CA 91786
Brumagen, Jerry, 2050 Idle Hour Center #191, Lexington, KY 40502
BrunckhorSt, C. Lyle, 23706 7th Ave SE, Bothell, WA 98021
Bruncetta, David, PO Box 4972, Laguna Beach, CA 92652
Bryan, Jack, 724 Highland Ave, Gardendale, AL 35071
Bryan, Tom, 14822 S Gilbert Rd, Gilbert, AZ 85296
Bryner, Barry, 448 N 1st Ave, Price, UT 84501
Buchman, Bill, 63312 South Rd, Bend, OR 97701
Buchner, Bill, PO Box 73, Idleyld Park, OR 97447
Bucholz, Mark A., 9197 W Parkview Terrace Loop, Eagle River, AK 99577
Buck, Bob, 582 Laurel St, Eagle Point, OR 97524
Buckbee, Donald M., 243 S Jackson Trail, Grayling, MI 49738
Buckner, Jimmie H., PO Box 162, Putney, GA 31782
Buebendorf, Robert E., 108 Lazy Brook Rd, Monroe, CT 06468
Bugden, John, RR 6 Box 7, Murray, KY 42071
Bullard, Randall, 7 Mesa Dr, Canyon, TX 79015
Bullard, Bill, RR 5 Box 35, Andalusia, AL 36420
Bullard, Tom, 117 MC 8068, Flippen, AR 72634
Bulauski, Rick, 21 Joles St, Sandwich, IL 60548
Bump, Bruce, 1103 Rex Ln, Walla Walla, WA 99362
Bumpus, Steve, 106 Bridle Ridge Rd, Collinsville, IL 62234
Bundick, Jim, PO Box 34875, Houston, TX 77234
Burden, James, 405 Kelly St, Burkburnett, TX 76354
Burke, Bill, 315 Courthouse Dr, Salmon, ID 83467
Burke, Dan, 22001 Ole Bard Rd, Edmond, OK 73034
Burkhart, Dan, 262 Mesa Dr, Camarillo, CA 93010
Burnett, Max, 537 Old Dug Mtn Rd, Paris, AR 72855
Burnette, Skip, 105 Hickory Hill Dr, Inman, SC 29349
Burns, Dave, 2825 SW 5th St, Boynton Beach, FL 33435
Burnstead, Dave, 1929 Burnstead Dr Apt 4, Billings, MT 59101
Burrows, Stephen R, 3532 Michigan, Kansas City, MO 64109
Burton, Bryan, 6218 Everglades Dr, Alexandria, VA 22312
Busfield, John, 153 Devonshire Cir, Roanoke Rapids, NC 27870
Busse, Jerry, 11651 County Rd E 12, Wauseon, OH 43567
Butler, D. L., 25 Mallard Lane, Wilmington, IL 60481
Butler, John, 777 Tyre Rd, Havana, FL 32333
Bybee, Barry, 795 Lock Rd E, Cadiz, KY 42211
Caffrey, Edward J., 2608 Central Ave West, Great Falls, MT 59404
Caldwell, Bill, 255 Rebecca Dr, West Monroe, LA 71292
Callahan, F. Terry, PO Box 880, Boeme, TX 78006
Callahan, Errett, 2 Fredonia Ave, Lynchburg, VA 24503
Callan, Peter, 7813 River Rd, Westwego, LA 70094
Calvert, Robert W. Jr., 911 Julia, Rayville, LA 71269
Cameron, Ron G., PO Box 183, Logandale, NV 89021
Camp, Jeff, 1621 Hwy 563, Dubach, LA 71235
Campbell, Dick, 20000 Silver Ranch Rd, Conifer, CO 80433
Campbell, Don, PO Box, Jerome, AZ 86331
Campbell, Irvin, Mile 20 Star Rt, Seward, AK 99664
Candrella, Joe, 1219 Barness Dr, Warminster, PA 18974
Cannady, Daniel, PO Box 301, Allendale, SC 29810
Cannon, Dan, 9500 Leon, Dallas, TX 75217
Cannon, Raymond W., PO Box 1412, Homer, AK 99603

Canter, Ronald E., 96 Bon Air Cir, Jackson, TN 38305
Cantini, Don, 3933 Claremont Pl, Weirton, WV 26062
Capdepon, Randy, 553 Joli Rd, Carencro, LA 70520
Capdepon, Robert, 829 Vatican Rd, Carencro, LA 70520
Carey Jr., Charles W., 1003 Minter Rd, Griffin, GA 30223
Cargill, Bob, RR 1 Box 383, Ocoee, TN 37361
Carlisle, Frank, 5930 Herford, Detroit, MI 48224
Carlson, Rudy, RR 1 Box 163, Moscow, ID 83843
Carnahan, Charles A., 10700 Wayfarer Rd, Germantown, MD 20876
Carnes, Wendel, PO Box 18, Whitesburg, GA 30185
Carothers, Harley, 17473 Via Susana, San Lorenzo, CA 94580
Carr, Tim, 3660 Pillon Rd, Muskegon, MI 49445
Carson, Harold J. (Kit), 1076 Brizendine Ln, Vine Grove, KY 40175
Carter, Fred, 5219 Deer Creek Rd, Wichita Falls, TX 76302
Carver, R. K., PO Box 29096, Atlanta, GA 30359
Casey, Dennis E., 2758 Devonshire Ave, Redwood City, CA 94063
Cash, Terry, 113 Sequoyah Cr, Canton, GA 30115
Cashen, Kevin R., 5615 Tyler Rd, Hubbardston, MI 48845
Casteel, Dianna, PO Box 63, Manchester, TN 37356
Casteel, Douglas, PO Box 63, Manchester, TN 37356
Catoe, David R., 4024 Heutte Dr, Norfolk, VA 23518
Caudell, Richard M., PO Box 602, Lawrenceville, IL 62429
Cellum, Tom S., 9 Cude Cemetary Rd, Willis, TX 77378
Centofante, Frank, PO Box 928, Madisonville, TN 37354
Centofante, Tony, PO Box 928, Madisonville, TN 37354
Chaffee, Jeff L., 14314 N Washington St, Morris, IN 47033
Chamberlain, Charles R., PO Box 156, Barren Springs, VA 24313
Chamberlain, John A., 11535 Our Rd, Anchorage, AK 99516
Chamberlain, Paul, Rt 2 Inverness Acres Unit, Inverness, FL 32650
Chamblin, Joel, 296 New Hebron Church Rd, Concord, GA 30206
Champagne, Paul, 48 Brightman Rd, Mechanicville, NY 12118
Champion, Robert, 1806 Plateau Lane, Amarillo, TX 79106
Channel, Tom, 7370 Peacock Way, Sacramento, CA 95820
Chapman, Gene, 27449 Baywood Dr NE, Kingston, WA 98346
Chapman, Mike, 907 Old Mill Ln, Houston, TX 77073
Chapo, William, 45 Wildridge Rd, Wilton, CT 06897
Chappel, Rod, 410 Walnut St, Edmonds, WA 98020
Chard, Gordon R., 104 S Holiday Ln, Iola, KS 66749
Chase, Alex, 208 E. Pennsylvania Ave, De Land, FL 32724
Chase, John E., 217 Walnut, Aledo, TX 76008
Chastain, Wade, RR 2 Box 137-A, Horse Shoe, NC 28742
Chauvin, John, 200 Anna St, Scott, LA 70583
Chavar, Edward, 1830 Richmond Ave, Bethlehem, PA 18018
Cheatham, Bill, PO Box 636, Laveen, AZ 85339
Cheatham, Don E., 22 E 61st St, Savannah, GA 31405
Chelquist, Cliff, PO Box 91, Arroyo Grande, CA 93421
Childress, D. W., RR 1 Box 240, Clinton, SC 29325
Childs, C. D., 1307 Bing St NW, Olympia, WA 98502
Choat, Milton, 1665 W County 17½, Somerton, AZ 85350
Christensen, Jon P., 7814 Spear Dr, Shepherd, MT 59079
Christian, Bennie, RR 3 Box 1925, Odessa, TX 79763
Churchman, T. W., 7402 Tall Cedar, San Antonio, TX 78249
Claiborne, Jeff, 1470 Roberts Rd, Franklin, IN 46131
Claiborne, Ron, 2918 Ellistown Rd, Knoxville, TN 37924
Clark, Roger, Rt 1 Box 538, Rockdale, TX 76567
Clark, Dave, 82 Valley View Manor Dr, Andrews, NC 28901
Clark, D. E. (Lucky), 314 Woodland St, Mineral Point, PA 15942
Clark, Howard F., 115 35th Pl, Runnells, IA 50237

Clark, Nate, 501 Churchill Dr, Oakland, OR 97462
Clark, W. R., 13009 Los Nietos Rd, Santa Fe Springs, CA 90670
Clay, J. D., 5050 Hall Rd, Greenup, KY 41144
Clay, Wayne, PO Box 125, Pelham, TN 37366
Cleaver, Merritt, 330 Race Hill Rd, Madison, CT 06443
Click, Gerald, 2410 N. Townleyn Ct, Santa Ana, CA 92706
Click, Joe, U344 Rd 2, Liberty Center, OH 43532
Coats, Eldon, PO Box 201, Bonanza, OR 97623
Cobb, Lowell D., 742 Alcazar Ave, Ormund Beach, FL 32114
Coberly, Ken, PO Box 1031, Petaluma, CA 94953
Cockrell, Dan, 7235 N Baldy Vista Ave, Glendora, CA 91741
Cofer, Ron, 188 Ozora Rd, Loganville, GA 30052
Coffman, Danny, 541 Angel Dr S, Jacksonville, AL 36265
Cohen, Terry A., PO Box 406, Laytonville, CA 95454
Cohen, Norman J., 2408 Sugarcone Rd, Baltimore, MD 21209
Coil, Jimmie J., 2936 Asbury Pl, Owensboro, KY 42303
Cole, Dave, 620 Poinsetta Dr, Satellite Beach, FL 32937
Cole, Welborn I., 3284 Inman Dr NE, Atlanta, GA 30319
Coleman, Keith E., 5001 Starfire Pl NW, Albuquerque, NM 87120
Coleman, Ken, 45 Grand St, Brooklyn, NY 11211
Coleman, Vernon W., 141 Lakeside Park Dr, Hendersonville, TN 37075
Collett, Jerry D., PO Box 296, Charlotte, TX 78011
Collins, Blackie, PO Box 100, North, SC 29112
Collins, Alex, 9651 Elon Ave, Arleta, CA 91331
Collins, Harold, 503 1st St, West Union, OH 45693
Collins, Jack, 112 Wedgewood Ln, Rocky Mount, VA 24151
Collins, Lynn M., 138 Berkley Dr, Elyria, OH 44035
Collins, Michael, 3075 Batesville Rd, Woodstock, GA 30188
Colter Wade, PO Box 2340, Colstrip, MT 59323
Comar, Roger N., 37 Camar Forge Dr, Marion, NC 28752
Combs Jr., Ralph, PO Box 1371, Naples, FL 33939
Compton, Paul E., 108 Overbrook Rd, Goldsboro, NC 27534
Compton, William E., 106 N Sequoia Ct, Sterling, VA 20164
Conable, Matt, PO Box 1329, Chino Valley, AZ 86323
Conkey, Tom, 9122 Keyser Rd, Nokesville, VA 22123
Conklin, George L., PO Box 902, Fort Benton, MT 59442
Conley, Bob, 1013 Creasy Rd, Jonesboro, TN 37659
Conn Jr., C. T., 206 Highland Ave, Attalla, AL 35954
Connell, Steve, 22117 Valley St, Adamsville, AL 35005
Connolly, James, 2486 Oro-Quincy Hwy, Oroville, CA 95966
Connor, Michael, PO Box 502, Winters, TX 79567
Conti, Jeffery, 4640 Feigley Rd W, Port Orchard, WA 98367
Coogan, Robert, 1516 Craft Center Dr, Smithville, TN 37166
Cook, James R., 3611 Hwy 26 W, Nashville, AR 71852
Cook, Louise, 475 Robinson Ln, Ozark, IL 62972
Cook, Mike, 475 Robinson Ln, Ozark, IL 62972
Cook, Mike A., 10927 Shilton Rd, Portland, MI 48875
Cook, R.C., 604 Phyllis Ct, Conroe, TX 77303
Cook, Ron, Rt 2 Box 5800, Superior, MT 59872
Coombs Jr., Lamont, 546 State Rt 46, Bucksport, ME 04416
Coon, Raymond C., 21135 SE Tillstrom Rd, Gresham, OR 97080
Cooper, George J., 1834 W Burbank Blvd, Burbank, CA 91506
Cooper, J. N., RR 8 Box 653, Lufkin, TX 75904
Copeland, Thom, 171 County Line Rd S, Nashville, AR 71852
Copeland, George S., 220 Pat Carr Ln, Alpine, TN 38543
Corbit, Gerald E., 1701 St John Rd, Elizabethtown, KY 42701
Corby, Harold, 218 Brandonwood Dr, Johnson City, TN 37604
Cordova, Joseph G., PO Box 977, Peralta, NM 87042

Corlee, Leonard, PO Box 143, Georgetown, GA 31754
Corrado, Jim, 255 Rock View Ln, Glide, OR 97443
Corwin, Don, 9324 Avedon Dr, Saline, MI 48176
Cosby, E. Blanton, 2954 Pierpoint Ave, Columbus, GA 31904
Cosgrove, Charles, 2314 W Arbook Blvd, Arlington, TX 76015
Costa, Scott, 409 Coventry Rd, Spicewood, TX 78669
Cottrill, James, 1776 Ransburg Ave, Columbus, OH 43223
Couchman, Don, RR 1 Box 283-A, La Mesa, NM 88044
Coughlin, Michael M., 74 Mainstreet N, Woodbury, CT 06798
Courtney Jr., Danny, RR 8 Box 237, Martinsville, VA 24112
Courtney, Eldon, 2718 Bullinger St, Wichita, KS 67204
Courtois, Bryan, 3 Lawn Ave, Saco, ME 04072
Cousino, George, 7818 Norfolk Dr, Onsted, MI 49265
Cover, Raymond A., RR 1 Box 194, Mineral Point, MO 63660
Cowles, Don, 1026 Lawndale Dr, Royal Oak, MI 48067
Cox, Colin J., 107 N Oxford Dr, Raymore, MO 64083
Cox, James O., 1203 Evergreen Dr, Smackover, AR 71762
Cox, Mike, RR 1 Box 69, Cowiche, WA 98923
Cox, Sam, 1756 Love Springs Rd, Gaffney, SC 29341
Crabtree, H. W., RR 1, Rudy, AR 72952
Craft, John M., PO Box 278, Peoria, AZ 85380
Craft, Richard C., 3045 Longwood Dr, Jackson, MS 39212
Craig, James H., 334 Novara Dr, Manchester, MO 63021
Craig, Roger L., 2815 Fairlawn Rd, Topeka, KS 66614
Crain, Frank, 127 W Dalke, Spokane, WA 99205
Crain, Jack W., PO Box 212, Granbury, TX 76048
Crane, Arnold H., 134 N La Salle St, Chicago, IL 60602
Crawford, Larry, 1610 Hutto Rd, Georgetown, TX 78626
Crawford, Pat, 205 N Center Dr, West Memphis, AR 72301
Crawford, Stewart, 504½ Front St, Morgan City, LA 70380
Crenshaw, Al, Rt 1 Box 717, Eufala, OK 74432
Crisp, Harold, 3885 Bow St NE, Cleveland, TN 37312
Crockford, Jack, 1859 Harts Mill Rd NE, Chamblee, GA 30341
Cross, John M., Rt 1 Box 351, Bryceville, FL 32009
Cross, Stuart, PO Box 1519, Alpine, TX 79831
Cross, Tim, 743 N Loma Vista Dr, Long Beach, CA 90813
Crosslen, Timothy J., PO Box 338, Grafton, WI 53024
Crowder, Robert, PO Box 1374, Thompson Falls, MT 59873
Crowell, James L., 7181 Happy Hollow Rd, Mountain View, AR 72560
Cruze, Dan, 14406 Winterset Dr, Orlando, FL 32832
Cullity, W. Daniel, Old Country Rd East, Sandwich, MA 02537
Culpepper, John, 2102 Spencer St, Monroe, LA 71201
Culver, Steve, 5682 94th St, Meriden KS 66512
Cumming, R. J., 35 Manana Dr, Cedar Crest, NM 87008
Cunningham, Jim, 1911 Madison Ave, Memphis, TN 38104
Cutchin, Roy D., 960 Hwy 169 South, Seale, AL 36875
Cute, Thomas, State Rt 90-7071, Cortland, NY 13045
D'Andrea, John, 501 Penn Estates, East Stroudsberg, PA 18301
D'Angelo, Laurence, 14703 NE 17th Ave, Vancouver, WA 98686
D'Elia, Frank, 2050 Hillside Ave, New Hyde Park, NY 11040
Dabbs, Bill, 18330 Wards Ferry Rd, Sonora, CA 95370
Dachtler, Orville, 35182 Cabral Dr, Fremont, CA 94536
Daconceicao, John M., 138 Perryville Rd, Rehoboth, MA 02769
Dagget, Dan, 1961 W Meteor Dr, Flagstaff, AZ 86001
Dahl, Cris W., RR 4 Box 558, Lake Geneva, WI 53147
Dailey, George E., 577 Lincoln St, Seekonk, MA 02771
Dake, Charles M., 19759 Chef Menteur Hwy, New Orleans, LA 70129
Damlovac, Sava, 10292 Bradbury Dr, Indianapolis, IN 46231

Daniels, Alex, 1416 County Road 415, Town Creek, AL 35672
Daniels, Travis E., 1655 Carrow Rd, Chocowinity, NC 27817
Darakis, Art, A., 18181 Quarry Rd, Wellington, OH 44090
Darby, Jed, 7878 E Co. Rd 50 N, Greensburg, IN 47240
Darby, Rick, 71 Nestingrock Ln, Levittown, PA 19054
Darcy, Chester L., 1608 Dominic Dr, College Station, TX 77840
Darpinian, Dave, 15219 W 125th, Olathe, KS 66062
Davenport, Jack, PO Box 451, Crystal Springs, FL 33524
Davenport, Steve, 15 Roman Ln, Alvin, TX 77511
Daves, Ken, 31 S Butler Ave, Indianapolis, IN 46219
Davidson, Edmund, 3345 Virginia Ave, Goshen, VA 24439
Davidson, Rob, 702 Indian Trl, Kerrville, TX 78028
Davis, Ken, 31 S Butler Ave #4, Indianapolis, IN 46219
Davis, Barry L., 4262 US 20, Castleton, NY 12033
Davis, Brothers, 1209 Woodlawn Dr, Camden, SC 29020
Davis, Charlie, PO Box 710806, Santee, CA 92072
Davis, Dixie, RR 3, Clinton, SC 29325
Davis, Don, 8415 Coyote Run, Loveland, CO 80537
Davis, Greg, PO Box 272, Fillmore, UT 84631
Davis, Jesse W., 7398-A Hwy 3, Sarah, MS 38665
Davis, John, 235 Lampe Rd, Selah, WA 98942
Davis, K. M., PO Box 267, Monroe, WA 98272
Davis, Gerald, PO Box 793, Camden, SC 29020
Davis, Larry, 411 Cedar Dr, Pierce, ID 83456
Davis, Steve, 3370 Chatsworth Way, Powder Springs, GA 30073
Davis, Syd, 1220 Courtney St, Richmond, TX 77469
Davis, Terry, PO Box 111, Sumpter, OR 97877
Davis, Vernon M., 2020 Behrens Circle, Waco, TX 76705
Davis, W. C., 19300 S School Rd, Raymore, MO 64083
Dawkins, Dudley L., 221 NW Broadmoor Ave, Topeka, KS 66606
Dawson, Barry, 10-A Town Plz Ste 303, Durango, CO 81301
Dawson, Lynn, 10 Town Plaza #303, Durango, CO 81301
Day, Phillip, Rt 1, Box 464 T Bay, Minetta, AL 35607
De Intinnis, Ed, 107 Summit Ave, Staten Island, NY 10306
Dees, Jay, Rt 1 Box 17-C, Collins, MS 39428
DeGrave, Richard, 329 Valencia St, Sebastian, FL 32958
Delarosa, Jim, 202 MacArthur Dr, Mukwonago, WI 53149
DeLong, Dick, 17561 E Ohio Circle, Aurora, CO 80017
DeMaria Jr., Angelo, 12 Boronda Rd, Carmel Valley CA 93924
DeYong, Clarence, 4140 Cripple Creek Way, Kennesaw, GA 30144
Dean, Harvey J., 3266 CR 232, Rockdale, TX 76567
Dearhart, Richard, RR 1, Lula, GA 30554
Dearing, John, 1569 Flucom Rd, Desoto, MO 63020
Defeo, Robert A., 403 Lost Trail Dr, Henderson, NV 89014
Defreest, William G., PO Box 573, Barnwell, SC 29812
Degraeve, Richard, 329 Valencia St, Sebastian, FL 32958
Del Pinto, Paul, 5901 Warner Ave Apt 3, Huntington Beach, CA 92649
Dellana, 168 Riverbend Blvd., St Albans, WV 25177
Delong, Dick, 17561 E Ohio Cir, Aurora, CO 80017
Demers, Roy, RR 1 Box 104, Wever, IA 52658
Dempsey, David, 103 Chadwick Dr, Macon, GA 31210
Dempsey, Gordon S., PO Box 7497, N Kenai, AK 99635
Dennard, J. R., 907 Greenwood Pl, Dalton, GA 30720
Dennehy, Dan, 13321 Hwy 160, Del Norte, CO 81132
Dennehy, John D., 3926 Hayes, Wellington, CO 80549
Denning, Geno, 135 Allenvalley Rd, Gaston, SC 29053
Dent, Douglas M., 1208 Chestnut St, Charleston, WV 25309
Derr, Herbert, 413 Woodland Dr, St Albans, WV 25177

Des Jardins, Dennis, PO Box 1103, Plains, MT 59859
Detloff, Larry, 130 Oxford Way, Santa Cruz, CA 95060
Detmer, Phillip, 14140 Bluff Rd, Breese, IL 62230
Dew, Norman, 742 Hobhollow, Channelview, TX 77530
De Yong, Clarence, 1448 Glen Haven Dr, Ft Collins, CO 80526
Di Marzo, Richard, 2357 Center Place, Birmingham, AL 35205
Diana, Julius S., PO Box 152, Carmichaels, PA 15320
Dias, Jack, PO Box 223, Palermo, CA 95968
Dickerson, Gordon S., 152 Laurel Ln, Hohenwald, TN 38462
Dickey, Charles, 803 NE A St, Bentonville, AR 72712
Dickison, Scott S., PO Box 357, Narragansett, RI 02882
Dickson, Jim, 2349 Eastway Rd, Decatur, GA 30033
Dietz, Howard, 421 Range Rd, New Braunfels, TX 78132
Dietzel, Bill, PO Box 1613, Middleburg, FL 32068
Digangi, Joseph M., PO Box 950, Santa Cruz, NM 87567
Dill, Dave, 7404 NW 30th St, Bethany, OK 73008
Dill, Robert, 1812 Van Buren Ave, Loveland, CO 80538
Dillon, Earl E., 8908 Stanwin Ave, Arleta, CA 91331
Dilluvio, Frank, 13611 Joyce Dr, Warren, MI 48093
Dingman, Scott, 4298 Parkers Lake Rd NE, Bemidji, MN 56601
Dion, Greg, 3032 Jackson St, Oxnard, CA 93033
Dion, Malcolm, 820 N Fairview Ave, Goleta, CA 93117
Dippold, A. W., 90 Damascus Ln, Perryville, MO 63775
Diskin, Matt, PO Box 653, Freeland, WA 98249
Dixon Jr., Ira E., PO Box 2581, Ventura, CA 93002
Doak, Charles A., PO Box 143, Saddle River, TN 37458
Dodge, Robert O., 1515 Braley St, Saginaw, MI 48602
Dodson Jr., Dr. Frank, RR 3 Box 372, Little Rock, AR 72211
Doggett, Bob, 1310 Vinetree Dr, Brandon, FL 33510
Dolan, Robert L., 220-B Naalae Rd, Kula, HI 96790
Dominy, Chuck, PO Box 593, Colleyville, TX 76034
Donaghey, John, PO Box 402021, Garland, TX 75045
Donovan, Patrick, 1770 Hudson Dr, San Jose, CA 95124
Doolittle, Mike, 13 Denise Ct, Novato, CA 94945
Dorough, Dick, 2624 Sunnydale Dr, Southside, AL 35901
Dotson, Tracy, 1280 Hwy C-4A, Baker, FL 32531
Douglas, John J., 506 Powell Rd, Lynch Station, VA 24571
Dow, Thomas G., 195 River Rd, Grandview, NY 10960
Dowell, T. M., 139 NW Saint Helens Pl, Bend, OR 97701
Downing, Larry, 12268 State Rt 181 N, Bremen, KY 42325
Downing, Tom, 2675 12th St, Cuyahoga Falls, OH 44223
Downs, James, 35 Sunset Rd, Londonderry, OH 45647
Dozier, Bob, PO Box 1941, Springdale, AR 72765
Draper, Audra, #10 Creek Dr, Riverton, WY 82501
Draper, Bart, PO Box 548, Big Piney, WY 83113
Draper, Kent, 23461 Highway 36, Cheshire, OR 97419
Draper, Mike, #10 Creek Dr, Riverton, WY 82501
Draw, Gerald, 2 Glenn Cable, Asheville, NC 28802
Drew, Frank, 729 Main St, Klamath Falls, OR 97601
Driskill, Beryl, PO Box 187, Braggadocio, MO 63826
Driscoll, Mark, 4115 Avoyer Place, La Mesa, CA 91941
Drost, Jason, Rt 2 Box 49, French Creek, WV 26218
Drost, Michael B., Rt 2 Box 49, French Creek, WV 26218
Dube, Paul, PO Box 122, Chaska, MN 55318
Duff, Bill, PO Box 694, Virginia City, NV 89440
Dufour, Arthur J., 8120 De Armoun Rd, Anchorage, AK 99516
Dugan, Brad, PO Box 693, Milford, DE 19963
Dugger, Dave, 2504 W 51st St, Westwood, KS 66205

Duke, R. D., 7160 Belgium Cir, Pensacola, FL 32526
Dumatrait, Gene, PO Box 3071, Beaumont, TX 77704
Dungy, Lawrence, 8 Southmont Dr, Little Rock, AR 72209
Dunkerley, Rick, PO Box 111, Lincoln, MT 59639
Dunn, Charles K, 17740 GA Hwy 116, Shiloh, GA 31826
Dunn, James E., 1560 Brookhollow Dr, Santa Ana, CA 92705
Dunn, Melvin T., 5830 NW Carlson Rd, Rossville, KS 66533
Dunn, Steve, 376 Biggerstaff Rd, Smiths Grove, KY 42171
Duran, Jerry T., PO Box 80692, Albuquerque, NM 87198
Durham, Kenneth, 10495 White Pike, Cherokee, AL 35616
Durio, Fred, 144 Gulino St, Opelousas, LA 70570
Duvall, Fred, 10715 Hwy 190, Benton, AR 72015
Duvall, Larry E., RR 3, Gallatin, MO 64640
Dyees, Eddie, 1005 Hamilton Dr, Roswell, NM 88201
Dyer, David, 4531 Hunters Glen, Granbury, TX 76048
Eagan, Tim, 118 Las Ondas Ct, Santa Cruz, CA 95060
Eaker, Allen L., 416 Clinton Ave, Paris, IL 61944
Easler, Paula, PO Box 301, Woodruff, SC 29388
Easler Jr., Russell O., PO Box 301, Woodruff, SC 29388
Eaton, Al, PO Box 43, Clayton, CA 94517
Eaton, Rick, 9944 McCrannie St, Shepherd, MT 59079
Echols, Roger, 46 Channing Rd, Nashville, AR 71852
Eck, Larry, PO Box 665, Terrebonne, OR 97760
Ecker, Dave, 110 Bleecker St, New York, NY 10012
Eckerson, Charley, 1117 Horseshoe Dr, Pueblo, CO 81001
Eden, Thomas, PO Box 57, Cranbury, NJ 08512
Edge, Tommy, PO Box 156, Cash, AR 72421
Edwards, Fain E., PO Box 280, Topton, NC 28781
Edwards, Homer W., 6429 W Camelback Rd, Phoenix, AZ 85033
Edwards, Lynn, RR 2 Box 614, West Columbia, TX 77486
Edwards, Mitch, 303 New Salem Rd, Glasgow, KY 42141
Edwards, Thomas W., 4513 N 56th Ave, Phoenix, AZ 85031
Ehrenberger, Daniel R., 6192 Hwy 168, Shelbyville, MO 63469
Ek, Gary Whitney, 1580 NE 125th St, North Miami, FL 33161
Elder, Ray, 121 E 11th St, Colorado City, TX 79512
Elder Jr., Perry B., 1321 Garrettsburg Rd, Clarksville, TN 37042
Eldridge, Allan, 7731 Four Winds Dr, Ft Worth, TX 76133
Elishwitz, Allen, 3960 Lariet Rd, New Braunfels, TX 78132
Elkins, R. Van, PO Box 156, Bonita, LA 71223
Ellefson, Joel, 310 S 1st St, Manhattan, MT 59741
Ellenberg, William C., 10 Asbury Ave, Melrose Park, PA 19027
Ellerbe, W. B., 3871 E Osceola Rd, Geneva, FL 32732
Elliott, Jim, 18175 Hwy 98 N, Okeechobee, WV 34972
Ellis, William Dean, 8875 N Barton, Fresno, CA 93720
Ellis, David, 3505 Camino Del Rio S #334, San Diego, CA 92108
Ellison, Don, 670 Browning St, Ypsilanti, MI 48198
Elmore, Clarence, 4944 Angeles Crest Hwy, La Canada, CA 91011
Embry, Brad, PO Box 1526, Valrico, FL 33565
Emerson, Ernest R., PO Box 4180, Torrance, CA 90510
Emery, Roger, 3514 S Central Ave, Phoenix, AZ 85040
Ence, Jim, 145 S 200 East, Richfield, UT 84701
Enders, Robert, 3028 White Rd, Cement City, MI 49233
Eneboe, James, 2860 Rosendale Rd, Schenectady, NY 12309
England, Mike, 608 W 4th St, Cordell, OK 73632
England, Virgil, 7133 Artic Blvd #5, Anchorage, AK 99518
Engle, William, 16608 Oak Ridge Rd, Boonville, MO 65223
Englebretson, George, 1209 NW 49th St, Oklahoma City, OK 73118
English, Jim, 14586 Olive Vista Dr, Jamul, CA 91935

Engnath, Bob, 1217 Cresent Dr Apt B, Glendale, CA 91205
Ennard, J. R., 907 Greenwood Pl, Dalton, GA 30720
Ennis, Ray W., 509 S 3rd St, Grand Forks, ND 58201
Enos, Thomas M., 12302 State Road 535, Orlando, FL 32819
Enton, W. F., 104 Lapine Dr, Eufaula, AL 36207
Epting, Richard, 4021 Cody Dr, College Station, TX 77845
Erickson, Curt, 449 Washington Blvd, Ogden, UT 84404
Erickson, L. M., PO Box 132, Liberty, UT 84310
Erickson, Walter E., 22280 Shelton Tr, Atlanta, MI 49709
Eriksen, James T., 3830 Dividend Dr, Garland, TX 75042
Essegian, Richard, 7387 E Tulare Ave, Fresno, CA 93727
Etienne, Serge, 14875 Esters Rd, Valley Ford, CA 94972
Etzler, John, 11200 N Island, Grafton, OH 44044
Evans, Bruce A., 409 CR 1371, Booneville, MS 38829
Evans, Carlton, PO Box 815, Aledo, TX 76008
Evans, John D., 5414 Grissom Dr, Arlington, TX 76016
Evans, Vincent K., 6301 Apache Trail, Show Lo, AZ 85901
Ewing, John H., 3276 Dutch Valley Rd, Clinton, TN 37716
Ewing, William S., 2724 Northcrest Dr, Plano, TX 75075
Falconer, Ralph, PO Box 1021, Frederick, OK 73542
Fannin, David A., 2050 Idle Hour Center #191, Lexington, KY 40502
Farr, Dan, 285 Glen Ellyn Way, Rochester, NY 14618
Farris, Cal, PO Box 41, Altoona, FL 32702
Fassio, Melvin G., 420 Tyler Way, Lobo, MT 59847
Faucheaux, Howard J., PO Box 206, Loreauville, LA 70552
Faulkner, Allan, Rt 11 Box 161, Jasper, AL 35501
Faust, Dick, 624 Kings Hwy N, Rochester, NY 14617
Fawcett, Alexander R., 3241 Kerner Blvd, San Rafael, CA 94901
Fecas, Stephen, 1312 Shadow Ln, Anderson, SC 29625
Feccia, Ron, 1600 Holloway Ave, San Francisco, CA 94132
Felfidel, Ralph, 15 Budlong Ave, Warrich, RI 02888
Felix, Alexander, 24011 Eshelman Ave, Lomita, CA 90717
Feragotti, Vince, Rt 1 Beechwood Dr, Industry, PA 15052
Ferdinand, Don, PO Box 1564, Shady Cove, OR 97539
Ferguson, Jim, 32131 Via Bande, Temecula, CA 92592
Ferguson, Jim, PO Box 764, San Angelo, TX 76902
Ferguson, Lee, 1993 Madison 7580, Hindsville, AR 72738
Ferguson, Lewis, 1200 Pico Blvd, Santa Monica CA 90405
Ferguson, Roy, PO Box 224, Wedderburn, OR 97491
Ferrara, Thomas M., 122 Madison Dr, Naples, FL 33942
Ferry, Tom, 16005 SE 322nd, Auburn, WA 98092
Fielder, William V., 8406 Knowland Circle, Richmond, VA 23229
Fikes, Jimmy L., PO Box 3457, Jasper, AL 35502
Filbrun, Robert, 3843 Beckwith Rd, Modesto, CA 95358
Finch, Ricky D., 2446 Hwy 191, West Liberty, KY 41472
Finger, L. C., 1001 113th N, Weatherford, TX 76086
Finley, C. H., 4176 Saint Patricks Ave, Redding, CA 96003
Fiorini, Bill, PO Box 237, Dakota, MN 55925
Fischer, Clyde E., HC 40 Box 133, Nixon, TX 78140
Fisher, Jay, PO Box 267, Magdalena, NM 87825
Fisher, Mike, RR 3, Beatrice, NE 68310
Fisher, Theo, 8115 Modoc Rd, Montague, CA 96064
Fisk, Jerry, 145 N Park Ave, Lockesburg, AR 71846
Fister, Jim, 5067 Fisherville Rd, Simpsonville, KY 40067
Fitch, C. S., 1755 Laurel St, Baton Rouge, LA 70802
Fitch, John S., 45 Halbrook Rd, Cllinton, AR 72031
Fitzgerald, Dennis M., 4219 Alverado Dr, Fort Wayne, IN 46816
Flemming, Jim, Yonna Valley Forge, Bonanza, OR 97623

Flint, Robert, 2902 Aspen Dr, Anchorage, AK 99517
Flood, James, PO Box 216, Chaska, MN 55318
Flournoy, Joe, 5750 Lisbon Rd, El Dorado, AR 71730
Flynn, Bruce, 8139 W County Rd 650 S, Knightstown, IN 46148
Fogg, Don, 40 Alma Rd, Jasper, AL 35501
Foley, Barney, 3M Reler Ln, Somerset, NJ 08873
Ford, Allen, 3927 Plumcrest Rd, Smyrna, GA 30082
Foreman, Bill, 1200 Catherine St, Metropolis, IL 62960
Forester, Del W., 7355 Sanborn Ln, Sacramento, CA 95823
Forge, H. B., RR 2 Box 24, Shiloh, OH 44878
Forrest, Brain, PO Box 203, Descanco, CA 91916
Forstall, Al, 38379 Aunt Massey Rd, Pearl River, LA 70452
Forthofer, Pete, 5535 Hwy 93 South, Whitefish, MT 59937
Foster, Al, 118 Woodway Dr, Magnolia, TX 77355
Foster, R. L., 745 Glendale Blvd, Mansfield, OH 44907
Foster, Ronnie E., 95 Riverview Rd, Morrilton, AR 72110
Foster, Timothy L., 723 Sweet Gum Acres Rd, El Dorado, AR 71730
Foust, Roger, 1925 Vernon Ave, Modesto, CA 95351
Fowler, C. Ronnie, 226 National Forest Rd 48, Ft McCoy, FL 32134
Fowler, Ed, Willow Bow Ranch Box 1519, Riverton, WY 82501
Fowler, Jerry, 610 FM 1660, Hutto, TX 78634
Fowler, Ricky, 22080 9th St, Silverhill, AL 36576
Fox, Jack L., 7085 Canelo Hills Dr, Citrus Heights, CA 95610
Fox, Paul, 4721 Rock Barn Rd, Claremont, NC 28610
Fox, Wendell, 1480 S 39th St, Springfield, OR 97478
Fraley, Derek, 1355 Fairbanks Ct, Dixon, CA 95620
France, Dan, PO Box 218, Cawood, KY 40815
Francis, Vance, 2612 Alpine Blvd, Alpine, CA 91901
Frank, Heinrich H., 13868 NW Keleka Pl, Seal Rock, OR 97376
Frankl, John M., 12 Holden St, Cambridge, MA 02138
Franklin, Mike, 9878 Big Run Rd, Aberdeen, OH 45101
Franks, Joel, 6610 Quaker Ave, Lubbock, TX 79413
Fraps, John, 3810 Wyandotte Tr, Indianapolis, IN 46240
Frazier, Ron, 2107 Urbine Rd, Powhatan, VA 23139
Freeman, Art F., 7542 St Philomena Way, Citrus Heights, CA 95610
Freeman, Douglas J., 4154 Dellwood Dr, Macon, GA 31204
Freer, Ralph, 114 12th St, Seal Beach, CA 90740
Freiling, Albert J., 3700 Niner Rd, Finksburg, MD 21048
Frese, William R., 5374 Fern Beach Rd, Saint Louis, MO 63128
Frey Jr., W. Frederick, 305 Walnut St, Milton, PA 17847
Friedly, Dennis, 12 Cottontail Ln, Cody, WY 82414
Fritz, Jesse, 900S 13th St, Slaton, TX 79364
Frizzell, Ted, 14056 Low Gap Rd, West Fork, AR 72774
Froehlick, R., 740 N California St, Lodi, CA 95240
Fronefield, Daniel, 137 Catherine Dr, Hapton Cove, AL 35763
Frost, Dewayne, 1016 Van Buren Rd, Barnesville, GA 30204
Fuegen, Larry, 617 N Coulter Circle, Prescott, AZ 86303
Fujisaka, Stanley, 45-004 Holowai St, Kaneohe, HI 96744
Fuller, Bruce A., 1305 S Airhart Dr, Baytown, TX 77520
Fuller, Burt, PO Box 734, Livingston, AL 35470
Fuller, Jack A., 7103 Stretch Ct, New Market, MD 21774
Fuller, Jim, PO Box 51, Burnwell, AL 35038
Fuller, John W., 6156 Ridge Way, Douglasville, GA 30135
Fuller, W. T., 400 S 8th St, East Gadsden, AL 35903
Fulton, Mickey, 406 S Shasta St, Willows, CA 95988
Funderburg, Joe, 1255 Bay Oaks Dr, Los Osos, CA 93402
Gaddy, Gary Lee, 205 Ridgewood Lane, Washington, NC 27889
Gaines, Buddy, 155 Red Hill Rd, Commerce, GA 30530

Gainey, Hal, 904 Bucklevel Rd, Greenwood, SC 29649
Gallagher, Barry, 135 Park St, Lewistown, MT 59457
Gallop, Bob, 44021 White Oak Ct, Rocklin, CA 95677
Gamble, Frank, PO Box 8169, Fremont, CA 94537
Gamble, Roger, 2801 65 Way N, St Petersburg, FL 33710
Gannaway, Woodson, 5402 Spicebush, Madison, WI 43714
Garbe, Robert, 33176 Klein, Fraser, MI 48026
Garcia, Raul, PO Box 693, Aberdeen, MD 21001
Garcia, Tony, 134 Gregory Pl, West Palm Beach, FL 33405
Gardner, Bob, 3828 Delhi Ct, Ann Arbor, MI 48103
Gardner, Mark, 11585 Lincoln St, Grand Haven, MI 49417
Gardner, Rob, 387 Mustang Blvd, Port Aransas, TX 78373
Garlits, Chuck, PO Box 577, Rosman, NC 28772
Garner, Larry W., 13069 PM 14, Tyler, TX 75706
Garner Jr., William O., 2803 E De Soto St, Pensacola, FL 32503
Gartman, M. D., Rt 4 Box 423-G, Gatesville, TX 76528
Gaston, Bert, PO Box 9047, North Little Rock, AR 72119
Gaston, Ron, 330 Peden Gaston Dr, Woodruff, SC 29388
Gaudette, Linden L., 5 Hitchcock Rd, Wilbraham, MA 01095
Gaugler, Earl W., 44 Center Grove Rd, Randolph, NJ 07869
Gault, Clay, 1225 Hwy 696 East, Lexington, TX 78947
Geisler, Gary R., PO Box 294, Clarksville, OH 45113
Genge, Roy E., PO Box 57, Eastlake, CO 80614
Genovese, Rick, 116 Fawn Dr, Sedona, AZ 86336
Genske, Jay, 283 Doty St, Fondulac, WI 54935
George, Harry, 3137 Old Camp Long Rd, Aiken, SC 29805
George, Les, 1703 Payne, Wichata, KS 67203
George, Tom, 6311 Shelton Ct, Magalia, CA 95954
Gepner, Don, 2615 E Tecumseh Rd, Norman, OK 73071
Gevedon, Hanners (Hank), 1410 John Cash Rd, Crab Orchard, KY 40419
Gibson Sr., James, RR 1, Box 177-F St Johns Park, Bunnell, FL 32110
Gilbreath, Randall W., 58 Crauswell Rd, Dora, AL 35062
Gillenwater, E. E. "Dick", 921 Dougherty Rd, Aiken, SC 29801
Gillis, C. R. "Rex", 2340 2nd Ave SW, Great Falls, MT 59404
Gilmore, Jon, 849 University Pl, Saint Louis, MO 63132
Gilpin, David, 902 Falling Star Ln, Alabaster, AL 35007
Giovannetti, Jim, 2710 S Denison Ave, San Pedro, CA 90731
Gladius, Terra, 1802 5th Ave SE, Olympia, WA 98501
Glaser, Ken, RR 1 Box 148, Purdy, MO 65734
Gleason, Roger, 13518 Grover St, Omaha, NE 68144
Glover, Ron, 7702 Misty Springs Ct, Mason, OH 45040
Glover, Warren, PO Box 475, Cleveland, GA 30528
Goddard, Wayne, 473 Durham Ave, Eugene, OR 97404
Goers, Bruce, 3423 Royal Ct S, Lakeland, FL 33813
Goertz, Paul S., 201 Union Ave SE Unit 207, Renton, WA 98059
Goff, Darrel W., 5725 NE Wholme Ave, Baltimore, MD 21206
Gofourth, Jim, 3776 Aliso Canyon Rd, Santa Paula, CA 93060
Goguen, Scott, 166 Goguen Rd, Newport, NC 28570
Goldberg, David, 1120 Blyth Ct, Blue Bell, PA 19422
Goldenberg, T. S., PO Box 238, Fairview, NC 28730
Golding, Robin, PO Box 267, Lathrop, CA 95330
Goltz, Warren L., 802 4th Ave E, Ada, MN 56510
Gonzalez, Gene, PO Box 33, Roma, TX 78584
Goo, Tai, 5920 W Windy Lou Ln, Tucson, AZ 85742
Goode, Bear, PO Box 6474, Navajo Dam, NM 87419
Goodwin, Butch, 1345 Foothill Dr, Vista, CA 92084
Gorenflo, James T., 9145 Sullivan Rd, Baton Rouge, LA 70818

Gottage, Dante, 43227 Brooks Dr, Clinton Twp, MI 48038
Gottage, Judy, 43227 Brooks Dr, Clinton Twp, MI 48038
Gottschalk, Gregory, 121st St (Ft. Pitt), Carnegie, PA 15106
Gouker, Gary B., PO Box 955, Sitka, AK 99835
Graber, Cliff C., 315 E 4th St, Ontario, CA 91764
Graffeo, Anthony I., 100 Riess Pl, Chalmette, LA 70043
Graham, Charles W., RR 1 Box 11, Eolia, MO 63344
Graham, Robert, 1632 Creighton Ave, Akron, OH 44310
Granquist, William R., 5 Paul St, Bristol, CT 06010
Grant, John B., 59 Wood Ln, Fairfax, CA 94930
Grant, Larry, PO Box 404, Auburn, WY 83111
Gravelle, Mike, 4710 Shabbona Rd, Deckerville, MI 48427
Gray, Bob, 1806 N Lucia Ct, Spokane, WA 99208
Gray, Daniel, 686 Main Rd, Brownville, ME 04414
Grebe, Gordon S., PO Box 296, Anchor Point, AK 99556
Greco, John, 100 Mattie Jones Rd, Greensburg, KY 42743
Green, Bill, 706 Bradfield, Garland, TX 75042
Green, David, 4640 Co Rd 1022, Joshua, TX 76058
Green, Larry G., 6911 NW 77th Ter, Kansas City, MO 64152
Green, Roger M., 4640 Co Rd 1022, Joshua, TX 76058
Green, Russ, 6013 Briercest Ave, Lakewood, CA 90713
Greene, Chris, 707 Cherry Ln, Shelby, NC 28150
Greene, David, 570 Malcom Rd, Covington, GA 30209
Greenfield, G. O., 2605 15th St, Everett, WA 98201
Greiner, Richard, 1073 E County Rd 32, Green Springs, OH 44836
Gregory, Michael, 211 Calhoun Rd, Belton, SC 29627
Grey, Bruce, 145 W 20th St, Chico, CA 95928
Greisi, Christian, 4122 S 'E' St, Springfield, OR 97478
Griffin Jr., Howard, 14299 SW 31st Ct, Davie, FL 33330
Griffin, Mark, 9706 Cedardale Dr, Houston, TX 77055
Griffin, Rendon, 9706 Cedardale Dr, Houston, TX 77055
Griffin, Thomas J., 591 Quevli Ave, Windom, MN 56101
Griffith, Lynn, PO Box 876, Glenpool, OK 74033
Grigg, Walt, 1303 Stetson St, Orlando, FL 32804
Grigsby, Ben, 318 E Main Mt View, AR 72560
Grigsby, John D., 5320 Circle Rd, Corryton, TN 37721
Grospitch, Ernie, 18440 Amityville St, Orlando, FL 32820
Gross, W. W., 325 Sherbrook Dr, High Point, NC 27260
Grossman, Stewart, 24 Water St # 419, Clinton, MA 01510
Grow, Jim, 1712 Carlisle Rd, Oklahoma City, OK 73120
Grubb, Richard E., 2759 Maplewood Dr, Columbus, OH 43231
Grussenmeyer, Paul G., 310 Dresson Rd, Cherry Hill, NJ 08034
Guess, Jack, 12 N Rockford Ave, Tulsa, OK 74120
Guess, Raymond L., 7214 Salineville Rd NE, Mechanicstown, OH 44651
Guignard, Gib, Box 3413, Quartzsite, AZ 85359
Gundersen, D. F., 5811 S Siesta Ln, Tempe, AZ 85283
Gunn, Nelson L., 77 Blake Rd, Epping, NH 03042
Gunter, Brad, 13 Imnaha Rd, Tijeras, NM 87059
Gurganus, Carol, 2553 NC 45 S, Colerain, NC 27924
Gurganus, Melvin H., 2553 NC 45 S, Colerain, NC 27924
Gutekunst, Ralph, 117 SW 14th St, Richmond, IN 47374
Guth, Kenneth, 35 E Wacker Dr Ste 1840, Chicago, IL 60601
Guthrie, George, 1912 Puetts Chapel Rd, Bessemer City, NC 28016
Gwozdz, Bob, 71 Starr Ln, Attleboro, MA 02703
Hagen, Philip (Doc), PO Box 58, Pelican Rapids, MN 56572
Haggerty, George S., PO Box 88, Jacksonville, VT 05342
Hagwood, Kellie, 9231 Ridge Town, San Antonio, TX 78250

Haines, Jeff, 302 N Mill St, Wauzeka, WI 53826
Hajovsky, Robert J., PO Box 77, Scotland, TX 76379
Halbrook, Gary R., 17564 Arrow Blvd, Fontana, CA 92335
Hall, Douglas A., 1450 Alta Vista Dr, Vista, CA 92084
Halligan, Ed, 14 Meadow Way, Sharpsburg, GA 30277
Halligan, Shawn, 14 Meadow Way, Sharpsburg, GA 30277
Hamby, Skip, PO Box 447, Portola, CA 96122
Hamlet Jr., Johnny, 300 Billington St, Clute, TX 77531
Hammock, Paul, 1433 S Broadway, Santa Maria, CA 93454
Hammond, Jim, PO Box 486, Arab, AL 35016
Hampton, William W, 7935 E D Robbins Rd, Howey in the Hills, FL 34737
Hancock, Tim, 10805 N 83rd St, Scottsdale, AZ 85260
Hancock, Ronald E., 3795 W Grover Cleveland Blvd, Lecanto, FL 34460
Hand, Bill, 1103 W 7th St, Spearman, TX 79081
Hand, James E., 1001 Mockingbird Ln, Gloster, MS 39638
Hansen, Lonnie, PO Box 4956, Spanaway, WA 98387
Hansen, Robert W., 35701 University Ave, Cambridge, MN 55008
Hanson, Travis, 651 Rangeline Rd, Mosinees, WI 54455
Hanson, Burt, 440 N 21st St, Las Vegas, NV 89101
Hanson III, Don, PO Box 13, Success, MO 65570
Hardin, Robert K., 814 Pamala Dr, Dalton, GA 30720
Hardy, Douglas E., 114 Cypress Rd, Franklin, GA 30217
Hardy, Scott, 639 Myrtle Ave, Placerville, CA 95667
Hargis, Frank, 321 S Elm St, Flora, IL 62839
Harkins, J. A., PO Box 218, Conner, MT 59827
Harless, Walt, PO Box 845, Stoneville, NC 27048
Harley, Larry W., 348 Deerfield Dr, Bristol, TN 37620
Harm, Paul W., 818 Yound Rd, Attica, MI 48412
Harmon, Joe, 8014 Fisher Dr, Jonesboro, GA 30236
Harmon, Jay, 462 Victoria Rd, Woodstock, GA 30189
Harn, Robert, 228 Pensacola Rd, Venice, FL 34285
Harper, D. J., 2817 W Glenrosa Ave, Phoenix, AZ 85017
Harrington, Mike, 408 S Cedar St, Abilene, KS 67410
Harris, Jay, 991 Johnson St, Redwood City, CA 94061
Harris, Ralph D., 2607 Bell Shoals Rd, Brandon, FL 33511
Harrison, Dan, PO Box 42, Edom, TX 75756
Harrison, Gene, 17731 Redding St, Hesperia, CA 92345
Harrison, Jim, 721 Fairington View Dr, St Louis, MO 63129
Harsey, William W., 82710 Howe Ln, Creswell, OR 97426
Hart, Bill, 647 Cedar Dr, Pasadena, MD 21122
Hartman, Arlan, 340 Ruddiman Dr, Muskegon, MI 49445
Hartsfield, Phill, PO Box 1637, Newport Beach, CA 92659
Harwood, Oscar, 903 S Cooper St, Memphis, TN 38104
Hatch, Ken, Rt 1 Box 83-A-5, Kooskia, ID 83539
Hawes, Chuck, PO Box 176, Weldon, IL 61882
Hawk, Gavin, Box 401, Idaho City, ID 83631
Hawk, Grant, Box 401, Idaho City, ID 83631
Hawk, Jack L., Rt 1 Box 771, Ceres, VA 24318
Hawk, Joe, Rt 1 Box 773, Ceres, VA 24318
Hawkins, Rade, 110 Buckeye Rd, Fayetteville, GA 30214
Hayes, Delores, PO Box 41405, Los Angeles, CA 90041
Hayes, Robert, PO Box 141, Rail Road Flat, CA 95248
Haynes, George, 906 S Wilson Ave, El Reno, OK 73036
Haynie, Charles, 125 Cherry Ln, Toccoa, GA 30577
Hays, Mark, 1008 Kavanagh Dr, Austin, TX 78748
Hearn, Terry L., RR 14 Box 7676, Lufkin, TX 75904
Heath, William, PO Box 131, Bondville, IL 61815
Hedgecock, Walter F., PO Box 175, Glen Daniel, WV 25844

Hedland, Gregory W., 736 Masonic Ave, San Francisco, CA 94117
Hedrick, Don, 131 Beechwood Hls, Newport News, VA 23602
Hegedus, Lou, PO Box 441, Cave Spring, GA 30124
Hegwald, J. I., 1106 Charles St, Humboldt, KS 66748
Hegwood, Joel, RR 4 Box 229, Summerville, GA 30747
Hein, L. T., 3515 Four Mile Rd, Racine, WI 53404
Heitler, Henry, PO Box 15025, Tampa, FL 33684
Heller, Henry, 12510 S Green Dr Apt 813, Houston, TX 77034
Helton, Roy L., 5650 District Blvd #128, Bakersfield, CA 93313
Helzer, Elwin, PO Box 898, Oracle, AZ 85623
Hembrook, Ron, PO Box 153, Neosho, WI 53059
Hemphill, Jesse, 896 Big Hill Rd, Berea, KY 40403
Henderson, Bert, Rt.1 Box 215, Eddyville, OR 97343
Hendricks, Samuel J., 2162 Van Buren Rd, Maurertown, VA 22644
Hendrickson, E. Jay, 4204 Ballenger Creek Pike, Frederick, MD 21703
Hendrickson, Shawn, 2327 Kaetzel Rd, Knoxville, MD 21758
Hendrix, Jerry, 175 Skyland Dr Ext, Clinton, SC 29325
Hendrix, Wayne, 5210 Burtons Ferry Hwy, Allendale, SC 29810
Hennon, Robert, 940 Vincent Lane, Ft Walton Beach, FL 32547
Henry, D. E., Star Rt Old Gulch Rd, Mountain Ranch, CA 95246
Hensley, Wayne, 2924 Glad Dale Dr SE, Conyers, GA 30094
Henson, Russell, PO Box 779, Jackson, WY 83001
Hergert, Bob, 12 Geer Circle, Port Orford, OR 97465
Herman, R., 4607 Pasadena Ave, Sacramento, CA 95821
Herman, Tim, 7721 Foster St, Overland Park, KS 66204
Hermes, Dana, 39594 Kona Ct, Fremont, CA 94538
Herndon, William R., 32520 Michigan Ave, Acton, CA 93510
Herron, George, 474 Antonio Way, Springfield, SC 29146
Hesser, David, PO Box 1079, Dripping Springs, TX 78620
Hethcoat, Don, PO Box 1764, Clovis, NM 88101
Hetmanski, Thomas S., 494 Orchard Dr, Mansfield, OH 44904
Hewitt, Ron, PO Box 632, Ludowici, GA 31316
Hibben, Daryl, PO Box 172, La Grange, KY 40031
Hibben, Gil, 2914 Winters Ln, La Grange, KY 40031
Hibben, Joleen, PO Box 172, La Grange, KY 40031
Hibben, Westley, 14101 Sunview Dr, Anchorage, AK 99515
Hickory, Beau, PO Box 34235, San Francisco, CA 94134
Hicks, Vernon W., 5211 Bauxite Hwy, Bauxite, AR 72011
Hielscher, Guy, HC34 PO Box 992, Alliance, NE 69301
High, Tom, 5474 S 1128 Rd, Alamosa, CO 81101
Hightower, C., RR 1, Beckville, TX 75631
Hilker, Tom, PO Box 409, Williams, OR 97544
Hill, Howard E., 111 Mission Ln, Polson, MT 59860
Hill, Rick, 20 Nassau Dr, Maryville, IL 62062
Hill, Steven E., 40 Rand Pond Rd, Goshen, NH 03752
Hillman, Charles, 225 Waldoboro Rd, Friendship, ME 04547
Hinderer, Rick, 5423 Kister Rd, Wooster, OH 44691
Hink III, Les, 1599 Aptos Ln, Stockton, CA 95206
Hinkle, John, PO Box 1793, Roswell, NM 88202
Hintz, Gerald, 5402 Sahara Ct, Helena, MT 59602
Hitchmough, Howard, 95 Old Street Rd, Peterborough, NH 03458
Hitt, Robert, 2111 Livingston Ave, Helena, MT 59601
Hobart, Gene, 100 Shedd Rd, Windsor, NY 13865
Hock, Ron, 16650 Mitchell Creek Dr, Fort Bragg, CA 95437
Hockensmith, Dan, PO Box E, Drake, CO 80515
Hodge, J. B., 1100 Woodmont Ave SE, Huntsville, AL 35801
Hodge, John, 422 S 15th St, Palatka, FL 32177
Hodges, Frank, 3710 85th St, Lubbock, TX 79423

Hodgson, Richard J., 9081 Tahoe Ln, Boulder, CO 80301
Hoel, Steve, PO Box 283, Pine, AZ 85544
Hoffman, Harold, 7174 Hoffman Rd, San Angelo, TX 76905
Hoffman, Kevin L., 14672 Kristenright Ln, Orlando, FL 32826
Hoffmann, Donald, PO Box 174, San Miguel, CA 93451
Hogstrom, Anders T., 2130 Valerga #8, Belmont, CA 94002
Hoke, Thomas M., 3103 Smith Ln, La Grange, KY 40031
Holbrook, H. L., RtBox 2017, Ridgecrest, CA 93555
Holder, D'Alton, 7148 W Country Gables Dr, Peoria, AZ 85381
Holguin, Paul, 2015 Lees Ave, Long Beach, CA 90815
Holland, John H, 1580 Nassau St, Titusville, FL 32780
Holland, Dale J., 4561 247th Pl SE, Issaquah, WA 98027
Hollar, Bob, 701 2nd St SW, Great Falls, MT 49404
Hollett, Jeff, 3077 Wildflower Way, Rockwall, TX 75032
Holloway, Paul, 714 Burksdale Rd, Norfolk, VA 23518
Holmes, Robert, 1431 S Eugene St, Baton Rouge, LA 70808
Holstrom, Ron, 615 W Alcott Ave, Fergus Falls, MN 56537
Homer, Glen, PO Box 2702, Bloomfield, NM 87413
Horn, Jess, 2526 Lansdown Rd, Eugene, OR 97404
Hornby, Glen, PO Box 444, Glendale, CA 91209
Horton, Scot, PO Box 451, Buhl, ID 83316
Hossom, Jerry, 3585 Schilling Ridge, Duluth, GA 30096
House, Gary, 2851 ierce Rd, Ephrata, WA 98823
Hover, Richard, 300 E Mineral King Ave, Visalia, CA 93291
Howard, Durvyn M., 4220 McLain St S, Hokes Bluff, AL 35903
Howard, Seth, PO Box 65051, Baton Rouge, LA 70896
Howell, Jason, 213 Buffalo Tr, Lake Jackson, TX 77566
Howell, Len, 550 Lee Rd 169, Opelika, AL 36804
Howell, Robert L, PO Box 1617, Kilgore, TX 75663
Howell, Ted, 1294 Wilson Rd, Wetumpka, AL 36092
Howie, David M., PO Box 615, Deer Park, TX 77536
Howser, John C., 54 Bell Ln, Frankfort, KY 40601
Hoy, Ken, 54744 Pinchot Ave, North Fork, CA 93643
Hrisoulas, Jim, 330 S Decatur Ave Ste 109, Las Vegas, NV 89107
Hubbard, Arthur J., 574 Cutlers Farm Rd, Monroe, CT 06468
Huckabee, Dale, 254 Hwy 260, Maylene, AL 35114
Huddleston, Joe D., 14129 93rd Ave SE, Yelm, WA 98597
Huddleston, Richard, 2965 S Fairview St, Santa Ana, CA 92704
Hudson, Rob, 340 Rousch Rd, Northumberland, PA17857
Hudson, C. Robbin, 22280 Frazier Rd, Rock Hall, MD 21661
Hudson, Robert, 3802 Black Crickett Ct, Humble, TX 77396
Hudson, Tommy, PO Box 2046, Monroe, NC 28110
Huelskamp, David, RR 1 Box 177, Breese, IL 62230
Huertas, Eppy, 1026 Thompson Ave Apt 3, Glendale, CA 91201
Hueske, Chubby, 4808 Tamarisk St, Bellaire, TX 77401
Huey, Steve, 5060 W Port St, Eugene, OR 97402
Huff, John, 2131 Keating St, Hillcrest Heights, MD 20748
Hughes, Dan, 13743 Persimmon Blvd, West Palm Beach, FL 33411
Hughes, Daryle, 10979 Leonard, Nunica, MI 49448
Hughes, Ed, 280½ Holly Lane, Grand Junction, CO 81503
Hughes, Lawrence, 207 W Crestway St, Plainview, TX 79072
Hull, Michael, 2118 Obarr Pl Apt C, Santa Ana, CA 92701
Hull, Michael J., 1330 Hermits Cir, Cottonwood, AZ 86326
Hulett, Steve, 115 Yellowstone Ave, West Yellowstone, MT 59758
Hulsey, Hoyt, 5699 Pope Ave, Steele, AL 35987
Hume, Don, 3511 Camino De La Cumbre, Sherman Oaks, CA 91423
Humenick, Roy, PO Box 55, Rescue, CA 95672

Humphreys, Joel, 3260 Palmer Rd, Bowling Green, FL 33834
Hunnicutt, Robert E., 2636 Magnolia Way, Forest Grove, OR 97116
Hunt, Alex, 1916 Simsbury Ct, Fort Collins, CO 80524
Hunt, Dick, 703 Eratz Brown, Moberly, MO 65270
Hunt, Jerry, 4606 Princeton Dr, Garland, TX 75042
Hunt, Maurice, 2492 N 800 E, Avon, IN 46123
Hunter, Hyrum, 285 N 300 W, Aurora, UT 84620
Hunter, Richard D., 7230 NW 200th Terrace, Alachua, FL 32615
Hurst, Cole, 1583 Tedford, E Wenatchee, WA 98802
Hurst, Gerald, 6205 Loftus Ave, Albuquerque, NM 87109
Hurst, Jeff, PO Box 247, Rutledge, TN 37861
Hurst, Jim, 4537 S Irvington Ave, Tulsa, OK 74135
Hurt, William R., 922 Oak Tree Circle, Fredrick, MD 21701
Husman, Dennis, PO Box 997, Patterson, CA 95363
Hyde, Jimmy, 5094 Stagecoach Rd, Ellenwood, GA 30049
Hyer, Jack, 4 Worthdale Ct, Winston Salem, NC 27103
Hytovick, Joe, 14872 SW 111th St, Dunellon, FL 34432
Iams, Richard D., PO Box 963, Mills, WY 82644
Imboden, Howard L., 620 Deauville Dr, Dayton, OH 45429
Imel, Billy Mace, 1616 Bundy Ave, New Castle, IN 47362
Inman III, Paul R., 3705 Artic Blvd, Anchorage, AK 99503
Irie, Michael, 1606 Auburn Dr, Colorado Springs, CO 80909
Isaacs, Dan, 3701 Eureka St Lot 59-A, Anchorage, AK 99503
Isgro, Jeffrey, 1516 First St, West Babylon, NY 11704
Jacks, Jim, 344 S Hollenbeck Ave, Covina, CA 91723
Jackson, Mark, 2405 33rd Ave S, Minneapolis, MN 55406
Jackson, David, 214 Oleander Ave, Lemoore, CA 93245
James, Clifton, Star Route Box 10, Atmore, AL 35611
James, Peter, 2549 W Golf Rd #200, Hoffman Estates, IL 60194
Janiak, John S., Rt 2 Park Rd, Colchester, CT 06415
Janiga, Matthew A., 15950 Xenia St NW, Andover, MN 55304
Jarvis, Paul M., 30 Chalk St, Cambridge, MA 02139
Jean, Gerry, 25B Cliffside Dr, Manchester, CT 06040
Jensen Jr., Carl, A., 8957 County Rd P-35, Blair, NE 68008
Jensen, John, PO Box 60547, Pasadena, CA 91116
Jeffries, Robert W., Rt 2 Box 227, Red House, WV 25168
Jernigan, Steve, 3082 Tunnel Rd, Milton, FL 32571
Jetton, Cay, PO Box 315, Winnsboro, TX 75494
Jirik, Sid, 11301 Patro St, Anchorage, AK 99516
Job, Robert, 1046 Goffle Rd, Hawthorne, NJ 07506
Jobs, S. R., 1513 Martin Chapel Rd, Murray, KY 42071
Johanning, Tom, 1735 Apex Rd, Sarasota, FL 34240
Johns, Rob, 1423 S Second St, Enid, OK 73701
Johnsen, Steve, PO Box 1015, Morro Bay, CA 93443
Johnson, Brad, 41046 Rue Chene, Ponchatoula, LA 70454
Johnson, David L., PO Box 222, Talkeetna, AK 99676
Johnson, Durrell, PO Box 594, Sparr, FL 32192
Johnson, Gene, 5648 Redwood Ave, Portage, IN 46368
Johnson, Gorden W., 5426 Sweetbriar St, Houston, TX 77017
Johnson, Harold C., 98 Penn St, Trion, GA 30753
Johnson, Herbert, 6515 Irving Ave S, Richfield, MN 55423
Johnson, Keith L., PO Box 382, Lyle, WA 98635
Johnson, Kenneth R., W3565 Lockington Rd, Mindoro, WI 54644
Johnson, Ronald B., PO Box 11, Clearwater, MN 55320
Johnson, Randy, 2575 E Canal Dr, Turlock, CA 95380
Johnson, Ruffin, 215 La Fonda Dr, Houston, TX 77060
Johnson, Ryan M., 7320 Foster Hixson Cemetery Rd, Hixson, TN 37343

Johnson, Steven R., PO Box 5, Manti, UT 84642
Johnson, W. C., 225 Fairfield Pike, Enon, OH 45323
Johnston, Frank, 11435 Ogle Rd NE, Poulsbo, WA 98370
Jokerst, Charles, 9312 Spaulding St, Omaha, NE 68134
Jones, Barry M., 221 North Ave, Danville, VA 24540
Jones, Bob, 6219 Aztec Rd NE, Albuquerque, NM 87110
Jones, Curtis J., 39909 176th St E, Palmdale, CA 93591
Jones, Enoch, 7278 Moss Ln, Warrenton, VA 22187
Jones, Fred, 858 E I St, Ontario, CA 91764
Jones, Franklin W., 6030 Old Dominion Rd, Columbus, GA 31909
Jones, Gomer G., 13313 E 13th St, Tulsa, OK 74108
Jones, John A., 779 SW 131 Hwy, Holden, MO 64040
Jones, Jolly, 1240 Abbott Ave, Campbell, CA 95008
Jones, Phillip G., 221 North Ave, Danville, VA 24540
Jones, Robert, 6219 Aztec Rd NE, Albuquerque, NM 87110
Juarer, Jacques, 1131 University Blvd W, Silver Spring, MD 20902
Justice, Shane, PO Box 251, Sheridan, WY 82801
Kalfayan, Edward N., 410 Channing St, Ferndale, MI 48220
Kapela, Robert A., 10060 Packard Rd, Temperance, MI 48182
Karlin, Don, PO Box 668, Aztec, NM 87410
Karp, Bob, PO Box 47304, Phoenix, AZ 85068
Kauffman, Dave, 120 Clark Creek Loop, Montana City, MT 59634
Kaufman, Scott, 302 Green Meadows Cr, Anderson, SC 29624
Kay, J. Wallace, 332 Slab Bridge Road, Liberty, SC 29657
Keeler, Bob, Sams Lane, Ijamsville, MD 21754
Keene, Harvey, 2135 Golden Gate Blvd W, Naples, FL 33964
Keeslar, Steven C., 115 Lane 216, Hamilton, IN 46742
Keeslar, Joseph F., 391 Radio Rd, Almo, KY 42020
Keeton, William, 6095 Rehobeth Rd SE, Laconia, IN 47135
Keidel, Gene W., 4661 105th Ave SW, Dickinson, ND 58601
Keidel, Scott J., 4661 105th Ave SW, Dickinson, ND 58601
Kelley, Gary, 17485 SW Pheasant Ln, Aloha, OR 97006
Kellogg, Brian R., 19048 Smith Creek Rd, New Market, VA 22844
Kellog, Robert, PO Box 2006, West Monroe, LA 71294
Kelly, Lance, 1723 Willow Oak Dr, Edgewater, FL 32132
Kelly, Stephen, 819 Flume St, Chico, CA 95928
Kelso, Jim, 577 Collar Hill Rd, Worcester, VT 05682
Kennedy, Jerry, 2104 SW 8-A, Blue Springs, MO 64015
Kennedy, Bill, PO Box 850431, Yukon, OK 73085
Kennedy, Kelly S., 9894-A W University Blvd, Odessa, TX 79764
Kennelley, J. C., 1114 N 'C' St, Arkansas City, KS 67005
Kern, R. W., 20824 Texas Trail W, San Antonio, TX 78257
Kersh, Todd, 1805 S Highview Ave, Joplin, MO 64804
Kessler, Ralph A., PO Box 61, Fountain Inn, SC 29644
Keyes, Dan, 6688 King St, Chino, CA 91710
Keys, Bill, 1398 Whitsett Dr, El Cajon, CA 92020
Khalsa, Jot Singh, 368 Village St, Millis, MA 02054
Ki, Shiva, 5222 Ritterman Ave, Baton Rouge, LA 70805
Kiefer, Tony, 112 Chateaugay Rd SW, Pataskala, OH 43062
Kilby, Keith, 1902 29th St, Cody, WY 82414
Kimble, Robert, 1100 E Main St, Visalia, CA 93292
Kimsey, Kevin, 198 Cass White Rd NW, Cartersville, GA 30121
King, Bill, 14830 Shaw Rd, Tampa, FL 33625
King, Fred, 430 Grassdale Rd, Cartersville, GA 30120
King, Jason, PO Box 151, Eskridge, KS 66423
King, Kemp, 6452 Paradise Point Rd, Flowery Branch, GA 30542
King, Randall, 54 Mount Carmel Rd Trlr 12, Asheville, NC 28806
King Jr., Harvey G., PO Box 184, Eskridge, KS 66423

Kinkade, Jacob, 197 Rd 154, Carpenter, WY 82054
Kinker, Mike, 8755 E County Rd 50 N, Greensburg, IN 47240
Kinney, R. W., 313 North 2nd Ave, Hailey, ID 83333
Kinniken, Todd, 8356 John McKeever Rd, House Springs MO 63051
Kious, Joe, 1015 Ridge Pointe Dr, Kerrville, TX 78028
Kirk, Jon W., 800 N Olive Ave, Fayetteville, AR 72701
Kirk, Ray, PO Box 1445, Tahlequah, OK 74465
Kirtley, George, Salina Star Route, Boulder, CO 80302
Kitsmiller, Jerry, 67277 Las Vegas Dr, Montrose, CO 81401
Klimaszewski, Bernard E., 2214 Spicewood Dr, Killeen, TX 76543
Klingbeil, Russell, 1120 Shaffer Tr, Oviedo, FL 32765
Knickmeyer, Hank, 6300 Crosscreek Rd, Cedar Hill, MO 63016
Knipschield, Terry, 808 12th Ave NE, Rochester, MN 55906
Knipstein, R. C., 731 N Fielder Rd, Arlington, TX 76012
Knott, Steve, 206 Academy St, Clinton, SC 29325
Knuth, Joseph E., 3307 Lookout Dr, Rockford, IL 61109
Kohler, J. Mark, 16430 Dawncrest Way, Sugarland, TX 77478
Kohls, Jerry, N 4725 Oak Rd, Princeton, WI 54968
Kolitz, Robert, 9342 Canary Rd, Beaver Dam, WI 53916
Kommer, Russ, 9211 Abbott Loop Rd, Anchorage, AK 99507
Kopp, Todd M., PO Box 3474, Apache Junction, AZ 85217
Kormanik, Chris, 6424 Stone Bridge Rd, Carnesville, GA 30521
Koster, Steven C., 16251 Birdie Ln, Huntington Beach, CA 92649
Koustopoulos, George, 41491 Biggs Rd, Lagrange, OH 44050
Koval, Michael T., 5819 Zarley St, New Albany, OH 43054
Kovar, Eugene, 2626 W 98th St, Evergreen Park, IL 60642
Kozlow, Kelly, 13860 Pioneer Rd, Apple Valley, CA 92307
Kraft, Elmer, 1358 Meadowlark Lane, Big Arm, MT 59910
Kraft, Steve, 315 SE 6th St, Abilene, KS 67410
Kramer, Bob, 1028 1st Ave S, Seattle WA 98134
Kranning, Terry L., 1900 W Quinn Rd Trlr 153, Pocatello, ID 83202
Krapp, Dennis G., 1826 Windsor Oak Dr, Apopka, FL 32703
Krause, Roy W., 22412 Corteville St, Saint Clair Shores, MI 48081
Kravitt, Chris, HC 31 Box 6484, Ellsworth, ME 04604
Kray, John S., 22451 Tula Dr, Saugus, CA 91350
Kreibich, Donald L., 6082 Boyd Ct, San Jose, CA 95123
Kreiger, G. J., PO Box 346, New Milford, NJ 07646
Kreimer, James J., Rt 2 Box 280, Milan, IN 47031
Kremzner, Raymond L., PO Box 31, Stevenson, MD 21153
Kretsinger, Philip W., 17536 Bakersfield Rd, Boonsboro, MD 21713
Krouse, Al, 918 Hodgkins St, Houston, TX 77032
Kruse, Martin, PO Box 487, Reseda, CA 91335
Kubaiko, Hank, 10765 Northvale, Beach City, OH 44608
Kubasek, John A., 74 Northampton St, Easthampton, MA 01027
Kuykendall, Jim, PO Box 539, Tulare, CA 93275
Kvitka, Dan, 17600 Superior St, Northridge, CA 91325
LaBorde, Terry, 26280 Guthridge Ln, Homeland, CA 92548
Ladd, Jim, 1120 Helen Dr, Deer Park, TX 77536
Ladd, Jimmie Lee, 1120 Helen Dr, Deer Park, TX 77536
Laduke, Ken, 1038 Pearl St, Santa Monica, CA 90405
Lainson, Tony, 114 Park Ave, Council Bluffs, IA 51503
Lairson Sr., Jerry, HC 68 Box 970, Ringold, OK 74754
Lake, Ron, 3360 Bendix Ave, Eugene, OR 97401
Lam, Brian, 1803 N 38th St, Phoenix, AZ 85008
Lambert, Jarrell D., 2321 FM 2982, Ganado, TX 77962
Lambert, Ronald S., 24 Vermont St, Johnston, RI 02919
Lamey, Robert M., 15800 Lamey Dr, Biloxi, MS 39532
Lampson, Frank, 3215 Saddlebag Cr, Rimrock, AZ 86335

Lance, Bill, PO Box 4427, Eagle River, AK 99577
Land, John, PO Box 917, Wadesboro, NC 28170
Landers, John, 758 Welcome Rd, Newnan, GA 30263
Landers, Steve, 3817 NW 125th St, Oklahoma City, OK 73120
Landrum, Leonard, 979 Gumpond Beall Rd, Lumberton, MS 39455
Lane, Ben, 4802 Massie St, North Little Rock, AR 72218
Lane, Don, RR 4 Box 291, Blackfoot, ID 83221
Lane, Ed, 440 N Topping Ave, Kansas City, MO 64123
Lane, Jerry, 1529 E Stafford Ave, Carbondale, IL 62901
Lang, Kurt, 4908 S Wildwood Dr, McHenry, IL 60050
Langbein, Jerry, 1670 River Dr, Fountain, CO 80817
Lange, Donald, RR 1 Box 66, Pelican Rapids, MN 56572
Lange, Kurt, RR 1 Box 1317, Trego, WI 54888
Langley, Gary, 1001 Powell Ave, Dumas, TX 79029
Langley, Gene H., 1022 N Price Rd, Florence, SC 29506
Langston, Bennie E., 2061 Pennington Gap, Memphis, TN 38134
Lankton, Scott, 8065 Jackson Ave R11, Ann Arbor, MI 48103
Laramie, Mark, 181 Woodland St, Fitchburg, MA 01420
Larson, Richard, 549 E Hawkeye Ave, Turlock, CA 95380
Lapen, Charles, PO Box 529, West Brookfield, MA 01585
Laplante, Brett, 4545 CR 412, MeKinney, TX 75071
Largin, Ken, PO Box 151, Metamora, IN 47030
Lary, Ed, 651 Range Line Rd, Mosinee, WI 54455
Lattimer, R. E., PO Box 3393, Glendale, CA 91221
Laughlin, Don, 190 Laughlin Dr, Vidor, TX 77662
Laurent, Kermit, 1812 Acadia Dr, LaPlace, LA 70068
Lawless, Charles, 611 Haynes Rd, Arab, AL 35016
Lawless, Ed, PO Box 277, New Hudson, MI 48165
Lawrence, Alton, 201 W Stillwell, De Queen, AR 71832
Lawson, Stephen M., RR 1 Box 398, Fredericksburg, TX 78624
Lay, L. J., 602 Mimosa St, Burkburnett, TX 76354
Layton, Jim, 2710 Gilbert Ave, Portsmouth, OH 45662
Lazo, Robert T., 11850 SW 181st St, Miami, FL 33177
Le Batard, Paul, 14700 Old River Rd, Van Cleave, MS 39565
Le Blanc, John, Rt 2 Box 22950, Winnsboro, TX 75494
Le Font, Mark, 3210 Oakley Dr, Hollywood, CA 90068
Leach, Mike J., 5377 Grand Blanc Rd, Swartz Creek, MI 48473
Leavitt Jr., Earl F., Pleasant Cove Rd, Boothbay, ME 04544
Lebatard, Paul M., 14700 Old River Rd, Vancleave, MS 39565
Leck, Dal, PO Box 1054, Hayden, CO 81639
Ledbetter, Randy, PO Box 897, Payette, ID 83661
Ledford, Bracy R., 3670 N Sherman Dr, Indianapolis, IN 46218
Lee, Randy, PO Box 1873, St. John, AZ 85963
Lee, Tommy, PO Box 572, Taylors, SC 29687
Leet, Larry W., 14417 2nd Ave SW, Burien, WA 98166
Leland, Steve, 2300 Sir Francis Drake Blvd, Fairfax, CA 94930
Lemery, Howard, PO Box 98, Knoxboro, NY 13362
Lenaze, Emmett, 4449 W Metairie Ave, Metairie, LA 70001
Lenderman, Cliff, RR 8 Box 653, Lufkin, TX 75904
Leone, Nick, 9 Georgetown Dr, Pontoon Beach, IL 62040
Lepore, Michael J., 66 Woodcutters Dr, Bethany, CT 06524
Leppert, A. R., 17718 Rhoda St, Encino, CA 91316
Lerch, Matthew, N88 W23462 N Lisbon Rd, Sussex, WI 53089
Letcher, William, 3909 South Trask St, Tampa, FL 33616
Levengood, Bill, 15011 Otto Rd, Tampa, FL 33624
Leverett, Ken, PO Box 696, Lithia, FL 33547
Levin, Yakov, 7216 Bay Parkway, Brooklyn, NY 11204

Levine, Bob, 101 Westwood Dr, Tullahoma, TN 37388
Levine, Norman, 34582 Farm Rd, Lake Elsinore, CA 92532
Lewis, K. J., 374 Cook Rd, Lugoff, SC 29078
Lewis, Mike, 111 W Central Ave, Tracy, CA 95376
Lewis, Tom R., 1613 Standpipe Rd, Carlsbad, NM 88220
Licata, Steven, 116 Front St, Mineola, NY 11501
Liegey, Kenneth R, 132 Carney Dr, Millwood, WV 25262
Lieneman, L. B., 625 Grand Ave, Billings, MT 59101
Likarich, Steve, 26075 Green Acres Rd, Colfax, CA 95713
Lile, Marilyn, 2721 S Arkansas Ave, Russellville, AR 72801
Lincoln, James, 5359 Blue Ridge Pkwy, Bartlett, TN38134
Lindsay, Chris, 1324 NE Locksley Dr, Bend, OR 97701
Lisk, Arlin J., PO Box 9711, Yakima, WA 98909
Lister Jr., Weldon E., 9140 Sailfish Dr, Boerne, TX 78006
Little, Gary M., HC 84 Box 10301, Broadbent, OR 97414
Little, Jimmy L., PO Box 871652, Wasilla, AK 99687
Lively, Tim, PO Box 8847 CRB, Tucson, AZ 85738
Livingston, Robert C., PO Box 6, Murphy, NC 28906
Lloyd, Richard, 520 S 500 W, Salt Lake City, UT 84101
Locke, Keith, PO Box 48363, Ft Worth, TX 76148
Lockett, Lowell C., 66653 Gunderson Rd, North Bend, OR 97459
Lockett, Sterling, 527 Amherst Dr, Burbank, CA 91504
Loflin, Bob, 5979 NW 151st St, Miami Lakes, FL 33014
Lokmor, Kevin, 2253 Lynbrook Ct, Pittsburg, CA 94565
Lonewolf, Juan A., 481 Hwy 105, Demorest, GA 30535
Long, Glenn A., 10090 SW 186th Ave, Dunnellon FL 33432
Longworth, Dave, 1811 SR 774, Hamersville, OH 45130
Loomis, Lewis A., 7120 SE Cavalier St, Milwaukie, OR 97267
Loos, Henry C., 210 Ingraham, New Hyde Park, NY 11040
Lorditch, Charles R., 7 Tollgate Rd, Johnstown, PA 15906
Loro, Gene, 2457 State Rt 93 NE, Crooksville, OH 43731
Louchard, Ed, 311 Jackson St, Port Townsend, WA 98368
Louis Jr., Tony, 7310 Stonemill Court, Louisville, KY 40291
Love, Ed, 3230 Sea Wolf Dr, Tallahassee, FL 32312
Loveless, R. W., PO Box 7836, Riverside, CA 92513
Lovestrand, Schuyler, 1136 19th St SW, Vero Beach, FL 32962
Lovett, Mike, PO Box 713, Killeen, TX 76540
Lozier, Don, 5394 SE 168th Ave, Oklawaha, FL 32179
Lozito, Joseph F., 6804 Burns St, Forest Hills, NY 11375
Lubrich, Mark, PO Box 122, Matthews, NC 28106
Luchak, Bob, 15705 Woodforest Blvd, Channelview, TX 77530
Luchini, Richard M., 6909 Pacific Ave, Stockton, CA 95207
Lucie, Jim, 4191 E Fruitport Rd, Fruitport, MI 49415
Luck, Gregory, PO Box 2255, Greeley, CO 80632
Luckett, Bill, 108 Amantes, Weatherford, TX 76088
Ludwig, Richard O., 57-63 65 St, Maspeth, NY 11378
Lui, Ronald, 4042 Harding Ave, Honolulu, HI 96816
Lum, Robert W., 901 Travis Ave, Eugene, OR 97404
Luman, James R., Clear Creek Tr, Anaconda, MT 59711
Lunn, Larry A., 6970 9th Ave North, St Petersburg, FL 33710
Lutes, Robert, 24878 US Highway # 6, Nappanee, IN 46550
Luttrell, Jay, 26255 Walker Rd, Bend, OR 97701
Lutz, Greg, 149 Effie Dr, Greenwood, SC 29649
Lyle, Ernest L., PO Box 1755, Chiefland, FL 32644
Lyle, Mac, 813 Evergreen Ln, Rock Hill, SC 29730
Lynds, Norman W., 1142 Marianas Ln, Alameda, CA 94502
Lyons, Randy, 572 Tannahill, Vidor, TX 77662

MacBain, Kenneth C., 30 Briarwood Ave, Norwood, NJ 07648
Mac Donald, John, 9 David Dr, Raymond, NH 03077
Madison II, Billy D., 2295 Tyler Rd, Remlap, AL 35133
Madison, Wes, 390 Crest Dr, Eugene, OR 97405
Madsen, Jack, 3311 Northwest Dr, Wichita Falls, TX 76305
Maestri, Peter A., S 11251 Fairview Rd, Spring Green, WI 53588
Mahon, Charles, 243 Millbrook Way, Vacaville, CA 95687
Maienknecht, Stanley, 38648 SR 800, Sardis, OH 43946
Maines, Jay, 5584 266th St, Wyoming, MN 55092
Malitzke, Jeffrey G., 4804 Lovers Ln, Wichita Falls, TX 76310
Malloy, Joe, 1039 Schwabe St, Freeland, PA 18224
Manabe, Michael K, 3659 Tomahawk Ln, San Diego, CA 92117
Mankel, Kenneth, PO Box 35, Cannonsburg, MS 49317
Manley, Cliff, 186 River St, Glenville, WV 26351
Manley, Clinton J., PO Box 326, Zolfo Springs, FL 33890
Manley, David W., 3270 Six Mile Hwy, Central, SC 29630
Mann, Michael L., PO Box 144, Sirit Lake, ID 83869
Manrow, Mike, 6093 Saddlewood Dr, Toledo, OH 43613
Mansfield, Dale, 1010 Woodleaf Dr, Forbestown, CA 95941
Manx, Ralph, 811 F St, San Diego, CA 92101
Maragni, Dan, RR 1 Box 106, Georgetown, NY 13072
Marchant, Larry, 2005 N Park Ave, Tifton, GA 31794
Mariacher, Robert R., PO Box 1836, Franklin, NC 28734
Maringer, Tom, 2692 S Powell St, Springdale, AR 72764
Markley, Ken, 7651 Cabin Creek Ln, Sparta, IL 62286
Marks, Chris, Rt 2 Box 527, Ava, MO 65608
Marlowe, Donald, 2554 Oakland Rd, Dover, PA 17315
Marshall, Glenn, 1117 Hoffman St, Mason, TX 76856
Martin, Bruce E., RR 6 Box 164-B, Prescott, AR 71857
Martin, Gene, PO Box 396, Williams, OR 97544
Martin, Jim, 1120 S Cadiz Ct, Oxnard, CA 93035
Martin, Joe, PO Box 6552, Lubbock, TX 79493
Martin, Michael W., PO Box 572, Beckville, TX 75631
Martin, Peter, 28220 N Lake Dr, Waterford, WI 53185
Martin, Randall J., 51 Bramblewood St, Bridgewater, MA 02324
Martrildonno, Paul, 140 Debary Dr, Debary, FL 32713
Marx, Dave, 40 Erie St, Tonawanda, NY 14150
Mase, Bill, 1740 W Orange Grove Rd, Tucson, AZ 85704
Masek, Dick, RR 3 Box 41, David City, NE 68632
Mason, Bill, 1114 Saint Louis Ave Trlr 33, Excelsior Springs, MO 64024
Massey, Richard, 1348 S. Viscay St, Aurora, CO 80017
Massey, Ronald J., 61638 El Reposo St, Joshua Tree, CA 92252
Massey, Roger, 4928 Union Rd, Texarkana, AR 71854
Mattis, James K, 500 N Central Ave Ste 740, Glendale, CA 91203
Maxfield, Lynn, 382 Colonial St, Layton, UT 84041
Maxwell, Don, 3164 N Marks Ste 122, Fresno, CA 93722
Maxwell, Gypsy, RR 2 Box 63, Beech Bluff, TN 38313
Maxwell, Lindsay, 4301 Main St, Springfield, OR 97478
May, Henry J., 1216 Odell Ave, Thermopolis, WY 82443
May, James E., 6513 State Road T, Auxvasse, MO 65231
Maynard, Larry Joe, PO Box 493, Crab Orchard, WV 25827
Maynard, William N, 2677 John Smith Road, Fayetteville, NC 28306
Mayo, Tom, 67-420 Alahaka St, Waialua, HI 96791
Mayville, Oscar L., 2130 E County Rd 910-S, Marengo, IN 47140
McAlpin, Jerry, PO Box 71, Bullard, TX 75757
McBee, William, 27275 Norton Grade, Colfax, CA 95713
McBurnette, Harvey, PO Box 227, Eagle Nest, NM 87718
McCarley, John, 4165 Harney Rd, Taneytown, MD 21787

McCarty, Harry, 1121 Brough Ave, Hamilton, OH 45015
McCarty, Zollan, 1011 Avenue E, Thomaston, GA 30286
McClung, Kevin, 29540 Ryder Cup Ln, Tehachapi, CA 93561
McClure, Leonard, 212 SW Avenue I, Seminole, TX 79360
McClure, Michael, 803 17th Ave, Menlo Park, CA 94025
McConnell, Charles R., 158 Genteel Ridge Rd, Wellsburg, WV 26070
McConnell, Loyd A., 1710 Rosewood, Odessa, TX 79761
McCormick, John, 9632 E 26th St, Tulsa, OK 74129
McCoun, Mark, 14212 jPine Dr, DeWitt, VA 23840
McCoy, Fred, 9937 Moss Ave, Silver Spring, MD 20901
McCrackin, Kevin, 3720 Hess Rd, House Springs, MO 63051
McCrackin, V. J., 3720 Hess Rd, House Springs, MO 63051
McCray, James F., PO Box 137, Loami, IL 62661
McCullough, Jerry, 274 W Pettibone Rd, Georgiana, AL 36033
McCullough, Larry E., RR 4 Box 556, Mocksville, NC 27028
McDearmont, Dave, 1618 Parkside Trl, Lewisville, TX 75067
McDonald, Richard, 4590 Kirk Rd, Columbiana, OH 44408
McDonald, Robin J., 6509 E Jeffrey Dr, Fayetteville, NC 28314
McDonald, Robert J., 14730 61 Court N, Loxahatchee, FL 33470
McDonald, W. J., 7173 Wilshire Cove E, Germantown, TN 38138
McElhannon, Marcus, 310 Darby Trails, Sugar Land, TX 77479
McFall, Ken, PO Box 458, Lakeside, AZ 85929
McFarland, Les, PO Box 2732, Opelika, AL 36803
McFarlin, Eric E., PO Box 2188, Kodiak, AK 99615
McFarlin, J. W., 3331 Pocohantas Dr, Lake Havasu, AZ 86404
McGill, John, PO Box 302, Blairsville, GA 30512
McGovern, Jim, 105 Spinnaker Way, Portsmouth NH 03801
McGowan, Frank E., 12629 Howard Lodge Dr, Sykesville, MD 21784
McGroder, Patrick J., 5725 Chapin Rd, Madison, OH 44057
McGuane IV, Thomas F., 410 S 3rd Ave, Bozeman, MT 59715
McHenry, W. J., PO Box 67, Wyoming, RI 02898
McIntosh, David, PO Box 948, Haines, AK 99827
McKendrick, Bob, PO Box F, Sausalito, CA 94965
McKissack, Tommy, PO Box 991, Sonora, TX 76950
McLane, Thomas, 7 N Tucson Ter, Tucson, AZ 85745
McLendon, Hubert W., 125 Thomas Rd, Waco, GA 30182
McLeod, James, 941 Thermalito Ave, Oroville, CA 95965
McLuin, Tom, 36 Fourth St, Dracut, MA 01826
McLurkin, Andrew, 2112 Windy Woods Dr, Raleigh, NC 27607
McMahon, John P., 44871 Santa Anita Ave, Palm Desert, CA 92260
McManus, Danny, 413 Fairhaven Dr, Taylors, SC 29687
McNabb, Tommy, 4015 Brownsboro Rd, Winston-salem, NC 27106
McNeil, Jimmy, 1175 Mt Moriah Rd, Memphis, TN 38117
McRae, J. Michael, 7750 Matthews-Mint Hill Rd, Mint Hill, NC 28227
McWilliams, Sean, 311 Gem Ln, Bayfield, CO 81122
Mead, Herbert, Star Rt 2 Box 171, Bonners Ferry, ID 83805
Mecchi, Richard, 4225 Gibraltar St, Las Vegas, NV 89121
Meeks, John, RR 9 Box 392-M, Glencoe, AL 35905
Meerdink, Kirt, 120 Split Rock Dr, Barryville, NY 12719
Meier, Daryl, 75 Forge Rd, Carbondale, IL 62901
Meloy, Sean, 7148 Rosemary Ln, Lemon Grove, CA 91945
Mendenhall, Harry E., 1848 Everglades Dr, Milpitas, CA 95035
Mensch, Larry, Rd #3 Box 1444, Milton, PA 17847
Mercer, Mike, 149 N Waynesville Rd, Lebanon, OH 45036
Merchant, Ted, 7 Old Garrett Ct, White Hall, MD 21161
Merritt, Jim, 3630 E Poppy St, Long Beach, CA 90805
Merz, Robert L., 20219 Prince Creek Dr, Katy, TX 77450
Meshejian, Mardi, 33 Elm Dr, E Northport, NY 11731

Messer, David T., 134 S Torrence St, Dayton, OH 45403
Messer, Glen David, RR#1, Sumrall, MS 39482
Metheny, H. A., 7750 Waterford Dr, Spotsylvania, VA 22553
Mettler, J. Banjo, 129 S 2nd St, North Baltimore, OH 45872
Meyers, Max, 418 Jolee St, Richardson, TX 75080
Middleton, Ken, 3023 Edison Ave, Sacramento, CA 95821
Milford, Brian A., RD 2 Box 294, Knox, PA 16232
Militano, Tom, 77 Jason Rd, Jacksonville, AL 36265
Millard, Fred G, 5317 N Wayne, Chicago, IL 60640
Miller, Bill, PO Box 434, Ashford, AL 36312
Miller, Bob, 7659 Fine Oaks Place, Oakville, MO 63129
Miller Jr., Chris, PO Box 15471, Gainesville, FL 32604
Miller, Don, 1604 Harrodsburg Rd, Lexington, KY 40503
Miller, Hanford J., PO Box 97, Cowdrey, CO 80434
Miller, James K., 226 E Hawthorne St Apt 1, Florence, AL 35630
Miller, James P., 9024 Goeller Rd RR 2 BOX 28, Fairbank, IA 50629
Miller, L. Maurice, PO Box 3064, Missoula, MT 59806
Miller, M. A., 8979 Pearl St, Apt 2005, Thornton, CO 80229
Miller, Michael E., 1508 Crestwod Dr, Wagoner, OK 74467
Miller, Michael K., 28510 Santiam Hwy, Sweet Home, OR 97386
Miller, R. D., 10526 Estate Ln, Dallas, TX 75238
Miller, Rick, 516 Kanaul Rd, Rockwood, PA 15557
Miller, Robert, PO Box 2722, Ormond Beach, FL 32175
Miller, Ronald T., 12922 127th Ave, Largo, FL 34644
Miller, Ted, PO Box 6328, Santa Fe, NM 87502
Miller, Terry, 450 S 1st St, Seward, NE 68434
Miller, Steve, 1376 Pine St, Clearwater, FL 34616
Mills, Andy, 414 E Schubert St, Fredericksburg, TX 78624
Mills, Louis G., 9450 W Waters Rd, Ann Arbor, MI 48103
Miltano, Tom, 77 Jason Rd, Jacksonville, AL 36265
Mink, Dan, 196 Sage Circle, Crystal Beach, FL 34681
Minnick, Jim, 144 N 7th St, Middletown, IN 47356
Mirabile, David, 1715 Glacier Ave, Juneau, AK 99801
Mitchell, Bobby, 511 Avenue B, South Houston, TX 77587
Mitchell, William Dean, 8438 County Rd 1, Lamar, OK 81052
Mitchell, James A., PO Box 4646, Columbus, GA 31904
Mitchell, Max, 3803 VFW Rd, Leesville, LA 71440
Mitchell, R. W., 24530 Bundy Canyon Rd, Wildomar, CA 92595
Miyakawa, Johnny, PO Box 43, Knippa, TX 78870
Mize, Richard, 2038 Fox Creek Rd, Lawrenceburg, KY 40342
Monk, Nathan P., 1304 4th Ave SE, Cullman, AL 35055
Montano, Gus A., 11217 Westonhill Dr, San Diego, CA 92126
Montegna, Delmar R., PO Box 6261, Sheridan, WY 82801
Montjoy, Claude, 706 Indian Creek Rd, Clinton, SC 29325
Moore, Bill, 806 Community Ave, Albany, GA 31705
Moore, Ed, 6829 N River Dr, Baltimore, MD 21220
Moore, James B., 1707 N Gillis St, Fort Stockton, TX 79735
Moore, Richard, 5413 Maple Ave, Rialto, CA 92377
Moore, Ted, 340 E Willow St, Elizabethtown, PA 17022
Moore, Tom W., Rt 7 Reece Church Rd, Columbia, TN 38401
Moran, William F., PO Box 68, Braddock Heights, MD 21714
More, Keith B., PO Box 164, Charlotte, MI 48813
Moreau, Kevin, 34 Western Ave, Brattleboro, VT 05301
Moretz, Jim, PO Box 2484, Boone, NC 28607
Morgan, Emil, 2690 Calle Limonero, Thousand Oaks, CA 91360
Morgan, Jeff, 9200 Arnaz Way, Santee, CA 92071
Morgan, Justin, 2690 Calle Limonero, Thousand Oaks, CA 91360
Morgan, Tom, 14689 Ellett Rd, Beloit, OH 44609

Morlan, Tom, 30635 S. Palm, Hemet, CA 92343
Morris, C. H., 1590 Old Salem Rd, Frisco City, AL 365445
Morris, Jason, 1590 Old Salem Rd, Frisco City, AL 365445
Morris, Eric, 306 Ewart Ave, Beckely, WV 25801
Morseth, Steve, 131 E Naches Ave, Selah, WA 98942
Mortenson, Ed, 2742 Hwy 93 N, Darby, MT 59829
Moser, James W., 17432 Marken Ln, Huntington Beach, CA 92647
Mosier, Joshua J., 802 6th St, St Edgar, NE 68935
Mosser, Gary E., 11827 NE 102nd Pl, Kirkland, WA 98033
Moulton, Dusty, 135 Hillview Ln, Loudon, TN 37774
Mount, Don, 4574 Little Finch Ln, Las Vegas, NV 89115
Moyer, Russ, HC 36 Box 57-C, Havre, MT 59501
Mulholland, Gary, PO Box 93, Davenport, CA 95017
Muller, Jody, PO Box 35, Pittsburg, MO 65724
Mullin, Steve, 500 Snowberry Ln, Sandpoint, ID 83864
Mumford, Peter, PO Box 3, Farisita, CO 81040
Munro, Paul, RR 1 Box 32, Franklin, ME 04634
Murphy, Dave, PO Box 256, Gresham, OR 97030
Murski, Ray, 12129 Captiva Ct, Reston, VA 22091
Myers, Mel, 611 Elmwood Dr, Spencer, IA 51301
Myers, Paul, 614 W Airwood Dr, East Alton, IL 62024
Myers, Ron, 100 Shady Acre Rd, Packwood, WA 98361
Naifeh, Woody, RR 13 Box 380, Tulsa, OK 74131
Naten, Greg, 1804 Shamrock Way, Bakersfield, CA 93304
Nativo, George, 15011 Florwood Ave, Hawthorne, CA 90250
Neal, Jerry C., PO Box 1092, Banner Elk, NC 28604
Nealey, Ivan F., Box 65 HC 87, Mountain Home, ID 83647
Nealy, Bud, 1439 Popular Valley Rd, Stroudsburg, PA 18360
Nedved, Dan, 206 Park Dr, Kalispell, MT 59901
Neeley, Vaughn, 666 Grand Ave, Mancos, CO 81328
Neely, Greg, 9605 Radio Rd, Houston, TX 77075
Neering, Walt, 4191 N Euclid Ave, Bay City, MI 48706
Neil, W. D., 579 White Ave, Chico, CA 95926
Neilson, Larry, 9520 S Emerald Dr, Port Orchard, WA 98366
Nelson, Keith, 18-D Chughole Ln, Los Lunas, NM 87031
Nelson, Ken, 11059 Hwy 73, Pittsville, WI 54466
Nelson, Roger S., PO Box 294, Central Village, CT 06332
Nevling, Mark, PO Box 9, Hume, IL 61932
Newcomb, Corbin, 628 Woodland Ave, Moberly, MO 65270
Newton, Larry, 1758 Pronghorn Ct, Jacksonville, FL 32225
Newton, Ron, 223 Ridge Ln, London, AR 72847
Nibarger, Charlie, 4908 E 15th St, Tulsa, OK 74112
Nicholson, R. Kent, PO Box 204, Phoenix, MD 21131
Nielson, Jeff V., POBox 365, Monroe, UT 84754
Niemuth, Troy, 3143 North Ave, Sheboygan, WI 53083
Nishiuchi, Melvin S., 6121 Forest Park Dr, Las Vegas, NV 89115
Nix, Robert T., 4194 Cadillac, Wayne, MS 48184
Nolen R.D., 1110 Lake Shore Dr, Estes Park, CO 80517
Nolen Steve, 1110 Lake Shore Dr, Estes Park, CO 80517
Nolfi, Tim, PO Box P, Dawson, PA 15428
Noren, Douglas E., 14676 Boom Rd, Springlake, MI 49456
Norfleet, Ross W., 3947 Tanbark Rd, Richmond, VA 23235
Norris, Don, 8861 N Shadow Rock Dr, Tucson, AZ 85743
Norris, Mike, 2115 W Main St, Albemarle, NC 28001
North, David, 105 Sharp, Chickamauga, GA 30707
Norton, Dennis, 5334 Ashland Dr, Ft Wayne, IN 46835
Norton, Don, 7517 Mountain Quail Dr, Las Vegas, NV 89146
Nott, Ron P., PO Box 281, Summerdale, PA 17093

Nowland, Rick, 3677 E Bonnie Rd, Waltonville, IL 62894
Nunn, Gregory, HC 64 Box 2107, Castle Valley, UT 84532
Nymeyer, Earl, 2802 N Fowler St, Hobbs, NM 88240
O'Ceilaghan, Michael, 1623 Benhill Rd, Baltimore, MD 21226
O'Leary, Gordon, 10911 Possom Trail Rd, Harrison, TN 37341
O'Neill, H. C., 9252 Deering Ave, Chatsworth, CA 91311
Ochs, Charles, 124 Emerald Ln, Largo, FL 34641
Oda, Kuzan, 629 W 15th Ave, Anchorage, AK 99501
Ogden, Bill, PO Box 72, Avis, PA 17721
Ogg, Robert G., 537 Old Dug Mtn Rd, Paris, AR 72855
Ogletree Jr., Ben R., 2815 Israel Rd, Livingston, TX 77351
Oliver, Anthony Craig, 1504 Elaine Pl, Fort Worth, TX 76106
Oliver, Milford, 3170 Angus Dr, Prescott, AZ 86301
Oliver, Todd, Tr 5 Box 659, Spencer, IN 47460
Olson, Darrold E., PO Box 1539, Springfield, OR 97477
Olson, Wayne C., 890 Royal Ridge Dr, Bailey, CO 80421
Onion, Kenneth, 91-990Oaniani St, Kapolei, HI 96707
Ortiz, Ron, 854 W B St, Ontario, CA 91762
Orton, Richard, PO Box 7002, La Verne, CA 91750
Osborne, Don, 5840 N Mccall Ave, Clovis, CA 93611
Osborne, Michael, 585 Timberridge Dr, New Braunfels, TX 78132
Osborne, Warren, PO Box 205, Waxahachie, TX 75168
Osterman, Daniel E., 1644 W 10th Ave, Junction City, OR 97448
Ottmar, Maurice, PO Box 657, Coulee City, WA 99115
Outlaw, Anthony L., 4115 Gaines St, Panama City, FL 32404
Overeynder, T. R., 1800 S Davis Dr, Arlington, TX 76013
Overholser, W. C., 235 NE 11th St, Newport, OR 97365
Owen, Bill, PO Box 161, Monterey, VA 24465
Owenby, John, 1716 Hastings Ct, Plano, TX 75023
Owens, Dan, PO Box 284, Blacksburg, SC 29702
Owens, Donald, 2274 Lucille Ln, Melbourne, FL 32935
Owens, John, 8755 SW 96th St, Miami, FL 33176
Owens, John, 13180 CR 280, Nathrop, CO 81236
Ownby, John C., 316 Springbridge Ln, Plano, TX 75025
Oyster, Lowell R., 543 Grant Rd, Corinth, ME 04427
Paback, Don, PO Box 318, Edgerton, WY 82635
Packard, Bob, PO Box 311, Elverta, CA 95626
Padgett Jr., Edwin L., 340 Vauxhall St, New London, CT 06320
Padilla, Gary, PO Box 6928, Auburn, CA 95604
Page, Larry, 165 Rolling Rock Rd, Aiken, SC 29803
Page, Reginald, 6587 Groveland Hill Rd, Groveland, NY 14462
Pagnard, Philip E., 2101 Garcia St NE, Albuquerque, NM 87112
Palmer, Howard, 2031 Tronjo Rd, Pensacola, FL 32503
Pankiewicz, Philip R., RFD #1 Waterman Rd, Lebanon, CT 06249
Papp, Robert, 252 Narseukkes Ave, Elyria, OH 44035
Pardue, Joseph, PO Box 693, Spurger, TX 77660
Pardue, Melvin M, RR 1 Box 130, Repton, AL 36475
Parker, Cliff, 6350 Tulip Dr, Zephyrhills, FL 33544
Parker, J. E., 1300 E Main, Clarion, PA 16214
Parker, James, P.O. 581, Alexis, NC 28006
Parker, Robert Nelson, 5223 Wilhelm Rd, Rapid City, MI 49676
Parks, Blane C., 15908 Crest Dr, Woodbridge, VA 22191
Parks, John, 3539 Galilee Church Rd, Jefferson, GA 30549
Parrish, Dwayne, PO Box 181, Palestine, TX 75802
Parrish, Gordon A., 940 Lakloey Dr, North Pole, AK 99705
Parrish, Robert, 271 Allman Hill Rd, Weaverville, NC 28787
Parsons, Michael R., 1600 S 11th St, Terre Haute, IN 47802
Pate, Lloyd D., 219 Cottontail Ln, Georgetown, TX 78626

Patrick, Chuck, PO Box 127, Brasstown, NC 28902
Patrick, Peggy, PO Box 127, Brasstown, NC 28902
Patrick, Willard C., PO Box 5716, Helena, MT 59604
Pattay, Rudy, 510 E Harrison St, Long Beach, NY 11561
Patterson, Alan W., RR 3 Box 131, Hayesville, NC 28904
Patterson, Karl, 8 Madison Ave, Silver Creek, NY 14136
Patton, Dick, 206-F W 38th St, Garden City, ID 83714
Pavack, Don, Elk Meadow Ranch—Leo Rt, Hanna, WY 82327
Peagler, Russ, PO Box 1314, Moncks Corner, SC 29461
Pearce, Hill Everett, PO Box 72, Gurley, AL 35748
Pease, W. D., 657 Cassidy Pike, Ewing, KY 41039
Peasley, David S., PO Box 604, Alamosa, CO 81101
Peel, W. K., 570 Ofarrell St Apt 204, San Francisco, CA 94102
Peele, Bryan, 219 Ferry St, Thompson Falls, MT 59873
Pendleton, Lloyd, 24581 Shake Ridge Rd, Volcano, CA 95689
Pendray, Alfred H., 13950 NE 20th St, Williston, FL 32696
Perry, Chris, 1654 W Birch, Fresno, CA 93711
Perry, John, 9 S Harrell Rd, Mayflower, AR 72106
Peters, Owen, 9008 Sparrow Dr, Richmond, VA 23229
Petersen, Dan L., 3015 SW Clark St, Topeka, KS 66604
Peterson, Chris, 2175 W Rockyford, Salina, UT 84654
Peterson, Eldon G., 260Haugen Heights Rd, Whitefish, MT 59937
Peterson, Lloyd, 64 Halbrook Rd, Clinton, AR 72031
Pfanenstiel, Dan, 1824 Lafayette Ave, Modesto, CA 95355
Pfeiffer, Kenneth, P.O. Box 551, Hagaman, NY 12086
Pharris, Glen, 6247 Whitecliff Way, North Highlands, CA 95660
Phelps, Paul S., 1306 Woodlawn Ave, Maryville, TN 37804
Philippi, D. A., 295 Holmes Rd, Pittsfield, MA 01201
Phillipini, Jim, 5448 Highview Ln, Citrus Heights, CA 95610
Phillips, Harold, RR 1 Box 37, Waukomis, OK 73773
Phillips, John, 31 Parker Way, Santa Barbara, CA 93101
Phillips, Randy, 759 E Francis St, Ontario, CA 91761
Phillips, Scott C., 671 California Rd, Gouvemeur, NY 13642
Phillips, Wayne, PO Box 78, Olancha, CA 9354
Pickens, Andrew, 8229 C.R. 334, Ignacio, CO 81137
Pickens, Selbert, Rt# 1 Box 216, Liberty, WV 25124
Pickering, Larry, 440 Belle Alliance Dr, Laplace, LA 70068
Pierce, Bruce M., 49 Laguna Way, Hot Springs, AR 71909
Pierce, Harold L, 106 Lyndon Ln, Louisville, KY 40222
Pierce, Jack L., 15945 SW Lake Forrest Blvd, Lake Oswego, OR 97034
Piergallini, Daniel E., 4011 N Forbes Rd, Plant City, FL 33565
Piorek, James S., PO Box 7733, Lakeside, MT 59922
Pitt, David F., 6812 Digger Pine Ln, Anderson, CA 96007
Pittman, Leon, 661 Hubert Pittman Rd, Pendergrass, GA 30567
Pixley, Jim, RR 1 Box 344, Pelican Rapids, MN 56572
Plunkett, Richard, 29 Kirk Rd, West Cornwall, CT 06796
Poag, James, Rt 1 Box 212-A, Grayville, IL 62844
Poehlman, Paul, PO Box 487, Stinson Beach, CA 94970
Pogreba, Larry, PO Box 861, Lyons, CO 80540
Pohlers, Rick, 4351 Toyon Rd, Riverside, CA 92504
Poletis, Jerry, PO Box 1582, Scottsdale, AZ 85252
Polk, Clifton, 4625 Webber Creek Rd, Van Buren, AR 72956
Polk, Rusty, 3225 Albert Pike Apt 11, Fort Smith, AR 72904
Polkowski, Al, 8 Cathy Ct, Chester, NJ 07930
Pollock, Wallace, 806 Russell Valley Dr, Cedar Park, TX 78613
Polzien, Don, 1912 Inler Suite L, Lubbock, TX 79407
Pomykalski, L. T., 15800 Le Claire Ave, Oak Forest, IL 60452
Ponzio, Doug, 3212 93rd St, Kenosha, WI 53142

Poole, Steve, 200 Flintlock Trl, Stockbridge, GA 30281
Poole, Marvin O., PO Box 5234, Anderson, SC 29623
Poplin, James L., 103 Oak St, Washington, GA 30673
Popp, Steve, 6573 Winthrop Dr, Fayetteville, NC 28311
Porter, James E., PO Box 2583, Bloomington, IN 47402
Porter, William R., 3403 Orchard Way, Oceanside, CA 92054
Portus, Robert, 130 Ferry Rd, Grants Pass, OR 97526
Posner, Barry E., 12501 Chandler Blvd Ste 104, N Hollywood, CA 91607
Poston, Alvin, 1197 Bass Rd, Pamplico, SC 29583
Poteet, Merle, 4616 W Cochise Dr, Glendale, AZ 85302
Potier, Timothy F., PO Box 711, Oberlin, LA 70655
Potocki, Roger, Rt 1 Box 333-A, Goreville, IL 62939
Potter, Frank, 25 Renfrew Ave, Middletown, RI 02842
Pou, Ed, 322 Cleveland St, New Albany, MS 38652
Powell, Robert C., 93 Gose Rd, Smarr, GA 31086
Powell, Wesley R., 7211 Tropicana St, Miramar, FL 33023
Poythress, John, PO Box 585, Swainsboro, GA 30401
Prater, Mike, 81 Sanford Ln, Flintstone, GA 30725
Pratt, Charles, 1953 Fillmans Bottom Rd SW, Port Washington, OH 43837
Presley, Vern, 3803 Alston Ln, Richmond, VA 23294
Pressburger, Ramon, 59 Driftway Rd, Howell, NJ 07731
Price, Jerry L., PO Box 782, Springdale, AR 72765
Price, Joel Hiram, RR1 Box 18GG, Interlochen, FL 32148
Price, Timmy, PO Box 906, Blairsville, GA 30514
Primos, Terry, 932 Francais Dr, Shreveport, LA 71118
Prince, Joe, 190 Bulman Rd, Roebuck, SC 29376
Pritchard, Ron, 613 Crawford Ave, Dixon, IL 61021
Prouty, Ralph, 5240 SW 49th Dr, Portland, OR 97221
Provenzano, Joseph D., 3024 Ivy Pl, Chalmette, LA 70043
Pryor, Stephen L., HC Rt 1 Box 1445, Boss, MO 65440
Pugh, Jim, PO Box 711, Azle, TX 76020
Pullen, Martin, 1701 Broken Bow, Granbury, TX 76049
Pulliam, Morris C., 560 Jeptha Knob Rd, Shelbyville, KY 40065
Pursley, Aaron, PO Box 1037, Big Sandy, MT 59520
Purvis, Bob, 2416 N Loretta Dr, Tucson, AZ 85716
Puterbaugh, Don, 3650 Austin Bluff Prkwy S, Colorado Springs, CO 80907
Putnam, Donald S., 590 Wolcott Hill Rd, Wethersfield, CT 06109
Quarton, Barr, PO Box 4336, Mc Call, ID 83638
Quattlebaum, Craig, 2 Ridgewood Ln, Searcy, AR 72143
Quenton, Warner, PO Box 607, Peterstown, WV 24963
Quick, Mike, 23 Locust Ave, Kearny, NJ 07032
Quinn, George, PO Box 692, Julian, CA 92036
Rachlin, Leslie S., 1200 W Church St, Elmira, NY 14905
Racy, Richard Ray, 8820 W Mescal St, Peoria, AZ 85345
Rados, Jerry F., 7523 E 5000 N Rd, Grant Park, IL 60940
Rafferty, Dan, PO Box 1415, Apache Junction, AZ 85217
Ragsdale, James D., 3002 Arabian Woods Dr, Lithonia, GA 30038
Rainville, Richard, 126 Cockle Hill Rd, Salem, CT 06420
Ralph, Darrel, 4185 S State Rt 605, Galena, OH 43021
Rambo, J. T., 113 Weber T.R.V., Rock Springs, WY 82901
Ramey, Marshall F., PO Box 2589, West Helena, AR 72390
Randall, Bill, 765 W Linberlost #30, Tucson, AZ 85705
Randall, Gary, PO Box 1988, Orlando, FL 32802
Randall Jr., James W., 11606 Keith Hall Rd, Keithville, LA 71047
Randall, W. D. "Bo", PO Box 1988, Orlando, FL 32802
Rapp, Steven J., 7273 S 245 East, Midvale, UT 84047
Rappazzo, Richard, 142 Dunsbach Ferry Rd, Cohoes, NY 12047
Rardon, A. D., 1589 S.E. Price Dr, Polo, MO 64671

Rardon, Archie F., 1589 S.E. Price Dr, Polo, MO 64671
Ratelle, Bill, 470 Raymond Dr, Benicia, CA 94510
Ray, Alan W., PO Box 479, Lovelady, TX 75851
Ray, Michael, 533 W 36th St N, Wichita, KS 67204
Raymond, Donald, PO Box 1141, Groveton, TX 75845
Raymond, Mary Jane, PO Box 1141, Groveton, TX 75845
Read, Bob, 916 Neartop Dr, Nashville, TN 37205
Read, Dick, 4616 N 5th St, Fresno, CA 93726
Rece, Charles V., PO Box 868, Paw Creek, NC 28130
Red, Vernon, 2020 Benton Cove, Conway, AR 72032
Redfearn, Dennis, 2542 Bobwhite Blvd, Mesquite, TX 75149
Redmon, Mark, 7946 Modesto Dr, Riverside, CA 92503
Ree, David, 816 E Main St, Van Buren, AR 72956
Reed, Dave, PO Box 132, Brimfield, MA 01010
Reed, Del, 13765 SW Parkway, Beaverton, OR 97005
Reed, John M., 1095 Spaulding Cr, Goose Creek, SC 29455
Reeve, Chris, 11624 W Presidents Dr, Boise, ID 83713
Reeves, Winfred M., PO Box 300, West Union, SC 29696
Reeves, James Gary, 416 Delta Ct, Gardondale, AL 35071
Reggio Jr., Sidney J., PO Box 851, Sun, LA 70463
Reh, Bill, 2061 Tomlinson Rd, Caro, MI 48723
Remington, David W., 12928 Morrow Rd, Gentry, AR 72734
Renner, Terry L., PO Box 15063, Bradenton, FL 34209
Reno, Lou, PO Box 253, Okeechobee, FL 34973
Repke, Mike, 4191 N Euclid Ave, Bay City, MI 48706
Revishvili, Zaza, 2102 Linden Ave, Madison, WI 53704
Rexroat, Kirk, 527 Sweetwater Circle Box 224, Wright, W 82732
Reynolds, Dave, RR 2 Box 36, Harrisville, WV 26362
Reynolds, John C., #2, Andover St HC77, Gillette, WY 82716
Rhea, David, RR 1 Box 272, Lynnville, TN 38472
Rhea, Jerry, 440 Clark St, Turlock, CA 95380
Rhodes, James D., 205 Woodpoint Ave, Hagerstown, MD 21740
Rial, Douglas, RR 2 Box 117-A, Greenfield, TN 38230
Rice, Adrienne, PO Box 252, Lopez, WA 98261
Richard, Ron, 4875 Calaveras Ave, Fremont, CA 94538
Richards Jr., Alvin, 2889 Shields Ln, Fortuna, CA 95540
Richards, Art, 1725 Bonita Ave, Burbank, CA 91504
Richards, Don T., 170 23rd St, Costa Mesa, CA 92627
Richardson, Charles, PO Box 38329, Dallas, TX 75238
Richardson Jr., Percy, PO Box 973, Hempill, TX 75948
Richardson, William J., 1026 W 1700 S Apt 1, Syracuse, UT 84075
Richter, John C., 932 Bowling Green Trl, Chesapeake, VA 23320
Richter, Scott, 516 E 2nd St South Boston, MA 02127
Ricke, Dave, 1209 Adams St, West Bend, WI 53095
Rigney, Willie, 191 Colson Dr, Bronston, KY 42518
Riker, Tom, 313 S Raleigh St, Martinsburg, WV 25401
Rippy, Robert, PO Box 425, Emory, TX 75440
Rizzi, Russell J., 37 March Rd, Ashfield, MA 01330
Roath, Dean, 3050 Winnipeg Dr, Baton Rouge, LA 70819
Robbins, Howard P., 1407 S 217 Ave, Elkhorn, NE 68022
Roberts, Asa, 1222 Willow Lane, Nampa, ID 83651
Roberts, Chuck, PO Box 7174, Golden, CO 80403
Roberts, Michael, 601 Oakwood Dr, Clinton, MS 39056
Robertson, Leo D., 3728 Pleasant Lake Dr, Indianapolin, IN 46227
Robertson, Ron, 6708 Lunar Dr, Anchorage, AK 99504
Robinson, Charles, PO Box 221, Vega, TX 79092
Robinson, Chuck, 1423 3rd Ave, Picayune, MS 39466
Robinson, Michael B., 860 Mcclelland St, Salt Lake City, UT 84102

Robinson III, Rex, 10531 Poe St, Leesburg, FL 34788
Robinson, Robert W., 1569 N Finley Point Rd, Polson, MT 59860
Rochford, Michael, PO Box 577, Dresser, WI 54009
Rodebaugh, James L., 9374 Joshua Rd, Oak Hills, CA 92345
Rodewald, Gary, 447 Grouse Ct, Hamilton, MT 59840
Rodkey, Daniel, 18336 Ozark Dr, Hudson, FL 34667
Rodrigues, Joe, 10606 San Gabriel Ave, South Gate, CA 90280
Roe Jr., Fred D., 4005 Granada Dr SE, Huntsville, AL 35802
Rogers, Richard, PO Box 769, Magdalena, NM 87825
Rogers, Robert P., 3979 S Main St, Acworth, GA 30101
Rogers, Rodney, 602 Osceola Ave, Wildwood, FL 34785
Rohmans, Mark, 607 Virginia Ave, La Grange, GA 30240
Rohn, Fred, 7675 W Happy Hill Rd, Coeur D Alene, ID 83814
Roland, Dan, 1966 W 13th Ln, Yuma, AZ 85364
Rollert, Steve, PO Box 65, Keenesburg, CO 80643
Romano, Richard, 31 Arlington Rd, Windsor Locks, CT 06096
Ronk, W. W., 511 W Boyd Ave, Greenfield, IN 46140
Root, George R., PO Box 6, Manchester, KY 40962
Root, Jon Paul, PO Box 474, Benson, AZ 85602
Roper, Mark H., 952 Deercrest Cir, Evans, GA 30809
Rose, Alex, 3624 Spring Valley Dr, New Port Richey, FL 34655
Rosenfeld, Bob, 955 Freeman Johnson Rd, Hoschton, GA 30548
Ross, Greg, 4556 Wenhart Rd, Lake Worth, FL 33463
Ross, Stephen, 534 Remington Dr, Evanston, WY 82930
Ross, Tom, 4962 Sierra Vista Ave, Riverside, CA 92505
Rossdeutscher, Robert N., 133 S Vail Ave, Arlington Hgts, IL 60005
Rotella, Richard A., 643 75th St, Niagara Falls, NY 14304
Roy, John, PO Box 191, Veneta, OR 97487
Royal, B. M., PO Box 934, Helen, GA 30545
Rozas, Clark D., 1436 W "G" St, Wilmington, CA 90744
Rua, Gary, 329 Snell St, Fall River, MA 02721
Ruana, Knifeworks, P.O. 520, Bonner, MT 59823
Rubley, James A., 4609 W Nevada Mills Rd, Angola, IN 46703
Rupert, Bob, 301 Harshaville Rd, Clinton, PA 15026
Ruple, William H., PO Box 370, Charlotte, TX 78011
Russ, Ron, 5351 NE 160th Ave, Williston, FL 32696
Russell, Roger, PO Box 27, Peralta, NM 87042
Russell, Tom, 6500 New Liberty Rd, Jacksonville, AL 36265
Rust, Charles C., PO Box 374, Palermo, CA 95968
Ryan, J. C., RR 5 Box 183-A, Lexington, VA 24450
Ryan, C. O., 902-A Old Wormley Creek Road, Yorktown, VA 23692
Rybar Jr., Raymond B., 277 Stone Church Rd, Finleyville, PA 15332
Ryder, Ben M., PO Box 133, Copperhill, TN 37317
Saindon, Bill, 11 Highland View Rd, Claremont, NH 03743
Sakmar, Mike, 2470 Melvin, Rochester, MI 48307
Salisbury, Joel, Rt 1 Box 6-A, Glorieta, NM 87535
Salley, John D., 3965 Frederick-Ginghamsburg Rd, Tipp City, OH 45371
Salpas, Bob, PO Box 117, Homewood, CA 96141
Sampogna, Michael, 45 E Argyle St, Valley Stream, NY 11580
Sampson, Lynn, 381 Deakins Rd, Jonesborough, TN 37659
Samson, Jody, 1834 W Burbank Blvd, Burbank, CA 91506
Sanders, Albert, 3850 72nd Ave NE, Norman, OK 73071
Sanders, Bill, 335 Baer Ave, Mancos, CO 81328
Sanders, Michael, PO Box 1106, Ponchatoula, LA 70454
Sanders, Sandy, 2358 Taylor Lane, Louisville, KY 40205
Sanderson, Ray, 4403 Uplands Way, Yakima, WA 98908
Sandlin, Larry, 4580 Sunday Dr, Adamsville, AL 35005
Sasser, Jim, 926 Jackson St, Pueblo, CO 81004

Sawby, Scott, 480 Snowberry Ln, Sandpoint, ID 83864
Sayen, Murad, PO Box 127, Bryant Pond, ME 04219
Scarrow, Lin, 16236 Chicago Ave, Bellflower, CA 90706
Scarrow, Will, 6012 Pierce, Lakewood, CA 90712
Schaller, Anthony B., 5609 Flint Ct NW, Albuquerque, NM 87120
Schedenhell, Jack, PO Box 307, Superior, MT 59872
Scheid, Maggie, 124 Van Stallen St, Rochester, NY 14621
Schell, Clude M., 4735 NE Elliott Circle, Corvallis, OR 97330
Schempp, Ed, PO Box 1181, Ephrata, WA 98823
Schempp, Martin, PO Box 1181, Ephrata, WA 98823
Schenck, Clifton, PO Box 1017, Bonners Ferry, ID 83805
Schepers, George B., PO Box 395, Sheldon, NE 68876
Schiffman, N. H., 963 Malibu St, Pocatello, ID 83201
Schiller, Arthur R., 143 Avenida Granada, San Clemente, CA 92672
Schirmer, Mike, PO Box 524, Twin Bridges, MT 59754
Schlomer, James E., 2543 Wyatt Pl, Kissimmee, FL 34741
Schlueter, David, PO Box 463, Syracuse, NY 13209
Schmidt, James A., 1167 Eastern Ave, Ballston Lake, NY 12019
Schmidt, Ray, PO Box 598, Whitefish, MT 59937
Schmidt, Rick, PO Box 1318, Whitefish, MT 59937
Schmier, Jack, 16787 Mulberry Cir, Fountain Valley, CA 92708
Schmoker, Randy, HC 63 Box 1085, Slana, AK 99586
Schneider, Craig M., 285 County Road 1400 N, Seymour, IL 61875
Schneider, Herman J., 10 Sun Hala, Pittsburg, TX 75686
Schneider, Karl A., 209 N Brownleaf Rd, Newark, DE 19713
Scholten, Bob, 511 Laguna Honda Blvd, San Francisco, CA 94127
Scholl, Tim, 1389 Langdon Rd, Angier, NC 27501
Schrock, Al, 1712 S Oak St, Pontiac, IL 61764
Schrock, Maurice, 1712 S Oak St, Pontiac, IL 61764
Schroder, Jeff, PO Box 794, Costa Mesa, CA 92627
Schroen, Karl, 4042 Bones Rd, Sebastopol, CA 95472
Schulds, John, 5711 Melvin Ave, Tarzana, CA 91356
Schulenburg, E. W., 406 Sunset Blvd, Carrollton, GA 30117
Schultz, Bob, 3650 Austin Bluffs Pky, Colorado Springs, CO 80918
Schultz, Richard, 22971 Triton Way, Laguna Hills, CA 92653
Schwartz, John J., 41 15th St, Wellsburg, WV 26070
Schwarzer, James, PO Box 4, Pomona Park, FL 32181
Schwarzer, Steve, PO Box 4, Pomona Park, FL 32181
Scofield, Everett, 2873 Glass Mill Rd, Chickamauga, GA 30707
Scott, Al, HC 63 Box 802, Harper, TX 78631
Scott, Winston, RR 2 Box 62, Huddleston, VA 24104
Scroggs, James, 108 Murray Hill Dr, Warrensburg, MO 64093
Sears, Mick, 1697 Peach Orchard Rd, Sumter, SC 29154
Seldomridge, John, 221 N 61st St, Kansas City, KS 66102
Selent, Chuck, PO Box 1207, Bonners Ferry, ID 83805
Self, Ernie, 950 O'Neill Ranch Rd, Dripping Springs, TX 78620
Selvey, W. H., 108 S 11th St, Blue Springs, MO 64015
Selvidio, Ralph, PO Box 1464, Crystal River, FL 34423
Sentz, Mark, 4084 Baptist Rd, Taneytown, MD 21787
Serafen, Steven E., 24 Genesse St, New Berlin, NY 13411
Serven, James, PO Box 1, Fostoria, MI 48435
Shadley, Eugene W., 26315 Norway Dr, Bovey, MN 55709
Sharp, Robert G., 17540 Saint Francis Blvd, Anoka, MN 55303
Sharpe, Philip, 483 Landmark Way, Austell, GA 30001
Sharp, Wes, 1220 N 18th Ave, Milton, FL 32583
Sharp, Margie, 1220 N 18th Ave, Milton, FL 32583
Sharrigan, Mudd, 111 Bradford Rd, Wiscasset, ME 04578
Shaw, David L., 2009 N 450 E, Ogden, UT 84414

Shearer, Robert A., 2121 Avenue T, Huntsville, TX 77340
Sheehan, Paul, 3985 E Montezuma Ave, Rimrock, AZ 83635
Sheehy, Thomas J., 4131 NE 24th Ave, Portland, OR 97211
Shelor, Ben, RR 14 Box 318-B, Richmond, VA 23231
Shelton, Paul, 1406 Holloway, Rolla, MO 65401
Shelton, Scott, 5230 Pressley Rd, Santa Rosa, CA 95404
Sherrill, Dave, 2905 F Rd 1/2, Grand Junction, CO 81504
Shinosky, Andy, 3117 Meanderwood Dr, Canfield, OH 44515
Shipley, Steven, 800 E Campbell Rd, Richardson, TX 75081
Shirley, Dave, 39723 Plumas Way, Fremont, CA 94538
Shoemaker, Carroll, 380 Yellowtown Rd, Northup, OH 45658
Shoemaker, Scott, 316 S Main St, Miamisburg, OH 45342
Shoger, Mark O., 14780 SW Osprey Dr Ste 345, Beaverton, OR 97007
Shore, John L., 2901-A Sheldon Jackson St, Anchorage, AK 99508
Shostle, Ben, 1121 Burlington, Muncie, IN 47302
Shuford, Rick, RR 8 Box 256-A, Statesville, NC 28677
Shulenberger, William E., RR 4 Box 312, Newville, PA 17241
Sibrian, Aaron, 4308 Dean Dr, Ventura, CA 93003
Sidelinger, Robert, 1365 Saint Francis Rd, Bel Air, MD 21014
Sigman, Corbet, RR 1 Box 212-A, Liberty, WV 25124
Sigman, James P., 10391 Church Rd, North Adams, MI 49262
Silva, Joe, 6829 Mayhews Landing Rd, Newark, CA 94560
Silva, Manuel, 829 Pine St, Ramona, CA 92065
Simmons, H. R., 1100 Bay City Rd, Aurora, NC 27806
Simonich, Rob, PO Box 278, Clancy, MT 59634
Simons, Bill, 6217 Michael Ln, Lakeland, FL 33811
Simons, Norman, HCR 4 Box 528, Burnet, TX 78611
Sims, Bob, PO Box 772, Meridian, TX 76665
Sinclair, J. E., 520 Francis Rd, Pittsburg, PA 15239
Sinyard, Cleston, 27522 Burkhardt Dr, Elberta, AL 36530
Sisemore, Charles, Hc 63 Box 5550, Hodgen, OK 74939
Siska, Jim, 6 Highland Ave, Westfield, MA 01085
Sites, David, 2665 Atwood Ter, Columbus, OH 43211
Sjostrand, Kevin, 1541 S Cain St, Visilia, CA 93292
Skirchak, Samuel, Rt 1 Lisbon Rd, Midland, PA 15059
Skorupa, Larry, RR 1 Box 1152, Bridger, MT 59014
Slee, Fred, 9 John St, Morganville, NJ 07751
Sloan, John, PO Box 486, Foxboro, MA 02035
Sloan, Shane, RR 1 Box 17, Newcastle, TX 76372
Slobodian, Scott, 4101 River Ridge Dr, San Andreas, CA 95249
Smale, Charles J., 509 Grove Ave, aukegan, IL 60085
Small, Ed, RR 1 Box 178-A, Keyser, WV 26726
Small, Jim, PO Box 67, Madison, GA 30650
Small, Michael, 332 Lindbergh Ave, Frederick, MD 21701
Smart, Steaten, 15815 Acom Circle, Tavares, FL 32778
Smart, Steve, 1 Meadowbrook Circle, Melissa, TX 75454
Smit, Glenn, 627 Cindy Ct, Aberdeen, MD 21001
Smith, Bobbie D., 802 W Hwy 90, Bonifay, FL 32425
Smith, Cary, 946 Marigny Ave, Mandeville, LA 70448
Smith, D. Noel, PO Box 1363, Canon City, CO 81215
Smith, D. W., RR 1 Box 141, Mars, PA 16046
Smith, Dan, 7334 Clear Creek Rd, Parkdale, OR 97041
Smith, David Lynn, 1946 W 550 S, Vernal, UT 84078
Smith, F. L., PO Box 817, Fair Oaks, CA 95628
Smith, Glenn L., 630 E 39th St, Hialeah, FL 33013
Smith, Gregory H., 8607 Codington Ct, Louisville, KY 40299
Smith, Harry R, 2105 27th Ave, Missoula, MT 59801
Smith, J. D., 516 East 2nd St, South Boston, MA 02128

Smith, Jack, 1404 Deerfield Ln, Woodbridge, VA 22191
Smith, James B., RR 2 Box 1525, Morven, GA 31638
Smith, Jim, 1608 Joann St, Wichita, KS 67203
Smith, John M., 3450 E Beguelin Rd, Centralia, IL 62801
Smith, John T., 8404 Cedarcrest Dr, Southaven, MS 38671
Smith, John W., 1416 Cow Branch Rd, West Liberty, KY 41472
Smith, Josh, PO Box 683, Lincoln, MT 59639
Smith, Michael J., 1418 Saddle Gold Ct, Brandon, FL 33611
Smith, Newman L., 676 Glades Rd, Gatlinburg, TN 37738
Smith, Ralph L., PO Box 1690, Greer, SC 29652
Smith, Raymond L., Box 370, Breesport, NY 14816
Smith, Rick, 1843 W Evans Creek, Rogue River, OR 97537
Smith, W. M., 802 Hwy 90, Bonifay, FL 32425
Smoker, Ray, 113 Church Rd, Searcy, AR 72143
Snare, Michael, 3352 E Mescal St, Phoenix, AZ 85028
Snell, Jerry L., 235 Woodsong Dr, Fayetteville, GA 30214
Snody, Mike, 7169 Silk Hope Rd, Liberty, NC 27298
Snow, Bill, 4824 18th Ave, columbus GA 31904
Soares, John, 3115 Ozark Ave, Port Arthur, TX 77640
Sokol, Richard, PO Box 90057, Indianapolis, IN 46290
Solomon, Marvin, 23750 Cold Springs Rd, Paron, AR 72122
Somerville, Jim, PO Box 165, Salem, IL 62881
Sonneville, W. J., 1050 Chalet Dr W, Mobile, AL 36608
Sonntag, Douglas W., 906 N 39 St, Nixa, MO 65714
Sontheimer, G. Douglas, 12604 Bridgeton Dr, Potomac, MD 20854
Sornberger, Jim, 25126 Overland Dr, Volcano, CA 95689
Sowell, Bill, 100 Loraine Forest Ct, Macon, GA 31210
Spano, Dominick, 2726 Rice Ave, San Angelo, TX 76904
Sparks, Bernard, PO Box 73, Dingle, ID 83233
Spencer, John E., HC 63 Box 267, Harper, TX 78631
Spencer, Velden L., 2664 Salton Vista Dr, Julian, CA 92036
Spendlove, Dale, 211 S 1000 E, Orem, UT 84058
Spicer, William F., 2213 Inverness Blvd, Rawlins, WY 82301
Spinale, Richard, 4021 Canterbury Ct, Lorain, OH 44053
Spivey, Jefferson, 9244 W Wilshire, Yukon, OK 73099
Spragg, Wayne E., PO Box 508 1314 3675 East Rd, Ashton, ID 83420
Sprouse, Terry, 1633 Newfound Rd, Asheville, NC 28806
St. Cyr, H. Red, 1218 Cary Ave, Wilmington, CA 90744
Stafford, Michael, 3109 Todd Dr, Madison, WI 53713
Stafford, Richard, 104 Marcia Ct, Warner Robins, GA 31088
Stahl, John, 2049 Windsor Rd, Baldwin, NY 11510
Stalter, Harry L., 2509 N Trivoli Rd, Trivoli, IL 61569
Stanley, John, 604 Elm St, Crossett, AR 71635
Stapel, Chuck, PO Box 1617, Glendale, CA 91209
Stapel, Craig, Box 1617, Glendale, CA 91209
Staples, Richard, 1904 Mifflin Rd, Beech Bluff, TN 38313
Stefani, Randy, 2393 Mayfield Ave, Montrose, CA 91020
Stegall, Keith, 2101 W 32nd, Anchorage, AK 99517
Stegall, Steve, 4588 Woodworth Rd, Mount Hood, OR 97041
Stegner, Wilbur G., 9242 173rd Ave SW, Rochester, WA 98579
Steigerwalt, Ken, 507 Sausagehill Rd, Orangeville, PA 17859
Steiger, Monte L., Box 186, Genesse, ID 83832
Steinberg, Al, 5244 Duenas, Laguna Woods, CA 92653
Steketee, Craig A., 871 N Hwy 60, Billings, MO 65610
Stephan, Daniel, 2201 S Miller Rd, Valrico, FL 33594
Stephani, Randy, 2393 Mayfield Ave, Montrose, CA 91020
Stephens, Kelly Lee, 4235 78th Ln N, Saint Petersburg, FL 33709
Sterling, Murray, 523 Round Peak Church Rd, Mt Airy, NC 27030

Stevens, Barry B., 901 Amherst Rd, Cridersville, OH 45806
Stewart, Charles, 2128 Garrick Ave, Warren, MI 48091
Stewart, Edward L., 4297 Audrain Rd 335, Mexico, MO 65265
Stewart, Patrick C., RR 3 Box 30075, Winchester, TN 37398
Stice, Douglas W., 446 W 6th St, Haysville, KS 67060
Stipes, Dwight, 2651 SW Buena Vista Dr, Palm city, FL 34990
Stites, Kay, 4931 Rands Rd, Bloomfield Hills, MI 48302
Stockwell, Walter, 368 San Carlos Ave, Redwood City, CA 94061
Stoddart, W. B., 917 Smiley Ave, Forest Park, OH 45240
Stokes, Ed, 22614 Cardinal Dr, Hockley, TX 77447
Stone, G. W., 610 N Glenville Dr, Richardson, TX 75081
Stone, Jerry, PO Box 1027, Lytle, TX 78052
Stormer, Bob, 10 Karabair Rd, St Peters, MO 63376
Stout, Johnny, 1205 Forest Trail, New Braunfels, TX 78132
Stover, James, 9130 Highway 140, Eagle Point, OR 97524
Stover, Terry, 1809 N 300 E, Kokomo, IN 46901
Straight, Don, PO Box 12, Points, WV 25437
Stranahan, Dan, 445 N Walch St, Porterville, CA 93257
Strickland, Dale, 1440 E Thompson View, Monroe, UT 84754
Strohecker, John J., PO Box 1411, Riverton, WY 82501
Strong, Bob, 1616 Camino Verde, Walnut Creek, CA 94596
Strong, Scott, 2138 Oxmoor Dr, Beaver Creek, OH 45431
Stroyan, Eric, Box 218, Dalton, PA 18414
Stuckey, Fred B., 1227 Baxley Ln, Longview, TX 75604
Stumpff, George, PO Box 2, Glorieta, NM 87535
Sturgeon, Jim, 1826 Delaware Ave, West Sacramento, CA 95691
Suedmeier, Harlan, RFD 2 Box 299-D, Nebraska City, NE 68410
Sullivent, Loyd, RR 1 Box 29, Clyde, TX 79510
Summers, Arthur L., 1310 Hess Rd, Concord, NC 28025
Summers, Dan, 2675 NY Rt 11, Whitney Point, NY 13862
Summers, Dennis, 827 E Cecil St, Springfield, OH 45503
Sutherland, Greg, PO Box 23516, Flagstaff, AZ 86002
Sutton, Russell S., 4900 Cypress Shores Dr, New Bern, NC 28562
Swain, Rod, 1020 Avon Pl, South Pasadena, CA 91030
Swan, Ed, 5107 95th Ave NE, Everett, WA 98205
Swyhart, Art, 509 Main St, Klickitat, WA 98628
Syslo, Chuck, 3418 S 116th Ave, Omaha, NE 68144
Szarek, Mark G., 94 Oakwood Ave, Revere, MA 02051
Szilaski, Joseph, 29 Carroll Dr, Wappingers Falls, NY 12590
Taglienti, Antonio, 164Rhodes Dr, Beaver Falls, PA 15010
Talley, Grant C., 14618 Cicotte, Allen Park, MI 48101
Tamboli, Michael, 12447 N 49th Ave, Glendale, AZ 85304
Tausher, Jeff, 9951 Windon, San Ramon, CA 94583
Taylor, Billy, 10 Temple Rd, Petal, MS 39465
Taylor, C. Gray, 560 Poteat Ln, Fall Branch, TN 37656
Taylor, David, 215 Hermosa Dr, Fall Branch, TN 37656
Taylor, Scott, 18124-B La Salle Ave, Gardena, CA 90248
Taylor, Shane, 18 Broken Bow Ln, Miles City, MT 59301
Tedder, Mickey, Rt 2 Box 22, Conover, NC 28613
Terrill, Stephen, 21363 Rd 196, Lindsay, CA 93247
Terzuola, Robert, 3933 Aqua Fina St, Santa Fe, NM 87501
Thayer, Danny, 4504 W 660 S, Lafayette, IN 47905
Thayer, Leroy, 15600 Pinto Way, Chino, CA 91709
Theis, Terry, HC 63 Box 213, Harper, TX 78631
Thill, Jim, 10242 Bear Run, Missoula, MT 59803
Thissell, Stiles B., PO Box 21, Inverness, CA 94937
Thomas, Daniel, 142 Clubhouse Dr SW #302, Leesburg, VA 20175
Thomas, David E., 8502 Hwy 91, Lillian AL 36549

Thomas, Devin, 90 N 5th St, Panaca, NV 89042
Thomas, Jerry, 6302 Holida Dr, Forest Park, GA 30050
Thomas, Kim, PO Box 631, Seville, OH 44273
Thomas, Rocky, 1716 Waterside Blvd, Moncks Corner, SC 29461
Thomason, Bill, 167 Lower Dawnville RD NE, Dalton, GA 30721
Thompson, Bruce Lee, 4101 W Union Hills Dr, Glendale, AZ 85308
Thompson, Kenneth, 4887 Glenwhite Dr, Duluth, GA 30136
Thompson, Leon, 45723 Saddleback Dr, Gaston, OR 97119
Thompson, Lloyd, PO Box 1664, Pagosa Springs, CO 81147
Thompson, Robert L., PO Box 23992, Phoenix, AZ 85063
Thompson, Tommy, 4015 NE Hassalo, Protland, OR 97232
Thomsen, Loyd W., HCR-46 Box 19, Oelrichs, SD 57763
Thornton, Danny, PO Box 334, Fort Mill, SC 29716
Thourot, Michael W., T814 Rt 1 Rd 11, Napoleon, OH 43545
Thuesen, Ed, 21211 Knolle Rd, Damon, TX 77430
Thuesen, Kevin, 10649 Haddington Dr Ste 190, Houston, TX 77043
Tiensvold, Alan L., PO Box 355, Rushville, NE 69360
Tiensvold, Jason, PO Box 795, Rushville, NE 69360
Till, Calvin E., 211 Chaping, Chadron, NE 69337
Tilton, John, 24041 Hwy 383, Iowa, LA 70647
Timm, Bob, 655 W Tomah Rd, Castle Rock, CO 80104
Tindera, George, 751 Hadcock Rd, Brunswick, OH 44212
Tinker, Carolyn D., PO Box 5123, Whittier, CA 90607
Tison, Robert E., 1844 Bartram Cir E, Jacksonville, FL 32207
Todd, Ed, 9 Woodlawn Rd, Putnam Valley, NY 10579
Todd, Richard C., RR 1, Chambersburg, IL 62323
Tokar, Daniel, PO Box 1776, Shepherdstown, WV 25443
Tollefson, Barry A., 177 Blackfoot Trail, Gunnison, CO 81230
Tomes, Anthony S., 8190 Loch Seaforth Ct, Jacksonville, FL 32244
Tomes, P. J., 594 High Peak Ln, Shipman, VA 22971
Tomey, Kathleen, 146 Buford Pl, Macon, GA 31204
Tompkins, Dan, PO Box 398, Peotone, IL 60468
Toner, John E., 5202 N 106 Dr, Glendale, AZ 85307
Toole, Bobby, L., 2 Briarwood Pl, Vicksburg, MS 39180
Topliss, M. W., 1668 Hermosa Ct, montrose, CO 81401
Towell, Dwight L., 2375 Towell Rd, Midvale, ID 83645
Townsend, J. W., PO Box 722, Watson, LA 70786
Trabbic, R. W., 4550 N Haven Ave, Toledo, OH 43612
Tracy, Bud B., 15500 Fawn Ln, Reno, NV 89511
Treiber, Leon, PO Box 342, Ingram, TX 78025
Treijs, Norm, 54 Browns Rd, Huntington, NY 11743
Treutel, Terry A., PO Box 187, Hamilton, MT 59840
Trindle, Barry, 1660 Ironwood Tr, Earlham, IA 50072
Triplett, Craig, 3524 Jug Factory Rd, Greer, SC 29651
Trisler, Kenneth W., 6256 Federal 80, Rayville, LA 71269
Trujillo, Adam, 3001 Tanglewood, Anchorage, AK 99517
Trujillo, Albert, 2035 Wasmer Cir, Bosque Farms, NM 87068
Trujillo, Miranda, 3001 Tanglewood, Anchorage, AK 99517
Trujillo, Thomas A., 3001 Tanglewood, Anchorage, AK 99517
Tsoulas, Jon, 1 Home St, Peabody, MA 01960
Turcotte, Larry, 1707 Evergreen, Pampa, TX 79065
Turecek, Jim, 12 Elliot Rd, Ansonia, CT 06401
Turnbull, Ralph A., 14464 Linden Dr, Spring Hill, FL 34609
Turner, Kevin, 17 Hunt Ave, Montrose, NY 10548
Tyce, William, 14 Hob St, Newbrug, NY 12550
Tycer, Art, 23820 N Cold Springs Rd, Paron, AR 72122
Tye, Virgil Dee, 901 S Chester Ave, Bakersfield, CA 93304
Tyer, Jerry L., Hc 67 Box 204, Everton, AR 72633

Tyser, Ross, 1015 Hardee Ct, Spartanburg, SC 29303
Underhill, Richard W., 1493 Sycamore Canyon Rd, Santa Barbara, CA 93108
Underwood, W. L., 1643 Pennsylvania Ave, East Liverpool, OH 43920
Urstadt, E. W., RR 4 Box 296, Deer Park, MD 21550
Vagnino, Michael, 38340 RD172, Visalia, CA 93292
Valachovic, Wayne, PO Box 4219, Kailua Kona, HI 96745
Valdes, Albert, 2708 Lakewood Ave, Los Angeles, CA 90039
Vallotton, Butch, 621 Fawn Ridge Dr, Oakland, OR 97462
Vallotton, Rainy D., 1295 Wolf Valley Dr, Umpkea, OR 97486
Vallotton, Shawn, 621 Fawn Ridge Dr, Oakland, OR 97462
Vallotton, Thomas, 621 Fawn Ridge Dr, Oakland, OR 97462
Valois, A. Daniel, 3552W Lizard Creek Rd, Lehighton, PA 18235
Van Eizenga, Jerry W., 14227 Cleveland, Nunica, MI 49448
Van Hoy, Ed, 1826 McCallum Rd, Candor, NC 27229
Vanderford, Carl G., RR 9 Box 238-B, Columbia, TN 38401
Vandeventer, Terry L., 3274 Davis Rd, Terry, MS 39170
Vans, John D., 5414 Grissom Dr, Arlington, TX 76016
Varnum, Fran, 1206 Cobblestone Ln, Santa Maria, CA 93454
Vaughan, Michael, 1610 Lisle St, Oildale, CA 93308
Vaughn, Eddie, 1905 Virginia St, Grand Prairie, TX 75051
Veatch, Richard, 2580 35th Pl, Springfield, OR 97477
Velarde, Ricardo, 7240 N Greefield Dr, Park City, UT 84098
Veit, Michael, 3289 E 5th Rd, La Salle, IL 61301
Viele, H. J., 88 Lexington Ave, Westwood, NJ 07675
Viniard, Billy, PO Box 644, Monticello, MS 39654
Vogt, Donald, 9007 Hogans Bend, Tampa, FL 33647
Von Boeckman, R., PO Box 40506, Memphis, TN 38174
Voorhies, Les, 14511 Lake Mazaska Tr, Faribault, MN 55021
Voss, Ben, 362 Clark St, Galesburg, IL 61401
Votaw, David, PO Box 327, Pioneer, OH 43554
Vought, Frank, 115 Monticello Dr, Hammond, LA 70401
Vunk, Robert, 3166 Breckenridge Dr, Colorado Springs, CO 80906
Waddle, Thomas, 11822 Lower River Rd, Louisville, KY 40272
Wade, James M., RR 1 Box 56, Wade, NC 28395
Wadeson, Joe, RR 1 Box 366, Interlachen, FL 32148
Wagaman, John K., 903 Arsenal Ave, Fayetteville, NC 28305
Waggoner, Les, 12542 Loraleen St, Garden Grove, CA 92641
Wagner, Dan, 112 Delaware St, New Castle, DE 19720
Wahlers, Herman F., Star Route Box 1, Austerlitz, NY 12017
Wahlster, Mark David, 1404 N 2nd St, Silverton, OR 97381
Waldrop, Mark, 14562 SE 1st Avenue Rd, Summerfield, FL 34491
Wallingford Jr., Charles W., 9024 US 42, Union, KY 41091
Walker, Bill, 431 Walker Rd, Stevensville, MD 21666
Walker, George A., 483 Aspen Hills, Alpine, WY 83128
Walker, Jim, 22 Walker Ln, Morrillton, AR 72110
Walker, John W., 10620 Moss Branch Rd, Bon Aqua, TN 37025
Walker III, John Wade, 2590 Gooch Pk, Paintlick, KY 40461
Walker, Michael, PO Box 1924, Taos, NM 87571
Wallace, Roger L., 4902 N Collins Ln, Tampa, FL 33603
Walters, A. F., 275 Crawley Rd, TyTy, GA 31795
Walters, Brian, PO Box 2124, Des Moines, IA 50310
Ward, A. R., 753 W Main St, Moore, OK 73160
Ward, Chuck, 1010 E North St, Benton, AR 72015
Ward, J. J., 7501 SR 220, Waverly, OH 45690
Ward, Ken, 5122 Lake Shastina Blvd, Weed, CA 96094
Ward, Ron, 409 Arrowhead Tr, Loveland, OH 45140
Ward, W. C., 817 Glenn, Clinton, TN 37716
Warden, Roy A., 275 Tanglewood Rd, Union, MO 63084

Wardian, Paul G., 460 SW Halsey Loop, Troutdale, OR 97060
Wardman, Dave, 9910 US Highway 23 S, Ossineke, MI 49766
Ware, D., RR 2 Box 2298, Benton City, WA 99320
Ware, J. D., 209 Cutbred St, Philadelphia, PA 19106
Ware, Tommy, PO Box 488, Datil, NM87821, 78606
Warenski, Buster, PO Box 214, Richfield, UT 84701
Warren, Al, 1423 Santa Fe Cir, Roseville, CA 95678
Warren, Daniel, 571 Lovejoy Rd, Canton, NC 28716
Warther, Dale, 418 E 10th St, Dover, OH 44622
Warzocha, Stanley, 32540 Wareham Ct, Warren, MI 48092
Washburn, Arthur D., 10 Hinman St, Pioche, NV 89043
Washburn Jr., Robert Lee, 244 Lovett Scott Rd, Adrian, GA 31002
Wasuta, Steve J., 1983 Jefferson St, San Francisco, CA 94123
Watanabe, Wayne, PO B3563, Montebello, CA 90640
Watson, Bert, PO Box 26, Westminster, CA 80030
Watson, Bill, 440 Forge Rd, Deatsville, AL 36022
Watson, Daniel, 350 Jennifer Ln, Driftwood, TX 78619
Watson, Thomas J., 1103 Brenau Ter, Panama City, FL 32405
Watt, Freddie, PO Box 1372, Big Spring, TX 79721
Wattelet, Michael A., PO Box 649, Minocqua, WI 54548
Watts, Mike, RR 1 Box 81, Gatesville, TX 76528
Watts, Wally, 9560 S Hwy 36, Gatesville, TX 76528
Weather, Ron, 4775 Memphis St, Dallas, TX 75207
Webb, Jim, RR 2 Box 435, Joplin, MO 64804
Weber, Fred E., 517 Tappan St, Forked River, NJ 08731
Weddle Jr., Del, 2703 Green Valley Rd, Saint Joseph, MO 64505
Weeber, Charles, 5285 E Tuave, Vicksburg, MI 49097
Weever, John S., 107-A Westmeadow Dr, Cleburne, TX 76033
Wehman, E. A., 104 Dr Ave, Summerville, SC 29483
Wehner, Rudy, 297 William Warren Rd, Collins, MS 39428
Weiland Jr., J. Reese, PO Box 2337, Riverview, FL 33568
Weiler, Donald E., PO Box 1576, Yuma, AZ 85366
Weinand, Gerome W., 14440 Harpers Bridge Rd, Missoula, MT 59802
Weinstock, Robert, PO Box 170028, San Francisco, CA 94117
Weiss, Charles L., 18847 N 13th Ave, Phoenix, AZ 85027
Weiss, Martin, 23 Bergwall Way, Vallejo, CA 94591
Weiss, Steven, 1465 Polk St, San Francisco, CA 94109
Welch, William H., 8232 Red Snapper Dr, Kimmell, IN 46760
Werner Jr., William A., 336 Lands Mill, Marietta, GA 30067
Werth, George W., 5223 Woodstock Rd, Poplar Grove, IL 61065
Wertz, Victor W., 1501 Arizona Ct, Woodbridge, VA 22191
Wescott, Cody, 5330 White Wing Rd, Las Cruces, NM 88012
Wescott, Jim, 4225 Elks Rd, Las Cruces, NM 88005
Wesolowski, Mike, 902-A Lohrman Lane, Petaluma, CA 94952
West, Charles, 1315 S Pine St, Centralia, IL 62801
West, Jim, 4504 Del Amo Blvd, Torrance, CA 90503
West, Pat, PO Box 9, Charlotte, TX 78011
Westberg, Larry, 305 S Western Hills Dr, Algona, IA 50511
Westwood, Tom, PO Box 177, Newberry, SC 29108
Wheat, Jon S., PO Box 323, Lakin, KS 67860
Whipple, Wesley A., PO Box 3771, Kodiak, AK 99615
Whitaker, Bob, 4633 Berta Rd, Memphis, TN 38109
White, Bryce, 1415 W Col Glenn Rd, Little Rock, AR 72210
White, Gene E., 6620Brierleigh Way, Alexandria, VA 22315
White, Robert, 641 Knox Rd 900 N, Gilson, IL 61436
White Jr., Robert J., Rt 1, Gilson, IL 61436
White, Scottie H., Rt 2 Box 556-G, Pecks Mill, WV 25547
Whitehead, James D., 1231 W 20th St, Florence, OR 97439

Whitley, Wayne, 210 E 7th St, Washington, NC 27889
Whitley, Weldon, 4308 N Robin Ave, Odessa, TX 79764
Whitman, Jim, 21044 Salem St, Chugiak, AK 99567
Whitmarsh, Jay, 19100 Dalton St, Newhall, CA 91321
Whitmire, Earl T., 725 Colonial Dr, Rock Hill, SC 29730
Whittaker, Robert E., PO Box 204, Mill Creek, PA 17060
Whittaker, Wayne, 2900 Woodland Ct, Metamora, MI 48455
Whitworth, Ken J., 41667 Tetley Dr, Sterling Heights, MI 48313
Wicker, Donnie R., 2544 E 40th Ct, Panama City, FL 32405
Wiggins, Horace, 203 Herndon St, Mansfield, LA 71052
Wiggins, James C., 1540 W Pleasant Ridge Rd, Hammond, LA 70403
Wilber, W. C., 400 Lucerne Dr, Spartanburg, SC 29302
Wilcher, Wendell L., RR6 Box 6573, Palestine, TX 75801
Wilding, L. R., 1485 Loretta Dr, Pittsburgh, PA 15235
Willey, W. G., RD 1 Box 235-B, Greenwood, DE 19950
Williams, Chip, 3519 Seneca Ave, Aiken, SC 29801
Williams, David, PO Box 75, Berea, WV 26327
Williams, Jack F., 4317 Boston Ave, La Crescenta, CA 91214
Williams, Jack H., 11803 NE 67th Pl, Kirkland, WA 98033
Williams, Jason, PO Box 67, Wyoming, RI 02898
Williams, Leonard, PO Box 162, Meadow Bridge, WV 25976
Williams, Michael L., PO Box 64-1, Broken Bow, OK 874728
Williams Jr., Richard, 1440 Nancy Cir, Morristown, TN 37814
Williams, Sherman A., 1709 Wallace St, Simi Valley, CA 93065
Williams, W. C., 711 Main St, Atlanta, TX 75551
Williamson, Tony, RR 3 Box 503, Siler City, NC 27344
Williamson, Walt, 10231 Ashford St, Rancho Cucamonga, CA 91730
Willis, Bill, Rt 7 Box 7549, Ava, MO 65608
Wills, Lowell, PO Box 452, Lake Forest, IL 60045
Willson, Harlan M., PO Box 2113, Lompoc, CA 93436
Wilson, Bob, 10116 Holman Rd SE, Port Orchard, WA 98366
Wilson, Gordon C., 6739 S 500 W, Trafalgar, IN 46181
Wilson, James G., PO Box 4024, Estes Park, CO 80517
Wilson, James R., PO Box 1285, Westcliffe, CO 81252
Wilson, Jon J., 1826 Ruby St, Johnstown, PA 15902
Wilson, Mike, 1416 McDonald Rd, Hayesville, NC 28904
Wilson, Philip C., PO Box 846, Mountain Ranch, CA 95246
Wilson, R. W., PO Box 2012, Weirton, WV 26062
Wilson, Ron, 2639 Greenwood Ave, Morro Bays, CA 93442
Wilson, Wayne O., 11403 Sunflower Ln, Fairfax, VA 22030
Wiman, Art, PO Box 92, Plumerville, AR 72127
Wine, Michael, 265 S Atlantic Ave, Cocoa Beach, FL 32931
Wingo, Gary, 240 Ogeechee, Ramona, OK 74061
Wingo, Perry, 22 55th St, Gulfport, MS 39507
Winkler, Daniel, PO Box 2166, Blowing Rock, NC 28605
Winn, Bill, Star Route, Gruver, TX 79040
Winn, Travis A., 558 E 3065 S, Salt Lake City, UT 84106
Winston, David, 1671 Red Holly St, Starkville, MS 39759
Wise, John, PO Box 994, Winchester, OR 97495
Witsaman, Earl, 3957 Redwing Circle, Stow, OH 44224
Wolf, William, 4618 N 79th Ave, Phoenix, AZ 85033
Wolfe, Jack, PO Box 1056, Larkspur, CA 94939
Womack, A. M., PO Box 1397, Coldspring, TX 77331
Wood, Barry, 3002 E Gunnison St, Colorado Springs, CO 80909
Wood, Dale, RR 1, Seymour, TX 76380
Wood, Larry B., 6945 Fishburg Rd, Huber Heights, OH 45424
Wood, Leonard J., 36 Sunrise Hill Rd, Fishkill, NY 12524
Wood, Owen, 6492 Garrison St, Arvada, CO 80004

Wood, Webster, 22041 Shelton Trail, Atlanta, MI 49709
Wood, William W., PO Box 606, Seymour, TX 76380
Woodard, Wiley, 4527 Jim Mitchell W, Colleyville, TX 76034
Woodcock, Dennis, PO Box 416, Nehalem, OR 97131
Woodward, Harold E., RR 3 Box 391, Woodbury, TN 37190
Woodworth, Al, RR 1 Box 13, Plainville, IL 62365
Wooldridge, Roy, 3106 Edgewood Dr SE, Jefferson, OR 97352
Worel, Joe, 3040 N Laporte, Melrose Park, IL 60164
Workman Jr., Hubert L., Tyree Rd, Williamsburg, WV 24991
Worrell, Morris C., 5625 S 25 W, Lebanon, IN 46052
Worthen, Richard, 834 Carnation Dr, Sandy, UT 84094
Wright, Harold C., 1710 Bellwood Dr, Centerville, TN 37033
Wright, Kevin, 671 Leland Valley Rd W, Quilcene, WA 98376
Wright, Ninda, 2643 Appian Way, Pinole, CA 94564
Wright, Richard S., 111 Hilltop Dr, Carolina, RI 02812
Wright, Tim, PO Box 3746, Sedona, AZ 86340
Wright, Tom, PO Box 54, Noel, MO 64854
Wyatt, William R., PO Box 237, Rainelle, WV 25962
Yancey, T. J., PO Box 943, Estes Park, CO 80517
Yates, Pat, PO Box 2047, Ridgecrest, CA 93556
Yaun, Christopher, 31240 Hwy 43, Albany, LA 70711
Yeates, Joe A., 730 Saddlewood Cir, Spring, TX 77381
Yopp, Col. D. C., Rt 3 Box 63, Old Town, FL 32680
York, David C., PO Box 3166, Chino Valley, AZ 86323
York, Ray, 815 Dadds Rd, Angels Camp, CA 95222
Yoshihara, Yoshindo, 49 Pt San Pedro Rd, San Rafael, CA 94901
Young, Charlie, 8252 Auburn Blvd, Citrus Heights, CA 95610
Young, Errol, 4826 Storeyland Dr, Alton, IL 62002
Young, George, 713 Pinoak Dr, Kokomo, IN 46901
Young, Paul A., 168 Elk Ridge Rd, Boone, NC 28607
Young, Raymond L., 2922 Hwy 188 E, Mt Ida, AR 71957
Yunes, Yamil R., PO Box 573, Roma, TX 78584
Yurco, Mike, PO Box 712, Canfield, OH 44406
Zaccagnino Jr., Don, 2256 Baucom Point Rd, Pahokee, FL 33476
Zahm, Kurt, 488 Rio Casa, Indialantic, FL 32903
Zakabi, Carl S., PO Box 3161, Mililani Town, HI 96789
Zalesky, Garry, 780 S. 14th St, Marion, IA 52302
Zboril, Terry, Rt 4 Box 318, Caldwell, TX 77836
Zeanon, Bill, 8612 Waxford Rd, Richmond, VA 23235
Zeleski, W. M., 83 Bradley St, East Hartford, CT 06118
Zeller, Dennis J., 1791 SW Lillyben Ave, Gresham, OR 97080
Zembko III, John, 140 Wilks Pond Rd, Berlin, CT 06037
Zima, Michael, 732 State St, Fort Morgan, CO 80701
Zinker, Brad, 1591 NW 17th St, Homestead, FL 33030
Zinmeister, Paul D., HC63 Box 53-B, Harper, TX 78631
Zowada, Tim, 4509 E Bear River Rd, Boyne Falls, MI 49713
Zscherny, Michael, 1840 Rock Island Dr, Ely, IA 52227

MILITARY KNIVES

One of the most dynamic knife collecting specialties during recent years has been military knives, especially those made for issue to U.S. troops. This listing includes utility-use pocketknives as well as the fighting-utility knives known to most knife enthusiasts and former military personnel.

Earlier editions of this book have included only knives issued by the several U.S. military services. Former members of the armed services, as well as students of military cutlery, recognize the prominence and reputation of some nonissue knives. This edition includes several models that were popular as privately purchased knives, often carried and used with or without government sanction.

It is unusual to see a military issue knife in true mint condition. While the condition standard of "mint" is used for most knives listed in this price guide, "excellent" condition is substituted for knives listed in this section. This means a knife that may have been carried and used but has not been damaged or heavily sharpened and is rust-free. If the knife is a type that was issued with a sheath, the price shown assumes that the original sheath is included with the knife. Leather, in handles or sheaths, may show only slight discoloration.

Collectors should be aware that several popular military knife models, particularly fighting/utility knives, have been reproduced. Most of these are appropriately identified as limited editions.

All illustrations of military knives are used with permission and courtesy of M. H. Cole, the late collector, maker and authority on U.S. military knives.

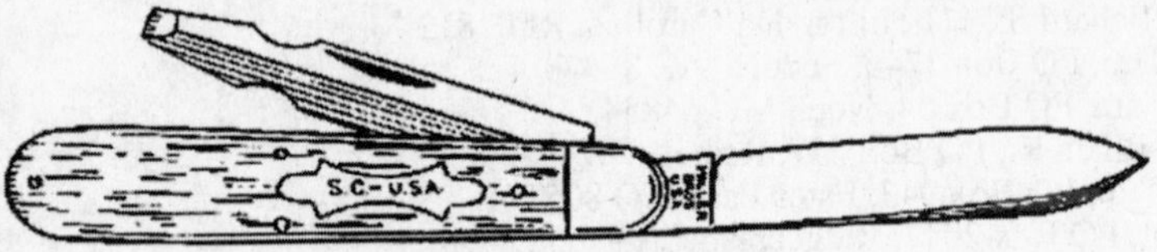

TL-29 Type Signal Corps Knives

These knives of the World War I era had no shackle and were slightly smaller than the better known TL-29. The screwdriver blade of this earlier version had an oval cutout on both sides.

Brand	*Handle*	*Markings*	*Variations*	*Value*
CAMILLUS	wood	shield stamped SC-USA		160
CASE	wood	shield stamped SC-USA/TL-29		160
EMPIRE	wood	shield stamped SC-USA		175
EMPIRE	wood	shield stamped SC-USA, blade etched	EZ open jack	180
KEEN KUTTER	wood	shield stamped US Signal Corps		200
MILLER BROS.	wood	shield stamped SC-USA	no shackle	200
MILLER BROS.	wood	shield stamped SC-USA	EZ open jack	235
ULSTER	wood	shield stamped US Signal Corps		140

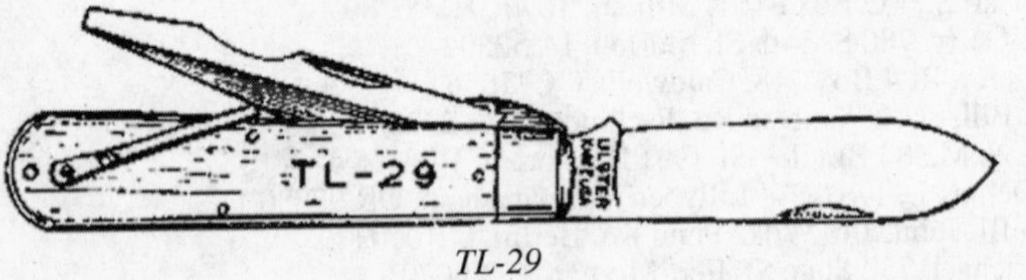

TL-29

These "Tool, Lineman" knives were issued to U.S. Signal Corps or military communications technicians after the smaller but similar knife listed above. Slightly larger and with only one oval cutout on the screwdriver blade, these models have a shackle.

Brand	*Handle*	*Markings*	*Variations*	*Value*
CAMILLUS	wood	shield stamped TL-29		55
CAMILLUS	wood	shield stamped U.S.M.C		85
CAMILLUS	wood	handle stamped TL-29		55
CAMILLUS	wood	handle painted TL-29		45
CAMILLUS	wood	handle stamped U.S.N.		65
CAMILLUS	wood	handle stamped U.S.M.C		65
CAMILLUS	wood	handle stamped R41-K-455		50
CAMILLUS	plastic	handle stamped TL-29		20
CASE	wood	handle stamped TL-29		80
CATTARAUGUS	wood	handle stamped TL-29	with shield	60

Brand	*Handle*	*Markings*	*Variations*	*Value*
CATTARAUGUS	wood	no TL-29 stamping	plain shield	50
COLONIAL	wood	handle stamped TL-29		50
IC Co	black plastic	handle stamped TL-29	made by Ka-Bar	35
IMPERIAL	plastic	handle stamped TL-29		25
KA-BAR	wood	handle stamped U.S. Army	no TL-29 marking	100
KA-BAR	wood	handle stamped TL-29		75
KA-BAR (Union Cut)		wood	shield stamped TL-29	80
KEEN KUTTER	wood	handle stamped TL-29		125
KINGSTON	wood	handle stamped TL-29		50
KUTMASTER	wood	handle stamped TL-29		50
KUTMASTER	wood	shield stamped TL-29		60
PAL	bone	blade tang stamped U.S. Army	no TL-29 marking	100
PAL	wood	handle stamped U.S. Army	no TL-29 marking	70
REMINGTON	wood	handle stamped TL-29		100
ROBESON	wood	handle stamped TL-29		60
SCHRADE	wood	handle stamped TL-29		50
SCHRADE	wood	shield stamped TL-29		65
ULSTER	wood	handle stamped TL-29		50
ULSTER	plastic	blade tang stamped TL-29		65
ULSTER	wood	handle stamped U.S.N.		65
ULSTER	plastic	blade etched	U.S. Govt TL-29	55
ULSTER	plastic	blade etched	Property of U.S. Govt	55
UNION CUT CO.	wood	shield stamped TL-29		70
UTICA CUTLERY	wood	handle stamped TL-29		50

Utility Pocketknives

Often called Navy Medical Department knives because of their first major use for this service, these knives have been issued within most branches of service since World War II. Most are of the typical four-blade scout/utility pattern. There are, however, some made in two- and three-blade variations as well as the five-blade version made as early as 1942 for the Eleventh Mountain Division. Bone-handled knives were common during the World War II era, but all-metal knives have replaced them beginning in the mid-1940s.

Brand	*Handle*	*Blades*	*Markings*	*Variations*	*Value*
CAMILLUS	bone	2	USA on blade tang	Easy opener jack	60
CAMILLUS	bone	4	U.S.A. on shield		100
CAMILLUS	bone	4	U.S.M.C. on shield		135
CAMILLUS	bone	4	M.D.-U.S.N. on shield		135
CAMILLUS	bone	3	U.S.N. on shield		100
CASE	bone	2	on blade	regular jack pattern	110
IMPERIAL	bone	4	USMC on shield		175
IMPERIAL	bone	2		Easy opener jack	55
IMPERIAL	metal	4		Vietnam War era	45
KINGSTON	metal	4	USMC on handle		60
ROBESON	bone	3	U.S.A. on shield		120
ULSTER	bone	5	US on bail	clip master blade	200
ULSTER	bone	5	US on shield	clip master blade	275
ULSTER	bone	5	US on bail	spear master blade	200

U.S. Model 1917–1918 Trench Knife

First of the two trench knives that were used by U.S. infantry troops during World War I, these knives featured a nine-inch triangular blade. Handle is one-piece wood, usually of walnut, with finger grooves. The metal guard wraps around the handle into a knuckle bow that ends at the pommel, which is capped with a "skull crusher."

Brand	*Blade*	*Markings*	*Variations*	*Value*
A.C. Co.	triangular	inside of guard		250
DISSTON	triangular	H.D. & S. front of guard		700
LF & C	triangular	LF & C. front of guard	six-point knuckles	240
LF & C	triangular	LF & C. front of guard	seven-point knuckles	300
O.C.L.	triangular	O.C.L. front of guard		500

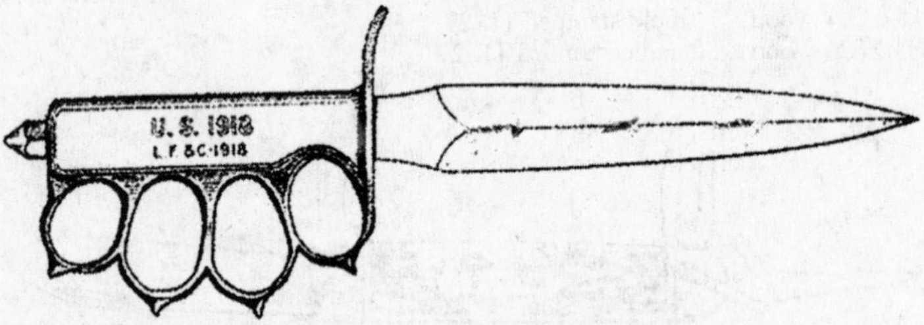

U.S. Mark 1 Trench Knife

This very distinctive military fighting knife is the one that most collectors visualize whenever the World War I period is considered. The first production of these knives for the U.S. government was accomplished in France, before U.S. manufacturers were able to tool up for the war effort. Later production was done domestically by companies such as Landers, Frary & Clark, Henry Disston & Sons, and Oneida Community Ltd.

The generic term "knuckle knife" is a natural one, derived from the cast brass handle that is used on all issue models and on which is stamped "U.S. 1918." The 6³/4″ blade is double edged and is housed in a metal scabbard.

Brand	*Blade*	*Markings*	*Variations*	*Value*
AU LION	bright	on blade tang	Lion logo on tang	350
DISSTON	bright	H.D. & S. on handle		800
LF & C	blackened	LF & C. on handle	scabbard marked	325
O.C.L.	bright	O.C.L. on handle	Oneida	1,000

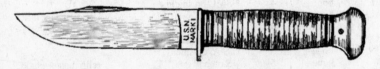

U.S.N. Mark 1

The original navy specifications for this knife called for a blade 5¹/8″ length, leather washer handles, aluminum pommel held by a threaded nut, as well as stampings of

"U.S.N." (mark side) and "Mark 1" (obverse side). In spite of these seemingly rigid specifications, the several manufacturers of this 1943 design used a great deal of latitude in fulfilling government contracts. As a result, there are great differences in the Mark 1s made by the various companies and there are even significant differences in some made by the same company.

Most knives did not vary from the blade length specified but blade finish varied from bright polished to parkerized and blued. Blade designs included flat grind, saber grind and fluted. Practically all were handled with leather washers and fiber spacers, but pommels varied in shape, size, materials and attachment method.

Brand	*Blade*	*Handle Type*	*Variations*	*Value*
BOKER	blued	smooth handle	plastic pommel	125
CAMILLUS	parkerized	smooth handle	plastic butt	125
CAMILLUS	bright finish	smooth handle	plastic butt	135
COLONIAL	parkerized	molded rubber		120
COLONIAL	parkerized	molded rubber-checkered		135
COLONIAL	parkerized	molded rubber-checkered	unmarked blade	125
GENEVA FORGE	parkerized	smooth handle	MARK 1 on tang	135
GENEVA FORGE	parkerized	smooth handle		120
GENEVA FORGE	bright finish	smooth handle	wood pommel	125
IMPERIAL	parkerized	grooved handle	bent guard	125
IMPERIAL	bright finish	grooved handle	bent guard	135
IMPERIAL	bright blade	smooth handle	half guard	160
KA-BAR	blued blade	smooth leather, iron pommel	w/o fuller	125
KA-BAR	blued blade	smooth leather, iron pommel	with fuller	135
KA-BAR	blued blade	smooth leather, wood	with fuller	150
PAL	parkerized	smooth handle		120
PAL	parkerized	smooth handle	tang marked PAL	160
PAL	parkerized	smooth handle	wood pommel	125
PAL	bright blade	smooth handle	$4\frac{7}{8}$ inch blade	135
ROBESON	bright finish	smooth handle	wood pommel	110
ROBESON	bright finish	smooth handle	wood pommel, half guard	125
ROBESON	blued	smooth handle	aluminum pommel	140
ROBESON	parkerized	smooth handle	aluminum pommel	130

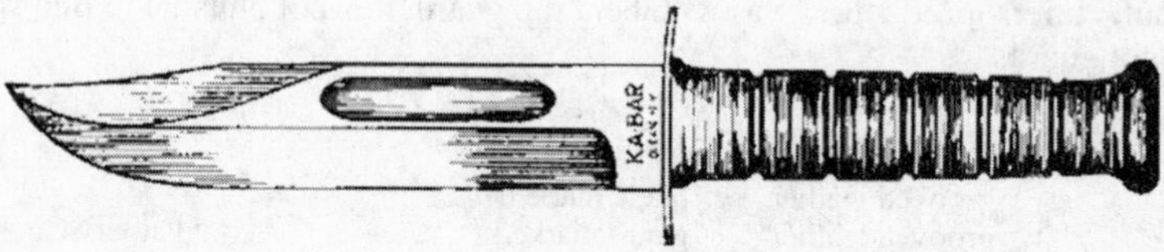

U.S.N. Mark 2

This fighting/utility knife is perhaps the most widely known military cutlery issue. Originally designated as the U.S.N. Mark 2, the sturdy knife has often been given the generic name of "Marine Ka-Bar" More than a million of these knives were made by manufacturers such as Ka-Bar, Camillus, Ontario, Pal Robeson and others.

The Mark 2 has a 7″ bowie-type clip blade, usually with fullers or "blood grooves." Handles are most always grooved leather. Pommels or butt caps are iron, which is either pinned or threaded onto the knife's hidden tang. Blade finish includes blued and plated, although most were parkerized. Most guards are bent on both sides.

Brand	*Blade*	*Handle Type*	*Variations*	*Value*
CAMILLUS	parkerized	grooved leather	Screw-type pommel	225
CAMILLUS	parkerized	grooved leather	blade marked USN	200
CAMILLUS	parkerized	grooved leather	blade marked USMC	275
CAMILLUS	parkerized	grooved leather	guard marked USN	200
CAMILLUS	parkerized	grooved leather	guard marked USMC	160
CAMILLUS	plated	grooved leather	guard marked USMC	500

Brand	*Blade*	*Handle Type*	*Variations*	*Value*
CAMILLUS	parkerized	grooved leather	post–World War II	65
KA-BAR/Olean NY	blued	grooved leather	blade marked USMC	500
KA-BAR	blued	grooved leather	blade marked USMC	275
KA-BAR	blued	grooved leather	blade marked USN	200
KA-BAR	blued	grooved leather	guard marked USN	150
KA-BAR	plated	smooth leather	UTD with fuller	375
KA-BAR	bright polished	smooth leather	UTD no fullers	500
KUTMASTER	parkerized	grooved leather	tan handle	200
KUTMASTER	parkerized	grooved leather	coated handle	200
PAL	parkerized	grooved leather	blade marked USN	200
PAL	parkerized	grooved leather	blade marked USMC	275
PAL	parkerized	grooved leather	Mark 1 pommel	400
ROBESON	blued	grooved leather	blade marked USMC	750
ROBESON	parkerized	grooved leather	blade marked USN	225
ROBESON	parkerized	grooved leather	guard marked USN	225

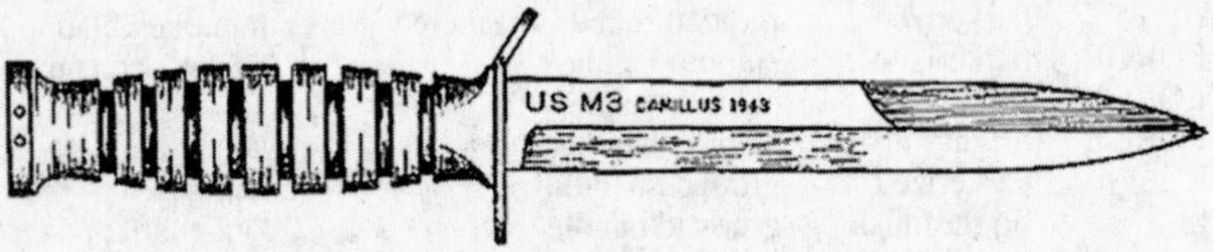

M3

This knife, often called the M3 Trench Knife, was developed in 1943 and manufactured in large numbers (approximately 2.5 million) by several different companies. Eighty percent of this high production was by Imperial, Utica, Camillus and Case. Although this knife was produced in high numbers, many were broken or lost on the battlefields, so they are hard to find on the collector market.

Early knives were stamped "U.S. M3" and maker's name on the blade. Later knives were stamped on the guard. Ordnance Department specifications were for grooved leather washer handles. In spite of this specification, some handles lacked the six to eight grooves commonly found and, instead, have smooth or ridged leather washer handles. Although most manufacturers' production was with bent top guard, it is not unusual to find specimens with straight guard.

Brand	*Handle Type*	*Markings*	*Comments*	*Value*
AERIAL	grooved leather	blade marked		325
A.C.C.	grooved leather	guard marked	Aerial Cutlery Co.	260
BOKER	grooved leather	blade marked		550
BOKER	grooved leather	guard marked		425
CAMILLUS	grooved leather	blade marked	marking dated	425
CAMILLUS	grooved leather	blade marked		250
CAMILLUS	grooved leather	guard marked		225
CASE	grooved leather	blade marked	marking dated	700
CASE	grooved leather	blade marked		400
CASE	grooved leather	guard marked		275
CASE	ridged handle	guard marked		650
CASE	grooved leather	guard marked	straight guard	450
CASE	grooved leather	guard marked	straight guard, bright blade	425
IMPERIAL	grooved leather	blade marked	marking dated	500
IMPERIAL	grooved leather	blade marked		320
IMPERIAL	grooved leather	guard marked		200
KINFOLKS	grooved leather	blade marked	marking dated	650
KINFOLKS	grooved leather	blade marked		425
KINFOLKS	grooved leather	guard marked		250
KUTMASTER	grooved leather	blade marked	marking dated	500
KUTMASTER	grooved leather	blade marked		350
KUTMASTER	grooved leather	guard marked		250

Brand	*Handle Type*	*Markings*	*Comments*	*Value*
KUTMASTER	smooth handle	blade marked		450
PAL	grooved leather	blade marked	marking dated	650
PAL	grooved leather	blade marked		425
PAL	grooved leather	guard marked		275
ROBESON	grooved leather	blade marked	marking dated	850
ROBESON	grooved leather	blade marked		550

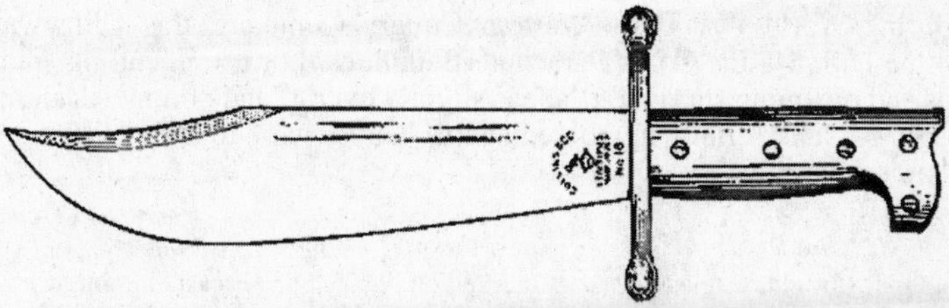

V-44 Survival Knife

This large bowie-type survival knife was originally designed in 1934 for use in the bailout kit of military personnel flying in jungle or tropical areas. The first issue of this model was made by Collins as the No. 18 machete. This 9$^{3}/_{8}$″ clip blade version became the standard knife used in pilot survival kits until 1942. The knife's greatest fame comes from its adoption by the Second Raider Battalion, U.S. Marine Corps, led by Lt. Col. Evans Carlson. The bitter and decisive actions of this group's fighting in the Pacific theater earned the knife its generic name: "Gung Ho Knife." Other U.S. manufacturers were Case, Kinfolks and Western.

Brand	*Blade*	*Handle Type*	*Variations/Markings*	*Value*
CASE	9$^{1}/_{4}$″	black bakelite		325
COLLINS	9$^{3}/_{8}$″	green horn	model No. 18	600
COLLINS	9$^{3}/_{8}$″	black bakelite	model No. 18	300
KINFOLKS	9$^{1}/_{4}$″	black bakelite		350
WESTERN	9$^{1}/_{4}$″	black bakelite		650

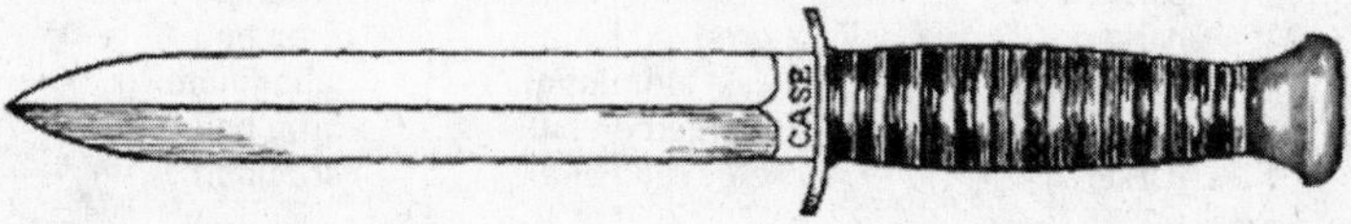

Stiletto

Made primarily by Case, these fighting knives have a double edge and are 7″ in length. Overall length should be 11$^{1}/_{2}$″, but variations in handle length means that some may be 12″. Handle is smooth leather washer type and guard is double with some straight and some slightly bent. Some obviously made by Case and verified by company records are unmarked.

Brand	*Blade*	*Markings*	*Pommel*	*Value*
CASE	bright	marked on blade	black plastic	900
CASE	blue	marked on blade	black plastic	925
CASE	parkerized	marked on blade	black plastic	900
CASE	bright	unmarked	cast aluminum	850
CASE	blue	unmarked	cast aluminum	875
CASE	parkerized	unmarked	cast aluminum	850
WESTERN	bright, single edge	marked on blade	cast aluminum	325
WESTERN	blued, single edge	marked on blade	black plastic	325
WESTERN	bright, double edge	marked on blade	cast aluminum	1,000

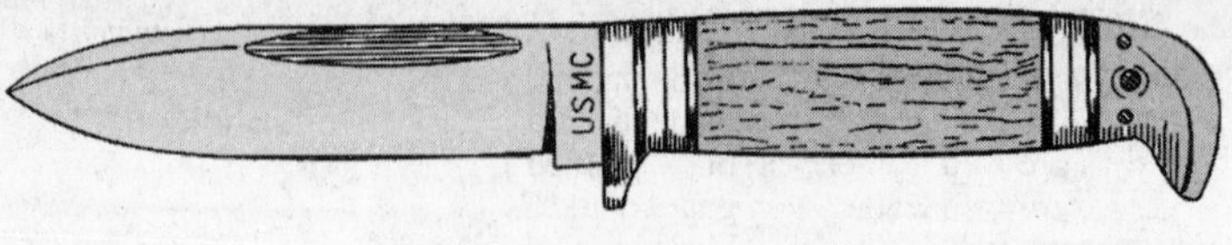

U.S.M.C. Parachutist Knife

Made during World War II by Western Cutlery Company, this knife was issued to trainees of the U.S. Marine Corps Parachute Battalions. For use in cutting entangled parachute cords and postjump survival. Blade is slightly over 4″ and pommel is aluminum. Tang stamped "USMC" and serially numbered guard. Knives were to remain with the school after completion of training.

Brand	*Blade*	*Markings*	*Pommel*	*Value*
WESTERN	bright, single edge	marked on blade	cast aluminum	1,500

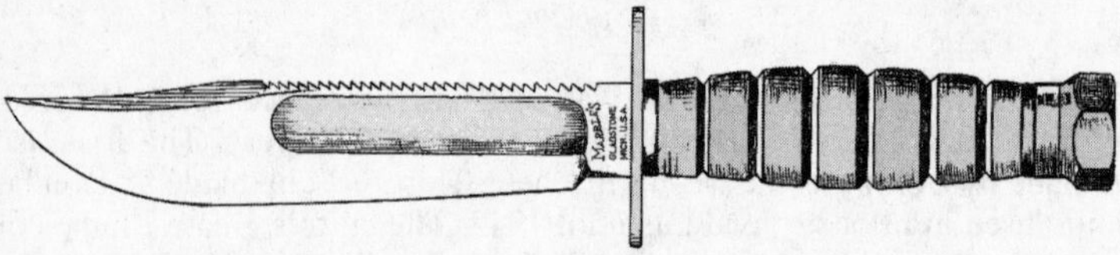

Pilot's Survival Knife

Developed after the Korean War by the U.S. Navy for use by pilots as an all-around survival knife. Earliest knives, with a 6″ blade, guard and pommel of blued metal, were made by Marble Arms. Later version knives had a 5″ blade and instead of being blued, metal was parkerized and often called Jet Pilot's Knife. Manufacturer's name is usually on blade tang and pommel. Though made by several cutlery manufacturers, most were made by Camillus.

Brand	*Blade*	*Markings*	*Pommel*	*Value*
CAMILLUS	parkerized	grooved handle	screw top	200
CAMILLUS	parkerized	grooved handle	iron butt	175
MILPAR	parkerized	grooved leather	iron butt	125
MILPAR	parkerized	cast aluminum	aluminum	500
ONTARIO	parkerized	marked on butt	iron butt	95
UTICA	parkerized	grooved handle	iron butt	600

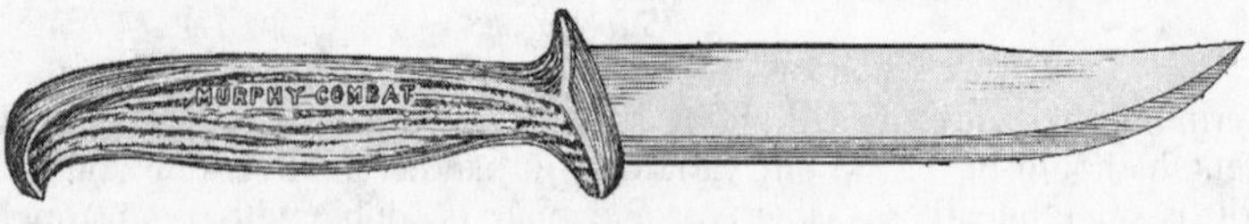

Murphy Combat Knife

David Z. Murphy, assisted by his son David M. Murphy and a few employees working in a small Oregon shop, made approximately 100,000 knives during World War II. Though not a military issue, these private-purchase fighting/utility knives were nonetheless popular and well respected by U.S. servicemen serving in all military branches.

Blades of approximate 6″ in length were made from saw blades and were handled in aluminum and cast with the Murphy name on one side. In addition to the standard size, some smaller but similar knives, marked "Murphy Combat Jr.," with a 5″ blade were made. Both models were marked "U.S.A." on reverse handle.

During the early 1990s, a small number of reproduction knives were made by David M. Murphy as a limited edition commemorative model. While these knives are in demand by collectors, prices shown below are for the earlier knives sold during the World War II and Korean War eras.

Brand	*Blade*	*Handle*	*Marking*	*Value*
Murphy Combat	6 1/8″	cast aluminum	Murphy Combat/USA	600
Murphy Combat Jr.	5″	cast aluminum	Murphy Combat Jr./USA	1,000

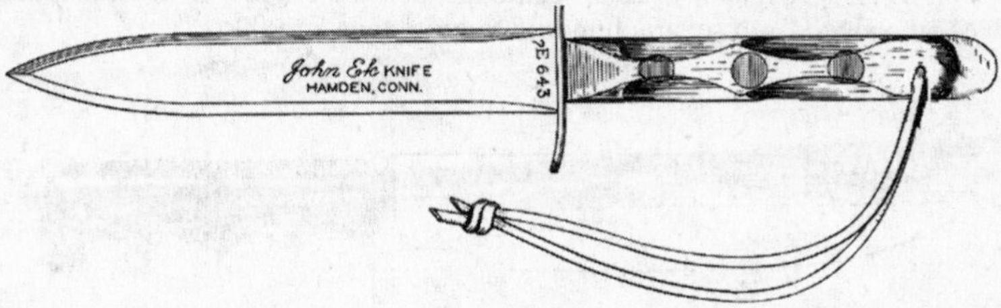

EK Commando Knives

"Made in America, by Americans, for Americans" was a motto of John Ek, who began making knives in 1941 at his Hamden, Connecticut, headquarters. During World War II and until he relocated to Miami, Florida, in 1949, Ek made over 100,000 knives for private sale to U.S. servicemen. He continued to make knives, but at a much lower volume, for military sales during the Korean and Vietnam conflicts.

Beginning early in his knife manufacturing career, Ek assigned a serial number to each knife sold. Sales of his knives were restricted to military personnel through a registration program, whereby the purchaser certified that he was an eligible combat-ready serviceman. A record-keeping program of serial number, model and knife buyer was instituted and maintained. Often called "The Silent Partner," each knife was accompanied by a booklet with the same title.

Ten models were made, handled with finger-grooved rock maple scales held by lead poured and hammered rivets. Blade tangs were stamped with the model number and a serial number. Blades were etched with the marking "John Ek" in script and location of manufacture.

"Camden" marked models 1 through 10 are valued in the $500 to $750 range; "Miami" marked knives are valued in the $600 to $900 range.

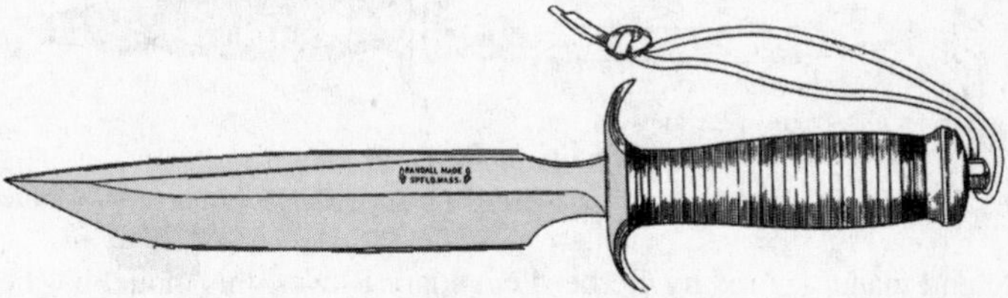

Randall Knives
Springfield Randall—Model 1

Of the very popular Model 1 design, those marked on the 8″ blade with the Randall logo and "SPFLD.MASS," are the rarest and most valued. Approximately 1,000 of these knives were manufactured under contract during World War II. Collector value of these knives, in excellent condition and with original sheath, begin at $2,000.

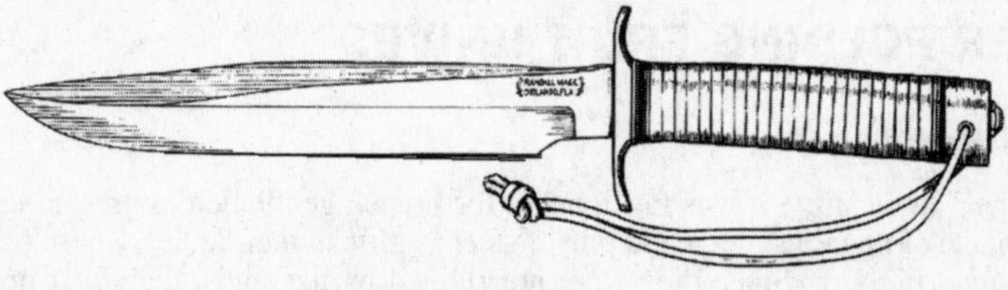

Randall—Model 1

The regularly produced Orlando, Florida, Model 1 has been one of the more popular and widely recognized designs from this respected producer of handforged knives. Having been in production for more than a half-century, several variations have been made in handle configuration, butt caps, sheaths, etc. Depending upon the era and its own characteristics, these knives are valued from several hundred to more than $4,000.

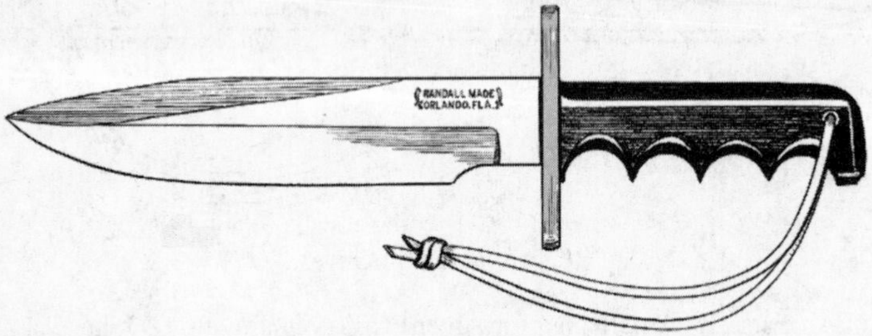

Randall Model—14

Similar in popularity to the Model 1 during World War II, Randall's Model 14 earned high regard as a privately purchased military sidearm during the Korean and Vietnam conflicts. The hefty bowie-type knife can be found handled in Micarta (black or brown) with leather thong. Blade is 7 1/2″ making the knife useful for combat and survival. Sheaths, with leather knife retaining thongs, were equipped with a sharpening stone in a sewn-on pocket.

As with the Model 1 and other Randall knives, there have been a number of subtle changes that affect the value of knives made during a particular era. Dependent upon these variations, these knives are valued from several hundred to more than $4,000.

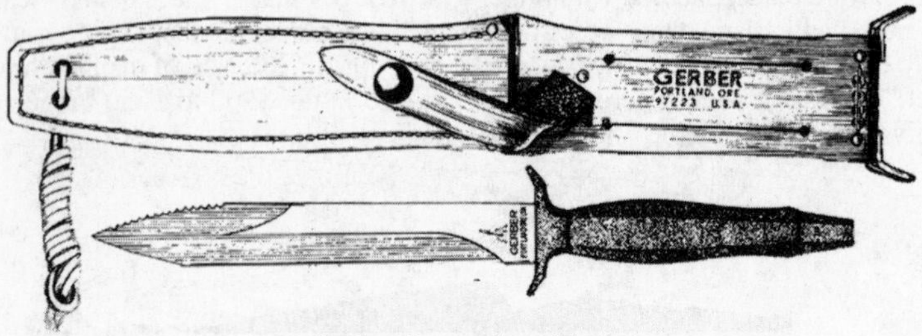

Gerber Legendary Blades
Gerber MK II

Designed and manufactured by Gerber Legendary Blades, this model has been produced in large quantities and in many variations since the mid-1960s. Never a military issue knife, the "Mark Two" was extremely popular as a private-purchase carry knife during the Vietnam War.

Blades are in the 6 1/2″ range, usually in bright steel and handles are molded texturized steel. Blade shapes, grinds, serrations or lack of same, and handle colors are among the many variations to be found. Dependent upon the variations, these knives are valued from $200 to $2,000, with the majority being valued at less than $1,000.

SILVER FOLDING FRUIT KNIVES

by Bill Karsten

During the 17th century, it was fashionable for French gentlemen to present knives featuring one blade of precious metal and one of steel as gifts to their ladies. These folding knives served a dual purpose. Since they were not stained by the acids, the silver or gold blades were used to cut fruit and the steel blade was used for general cutting purposes.

Some years later, about 1760, the English began to follow suit. After silver assay offices were established at Sheffield and Birmingham in 1773, the manufacture of fruit knives and forks flourished.

Silver hallmarks were first introduced in London during the 14th century and eventually there were five. Hallmarks are a very effective means for evaluating fruit knives. The complete series disclosed the city of origin, the maker's initials, the year of assay, the sterling silver (92.5%) content and a duty stamp. After 1890, when Queen Victoria revoked the duty on silver, four marks remained in the hallmark system.

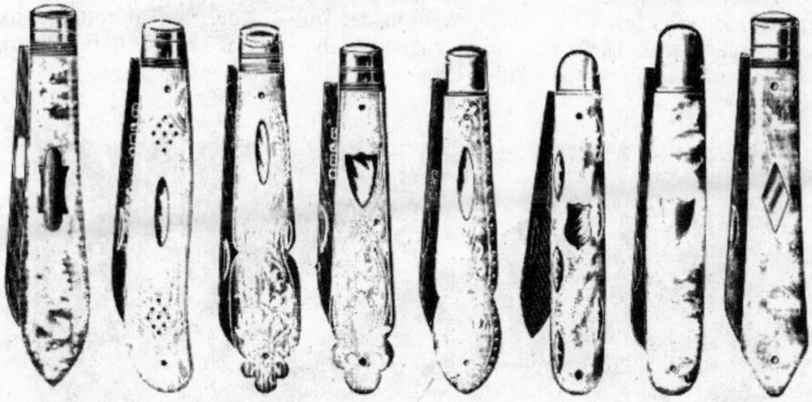

Illustrations from an old English trade catalogue feature the knives of William Needham, 13 Jeasop Street, Sheffield, c. 1891.

A beautifully engraved knife by Sheffield makers Ashforth and Harthorn. Although it was made in 1847, it does not bear the profile of Queen Victoria, an unusual but rather common practice.

This handsomely engraved knife was made by Henry Cook, Sheffield, in 1872.

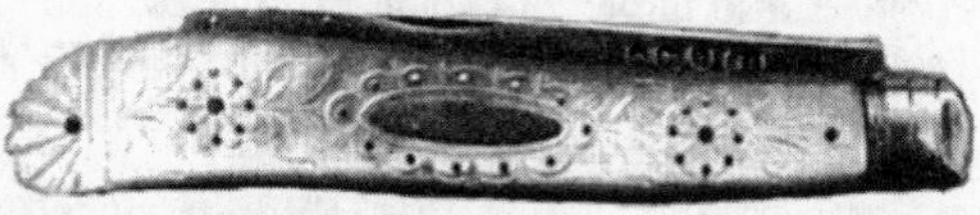

J. Y. Coulishaw made this exceptional knife in 1915. Although this was late in his career, the knife resembles his earlier Victorian work.

During the later Georgian period (1773–c.1830), the duty mark, a stamping of the reigning monarch's profile, and the sterling mark, a lion passant, were usually the only marks stamped on the blade. The maker's mark and that of the year of assay have been found on the blade tang, covered by the bolster. Eventually, by making the marks smaller, there was room for all five on the face of the blade.

Georgian period knives were elegant, featuring slim lines with handles usually of mother-of-pearl and very often a bright cut design along the top of the blade. The springs were usually chased, the earliest being of a diagonal pattern.

There came slow but definite changes in fruit knife design during the reign of William IV, which started in 1830. They continued through the reign of Queen Victoria (1837–1901). More shapely handles, engraved in a variety of pleasing geometric and floral themes, were introduced. Possibly the Georgian designs were thought to be too austere. Toward the end of Queen Victoria's reign, the handles were made thick and almost too cumbersome.

Around the time of King Edward's reign (1901–1910), mass production methods resulted in diminished quality.

After World War I fewer fruit knives were made. This was due, in part, to the introduction of stainless steel. There was also a change in the style of English living. One very seldom finds a fruit knife dated 1925 or later.

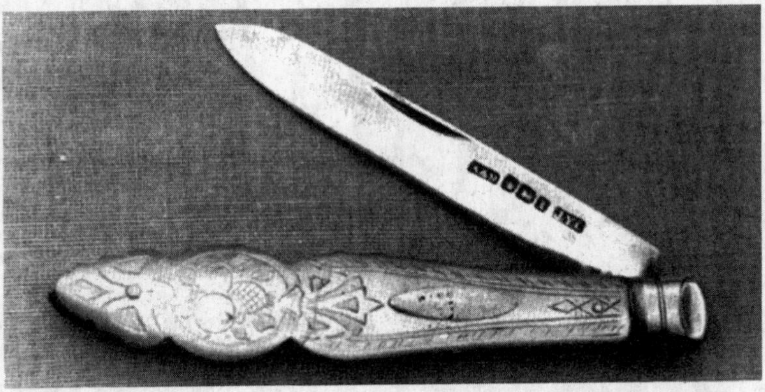

This beautiful knife, with engraving and pique work, was made by James Fenton of Sheffield in 1891.

American Folding Fruit Knives

In America, with the exception of one brief period (1814–1830), we had no hallmark system. Early silversmiths used their initials, names or marks. Occasionally, pseudo hallmarks featuring symbols such as a lion passant or a crown were used, probably to lead a buyer to assume he had bought an article of English origin.

A number of American silver firms, particularly those of the New England area, made these knives. The collector will find some beautiful examples made and identified by Gorham or Albert Coles, but Rogers Cutlery, Meriden, Brittania, Wallace Bros., Empire Knife Co., Miller Bros. and others also turned out some fine pieces. Some bore marks similar to those of England and some were not identified or were only stamped "Coin" or "Sterling."

This pretty silver fruit knife shows a pseudo hallmark. The owner's initials are engraved on the handle.

Made by the Meriden Brittania Company, this plated knife was an advertising gift. The reverse side of the blade is engraved "Bon Voyage."

Usually, American knives were handled in silver, but other materials such as ivory were also used. Some beautiful pieces were silver plated. There were no date marks, but one can be fairly certain that these knives were made beginning in the early part of the 19th century and continued for approximately 100 years.

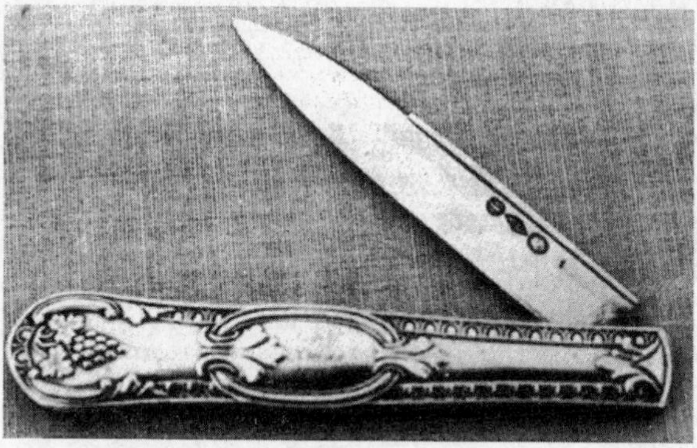

With typical heavily embossed handles, this silver knife illustrates the mark of Albert Coles, a New York maker.

Price estimates are for knives and forks in excellent condition as defined elsewhere in this book.

English Knives and Forks

Late Georgian Era 1773–c.1830

Single knife or fork	$150–$200 each
Matching knife and fork	$275–$350 pair
Gold-bladed knives	$600–$900 each

Era of William IV 1830–1837 and Victoria 1837–1901

Single knives and forks	$125–$175
Take-apart knife and fork combination	$250–$300
Knives with a blade and seed pick	$125–$175
Matching knife and fork	$225–$375 pair

Era of Edward VII 1901–1910 and George V 1910–1936

Excepting knives of the quality of the previous period, those of this era may be bought for $80 or less.

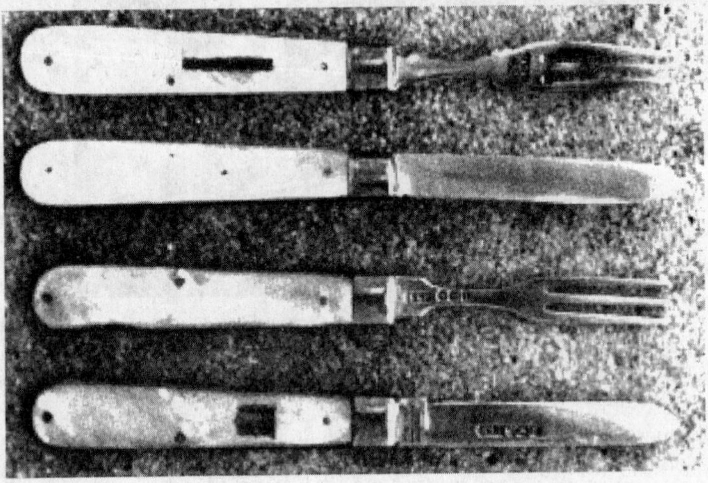

American Fruit Knives

Knives by Coles or Gorham	$90–$150
Knives by other companies	$80–$125
Silver fruit knives marked "Coin" or "Sterling"	$85–$125
Silver fruit knives bearing only pseudo hallmark	$75–$100
Plated fruit knives identified	$60–$85
Plated fruit knives not identified	$40–$65
Knives bearing advertising or other odd features	$30–$100

(W. C. "Bill" Karsten is a collector and researcher of several types of knives. He has written a number of articles which have been published in *Knife World* and other magazines. Recognized in the U.S. and several other countries as an authority on the subject, he is the author of the book *Silver Folding Fruit Knives*.)

Sheffield Hallmarks 1773–1960

Year						Year			Year	
1773			E			1876	J	"	1921	d
1774			F	Mark shown in col. 6 was used on small objects to replace those in 3 and 4		1877	K	"	1922	e
1775			H			1878	L	"	1923	f
1776			R			1879	M	"	1924	g
1777			h			1880	N	"	1925	h
1778			S			1881	O	"	1926	i
1779			A			1882	P	"	1927	k
1780			Z			1883	Q	"	1928	l
1781			D			1884	R	"	1929	m
1782			G						1930	n
1783			B			1885	S	"	1931	o
1784			J			1886	T	"	1932	p
1785			V			1887	U	"	1933	q
1786			k			1888	V	"	1934	r
1787			T			1889	W	"	1935	S
1788						1890	X	"	Edw. VIII 1936	t
1789						1891	Y	"	Geo. VI 1937	u
1790			L			1892	Z		1938	V
1791			P						1939	W
1792			W			1893	a		1940	X
1793			O			1894	b		1941	y
1794			M			1895	c		1942	Z
1795			q			1896	d		1943	A
1796			Z			1897	e		1944	B
1797			X			1898	f		1945	C
1798			V			1899	g		1946	D
1799			E			1900	h		1947	E
1800			N			Edw. VII 1901	i		1948	F
1801			H			1902	k			
1802			M			1903	l			
1803			F			1904	m			
1804			G			1905	n			
1805			B			1906	o		1949	G
1806			A			1907	p		1950	H
1807			S			1908	q		1951	I
1808			P			1909 Geo. V 1910	r		Eliz. II 1952	K
1809			K			1911	t		1953	L
1810			L			1912	u		1954	M
1811			C			1913	v		1955	N
1812			D			1914	w		1956	O
1813			R			1915	x		1957	P
1814			W			1916	y		1958	Q
1815			O			1917	z		1959	R
1816			T						1960	S
1817			X			1918	a			
1818			I			1919	b			
1819 Geo. IV 1820			V Q			1920	C			
1821			Y							
1822			Z							
1823			U							

Year						Year			
1824			a			1848	E		
1825			b			1849	F		
1826			C			1850	G		
1827			d			1851	H		
1828			e			1852	I		
1829 Wm. IV 1830			f			1853	K		
1831			h			1854	L		
1832			k			1855	M	"	
1833			l			1856	N	"	
1834			m			1857	O	"	
1835			P			1858	P	"	
1836 Vict. 1837			q T			1859	R	"	
1838			S			1860	S	"	
1839			t			1861	T	"	
1840			u			1862	U	"	
1841			V			1863	V	"	
1842			X			1864	W	"	
1843			Z			1865	X	"	
1844			A			1866	Y	"	
1845			B			1867	Z	"	
1846			C			1868	A	"	
1847			D			1869	B	"	
						1870	C	"	
						1871	D	"	
						1872	E	"	
						1873	F	"	
						1874	G	"	
						1875	H	"

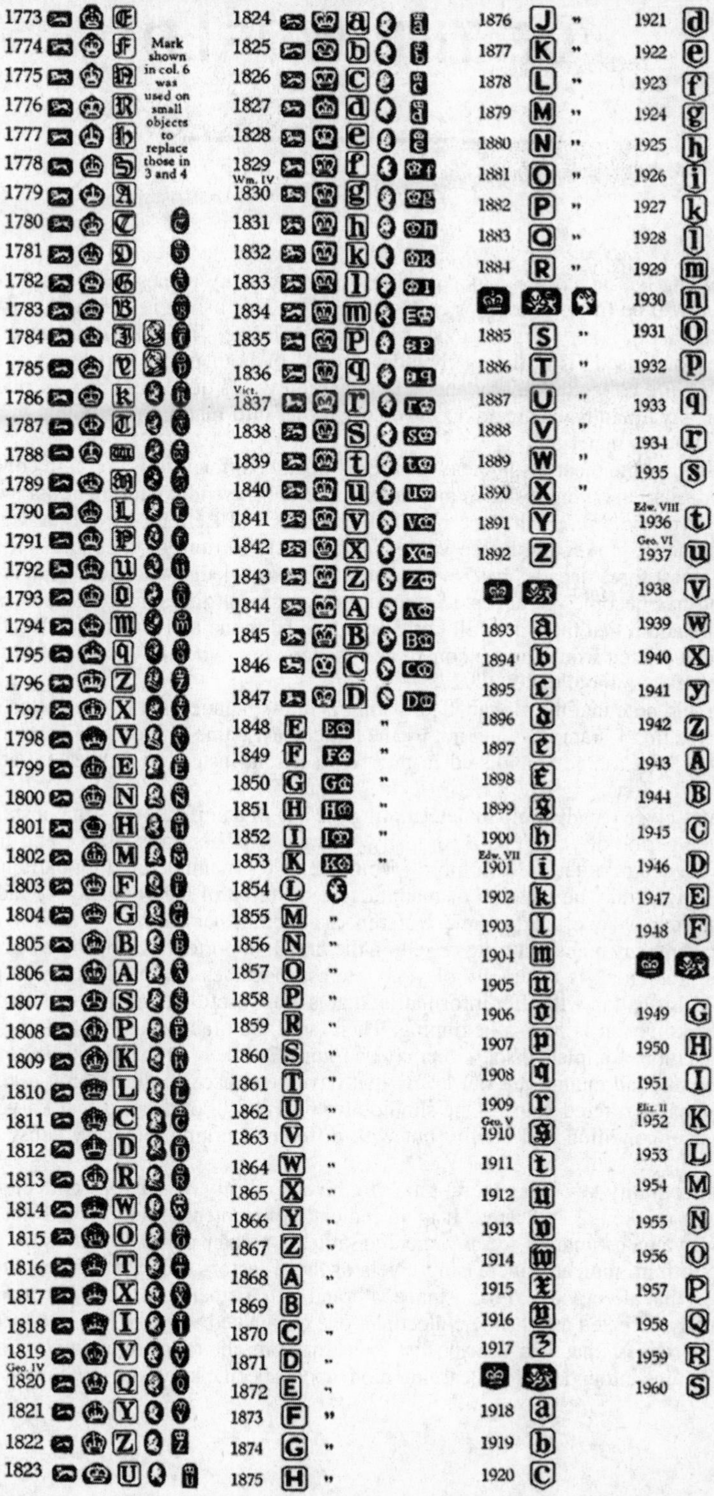

KNIFE BRANDS OF THE WORLD

The following list includes a major portion of the company names and/or trademarks for knives that will be found in today's collector market. This listing is designed to offer basic information about a very large number of brands and space limitations dictate that such a listing be condensed. This listing includes brands of both major and lesser importance within the knife collecting hobby and is intended only as a quick reference. Collectors interested in any brand listed are advised to seek further information from within this book or in other reference materials.

This listing is the most complete ever offered in any edition of this book. In compiling it, the author relied upon the research and knowledge of others to compliment his own. Especially noteworthy is research done by John E. Goins and Bernard Levine as well as that done by James F. Parker and Bruce Voyles in their early editions of this guide. Goins' work during the past three decades has revolutionized the knowledge of cutlery brands or trademarks and has become the accepted standard reference on the subject. Knife researchers will readily admit that there are still knife brands to be found and documented. Information on brands not listed would be welcomed and readers are invited to write to Houston Price, P.O. Box 3395, Knoxville, TN 37927.

One should note that the alphabetical listing is in the manner that is most often found on a knife's trademark stamping, and not by the typical last-name-first order. For example, one will find W. R. Case & Sons listed in the "W" section, instead of in the "C" section for Case, W. R. & Sons.

The dates given usually help in determining the age of a knife, but in some instances they indicate the period of years that a company or brand has been in existence and further research is needed in order to learn more specific dates for manufacture of a particular knife. Locations given may be location of manufacture, location of the company's headquarters, or both, since they are often the same. References are brands or trademarks used by the listed company, company manufacturing or selling the brand, importer or company ownership.

Reading this book is testimony of your interest in knives and particularly in their values. While this listing will offer information that is quite useful in arriving at collector value of specific knives, it is only a beginning. There are many factors that determine collector value and a more complete discussion may be found elsewhere in this book. Factors such as rarity, demand and quality are but a few that have been used in developing a key to collectibility that is offered below. One should also be mindful of the fact that knives of near identical age, condition and quality but with different marking will vary substantially in value.

The collectibility key is a general guide to the desirability of—that is, collector demand for—knives marked as indicated. It is an indication of potential and should not be interpreted as a value estimation for any specific knife. A greater number of stars (★), ranging from one to four, indicates increasing levels of those factors (rarity, collector interest, demand, etc.) that affect value. For instance, a brand or trademark designated ★★★★ is one that is widely accepted as a prime collectible; one designated ★ ranks low in collectible potential. We suggest that you use the list to learn more about collector knives in general, thereby building a foundation for learning more about specific knives or knife manufacturers.

Brands/Manufacturers/Location	*Reference or Trademarks*	*Dates*	*Collectibility*
20TH CENTURY CUTLERY CO.	A. J. Jordan	c.1890–1906	★★
AARON BURKINSHAW (Pepperell, MA)	Exile, Pain, X-L	1853–1920	★★★★
ABERCROMBIE & FITCH (New York, NY)	A. & F. Co.	1892–c.1978	★★★
ABRAHAM DAVY (Sheffield)		c.1836–1856	★★★
ABRAHAM DAVY & SONS (Sheffield)		c.1856–1870	★★★
ABRAM BROOKSBANK (Sheffield)	Defiance	c.1849–1864	★★
ACCO (Atlanta, GA)		c.1970	★
ACE (San Francisco, CA)	Bauer Mfg. Co.	c.1910–1930	★
ACE CUTLERY CO.	Fremont, OH	c.1920–1930	★
ACME KNIFE CO. (Walden, NY)	Taylor patent, all metal knives	c.1920s	★
ACME (New York, NY)	F. Westpfal	c.1884–1928	★
ADMIRATION	E. Morris	c.1919–1921	
ADOLPH BLAICH, INC. (San Francisco, CA)	Reno, NV 1954	1885–1954	★★★
ADOLPH BLAICH/J. S. HOLLER (San Francisco, CA)	Arrow Brand	c.1880–1906	★★★
ADOLPH KASTOR & BROS (Germany)	X.L.N.T., Clover, Morley	c.1876–1947	★★
ADOLPHUS BUSCH (St. Louis MO)	Anheuser Busch	1932–1948	★★★
ADOLPHUS CUTLERY CO. (England & Germany)	A. J. Jordan	c.1882–1891	★★
AERIAL CUTLERY CO. (DULUTH, MN (Duluth, MN)	Jaeger Bros.	1909–1912	★★★
AERIAL CUTLERY CO. (MARINETTE, WI (Marinette, WI)	Jaeger Bros.	c.1912–1950	★★★
AERIAL MFG. CO. (Marinette, WI)	Jaeger Bros.	1912–1950	★★★
AINSLIE-MARTIN (Lynchburg, VA)	hardware dist.	1900–1922	★★
AITOR	made in Spain	c.1939–present	
AKRON CUTLERY CO. (Akron, OH)		c.1911–1928	★★
AL MAR KNIVES (Lake Oswego, OR)	made in Japan	1979–present	★★★
ALAMO (Japan)		c.1960s	★
ALBERT COLES (New York, NY)	silver fruit knives	1844–1880	★★★
ALBERTSON CO. (Kane, PA)	formerly Hollingsworth	c.1930–1938	★★
ALBION CUTLERY (Akron, OH)	"Blue Steel Made in Germny"	c.1920–1940	★
ALCAS CUTLERY CO. (Olean, NY)	Cutco, WearEaver	1941–present	★
ALCOSO (Solingen)	Alexander Coppel	c.1933–present	★
ALEY BUSSIFF BROS (Olean, NY)	"Magnetic Steel"	c.1900–1923	★★
ALLEN & SON (Sheffield)	square and compass logo	1818–1902	★★
ALLENTOWN CUTLERY WORKS	C. F. Wolfertz & Co.	c.1862–1900	
ALEX FRASER & CO. (England)		c.1911	★★
ALEXANDER (Sheffield)	R. H. Alexander, importer	c.1850–1878	★★★
ALEXANDER COPPEL (Solingen)	Balance, Alcosco, A. C. S.	1884–1892	★★
ALFRED FIELD & CO. (England & Germany)	Criterion	1855–1942	★★
ALFRED HOBSON & SONS (Sheffield)		c.1880s	★★★
ALFRED HUNTER (New York, NY)	bowie-type knives	1830–1865	★★★★
ALFRED WILLIAMS (Sheffield)	EBRO, imported by Kastor	c.1890–1920	★★
ALFRED & SON CELEBRATED CUTLERY		c.1850–1875	★★
ALLDIS		1884	★
ALLEN CUTLERY CO. (Newburgh, NY)		1917–1925	★★
ALLEN & SON (Sheffield)		1917–1925	★★
ALLIANCE CUTLERY WORKS	Philadelphia, PA	c.1875–1900	★★
ALLIGATOR BRAND (Jacksonville, FL)	Florida Hardware Co. trademark	c.1939	★
ALLMAN (Germany)		c.1915–1930	★

Brands/Manufacturers/Location	*Reference or Trademarks*	*Dates*	*Collectibility*
ALOISE		1920–1940	★
ALPHA (England)	Harrison Brothers & Howson	c.1900	★★★
ALTENBACH (Germany)		1906–1996	★
AMBASSADOR (Providence, RI)	Colonial Knife Co.	1951–2002	★
AMERICAN ACE	Simmons Hdwe brand	c.1939–1960	★★
AMERICAN ACE/U.S.A.	New Jersey Cutlery Co.	c.1919–1920	★
AMERICAN AUTOMATIC KNIFE CO.	Brooklyn, NY	c.1892–1902	★★
AMERICAN BLADE CUTLERY CO. (Chattanooga, TN)	Parker Cutlery Co.	1981–1991	★★
AMERICAN CUTLERY CO. (Chicago, IL)	pocketknives date before 1900	1879–1928	★★★
AMERICAN HARDWARE & SUPPLY CO. (Pittsburg, PA)	American Beauty	c.1911–1935	★★★
AMERICAN IMPORT CO. (Germany)	Arrow Brand	1920–1960	★
AMERICAN KNIFE CO./GERMANY (Germany)	Sabre	c.1960–1980	★
AMERICAN KNIFE CO./JAPAN (Japan)	Cole National	c.1960–1980	★
AMERICAN KNIFE CO./ PLYMOUTH (Plymouth, MA)	Plymouth Hollow	c.1849–1875	★★★★
AMERICAN KNIFE CO./ THOMASTON (Thomaston, CT)	called Plymouth Hollow to 1875	1875–1895	★★★★
AMERICAN KNIFE CO./ WINSTED CONN (Winsted, CT)		1919–1950	★★★★
AMERICAN MAID	J. Chatillon & Sons	c.1915	★★★★
AMERICAN MAID	Utica Cutlery Co.	c.1950's	★★
AMERICAN POCKETKNIFE CO.	Massilon, OH	1930s	★★
AMERICAN SHEAR & KNIFE CO. (Hotchkissville, CT)	first pocketknives 1870	1853–1914	★★★
AMERICA'S BEST	New York	c.1930	★
AMES CUTLERY CO.	Ames Manufacturing	c.1860s–1890s	★★★★
AMES MANUFACTURING CO. (Chelmsford, MA)		c.1829–1935	★★★★
AMOS BELKNAP	blacksmith	1839–1883	★★★★
ANDOVER CUTLERY CO.	Andover, NY	c.1920	★★
ANDREW & TREADWAY (Dubuque, IA)	hardware dist.	1853–1873	★★★
ANGLO-PACIFIC (Sheffield)		c.1880s	★★
ANHEUSER-BUSCH/GERMANY		c.1881–1914	★★★
ANHEUSER-BUSCH (St. Louis, MO)	Kastor, Wester Bros., Camillus	1932–1948	★★★
ANTELOPE (Germany)		c.1950–1970	★
ANTON WINGEN, JR. (Solingen)	Othello	1888–present	★
ANVIL CUTLERY CO.	Jersey City, NJ	1920–1921	★★
ANVIL/USA	Colonial	c.1971–2002	★
ARDOBO CUTLERY CO. (Germany)		c.1930	★
ARGYLE CUTLERY CO. (Germany)	Brown Bros.	c.1910–1930	★
ARISTOCRAT	McCrory Stores brand	c.1932–1950s	★
ARKANSAS TRAVELER (Little Rock, AR)	Fones Bros.	c.1881–1914	★★★
ARMSTRONG CUTLERY CO./U.S.A.		c.1901	★
ARNEX (Solingen)		c.1920–1940	★
ARROW BRAND KNIFE CO.	American Import Co., A. Blaich	c.1885–1954	★★
ART KNIFE CO. (Nicholson, PA)	Made in USA	c.1915–1917	★★
ASKHAM & MOSFORTH (New York, NY)	importer, Sheffield made	1856–1920s	★★★
ATCO (Japan)		c.1987–present	★
ATLANTIC CUTLERY CO. (Germany)	Wiebusch import	1898–1914	★

Brands/Manufacturers/Location	*Reference or Trademarks*	*Dates*	*Collectibility*
ATLAS CUTLERY CO. (Bradford, PA)	made in Japan	c.1961–1965	★
ATLAS WORKS (Turner Falls, MA)	John Russell & Co.	c.1880	★★★
AUG. MULLER SOHNE (Solingen, Germany)	"M.B.K."	c.1980s	★
AUTO KNIFE CO. (Middletown, CT)	(Automatic) Wilizin's patent	c.1891–1893	★★★
AUTOMATIC	Eagle Pencil Co.	c.1883–1945	★★
AUTOPOINT (Chicago, IL)	advertising specialty knives	c.1911–1980s	★
AXEL NIELSSON (Germany)	imported by Thompson Hdw.	pre-1914	★
A–1 NOVELTY CUTLERY (Canton, OH)		c.1920s	★★
A. A. A. 1 (St. Louis, MO)	A. J. Jordan, Sheffield made	c.1886	★★
A. BURKINSHAW (Pepperell, MA)	"Exile"	1856–1881	★★★★
A. DINCER (Germany)		c.1930s	★★
A. FEIST & CO. (Solingen)	Omega, Lunawerk, English Steel	c.1870–1948	★★
A. FIELD & CO. (Prussia/Germany)	Criterion, Progress	c.1886–1942	★★
A. FISHER (Solingen)		c.1930s	★
A. HERMES (Germany)		c.1908–1913	★
A. KASTOR & BROS. (New York, NY)	XLNT, EBRO, Clover, Morley	1876–c.1947	★★
A. PAOLANTONIO CUTLERY CO. (Providence, RI)	forerunner of Colonial	1920–1926	★★
A. STRAUSS COMPANY (New York, NY)	bought by William Elliot	c.1907–1918	★
A. TILLES & CO. (Philadelphia, PA)			★
A. ULMER (Portland, ME)	C. F. Ulmer after 1890	1869–1928	★★
A. WINGEN (Solingen)		c.1875–present	★
A. A. FISHER CO. (New York, NY)		c.1919	★
A. B. CALDWELL CUTLERY CO. (Indianapolis, IN)	Van Camp Hdwe. Co.	c.1910	★★
A. CO. (Kane, PA)	Albertson Co.	c.1930–1938	★
A. C. (Nashville, TN)			★
A. C. MFG. CO. (Marinette, WI)	Aerial Cutlery Co.	c.1912–1950	★★★
A. C. M. COMPANY (Marinette, WI)	Aerial Cutlery Mfg. Co.	c.1912–1950	★★★
A. C. PENN (New York, NY)		c.1914–1921	★★
A. C. S. (Solingen)	Alexander Coppel	1884–1892	★★
A. E. MERGOTT & CO. (Newark, NJ)		1888–1950	★
A. F. BANNISTER & CO. (New Jersey)		c.1867–1915	★★
A. F. S & Co.	A. F. Shapleigh Hardware	c.1883	★★
A. F. SHAPLEIGH HDW. CO. (St. Louis, MO)	Diamond Edge (after 1888)	1843–1960	★★
A. G. RUSSELL (Springdale, AR)	Germany, USA, Japan	c.1974–present	★★
A. J. JORDAN (St. Louis, MO)	AAA1, Adolphus, Old Faithful	c.1870–1926	★★
A. J. JORDAN CUTLERY CO.	Sheffield & Solingen	c.1878–1926	★★
A. J. WESTERSSON	Sweden	c.1900	★
A. K. & B.	A. Kastor & Brothers	1875–1900	
A. M. LEONARD, INC. (Piqua, OH)	made by Schrade prior 1960	1885–present	★★
A. P. CO. (New York, NY)			★
A. P. S. (Germany)			★
A. R. JUSTICE (Philadelphia, PA)	Battle Axe Cutlery Co.	c.1897–1937	★★
A. K. BELKNAP (St. Johnsbury, VT)	Amos Belknap, blacksmith	1839–1883	★★★★
A. W. BRADSHAW & SONS (Germany)		c.1856–1860	★
A. W. WADSWORTH & SONS (Germany)	XLNT (A. Kastor & Bros.)	c.1905–1936	★★
A. W. WADSWORTH & SONS (Austria)		c.1905–1936	★★
A. W. WADSWORTH & SONS (New York, NY)	part of A. Kastor & Bros.	c.1905–1922	★★
BADGER STATE KNIFE CO. (Germany)		c.1900–1920	★

Brands/Manufacturers/Location	*Reference or Trademarks*	*Dates*	*Collectibility*
BAKALAR CUTLERY CO. (New York, NY)		1917–1918	★★
BAKER (New York, NY)			★
BAKER & HAMILTON (San Francisco, CA)	Damascus, Eclipse, Golden Gate	1853–1981	★★★
BAKER, HAMILTON & PACIFIC (San Francisco, CA)	Stiletto	1918–c.1945	★★★
BALDWIN CUTLERY CO (New Orleans, LA)	"Southern Belle" "I Cut Kleen"	1874–1939	★★★
BALDWIN CUTLERY CO. (Jamestown, NY)	also Tidioute, PA.	c.1912–1932	★★
BALISONG (Los Angeles, CA)	"Butterfly" knives	1979–1982	★★
BALL BROTHERS (Sheffield)	"Sucess"	1865–1953	★★
BANNER CUTLERY CO. (New York, NY)	importer	pre 1915	★
BANNER KNIFE CO. (Germany)	imported by Kastor	pre 1915	★
BANNER KNIFE CO.	Simmons Hdwe. trademark	c.1939	★
BANTAM	Colonial trademark	c.1954–1955	★
BARKER-JENNINGS HARDWARE (Lynchburg, VA)	hardware dist.	1887–1900s	★
BARLOW (Sheffield)	Samuel Barlow	c.1780–1840	★★★★
BARNES & MILLER HARDWARE (Memphis, TN)		c.1913	★★
BARNSLEY BROS./USA (Monett, MO)		1898–1906	★★★
BARON (Solingen)		c.1950–1968	★
BARR BROS. (Eugene, OR)		1893–1911	★★★
BARR BROS. (Oakland, CA)		1911–1939	★★★
BARRETT & SONS (England)		c.1920s	★
BARRETT-HICKS CO.	Fresno, CA	c.1913–1938	★★
BARRY & CO. (Germany)		c.1919–1925	★
BARTLETT TOOL CO.	Geneva, NY	c.1915	★
BARTON BROS. (Sheffield)		c.1843–1855	★
BASSETT	Derby, CT	c.1920–1940	★
BASTIAN BROS. CO.	Rochester, NY	c.1895–present	★
BATES & BACON	New York	c.1900–1930	★★
BATTLE AXE (Winston-Salem, NC)	made in (Germany)	1975–1987	★★
BATTLE AXE CUTLERY CO. (Philadelphia, PA)	A. R. Justice Co.	c.1897–1937	★★
BATTLE AXE KNIVES (Winston-Salem, NC)	Hickey & Shouse	1975–1990	★
BAUER MFG. CO (San Francisco, CA)	"Ace"	1910–1930	★
BAY RIDGE WORKS (Solingen)		c.1905–1920s	★
BAY STATE MFG. CO. (Worcester, MA)		c.1875–1900	★★
BAYONNE KNIFE CO. (Bayonne, NJ)		1888–1910	★★
BAZAR (Solingen)	diamond outline with fish	1950–1960	★
BEAR MGC (Jacksonville, AL)	formerly Parker-Edwards	1990–present	★
BEARDSLEY & ALVORD	became Empire Knife Co.	c.1853–1856	★★★
BEAVERBROOK KNIFE CO. (Beaver Brook, MA)	B. B. Knife Co.	c.1880s	★★★
BEAVER FALLS CUTLERY CO. (Beaver Falls, PA)		1866–1886	★★★
BECK & GREGG HDWE. CO. (Atlanta, GA)	Dixie Knife	1888–1938	★★
BEE-KAY (Evansville, IN)	Boetticher & Kellog Co	1923–1929	★★
BELKNAP HARDWARE CO. (Louisville, KY)	Primble, Blue Grass, Pine Knot	c.1840–1986	★★
BELL & DAVIS (Atlanta, GA)	maker of Confederate bowies	c.1861	★★★
BELMONT KNIFE CO.	E. Morris	c.1920–1930	★

Brands/Manufacturers/Location	*Reference or Trademarks*	*Dates*	*Collectibility*
BEN HUR (Indianapolis, IN)	Van Camp Hdwr. brand	c.1927–1954	★★
BENCHMADE	formerly Pacific Cutlery Co.	1987–present	★★
BENCHMARK KNIVES (Gastonia, NC)	Rolox, Com-Belt, Ninja Jenkins Metal Corp.	1978–1984	★★
BENCHMARK KNIVES (Portland, OR)	Gerber owned	1984–1992	★
BENCHMARK KNIVES (Gastonia, NC)	Jenkins Metal Corp.	1992–1998	★
BENEDICT, WARREN DAVIDSON & CO.	Memphis, TN	1902–1913	★
BENNETT CUTLERY WORKS	Canton, NY	c.1922	★★
BENOIT	French farmers knife	1900–1958	★★
BERING-CORTES HARDWARE CO.	Houston, TX	c.1905–1947	★★
BERKSHIRE CUTLERY CO. (Germany)	O-U-NO	c.1890	★
BERETTA (Accokeek, MD)	Beretta USA Corp.	1984–present	★★
BERTRAM/GERMANY (Solingen)	Hen & Rooster, A. G. Russell	1975–1980	★★★
BERTRAM CUTLERY GERMANY (Solingen)	Hen & Rooster, made by Klaas	1981–present	★★
BEST ENGLISH CUTLERY		c.1800–1860	★★
BESTEEL WARRANTED		c.1945–1960	★
BETA BOS'N (Germany)		1940–1950	★
BETZ BIFFMAN (Germany)		1920–1940	★
BIDDLE HARDWARE (Philadelphia, PA)	Robbins, Clark & Biddle	c.1837–1920	★★
BIG HORN	Italy	1971–present	★
BIGELOW & DOWSE (Boston, MA)	Hdwe, Cutlery, Adv. spec.	1839–1954	★
BILLINGS & SPENCER (Hartford, CT)	knives c.1869–1914	1869–1963	★★★
BINGHAM CULTERY CO. (Cleveland, OH)	BBB, XLCR	1841–1930	★★
BINGHAM & OGDEN (Sheffield)	Select, Arrow	1858–1938	★★
BIRMINGHAM KNIFE FACTORY (Birmingham, CT)		c.1849	★★★★
BINGHAMPTON CUTLERY CO.	"The Very Best"	c.1888–1894	★★★
BINNS & MASON	Rochester, PA	c.1866	
BIRD/KNOXVILLE	hardware brand	c.1920–1950	★★
BISON (Japan)		c.1950–1960	★
BLACKJACK (Effingham, IL)		1986–1997	★
BLAKE & LAMB (Utica, NY)	made by Utica Cutlery	c.1930	★★
BLISH-MIZE-SILLIMAN HDWE. CO. (Atchison, KS)	Mohawk	1871–present	★★
BLITZKNIFE (Charlotte, NC)	W. F. Harwell	c.1947	★★
BLUE GRASS (Louisville, KY)	Belknap Hdw. Co.	c.1898–1986	★★
BLUE GRASS CUTLERY CO. (Manchester, OH)	Winchester, Primble	c.1985–present	★★
BLUE RIBBON (Louisville, KY)	Belknap Hdw. Co.	1910–1950	★
BOB WHITE CUTLERY (Santa Fe, TN))	Quail logo	1979	★
BOENTGEN & SABIN (Solingen)	Bonsa or Bonsa-Werk	c.1968–1983	★★
BOKER, U.S.A. (Maplewood, NJ)	Tree Brand, Valley Forge	1899–1921	★★★
BOKER, U.S.A. (Maplewood, NJ)	sold to J. Wiss 1969	1917–1986	★★
BOKER, U.S.A. (Apex, NC)	Cooper Group	1978–1986	★
BOKER CUTLERY CO. (Golden, CO)	Henr. Boker importer	1986–present	★★
BOKER/SOLINGEN GERMANY	tree brand	c.1960–present	
BON KNIFE CO.		c.1900–1920	★
BONSA (Solingen)	Boentgen & Sabin	1867–1983	★
BONZER INC. (Germany)		c.1950–1980	★
BOOTH BROS. (Newark, NJ)		1864–1879	★★★
BOOTH BROS. (Boonton, NJ)		1879–1889	★★★
BOOTH BROS. (Stockholm, NJ)		1889–1903	★★★

Brands/Manufacturers/Location	*Reference or Trademarks*	*Dates*	*Collectibility*
BOOTH BROS. (Sussex, NJ)		1903–1909	★★★
BOOTH BROS. CELEBRATED (Newark, NJ)	Crown and wings	1900–1909	★★★
BOSTWICK BRAUN CO.	Toldeo, OH	1873–present	★★
BOWEN KNIFE CO. (Waycross, GA)	Bullet shields, Collins Bros.	1973–present	★★
BOWER IMPLEMENT CO. (Germany)	F. A. Bower	c.1950–1980	★
BOWN & TETLEY (Pittsburg, PA)	bowie-type knives	1848–1862	★★★★
BOWMAN CUTLERY CO. (Germany)		c.1900–1920	★
BRADFORD & ANTHONY (Boston, MA)	Dame, Stoddard & Kendall	1867–1881	★★★
BRANTFORD CUTLERY CO./USA	Warranted Never Dull, Butler Bros.	c.1900	★★
BRIDGE CUTLERY CO. (St. Louis, MO)	Shapleigh Hdwe. brand	c.1915	★★★
BRIDGEPORT KNIFE CO. (Bridgeport, CT)	Bridgeport Hdwe. Mfg. Corp.	c.1904	★★
BRIDGEPORT TOOL CO. (New Haven, CT)	Pequot	c.1910–1920	★★
BRIGHTON CUTLERY WORKS (Germany)		c.1900	★
BRISTOL LINE (Germany)		c.1950s	★
BRISTOL KNIFE CO (Bristol, CT)		1868–1874	★★★
BRIT-NIFE (St. Louis, MO)		c.1930–1950	★
BROCH & KOCH		c.1880s	★
BROCH & THIEBES CUTLERY CO. (St. Louis, MO)	Climax	c.1882–1892	★★
BRONSON & TOWNSEND CO. (New Haven, CT)	"Pequot"	1923–1938	★★★
BROOKES & CROOKES (Sheffield)	Bell logo	c.1858–1957	★★★
BROOKLYN KNIFE CO.	New York	c.1895–1920	★★
BROWN & BIGELOW (St. Paul, MN)	B & B, made by Colonial	1931–1950s	★
BROWN BROS. KNIFE CO. (Tidioute, PA)	Union Cutlery Co.	prior 1902	★★★
BROWN BROS. KNIFE CO. (Olean, NY)	Union Cutlery Co.	after 1911	★★★
BROWN BROS. MFG. CO. (Tidioute, PA)	became Union Razor Co.	c.1890–1902	★★★
BROWN BROS./GERMANY (Germany)	Union Cut	prior 1902	★★
BROWN CAMP HARDWARE CO. (Des Moines, IA)	I.O.A.	c.1907–1959	★★
BROWN-CAMP HDWE. CO. (St. Louis, MO)		1907–1959	★★
BROWNING/USA (Morgan, UT)		c.1969–1983	★★
BROWNE & PHARR (Atlanta, GA)	handmade pocketknives	1972–1989	★★★
BRUNSWICK CUTLERY CO. (San Francisco, CA)	Dunham-Carrigan-Hayden	c.1897–1907	★
BUCK (El Cajon, CA)	started by H. H. Buck c.1900	1963–present	★★
BUCK BROS.	Worcester, MA	c.1853–1927	★★★★
BUCK CREEK (London, KY)	made in (Germany)	1970–1989	★★
BUCK CREEK (Kingsport, TN)	made in Japan for Taylor	1989–1993	★
BUD BRAND CUTLERY CO. (Winstead, CT)		c.1922	★★★
BUFFALO CUTLERY CO. (Germany)	Buffalo Wholesale Hdwe. Co.	c.1915	★★
BUHL & SONS CO.	Detroit, MI	c.1898–1938	★
BULL BRAND (Germany)	Lauderdale, Castilian Springs, TN	1985–1996	★
BULLDOG (Solingen)	S & D Products	c.1980–1993	★★
BULLDOG (Solingen)	Parker KCS	c.1993–present	★★
BURGON & BALL (Sheffield)	Sound	c.1873–1917	★★

Brands/Manufacturers/Location	*Reference or Trademarks*	*Dates*	*Collectibility*
BURKINSHAW KNIFE CO. (Pepperell, MA)	Exile, Pain	1853–1881	★★★★
BUSTER BROWN SHOE CO. (St. Louis, MO)	by Camillus via Shapleigh	c.1930s	★★
BUTLER BROS. (Chicago, IL)	Warranted Never Dull	1865–1952	★★
BUTLER & CO. (Sheffield)		1865–1952	★
BUTTERICK PATTERN CO.	B. P. Co. Ltd.	c.1910	★
B. ALTMAN & CO. (New York, NY)		c.1900	★
B.B.B. (Monet, MO)	Barnsley Brothers	c.1898–1906	★★
B. B. KNIFE CO. (Beaverbrook, MA)	Beaver Brook Knife Co.	c.1880s	★★★
B. H. MORSE (Waterbury, CT)	Waterville Co.	c.1857	★★
B. H. SPECIAL (Germany)	Biddle Hardware	c.1910	★
B. J. EYRE CO. (Germany)	Wiebusch trademark	c.1876–1910	★★
B. J. EYRE & CO. (Sheffield)	Late W. Greaves & Son	1850–c.1876	★★
B. SVOBODA (Montrose, CA)	imported by Liberty	c.1950–present	★
B. T. CO. (New Haven, CT)	Bridgeport Tool Co.	c.1922	★★
B. WORTH & SONS (Sheffield)		c.1874–1919	★★
B. & A. (Boston, MA)	Bradford & Anthony	c.1867–1881	★★★
B. & B. (St. Paul, MN)	Brown & Bigelow	c.1931–1952	★
CALDWELL CUTLERY CO. (Indianapolis, IN)	Van Camp Hdwe.	c.1879–1929	★★
CALIFORNIA NOTION & TOY CO. (San Francisco, CA)		1894–c.1930	★
CAM III	Vacaville, CA	1977–1990s	★
CAMBRIDGE CUTLERY CO. (Sheffield)	U.S. Navy contractor	c.1865	★★★
CAMCO (Camillus, NY)	Camillus Cutlery Co.	1948–present	★
CAMERON KNIFE CO.		c.1920s	★
CAMILLUS (New York, NY)		c.1902–present	★★
CAMILLUS CUTLERY CO. (Camillus, NY)	(mark used through World War II)	1902–present	★★
CAMILLUS/NEW YORK/USA (Camillus, NY)	(mark used after World War II)	1902–present	★★
CAMP BUDDY/U.S.A.	Camillus Cutlery Co.	1902–present	★
CAMP KING (Germany)			★
CANASTOTA KNIFE CO. (Canastota, NY)	dist. by Cornwall	1875–1895	★★★★
CANTON CUTLERY CO. (Canton, OH)	W. S. Carnes, Car-Van	1879–c.1930	★★
CANTON HARDWARE CO. (Canton, OH)	Keen Edge	c.1910	★★
CAPITOL CUTLERY CO. (Indianapolis, IN)	Van Camp Hdwe.	1904–1948	★★
CAPITOL KNIFE CO. (Winsted, CT)		c.1920s	★★
CARBO-MAGNETIC	trademark by Griffon Cutlery	1895–1966	★
CARL BERTRAM (Solingen)	Hen & Rooster	1864–1983	★★★
CARL KAMMERLING & CO. (Germany)	P. L. Schmidt, Wintgen	1904–present	★
CARL KLAUBERG & BROS. (New York, NY)		c.1883–1940	★
CARL LINDER (Solingen)	Rehwappen	1980–present	★
CARL SCHLIEPER (Solingen)	Eye Brand, Fan, El Gallo, Jim Bowie	1796–present	★★
CARL SCHMIDT SOHN (Solingen)		1829–present	★★
CARL WUSTHOF (Solingen)	Gladiator, Hejo, James	1895–present	★★
CARRIER CUTLERY CO. (Elmira, NY)	Cronk & Carrier	1900–1921	★★★
CARTER BLADE MASTER	Cleveland, OH	c.1939	★
CARTERS (Scottsville, KY)	Bertram's Hen & Rooster logo	1969–1983	★★
CAR-VAN S P (Canton, OH)	Canton Cutlery Co.	1911–1930	★★
CASE BROS.	Little Valley, NY	1900–1914	★★★★
CASE BROS.	Springville, NY	c.1912	★★★★
CASE BROTHERS (Little Valley, NY)	Tested XX	1900–1912	★★★★

Brands/Manufacturers/Location	*Reference or Trademarks*	*Dates*	*Collectibility*
CASE BROTHERS (Springville, NY)	Tested XX	1912–1915	★★★★
CASE BROTHERS & CO. (Gowanda, NY)	made by C. Platts & Sons	1869–1900	★★★★
CASE CUTLERY COMPANY (Kane, PA)	Case Bros. 1907–1911	1907–1911	★★★★
CASE MFG. CO.	Little Valley, NY	c.1898–1899	★★★★
CASE XX METAL STAMPING LTD. (Bradford, PA)	by Case for Canadian govt.	1940s	★★★
CATSKILL KNIFE CO.	Camillus contract brand	c.1930s	★
CATTARAUGUS (Springdale, AR)	A. G. Russell	1984–present	★
CATTARAUGUS CUTLERY CO. (Little Valley, NY)	Indian logo	1886–1963	★★★★
CEB MULLER (Germany)		c.1950s	★
CENTAUR CUTLERY (Germany)	Sperry & Alexander	c.1893–1913	★
CENTENNIAL MILLS (Solingen)		c.1900–1930	★
CENTRAL CITY KNIFE CO. (Phoenix, NY)	C. C. Knife Co.	1880–1892	★★★
CENTRAL CUTLERY CO.	Elizabeth, NJ	c.1926	★★
CHALLENGE CUTLERY CO. (Sheffield)	B. J. Eyre Co.	1867–1877	★★★
CHALLENGE CUTLERY CO. (Germany)	Wiebusch & Hilger	1877–1891	★★★
CHALLENGE CUT. CORP. (Bridgeport, CT)	Wiebusch & Hilger	c.1891–1928	★★★
CHALMERS & MURRAY (New York, NY)		c.1890s	★★
CHAMPION (Birmingham AL)	Moore-Handley Hardware	c.1925–1932	★
CHAPMAN CUT. CO. (Muncie, IN)	Chapman Hand Forged	1915–1931	★★
CHARLES HALL (Sheffield)	C. Hall	c.1836–1872	★★
CHARLES LANGBEIN	New York	c.1880–1890	★★
CHARLES R. RANDALL (Germany)		c.1930s	★
CHERO-COLA CO.		c.1940s	★
CHICAGO CUTLERY	Minneapolis, MN	current	★
CHICAGO KNIFE WORKS (Chicago, IL)		c.1911	★
CHICAGO POCKET KNIFE CO. (Chicago, IL)		c.1945	★
CHIPAWAY CUTLERY CO. (England)	for E. C. Simmons Hdwe.	c.1891–1907	★★★
CHRISTOPHER JOHNSON & CO. (Sheffield)	CJ in flag; to I*XL 1955	1865–c.1977	★★
CHRISTY (Fremont, OH)	Russ J. Christy Knife Co.	1890–present	★
CHRISTIANS (Solingen)	knife pistols and pocketknives	1824–present	★★
CLARK BROTHERS (Kansas City, MO)	bought Northfield in 1919	1895–1929	★★
CLARKS CUTLERY/USA	Baker & Hamilton, XLT on blade	1899–1926	★★
CLAUBERG CUTLERY CO. (Germany)		1857–1926	★
CLAUSS (Freemont, OH)	made by Shatt & Morgan	1887–present	★★
CLAY CUTLERY CO. (Andover, NY)	probably by Robeson	c.1930s	★★
CLEAN CUT (San Francisco, CA)	Clover logo, D. C. & H.	c.1884–1912	★★
CLEARCUT/U.S.A.	George Worthington	1835–1949	★
CLEMENTS (Sheffield)	Hand Forged, 20th Century	c.1850–1875	★
CLEVELAND CUTLERY CO. (Cleveland, OH)	Made in Japan & Germany	c.1925	★
CLIM (Germany)	Schmachtenberg	c.1887–1939	★
CLIPPER CUTLERY CO (Richmond, VA)	Watkins-Cottrell Co.	c.1901	★★
CLOVER BRAND (Syracuse, NY)	Kastor & Camillus	c.1941–42	★
CLYDE CUTLERY CO.	Clyde, OH	c.1929–1949	★★

Brands/Manufacturers/Location	*Reference or Trademarks*	*Dates*	*Collectibility*
COAST CUTLERY CO.	Portland, OR	1919–present	★
COCA COLA (Atlanta, GA)	made by Camillus	1930–1940s	★
COHELLE COIN			★
COLD STEEL	Japan import specialty	1980–present	
COLEMAN CUTLERY CO.		c.1910–1920	★
(Titusville, PA)			
COLEMAN-WESTERN	formerly Western Cutlery	1984–1990	★
COLES (New York)	Hand Forged	c.1960s	★
COLLINS BROS. (Atlanta, GA)	made by Camillus	c.1970–1973	★★
COLLINS CO.	Collinsville, CT	c.1826–1966	★★
COLONIAL KNIFE CO.	Old Cutler, Ranger, Topper	1926–2002	★
(Providence, RI)			
COLT (Germany		c.1969–1973	★
COLT (Hartford, CT)	by Barry Wood, Venice, CA	1969–1973	★★★
COLUMBIA KNIFE CO.	New York	c.1900	★
COL COON (Columbia, TN)	Racoon, Tenn. Knife Works	c.1978–1988	★★
COMMANDER (Little Valley, NY)	Metropolitan Cutlery Co.	c.1891–1928	★★
CONCORD CUTLERY CO.		c.1880	★★
CONN. CUTLERY CO.	Naugatuck, CT	1867–1883	★★★
CONTINENTAL CUTLERY CO.	Clark Bros.	1915–1920	★
(Kansas City, MO)			
COOK BROTHERS (Sheffield)		c.1890	★★
COOPER BROTHERS (Sheffield)		c.1953	★
COOPERATIVE KNIFE CO.	became Ulster, Walden	1871–1876	★★★★
(New York)			
CORA (Germany)		c.1950s	★
CORLISS CUTLERY (Germany)		c.1900–1910	★
CORNING KNIFE CO.		c.1930s	★
(New York, NY)			
CORNWALL KNIFE CO.	Cornwall, CT	1800s	★★★
CORSAN DENTON BURDEKIN		c.1860	★★★
(Sheffield)			
CRAFTSMAN (Chicago, IL)	by Camillus, Schrade Ulster	1940s–present	★
CRANDALL CUTLERY CO.	merged with W. R. Case	1905–1912	★★★
(Bradford, PA)			
CRESCENT CUTLERY CO.	Fremont, OH	c.1917–1950	★
CRIPPLE CREEK (Lockport, IL)	Bob Cargill	1981–1986	★★★
CRIPPLE CREEK (Old Fort, TN)	Bob Cargill	1986–1993	★★
CRIPPLE CREEK (Effingham, IL)	Blackjack Knives	1993–1996	★
CRITERION (Sheffield)	Alfred Field	1886–1942	★★
CRONK & CARRIER MFG. CO.	Carrier Cutlery Co.	1900–1921	★★
(Elmira, NY)			
CRONK & CARRIER MFG. CO.	Nontour Falls, NY	1920–1928	★★
CROSMAN BLADES	Wichita, KS	1982–1985	★
CROWN CUTLERY CO.		1910s–20s	★
(New York, NY)			
CRUCIBLE KNIFE CO.	sold by W. T. Grant, NYC	1926–1932	★
(Lynn, MA)			
CUTWELL	A. Kastor & Bros. trademark	1920–1940	★
CULF & KAY (Sheffield)			★★
CUMBERLAND CUTLERY CO.	Gray & Dudley,	c.1897–1948	★
(Sheffield)	C. M. McClung		
CURLEY BROS.	New York	c.1885–1905	★
CURTIN & CLARK CUTLERY CO.	C.C.C.	c.1898–1910	★★
(St. Joseph, MO)			
CUSSINS & FEARN	U.S.A.	1930s	★
CUT SURE	Kruse & Bahlman	c.1889–1962	★
CUTINO CUTLERY CO.	some made by Challenge	c.1914–1935	★★
(Kansas City, MO			
CUTWELL CUTLERY CO.	A. Kastor & Bros.	c.1886–1945	★★
(Germany)			
C. BERTRAM (Solingen)	Hen & Rooster brand	c.1865–1980	★★★
C. B. BARKER & CO.	Owl, Howard trademarks	c.1880–1905	

Brands/Manufacturers/Location	*Reference or Trademarks*	*Dates*	*Collectibility*
C. B. S. (Solingen)			★
CCC (Little Valley, NY)	Cataraugus Cutlery Co	1886–1963	★★★
C. CONGREVE (Sheffield)		1829–1843	★★★
C. C. KNIFE CO. (Phoenix, NY)	Central City Knife Co.	c.1880–1892	★★★
C. FRIEDR. ERN & CO. (Germany)		1874–1926	★
C. F. WOLFERTZ & CO. (Allentown, PA)	(Mfr. 1862–c.1920)	c.1862–1873	★★
C. J. & CO. (Sheffield)		1836–1956	★
C. K. CO. (Germany)	Colonial Knife Co.	c.1933	★
C. P. WRENCH CO. (Briston, TN)	pat. 6/26/08	c.1908	★★★
C. LUTTERS & CO. (Solingen)	reclining lion trademark	1840–present	★★
C. M. MCCLUNG & CO. (Knoxville, TN)	Cranberry, Keener Edge	1882–c.1960	★★
C. PLATTS & SONS Gowanda, NY)	in old S. & M. plant	1896–1900	★★★★
C. PLATTS & SONS (Elred, PA)	became C. Platts' Sons	1897–1900	★★★★
C. PLATTS' SONS (Elred, PA)	merged with W. R. Case 1905	1900–1905	★★★★
C. PRADEL	1er Choix (first choice)		★
C. SARRY	Thiers France	c.1910–1930	★
C. T. ERVIN CO. (Germany)		c.1900–1930	★
C. & R. LINDER (Solingen)	crown/pruning knife	1842–1971	★
DAHLIA (Germany)			★
DAMASCUS STEEL PRODUCTS CORP. (Rockford, IL)	DASCO	1922–1962	★★
DAME STODDARD & CO. (Boston, MA)	D S & C	c.1901–1930	★★★
DAME STODDARD & KENDALL (Boston, MA)	(DS&K, Hub)	c.1881–1901	★★★
DANCE CUTLERY CO. (Germany)			★
DANIEL PERES & CO. (Solingen)	Ale Barrel	1792–present	★★
DART	U.S.A.		★
DASCO (Rockford, IL)	Damascus Steel Products	c.1922–1962	★★
DAWES & BALL (Sheffield)		1925–1962	★★
DECORA (Germany)			★
DEERSLAYER BRAND	Precise		★
DEFENDER	.22 cal. knife-pistol	c.1912	★★★★
DELMAR CUTLERY CO.		c.1910	★★
DELTA (Germany)	Hugo Linder	1878–1953	★
DELUXE (Torrence, CA)	Salm	1918–1925	★★
DEPEND-ON-ME CUTLERY CO. (New York, NY)		c.1945	★
DIAMOND EDGE (St. Louis, MO)	Shapleigh Hardware <D-E>	1864–1960	★★
DIAMOND EDGE VAL-TEST (Chicago, IL)	Schrade trademark	1960–1967	★
DIAMOND EDGE (IMPERIAL) (Providence, RI)	Imperial Knife Co. trademark	c.1967–present	★
DICTATOR		c.1930s	★
DISSTON STEEL (Philadelphia, PA)	commemorative knife	1940	★★
DIXIE KNIFE (Atlanta, GA)	Beck & Gregg Hdwe.	c.1890–1894	★★
DIXON CUTLERY CO. (Germany)		c.1920s	★
DODSON MFG. CO. (Chicago, IL)		c.1937	★
DOLLAR KNIFE CO. (Atlanta, GA)		c.1922	★★
DOLLAR KNIFE CO. (Titusville, PA)	Schatt & Morgan	c.1927	★★★
DOLMETACH	Zurich Sweden	c.1900–1920	★
DOLPHIN CUTLERY CO. (New York, NY)		1918–1920s	★★
DOMAR CUTLERY CO. (Oklahoma City, OK)	Theodore M. Green Co.	c.1916–1920	★★
DOUBLE COLA	U.S.A.	c.1930–1940s	★
DOUBLE SHARP (Sheffield)	G. Ibberson	c.1932–1942	★
DOUGLAS	Brockton, MA	c.1930–1940	★
DRAKE HARDWARE CO.	Burlington, IA	c.1890	★★
DREITIUM (Germany)		1829–present	★

Brands/Manufacturers/Location	*Reference or Trademarks*	*Dates*	*Collectibility*
DRESDEN (Germany)			★
DRIEZACK (Germany)	Wusthof trademark	1814–present	★
DRITTES (Germany)			★
DUANE CUTLERY CO. (Germany)	A. Kastor	c.1910	★
DUKE PETERSON HDWE. CO.		c.1920s	★★
DUKES	"Father of Barlows" on bolster	c.1875–1900	★
DUNHAM CARRIGAN & HAYDEN (San Francisco, CA)	Clean Cut, Springbrooke, Volka	1848–1927	★★
DUNLOP	Sears brand by Camillus	1938–1942	★★
DUNN BROS.	Providence, RI	1927–present	★
DURANGO	Case brand by Colonial	c.1975	★
DURO-EDGE (Utica, NY)	Montgomery Ward	c.1928–1930	★
DWIGHT DIVINE & SONS (Ellenville, NY)	Ulster Knife Co., Kingston	1876–1941	★★★
D. C. & H. (San Francisco, CA)	Dunham Carrigan & Hayden	c.1849–1964	★★
D. PERES (Germany)		c.1885–present	★
D. S. & CO. (Boston, MA)	Dame Stoddard & Co.	c.1901–1930	★★★
D. S. & K. (Boston, MA)	Dame Stoddard & Kendall	c.1881–1901	★★★
EAGLE BRAND (Japan)	Parker Cutlery	c.1974–1991	★★
EAGLE CUTLERY CO.	Eagle Pencil Co.	c.1883–1945	★
EAGLE KNIFE CO. (New Haven, CT)	Hemming Pat. 10/1/1918	1916–1919	★★
EAGLE PENCIL CO. (New York, NY)		c.1883–1945	★
EAGLETON KNIFE CO. (Germany)	Wester & Butz	c.1890	★★
EAGLE/PHIL'A (Philadelphia, PA)	Creutzberg	c.1883–1945	★
ECLIPSE CUTLERY CO. (San Francisco, CA)	Baker & Hamilton, by Boker	c.1897–1918	★★
EDER & CO. (Germany)			★
EDGAR CUTLERY CO. (Germany)			★
EDGE MARK (Japan & Germany)	Gutmann Cutlery, Inc.	c.1950–1997	★
EDGEMASTER (U.S.A.)	switchblade knife by Schrade	c.1940s	★★
EDIRLAM (Solingen)			★
EDITHWERKS (Solingen)			★
EDUARD WUSTHOF (Solingen)	Dreizack (Trident)	1814–present	★
EDULON (Solingen)			★
EDWARD BARNES/US (Sheffield)	made in (Sheffield)	c.1850s	★★★
EDWARD BARNES & SONS (Sheffield)		c.1853–1865	★★★
EDWARD K. TRYON (Philadelphia, PA)	3/T. Some by Utica.	c.1811–1952	★★★
EDWARD PARKER & SONS (New York)	Germania Cutlery Works	c.1900	★
EDWARD WECK (New York, NY)	also Pauls Bros.	1893–1943	★
EDWARD WECK & SONS (New York, NY)	New York, NY	c.1893–1943	★
EDWARD ZINN (New York, NY)	made in (Germany)	c.1920	★
EDWIN BLYDE (Shefield)	bowies	1798–present	★★
EKCO (Chicago, IL)	EKCO Products, Geneva Forge	1908–1948	★★
EL GALLO	Schlieper brand made in Germany	1954–1972	★
ELBERFIELD CUTLERY CO. (Germany)	made by Wester & Butz	c.1866–1891	★
ELBERON CUTTING WORKS (Germany)			★
ELDER & CO. (Germany)			★
ELECTRIC (Germany)	Friedmann & Lauterjung	c.1873–1901	★★★
ELECTRIC CUTLERY CO./ NEWARK N.J.(New York, NY)	Friedmann & Lauterjung	1873–c.1901	★★★
ELECTRIC CUTLERY CO./ WALDEN N.Y.(New York, NY)	Friedmann & Lauterjung	after 1901	★★
ELGIN A M MFG. CO.	U.S.A.		★
ELIKSCH KADISON (Germany)			★
ELINOX	Victorinox marking	1891–present	★

Brands/Manufacturers/Location	*Reference or Trademarks*	*Dates*	*Collectibility*
ELLENVILLE KNIFE CO. (Ellenville, NY)	Dwight Divine & Sons	1876–1920	★★★
ELLIOTT CUTLERY CORP. (Germany)			★
ELYRIA CUTLERY CO. (Elyria, OH)	became Clauss Cutlery Co.	1878–1887	★★★
ELYTE (Germany)		c.1840–1880	★
EM-HAW-CO (Huntington, WV)	Emmons-Hawkins Hdwe. Co.	1875–1969	★★
EMIL OLSSON (Eskilstuna, Sweden)	Sea Serpant insignia	c.1890–c.1965	★
EMPIRE KNIFE CO. (Winsted, CT)	West Winsted after 1880	1856–1930	★★★★
ENDERSES	Albert Lea, MN	c.1918	★★
ENDURE (Sheffield)	J. Beal	1870–1890	★★
ENGELSWERK (Germany)		1909–1943	★
ENGLISH CUTLERY CO. (Sheffield)		c.1950s	★
ENTERPRISE CUTLERY CO. (St. Louis, MO)	Shapleigh brand by Camillus	1918–1920s	★
ERA (Sheffield)	James Barber	1870–1880s	★★
ERBER	Austria	c.1890	★
ERMA (Germany)		c.1950s	★
ERN (Solingen)		1916–1926	★
ERNEST BRUECKMANN (Solingen)	Bridge logo	1891–c.1956	★★★
ERNEST G. AHRENS (Solingen)		1930s	★
ERNEST WARTHER	Dover, OH	1920s–1940s	★★★★
ESKILSTUNA (Eskilstuna, Sweden)	Crown, Anchor and "E" trademark	1885–1949	★★
ESSEM CO.	Shiman Mfg. Co.	1921–1949	★
ESSEX CUTLERY CO.		c.1900–1920	★
EUREKA CUTLERY CO (Nicholson, PA)	became Lackawanna	1911–1915	★★
EVER-SHARP (Baltimore, MD)	American Wholesale Co.	1923–1925	★★
EXCELSIOR KNIFE CO. (Torrington, CT)	sold to Northfield c.1884	1880–1884	★★★
EXECUTIVE (U.S.A)	Colonial brand	c.1960s–1980	★
EXPLORER (Germany)	Gutmann Cutlery Co.	current	★
EYE BRAND (Germany)	Carl Schlieper	c.1769–present	★★
EYRE WARD & CO. (Sheffield)	Sheaf Works	c.1840–1869	★★★
E. BARNES & SONS (Sheffield)		c.1856–1865	★★★
E. BRUCKMANN (Solingen)	Mann	c.1920–1956	★★
E. B. EXTRA (Germany)	Hartford Cutlery Company	c.1914	★
E. C. ATKINS & CO. (Indianapolis, IN)	saw logo, daggers World War II	1857–1950	★★
E. C. SIMMONS HDW. CO. (St. Louis, MO)	Keen Kutter/Shapleigh after 1940	1868–1960	★★★
E. DIRLAM (Solingen)		c.1900–1920	★
E. DULON (Solingen)		c.1900–1910	★
E. FABER (Germany)		c.1880	★
E. FELSENHELD	New York	c.1900–1920	★
E. MOULIN	Greenville, IL		★
E. M. DICKINSON (Sheffield)		c.1870–1912	★★
E. T. ALLEN (San Francisco, CA)	The Club	1878–1899	★★
E. WILD & SONS (Germany)		c.1850s	★
E.A.A. (Solingen)		c.1920–1940	★
E.F. & S. (England)	Furness	c.1870–1915	★★
EIG	Tipps Hardware brand	c.1940s–1960s	★
E.K.A	Eskilstuna Sweden	1885–present	★
FABICO (Germany/Japan)	import by Bower	1970–1980	★
FABYAN KNIFE CO. (Germany)	Q.E.D.	c.1890	★★
FAIRMONT CUTLERY CO. (Camillus, NY)	Camillus brand	1930s	★
FALCON KNIFE CO.		c.1810–1930	★
FALL RIVER KNIFE CO. (Fall River, MA)	made in Germany	c.1900	★
FARWELL OZMUN KIRK & CO. (St. Paul, MN)	Henry Sears & Son	1881–1959	★★
FAULKHINER & CO. (Germany)		c.1910–1930	★

Brands/Manufacturers/Location	*Reference or Trademarks*	*Dates*	*Collectibility*
FAVORITE KNIFE CO. (Germany)		c.1939	★
FAYETTEVILLE KNIFE CO. (Fayetteville, NY)	F. K. Co.	c.1911	★★
FEDERAL KNIFE CO. (Syracuse, NY)	made by Camillus	c.1920s	★★
FIDELITY KNIFE CO.	New York	c.1939	★
FIFE CUTLERY CO. (Mount Sterling, KY)	made by C. Bertram	1968–1974	★★
FIGHT'N ROOSTER (Lebanon, TN)	Frank Buster Cutlery	1973–present	★★
FILLMORE CUTLERY CO. (Genesee, NY)	Gennesee	1891–1895	★★★
FINEDGE CUTLERY CO. (New York, NY)	Ostiso Hardware	c.1921–1923	★★
FLETCHER KNIFE CO. (Detroit, MI)	Fletcher Hardware Co.	c.1863–1913	★★
FLOYD & BOHR CO.	Louisville, KY	c.1900–1920	★★
FLYLOCK KNIFE CO. (Bridgeport, CT)	by Challenge Cutlery	1918–1928	★★★
FONES BROTHERS (Little Rock, AR)	Arkansas Traveler	c.1881–1914	★★★
FORD & MEDLEY (Sheffield)	Emu logo	1872–c.1930	★★
FOREST MASTER (Providence, RI)	Colonial	1934–2002	★
FOSTER BROS. & CHATILLON CO.	Fulton, NY	c.1930–1937	★
FOX CUTLERY (Milwaukee, WI)	Koeller & Schmidt	c.1884–1955	★★
FRANCE & RUSSIE			★
FRANCIS NEWTON & SONS (Sheffield)	J. & R. Dodge	c.1838–present	★★
FRANK BUSTER CELEBRATED CUTLERY (Solingen)	Fight'n Rooster logo	c.1973–present	★★
FRANK BUSTER CUTLERY CO. (Lebanon, TN)	Fight'n Rooster logo	1977–present	★★
FRANK MILLS & CO. (England)		c.1860	★
FRANKFURTH HDWE. CO.	Milwaukee, WI	c.1862–present	★
FRARY CUTLERY CO. (Bridgeport, CT)	A–1 Warranted	1876–1884	★★★
FRARY & SON (Bridgeport, CT)	became LaBelle	c.1881–1884	★★★
FRED BIFFAR (Chicago, IL)	Dixie Switch, Dixie Guard	1917–1922	★★
FRED KRONER HDWE. (Germany)	Lacrosse, WI	1865–c.1920s	★
FRIEDRICH OLBERTZ (Solingen)	crown and wings trademark	1915–present	★
FREDERICK FENNEY (Sheffield)	Fox, Tally-Ho	1824–1852	★★
FREDERICK REYNOLDS (Sheffield)		1919–1926	★★
FREDERICK WESTPFAL (New York, NY)	Acme	c.1884–1940	★★
FRIEDMANN & LAUTERJUNG (New York, NY)	"Electric," import firm	1864–1909	★★
FRITZ ERN & CO. (Solingen)		c.1924–present	★
FRONTIER (Providence, RI)	for Imperial by Camillus	1975–present	★
FROST CUTLERY CO. (Chattanooga, TN)	made in Japan	1978–present	★
FRYE PHIPPS & CO.	Boston, MA	1901–1920	★★
FULTON CUTLERY CO. (New York, NY)		c.1910	★★
F. A. KOCH & CO. (New York, NY)		c.1880–1933	★★
F. STERLING (Germany)			★
F. WARD & CO. (Sheffield)	B 4 * ANY (regis. 1867)	c.1850s–1879	★★★
F. WIEBUSCH (New York, NY)	Challenge, Wester, Monument	c.1874–1928	★★
F. W. JORDAN (New York)	probably by Krusius Bros.	c.1920s	★★
F. W. SHELDON & CO. (Germany)			★
F. & K. (Solingen)			★
F. & L. (New York, NY)	Friedmann & Lauterjang	c.1866–1910	★★★

Brands/Manufacturers/Location	*Reference or Trademarks*	*Dates*	*Collectibility*
F. & L. CELEBRATED CUTLERY (Germany)	Friedmann & Lauterjung	c.1864–1909	★★★
GAMBLE STORES (Minneapolis, MN)	made by Camillus	c.1930s–1950s	★
GARDEN CITY CUTLERY CO.		c.1890–1910	★
GARLAND CUTLERY CO. (Germany)		c.1913	★
GATEWAY CUTLERY CO.			★
GEBRUDER CHRISTIANS (Solingen)	Fork logo, Christians Bros.	1824–present	★
GEBRUDER KRUSIUS (Solingen)	Krusius Bros.	1856–1983	★
GEBRUDER RICHARTZ & SOEHNE (Solingen)	Whale logo	1900–present	★
GELBROS. CO. (Germany)	Gellman Brothers	c.1920	★
GELLMAN BROS.	Minneapolis, MN	c.1920	★
GENERAL (Chicago, IL)			★
GENESSE	Robeson	1891–1895	★★★
GENEVA CUTLERY CO. (Geneva, NY)	became Geneva Forge 1934	1902–1934	★★
GENEVA FORGE, INC. (Geneva, NY)	div. of E. Katzinger (EKCO)	1934–c.1948	★★
GEORGE BARNSLEY & SONS (Sheffield)	Wide Awake, Stoic	c.1839–1950s	★★★
GEORGE DOBSON (Sheffield)		c.1880s	★★
GEORGE F. CREUTZBERG (Philadelphia, PA)	Eagle/Phil'a	c.1875–1943	★★
GEORGE HANCOCK & SONS		c.1834	★
GEORGE IBBERSON & CO. (Sheffield)	Violin (after 1880)	1700–1988	★★★
GEORGE JOHNSON & CO. (Sheffield)	Seven stars logo	1810–1855	★★★
GEORGE SAVAGE & SONS (Sheffield)		c.1855	★★
GEORGE SCHRADE KNIFE CO. (Bridgeport, CT)	Presto [H], Commando	c.1925–1945	★★
GEORGE TRITCH HDW. CO. (Denver, CO)	made by Ulster	c.1910	★★
GEORGE WOLSTENHOLME (Sheffield)		c.1745–1775	★★★★
GEORGE WOODHEAD & SON (Sheffield)	G. W.*I.	c.1845–1870s	★★★★
GEORGE WOSTENHOLM (Sheffield)	I*XL, Oil The Joints	c.1930s–1977	★★★
GEORGE WOSTENHOLM (Sheffield)	Rockingham Works	1815–1848	★★★★
GEORGE WOSTENHOLM (Sheffield)	I*XL, ENGLAND on blade	c.1891–1971	★★★
GEORGE WOSTENHOLM (Sheffield)	I*XL Celebrated	c.1860s–1890s	★★★★
GEORGE WOSTENHOLM (Sheffield)	I*XL Washington Works	1848–1870s	★★★★
GEORGE WOSTENHOLM (Sheffield)	I*XL (see other listings)	1745–c.1971	★★★
GEORGE WOSTENHOLM IMPROVED CUTLERY (Sheffield)		c.1832–1837	★★★★
GEORGE WOSTENHOLM & SON CUTLERY CO.(Sheffield)		c.1815–1971	★★★
GEORGE WOSTENHOLM & SONS (RKS)	Washington Works	c.1848–1890	★★★★
GEORGE W. KORN (New York, NY)		c.1880–1925	★★★
GEO. SCHRADE KNIFE CO. (Bridgeport, CT)	Wire Jack knives	c.1940–1956	★★

Brands/Manufacturers/Location	*Reference or Trademarks*	*Dates*	*Collectibility*
GEO. W. MILLER (Meriden, CT)	co-owner of Miller Bros.	c.1886	★★★
GERBER (Portland, OR)	Legendary Blades	1939–present	★★
GERBER-SAKAI (Seki City, Japan)	Silver Knight	1977–1995	★★
GERBR HOPPE (Germany)	Hoppe Bros.	1919–present	★
GERLACH	Poland		★
GERMANIA CUTLERY CO. (Germany)	O.N.B. on bolster, Kastor	1896–1938	★
GERMO MFG. CO. (Germany)			★
GERSON CO. (Germany)		c.1950–1970	★
GESCO (Japan/Ireland)		c.1970–1980	★
GIANT GRIP			★
GIESEN & FORSTHOFF (Solingen)	G(man)F. Timor	1920–present	★
GILBERT (Sheffield)	Saville Works	c.1900	★
GITSNIFE	Gits Bros. Mfg. Co	1923–1950	★★
GITS RAZOR NIFE (Chicago, IL)	by Gits Molding Co.	c.1938	★
GLADSTONE			★
GLASNER & BARZEN (Germany)			★
GLEN FALL CUTLERY CO. (England)		c.1898	★★
GLOBE CUTLERY CO. (New York, NY)	Pat. 4-25-05	c.1922	★★
GLOBRISMEN (Germany)			★
GOLD SEAL	F. M. O'Brian	c.1927–1948	★
GOLD TOP (N. Attlebury MA)	P. J. Cummings	c.1924–1948	★
GOLDEN GATE CUTLERY CO. (San Francisco, CA)	Baker & Hamilton	c.1890s	★★★
GOLDEN RULE CUTLERY CO. (Chicago, IL)	G. R. C. Co. or G. R. K.	1911–c.1924	★★★
GOODELL CO.	Antrim, NH	1913–1948	★★
GRACE BROS. (Germany)	Graef & Schmidt		★
GRAEF & SCHMIDT (New York, NY)	Welkut, Spider logo	1883–c.1948	★★
GRAHAMSVILLE CUTLERY	Grahamsville, NY	c.1900–1920	★★
GRAND LEADER (Germany)			★
GRAVELEY & WREAKS (New York, NY)	importer, retailer	1830–1837	★★★★
GRAY & DUDLEY HARDWARE CO. (Nashville, TN)	"Washington," "Hermitage"	1895–1938	★★
GRIFFON (New York, NY)	Griffon XX. Carbomagnetic	c.1918–1966	★★
GRIFFON XX (Worchester, MA)	Griffon Cutlery Works	c.1918–1966	★★
GROVE MFG. CO. (Chicago, IL)		c.1940–1960	★
GUSTAV FELIX (Solingen)	Gloria-Werke	1850–present	★
GUTTMAN CUTLERY CO. (Mount Vernon, NY)	Explorer; Edge; G. C. CO.	1947–1997	★
GUY M. THOMPSON. (Minneapolis, MN)	probably Thompson Hdwe. Co.	1910–1922	★
G. C. KNAUTH	Spring Valley, NY	c.1900–1941	★★
G. D. ABRAMS & SON (Wayland, NY)	Blue Bird	c.1920–1939	★
G. DUNBAR (Germany)		c.1901	★
G. HANNESFAHR		1684–present	★
G. IBBERSON (Sheffield)	violin logo	1700–1988	★★★
G. H. LAWRENCE (Sheffield)	Laurel	c.1919–1952	★
G. OR H. CROOKES & CO. (Sheffield)		c.1836–1867	★★
G. R. C. CO. (Chicago, IL)	Golden Rule Cutlery Co.	c.1911–1924	★★★
G. R. SPRINGER	Kansas City, MO	c.1894–1906	★★
G. TIEMANN	New York	1826–present	★
G. WOODHEAD WARRANTED (Sheffield)		1850–1876	★★★★
G. W. & H. HDWE. CO. (St. Louis, MO)	Geller-Ward-Hosner Hdwe. Co.	c.1903–1937	★★
HACKET-WALTER GATES	Minnesota hdwr. dist.	1902–1912	★★

Brands/Manufacturers/Location	*Reference or Trademarks*	*Dates*	*Collectibility*
HALE BROTHERS (Sheffield)	horse head logo	c.1871–1907	★★
HALL			★
HAMMER BRAND (Walden, NY)	New York Knife Co.	c.1878–1932	★★★
HAMMER BRAND (Providence, RI)	Imperial	c.1936–present	★
HAPPY JACK	Chuck Garlits, maker	1987–1889	★
HARCO	by Harwi Hardware	1875–1915	★★
HARGREAVES SMITH & CO. (Sheffield)		c.1866–1920	★★
HARRIS BROS. SHEFFIELD	(Chicago, IL)	c.1920–1940	★★
HARRIS BROS (Chicago, IL)		c.1915–1926	★★
HARRISON BROTHERS & HOWSON (Sheffield)	Alpha, crown logo	c.1853–1919	★★★
HART CUTLERY CO. (New York, NY)	probably by Camillus	c.1920s	★
HARTKOPT & CO. (Solingen)		1855–1957	★
HARTFORD CUTLERY CO. (Duluth, MN)	Marshall Wells Hdwe.	c.1928	★
HARTFORD CUTLERY CO. (Tariffville, CT)		c.1880	★★★
HARWI	Harco, hdwe. distributor	1875–1915	★★
HASSAM BROTHERS (Boston, MA)	formerly N. Hunt & Co.	c.1853–1872	★★★★
HATCH CUTLERY CO. (Bridgeport, CT)	moved to Michigan and Wisconsin	1885–1899	★★★★
HAWTHORNE CUTLERY CO. (Germany)		c.1900–1920	★
HAYNES STELLITE	Kokomo, IN	1911–1919	★★★
HAYWARD KEY KNIFE	Empire	1856–1930	★★
HEATHCOTE (England)	Shefield	c.1893	★★
HEINRICH KAUFMANN & SOHNE (Solingen)	Mercator, K55K, Indiawerk	1856–1995	★
HELLER BROS. CO.	Newark, NJ	1900–1930	★★
HEMMING BROS. (New Haven, CT)	had operated Eagle Knife Co.	1923–1924	★★
HEN & ROOSTER (Solingen)	Carl Bertram	1872–1975	★★★
HEN & ROOSTER (Solingen)	A. G. Russell	1975–1980	★★★
HEN & ROOSTER (Solingen)	by Robt. Klaas for Frost Cutlery	1881–present	★★
HENCKELS INTERNATIONAL (Solingen)	Half Twin with halberd	c.1970s	★
HENDINGTAN & SONS ESHILSTUNA	Sweden		★
HENKLE & JOYCE HDW. CO.	Lincoln, NE	c.1900–1934	★★
HENRICH BOKER (Solingen)	Tree Brand, Arbolito	1868–present	★★
HENRY BARGE (Sheffield)		c.1850	★★★
HENRY COWLISHAW (Hartford, CT)	"The Pearl"	1881–1911	★★★★
HENRY HARRINGTON	Cutler to the People	1818–1876	★★★★
HENRY HOBSON & SONS (Sheffield)	Express	c.1860s	★★★
HENRY ROGERS SONS & CO. (Sheffield)	H.R.S.& CO./flag/crown	c.1880–c.1930	★★★
HENRY SEARS 1865 (St. Paul, MN)	Farwell-Ozmun-Kirk	c.1897–1959	★★
HENRY SEARS CO.	Prussia		★★
HENRY SEARS & CO. (Chicago, IL)		1865–1878	★★★
HENRY SEARS & SON (Chicago, IL)	(1865) Farwell Ozmun Kirk	1878–c.1959	★★
HENRY TAYLOR (Sheffield)	Acorn	c.1858–1927	★★★
HERBERT M. SLATER (Sheffield)	Venture, Bee Hive, H. G. Long	1853–1993	★★
HERBERT ROBINSON (Sheffield)	Grinder logo	c.1873	★★
HERDER & CO. (Germany)		c.1872–1992	★★
HERDER'S	Philadelphia, PA	1847–1992	★★
HERMITAGE CUTLERY (Nashville, TN)	Gray & Dudley Hdwe.	c.1895–1927	★

Brands/Manufacturers/Location	*Reference or Trademarks*	*Dates*	*Collectibility*
HERMS(Germany)		1908–1913	★
HIBBARD (Chicago, IL)	Hibbard, Spencer, Bartlett	c.1913–1927	★★★
HIBBARD SPENCER BARTLETT & CO. (Chicago, IL)	O.V.B., Tru Value	1855–c.1960	★★★
HICKORY (Duluth, MN)	Kelly How Thomson	c.1902–1947	★
HIGH CARBON STEEL (Camillus, NY)	Camillus made for Sears and/or Montgomery-Ward	1928–1940	★
HIKE CUTLERY CO. (Solingen)	Hickut, Hikenife	c.1923–1924	★
HILLARD & CHAPMAN	Glasgow Scotland	c.1850	★★★
HIT	Colonial U.S.A.	c.1950s	★
HOFFRITZ (New York, NY)	some made by Schrade	c.1930–present	★
HOLLEY	Lakeville	c.1854–1930s	★★★★
HOLLEY MFG. CO.	Lakeville, CT	c.1846–1930s	★★★★
HOLLEY & CO.	Salisbury, CT	1844–1846	★★★★
HOLLINGER	Fremont, OH	1905–1958	★★
HOLLINGSWORTH KNIFE CO. (Kane, PA)	formerly Kane Cutlery	c.1916–1930	★★★
HOLUB	Sycamore, IL	1974	★
HOME	Holley & Merwin, Lakeville, CT	1850	★★★★
HONK FALLS KNIFE CO. (Napanoch, NY)	old Napanoch factory	1921–1929	★★★★
HORNET	Simmons Hdwe brand	c.1891–1960	★★
HORNIS CUTLERY CO.			★
HOWARD BROS. (Germany)		1885–1905	★
HOWARD CUTLERY CO. (New York, NY)	Owl, Howard— (C. B. Barker Co.)	c.1890–1905	★★★
HOWARD W. SHIPLEY (Philadelphia, PA)	Coquanoc Works	c.1876	★★★
HOWES CUTLERY CO. (Germany)		c.1900	★
HUBERTUS (Solingen)	Kuno Ritter	1932–present	★★
HUDSON KNIFE CO. (Germany)		c.1927	★
HUDSON VALLEY CUTLERY CO.	New York	c.1890s	★★★
HUDSON'S BAY COMPANY (Winnipeg, MB)	pocketknives date to c.1880	1670–present	★★★
HUGAL 7 WORKS (Germany)			★
HUGO KOLLER (Solingen)	Eagle	1861–1980s	★
HUGO LINDER (Solingen)	Deltawerk	1878–1957	★★
HUMASON & BECKLEY (New Britain, CT)	H. & B.	1852–1914	★★★
HUMASON & BECKLEY MFG. CO. (New Britain, CT)	H. & B., sold to L. F. & C. 1912	1852–1916	★★★
HUNKILL-HUNTER	Pittsburgh, PA		★★
HUNTER CUTLERY CO. (Germany)	Radigan-Rich	1905–1907	★
HY KAUFFMANN (Solingen)	"Mercator" and "K55K"	1856–1995	★
H'VILLE KNIFE CO. (Hotchkissville, CT)	Hotchkissville Knife Co.	c.1870s	★★★
H. A. DREER	Philadelphia, PA	c.1900–1910	★
H. BOKER CO.'S CUTLERY/ GERMANY	tree logo	c.1869–1914	★★
H. BOKER & CO./SOLINGEN GERMANY	tree brand on blade back	c.1919–1932	★★
H. BOKER & CO./SOLINGEN GERMANY	tree brand on blade front	c.1932–1950	★★
H. BOKER'S IMPROVED CUTLERY (Newark, NJ)	merged into Broker U.S.A.	1837–1917	★★
H. BOKER & CO IMPROVED CUTLERY	tree on back of tang	c.1920–1930	★★
H. G. LIPSCOMB & CO. (Nashville, TN)	Watauga	1891–1913	★★
H. G. LONG & CO. (Sheffield)		c.1846–1991	★★
H. HOWSEN & SONS			★★
H. H. TAYLOR & BROS. (Sheffield)	(U.S. Navy contractor)	c.1855–1890	★★★

Brands/Manufacturers/Location	*Reference or Trademarks*	*Dates*	*Collectibility*
H. KESCHNER (Germany)	Diamond	c.1920s	★
H. K. CO. (Kane, PA)	Hollingsworth Knife Co.	c.1916–1930	★★★
H. M. SLATER, LTD (Sheffield)	Heaart & Pistol, Crookes	c.1853–1993	★★
H. SEARS MFG. CO. (Chicago, IL)		c.1865–1883	★★★
H. SEYMOUR CUTLERY CO.		c.1865–1917	★
H. S. B. & CO. (Chicago, IL)	Hibbard Spencer Bartlett	1855–1960	★★★
H. UNDERWOOD (London England)	56 Haymarket	c.1820–1900	★★★
H. & B. MFG. (New Britain, CT)	Humason & Beckley	c.1852–1914	★★★
H. & J. W. KING		1857–1876	★
H. & L. MFG. CO.	Bridgeport, CT	c.1930s	★
IBBOTSON BROTHERS & CO. (Sheffield)	Globe	1841–c.1925	★★★
IBBOTSON PEACE & CO. (Sheffield)	became W. K. Peace & Co.	c.1847–1864	★★★
IBBOTSON & SONS (Sheffield)		c.1870s	★★★
IBBOTSON, CHARLES, & CO. (Sheffield)		c.1868–1896	★★★★
IDEAL (Louisville, KY)	I-D-L, Belknap Hdwe. Co.	1890s	★
IDEAL KNIFE CO. (Providence, RI)	IDEAL/U.S.A.	1924–1986	★★
IKCO (U.S.A) Imperial Knife Co.		c.1920s–1940s	★
ILLINOIS CUTLERY CO. (Chicago, IL)	probably made by Golden Rule	c.1911–1912	★★
IMPERIAL			★
IMPERIAL (Germany)	Mexico	c.1980s	★
IMPERIAL KNIFE CO. (Providence, RI)	IKCO, Crown, Hammer	1917–1987	★
IMPERIAL KNIFE ASSOCIATED CO.(Providence, RI)	Schrade, Imperial	1947–present	★
INDIA STEEL WORKS (Louisville, KY)	Belknap Hdwe. Co.	1890–1940	★★
INDIANA CUTLERY CO. (Terre Haute, IN)	Wabash Cutlery Co.	c.1932	★★★
INDUSTRY NOVELTY CO. (Chicago, IL)		1908–1917	★★
INTERNATIONAL CUTLERY CO.	Clauss Cutlery Co.	c.1920s	★★
INTRINSIC JOHN MILNER & CO. (Sheffield)		1850–1860	★
IROQUOIS CUTLERY CO. (Utica, NY)	Utica Cutlery Co.	c.1930–1940	★
IROS	Keen, NY	1924–1925	★
IRVING CUTLERY CO. (Germany)		1926–1927	★
ISAAC BARNES (Sheffield)		c.1837–1870	★★★
ISSAC MILNER (Sheffield)		c.1850–1860	★★
IVER JOHNSON S. G. CO. (Boston, MA)	Russell, New York Knife Co.	c.1912	★★
IVY (Germany)	S. Hecht & Son	1900–1901	★
I*XL (Sheffield)	George Wostenholm	1890–1971	★★★
I-KUT (Louisville, KY)	Belknap Hdwe. Co.	c.1898–1907	★
I. ELLIS & SONS LTD. (England)	Primus	1839–1932	★★
I. K. CO. OR IKCO (Providence, RI)	Imperial Knife Co.	1920s–1940s	★
I. MANSON (Sheffield)		1800s	★★
I. Wilson (Sheffield)	"Green River"	1750–1952	★★
I.N.C. CO. (Cedar Rapids, IA)	Iowan Novely Cutlery Co.	c.1910s	★★
I. & J. MFG. CO. (Plainfield, NJ)	Shur-Lock	c.1950	★
I. G. ELY CO. (Atlanta GA)	Elyte	c.1960–1980	★
JACK KNIFE BEN (Chicago, IL)	Benjamin Chon	1887–1940s	★★★
JACK KNIFE SHOP (Chicago, IL)	Union Stockyard	c 1900s	★★★
JACKMASTER (Providence, RI)	Imperial Knife Co.	1938–present	★
JACKSON KNIFE & SHEAR CO.	Fremont, OH	c.1900–1914	★★
JACK-O-MATIC (Providence, RI)	made by Imperial Knife	1943–1958	★
JACOBY & WESTER	New York	c.1891–1904	★★★
JAEGER BROS. (Marinette, WI)	Aerial Cutlery Co.	c.1912–1944	★★
JAMES & LOWE (Sheffield)	bowies stamped IX*L	1945–1985	★★

Brands/Manufacturers/Location	*Reference or Trademarks*	*Dates*	*Collectibility*
JAMES BARBER (Sheffield)	Era	1870–1880s	★★
JAMES BARLOW & SON (Sheffield)		c.1828–1856	★★★
JAMES BODEN (Sheffield)		c.1860	★★
JAMES BURNAND & SONS (Sheffield)	Indian logo, Self Defence	c.1865–1970s	★★
JAMES CRANSHAW	successor to Nowill & Kippax	c.1826	★★★
JAMES JOHNSON (Sheffield)		c.1818–1853	★★
JAMES RODGERS (Sheffield)		c.1830s–1950s	★★★
JAMES W. PRICE	Pine Knott, Belknap Hdwe. Co.		★★
JEAN CASE	Little Valley, NY	1928–1948	★★★★
JEFFREY(Germany)	by C. Bertram	c.1971	★★
JENSEN-KING BYRD CO.	Spokane, WA, hdwe. dist.	c.1900–1930	★★
JET KNIFE CORP.	New York NY	1947–1980s	★
JETTER & SCHEERER (Germany)		c.1880–1932	★★
JET-AIRE CORP. (Paterson, NJ)	G-96	1973–present	★
JIM BOWIE (Solingen)	Carl Schlieper	1972–1975	★
JIM DANDY		c.1920–1940	★
JOHN ALDEN	Eisenstadt Mfg. Co	c.1940–1950	★
JOHN ASHMORE (Philadelphia, PA)	manufacturer	1832–1858	★★★★
JOHN ASKHAM (New York, NY)	Toboggan, Sheffield made	1856–1920s	★★★
JOHN BAKER (Sheffield)	"Real Phoenix"	1837–1953	★★
JOHN BARBER (Sheffield)		1810–1834	★★★
JOHN BARBER & SON (Sheffield)		1834–c.1852	★★★
JOHN BEDFORD & SONS	Defiance, bear logo, "in mind"	c.1865–present	★★
A. BELKNAP	St. Johnsbury, VT, blacksmiths	c.1839–1883	
JOHN BLYDE (Sheffield)	Genius	c.1875	★★★
JOHN BROWN (Sheffield)		c.1830–1880s	★★★
JOHN CHATILLION & SONS (New York, NY)		c.1894–1937	★★★
JOHN D. CHEVALIER (New York, NY)	bowie-type knives	1835–1872	★★★★
JOHN CLARKE & SON (Sheffield)	Wm. Rodgers, John Holmes	1848–1980	★★★
JOHN ENGSTROM (Eskilstuna Sweden)	Wiebusch import	1874–c.1893	★★
JOHN FARR (Sheffield)		c.1821–1852	★★
JOHN HINCHCLIFFE (Sheffield)		c.1850	★★★
JOHN HOLMES & CO. (Sheffield)	sold to J. Clarke before 1900	1860–present	★★
JOHN JOWETT (Sheffield)		c.1870s	★★
JOHN KAY	New Haven, CT	c.1857	★★★
JOHN KENYON & CO. (Sheffield)	Fulton, Fulltone, IL	c.1870–1920	★★
JOHN McCLORY & SONS (Sheffield)	Scotia, Thistlelogo	c.1870–present	★★
JOHN NEWTON (Sheffield)	H. Boker, Newark, NJ	c.1906	★★
JOHN NOWILL & SONS (Sheffield)	Krosskeys, *D	c.1848–present	★★★
JOHN PETTY & SON (Sheffield)		1858–1953	★★
JOHN PRIMBLE (Louisville, KY)	Belknap Hdwe. Co.	1940–1986	★★
JOHN PRITZIAFF KNIFE CO. (Milwaukee, WI)	Everkeen	c.1850–1957	★★
JOHN SALM (Torrance, CA)	DeLuxe	1918–1935	★★
JOHN SELLERS & SONS (Sheffield)	Signal	1820–c.1900	★★
JOHN WALTERS & CO. (Sheffield)	Globe Works	c.1846–1862	★★
JOHN WATTS (Sheffield)	"Estb. 1765"	c.1855–present	★★
JOHN M. HOBSON (Sheffield)		c.1840s–1850s	★★
JOHN WEISS & SONS	London, England	1878–present	★★★
JOHN WILTON (Sheffield)			★★
JOHNNY MUSKRAT	Ulster trademark	1920–1940	★★
JONATHAN CROOKES (Sheffield)	Heart and Pistol	c.1780–1827	★★★
JONATHAN CROOKES & SON (Sheffield)	sold to H. Slater 1947	1827–present	★★
JONATHAN HALL (Sheffield)	I. Hall	1795–1830	★★★
JONES & SON (Germany)		c.1970	★
JOSEPH ALLEN & SONS (Sheffield)	NON-XLL	1886–1947	★★

Brands/Manufacturers/Location	*Reference or Trademarks*	*Dates*	*Collectibility*
JOSEPH ELLIOTT & SONS (Sheffield)		1795–present	★★
JOSEPH FEIST (Germany)		1898–1924	★
JOSEPH FENTON & SONS (Sheffield)		c.1860	★★
JOSEPH GARDNER (Shelburne Falls, MA)	Gardner 1876	1876–1883	★★★
JOSEPH HAYWOOD (Sheffield)	Tea-kettle logo	c.1850–1869	★★★
JOSEPH JAEGER (Los Angeles, CA)	Palm	c.1891–1909	★★
JOSEPH LAW (Sheffield)	LIBERTY on bolster	c.1820	★★★
JOSEPH LINGARD (Sheffield)	I-Fly Shuttle logo	c.1842–1925	★★
JOSEPH RODGERS & SONS (Sheffield)		c.1837–1901	★★★★
JOSEPH RODGERS & SONS (Sheffield)	Cutlers to His Majesty	c.1901–1948	★★★★
JOSEPH RODGERS & SON (Sheffield)	No. 6 Northfolk St.	1682–1971	★★★★
JOSEPH SWIFT& CO.	Sheffield	c.1893	★★
JOSEPH THORPE (Sheffield)		c.1853–1873	★★
JOSH. BEAL & SONS (Sheffield)	Endure, Sound, Boar	c.1870s–1890s	★★
JUDSON CUTLERY CO. (New York, NY)		c.1900–1940	★
JUSTUS BIERHOLFF (Solingen)		c.1901–1930	★
J. AMBACHER (Sandusky, OH)	Pat. April 27, 1880	c.1869–1891	★★
J. A. HENCKELS (Solingen)	Twinworks	1731–present	★★★
J. A. SCHMIDT & SOHNE (Solingen)	Dreiturm (Three Spires)	1829–present	★★
J.B.F. CHAMPLIN & SON	Little Valley, NY	1882–1886	★★★★
J.B.F. CHAMPLIN (Little Valley, NY)	"Warranted" "Galvanic"	1880–1886	★★★★
J. BUNGER & SONS CELEBRATED CUTLERY		c.1876–1900	★★
J. COPLEY & SONS (Sheffield)	XX	c.1876–1924	★★
J. CURLEY & BROS. (New York, NY)		c.1864–1921	★★
J.C.N. CO. (Jersey City, NJ)	made by G. Schrade	c.1940	★
J. DIXON CUTLERY CO. (Germany)	XTRA on blade	c.1920	★
J. DUNLAP (New York, NY)	Schmachtenberg	1916–c.1939	★
J. DUNN (New York, NY)		c.1879–1922	★★
J. D. CASE (Little Valley, NY)	Case Mfg. Co.	c.1898–1899	★★★★
J. E. BASSETT & CO.	New Haven, CT	c.1784–1897	★★
J. E. MERGOTT CO.	Newark, NJ	1888–1950	★★
J. H. ANDREW & CO., LTD. (Sheffield)		c.1860	★★
J. H. SUTCLIFFE & CO. (Louisville, KY)	Hickory Hand Forged	c.1900	★★
J. H. THOMPSON CUTLER LTD. (Sheffield)		c.1953	★★
J. K. ABBOT & CO.	Oxford, ME	c.1860	★★★
J. KOESTER & SONS (Ohligs Germany)	imported by Kastor	c.1930s	★
J. LEE	Medway, MA	c.1830	★★★★
J. M. SCHMID & SON	Providence, RI	1857–1964	★★
J. M. ABBOT & CO. (Welchville, ME)	"Thyme" in horse logo	c.1860s	★★
J. M. THOMPSON HDW. CO. (Minneapolis, MN)	Sterling Service	c.1910–1922	★★
J. PRITXLAFF HDWE. CO. (Milwaukee, WI)	Everkeen	c.1850–1957	★
J. P. SNOW CO. (Chicago, IL)		c.1861	★★
J. RUSSELL & CO. GREEN RIVER WKS. (Turner Falls, MA)	R(arrow)	1834–present	★★★

Brands/Manufacturers/Location	*Reference or Trademarks*	*Dates*	*Collectibility*
J. RUSSELL & CO. GRW	Turner Falls, MA	c.1884–1941	★★★
J. R. TORREY RAZOR CO.	Worchester, MA	1858–1963	★★
J. S. HOLLER (New York, NY)	A. Blaich	c.1867–1906	★★
J. T. MOUNT & CO.	Newark, NJ	1885–1911	★
J. W. BILLINGS (Sheffield)	X. X. L. Cutlery	c.1880s	★★
J. W. HICKEY & SONS (Solingen)		c.1976–1985	★
J. Y. COWLISHAW (Sheffield)	maker of silver fruit knives	1853–1927	★★★
KA-BAR (Olean, NY)	Kabar, Union Cutlery Co.	1923–1951	★★★★
KA-BAR (Olean, NY)	KA-BAR, KA-BAR/U.S.A.	1951–c.1966	★★★
KA-BAR UNION CUTLERY CO. OLEAN	Little Valley, NY	c.1923–1951	★★★
KA-BAR/OLEAN N.Y. (Olean, NY)	KA-BAR/UNION CUT. CO.	1923–1950	★★★★
KA-BAR/UNION CUT. CO. (Olean, NY)	Union Cutlery Co.	1923–1950	★★★★
KA-BAR/U.S.A. (Olean, NY)	Kabar Cutlery Co.	1923–present	★★★
KA-BAR/(NUMBER) USA (Olean, NY)	Kabar (Cole National)	c.1975–1997	★
KAMP CUTLERY CO. (Germany)		c.1910	★
KAMP HAUSER (Germany)		c.1930s	★
KAMP KING (Providence, RI)	Imperial Knife Co.	1935–present	★
KANE CUTLERY CO. (Kane, PA)	became Hollingsworth	c.1910–1916	★★★
KANE GERMANY (Solingen)	made by C. Bertram	c.1971	★
KAN-DER (Germany)			★
KEEN CUTLERY CO. (New York)	made by Napanoch	c.1910	★★★
KEEN CUTTER (VALTEST) (Chicago, IL)	Schrade Cutlery Co.	1960–1965	★
KEEN EDGE (Nashville, TN)	Keith Simmons & Co.	1901–1927	★★
KEEN KUTTER (St. Louis, MO)	E. C. Simmons	c.1870–1940	★★★
KEEN KUTTER (St. Louis, MO)	Shapleigh	c.1940–1960	★★
KEENER EDGE (Knoxville, TN)	C. M. McClung Hdw.	c.1932	★★
KEENIFE	Boston, MA	c.1939	★
KEENWELL MFG. CO. (Olean, NY)	by Union Cutlery Co.	c.1910	★★
KEITH SIMMONS & CO. (Nashville, TN)	Keen Edge	c.1901–1927	★★
KELLY HOW THOMSON CO. (Duluth, MN)	Hickory	1902–1947	★★★
KENDALL MFG. CO. (Camillus, NY)	Winsted, CT	c.1948	★
KENT/NY CITY/USA	made for F. W. Woolworth Co.	c.1934	★
KERSHAW (Portland, OR)	by Kai Cutlery, Japan	1974–1998	★
KEYES CUTLERY CO.	Unionville, CT	prior to 1893	★★★
KEYSTONE CUTLERY CO.	Milwaukee, WI	c.1925–1938	★★
KEYSTONE KNIFE CO.	Titusville, PA	c.1925–1938	★★★
KHYBER (Cleveland, OH)	Cole National (Kabar)	1980s	★
KINFOLKS INC. (Little Valley, NY)	Kinfolks, K. I., Jean Case	1925–c.1951	★★★
KING CUTLERY CO. (Germany)			★
KING HARDWARE CO. (Atlanta, GA)	King Bee	1886–1952	★
KINGS KWALITY	U.S.A.		★
KINGSTON (Ellenville, NY)	Joint venture by Ulster & Imperial	1943–1947	★
KINGSTON USA (Ellenville, NY)	D. Divine & Sons & Ulster	c.1915–1958	★
KIPSI KUT (Poughkeepsie, NY)	Poughkeepsie Cutlery trademark	c.1918–1925	★★
KIRKAN & CO. (Germany)			★
KISSING CRANE (Solingen)	Robt. Klass	1896–1988	★★
KIT CARSON	trademark by Imperial	1969–1971	★
KLICKER (St. Louis, MO)	Shapleigh Hdwe.	c.1958	★
KLOSTERMEIER BROS.	Atchison, KS	c.1900	★★
KNAPP & SPENCER (Sioux City, IA)	Regent	c.1895–1905	★★
KNIFE CRAFTERS	H. C. James	c.1944–1945	★★
KNOXALL	Simmons Hdwe. brand	c.1939–1960	★★
KOELLER BROS. (Solingen)	F. Koeller & Co.	c.1905–1927	★★
KOELLER & SCHMIDT	Milwaukee, WI	c.1884–1916	★★
KOESTER & SONS		1910–1930	★
KORN'S PATENT	G. W. Korn, New York	1880–1919	★★★

Brands/Manufacturers/Location	*Reference or Trademarks*	*Dates*	*Collectibility*
KREMITZ			★
KRUSE & BAHLMAN HDWE. CO. (Cincinnati, OH)	K. & B., Cut Sure	c.1896–1962	★★
KRUSIUS BROTHERS (New York, NY)	K. B. Extra, Primrose	c.1888–1927	★★
KRUSIUS CUTLERY CORP. (Germany)		c.1856–1983	★★
KUNDE & CO. (Germany)		current	★
KUTMASTER (Utica, NY)	Utica Cutlery Co.	1937–present	★
KUTWELL (Olean, NY)	Union Cutlery	c.1930s	★★
KWIK CUT (St. Louis, MO)	Sears brand by Camillus	1930–1941	★
K. & B. CUTLERY CO. (Cincinnati, OH—made in Germany)	Kut Sure, Kruse & Bahlman Hdwe.	1884–1962	★★
LABELLE CUTLERY WORKS (Bridgeport, CT)	formerly Frary & Son	c.1884–1888	★★★
LACKAWANNA CUTLERY CO. (Nicholson, PA)	formerly Eureka Cutlery	1917–c.1930	★★★
LAFAYETTE CUTLERY CO.	New York	c.1910–1920s	★
LAKESIDE CUTLERY CO. (Chicago, IL)	Challenge, Montgomery Ward	c.1922–1928	★★★
LAKOTA CORP.	Riverton WY	c.1980s–present	★
LALLI BROS. CELEBRATED CUTLERY	Germany		★★
LAMSON & GOODNOW (Shelburne Falls, MA)	pocketknives date to c.1870s	1844–present	★★
LANDERS FRARY & CLARK (New Britain, CT)	Universal	1863–1954	★★
LANDIS BROTHERS (Canton, OH)	Pat. Nov. 11, 1879	c.1879	★★★
LANGSTAFF HDWE. CO.	Prussia	c.1910	★
LAUTERJUNG & CO. (Solingen)	Tiger Brand, Cervo	1813–present	★★★
LAUTERJUNG & SOHN (Solingen)	now Puma-Werk	1769–1890s	★★★
LAW BROTHERS	Celebrated Cutlery	c.1890s	★★★
LAWTON CUTLERY CO. (Chicago, IL)		c.1895	★★
LAYMAN CAREY CO.	Independence, IN	1865–1920	★★
LEADER	U.S.A.	1903–present	★
LEE HARDWARE CO.	Salina, KS		★★
LEHENBERG (Solingen)			★
LENOX CUTLERY CO. (Germany)		1909–1920	★
LEVERING KNIFE CO.	New York	1900–1930	★★
LEVI ABBOT (Welchville, ME)	J. M. Abbot & Co	c.1860s	★★
LIBERTY KNIFE CO.	New Haven, CT	c.1919–1925	★★
LINCOLN NOVELTY CO.		1921–1923	★
LINDER & CO. (Solingen)	Junkerwerk	1887–present	★★
LION CUTLERY CO. (Sheffield)		1903–1929	★
LIPSCHULTZ (Nashville, TN—made in Solingen)	by Bertram, Mutt	c.1975	★★
LITTLE VALLEY KNIFE ASSOCIATION (Little Valley, NY)	L.V.K.C.	1900–1905	★★★
LOCKWOOD BROS. (Sheffield)	C + X, Pampa, Rhea logo	c.1849–1993	★★
LOCKWOOD LUETKEMEYER HENRY (Cleveland, OH)	Thelco, L.L.H. Co.	1848–c.1970	★★
LONG	Oxford, England	c.1880	★★
LORD BROS.		c.1880s	★★
LUBOT CO.	Hamilton or Cincinnati, OH	c.1930s–1950s	★
LUKE FIRTH (Sheffield)		c.1850	★★
LUNA (Germany)	A. Feist & Co.	1928–1948	★
LUKE OATES	arrow, heart and bugle logo	c.1800–1850	★★★
LUX (Solingen)	imported by Louis Lux	c.1920	★
LUXRITE	Hollywood, CA		★
LYON CUTLERY CO.	Bridgeport, CT	1880s	★★★
L. BRADLEY & CO. (Naugatuck, CT)	Salem became Naugatuck	1841–1876	★★★★
L.C.A. HARDWARE	Omaha, NE	1881–1923	★

Brands/Manufacturers/Location	*Reference or Trademarks*	*Dates*	*Collectibility*
L. F. & C. CO. (New Britian, CT)	Landers, Frary & Clark	c.1912–1950	★★
L. K. CO. (New Britain, CT)	Liberty Knife Co.	1919–1925	★
L. L. BEAN	Freeport, ME	1912–present	★
L. L. H. CO. (Cleveland, OH)	Lockwood Luetkemeyer Henry	c.1911	★
L.V.K. ASSN. (Little Valley, NY)	Little Valley Knife Association	1900–1905	★★★★
MADDEN & SONS (Sheffield)		c.1900–1930	★★
MADE IN USA	Sears & Roebuck by Camillus	1924–1941	★
MAGNETIC CUTLERY CO. (Philadelphia, PA)	Otto and Frank Maussner	c.1900–1932	★★
MAHER & GROSH (Toledo, OH)	to Clyde, OH 1963	1877–1988	★★★
MAJESTIC CUTLERY CO. (Germany)	Matthews & Lively	c.1910	★★
MANCHESTER	USA	c.1920s	★★
MANHATTAN CUTLERY CO. (Sheffield)	H. Boker's, Newark, NJ	c.1868–1906	★★
MAPPIN BROTHERS (Sheffield)	Queen's Cutlery Works, Sun	c.1841–1902	★★★★
MANSON (Sheffield)	Dirks and Bowies	c.1860s	★★★
MAPPIN & WEBB (Sheffield)	Trustworthy, Sun	c.1835–1964	★★★★
MARBLE'S SAFETY AXE CO. (Gladstone, MI)	knives c.1900–1942	1898–present	★★★★
MARSH BROS. (Sheffield)	W. & T. Marsh, Pond Works	c.1850–1947	★★★
MARSHALL FIELD & CO. (Germany)		c.1909–1923	★
MARSHALL WELLS HDWE. CO. (Duluth, MN)	M.W.H. Co., Zenith	1888–1963	★★★
MARSHES & SHEPHERD (Sheffield)	Pond Works, Marsh Bros.	1818–1850	★★★
MARTIN BROS. & NAYLOR (Sheffield)		c.1849–1854	★★
MARTIN L. BRADFORD & SON (Boston, MA)	became Bradford & Anthony	1845–1856	★★★
MARX & CO.		c.1876	★★
MASON & SONS		1870–1871	★★
MASSILLON CUTLERY CO. (Massillon, OH)	was Ohio Cutlery Co.	c.1924	★★
MAUSSNER (Germany)		1900–1932	★
MAYER (Germany)	diamond logo	c.1920	★
MCINTOSH HDWE. CO. (Cleveland, OH)	Heather; became L.L.H.	1875–1911	★★
MCL HDWE. CO. (Waco TX)	by S & M for McLendon Hdwe.	c.1890–1945	★★
MERCATOR (Solingen)	Heinrich Kauffmann	c.1856–present	★
MERIDAN CUTLERY CO. (Meriden, CT)	Southington, Valley Forge	1855–c.1925	★★
MERIDEN KNIFE CO. (Meriden, CT)	made for Miller Bros.	1917–c.1932	★★
MERRIMAC CUTLERY CO. (Germany)	Knox-All on blade	c.1939	★★
METROPOLITAN CUTLERY CO. (New York, NY)	Commander	c.1918–1951	★
MILLER BROS. CUT. CO.	Meriden, CT	c.1872–1926	★★★
MILLER BROTHERS	Yalesville, CT	c.1863–1926	★★★
MILLER, SLOSS & SCOTT (San Francisco, CA)	Stiletto, Pacific Hdwe. & Steel	1891–1901	★★★
MISSOULA MERCANTILE CO. (Missoula MT)	Buffalo brand	1885–c.1972	★★★
MITCHELL & CO. LTD.	Manchester, England	c.1910	★★
MIZZOO CUTLERY CO. (St. Louis)	Norvell-Shapleigh	c.1906–1918	★★
MONROE CUT. CO. (Germany)	Monroe Hdwe., Feather Edge	c.1904–1916	★
MONUMENTAL CUTLERY CO. (New York, NY)	F. Wiebusch	c.1874–1893	★★
MOORE HANDLEY HDWE. CO. (Birmingham AL)	Champion, America's Best	c.1882–1989	★★
MORLEY BROS. (Saginaw, MI)	Wedgeway Cutlery Co.	1863–present	★★
MORRIS CUTLERY CO.	Morris, IL	1882–c.1930	★★★
MOSLEY CUTLERY CO.		c.1870s–1960	★
MOUNT VERNON CUTLERY CO.		c.1890	★★

Brands/Manufacturers/Location	*Reference or Trademarks*	*Dates*	*Collectibility*
MSA (Gladstone, MI)	Marbles Safety Axe Co.	c.1898–1942	★★★★
MUELLER & SCHMIDT (Solingen)	Five arrows around circle	1896–present	★
MUMBLEY PEG (Camillus, NY)	Camillus brand	c.1937–1948	★★★
MUTUAL CUTLERY CO.	Canton, OH	1921–1926	★
M. B. CO.		1852–1983	★★★
M. F. & S. (England)		c.1913	★★
M. F. ROBESON (England) (Elmira, NY)		1880–1884	★★★
M. KLEIN & SONS (Chicago, IL)		c.1911–present	★
M. MOGAL, INC. (Germany)		1924–1951	★
M. PRESSMAN & CO.	New York		★★
M. PRICE (San Francisco, CA)	bowies, dirks, tableware	1856–1889	★★★★
M.S.A. CO. (Gladstone, MI)	Marble's Safety Axe	1898–1911	★★★★
M. S. LTD. XX (Canada)	Case XX Metal Stamping Ltd.	c.1940s	★★★
M.W.H. CO. (Duluth, MN)	Marshall Wells Hdwe.	1893–1963	★★★
M. & C. CO.	Anvil, Meriden Cut.	1855–1925	★★
NAGLE REBLADE KNIFE CO.	Poughkeepsie, NY	1912–1916	★★★★
NANTUCKET CUTLERY CO (Nantucket, RI)	bow & arrow logo, "B M"	c.1900–1920	★★★
NAPANOCH KNIFE CO. (Napanoch, NY)	became Winchester & Honk Falls	1900–1919	★★★★
NAPANOCH KNIFE CO.	made by J. Cushner	1931–1939	★★★
NASH HARDWARE CO.	Fort Worth, TX	1873–1975	★
NATHAN JOSPEH (San Francisco, CA)	Queen's Own Co.	c.1873–1894	★★★
NATIONAL SILVER CO.	New York		★
NAUGATUCK CUTLERY CO.	Naugatuck, CT	1872–1888	★★★
NAYLOR & SANDERSON (Sheffield)	N & S	c.1810–1830	★★★★
NEEDHAM BROS. (Sheffield)	Repeat, Wiebusch import brand	c.1860–1900	★★★
NEEDHAM, VEALL & TYZACK (Sheffield)	"Taylor Eye Witness"	1895–1975	★★
NEFT SAFETY KNIFE	Newark, NJ	c.1920–1930s	★★★
NELSON KNIFE CO.		c.1894	★
NEVER DULL CUT. CO. (Chicago, IL)	Butler Bros.	c.1896–1940	★
NEW BRITAIN KNIFE CO. (New Britain, CT)	The N. B. Knife Co.	c.1910–1930	★★
NEW CENTURY CUTLERY CO. (Germany)		c.1900	★★
NEW ENGLAND CUTLERY CO.	Wallingford, CT	1852–1860	★★★
NEW ENGLAND KNIFE CO.		c.1910	★★
NEW HAVEN CUTLERY CO. (San Francisco, CA)	Baker & Hamilton, Damascus	c.1890s	★★★
NEW JERSEY KNIFE CO. (Newark, NJ)	American Ace	c.1921	★★
NEW YORK CUTLERY CO. (Gowanda, NY)	became Schatt & Morgan	1890s	★★★
NEW YORK KNIFE CO. (Matteawan, NY)		1852–1856	★★★★
NEW YORK KNIFE CO. (Walden, NY)	Hammer Brand	1856–1931	★★★
NEWTON PREMIER (Sheffield)		1838–present	★
NIFTY (New York, NY)	G. Borgfeldt	c.1913–1914	★
NON-XLL (Sheffield)	Joseph Allen	c.1886–1947	★★
NORMARK (Minneapolis, MN)	Mfd. by E.K.A.	1959–present	★
NORSHARP			★
NORTH AMERICAN KNIFE CO.	Wichita, KS	c.1920s	★★
NORTH WEST CUTLERY CO.		c.1890	★
NORTHFIELD KNIFE CO. (Northfield, CT)	UN-X-LD	1858–1919	★★★
NORTHHAMPTON CUTLERY CO.	Northhampton, VT	1871–present	★★
NORVELL'S BEST (St. Louis, MO)	Norvell-Shapleigh	c.1902–1917	★★

Brands/Manufacturers/Location	*Reference or Trademarks*	*Dates*	*Collectibility*
NORVELL-SHAPLEIGH HDWE. CO. (St. Louis, MO)	Shapleigh Hardware Co.	c.1902–1917	★★
NORWICH CUTLERY CO.			★
NOVELTY CUTLERY CO. (Canton, OH)	Canton Knife Co., A. Vignos	1879–1949	★★★
NOVCO USA	Novelty Cutlery trademark	1917–1948	★★
NOXALL CUTLERY CO. (Germany)	Kastor Bros.	c.1907	★
N. C. CO. (Canton, OH)	Novelty Cutlery Co.	1879–1949	★★★
N. HUNT & CO. (Boston, MA)	sold to Kingman & Hassam	c.1840–1853	★★★
N. Y. KNIFE CO. (Walden, NY)	New York Knife Co.	1856–1931	★★★★
OAK LEAF (St. Louis, MO)	Wm. Enders, Simmons Hdwe. Co.	c.1888–1920	★★★
OAKMAN BROS. (New York, NY)		c.1900	★★
OCCIDENT CUTLERY CO. (Seattle WA)	Seattle Hdwe. Co.	c.1910	★★
ODELL HDWE. CO. (Greensboro, NC)	Southern (cross) Cutlery	1873–1900s	★★
OEHM & CO. (Baltimore, MD)	Some made by Miller Bros.	c.1860–1936	★★
OHIO CUTLERY CO. (Massillon, OH)	O. C. Mfg. Co. Tru-Temper	1919–1923	★★★
OKLAHOMA CITY HARDWARE	Oklahoma City, OK	1901–1951	★★
OLBOS (Germany)	F. Obertz	1915–present	★
OLCUT (Olean, NY)	Olean Cutlery Co.	c.1911–1920s	★★
OLD CUTLER (Providence, RI)	Colonial Knife Co.	c.1978–1986	★★
OLD HICKORY	Ontario Knife Co. trademark	1971–present	★
OLD TIMER (Ellenville, NY)	Schrade Cutlery Co.	1959–present	★
OLEAN CUTLERY CO.	Olcut. Div. of Union Cut.	c.1911–1920s	★★★
OLSEN KNIFE CO. (Howard City, MI)	sheath knives	c.1960–1983	★★
OMEGA (Germany)	Joseph Feist	c.1898–1924	★
ONTARIO KNIFE CO. (Franklinville, NY)	Old Hickory	1889–present	★★
OPINEL (France)	Crowned Hand	c.1890–present	★
ORANGE CUTLERY CO. (Walden, NY)	former Walden Knife employees	1923	★★★
OSGOOD BRAY & CO.	(Three Stars) by Burkinshaw	1800s	★★★
OTHELLO (Solingen)	A. Wingen, Moor's head logo	c.1923–present	★
OVERLAND (Solingen)	Fred Mac Overland	1951–1953	★★
OWL CUTLERY CO. (Sheffield)	C. B. Barker import brand	1880–1910	★★
O. BARNETT TOOL CO. (Newark, NJ)	Patent; H.H.H.	1900–c.1915	★★★
O. D. GRAY & CO.			★★
O.N.B. (Germany)	A. W. Wadsworth & Sons	c.1910	★★★
O.S.T. CUTLERY CO.	Newark, NJ		★
O.V.B. (OUR VERY BEST) (Chicago, IL)	Hibbard, Spencer & Bartlett	1884–1960	★★★
PACIFIC CUTLERY CO. (Los Angeles, CA)	formerly Balisong	1982–1987	★★
PACIFIC HDWE. & STEEL CO. (San Francisco, CA)	Stiletto	1901–1918	★★★
PAL (Germany)	imported by Mailman Bros.	c.1924–1939	★★
PAL BLADE CO. (Plattsburg, NY)	imported by Utica	c.1939–1945	★★
PAL CUTLERY CO. (Plattsburg, NY, and Holyoke, MA)	bought Remington 1940	c.1929–1953	★★
PAPES-THIEBES CUTLERY CO. (St. Louis, MO)	Unitas	c.1903–1929	★★
PARIS BEAD (Chicago, IL)		c.1920s	★
PARISIAN NOVELTY CO. (Chicago, IL)	advertising specialties	c.1905–1985	★
PARKER BROS. (Chattanooga, TN)	made in Japan	c.1980–1983	★★
PARKER CUTLERY CO. (Chattanooga, TN)	Eagle, Parker Bros., Amer. Blade	c.1970–1991	★★
PARKER-EDWARDS CUTLERY CO.	Jacksonville, AL	c.1984–1987	★★
PARKER-FROST CUTLERY CO.	Chattanooga, TN	1976–1978	★★

Brands/Manufacturers/Location	*Reference or Trademarks*	*Dates*	*Collectibility*
PAVIAN-ADAMS CUTLERY CO. (St. Paul, MN)	Summit	1906–c.1920	★★
PAXTON & GALLAGHER (Omaha, NE)	CutAway	c.1864–1959	★★
PEERLESS (Wichita, KS)	Peerless Cutlery Co., importer	1930s	★
PENNSYLVANIA KNIFE CO. (Tidioute, PA)		c.1914–1921	★★
PENN. CUTLERY CO. (Tidioute, PA)		c.1914–1921	★★
PERRY CUTL. CO. (Perry, NY)	Robeson	1919–1929	★★★
PETERS BROS. CELEBRATED CUTLERY (Solingen)		c.1876–1886	★★
PETERS CUTLERY MFG. CO. (Solingen)		c.1876–1886	★★
PETERS CUTLERY CO. (Chicago, IL)		c.1876–1886	★
PHOENIX KNIFE CO. (Phoenix, NY)	was Central City Knife Co.	1892–1916	★★★
PINE KNOT JAS. W. PRICE (Louisville, KY)	Belknap Hdwe. Co., bird logo	1930s	★★★
PLATTS BROS.	Union, NY	1905–1907	★★★★
PLATTS BROTHERS CUTLERY CO.	Andover, NY	1907–c.1911	★★★★
PLATTS N'FIELD (Northfield, CT)	from parts—by Ray Platts	post–1919	★★★
PLI-R-NIF CO. (San Francisco, CA)	San Francisco/Berkley	1905–c.1908	★★★★
POCKETEZE (Rochester, NY)	Robeson	1914–1977	★★★
POTTER-HOY HDWE. CO.	Bellfountain, PA	1865–1900s	★★
POWER KRAFT (Chicago, IL)	made for Montgomery-Ward	c.1939–present	★
PRADEL	France		★
PRATT & CO.		1830–1900s	★★
PRATT, ROPES & WEBB CO. (Meriden, CT)	became Meriden Cutlery	1846–1855	★★★
PRECISE (Suffern, NY)	Deerslayer	1954–present	★
PREMIER (New York & Toronto)	import brand/Germany	1921–1955	★
PREMIER CUTLERY CO. (New York, NY)	Elk, Lifetime	c.1921–1955	★
PRENTISS KNIFE CO. (New York, NY)		c.1910	★★★
PRESS BUTTON KNIFE CO. (Walden, NY)	Geo. Schrade/ Walden Knife Co.	c.1892–1923	★★★
PRESTO (Bridgeport, CT)	George Schrade Knife Co.	c.1925–1945	★★★
PRIBYL BROS. (Chicago, IL)		1880–1905	★★★
PRIMBLE (Louisville, KY)	Belknap Hdwe. Co.	1890–1985	★★
PROGRESS (Sheffield)	Alfred Field	1886–1942	★★
PRONTO (Providence, RI)	Colonial Kinfe Co.	c.1926–1952	★
PROVIDENCE CUTLERY CO.	Providence, RI	c.1890s–1980s	★★
PUMA (Solingen)	was Lauterjung & Sohn	1769–present	★★★
PUTMAN CUTLERY CO.	New Britain, CT	c.1886–1909	★★
P. HOLMBERG	Eskilstuna, Sweden	c.1900	★★
P. KAMPHAUS (Solingen)	Granate	c.1797–present	★★
QUEEN	U.S.A.		★★
QUEEN CITY	Titusville, PA	c.1922–1945	★★★
Q/CROWN (Titusville, PA)	Queen Cutlery Co.	1932–1955	★★
QUEEN CUTLERY CO. (Titusville, PA)	Q/Crown, Queen Steel	1945–present	★★
QUICK POINT (St. Louis, MO)	Advertising specialty dist.	c.1930s	★
QUICK-KUT, INC.	Freemont, OH	c.1930–1950	★
Q.C.C.C. (Titusville, PA)	Queen City Cutlery Co.	c.1922	★★★
Q. C. MFG. CO.	Massillon, OH		★★
RACE BROS.	Celebrated Cutlery	1880s	★★
RAINBOW (Providence, RI)	Boker USA	c.1933–1954	★
RANDAL, HALL & CO. (Chicago, IL)	made in Germany	c.1875	★
RANGER (Providence, RI)	Colonial	1938–2002	★
RAOLA CUTLERY	Raola Hardware & Iron	c.1939	★
RAWSON BROS. (Sheffield)	winged cross logo	1870–1980	★★★

Brands/Manufacturers/Location	*Reference or Trademarks*	*Dates*	*Collectibility*
REC-NOR CO.	Boston, MA	1950–1970	★
RED STAG (Chattanooga, TN)	Goodwin Enterprises	1983–present	★★
REMINGTON/U.M.C. (Bridgeport, CT)	Remington Arms Co.	c.1919–1940	★★★★
REV-O-NOV (Chicago, IL)	Hibbard Spencer Bartlett brand	1905–1960	★★
RICH-CON USA (Kansas City, MO)	Richards & Conover Hdwe.	1857–1956	★★
RICHARD ABR. HERDER (Solingen)	4-pointed star	1885–present	★★
RICHARDS	Southbridge, MA	1862–1908	★
RICHARDS BROS. & SONS LTD. (Sheffield)	street lamp logo	c.1934–1982	★
RICHARDS & CONOVER HDWE. CO. (Kansas City, MO)	Rich-Con., R. & C.	c.1875–1956	★★
RICHMOND CUTLERY CO.	Germany	late 1800s	★★
RIGID KNIVES	Santee, CA	c.1970–1980	★★
RIGID KNIVES	Lake Hamilton, AR	c.1980–1987	★
RIGID KNIVES	Sevierville, TN (Smoky Mtn KW)	c.1988–present	★
RIVERSIDE CUTLERY	New York	c.1918	★★
RIVERSIDE CUT. CO. N.Y. (San Francisco, CA)	by Boker USA	c.1918	★
RIVINGTON WORKS (Sheffield)	Alfred Williams	1900–1946	★
ROBBINS CLARK & BIDDLE (Philadelphia, PA)	became Biddle Hdwe.	1830s	★★
ROBERT HARTKOPF & CO. (Solingen)	Winged lions trademark	c.1855–1957	★★
ROBERT HERDER (Solingen)	4-leaf clover, Windmill	1872–present	★★
ROBERT KLAAS (Solingen)	Two Cranes "Kissing" logo	1834–present	★★
ROBERT LINGARD (Sheffield)		1800s	★★★
ROBERT WADE (Sheffield)	Wade	c.1810–1819	★★
ROBESON (Rochester, NY)	Robeson Cut. marking	1894–1922	★★★
ROBESON DEMONSTRATOR (Rochester, NY)	Salesman sample mark	1911–1916	★★★
ROBESON/ (Germany)		c.1894–1896	★★
ROBESON CUTLERY (Rochester, NY)		1894–1922	★★★
ROBESON CUTLERY CO. (Rochester/Perry, NY)	ShurEdge, PocketEze, Premier	c.1894–1977	★★★
ROBESON-ROCHESTER CORP.	Rochester, NY	c.1940s	★★
ROBINSON BROS. & CO. (Louisville, KY)	hdwe. dist.	c.1878–1925	★★
RODGERS WOSTENHOLM LTD. (Sheffield)	Division of Imperial 1977–1982	1971–1984	★
ROGERS CUTLERY	Hartford, CT	1873–1879	★
ROMO (Germany/Japan)	Rosenbaum & Mogal, dist.	1917–present	★
ROYAL CUTLERY CO.		1814–1954	★
RUNKEL BROS.	made by Wester & Butz	c.1920s	★
RUSSELL USA (CURVED) (Turner Falls, MA)	John Russell Co.	c.1875–1941	★★★★
RUSSELL & CO. GREEN RIVER WORKS (Turner Falls, MA)	R/arrow logo	c.1875–1941	★★★★
R. BUNTING & SONS (Sheffield)	Wells Ayer, distributor	c.1841–1850	★★★★
R. C. CO.	Genesee, NY	1891–1895	★★★
R. C. CO.	Rochester, NY	1922–1939	★★★
R. C. KRUSCHIL	Duluth, MN		★
R. I. KNIFE CO.	Rhode Island Knife Co.	1920–1921	★
R. J. RICHTER (Germany)	Nazi penknives, switchblades	1963–1978	★
R. J. & R. S. CO. (Germany)	Johnson & Rand Shoe Co.	c.1920–1940	★
R. KELLEY & SONS (Liverpool, England)	Bulldog on tang		★
R. MURPHY	Boston, MA	1890–1895	★

Brands/Manufacturers/Location	*Reference or Trademarks*	*Dates*	*Collectibility*
R. & W. BRADFORD (Cork, Ireland)	9 Patricks Road	c.1850	★★★
SABATIER	France	1679–1941	★
SABRE (Japan and Germany)	Cole National economy line	1960–1980	★
SALM (Torrence, CA)	Salm Mfg. Co., Deluxe brand	1918–1935	★★
SAM L. BUCKLEY & SON (Sheffield)		c.1920–1940	★
SAMCO (Nashville, TN)	Sanders Mfg. Co. brand	current	★
SAMUEL BARLOW (Sheffield)	BARLOW Z Scimitarlogo	c.1780–1840	★★★★
SAMUEL BRADFORD	Ireland	c.1850	★★★
SAMUEL BRADLEE (Boston, MA)	sold to M. L. Bradford	1799–1845	★★★
SAMUEL BELL (Knoxville, TN)	silversmith and bowie maker	1819–1852	★★★★
SAMUEL E. BERNSTEIN (New York, NY)	Royal Brand Sharp Cutter	c.1890–1950s	★★
SAMUEL HAGUE (Sheffield)		c.1830s–1950s	★★
SAMUEL HANCOCK & SONS (Sheffield)	Mazeppa, Zephyr	c.1836–1924	★★
SAMUEL NORRIS (Sheffield)	*P Cast Steel	c.1795–1815	★★★
SAMUEL OSBORN & CO. (Sheffield)	Hand & Heart logo	c.1841–1928	★★★
SAMUEL ROBINSON (Sheffield)		1800s	★★★
SAMUEL WRAGG & SONS (Sheffield)	Sheaf Island Works	c.1930s–1960s	★★★★
SANDERS MANUFACTURING CO. (Nashville, TN)	Samco, advertising specialties	current	★
SARCO (Florence, AL)	Sargent Cutlery Co.	1980–present	★
SAXONIA CUTLERY CO. (Germany)		c.1936	★
SAYNOR COOKE & RIDAL (Sheffield)	Rainbow, Saynor, Obtain	c.1840–1868	★★
SCHATT & MORGAN (Gowanda, NY)	was N. Y. Cutlery Co.	1890–1896	★★★
SCHATT & MORGAN (Titusville, PA)	S. & M.; sold to Queen City	1896–1931	★★★
SCHMACHTENBERG BROS. (Solingen)	Clim(Axe), Anchor/ Swords logo	1887–1939	★★
SCHMIDT & ZIEGLER (Solingen)	Bull head logo, El Toro	c.1930s	★★
SCHRADE (Ellenville, NY)	div. of Imperial-Schrade	c.1973–present	★
SCHRADE CUTLERY CO. (Walden, NY)	Albert & Henry Baer	1904–1946	★★★
SCHRADE-WALDEN (Walden, NY)	Imperial owned	1946–1973	★★
SCHWABACHER HARDWARE CO. (Seattle WA)	Colonial Cutlery Co.	1864–present	★★
SEABOARD STEEL CO. (France)	tool knives	c.1948	★
SEARS ROEBUCK & CO. (Chicago, IL)	Wilbert, Dunlap, Craftsman	1886–present	★★
SEATTLE HARDWARE CO. (Seattle WA)	Occident Cutlery Co.	1885–1908	★★
SECO WORKS	New Orange, NJ	1912–1939	★
SENECA CUTLERY CO. (Utica, NY)	by Utica Cutlery Co.	c.1932–1942	★★
SEVERIN R. DROESCHERS (New York, NY)	S.R.D./Arrow	c.1891–1924	★
SHAPLEIGH HWDE. CO. (St. Louis, MO)	Diamond Edge, Keen Kutter	1843–1960	★★
SHELBURNE FALLS CUTLERY CO. (Shelburne Falls, MA)	for Lamson & Goodnow	c.1870s–80s	★★★★
SHELDON (Sheffield)		c.1893	★★
SHERWOOD	became Camillus Cutlery	1894–1901	★★
SHUMATE CUTLERY CORP (St. Louis, MO)	John & Thomas Shumate	1884–1928	★★
SHUREDGE (Rochester, NY)	Robeson Cutlery Co.	c.1916–1977	★★★
SHUR-SNAP (Providence, RI)	Colonial Knife Co.	c.1949	★

Brands/Manufacturers/Location	*Reference or Trademarks*	*Dates*	*Collectibility*
SILBERSTEIN LAPORTE & CO. (Germany)	S.B. & C. Co. Diamond	c.1900–1910	★
SIMMONS BOSS	Simmons Hdwe.	c.1940–1960	★
SIMMONS HARDWARE CO. (St. Louis, MO)	Keen Kutter, ChipAway	c.1890–1940	★★★
SIMMONS HDWE. CO. (Germany)	Hornet	c.1868–1960	★★
SIMMONS, WARDEN, WHITE CO. (Dayton, OH)	SWWCo., made by Camillus	1937–1946	★★
SINGLETON & PRIESTMAN (Sheffield)		c.1861–1936	★★
SLASH (Sheffield)	C. Ibbotson & Co.	1868–1896	★★
SMETHPORT CUTLERY CO. (Smethport, PA)	sold to W. R. Case	1907–1909	★★★
SMITH BROTHERS HDWE. CO. (Columbus, OH)	CutEasy	1893–1959	★★
SMITH & CLARK (Bronxville, NY)	fruit knives	c.1850	★★★
SMITH & HEMENWAY (Utica, NY)	Red Devil, S. & H. Co.	c.1890–1936	★★
SMITH & HOPKINS	Naugatuck, CT	c.1850	★★★
SMITH & WESSON (Springfield, MA)	S & W	c.1974–1986	★
SMITH & WESSON	dist. by Taylor Cutlery	c.1993–present	★★
SMOKY MOUNTAIN KNIFE WORKS (Sevierville, TN)	Klaas, Rigid—mail order dist.	1982–present	★★
SOG SPECIALTIES (Edmonds, WA—made in Japan)	Tom Cat, Air-Sog, Stingray	1985–present	★
SOUTHERN & RICHARDSON (Sheffield)	Nest, Cigar, Squatter	1846–1975	★
SOUTHINGTON CUTLERY CO. (Southington, CT)	dist. by Meriden Cut. Co.	1867–c.1914	★★
SPEAR CUTLERY CO. (Germany)		pre-1915	★
SPERRY & ALEXANDER (New York, NY)	Centaur, S. & A.	1893–1920s	★★
SPRING CUTLERY CO. (Sheffield)		c.1890	★★
SPRINGBROOKE KNIFE CO. (San Francisco, CA)	D. C. & H., by N. Y. Knife Co.	c.1849–1927	★★★
SPYDERCO (Goldon CO)	importer, Clipit	1977–present	★★
STA SHARP for Sears by Camillus		1927–1940	★
STACY BROS. & CO. (Sheffield)	Arkansas dist.	1847–1941	★★
STAINLESS CUTLERY CO. (Camillus, NY)	Camillus, Kastor	1924–1930s	★
STANDARD CUTLERY CO. (Sheffield)			★
STANDARD CUTLERY CO. (U.S.A)	Dean & Elliott Case	1901–1903	★★
STANDARD KNIFE CO. (Little Valley, NY)	owned by two Case Brothers	1901–1903	★★★
STANDARD KNIFE CO. (Bradford, PA)	made by W. R. Case & Sons	1920–1923	★★★
STAR (Knoxville, TN)	Star Sales, Inc. made in Japan	1978–1988	★
STELLITE (Kokomo, IN)	Haynes Stellite	1911–1920	★★★
STERLING (New York, NY)	McIlwaine, Linn & Hughes	1896–1914	★★
STIDHAM KNIVES (Made in Germany)	"Bird Dog Whittler"	1976–1977	★★
STILETTO (San Francisco, CA)	Miller, Sloss & Scott	1896–1905	★★
STILLETTO CUTLERY CO. (New York)	M. S. & S., later B. H. & P.	1896–1926	★★★
STOCKER & CO. (Solingen)	S.M.F. (after 1933)	1897–1970s	★
STRAUSS BROS. & CO. (Germany)	formerly Wm. Elliott	1907–1918	★
STREAMLINE (Camillus, NY)	made by Camillus	1935–1936	★
STRINGER	Philadelphia, PA	1893	★★
ST. LAWRENCE CUTLERY CO. (St. Louis, MO)	Schmachtenberg	1886–1916	★★
SUMMIT KNIFE CO. (St. Paul, MN)	Pavian-Adams	1906–1920	★
SUPERIOR CUTLERY (Solingen)	Austria & Germany	c.1910–1980s	★

Brands/Manufacturers/Location	*Reference or Trademarks*	*Dates*	*Collectibility*
SUPPLEE HDWE. CO. (Philadelphia, PA)	crown and arrow logo	1905–1914	★
SWAN WORKS (Germany)	Altenbach	1901–1996	★
SWANK	advertising specialty brand	c.1950–1980s	★
SWANNER (Fairfield, OH)	made in Japan, swans logo	1980s	★
SWORD BRAND (Camillus, NY)	Kastor and Camillus	c.1906–present	★
SYRACUSE KNIFE CO. (Camillus, NY)	Camillus brand	1930s	★
S. B. LUTTRELL & CO. (Knoxville, TN)	Samuel Bell Luttrell Hardware	c.1880	★★
S. E. OATES & SONS (Sheffield)	S. E. O. & S.	pre-1915	★★
S. & A. (New York)	Sperry & Alexander	1893–1913	★
S. & CO.			★
S. & C. WARDLOW (Sheffield)	Terrifik	1855–c.1920	★★
S. & M. (Gowanda, NY)	Schatt & Morgan	c.1890–1895	★★★
S. & M. (Titusville, PA)	Schatt & Morgan	1895–1928	★★★
TAMPA HDWE. CO. (Tampa, FL)	W.C.T.	1900–1930	★★
TARRY (Thiers, France)	Lizzard logo	1864–1930s	★
TAYLOR CUTLERY CO. (Kingsport, TN)	Made in Japan	1978–present	★
TAYLOR (EYE) WITNESS (Sheffield)	Needham Veall Tyzack	c.1879–1975	★
TELL (Germany)		c.1945–1960	★
TENK HARDWARE (Quincy, IL)	Clipper, Tenk's Clipper	1865–1920	★★
TENNESSEE KNIFE WORKS (Columbia, TN)	Colonel Coon	1978–1987	★★
TERRIER CUTLERY CO. (Rochester, NY)	made by Robeson	c.1910–1916	★★
THE RALPH BROWN CO. (San Francisco, CA)	wholesale distributor	c.1910	★
THEILE & QUACK (Elberfeld, Germany)	Wester, Wade Bros., Tyler, A*1	c.1866–1890	★★
THELCO (Cleveland)	Lockwood Luetkemeyer	1848–1970	★★
THEO M. GREEN CO. (Oklahoma City, OK)	later named Domar Cutlery	c.1916–1920	★★
THOMAS ELLIN (Sheffield)	J. Barber ERA, Vulcan	c.1840–1970	★★
THOMAS FENTON		1854–1907	★
THOMAS MFG. CO. (Dayton, OH)	HHH, American Shear & Knife	1907–1911	★★
THOMAS TURNER & CO. (Sheffield)	Encore, Suffolk, Haywood	1802–1932	★★
THOMAS WARD & SONS (Sheffield)	Stacey Bros.	1850–present	★★
THOMASTON KNIFE CO. (Thomaston, CT)		1884–1930	★★★
THOMPSON CENTER ARMS CO.	stock knife by Camillus	c.1970s	★★
THOMPSON & GASCOIGNE (Winsted, CT)	became Empire Knife Co.	1852–1856	★★★★
THORNTON/U.S.A.	Federal Knife Co.	c.1950s	★
TIDIOUTE CUTLERY CO. (Tidioute, PA)	Union Razor Co., Baldwin Cut.	1897–1916	★★★
TIGER CUTLERY (Solingen)	Herfarth Bros.	1905–1931	★
TILLOTSON & CO. (Sheffield)	Columbia Place, mfg.	1760s–1863	★★★
TINA		c.1890–present	★
TIP TOP (Germany)	A. Kastor Bros.	1904–1941	★
TOLEDO CUTLERY CO. (Germany)	import brand	1890s	★
TOM RAY CUTLERY CO.	Kansas City, MO	c.1910	★★
TOPPER	Colonial trademark	1938–1950	★
TORREY (Worcester, MA)	J. R. Torrey, razors	c.1858–1963	★★
TOWNLEY HDWE. CO. (Kansas City, MO)		1884–present	★★
TRENTON CUTLERY CO. (Sheffield)	metal works, wholesaler	1880–1906	★

Brands/Manufacturers/Location	Reference or Trademarks	Dates	Collectibility
TROUT HARDWARE CO. (Chicago, IL)	Square Deal	c.1896–1907	★★
TURTON BROTHERS & MATTHEWS (Sheffield)	Torpedo, Locomotive	c.1860–1950	★★
TWENTY GRAND	U.S.A.	1932–1948	★
TWIG BRAND (New York, NY)	G. Borgfeldt	c.1911	★
TWITCHELL BROS.	Naugatuck, CT	1883–1890	★★★
T. C. BARNSLEY MFG. CO.	Oklahoma City, OK	c.1898	★★★
T. E. ROWBOTHAM & SON (Sheffield)		c.1820	★★★
T. HESSENBRUCH (Philadelphia, PA)	Bear with cane logo	1873–1926	★
T. RENSHAW & SON (Sheffield)	Stand	1840–1900	★★★
T.T.C. DIAMOND BRAND, N.Y. (Chicago, IL)	sold by Sears Roebuck	c.1909	★★
ULERY (New York, NY)	U. J. Ulery Co.	c.1902–1919	★
ULSTER KNIFE CO. (Ellenville, NY)	Dwight Divine & Sons	1876–1941	★★★
ULSTER USA (Ellenville, NY)	Albert and Henry Baer	1941–1943	★★★
UNCLE HENRY (Walden, NY)	Schrade-Walden, Imperial-Schrade	1967–present	★
UNION CUTLERY CO. (Olean, NY)	KA-BAR	1911–1951	★★★★
UNION CUTLERY CO. (Tidioute, PA)		1909–1911	★★★★
UNION CUTLERY & HDWE. CO.	Unionville, CT	1877–1925	★★
UNION KNIFE CO.	Naugatuck, CT	1851–1885	★★★★
UNION KNIFE WORKS	Union, NY	c.1911–1913	★★★
UNION RAZOR CO. (Tidioute, PA)	became Union Cutlery	1898–1909	★★★★
UNION STOCK YARDS	mark used by Jack Knife Ben	1887–1940	★★★
UNITED CUTLERY (New York, NY)	made in Germany	1901–1920	★
UNITED CUTLERY CO. (Canton, OH)	picture handle knives	1919	★★
UNITED CUTLERY CO. (Germany)	None Better	1908–1920	★
UNITED CUTLERY CO. (Sevierville, TN)	Colt, Hibben, importer	1908–1920	★
UNIVERSAL (New Britain, CT)	L. F. & C.	1898–1950	★★
UNIVERSAL KNIFE CO. (Germany)	L. T. Snow	c.1897–1909	★★
UNWIN & ROGERS (Sheffield)	knife-pistols	c.1848–1867	★★★★
UN-X-LD	Northfolk Knife Co.	1858–1919	★★★
UTICA CUTLERY CO. (Utica, NY)	Kutmaster, Seneca	1910–present	★★
UTICA K. & R. CO. (Utica, NY)	importer, made in Germany	1924–1935	★★★
U. K. & R. CO. (Germany)	Utica Knife & Razor	1924–1935	★★
U. S. CUTLERY CO.	Belleville, NJ	c.1929	★★
U. S. KNIFE CO.	Terre Haute, IN	c.1904	★★
U. S. SMALL ARMS CO. (Chicago, IL)	small knife-pistol	c.1914–1923	★★★
VALLEY FALLS CUTLERY CO.	USA	c.1915	★★
VALLEY FORGE CUTLERY CO.	Newark, NJ	1892–1899	★★★
VALLEY FORGE (VF IN CIRCLE) (Newark, NJ)	owned by Boker	1899–c.1950	★★
VALOR (Miami, FL)	importer-Japan, Germany, etc.	c.1970–present	★
VAN CAMP HDWE. CO.	Indianapolis, IN	c.1888–1960	★★
VAN CAMP HDWE. & IRON CO. (Indianapolis, IN)	owned Capitol Cut. Co.	c.1876–1960	★★
VANCO (Indianapolis, IN)	Van Camp Hardware	1888–1940	★
VERINDER	St. Paul, MN—Sheffield made	c.1900	★
VERITABLE PRADEL	Anchor on blade	c.1880s–1900s	★
VERMONT CUTLERY CO. (Burlington, VT)	German-made hardware brand	1871–1900s	★★
VICTOR	knife tool kit	c.1907–1913	★
VICTORINOX (Switzerland)	Karl Elsener	c.1891–present	★
VICTORY CUTLERY CO.	New Haven, CT	c.1925	★★

Brands/Manufacturers/Location	*Reference or Trademarks*	*Dates*	*Collectibility*
VIGNOS CUTLERY CO. (Canton, OH)	August Vignos, Novelty Cut. Co.	c.1879–1948	★★★
VIKING (New York, NY)	Eric Wedemeyer	c.1931–1934	★
VINTERS (Sheffield)			★
VOM CLEFF & CO. (New York, NY)	importer, V. C. & Co.	1887–c.1930	★★
VOOS CUTLERY CO. (New Haven, CT)	Voos/Arrow, New Haven Hdwe.	c.1923–1981	★★
VOSS CUTLERY CO. (New York, NY)	Solingen, Hen & Rooster	c.1968–1975	★★
VOYLES CUTLERY	Bruce Voyles	c.1970s	★
VULCAN (Sheffield)	T. Ellin & Co.	1886–1944	★★
VULCAN KNIFE CO. (Germany)	Thomas Ellin, importer	c.1920–1940	★
VULCAN & TELLIN & CO.		c.1875–1900	★
V. K. CUTLERY CO. (Germany)			★
WABASH CUTLERY CO. (Terra Haute, IN)	Indiana Cut Co. c.1932	1921–1935	★★
WADE BROS. (Germany)	Theile & Quack	1866–1876	★★★
WADE & BUTCHER (Sheffield)	W. & S. Butcher	c.1819–1947	★★★
WADSWORTH (Germany)	Kastor import brand	1905–1922	★
WADSWORTH & SONS	Austria	1905–1917	★
WALDEN KNIFE CO. (Walden, NY)	to E. C. Simmons 1902	c.1870–1923	★★★
WALKER & HALL (Sheffield)	W. & H. in flag logo	1845–1960	★★
WALKILL RIVER WORKS (Walden, NY)	N. Y. Knife Co.	1928–1931	★★
WALL BROS. (Sheffield)			★★
WALLACE BROS. (Wallingford, CT)	primarily tableware	c.1895–1955	★
WALSH & LOVETT (Sheffield)			★★
WALTCO.	U.S.A.	c.1956	★
WALTER BROS. (New York, NY)	Germany-Boy's Own, Dime Knife	1904–1914	★
WALTHAM CUTLERY (Waltham, MA)	made in Germany	c.1910	★
WANDY	Italy	1950s	★
WARD BROS.	(Sheffield)	c.1890s	★
WARD & CO. (Bronxville, NY)	fruit knives	c.1860s	★★★
WARDS (Chicago, IL)	Montgomery-Ward	c.1935–1950s	★★
WARREN (Baker, OR)	refurbished old Remingtons	1930s	★★
WARWICK KNIFE CO.	Warwick, NY	c.1907–1928	★★
WASHINGTON CUTLERY CO. (Tidioute, PA)	Anchor logo, Gray & Dudley	c.1885–1927	★★
WASHINGTON CUT. CO. (Nashville, TN)	hardware brand	c.1885–1927	★★
WATAUGA (Nashville, TN)	H. G. Lipscomb & Co.	1891–1950s	★★
WATER BROS. CUTLERY (Germany)			★
WATERVILLE MFG. CO. (Waterbury CT)		1843–1913	★★★
WATKINS COTTRELL CO. (Richmond, VA)	Clipper	1867–present	★★
WEBSTER	Sycamore Works	c.1900–1920	★
WEDGEWAY CUTLERY CO. (Saginaw, MI)	Morley Bros. Hdwe. Co.	1887–1933	★
WEED & CO.	Buffalo, NY	1818–1900s	★★
WENGER (Switzerland)	Wengerinox, Swiss Army	c.1908–present	★★
WERWOLF CUTLERY WORKS (Germany)	Dixon Cutlery Co.	c.1920	★
WESKE CUTLERY CO. (Sandusky, OH)	hunting knives	c.1946–1952	★
WEST VIRGINIA CUTLERY CO.	hardware dist. brand	c.1970s	★
WESTER BROS. (New York, NY)	Anchor-Star-Arrow logo	1902–c.1967	★★
WESTER & BUTZ (Solingen)	Wester Bros.	1832–1966	★★
WESTERN	Boulder, CO	c.1911–1978	★★

Brands/Manufacturers/Location	*Reference or Trademarks*	*Dates*	*Collectibility*
WESTERN (Camillus, NY)	Camillus Cutlery Co.	1991–present	★
WESTERN CUTLERY CO. (New York, NY)	imported by Wiebusch & Hilger	c.1874–1914	★★
WESTERN CUTLERY CO. (Longmont, CO)	sold to Coleman 1984	1956–1978	★★
WESTERN STATES CUTLERY CO. (Boulder, CO)	Tested-Sharp-Temper logo	1911–1956	★★★
WESTMARK (Longmont, CO)	Western Cutlery Co.	1970s–1980s	★
WESTPFAL CUTLERY CO. (New York, NY)	Standpoint	c.1920–1951	★★
WEYHAND (Solingen)			★
WHITEHEAD & HOAG CO. (Newark, NJ)	made by Boker USA	1870–1959	★★
WILBERT CUTLERY CO. (Chicago, IL)	for Sears by Napanoch, Empire	c.1909	★★★
WILHEIM CLAUBERG (Solingen)	A. Wingen brand	1810–1996	★★
WILKINSON SWORD LTD. (London and Sheffield)		c.1905–present	★
WILL ROLL BEARING CO. (Terre Haute, IN)	W.R.B. Co.	c.1920s	★★
WILL & FINCK (San Francisco, CA)	mfg., also imported	1863–1932	★★★★
WILLIAM ATKINS (Sheffield)	Turtle logo	c.1848–1913	★★
WILLIAM BAGSHAW (Sheffield)	Spring Street, Sheffield	c.1817–1852	★★★
WILLIAM BROKHAHNE (New York, NY)	W. B. Speed	c.1875–1906	★★
WILLIAM J. DONOVAN	Springfield, MA	c.1893–1901	★★
WILLIAM ELLIOT (New York, NY)	Adloph Strauss, owner	c.1880–1918	★★
WILLIAM LANGBEIN & BROS. (New York, NY)	"L" in swastika logo	c.1900–1960	★★
WILLIAM W. MARSDEN (Sheffield)		c.1850–1870	★★★
WILLIAM NICHOLSON (Sheffield)		c.1836–1864	★★★
WILLIAM RODGERS (Sheffield)	"I Cut My Way" logo	1830–185	★★
WILLIAM SHAW (Sheffield)	W. S. logo	c.1847–1871	★★★
WILLIAM THOMAS STANIFORTH (Sheffield)	Ascend, wings logo	1849–c.1920	★★★
WILLIAM & J. R. PARKER (Sheffield)		c.1890–1920	★★
WILLIAMS CUTLERY CO. (San Francisco, CA)		c.1900–present	★★
WILMINGTON CUT. CO. (Wilmington, IL)	J.C. & Charles Cogan	c.1940s	★
WILSON, HAWKSWORTH & MOSS (Sheffield)	Joshua Moss	1832–1846	★★★
WINCHESTER (New Haven, CT)	Winchester Arms Co.	c.1919–1942	★★★★
WINCHESTER (Manchester, OH)	Blue Grass Cutlery	c.1985–present	★★
WINGFIELD & ROWBOTHAM (Sheffield)	sold to Thomas Turner	c.1825–1898	★★★
WITTE HDWE. CO. (St. Louis, MO)		c.1880–1900s	★★
WM. ENDERS (St. Louis, MO)	Oak Leaf—Simmons Hdwe. later Shapleigh Hdwe.	1908–1929	★★
WM. JACKSON (Sheffield)	Sheaf Island Works	1859–1890s	★★★
WOODBURY CUTLERY CO.	Woodbury, CT	1800s	★★★
WYETH HDWE. & METAL CO. (St. Joseph, MO)	Wyeth's Warranted Cutlery	c.1884–present	★★
WYETH'S CUTLERY USA	hardware brand	c.1884–1934	★★
W. A. IVES MFG. CO.	Meriden, CT	1800s	★★★
W. A. TYZACK & CO. (Sheffield)	Horseman, Stella	c.1850–1953	★★
W. BINGHAM & CO. (Cleveland, OH)	XLCR, BBB. Ulster agent	c.1841–1940	★★
W. F. FORD (New York, NY)	Shepards & Dudley brand		★★

Brands/Manufacturers/Location	*Reference or Trademarks*	*Dates*	*Collectibility*
W. GREAVES WARRANTED (Sheffield)	Fame	c.1780–1816	★★★★
W. GREAVES & SONS (Sheffield)	sold to B. J. Eyre	c.1816–1870	★★★★
W. H. MORLEY & SONS (New York, NY)	A. Kastor & Bros.	c.1913–1927	★★
W. H. PARKER (Sheffield)			★★
W. JNO. BAKER	Sydney Australia	1888–present	★★
W. K. PEACE & CO. (Sheffield)	Eagle, Ibbotson Peace	c.1867–present	★★
W.R.B. CO. (Terre Haute, IN)	Will Roll Bearing Co.	1920–1929	★★
W. R. CASE & SON CUTLERY CO. (Little Valley, NY)	made by Platts & Napanoch	1902–1905	★★★★
W. R. CASE & SONS (Bradford, PA)		1905–1920	★★★★
W. R. CASE & SONS (Bradford, PA)	Case/Tested XX	1920–1940	★★★★
W. R. CASE & SONS (Bradford, PA)	CASE XX	1905–present	★★★
W. R. CASE & SONS (Bradford, PA)	CASE XX/Made in USA	1905–present	★★★
W. R. HUMPHREYS & CO. (Sheffield)	Radiant	c.1875–present	★
W. THORNHILL (England)	tree logo	1800s	★★★
W. WILKINSON & SON (Sheffield)		c.1760–1892	★★
W. W. BINGHAM	Cleveland, OH	1841–1930	★★
W. & A. CO. (Providence, RI)		c.1911	★
W. & H. CO. (Newark, NJ)	Whitehead & Hoag	1870–1959	★★
W. & S. BUTCHER (Sheffield)	Wade & Butcher, X.C.D.	c.1819–1947	★★★
W. & T. MARSH (Sheffield)	Marsh Bros.	c.1780–1840	★★★
W. & W. (Sheffield)	Walter Warrington		★
X.C.D. (Sheffield)	W. & S. Butcher	1830–1947	★★
X.L.N.T. (Germany)	Adolph Kastor, A. Kastor & Bros.	1876–1947	★★
YALE CUTLERY CO. (Meriden, CT)	owned by Son Bros. S.F.C.A	1883–1900s	★★
YANKEE CUTLERY CO. (New York, NY)	Colonial Knife Co.	1903–1950s	★
ZENITH (Duluth, MN)	Marshall Wells Hdwe.	c.1893–1917	★★★

HISTORIES AND LISTINGS OF FACTORY KNIVES

AERIAL CUTLERY COMPANY

The story of Aerial begins with an industrious salesman named Fred Jaeger who began selling knives and razors to his fellow papermill laborers near the turn of the 20th century. Motivated by his success, Jaeger quit his job and took to the road with his cutlery satchel seeking business in backcountry mills, mines and lumber camps. Before long, his growing sales exceeded the capability of his supplier, Morris Cutlery Company, to furnish the quantity sold.

In 1910, Fred "Fritz" Jaeger was joined by his brothers, Chris and Richard, and by Thomas Madden in forming a company to buy the Morris factory. The purchased company was reorganized in Duluth, Minnesota, and was given a new name: Aerial Cutlery Manufacturing Company. It was an unusual name but one which held a great deal of significance for the new owners. The Aerial Bridge, located in Duluth, was the first suspension bridge of its kind in the country. The name and a bridge trademark was selected by the company's owners as a symbol of stamina, hard work and determination against all odds.

The name, Aerial, would remain as a part of the company name when it was shortened in 1912 to Aerial Cutlery Company. At that time, a major move of manufacturing facilities was made from Duluth to Marinette, Wisconsin. According to Jaeger family records, the old factory was moved "lock, stock and barrel." Equipment and tools, whether large or small, were loaded onto a trainload of flat cars for the journey. As late as 1982, some of that old equipment was still in use at Olsen Knife Company.

During the early part of the 20th century, one of the popular types of pocketknives were those that featured pictures within transparent handles. Although picture knives were made by a few other companies, Aerial was the most prolific producer and the one with the longest history. These picture handled knives were made in practically all sizes and patterns, from small pen knives to folding hunters and sheath knives. The pictures used in decorating the handles included but were not limited to natural scenes such as farm animals, lodge and fraternal emblems, bathing beauties, comic strip characters, political slogans and made-to-order advertising messages. In fact, Aerial's customers could even order their own special knife with its handle displaying their favorite personal picture. The company claimed that the knife handles were practically indestructible, especially when compared to other commonly used materials such as ivory, stag, horn or wood.

In addition to picture handled knives, Aerial made a number of other knife types. Some of them were stamped with the Aerial trademark, while others used other Aerial brand names such as Jaeger Bros. and A. C. Mfg. Co. as well the tradenames of customers such as Belknap Hardware and Butler Brothers.

One of Aerial's major undertakings was the manufacture of the military trench knife and M-1 bayonet during World War II. But, shortly after the war's end, the company's cutlery business began to falter—due in no small part to celluloid falling into disfavor. In the last known Aerial cutlery catalog, dating to the later half of the 1940s, the previously extensive line of knives had been reduced to a few pocketknife patterns with Pyralin handles and leather washer handled fixed blade knives. By 1950, the company had ceased knife production but continued in its growing business of barber and beauty shop supplies. Although it has been more than half a century since Aerial made picture handled knives, finding one in mint condition is still possible. In 1973, well over 2,000 mint knives were found in storage and were sold within the collector market.

BAKER & HAMILTON

A product of the California Gold Rush, Baker and Hamilton was formed in 1853 by Livingston L. Baker and Robert M. Hamilton, who had worked together in the mining supply business. During its early years, the company was a supplier of agricultural hardware and supplies. Its knife line was primarily made up of butcher knives, hay knives and other farm-type utility cutlery. Later, the company became a major hardware wholesaler serving the far western part of the country and cutlery represented an important part of its business.

Pocketknives were first offered in 1879, but it is doubtful that these products were actually available for sale since their arrangement with an eastern manufacture failed to materialize. By 1895, the company's full line of cutlery products included pocketknives.

Brands sold by the company near the turn of the 20th century include "Damascus," "New Haven Cutlery Company" and "Ecilpse Cutlery Company." These were followed in the early 1900s by knives stamped with the "Baker & Hamilton" name.

In 1917, Baker and Hamilton merged with Pacific Hardware & Steel to form Baker, Hamilton & Pacific. Pacific's established "Stiletto Cutlery Co., New York" brand was added to the company's line of pocketknives and remained along with nationally known brands until the early 1940s.

BELKNAP HARDWARE COMPANY, INC.

In 1840, W. B Belknap formed a company in Louisville, Kentucky, that was to grow into one of the nation's larger hardware firms. Originally, the company sold items such as carriage supplies, horseshoes and blacksmith supplies, but eventually it added cutlery as well. By the late 1800s, pocketknives had been established as one of Belknap's primary lines and names such as "Blue Grass" and "John Primble" were introduced. Although they would survive to current times, another company trademark stamping of "Pine Knot" and "Pine Knot, Jas. W. Price" would only be sold during the 1930–1934 period.

Pine Knot knives were probably made for Belknap by Robeson and most knives were handled in bone, redwood and celluloid.

Except for the barlow pattern, the Blue Grass knives were discontinued in the 1950s. Any knife pattern other than the currently made barlow is considered collectible.

The best known of Belknap's stampings is that of Primble and, except for the knives stamped "Prussia" or "Germany," have been manufactured under contract by companies such as Camillus, Boker and Schrade. Primble stampings include the following:

JOHN PRIMBLE (c.1890–1986)
JOHN PRIMBLE EAST INDIA WORKS
JOHN PRIMBLE INDIA STEEL WORKS (c.1890–1940)
JOHN PRIMBLE INDIA STEEL WORKS PRUSSIA (c.1890–1914)
J. PRIMBLE BELKNAP GERMANY
JOHN PRIMBLE BELKNAP HDWE. & MFG. CO. (c.1940–1968)
JOHN PRIMBLE BELKNAP INC. (c.1968–1986)

Belknap Hardware went out of business in 1986. The Primble India Steel Works trademark was transferred to Blue Grass Cutlery Corporation, who has recently released new knives bearing that marking. Beginning in 1992, the Primble reproduction knives were produced in 6 patterns, and 200 pieces of each pattern are released in varying handle materials. Other patterns and additional handle materials have been and continue to be used on newly manufactured Primble knives. Still, the releases are in very limited quantities. The limited production, coupled with the obvious quality of workmanship and materials, makes these knives worthy of attention by collectors of reissue knives.

BENCHMARK KNIVES

Originally formed by knife designer and custom maker Walter "Blackie" Collins in the mid-1970s, Benchmark has changed ownership several times. Shortly after the company's founding, it became a division of Jenkins Metal Company of Gastonia, North Carolina. In 1985, the Benchmark business was sold to Gerber Legendary Blades, who continued to market a few of the models. The new Benchmark parent in turn sold, in 1987, to Fiskars.

Benchmark went near full cycle in 1993 when ownership of the brand name, design patents, etc. was again purchased by Jenkins Metal. Marketing the Benchmark line through Heritage Knives, the majority of Benchmark production has returned to Gastonia.

Of special interest to collectors are the older (pre-Gerber) Benchmark knives, especially the patented Rolox knife made by Jenkins Metal and those made by both Collins and Jenkins known as the Ninja and the Com-Belt. The unique Rolox knives are again marketed through acquisition of the brand by former Atlanta Cutlery owners.

C. BERTRAM—HEN AND ROOSTER

The Hen and Rooster knife was produced by a Solingen, Germany, company established in 1872 by Carl Bertram. Knives were stamped with the words C. BERTRAM/GERMANY plus the logo of a hen and a rooster. The Hen & Rooster name and logo soon became recognized for very high quality knives, a reputation that continues to the present. Early knives were handled in stag and pearl and were primarily congress patterns. The firm also made a considerable number of knives on a contract basis and these were stamped with the trademark logo plus the importers name.

The firm, its factory and trademark was owned by Bertram family members until 1975, when it was sold to A. G. Russell of Springdale, Arkansas. Production was ceased in the early 1980s and the business was liquidated in 1983. Russell was able to obtain a number of knives from the factory's inventory and offered them to his customers. Meanwhile, their value has continually increased.

At that time, the trademark and Bertram name for cutlery was purchased by Tennessee businessmen James Frost and Howard Rabin, operating as Bertram, USA. Knives made since 1983 have been manufactured at other German factories, probably Robert Clauss. Although the Hen & Rooster trademark continues, these knives should not be confused with the earlier knives made by C. Bertram, which are valued higher within the collector market. The trademark is now the sole property of Frost Cutlery Company.

BOKER

The name "Boker" is one of the oldest in American cutlery and had its beginning during the early part of the 19th century. Hermann and Robert Boker had begun a cutlery manufacturing operation, located in Remscheid, Germany, in 1829. The brothers came to North America in 1837 to develop a market for knives branded with their name. Hermann Boker established the importing firm H. Boker & Company, with headquarters in New York City. Robert Boker at first concentrated on the Canadian market and later opened headquarters for his importing firm in Mexico City.

Along with Herman Heuser, Heinrich Boker started Heinrich Boker & Co. in 1869. This Solingen, Germany, manufacturing operation was built to make Boker's "Tree Brand" cutlery products for the companies owned by Heinrich's cousins in the U.S. and Mexico. Although the Heinrich Boker & Co. manufacturing facilities had large production capacity, the H. Boker company also imported knives made in Sheffield.

When protective tariffs increased the U.S. cost of German and other foreign-made cutlery, H. Boker & Co. began acquiring U.S. manufacturing facilities about 1916. One factory used to produced Boker's knives was the Valley Forge Cutlery Company of Newark, New Jersey. Whether H. Boker & Co. acquired the factory about that time or had owned it earlier is unknown. Valley Forge stampings have been traced to 1892 and Hermann Boker had established a warehouse at that location shortly after his arrival in the states. In either case, knives branded VALLEY FORGE CUTLERY CO. NEWARK N.J. and BOKER USA were both made at the factory.

In 1921, H. Boker & Co. established a manufacturing facility in Maplewood, New Jersey, probably to supplement production of the Newark and German factories. This facility was expanded in 1930, making it one of the nation's larger cutlery manufacturing factories.

Boker stampings used during its long history have included but are not limited to H. BOKER & CO.'S CUTLERY, H. BOKER & CO. IMPROVED CUTLERY, H. BOKER & CO. SOLINGEN GERMANY, HEINR. BOKER & CO. AND BOKER USA. Typical handle materials for Boker knives have been bone, stag, celluloid, pearl, hard rubber and wood.

The Boker U.S.A. business was purchased in 1969 by J. Wiss and Sons, a shear manufacturer since 1847. In 1978, the Boker cutlery business was sold to the tool manufacturing Cooper Group, headquartered in Apex, North Carolina. Another transfer of the cutlery business came in 1986 when it reverted back to the Heinrich Boker firm in Germany. Boker's U.S. business, Boker USA, is now headquartered in Golden, Colorado.

ERNST BRUCKMAN

Using the MANN trademark, the German firm of E. Bruckman produced a large number of high-quality knives during the 1920 to the 1956 era. In the early 1970s, a considerable quantity of fine old knives in mint condition were discovered. For several years they were largely unappreciated by collectors, but that has changed. Now that they are more difficult to find and their excellent quality is recognized, their value has appreciated considerably.

BUCK KNIVES

The first knives made by a member of the family owning Buck Knives were made about 1900 by Hoyt Heath Buck, a blacksmith's apprentice. Young Buck had developed an effective method of tempering and had used it in his work of rebuilding worn out grub hoes used by local farmers and gardeners. Those for whom he had worked recognized that the rebuilt hoes were superior to new ones. Because of this, one of his customers ask Buck to forge a knife.

Using the same type of worn farriers files that he used to rebuild the cutting edges of hoes, Buck made his first knife and personal recommendations led to his making others. As the reputation of his knives spread, he began to custom make knives on a regular but part-time basis. During the years from 1907 until 1930, Hoyt Buck earned the family's livelihood by working in the logging industry, but supplemented his income by making knives in his spare time.

A son, Alfred Charles, was born to Hoyt and Daisy Buck in 1910. After his discharge from the U.S. Coast Guard in 1940, Al Buck settled in San Diego, California. Meanwhile, Hoyt Buck had been ordained a minister and had moved to Mountain Home, Idaho, to pastor a small church. His forge was set up in the church basement and he continued to forge knives for local customers. With our nation's involvement in World War II, a growing number of the area's young men would leave for military service with their own knife made by Buck. For the first time, knives made at the Buck forge would gain more than a local reputation for quality as the few fortunate servicemen proudly showed their knives to their comrades-in-arms.

In 1945, Hoyt and Daisy Buck moved to San Diego to join their son. Hoyt began to make knives full-time and Al made knives part-time whenever he was not at his regular job as a bus driver. The Bucks had reasoned that their knives could be sold mail order via advertisements in outdoor magazines, since some of their readers could well have been former servicemen who had already learned of the knives made by H. H. Buck. Continuing in the four-decade tradition, most of the early Buck knives were made from old files or power hacksaw blades. They were usually handled in Lucite plastic of various colors, South American lignum vitae, or local desert ironwood. Their reasoning had been sound and business during the 1945–1950 period was good.

Hoyt Buck died in 1949, but his son, Al, continued to make knives at his San Diego shop. In 1959, he was joined in the business by his own son, Charles T. Buck. In 1961, incorporation of the business and sale of stock allowed for expansion of the knife business by moving to a larger workshop and employing three knife makers.

Buck's line was still limited to fixed blade hunting and filet knives made from files and sawblade steel. Soon, however, a nearby commercial forging company made the blades which were finished into knives and stamped "Buck" at the company shop. Models produced at this time included #102—Woodsman, #103—Skinner, #105—Pathfinder, #116—Caper, #118—Personal, #119—Special, #120—General and #121—Fisherman.

Some general determination of a fixed blade Buck knife's age may be made by noting tang style. The earlier production knives followed the system of their handmade predecessors in that their tangs were threaded and a barrel nut was used to hold on the handle and butt cap. Knives produced after 1962 had a flat tang with the butt pressed on and held with a pin.

The knife that would bring fame and fortune to Buck knives was the Model 110. Although it has become synonymous with the term "folding hunter" and is the most copied knife made today, the basic locking design was not new when Al Buck designed it in 1962. But, the phenomenal demand for knives of this type was created through the qualities of the Buck 110 and it remains today as the market leader. The company's success with the 110 led to production, in 1969, of the slightly smaller version Model 112.

During the 1960s, the company expanded its line of pocketknives through contracting for its manufacture by Schrade and Camillus. In 1975, the 500 series models were introduced and were made for Buck by Camillus. Production of Buck pocketknives was moved to the company's own factory in 1979.

When Buck began to market knives in Canada in 1968, the stamping was changed to "Buck/U.S.A." or "Buck, Made in U.S.A.." Older Buck fixed blade knives and Model 110 folding hunters are becoming more popular with collectors as are several recently marketed limited editions. The brand's contract-made pocketknives and recent standard production models are of little interest to collectors.

BULLDOG KNIVES

In 1980, Charles Dorton introduced the Bulldog brand of quality German-made knives to the collector market. The foundation for the brand had been laid a couple of years earlier when Dorton had a very few special issue knives made bearing the "Pit Bull" trademark as well as some saluting the Henry Repeater rifle.

S & D Enterprises of Manchester, Ohio, assumed marketing responsibility for the brand a short time later when Dorton and his partner, George Smith, joined with David Scott. Production of the brand ceased in 1986 when a new company, Blue Grass Cutlery, was formed to concentrate on the reintroduction of Winchester brand knives.

No Bulldog knives were made during the 1988–1990 period. In 1991 and 1992, Bulldog knives that had been made during the earlier period or knives assembled from parts that had been made prior to 1988 were shipped into the U.S. Manufacture of Bulldog knives began again in 1993 when marketing rights for the brand became the property of Billie (Mrs. James) Parker.

During the past decade of Parker ownership, the brand has become widely recognized for its quality, collector interest and rapidly expanding product line. The following prices apply to the earliest made Bulldog knives from the 1980–1987 period.

Etching	*Handle*	*Shield*	*Mint Price*
3½″ Gunstock Jack			
"Pit Bull"	Brown Bone	Banner	125
"Bulldog Brand"	Pearl	None	160
3½″ Gunstock Stockman			
"Henry Repeater"	Butter & Molasses	Rifle	200
3¾″ Gunstock Stockman			
"Pit Bull"	Stag	Heart	125
"Saddle Tramp"	Stag	Heart	140
"Pit Bull"	Various Celluloid	Heart	95

Etching	*Handle*	*Shield*	*Mint Price*
4″ Gunstock Stockman			
"Pit Bull"	Stag	Spear	130
"Pit Bull"	Various Celluloid	Spear	100

4″ Premium Stockman

Etching	*Handle*	*Shield*	*Mint Price*
4″ Premium Stockman			
"Cowboy's Pet"	Celluloid	Spade	110
"Cowboy's Pet"	Green Bone	Spade	115
"Cowboy's Pet"	Stag	Spade	140
"Pit Bull"	Stag	Spear	140
"Quarter Horseman"	Stag	Spear	145
"S & D"	Stag	Spear	140
"Pit Bull"	Various Celluloid	Spear	110

4″ Moose—Square Bolsters

Etching	*Handle*	*Shield*	*Mint Price*
4″ Moose—Square Bolsters			
“Lumber Jack”	Stag	Diamond	130
“Lumber Jack”	Celluloid	Diamond	100
“Lumber Jack”	Purple Celluloid	Peacock	250

3¾″ Stockman

Etching	*Handle*	*Shield*	*Mint Price*
3¾″ Stockman			
“Pit Bull”	Brown Bone	Banner	100
“Pit Bull”	Stag	Banner	125
“Pit Bull”	Celluloid	Banner	90
“Bulldog Brand”	Celluloid	Banner	75
“Coal Miner”	Brown Bone	Coal Miner	110
“Coal Miner”	Stag	Coal Miner	120
3¾″ Stockman—Square Bolsters			
“Pit Bull” (Winchester stamp)	Brown Bone (28 made in 1978)	Crest	300
“Pit Bull” (Pit Bull tang stamp)	Brown Bone (138 made in 1979)	Crest	200
3¼″ Stockman—Square Bolsters			
“Pit Bull”	Brown Bone	Crest	100
“Pit Bull”	Tortoise	Heart	150
“Pit Bull”	Celluloid	Heart	120
3½″ Stockman—Square Bolsters			
“Pit Bull”	Stag	Heart	125
“Pit Bull”	Brown Bone	Heart	110
“Pit Bull”	Celluloid	Heart	95
3⅞″ Stockman—Round Bolsters			
“S & D Enterprises”	Stag	Crest	120
“Pit Bull”	Stag	Banner	110
“Pit Bull”	Celluloid	Banner	80
“Pick & Shovel”	Black Celluloid	Coal Miner	110
3½″ Stockman—Square Bolsters			
“S & D Our Best”	Stag	Crest	125
“Pit Bull”	Stag	Spade	110
“Pit Bull”	Brown Bone	Spade	90
“Pit Bull”	Celluloid	Spade	80
“Bulldog Knife Club”	Pearl	None	160

4¼″ Cattle Knife

Etching	*Handle*	*Shield*	*Mint Price*
4¼″ Cattle Knife			
"Cattle King"	Stag	Bar	150
"Cattle King"	Bone	Bar	125
"Cattle King"	Celluloid	Bar	100
3⅜″ Serpentine Stockman			
"Run for the Roses"	Stag	Horseshoe	135
"Run for the Roses"	Celluloid	Horseshoe	100
"Oktoberfest"	Celluloid	Beer Stein	150
3⅝″ Serpentine Stockman			
"Tobacco King"	Stag	Leaf	130
"Tobacco King"	Celluloid	Leaf	100

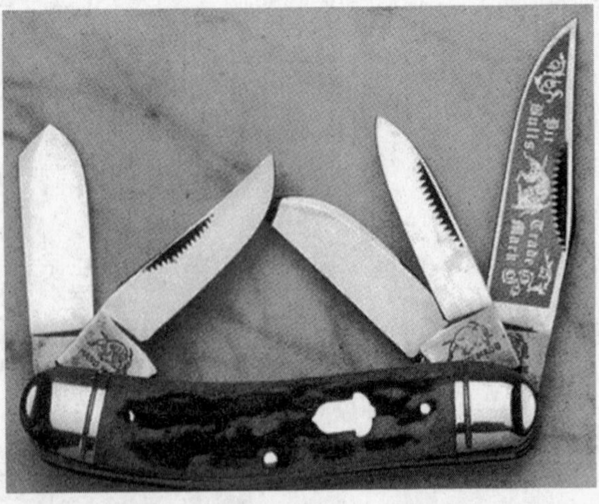

3⅝″ Serpentine Stockman—Five Blade

3⅝″ Serpentine Stockman—Five Blade			
"S & D Our Best"	Stag	Crest	200
"Pit Bull"	Stag	Acorn	250

Etching	*Handle*	*Shield*	*Mint Price*
3⅞″ Serpentine Stockman			
"S & D Our Best"	Stag	Crest	180
"Cutting Horse"	Stag	Club	195
"Cutting Horse"	Green Bone	Club	180
"Cutting Horse"	Celluloid	Club	115
4⅛″ Trapper			
"Old Dominion"	Stag	OKCA	125
"Dog & Coon"	Celluloid	Raccoon	110
"Trapper Jack"	Celluloid	Mountain Man	120
"S & D Buckeye Special"	Stag	Banner	150

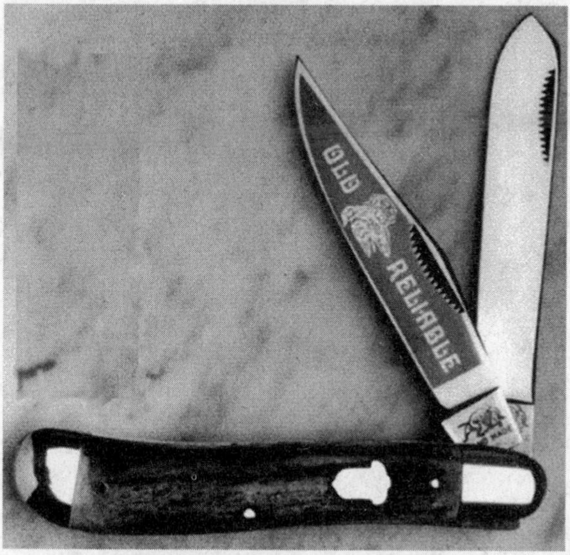

3⅞″ Serpentine Trapper

3⅞″ Serpentine Trapper			
"Old Reliable"	Stag	Acorn	125
"Old Reliable"	Green Bone	Acorn	110
"Old Reliable"	Celluloid	Acorn	90
"Our Best"	Stag	Crest	135
"Pit Bull"	Stag	Crest	110
"Pit Bull"	Celluloid	Banner	85
"Pit Bull"—3 blade	Stag	Banner	150

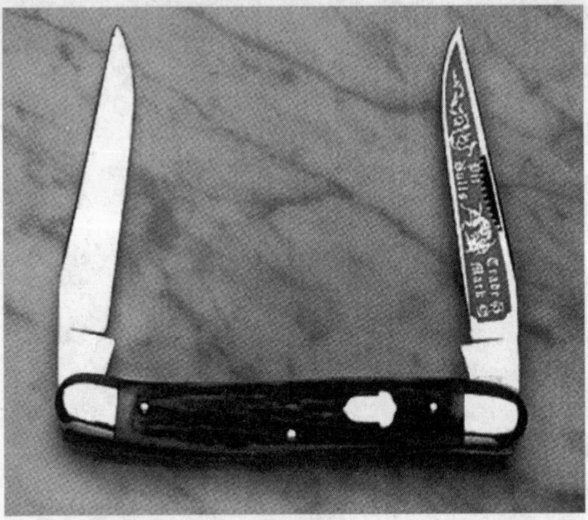

3 7/8" Muskrat

Etching	*Handle*	*Shield*	*Mint Price*
3 7/8" Muskrat			
"Johnny Muskrat"	Celluloid	Muskrat	110
"Dog & Coon"	Celluloid	Raccoon	120
"S & D Buckeye Special"	Stag	Banner	150
3 3/4" Copperhead			
"Rabbit Hound"	Celluloid	Heart	90
"Rabbit Hound"	Stag	Heart	115
"S & D Our Best"	Stag	Heart	130

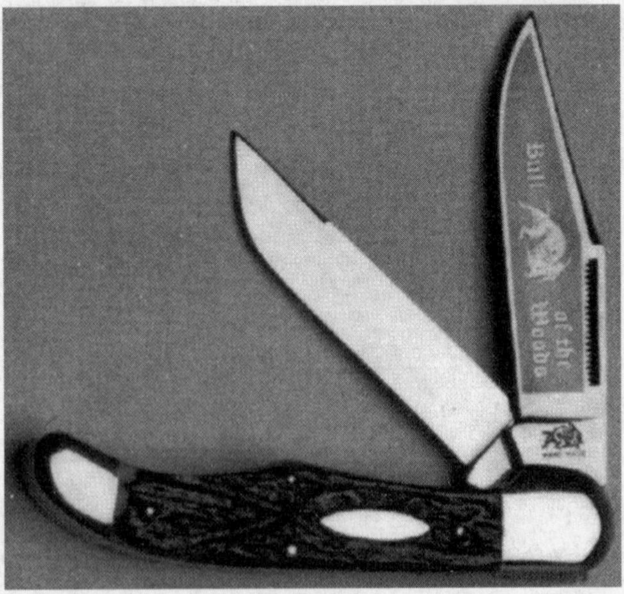

4 7/8" Folding hunter

4 7/8" Folding hunter			
"War Hawk"	Stag	Spear	175
"War Hawk"	Brown Bone	Oval	150

Etching	*Handle*	*Shield*	*Mint Price*
"Mountain Hunter"	Brown Bone	Oval	125
"Bull of the Woods"	Brown Bone	Oval	130
"Hunter's Pride"	Brown Bone	Oval	160
$4^7/_8$″ Lockback Folding Hunter			
"Bulldog"	Stag	None	250
$3^1/_2$″ Barlow—Fancy Tobacco Bolster			
"S & D Our Best"	Stag	S & D	100
"S & D Our Best"	Brown Bone	S & D	85
"Kentucky Burley"	Bone	None	75
"Tennessee Burley"	Bone	None	75
"North Carolina Flue Cured"	Bone	None	80
"South Carolina Flue Cured"	Bone	None	75
"Virginia Flue Cured"	Bone	None	75
"Kentucky Burley"	Stag	None	100
"Tennessee Burley"	Stag	None	95
"North Carolina Flue Cured"	Stag	None	90
"South Carolina Flue Cured"	Stag	None	75
"Virginia Flue Cured"	Stag	None	80

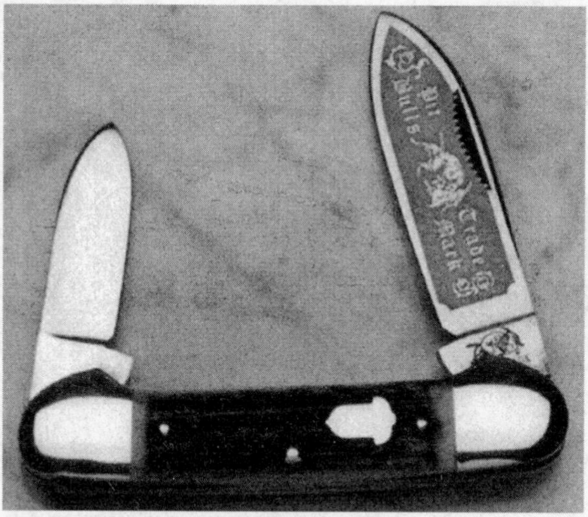

$3^5/_8$″ Canoe

$3^5/_8$″ Canoe			
"Tobacco"	Stag	Leaf	165
"Tobacco"	Bone	Leaf	140
"Tobacco"	Celluloid	Leaf	125
"S & D"	Stag	Crest	165
"S & D"—3 blades	Stag	Crest	175
"Tobacco"—3 blades	Bone	Crest	175

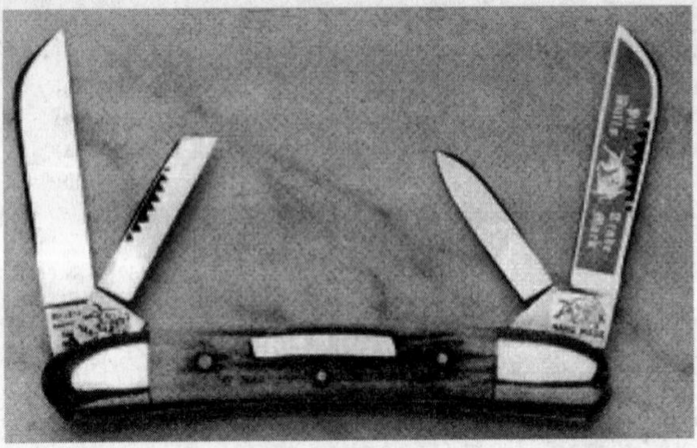

3⅞" Congress—Round Bolsters

Etching	*Handle*	*Shield*	*Mint Price*
3⅞" Congress—Round Bolsters			
"Pit Bull"	Stag	Bar	140
"S & D Enterprises"	Stag	Crest	150
"Tobacco"	Celluloid	Leaf	90
"Tobacco"	Pearl	None	165
3⅞" Congress—Grooved Bolsters			
"Tobacco"	Stag	Bar	150
"Tobacco"	Celluloid	Bar	85
"Tobacco"	Pearl	None	170
"Tennessee Walking Horse"	Pearl	Heart	175
"S & D Our Best"	Stag	Crest	150
"Cut Plug"	Stag	Bar	135
"Cut Plug"	Celluloid	Leaf	85
3⅝" Congress—Round Bolsters			
"S & D Our Best"	Stag	Crest	145
"Old Chum"	Stag	Diamond	135
"Old Chum"	Celluloid	Diamond	95
"Fulton Hardware"	Celluloid	Diamond	110
"Pit Bull"	Stag	Spade	130
"Pit Bull"	Bone	Spade	90
"Pit Bull"	Celluloid	Spade	75

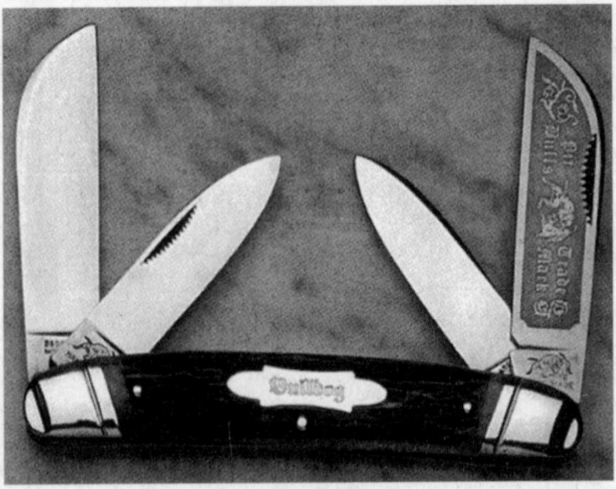

4¼" Jumbo Congress

Etching	*Handle*	*Shield*	*Mint Price*
4¼″ Jumbo Congress			
"Our Best"	Torched Stag	Leaf	180
"Tobacco"	Torched Stag	Leaf	185
"Tobacco"	Bone	Leaf	125
"Tobacco"	Tortoise Celluloid	Leaf	110
"Tobacco"	Purple Celluloid	Leaf	150
9⅞″ Boot Knives			
Miscellaneous blade etchings	Stag	none	100
Miscellaneous blade etchings	White Micarta	none	85
15½″ Bowie			
"Simon Kenton's Ride 1785"	Stag	none	250

CAMILLUS CUTLERY COMPANY

The company that was to be the forerunner of this cutlery giant was founded in Camillus, New York, by Charles Sherwood as the Sherwood Cutlery Company. In 1894, Sherwood's company made its first shipment of knives, a total of thirty dozen pieces. The small cutlery manufacturing operation lasted only a couple of years before the factory was leased to Robeson Cutlery Company. Sherwood remained as manager during the two-year occupancy and reopened his business in 1901.

Some twenty years prior to Sherwood's venture, Adolph and Nathan Kastor had formed a hardware wholesale and knife importing business known as A. Kastor & Bros. The Kastor business grew to the point that it had become the country's largest knife importer, but the 1897 Tariff Act passage caused a substantial increase in the cost of his imported knives. Adolph Kastor & Bros. purchased Sherwood's manufacturing facility in 1902 and renamed it Camillus Cutlery Company. In addition to pocketknives, wartime saw the company making military knives for the U.S. as well as other allied countries.

After the war, renewed emphasis was placed upon the manufacture and sale of pocketknives and a new Camillus salesman, Albert Baer, was hired in 1922. Within his first year, Baer was successful in landing the large Sears, Roebuck account and Camillus began manufacturing the Sears STA-SHARP brand. Other large contracts, such KENT knives made for Woolworth, would become a major portion of the company's business.

Camillus adopted a number of its own brand names and stampings and large quantities of knives marked CAMILLUS CUTLERY CO./CAMILLUS NY USA, CAMCO, SWORD BRAND, and MUMBLY PEG have been sold over the years. Although these brands have not become particularly desirable in the collector market, the company has been the major contract manufacturer of dozens of other brands that are in demand. Brand stampings such as O.V.B., KEEN KUTTER, DIAMOND EDGE, VAN CAMP HARDWARE, HENRY SEARS & SONS, and BUCK are but a few that reflect the manufacturing capabilities of this cutlery giant.

Albert Baer remained with the company until 1941 and, in 1963, purchased the firm on behalf of his two daughters. Operational control now comes under the Baer-owned conglomerate Imperial Knife Associated Companies.

CANASTOTA KNIFE COMPANY

This firm was incorporated in the town of Canastota, New York, in 1875. Its knives, which were of high quality, were stamped CANASTOTA KNIFE CO. N.Y. and were marketed by the William Cornwall firm of New York City. Prominent handle materials for the company's knives were bone and wood. In addition to its own brand, the factory produced other brands under contract. The company went out of business in 1895. Canastota knives are quite rare and are desirable collectibles.

CANTON CUTLERY COMPANY

Knives stamped CCC, CANTON CUTLERY CO., and CAR-VAN were made by this company, which was formed around 1879. W. Stuart Carnes of Canton, Ohio, was one of two local businessmen licensed to make picture handled knives by their inventors, Henry and Rueben Landis. Recognizing an opportunity, Carnes produced these knives under his own tradenames and was successful in their sale for a number of years. Canton Cutlery Co. ceased knife manufacture in the 1930s.

CASE

W. R. Case & Sons and Related Companies

The story of knives branded with the name Case encompasses dozens of markings and as many members of a family who would make cutlery history. To study the brand that is recognized by most collectors as king of factory knife collectibles, W. R. Case & Sons Cutlery, it is important to include information on other companies—some of which may be discussed in greater detail elsewhere in this book.

Although Job Russell Case was never directly involved with the manufacture or the sale of knives, he is considered by many to be the grandfather of the several knife brands that carried his name. And, the name Case is near magic to the ears of collectors of factory-made knives. It's a name that is best known, widely respected and intertwined with the American cutlery industry. Grandpa Job Case was born in 1821 and spent his adult years as a farmer, horse trader, freighter and lumberman. It is through his descendants that he exerted so much influence upon the knives we collect today. These descendants were introduced to the cutlery business by their relatives who were knife makers and, in turn, they influenced several other family members to become part of what was to become a knife manufacturing dynasty.

The story of Case knives begins in the latter part of the 19th century and continues through at least a half-dozen significant stages in the history of the knives and the family that created them. To make them more meaningful to collectors, the knife stampings associated with these periods are included.

THE EARLY YEARS

The Case family was introduced to knife making when Job's daughter, Theresa, married a cutlery salesman named John Brown Francis Champlin. In 1882, Champlin resigned from the cutlery importing firm of Friedman and Lauterjung to begin his own business as a knife broker. In this capacity, he contracted for knives to be made and then sold them under his own brand name. The brand, J.B.F. Champlin Little Valley New York, was so successful that four of his wife's brothers joined the business in 1886. When Champlin's brothers-in-law, William R., Jean, John D. and Andrew Case, joined his firm, it was renamed Cattaraugus Cutlery Company. The company continued to do well with Champlin and his son, Tint, directing its manufacturing. For further information about this era and the knife stampings, see the section on Cattaraugus Cutlery Company.

The Case brothers' employment with Cattaraugus was short lived but its impact upon their lives was not. When they left, in 1887, they took with them the desire to be involved in the cutlery industry.

ENTERING THE KNIFE BROKERAGE BUSINESS

The first cutlery company to use the family name was Case Brothers Cutlery Company, a brokerage firm also located in Little Valley, New York. The company's owners were Jean, John, and Andrew but did not include their brother and former Cattaraugus associate, William R. Case. The new company contracted with various knife manufacturers to make knives and sold them marked with several tang stampings such as:

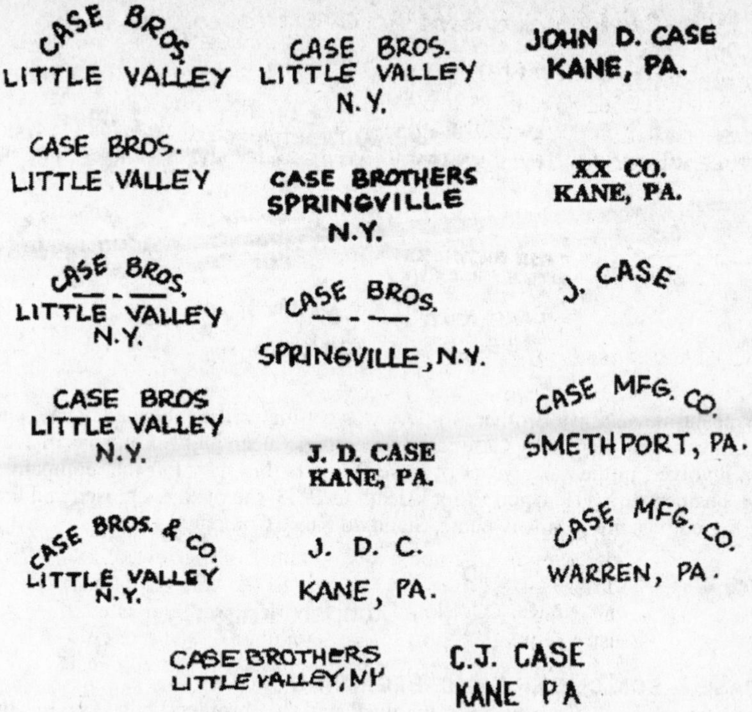

All Case and related trademark sketches are by Allen Swayne

BEGINNING THE MANUFACTURE OF KNIVES

The Case Brothers' cutlery business was so successful that, in 1900, they built their own factory. Sales responsibility belonged to Jean Case and he apparently was doing an outstanding job because sales continued to increase along with the number of knife models produced. The brothers' specialty was hand-forged cutlery and they were justly proud of the company's high-quality products. Desiring to impress their customers with a trademark signifying excellent quality, the brothers began to use the XX mark that is so well known today. Knives of this 1900–1914 period were stamped with the XX mark usually near the middle of the blade but sometimes on the reverse tang. It would also occasionally appear as Tested XX.

Further expansion came as Case Brothers knives were manufactured briefly in a few other locations such as the Pennsylvania towns of Kane, Smethport and Warren. Whether this diversification of manufacturing was the cause or the effect is not known, but there was disagreement between the brothers and Andrew withdrew from the firm in 1911. He did retain an interest in the industry, however, as evidenced by his 1940 obituary stating that he held a proprietary interest in Union Cutlery Company—later known as Ka-Bar. It also indicated that he had been a salesman for W. R. Case & Sons Cutlery Company until a few years before his death.

Not only did the Case Brothers factory produce high-quality knives, but it also served as a training ground for the family's succeeding generation. When, in 1912, the Little Valley factory burned, a relocation to Springville, New York, was attempted. Within a couple of years, the company had failed and, in 1914, the famous XX trademark was transferred to the competing family firm of W. R. Case & Sons Cutlery Company. During the tenure of the Case Brothers company, a large number of tang marks were used and included:

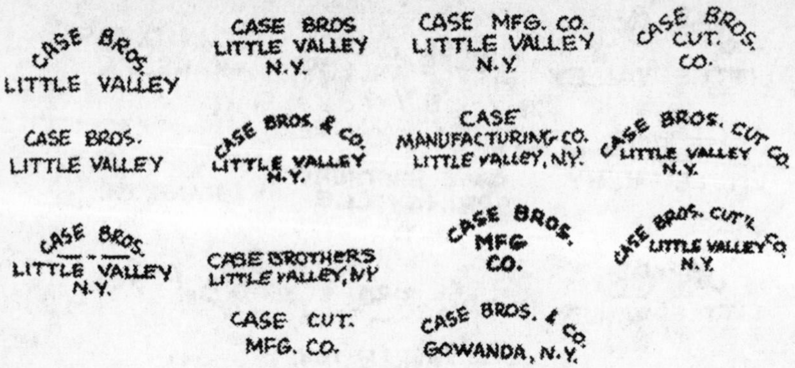

In the meantime, as Case Brothers Cutlery was getting well established, a new knife brokerage company was started by Case family members. Dean and Elliot, sons of Jean Case, had been involved in the early years of Case Brothers, but they left that company to start their own business in 1901. Upon Elliot's death in 1903, the business closed and their only trademark used was the company name, Standard Knife Company.

STANDARD
KNIFE CO. Standard Knife Co.

W. R. CASE & SON CUTLERY—THE BEGINNING

As stated earlier, W. R. Case was not involved with his brothers' business, but the Case Brothers company had served to train his son. During the years of 1900 to 1902, John Russell Case had worked for his uncles and earned his indoctrination into the cutlery business. Through the support and financial assistance of his father, "Russ" Case founded a knife brokerage firm in Little Valley, New York, in 1902. In an effort to have customers perceive his new business as being well established, he not only used his grandfather's (Job R. Case) picture in the company's advertising, but he also used his father's name in naming the company W. R. Case & Son.

Russ Case purchased knives for his brokerage business on contract from Platts Brothers Cutlery Co., Cattaraugus Cutlery Co. and others. Consequently, there were many pattern variations during this 1902–1905 period preceding his own factory. Various tang marks on the contract knives of this period include

W. R. CASE & SONS—KNIFE MANUFACTURERS

Russ Case was an excellent salesman and flourishing business encouraged him to move to Bradford, Pennsylvania, and to build a knife factory there. Another family member, by marriage, would provide the manufacturing expertise needed to compliment Case's sales ability. The husband of Russ's sister, Debbie, had come from a family well established in knife making, so, in 1905, H. N. Platts joined with his brother-in-law in combining their operations under one company name. Since Platts was a son-in-law of W. R. Case, and since Russ Case had established strong brand recognition, the letter S was added to his former company's name. The new combined company became W. R. Case & Sons Cutlery Company.

Business was excellent and many new knife patterns were introduced during the 1905–1914 period, but the prestigious XX symbol still belonged to Case Brothers. With the failure of that company in 1914, W. R. Case & Sons was able to acquire the trademark—one which has been a standby for the company to this day.

Due to his failing health, H. N. Platts left the company about 1910 and moved to Colorado where he started a new cutlery company. For further information, see the section on Western Cutlery Company. At about the same time, Russ Case's other brother-in-law, Herbert Crandall, merged his Crandall Cutlery Company with W. R. Case & Sons.

Russ Case had no children but, for many years, his company would remain under the ownership and leadership of family members. When he died in 1953, majority ownership of W. R. Case & Sons Cutlery Company passed to his niece. Rhea Crandall was the daughter of Theresa (Case) and Herbert Crandall, Russ Case's early partner. Rhea was first married to Harold Osborne, to whom she bore a son. After the elder Osborne's death, she married John O'Kain. O'Kain led the company as president until his retirement in 1971. At that time, he became chairman of the board and Rhea's son, Russell B. Osborne, became the company's president.

ENDING OF CASE FAMILY OWNERSHIP

In 1972, ownership of the W. R. Case & Sons Cutlery Company was passed from the Case family members to American Brands, Inc., but leadership influence of the Case family would remain for yet a while. Russell B. Osborne continued as president until his death in 1975 and his son, John, served as vice president and new products manager.

American Brands ownership of the famed cutlery giant continued until the end of 1988. The cutlery business which the conglomerate had purchased sixteen years earlier had enjoyed a reputation built over several decades. Although it may not have been recognized by the average consumer, many dedicated knife enthusiasts perceived a dwindling interest by the parent company in maintaining that image. They were, therefore, not surprised when American Brands had made public its interest in selling the old company. By the beginning of 1989, W. R. Case & Sons Cutlery Company was under the ownership and leadership of James F. Parker, an enterprising businessman who had already built a thriving cutlery business of his own.

The Case family had made a tremendous impact on the knife industry over a period of 100 years. At the beginning of the 1990s, Case was again guided by cutlery-oriented ownership and leadership. The change marked a turning point that would likely be significant for generations to come.

Knife patterns, stampings and handle materials used many years ago but discontinued over the past several decades were reintroduced. Among the handle materials used on "the new Case" knives was Rogers Bone, Christmas Tree Celluloid, Gold Stone Celluloid, Red Bone, Green Bone, Curly Maple and India Stag. The reintroduction of old-time patterns and stampings was accomplished through a series started in 1989 and known as Commemorative Case Classics. This series was announced as "basically handmade just as they were in the late 1800s" and were made using many of the original dies. Collectors should be aware that knives in the Classic series were made for Parker by a company other than Case. After Parker's ownership of the cutlery company ceased, he retained marketing rights for the Classics for several years.

Earliest knives with revived stampings were patterns ROG639—(Case Brothers), G6391—(W. R. Case & Sons), CT1072—(Case Tested XX), ROG61050SAB—(Case Brothers), 51050SAB—(W. R. Case), G62075—(W. R. Case & Sons) and ROG62075—(Case Brothers). The handle materials, shields, blade pulls and blade marks were matched to the original period of the knife's production by the old companies. Their stamping includes the year of manufacture. These knives were limited in production to 3,000 of each and 500 of each was reserved for the Centennial Mint Set. Retail prices of these early Classics releases ranged from $120 to $150.

The Centennial Mint Set contained a total of 100 knives with a wide variety of patterns and handle materials. Most of their blades were etched "Case XX Tested Centennial 1889–1989." Retail price of the complete matching serial number sets was $5,000.

Beginning in 1990, the new tang stamping for regular production knives was changed to "Case XX Bradford, PA 19 USA 90" and the intent was for subsequent years' production to reflect the year made in the tang marking. By 1993, however, the dot system was revived by the company's new owner; a "long-tail C" and dots stamping would be used through the 1990s.

Perhaps one of the more significant actions taken during this time was the sale of the Case Factory Collection of knives, along with other knife-related items of historical and collector value. A considerable number of extremely rare knives were sold into the collector market. They quickly found "homes" in the collections of a number of lucky Case fans. Some, of course, have since been traded or sold, thus adding several fine and expensive old knives to the marketplace.

Case's tenure as a Parker company was relatively short lived. In March 1990, Case joined other of his companies in bankruptcy proceedings. The company was sold to a Chattanooga-based investment firm known as River Associates and operations of the Bradford factory resumed. In 1993, ownership of the company went to Zippo Manufacturing Company. Ironically, the company known best for its cigarette lighters had been Case's sister subsidiary when they were both owned by American Brands.

Although short, the Case-Parker years were significant ones for the famous old brand. For too many years preceding the Parker ownership, many collectors believed that the knife manufacturer had failed to live up to its generations-long reputation for quality. The turn into the 1990s marked the beginning of a turnaround in product quality. Once again, collectors and users alike could join the company's employees in their pride for their knives marked "Case."

W. R. Case & Sons Stampings

During the long history of W. R. Case & Sons, there have been about three dozen different stamps used on its knives. These include but are not limited to the following:

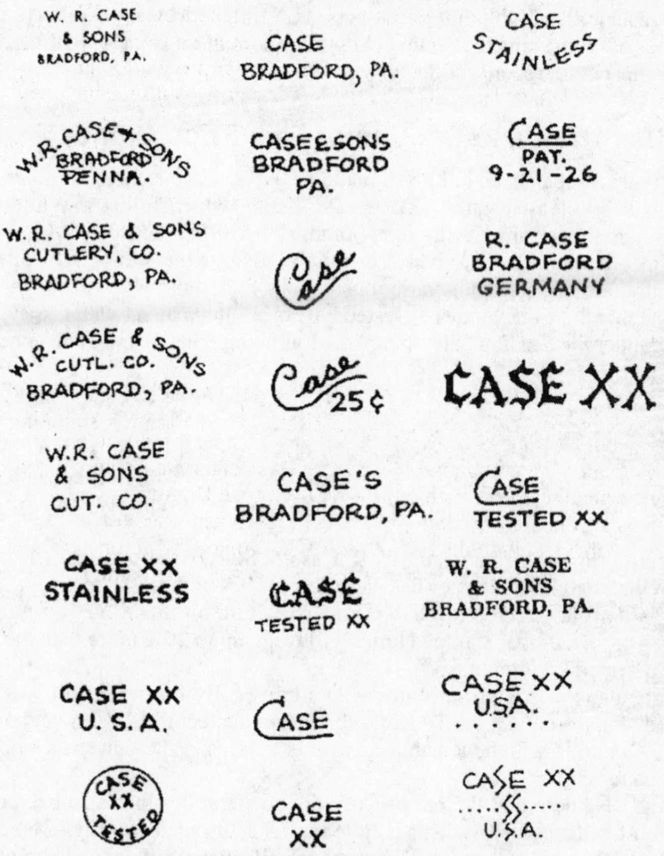

The "Case XX" stamping on pocketknives was used from 1940 to 1965 with pattern numbers added to the reverse side of the tang in 1949. In 1965, the company began stamping its knives "Case XX U.S.A." In 1970, the logo was again changed, this time to "Case XX U.S.A." but with ten dots under the logo. Each year after that, a dot was removed so that a 1975 knife would have five dots and a 1979 knife would have one dot. In 1980, the stamping was again changed. The dotting system, beginning with ten dots, was renewed, but the name stamp was modified to what was to become known as "the Lightning S"—the "S" in the company name was no longer curved and resembled a lightning bolt. In 1990, the system of dots was stopped and the year of manufacture was stamped onto knife tangs.

On the occasion of some of these logo changes, there were large numbers of collectors who bought store displays of the old logo knives. Some of these displays can still be found intact, but individual knives that have been on those boards usually fade on one side and do not bring as much as knives of the same stamping that were not on a board.

TRANSITIONS

With each logo change there were some knives, such as the 6488 and the 64052, that had two blades stamped with the logo. Sometimes one blade with the old logo and one blade with the new logo were used in the same knife. These knives with transitory markings can be found in XX to USA, USA to ten dots, and in various combinations of dots, with eight to ten dots being most common for the 6488. The knife in question would be considered a

USA, XX, ten dot, etc. by the tang stamping on the master blade—the blade closest to the shield.

The collector should be aware that minor variations in many of these stampings is not so unusual. Whenever a worn-out or broken die was replaced, the replacement die was occasionally not identical to its predecessor. One may see this variation on some Tested XX knives. For instance, the top point of the large "C" often varies in its relative position with the top of the "a." Most knife collectors chose to ignore these small variations as being relatively insignificance as regards collector values.

How to Use the Case Section of This Price Guide

The collector who specializes in knives made by W. R. Case & Sons or other Case-related companies will be pleased with the extensive listing which follows. While the listing is much larger than that of any other single brand, it is justified because of Case's undisputed leadership in collectible pocketknives. The field is so large that most Case collectors further specialize into patterns, stamping variations, handle materials, etc.

Please note that the value guides to Tested knives is shown along with Case XX, USA, and Dot knives. Under the heading "Stamping" the following criteria should be remembered:

Tested . . . . Case Tested XX stamping (prior to 1940)
XX. . . . . Case XX stamping (1940–1965)
U.S.A. . . . . Case XX U.S.A. stamping (1965–1970)
Dots . . . . Case XX U.S.A. with dots beneath (1970–1980)
Lightning S Dots . . . . Case XX U.S.A. with dots and stylized "S" (1980–1990)

A price guide for knives stamped "W. R. Case & Sons, Bradford, PA." (last used around 1920) is not included in the master list. Very few knives with this stamping will be encountered, so it is hard to develop a reliable price structure on them; but, on most patterns, a "W. R. Case" or "Bradford" stamped knife will bring up to 20% more than the same pattern with a "Case Tested" stamping.

Please note also the pricing structure of Dot knives. By far the majority of collectors of Case "dotted" knives collect the 10 Dot only or they collect the 9,8,7,6, and 5 Dots only as a group. A 5 Dot knife with bone handles is valued basically the same as a 9 dot of the same handle and pattern.

One should also note that the era of Case-dotted stampings has also been one of Delrin handles on quite a few patterns. This handle material, although worthy of hard use, has not been popular with knife collectors. The average collector would value them at less than retail price, although a person seeking a using knife may be happy to have purchased the knife at full retail.

All Tested knives are priced as though they are handled in green bone since that is true for approximately 90% of this era's patterns. The remaining small percentage is handled in red bone and rough black. While red bone handled knives will sell for only slightly less than green bone, rough black handled knives will be valued at 20–30% below green bone tested knives.

LININGS ON CASE KNIVES

Case used iron liners until the late 1920s, when a change was made to nickel silver. At times, the company would substitute brass for nickel silver. The exception to this note of interest is the "Big Daddy Barlow," which was lined with iron until 1973, when the pattern was changed to Delrin handles with brass liners.

PATTERN NUMBERS

Case's knife numbering system offers the collector quite a bit of information about a knife, allowing one to determine whether the knife has the proper handle, number of blades, etc. These pattern numbers can only be relied upon, however, on Case knives made after 1949, when the pattern numbers were stamped on each knife produced.

A Case pattern number usually consists of four digits. The first indicates the handle material, the second digit represents the number of blades and the last two digits are the factory pattern numbers and a zero between the second and third digits represents a variation of an existing pattern.

THE FIRST DIGIT

The handle material numbers and letters are listed below. An "*" will be used to show a handle material found only on Case Tested XX knives (1920–1950):

1—Walnut
2—Black Composition
3—Yellow Composition
4—White Composition
5—Genuine Stag
6—Bone and Delrin, also used for Second Cut Stag and Rough Black Composition
7—* Tortoiseshell
8—Genuine Mother-of-Pearl
9—Imitation Pearl
B—* Imitation Onyx
CI—Cracked Ice
G—* Green and Red Metal Flake ("Christmas Tree")
GS—Gold Stone (Gold Metal Flake)
H—* Mottled Brown and Cream Composition
HA—* A bathing beauty under clear celluloid
I—Imitation Ivory
M—Metal
P—Pakkawood
S—Silver
R—* Red Striped Celluloid ("Candy Stripe")
RM—Red Mottled
W—*Wire

Although "7" denoted imitation tortoiseshell during Tested XX days, when Case introduced the "Sharkstooth" knife it originally planned to use curly maple and to use the number 7 for its designation. A few blades were already stamped "7" when the company decided to use black dyed Pakkawood instead. Some blades stamped "7" were put into the Pakkawood handled knives and will sometimes be found in a Sharkstooth.

The designation "R" now indicates "Red Bone" rather than the early designation of "Candy Stripe." "G" indicates "Green Bone," instead of the earlier designation of "Christmas Tree."

Since Case has used so many handle materials, the following discussion is offered as additional information on the materials, their origin and usage.

Appaloosa is smooth mottled brown bone first used in 1979.

Black Composition has a smooth texture and usually glossy appearance. Its use began before 1940.

Bone, also known as Bone Stag, comes from the shin bone of a cow and at one time almost every knife manufacturer used this material to handle its knives. With much of the bone used on knives coming from South America, it has become more difficult to get and shortages sometimes cause Case to resort to delrin.

Celluloid-based materials have often been impregnated with colors and metal flakes, offering unusual handle designs. Called by names such as Candy Stripe, Christmas Tree, Goldstone, and Metal Flake, these and other celluloid materials were used on Case Tested knives.

Delrin is a man-made material first used by Case in 1967. It looks much like genuine bone. Since 1974, the shield of a genuine bone stag handled knife will have a circle around the word "CASE" on the shield, while a Delrin or laminated wood handle will not have a circle. Prior to 1974, all shields had the circle around the name.

Genuine Mother-of-Pearl comes from the shell of an oyster. Due to shortages of this material, Case has significantly curtailed production of pearl handled knives except for special issues. The first cutback came in 1967, and the company's 1968 catalog listed no pearl handled knives. In 1970, it again made the 8261, $8279^{1}/_{2}$, 82053SC SS and 8364SC SS patterns, only to again discontinue all pearl handled knives (except $82079^{1}/_{2}$) in 1975.

Genuine Stag has been used since Case's earliest days. It was temporarily discontinued in 1971, but the company still puts stag handles on the Kodiak sheath knife and has issued collector's sets of stag handled knives.

Green Bone is bone stag with a deep green or brown-green tint. It was quite commonly used on Tested knives and is found on the older XX knives. Used between 1940 and 1955, knives handled with green bone are now one of the more desirable Case collectibles.

High Art is a handle type similar to those made famous by Canton Cutlery Co., Aerial Cutlery Co. and others. It features a photo under a transparent plastic cover and is found on a few extremely old Case knives and on a 1980 limited issue knife, the HA$199^{1}/_{2}$.

Imitation Pearl is produced in several variations with the more usual one having a flaked appearance and popularly known as "Cracked Ice."

Red and Green Bone in a different shading has been used on some special Case contract knives and regular production in recent years.

Red Bone in its true form is found only on XX or Tested knives and its color was probably caused by a particular dye that Case was using at the time. A true red bone should have the front handle the same tint as the back handle. Knives that have been displayed in sunlight sometimes fade to a red color, but one that is usually dull and does not match the back handle. This isn't a true red bone. Some USA and Dot knives have red handles that would be the true red bone if they were on a Case XX. These knives are valued slightly higher than knives of the same pattern handled with regular bone.

Red Stag is genuine stag with a reddish cast, usually found on pre-1940 Case knives. It was also used in some limited production knives during the late 1900s.

Rough Black was used as a substitute for bone stag during and shortly after World War II. Called Plastag by W. R. Case & Sons, it has a rubber-like base and has no set pattern of jigging.

Second Cut Stag is made from the remaining antler after the stag slabs have been removed for use as "genuine stag." Jigged, as is bone, it can be found on knives stamped both "5" and "6." This type of handle has been usually been used on patterns 5254, 6254, 5375, 6375, 6488 and 5488, hence some occasional misrepresentation of handle material and pattern numbers among knife traders.

Smooth Bone is a red bone handle that is not jigged, first used by Case in 1979.

Walnut has been used on Case knives since 1920.

White Composition was discontinued about 1974. White in color but in texture the same as black composition.

Yellow Composition may be seen in two variations. One has a deep glossy yellow color handle with a white line around its outer edge, sometimes referred to as a white liner. This variation, when found, is only on XX or older knives. The other variation lacks the white liner and can be found on knives today.

THE SECOND DIGIT

The second digit of the Case pattern numbers indicates the number of blades. W. R. Case & Sons made a few patterns with five blades in the Tested XX and Bradford days but, since that time, has primarily made one, two, three, and four blade knives.

FACTORY DESIGN NUMBERS

The remaining digits of a Case pattern number denote the factory designation for that handle pattern. A "0" as the first digit denotes a variation from an existing pattern. For example, 06247 is a two blade variation of the 6347 pattern.

A few Case knives omit the handle material and blade number digits, leaving only the factory pattern number. An example is the $6225^{1}/_{2}$ stamped $25^{1}/_{2}$.

BLADE ABBREVIATIONS

After many pattern numbers, there are abbreviations for the various blades or a description of the knife, such as:

DR—Drilled through bolster for lanyard
EO—Easy open
F—File blade
I—Iron liners
L—Blade locks open
P—Punch blade
PEN—Pen blade
R—Bail in handle
RAZ—One arm man blade or razor blade
SAB—Saber ground master blade
SH—Sheepfoot blade
S or SHAD—indicates no bolsters
SC or SCIS—indicates scissors
SP—Spey blade
SS—Stainless steel blades and springs
SSP—Stainless steel blades and springs, polished edge
T—Tip bolsters
1/2—Clip master blade
3/4—Saber ground blade

Sheath Knives

The collector interested in Case sheath knives should recognize several peculiarities relating to their collector value and stampings. Sheath knives have not been in nearly so great demand by Case collectors as pocketknives. Consequently, they are not valued as highly as pocketknives of the same period. For example, when Case issued its collector's sets, there were five stag handled sheath knives in each set. When the knives were sold individually, the fixed blade knives were sold for about half the amount realized by pocketknives. As older pocketknives have become more difficult to find and more expensive to buy, sheath knives may be future"sleepers." Consequently, it may be wise for collectors to occasionally purchase Case sheath knives that are reasonably priced. Case-related knives marked "Jean Case Cutlery Co." and "Kinfolks" are noteworthy for any collector of Case sheath knives.

Case did stamp sheath knives with "Case Tested XX" but, when the pocketknife stamping was changed to "Case XX" about 1940, the stamping on the sheath knives was changed from "Case XX" to "Case." When the pocketknife stamping was again changed from "Case XX" to "Case XX, U.S.A." in 1965, the sheath knives stamping was changed to "Case XX Made in U.S.A." When pocketknife stamping was changed to the dot system in 1970, sheath stamping was not changed. Specific stampings/markings on sheath knives do differ from pocketknives made during the same periods. Still, the following letter codes listed with the stamping examples offer insight as to dates of manufacture.

W.R.CASE &SONS
BRADFORD,PA.
(Until 1932)
(A)

CASE
BRADFORD, PA.
(Until 1932)
(B)

Case
STAINLESS
(Mid 1930s)
(C)

CASE
(About 1932 - 1940)
(D)

CASE
TESTED XX
(About 1932 - 1940)
(E)

CASE'S
TESTED XX
(About 1932 - 1940)
(F)

CASE
(About 1932 - 1940)
(G)

CASE'S
STAINLESS
(About 1945 - 1955)
(H)

CASE
(About 1940 - 1965)
(I)

CASE
(About 1940 - 1965)
(J)

CASE XX
(About 1940 - 1965)
(K)

CASE XX
U.S.A.
(1965 to Date)
(L)

CASE XX
•••••••••
USA
(1980)
(M)

Sketches by Allen Swayne

Fixed Blade Knives

Pattern	*Stamping*	*Years Made*	*Handle*	*Variation/Blade*	*Mint Price*
M-15	D	1940–1965			150
M-15	I	1940–1965			90
M-15	J	1940–1965			150
M-15	K	1940–1965			90
E-22-5	D	1937–1940			150
E-22-5	E	1937–1940			150

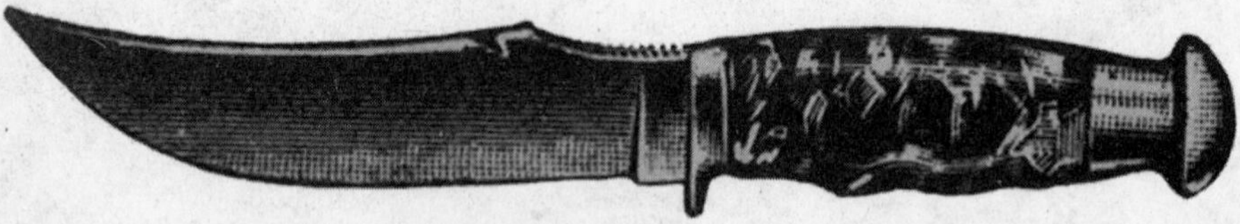

E-23-5	D	1937–1940	Pearl/Black/Red	Chromed	250
E-23-5	E	1937–1940	Pearl/Black/Red	Chromed	250
E-23-5	F	1937–1940	Pearl/Black/Red	Chromed	250
E-23-5	G	1937–1940	Pearl/Black/Red	Chromed	250
E-23-5	H	1945–1949	Pearl/Black/Red	Chromed	225

Pattern	*Stamping*	*Years Made*	*Handle*	*Variation/Blade*	*Mint Price*
C-23-5	D	1937–1940			170
C-23-5	E	1932–1942			170
34	D	1937–1949			100
34	E	1937–1942			100
	F	1937–1942			200
RE-62	F	1937–1940			175
62-5	F	1934–1949	Bone	5″ Chromed	250

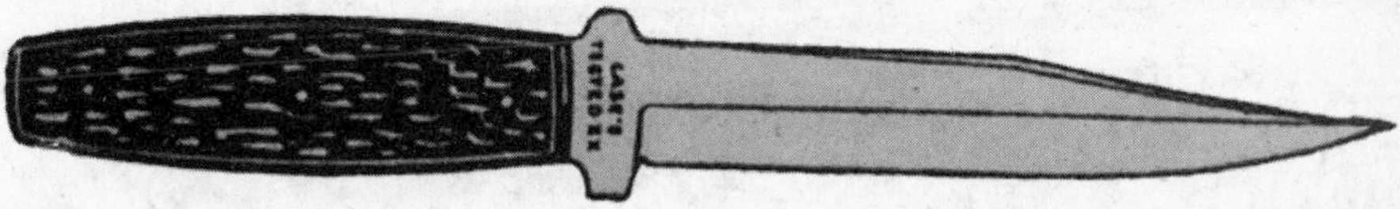

62-6	F	1934–1949	Bone	6″ Chromed	250
63-5	D	1934–1940	Bone	5″ Chromed/Saber	255
63-5	J	1940–1942	Bone	5″ Chromed/Saber	225
63-6	B	1926–1934	Bone	5″ Chromed	275
63-6	D	1934–1940	Bone	5″ Chromed	250
63-6	I	1940–1942	Bone	5″ Chromed	175

64	F	1934–1940	Bone	4″ Chromed/Straight	155
64	H	1940–1949	Bone	4″ Chromed/Straight	150
64	K	1940–1949	Bone	4″ Chromed/Straight	115
E66	F	1934–1940	Bone	4″ Chromed	165
E66	I	1940–1941	Bone	4″ Chromed	165

RE66	F	1934–1940	Pearl and Brown	4″ Chromed	160
RE66	I	1940–1941	Pearl and Brown	4″ Chromed	160
67	D	1934–1940	Bone	4″ Chromed/Skinning	150
67	F	1934–1940	Bone	4″ Chromed/Skinning	140
67	I	1940–1949	Bone	4″ Chromed/Skinning	115
67	K	1940–1949	Bone	4″ Chromed/Skinning	115

92	D	1934–1940	Leather/Fiber	4 1/2″ Chromed	90
92	E	1934–1940	Leather/Fiber	4 1/2″ Chromed	90
92	F	1934–1940	Leather/Fiber	4 1/2″ Chromed	85
92	G	1934–1940	Leather/Fiber	4 1/2″ Chromed	85
92	I	1940–1949	Leather/Fiber	4 1/2″ Chromed	75
92	J	1940–1949	Leather/Fiber	4 1/2″ Chromed	80
92	K	1940–1949	Leather/Fiber	4 1/2″ Chromed	75
147	D	1937–1940	Walnut	Chromed	120

Pattern	*Stamping*	*Years Made*	*Handle*	*Variation/Blade*	*Mint Price*
147	E	1937–1940	Walnut	Chromed	120
147	F	1937–1940	Walnut	Chromed	120
147	G	1937–1940	Walnut	Chromed	110
147	H	1945–1955	Walnut	Chromed	85
147	I	1940–1965	Walnut	Chromed	70
147	J	1940–1965	Walnut	Chromed	70
147	K	1940–1965	Walnut	Chromed	70
147	L	1965–1975	Walnut	Chromed	50

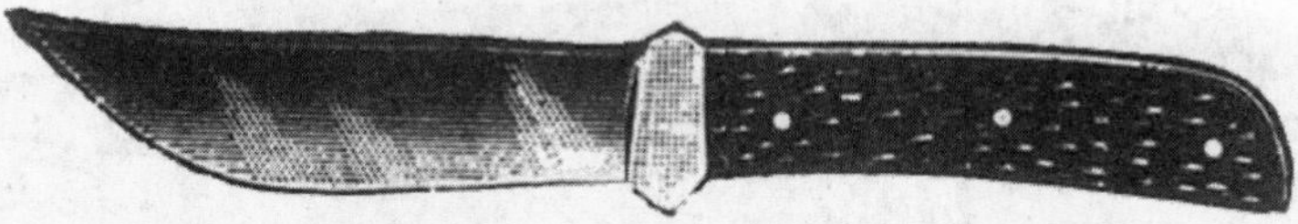

161	D	1934–1940	Bone Stag	Chromed	165
161	E	1934–1940	Bone Stag	Chromed	160
161	F	1934–1940	Bone Stag	Chromed	160
161	G	1934–1940	Bone Stag	Chromed	160
161	I	1940–1949	Bone Stag	Chromed	130
161	J	1940–1949	Bone Stag	Chromed	125
161	K	1940–1949	Bone Stag	Chromed	125
2FINN	L	1968–1988	Black Plastic	Chromed	35
206	I	1940–1949			120
206	J	1940–1949			120

208-5	E	1934–1940	Black Rubber	Chromed	95
208-5	I	1940–1949	Black Rubber	Chromed	85
209	H	1942–1949	Brn/Blk Rubber	Chromed/Saber	100
209	J	1942–1949	Brn/Blk Rubber	Chromed/Saber	90
216-6	L	1972–1988	Black Plastic	Chromed	40
223-5	L	1965–1988	Black Plastic	Chromed/Saber	55
223-6	L	1968–1988	Black Plastic	Chromed/Saber	45

Pattern	Stamping	Years Made	Handle	Variation/Blade	Mint Price
261-KNIFAX	E	1934–1940	Walnut	Chromed	400
261-KNIFAX	F	1934–1940	Walnut		400
261-KNIFAX	K	1940–1965	Walnut		325
261-KNIFAX	L	1965–1968	Walnut		250
261 Deluxe	J	1940–1964	Walnut	Chromed/Large Axe	400
261 Deluxe	K	1960–1964	Walnut	Chromed/Large Axe	350
262	D	1932–1940	Rubber	Chromed/Skinning	155
013-FINN	H	1949–1955	Leather	4 1/2″ Carbon Steel	50
3-FINN	D	1937–1940	Leather	4 1/2″ Chromed/Saber	60
3-FINN	I	1940–1965	Leather	4 1/2″ Chromed/Saber	45
3-FINN	L	1965–1988	Leather	4 1/2″ Chromed/Saber	35
3-FINN	H	1949–1955	Leather	4 1/2″ Carbon Steel	55
3-FINNSSP	L	1966–1988	Leather	4 1/2″ Carbon Steel	40
3-TWINFINN	I	1942–1965	Leather	4 1/2″ Carbon Steel	70
3-TWINFINN	L	1965–1977	Leather	4 1/2″ Steel	45

Pattern	Stamping	Years Made	Handle	Variation/Blade	Mint Price
M3-FINN	I	1942–1965	Leather	3″ Chromed/Saber	40
M3-FINN	L	1965–1973	Leather	3″ Chromed/Saber	30
M3-FINN	H	1949–1955			45
M3-FINNSSP	L	1966–1988			35

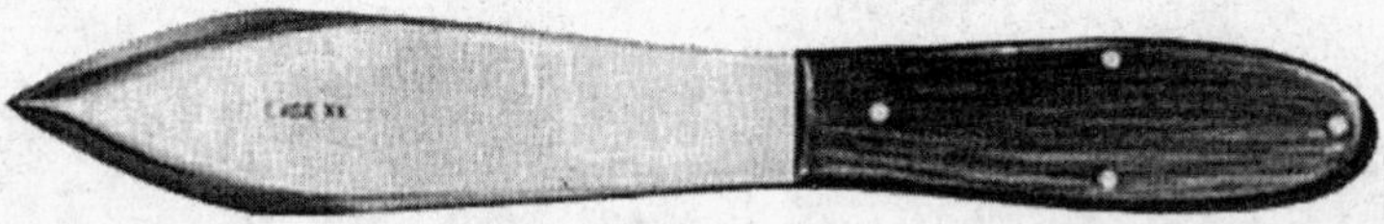

Pattern	Stamping	Years Made	Handle	Variation/Blade	Mint Price
303	D	1934–1940	Fiber	Chromed	50
303	K	1940–1980	Fiber	Chromed	35
309	D	1932–1940	Leather/Aluminum	Chromed/Saber	160
309	G	1937–1949	Leather/Aluminum	Chromed/Saber	150

Pattern	Stamping	Years Made	Handle	Variation/Blade	Mint Price
315-4″	D	1934–1940	Leather/Fiber	Chromed	85
315-4″	K	1940–1965	Leather/Fiber	Chromed	65
315-4″	L	1965–1975	Leather/Fiber	Chromed	45
315-4 1/4″	I	1942–1949	Leather/Fiber	Chromed	60
315-4 1/4	K	1940–1949	Leather/Fiber	Chromed	60
315-4 1/2″	I	1955–1965	Leather/Fiber	Chromed	55
315-4 1/2″	L	1965–1996	Leather/Fiber	Chromed	35
316-5″	I	1942–1965	Leather/Fiber	Chromed	55
316-5″	J	1940–1965	Leather/Fiber	Chromed	55
316-5″	K	1940–1965	Leather/Fiber	Chromed	40
316-5″	L	1965–1973	Leather/Fiber	Chromed	30
316-5″ SSP	L	1966–1980	Leather/Fiber	Stainless Steel	35
317	D	1932–1940			130
317	E	1932–1940			130
317	F	1932–1940			130
317	G	1932–1940			130
322-5″	D	1937–1940	Leather/Fiber	Chromed	145
322-5″	E	1937–1940	Leather/Fiber	Chromed	145
322-5″	F	1937–1949	Leather/Fiber	Chromed	140
322-5″	G	1937–1949	Leather/Fiber	Chromed	140

Pattern	*Stamping*	*Years Made*	*Handle*	*Variation/Blade*	*Mint Price*
322-5½″	I	1942–1949			110
322-5½″	J	1942–1949			110
322-5½″	K	1942–1949			110
323-3¼″	I	1959–1965	Leather		40
323-3¼″	J	1959–1965	Leather		40
323-3¼″	K	1959–1965	Leather		40
323-3¼″	L	1965–1988	Leather		30
323-5″	D	1934–1940	Leather		70
323-5″	E	1934–1940	Leather		70
323-5″	F	1934–1940	Leather		70
323-5″	G	1934–1940	Leather		70
323-5″	I	1940–1965	Leather		60
323-5″	J	1940–1965	Leather		60
323-5″	K	1940–1965	Leather		45
323-5″	L	1965–1988	Leather		35
323-6″	D	1934–1940	Leather/Fiber		75
323-6″	E	1934–1940	Leather/Fiber		75
323-6″	F	1934–1940	Leather/Fiber		75
323-6″	G	1934–1940	Leather/Fiber		75
323-6″	I	1940–1965	Leather/Fiber		65
323-6″	J	1940–1965	Leather/Fiber		60
323-6″	L	1965–1985	Leather/Fiber		45
324	D	1934–1940	Leather/Fiber	4⅝″ Skinning	80
324	E	1934–1940	Leather/Fiber	4⅝″ Skinning	80
324	F	1934–1940	Leather/Fiber	4⅝″ Skinning	80
324	G	1934–1940	Leather/Fiber	4⅝″ Skinning	80

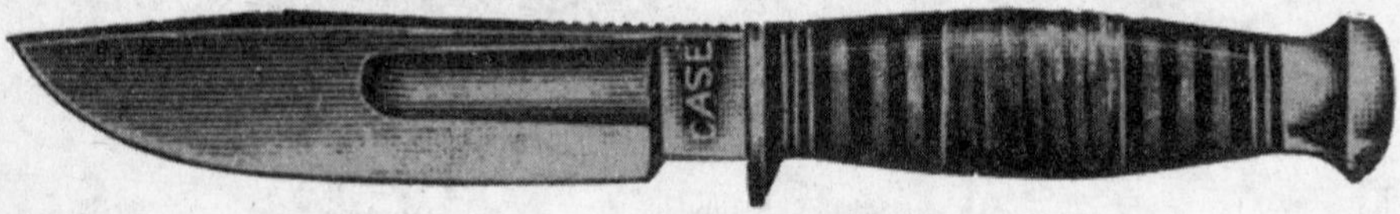

Pattern	*Stamping*	*Years Made*	*Handle*	*Variation/Blade*	*Mint Price*
325-4″	D	1934–1940	Leather/Fiber/Brass	Chromed	80
325-4″	E	1934–1940	Leather/Fiber/Brass	Chromed	80
325-4″	F	1934–1940	Leather/Fiber/Brass	Chromed	80
325-4″	G	1934–1940	Leather/Fiber/Brass	Chromed	80
325-4″	I	1940–1965	Leather/Fiber/Brass	Chromed	65
325-4″	J	1940–1965	Leather/Fiber/Brass	Chromed	65
325-4″	K	1940–1965	Leather/Fiber/Brass	Chromed	60
325-4″	L	1965–1974	Leather/Fiber/Brass	Chromed	40
3025-5″	C	1932–1938	Leather/Fiber/Brass	Chromed	160
3025-5″	D	1932–1940	Leather/Fiber/Brass	Chromed	155
3025-5″	E	1932–1940	Leather/Fiber/Brass	Chromed	145
3025-5″	F	1932–1940	Leather/Fiber/Brass	Chromed	125
3025-5″	K	1940–1959	Leather/Fiber/Brass	Chromed	100
3025-6″	D	1937–1940	Leather/Fiber/Brass	Chromed	125
3025-6	K	1940–1965	Leather/Fiber/Brass	Chromed	90
3025-6	L	1965–1966	Leather/Fiber/Brass	Chromed	100
326	D	1937–1940	Leather/Fiber/Brass	4½″ Chromed	85
326	E	1937–1940	Leather/Fiber/Brass	4½″ Chromed	85
326	F	1937–1940	Leather/Fiber/Brass	4½″ Chromed	85
326	G	1937–1949	Leather/Fiber/Brass	4½″ Chromed	85
352	D	1934–1940	Cream Composition	5″ Chromed/Saber	125
352	E	1934–1949	Cream Composition	5″ Chromed/Saber	125
352	F	1934–1949	Cream Composition	5″ Chromed/Saber	125
352	G	1934–1939	Cream Composition	5″ Chromed/Saber	125
361	D	1934–1937	Leather/Fiber	4½″ Chromed/Skinning	125
361	E	1934–1937	Leather/Fiber	4½″ Chromed/Skinning	125
361	F	1934–1937	Leather/Fiber	4½″ Chromed/Skinning	125
361	G	1934–1937	Leather/Fiber	4½″ Chromed/Skinning	125

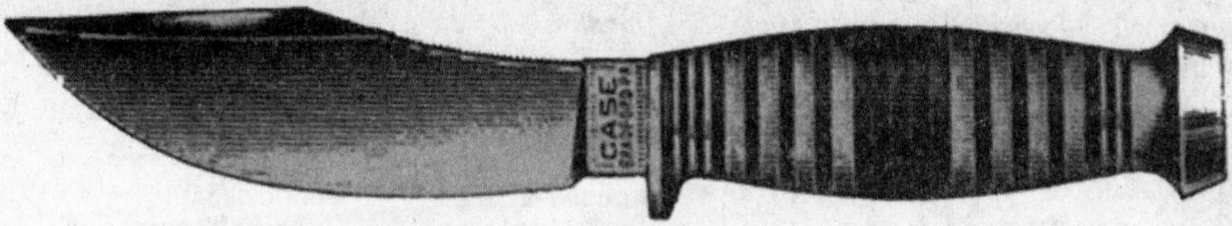

Pattern	*Stamping*	*Years Made*	*Handle*	*Variation/Blade*	*Mint Price*
362	D	1934–1940	Leather/Fiber/Brass	4$^{1}/_{2}$″ Chromed	175
362	J	1940–1965	Leather/Fiber/Brass	4$^{1}/_{2}$″ Chromed	140
362	L	1965–1974	Leather/Fiber/Brass	4$^{1}/_{2}$″ Chromed	75

364SAB	D	1934–1940	Leather/Fiber	4$^{1}/_{2}$″ Chromed/Saber	65
364SAB	I	1940–1965	Leather/Fiber	4$^{1}/_{2}$″ Chromed/Saber	55
364SAB	L	1965–1988	Leather/Fiber	4$^{1}/_{2}$″ Chromed/Saber	40
365	D	1934–1940	Leather/Fiber/Brass	5″ Chromed	60
365	I	1940–1965	Leather/Fiber/Brass	5″ Chromed	50
365	L	1965–1974	Leather/Fiber/Brass	5″ Chromed	30
365SAB	I	1942–1965	Leather/Fiber/Brass	5″ Chromed/Saber	60
365SAB	J	1942–1965	Leather/Fiber/Brass	5″ Chromed/Saber	60

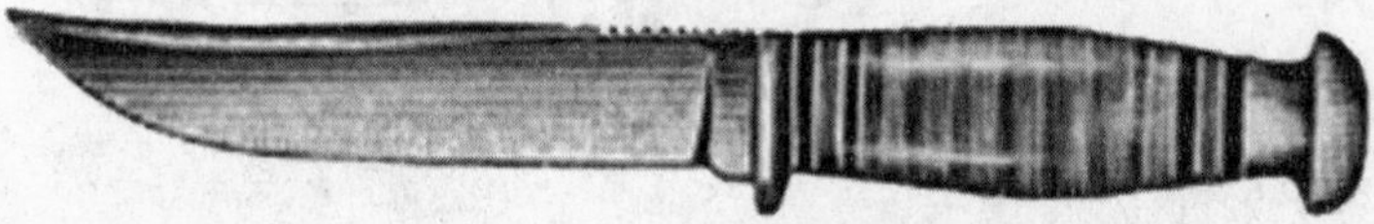

365SAB	L	1965–1988	Leather/Fiber/Brass	5″ Chromed/Saber	40
366	D	1937–1940	Leather/Fiber/Brass	4″ Chromed	65
366	I	1940–1965	Leather/Fiber/Brass	4″ Chromed	55
366	L	1965–1985	Leather/Fiber/Brass	4″ Chromed	35

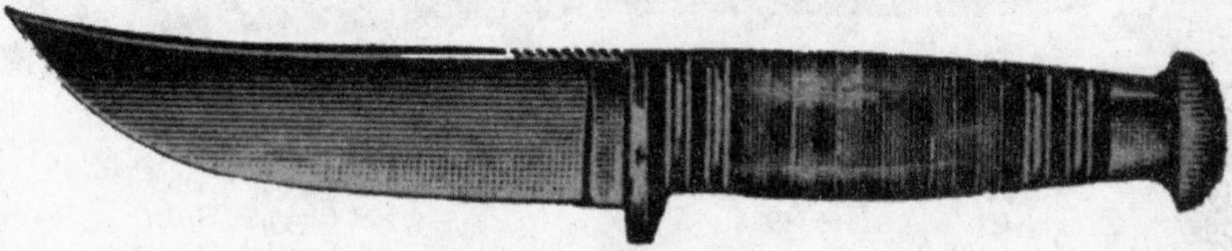

378	D	1934–1940	Leather/Fiber	4$^{1}/_{2}$″ Chromed	80
378	I	1940–1959	Leather/Fiber	4$^{1}/_{2}$″ Chromed	55
378	J	1940–1959	Leather/Fiber	4$^{1}/_{2}$″ Chromed	60
378	K	1940–1959	Leather/Fiber	4$^{1}/_{2}$″ Chromed	50
380 COMBO	L	1968–1974	Leather	Axe and 5″ Blade Hunter	150
392	D	1934–1940	Ivory Composition	4$^{1}/_{2}$″ Chromed/Skinning	160
392	E	1934–1940	Ivory Composition	4$^{1}/_{2}$″ Chromed/Skinning	160
392	F	1934–1940	Ivory Composition	4$^{1}/_{2}$″ Chromed/Skinning	160
392	G	1934–1940	Ivory Composition	4$^{1}/_{2}$″ Chromed/Skinning	160
3361	D	1934–1942	Ivory Composition	4$^{1}/_{2}$″ Chromed/Skinning	165
	J	1940–1942	Ivory Composition	4$^{1}/_{2}$″ Chromed/Skinning	165
457	D	1934–1940	Ivory Composition	3$^{3}/_{4}$″ Chromed/Saber	140
457	E	1934–1940	Ivory Composition	3$^{3}/_{4}$″ Chromed/Saber	140

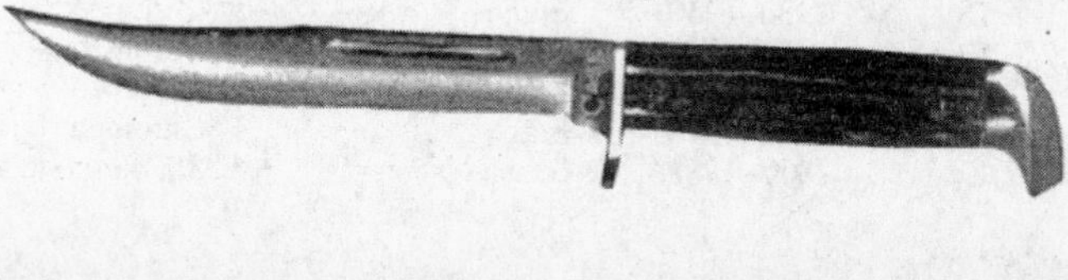

Pattern	*Stamping*	*Years Made*	*Handle*	*Variation/Blade*	*Mint Price*
5-FINN	D	1937–1940	Stag	4 1/4″ Chromed/Saber	140
5-FINN	I	1940–1965	Stag	4 1/4″ Chromed/Saber	85
5-FINN	L	1965–1987	Stag	4 1/4″ Chromed/Saber	55
5-FINN	I	1962–1975	Second cut Stag	5″ Chromed/Saber	150
5-FINNCCSS	H	1949–1955	Second cut Stag	5″ Chromed/Saber	85
5-FINNCCSS	I	1949–1955	Second cut Stag	5″ Chromed/Saber	80
5-FINN-SS	H	1949–1955	Second cut Stag		75
5-FINN-SS	I	1949–1955	Second cut Stag		70
5-FINN-SSP	L	1972–1982	Stag	4 1/4″ Stainless Steel	50
M-5-FINN	G	1940–	Stag		100
M-5-FINN	I	1940–1965	Stag		95
M-5-FINN	L	1965–1988	Stag		80
M-5FINNSS	I	1949–1955	Stag	5″ Stainless Steel	100
F52	D	1934–1940			110
F52	E	1934–1940			110
F52	F	1934–1940			110
F52	G	1934–1940			110
501	D	1937–1940			110
501	E	1937–1940			110
501	F	1937–1949			110
501	G	1937–1949			100

515	D	1934–1940	Stag	4″ Chromed	95
515	E	1934–1940	Stag	4″ Chromed	95
515	F	1934–1940	Stag	4″ Chromed	85
515	G	1934–1940	Stag	4″ Chromed	95
515	I	1940–1965	Stag	4″ Chromed	85

516-5	I	1940–1965	Stag	5″ Chromed/Saber	115
516-5	J	1940–1965	Stag	5″ Chromed/Saber	110
516-5	K	1940–1965	Stag	5″ Chromed/Saber	95
516-5	L	1965–1988	Stag	5″ Chromed/Saber	70
516-5-SSP	L	1972–1982	Stag	5″ Stainless Steel	50
523-3 1/4″	I	1959–1965	Leather		65
523-3 1/4″	J	1959–1965	Leather		65
523-3 1/4″	K	1959–1965	Leather		60
523-3 1/4″	L	1965–1977	Leather		45

523-5″	D	1934–1940	Stag	5″ Chromed	140
523-5″	E	1934–1940	Stag	5″ Chromed	120
523-5″	I	1940–1965	Stag	5″ Chromed	160
523-5″	L	1965–1974	Stag	5″ Chromed	75
523-5-SSP	L	1972–1988	Stag	5″ Stainless Steel	50

Pattern	*Stamping*	*Years Made*	*Handle*	*Variation/Blade*	*Mint Price*
523-6″	D	1934–1940	Stag	6″ Chromed	160
523-6″	J	1940–1965	Stag	6″ Chromed	125
523-6″	K	1965–1974	Stag	6″ Chromed	75

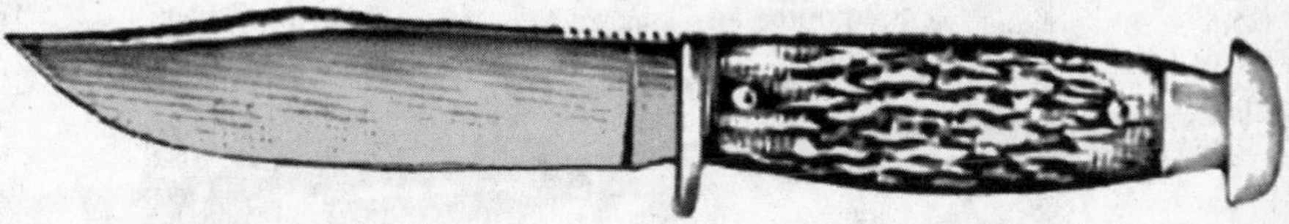

Pattern	*Stamping*	*Years Made*	*Handle*	*Variation/Blade*	*Mint Price*
5025-5	D	1934–1940	Stag	5″ Chromed	150
5025-5	E	1934–1940	Stag	5″ Chromed	150
5025-5	F	1934–1940	Stag	5″ Chromed	145
5025-5	G	1934–1940	Stag	5″ Chromed	150
5025-5	K	1940–1962	Stag	5″ Chromed	130
5026-6	K	1964	Stag	6″ Chromed	215
5026-6	L	1965–1968	Stag	6″ Chromed	225
551	I	1940–1941	Stag	Blade folds into handle	900
552	I	1959–1962		5 3/4″ Chromed	95
552	J	1959–1962		5 3/4″ Chromed	100
552	K	1959–1962		5 3/4″ Chromed	85

Pattern	*Stamping*	*Years Made*	*Handle*	*Variation/Blade*	*Mint Price*
557	D	1934–1940	Stag	3 3/4″ Chromed	145
557	E	1934–1940	Stag	3 3/4″ Chromed	145
557	I	1940–1965	Stag	3 3/4″ Chromed	120
557	L	1965–1968	Stag	3 3/4″ Chromed	125
557SAB	D	1937–1940	Stag	3 3/4″ Chromed/Saber	110
557SAB	E	1937–1940	Stag	3 3/4″ Chromed/Saber	110
557SAB	I	1940–1949	Stag	3 3/4″ Chromed/Saber	100
557SAB	J	1940–1949	Stag	3 3/4″ Chromed/Saber	110
557SAB	K	1940–1949	Stag	3 3/4″ Chromed/Saber	90
Knife-Axe Combo					
561Deluxe	E	1937–1940	Stag	5″ Blade/Large Axe Head	500
561Deluxe	F	1937–1940	Stag	5″ Blade/Large Axe Head	500
561Deluxe	K	1940–1965	Stag	5″ Blade/Large Axe Head	425
561Deluxe	L	1965–1974	Stag	5″ Blade/Large Axe Head	400
578	D	1934–1940	Stag		95
578	E	1934–1940	Stag		95
578	J	1940–1959	Stag		95
578	K	1940–1959	Stag		60
580 COMBO	L	1968–1974	Walnut	Axe and 5″ Blade Hunter	130
5324	D	1934–1940	Stag	4 5/8″ Skinning	220
5324	E	1934–1940	Stag	4 5/8″ Skinning	220
5324	I	1940–1941	Stag	4 5/8″ Skinning	190
5324	J	1940–1941	Stag	4 5/8″ Skinning	180
5324	K	1940–1941	Stag	4 5/8″ Skinning	170

Pattern	*Stamping*	*Years Made*	*Handle*	*Variation/Blade*	*Mint Price*
5325-5	D	1934–1940	Stag	5″ Chromed	160
5325-5	E	1934–1940	Stag	5″ Chromed	165
5325-5	I	1940–1965	Stag	5″ Chromed	120

Pattern	*Stamping*	*Years Made*	*Handle*	*Variation/Blade*	*Mint Price*
5325-5	K	1940–1965	Stag	5″ Chromed	120
5325-5	L	1965–1966	Stag	5″ Chromed	160
5325-6	D	1934–1940	Stag	6″ Chromed Blade	220
5325-6	E	1934–1940	Stag	6″ Chromed Blade	220
5325-6	I	1940–1965	Stag	6″ Chromed Blade	180
5325-6	K	1940–1965	Stag	6″ Chromed Blade	180
5325-6	L	1965–1968	Stag	6″ Chromed Blade	175

5361	D	1934–1940	Stag	4½″ Chromed/Skinning	220
5361	J	1940–1965	Stag	4½″ Chromed/Skinning	185
5361	K	1940–1965	Stag	4½″ Chromed/Skinning	180
5361	L	1965–1975	Stag	4½″ Chromed/Skinning	125
5362	D	1934–1940	Stag	4½″ Chromed	200
5362	I	1940–1949	Stag	4½″ Chromed	150

652	D	1934–1940	Bone	5″ Chromed/Saber	140
652	I	1940–1949	Bone	5″ Chromed/Saber	120
652	K	1940–1949	Bone	5″ Chromed/Saber	120
652-5	J	1962–1965	Bone	5″ Chromed/Saber	130
652-5	K	1962–1965	Bone	5″ Chromed/Saber	125
652-5	L	1965–1968	Bone	5″ Chromed/Saber	100
Knife-Axe Combo					
661-KNIFAX	D	1934–1942	Bone	5″ Blade/4¼″ Axe Chromed	500
661-KNIFAX	E	1934–1942	Bone	5″ Blade/4¼″ Axe Chromed	500
661-KNIFAX	F	1934–1942	Bone	5″ Blade/4¼″ Axe Chromed	500
661-KNIFAX	G	1934–1942	Bone	5″ Blade/4¼″ Axe Chromed	500
F78	E	1934–1937			150
F78	G	1934–1937			150
PS78	E	1934–1937			150
PS78	G	1934–1937			150

709	E	1934–1942	Metal	5″ Blade/Handle compass	250
M-8-FINN	I	1940–1949			75
M-8-FINN	K	1940–1949			75
9-FINN	F	1934–1940	Pearl Composition	4½″ Chromed/Saber	90
9-FINN	K	1940–1955	Pearl Composition	4½″ Chromed/Saber	75

M-9-FINN	E	1934–1955	Pearl Composition	3″ Chromed/Saber	95
M-9-FINN	K	1940–1955	Pearl Composition	3″ Chromed/Saber	75
PS97	D	1934–1937			150

Pattern	*Stamping*	*Years Made*	*Handle*	*Variation/Blade*	*Mint Price*
PS97	E	1934–1937			140
903	E	1934–1937			140
923-5″	D	1934–1940	Leather		125
923-5″	I	1940–1949	Leather		100
923-5″	J	1940–1949	Leather		110
923-5″	K	1940–1949	Leather		100
923-6″	D	1934–1940	Leather		125
923-6″	I	1940–1949	Leather		90
923-6″	J	1940–1949	Leather		120
923-6″	K	1940–1949	Leather		90
952	D	1934–1940			95
952	E	1934–1942			110
952	G	1934–1943			100
957	D	1934–1940			125
957	E	1934–1940			125
957	G	1934–1940			120
957	I	1940–1942			100
957	J	1940–1942			110
957-SAB	D	1937–1940			120
957-SAB	E	1937–1940			115
957-SAB	G	1937–1940			110
957-SAB	I	1940–1949			110
961	E	1934–1940	Imitation Pearl		425
961	F	1934–1940	Imitation Pearl		425
961	K	1940–1949	Imitation Pearl		375
5″ Blade Knife/Axe					
961-Deluxe	E	1932–1040	Imitation Pearl		500
961-Deluxe	F	1932–1940	Imitation Pearl		475
964	F	1932–1940	Fancy Composition	4″ Chromed/Straight	160
964	I	1940–1965	Fancy Composition	4″ Chromed/Straight	150
964	K	1940–1965	Fancy Composition	4″ Chromed/Saber	145
978	F	1932–1940	Pearl Composition	4 1/2″ Blade	125
9235-5	F	1932–1940		5″ Blade	150
9235-5	I	1940–1965		5″ Blade	125
9362	F	1932–1940	Deer Horn	4 1/2″ Chromed/Straight	140
9362	I	1940–1965	Deer Horn	4 1/2″ Chromed/Straight	130
APACHE	L	1966–1980	Stag	5 1/4″ Stainless Steel	60
APACHE	M	1981	Stag	5 1/4″ Stainless Steel	50
BOWIE	L	1967–1988	Black	11 1/2″ Blade	200
CHEROKEE	L	1967–1980	Stag	4 1/4″ Stainless Steel	45
CHEYENNE	L	1967–1980	Stag	5″ Stainless Steel	50
CHEYENNE	M	1981	Stag	5″ Stainless Steel	75
FINN	D	1934–1937	Pearl Composition	4 3/8″ Chromed	125
KODIAK	I	1964–1966	XX Model	4 3/8″ Chromed	150
KODIAK	K	1966–1967	Transitional Model		150
KODIAK	L	1967–1973	No Stars Model		110
KODIAK	M	1973–1988			95
MACHETE	K	1942	Military		170
MIDGET	D	1934–1940	Pearl Composition	2 1/4″ Chromed	175
	I	1940–1948	Pearl Composition	2 1/4″ Chromed	175

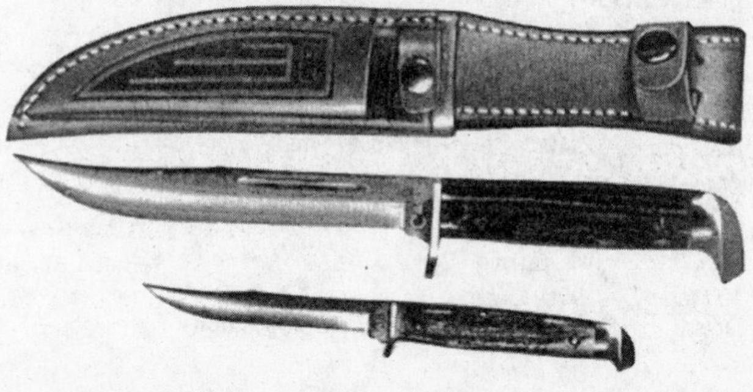

Pattern	Stamping	Years Made	Handle	Variation/Blade	Mint Price
TWIN-FINN	D	1940–1949	Stag	5″ & 3″ Chromed	250
TWIN-FINN	K	1950–1964	Stag	5″ & 3″ Chromed	170
TWIN-FINN	L	1965–1974	Stag	5″ & 3″ Chromed	130
SPORTSMAN	A	1930	Stag	5 Piece Set	2500

Pocket Knives

Pattern	Stamping	Years Made	Handle	Variation/Blade	Mint Price

2³/₁₆″ Watch Fob

Watch Fob	Tested	Prior 1940	Pearl		200

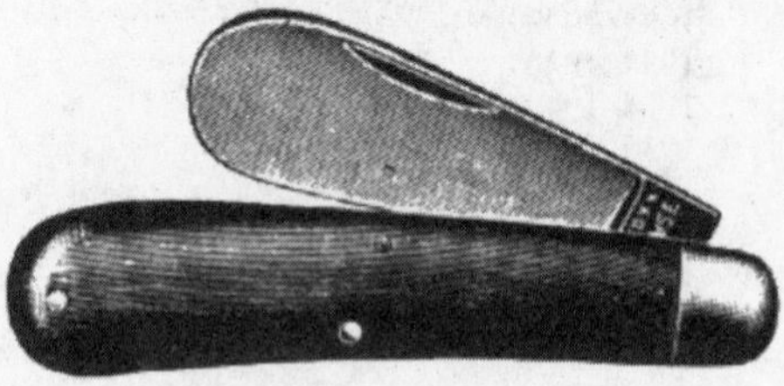

Maize Knife

Maize Knife

Maize #1	Tested	Prior 1940	Cocobolo	3⁵/₈″	400
Maize #2	Tested	Prior 1940	Cocobolo	4″	400

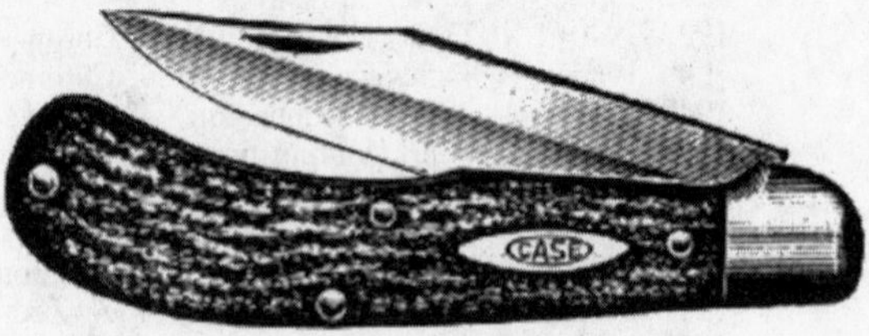

4¹/₂″ Saddlehorn

4¹/₂″ Saddlehorn

3100	Tested	Prior 1940	Yellow Composition		775
6100	Tested	Prior 1940	Green Bone		1250

3¹/₄″ Press Button Slide Blade

3¹/₄″ Press Button Slide Blade

M100	Tested	Prior 1940	Metal		155
M100	Tested	Prior 1940	Green Bone		250
M100	Tested	Prior 1940	Blue Celluloid		175
M100	XX	1940s	Nickel Plated		150
M100	XX	1940s	Gold Plated		200

5¹/₂″ Melon Tester

4100	XX	1960–1965	White Composition		200
4100	USA	1965–1970			160
4100SS	USA	1965–1970		Serrated Blade	700
4100SS	10 Dots	1970–1971			185
4100SS	Dots	1971–1974	White Composition		65

Pattern	Stamping	Years Made	Handle	Variation/Blade	Mint Price
$2\frac{7}{8}$″ Press Button Slide Blade					
M101	Tested	Prior 1940	Metal		150
$3\frac{1}{4}$″ Budding Knife					
4103B&G	Tested	Prior 1940	White Composition		275
6103B&G	Tested	Prior 1940	Bone		600

$3\frac{3}{8}$″ Budding Knife

$3\frac{3}{8}$″ Budding Knife					
6104B	Tested	Prior 1940	Green Bone		650
4104SS	XX	1940–1955	Green Bone		500

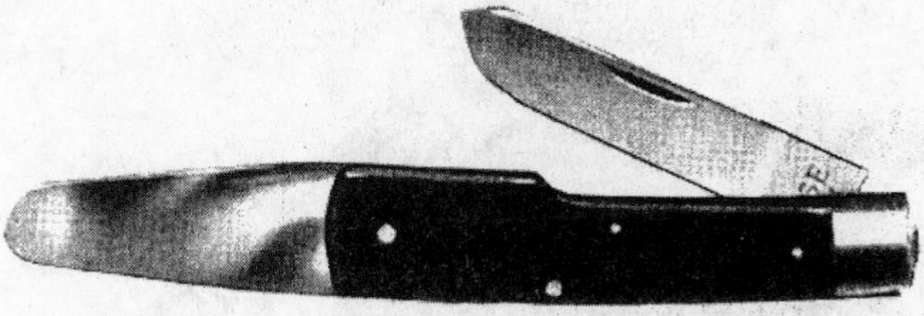

$3\frac{1}{4}$″ Budding Knife

$3\frac{1}{4}$″ Budding Knife					
2109B	Tested	Prior 1940	Black Composition		200
2109B	XX	1940–1965	Black Composition		120
2109B	USA	1965–1968	Black Composition		135
6109B	Tested	Prior 1940	Bone		600

$3\frac{1}{8}$″ Speying Knife

$3\frac{1}{8}$″ Speying Knife					
M110	Tested	Prior 1940	Nickel Silver		150
M110	XX	1940s	Nickel Silver		120
$3\frac{3}{8}$″ Switchblade					
$91210\frac{1}{2}$	Tested	Prior 1940	White Onyx		775

4″ Pruning Knife

Pattern	Stamping	Years Made	Handle	Variation/Blade	Mint Price
4″ Pruning Knife					
11011	Tested	Prior 1940	Walnut		110
11011	XX	1940–1965	Walnut		70
11011	USA	1965–1970	Walnut		40
11011	5 Dots	1974	Pakkawood		40
11011	10 Dots	1970–1971	Walnut		55
11011	Dots	1970s	Walnut		35
61011	Tested	Prior 1940	Green Bone		250
61011	XX	1940s	Green Bone		250
61011	XX	1940s–1965	Bone		125
61011	XX	1964–1965	Laminated Wood		100
61011	USA	1965	Bone		150
61011	USA	1965–1970	Laminated Wood		40
61011	10 Dots	1970–1971	Laminated Wood		45
61011	Dots	1970s	Laminated Wood		30
61011	"S" Dots	1980s	Laminated Wood		25

4″ Bow-Tie Switchblade

Pattern	Stamping	Years Made	Handle	Variation/Blade	Mint Price
4″ Bow-Tie Switchblade					
31211½	Tested	Prior 1940	Yellow Composition		850
H1211½	Tested	Prior 1940	Brn/Cream Celluloid		900
R1212½	Tested	Prior 1940	Red/White Celluloid		925

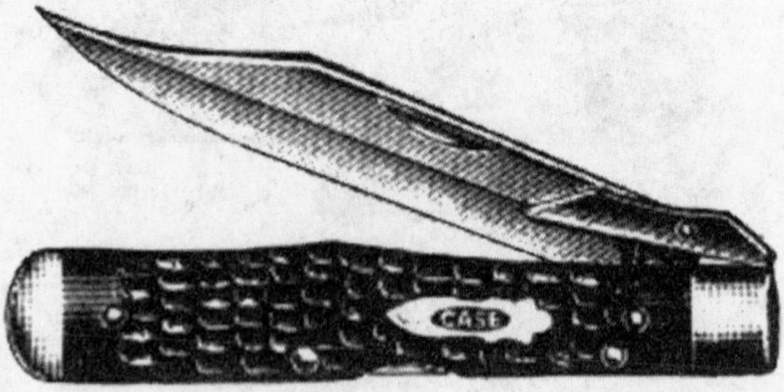

4⅜″ Lockback

Pattern	Stamping	Years Made	Handle	Variation/Blade	Mint Price
4⅜″ Lockback					
3111½	Tested	Prior 1940	Yellow Composition		1000
5111½	8 Dots	1973	Stag	Small Stamp	300
5111½	8 Dots	1973	Stag	Large Stamp	325
5111½	4 Dots	1977	Stag	"Case Razor Edge"	150
5111½	3 Dots	1978	Stag	Blue Scroll	175
5111½	10 Dots	1970	Stag	"Cheetah"	1500
6111½	Tested	Prior 1940	Green Bone		1250
6111½	Tested	Prior 1940	Green Bone	Long Pull	1300

Pattern	Stamping	Years Made	Handle	Variation/Blade	Mint Price
6111½L	XX	1940–1945	Green Bone		1100
6111½L	XX	1955–1965	Bone		500
6111½L	USA	1965–1970	Bone		275
6111½L	10 Dots	1970–1971	Bone		275
6111½L	Dots	1970s	Bone		110
6111½L	Dots	1970s	Delrin		125
6111½L	"S" 10 Dots	1980	Bone		85

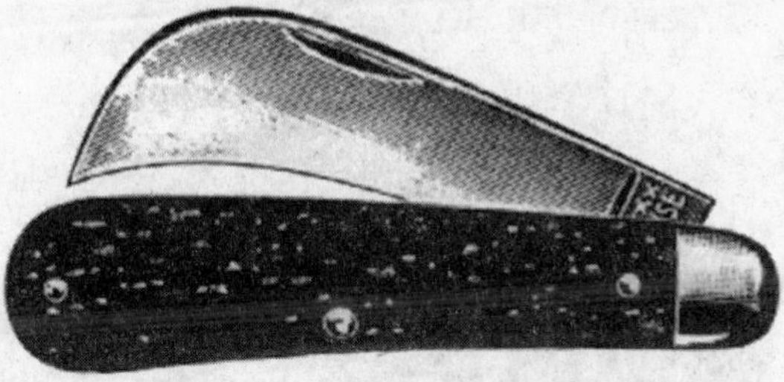

4″ Pruner

4″ Pruner					
61013	Tested	Prior 1940	Green Bone		425
5½″ Swell Center					
61213	Tested	Prior 1940	Green Bone		1400

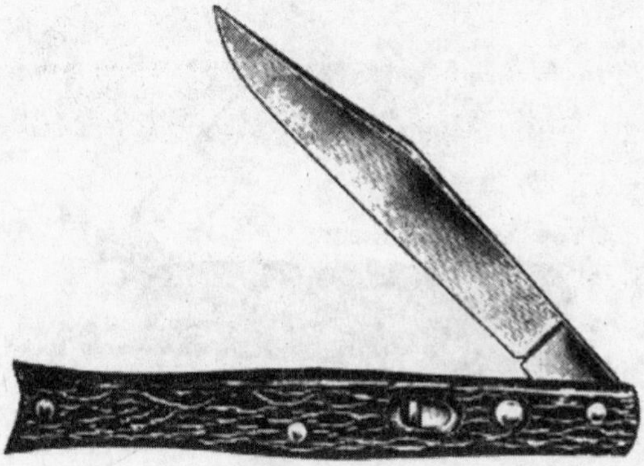

4″ Switchblade

4″ Switchblade					
61213½	Tested	Prior 1940	Rogers Bone		1600

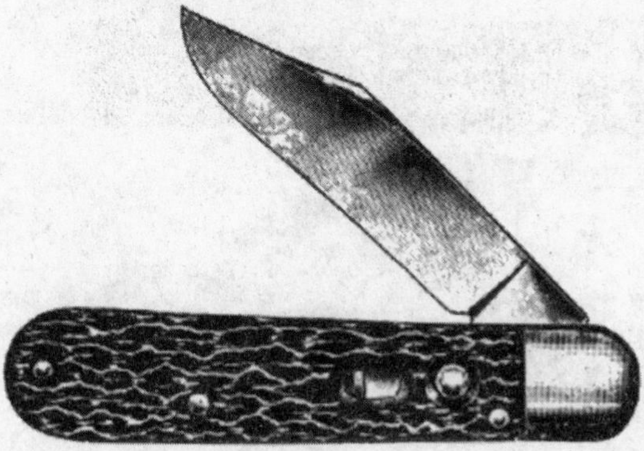

4⅛″ Switchblade

Pattern	Stamping	Years Made	Handle	Variation/Blade	Mint Price
4 1/8″ Switchblade					
61214 1/2	Tested	Prior 1940	Bone		1700
61215 1/2	Tested	Prior 1940	Bone	As above but 5″	1700

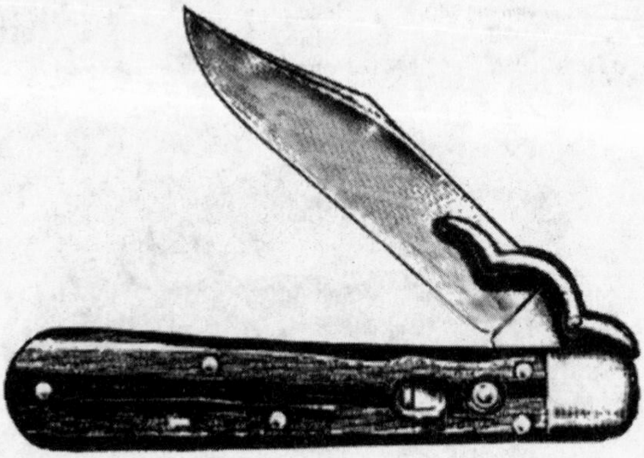

5″ Switchblade

Pattern	Stamping	Years Made	Handle	Variation/Blade	Mint Price
5″ Switchblade					
51215G	Tested	Prior 1940	Stag	Folding guard	3600
51215 1/2F	Tested	Prior 1940	Stag	Fish scaler	3700

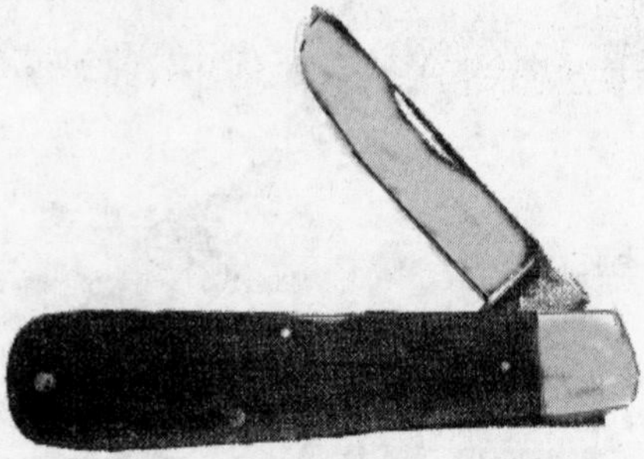

3 1/2″ Budding Knife

Pattern	Stamping	Years Made	Handle	Variation/Blade	Mint Price
3 1/2″ Budding Knife					
1116SP	XX	1960s–1965	Walnut		60
1116SP	USA	1965–1970			45
1116SP	10 Dots	1970–1971			50
1116SP	9 Dots	1971–1972			40
3 3/8″ Jack					
6116 1/2	Tested	Prior 1940	Green Bone		250
6116SP	Tested	Prior 1940	Green Bone		300
6116	Tested		Green Bone		275

3 1/8″ Wire Jack

Pattern	*Stamping*	*Years Made*	*Handle*	*Variation/Blade*	*Mint Price*
3 1/8″ Wire Jack					
W1216	Tested	Prior 1940	Wire	One-piece handle/back	175
W1216K	Tested	Prior 1940	Wire	Cap lifter in blade	175
W1216Pr	Tested	Prior 1940	Wire	Pruner blade	175
M1217	Tested	Prior 1940	Metal	Pull ball opener	400

3″ Pen Knife

Pattern	*Stamping*	*Years Made*	*Handle*	*Variation/Blade*	*Mint Price*
3″ Pen Knife					
M1218K	Tested	Prior 1940	Metal		150

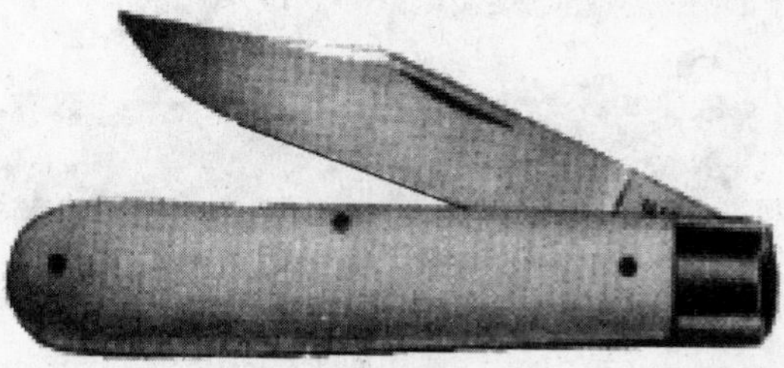

3″ Jack

Pattern	*Stamping*	*Years Made*	*Handle*	*Variation/Blade*	*Mint Price*
3″ Jack					
3124	Tested	Prior 1940	Yellow Composition		150
6124	Tested	Prior 1940	Green Bone		225
31024	Tested	Prior 1940	Yellow Composition		200
61024	Tested	Prior 1940	Green Bone		275
31024½	XX	1955–1965	Yellow Composition		65
61024½	XX	1955–1965	Bone		75
61024½	USA	1965–1967	Bone		60

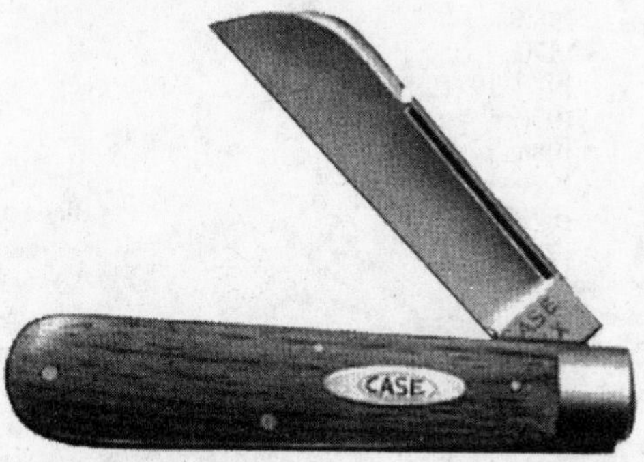

3 1/16″ Jack

Pattern	*Stamping*	*Years Made*	*Handle*	*Variation/Blade*	*Mint Price*
3 1/16″ Jack					
11031SH	Tested	Prior 1940	Walnut		125
11031SHCC	Tested	Prior 1940	Walnut	Concave ground blade	175
11031SHCC	XX	1940–1952	Walnut	Concave ground blade	60
11031SH	XX	1940–1965	Walnut		60

Pattern	*Stamping*	*Years Made*	*Handle*	*Variation/Blade*	*Mint Price*
11031SH	USA	1965–1970	Walnut		45
11031SH	10 Dots	1970–1971	Walnut		45
11031SH	Dots	1970s	Walnut		30

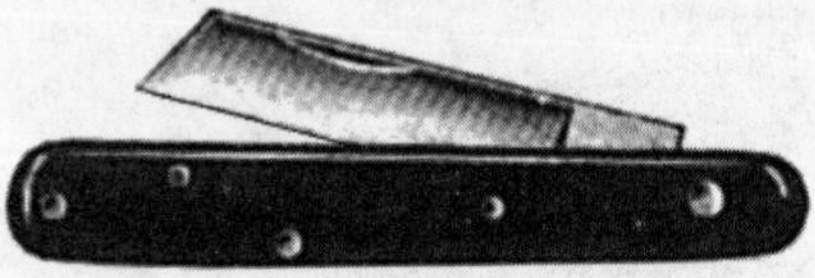

4¹/₈″ Budding Knife

4¹/₈″ Budding Knife

2136	Tested	Prior 1940	Black Composition	Not made in XX	175

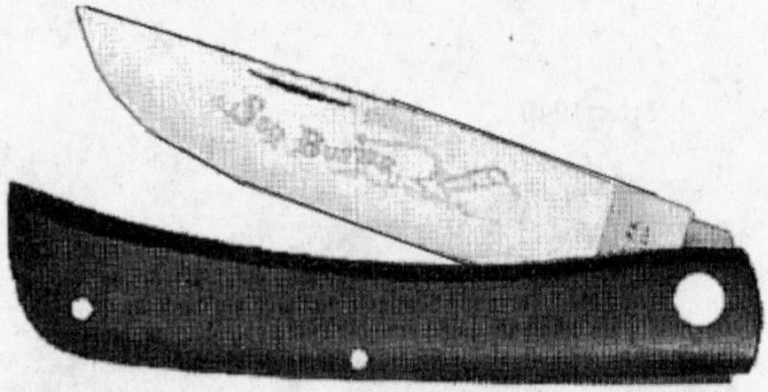

3⁵/₈″ Sodbuster Jr.

3⁵/₈″ Sodbuster Jr.

2137SS	10 Dots	1970–1971	Black Composition		40
2137SS	Dots	1970s			30
2137SS	"S" Dots	1980s			25
2137	10 Dots	1970–1971			80
2137	Dots	1970s			25
2137	"S" Dots	1980s			20
P137SS	Dots	1970s	Pakkawood	Kentucky Bicentennial	35
G137SS	Dots	1970s	Green Delrin	Kentucky Bicentennial	45
5137SS	Dots	1970s	Stag	Kentucky Bicentennial	65

5⁵/₈″ Sodbuster

2138	USA	1967–1970	Black Composition		35
2138	10 Dots	1970–1971			40
2138	"S" Dots	1980s			25
2138	Dots	1970s			30
2138SS	10 Dots	1970–1971			40
2138SS	Dots	1970s			25
2138SS	"S" Dots	1980s			25
2138SSL	10 Dots	1970–1971		Blade locks open	65
2138SL	Dots	1970s		Blade locks open	50
2138LSS	"S" Dots	1980			25
P138LSS	Dots	1970s		Alyeska	150

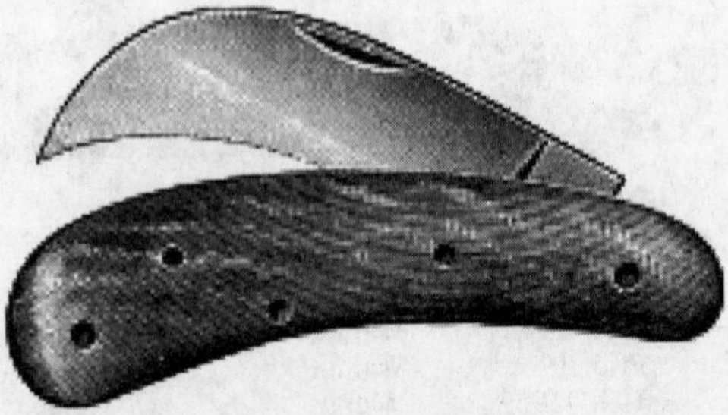

4¹/₄″ Banana Knife

Pattern	*Stamping*	*Years Made*	*Handle*	*Variation/Blade*	*Mint Price*
4¼″ Banana Knife					
1139	Tested	Prior 1940	Walnut		190
1139	XX	1955–1965	Walnut		165

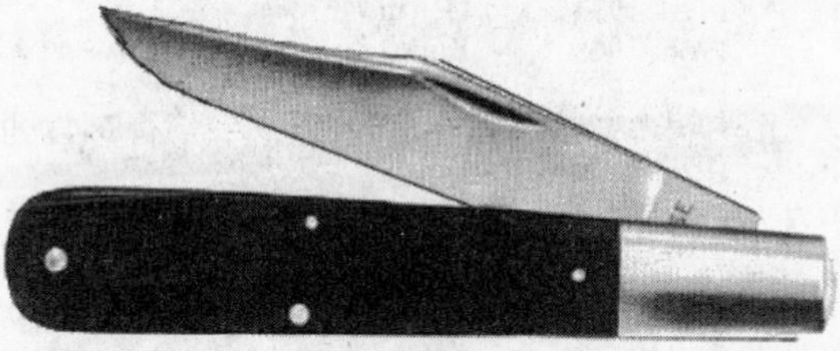

5″ Daddy Barlow

5″ Daddy Barlow					
6143	Tested	Prior 1940	Brown Bone		350
2143	XX	1940s	Slick Black	Iron liners	145
6143	XX	1941s	Green Bone	Iron liners	300
6143	XX	1940–1965	Bone	Iron liners	125
6143	USA	1965–1970	Bone	Iron liners	75
6143	10 Dots	1970–1971	Bone	Iron liners	75
6143	Dots	1970s	Bone	Iron liners	50
6143	Dots	1970s	Delrin	Brass liners	45
6143	"S" 10 Dots	1980	Delrin	Brass liners	45
6143	"S" Dots	1980s	Delrin		40

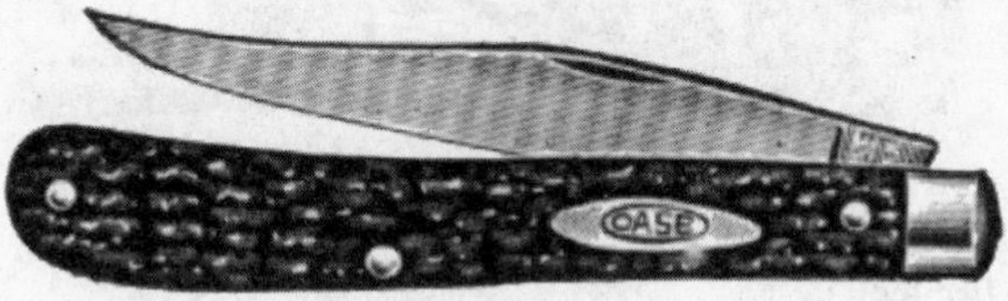

4⅛″ Farmer's Knife

4⅛″ Farmer's Knife					
21048LS	XX	1940–1965	Black Composition	Etched	100
31048SHR	XX	1940–1965	Yellow Composition	Florist's knife	125
31048	XX	1940s–1965			100
31048	USA	1965–1970			65
31048	10 Dots	1970–1971			65
31048	Dots	1970s			35
31048	"S" Dots	1980s			30
31048SP	XX	1958–1965	Yellow Composition		100
31048SP	USA	1965–1970			70
31048SP	10 Dots	1970–1971			70
31048SP	Dot	1971–1972			40
B1048	XX	Prior 1940	Imitation Onyx		325
61048	Tested	Prior 1940	Green Bone		475
61048	XX	1940–1965	Green Bone		275
61048	XX	1940–1965	Red Bone		225
61048	XX	1940–1965	Bone		120
61048	USA	1965–1970	Bone		75
61048	USA	1965–1970	Delrin		40
61048	10 Dots	1970–1971	Bone		220
61048	10 Dots	1970–1971	Delrin		45
61048	Dots	1970s	Delrin		25
61048	"S" 10 Dots	1980	Delrin		25
61048	"S" Dots	1980s	Red Bone		55

Pattern	Stamping	Years Made	Handle	Variation/Blade	Mint Price
61048SP	XX	1957–1963	Bone		125
61048SP	XX	1963–1965	Delrin		125
61048SP	USA	1965–1970	Bone		90
61048SP	USA	1965–1970	Delrin		45
61048SP	10 Dots	1970–1971	Delrin		45
61048SSP	USA	1966–1969	Bone	"Tested XX Stainless"	85
61048SSP	USA	1966–1969	Bone		60
61048SSP	USA	1965–1970	Bone	Blade polished	75
61048SSP	10 Dots	1970–1971	Delrin		45
61048SSP	Dots	1970s	Delrin		30

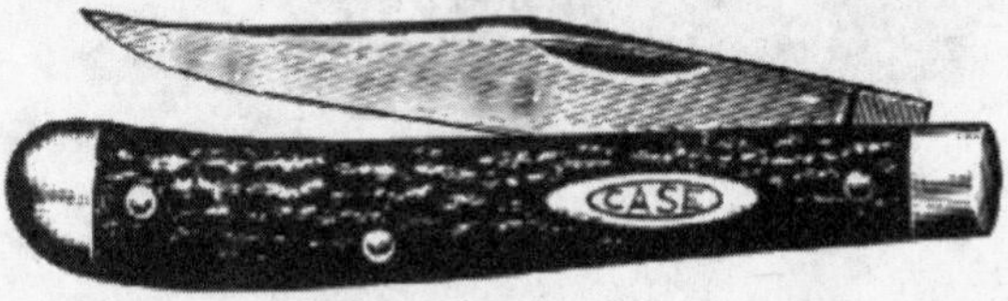

$4\frac{1}{16}$" Farmer's Knife

$4\frac{1}{16}$" Farmer's Knife

61049	Tested	Prior 1940	Green Bone		1050

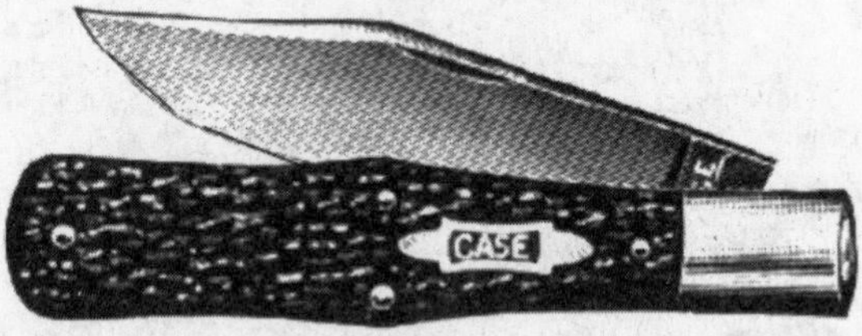

$5\frac{3}{8}$" Swell Center Hunter

$5\frac{3}{8}$" Swell Center Hunter

61050	Tested	Prior 1940	Green Bone		1000

$5\frac{3}{8}$" Press Button Slide Blade

PBB1050	Tested	Prior 1940	Imitation Onyx		750
PB31050F	Tested	Prior 1940	Cream Composition	Fish scaler blade	725

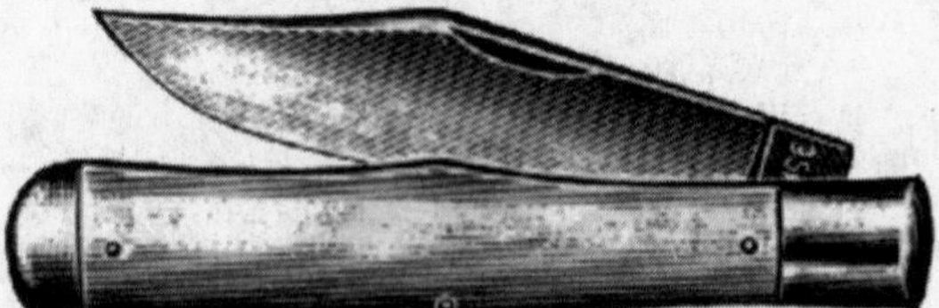

$5\frac{1}{8}$" Swell Center Hunter

$5\frac{1}{8}$" Swell Center Hunter

310050	Tested	Prior 1940	Yellow Composition		675
610050	Tested	Prior 1940	Green Bone		1050
B10050	Tested	Prior 1940	Christmas Tree Stripe		1050

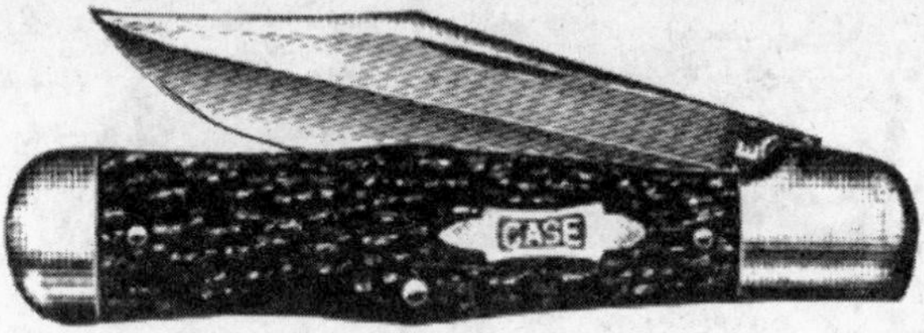

5$^3/_8$″ Swell Center Hunter

Pattern	Stamping	Years Made	Handle	Variation/Blade	Mint Price
5$^3/_8$″ Swell Center Hunter					
C51050-SAB	Tested	Prior 1940	Stag		2000
C61050-SAB	Tested	Prior 1940	Green Bone		1000
C61050-SAB	Tested	Prior 1940	Red Bone		750
C61050-SAB	XX	1940s	Green Bone		575
C61050-SAB	XX	1940–1965	Red Bone		500
C61050-SAB	XX	1940–1965	Bone		275
C61050-SAB	XX	1964–1965	Laminated Wood		150
C61050-SAB	USA	1965–1970	Laminated Wood		75
C61050-SAB	10 Dots	1970–1971	Laminated Wood		75
C61050-SAB	Dots	1970s	Laminated Wood		60
C61050-SAB	USA		Bone		300

5$^1/_2$″ Swell Center Hunter

Pattern	Stamping	Years Made	Handle	Variation/Blade	Mint Price
5$^1/_2$″ Swell Center Hunter					
C61050L	Tested	Prior 1940	Green Bone		4500

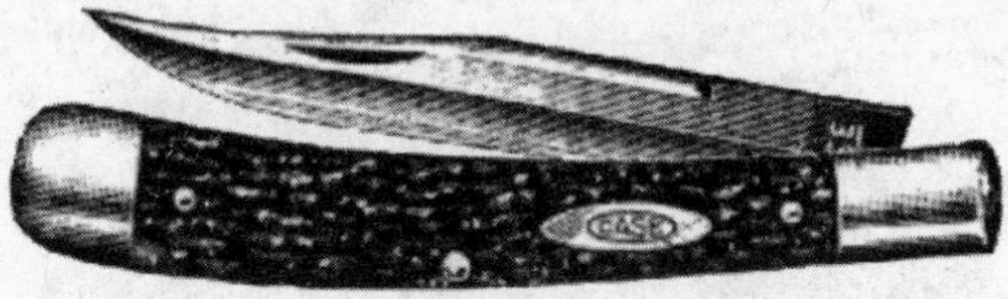

5$^1/_4$″ Hobo

Pattern	Stamping	Years Made	Handle	Variation/Blade	Mint Price
5$^1/_4$″ Hobo					
3151	Tested	Prior 1940	Yellow Composition		600
6151	Tested	Prior 1940	Green Bone		1000
6151L	Tested	Prior 1940	Green Bone		1050
8151L	Tested	Prior 1940	Genuine Pearl		2000
9151	Tested	Prior 1940	Imitation Pearl		800
3$^3/_4$″ Lockback					
M1051L	4 Dots	1976	Metal		20
21051L	4 Dots	1976	Black Composition		30
61051L	4 Dots	1976	Jigged Laminated Wood		25
61051L	Dots	1970s	Jigged Laminated Wood		75
61051L	“S” Dots	1980s	Jigged Laminated Wood		65

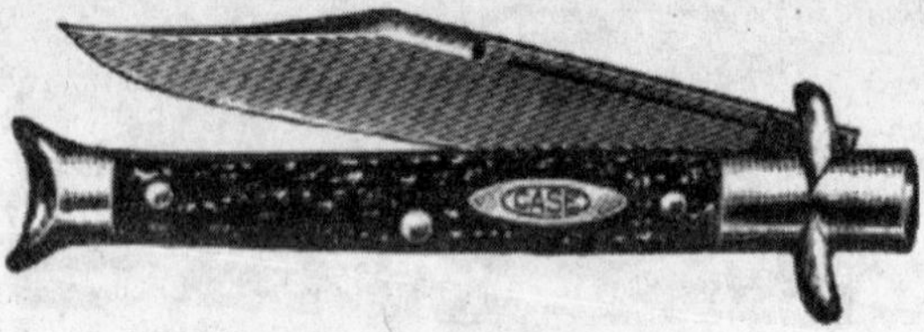

3⁷/₈″ Bow Tie

Pattern	Stamping	Years Made	Handle	Variation/Blade	Mint Price
3⁷/₈″ Bow Tie					
61051	Tested	Prior 1940	Green Bone		900
B1051	Tested	Prior 1940	Celluloid		750
GS1051	Tested	Prior 1940	Celluloid		800
Mako					
P158LSSP	3 Dots	1977	Black Pakkawood		60
5158LSSP	1 Dot	1979	Stag		85
P158LSSP	"S" 10 Dots	1980	Pakkawood		70
5158LSSP	"S" Dots	1980s	Stag		50
Hammerhead					
2159LSSP	"S" 10 Dots				60
5158LSSP	3 Dots	1977	Black Pakkawood		75
P159LSSP	"S" 3 Dots	1977	Black Pakkawood		55
5159LSSP	1 Dot	1979	Stag		95
5159LSSP	"S" 10 Dots	1980	Stag		90

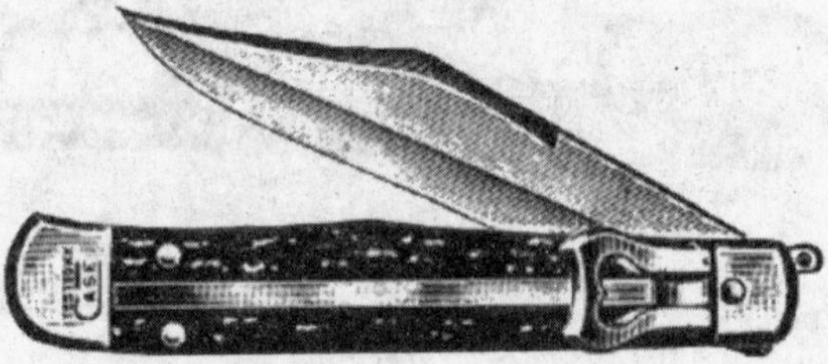

4³/₈″ Switchblade

4³/₈″ Switchblade					
5161L	Tested	Prior 1940	Stag		3200
6161L	Tested	Prior 1940	Green Bone		3000

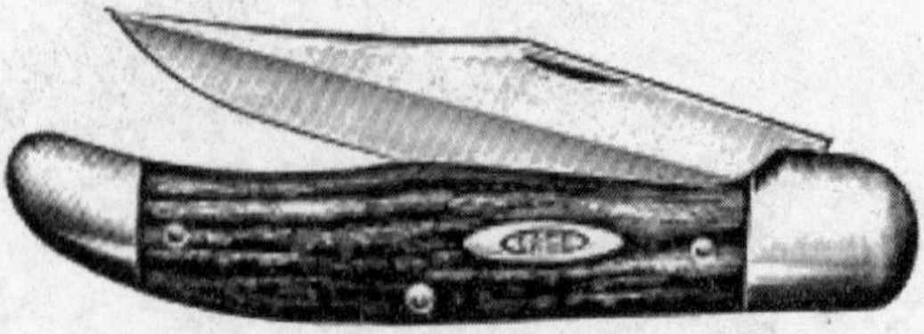

5¹/₂″ Folding Hunter

5¹/₂″ Folding Hunter					
2165	"S" Dots	1984	Black Composition	Etched	75
3165	Tested	Prior 1940	Yellow Composition		525
5165	Tested	Prior 1940	Stag		900
5165	XX	1940s	Stag	Flat ground blade	700
5165SAB	Tested	Prior 1940	Stag		825

Pattern	*Stamping*	*Years Made*	*Handle*	*Variation/Blade*	*Mint Price*
5165SAB	XX	1940–1965	Stag	Bolster drilled	450
5165SAB	XX	1964–1965	Stag	Bolster not drilled	400
5165SAB	USA	1965–1968	Stag	XX frame, small stamp	425
5165SAB	USA	1965–1966	Stag	XX frame, large stamp	450
6165	Tested	Prior 1940	Green Bone		850
6165	XX	1940s–1965	Green Bone	Flat ground blade	500
6165	XX	1940s	Bone	Flat ground blade	425
6165SAB	XX	1940–1955	Green Bone		650
6165SAB	XX	1940–1965	Bone		275
6165SAB	XX	1940–1960	Red Bone		425
6165SAB	XX	1940s	Rough Black		400
6165SAB	XX	1964–1965	Laminated Wood		150
6165SAB	USA	1965–1966	Bone		325
6165SAB	USA	1965–1966	Laminated Wood	XX Frame not drilled	95
6165SAB	USA	1965–1966	Laminated Wood	XX Frame	80
6165SAB	USA	1965–1970	Laminated Wood		75
6165SAB	10 Dots	1970–1971	Laminated Wood		65
6165SAB	Dots	1970s	Laminated Wood		45
6165SAB	"S" Dots	1980s	Laminated Wood		40
6165LSSP	2 Dots	1978	Laminated Wood		45
6165SAB	"S" Dots	1980s	Laminated Wood		35
9165	Tested	Prior 1940	Imitation Pearl		650
9165SAB	Tested	Prior 1940	Imitation Pearl		650

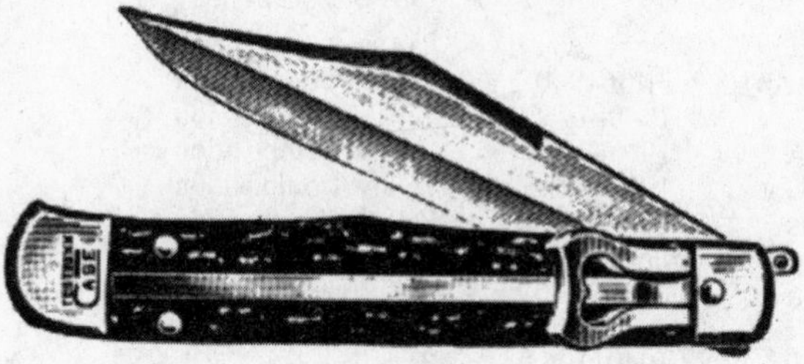

5½″ Switchblade

5½″ Switchblade

5171L	Tested	Prior 1940	Stag	5⅜″	4000
6171L	Tested	Prior 1940	Green Bone		3500

5½″ Switchblade

5172	Tested	Prior 1940	Stag	"Zipper"	8000
6172	Bradford	Prior 1940	Green Bone	"Zipper"	7500

5½″ Clasp Knife

5½″ Clasp Knife

3172	Tested	Prior 1940	Yellow Composition		1550
5172	Tested	Prior 1940	Stag		3000
6172	Tested	Prior 1940	Green Bone		2500
7172	Tested	Prior 1940	Imitation Tortoise Shell		2200
5172	XX	1940s	Stag	"Handmade in USA"	650
5172	XX	1957–1965	Stag		500
5172	USA	1965–1970	Stag		350
5172	Transition	1964–1965	Stag	XX to USA	350

Pattern	*Stamping*	*Years Made*	*Handle*	*Variation/Blade*	*Mint Price*
5172	4 Dots	1978	Stag	Part of 1978 set	225
5172	3 Dots	1979	Stag	Blue scroll	200
5½″ Buffalo					
P172	USA	1969–1970	Pakkawood		125
P172	9 Dots	1971–1972	Pakkawood		100

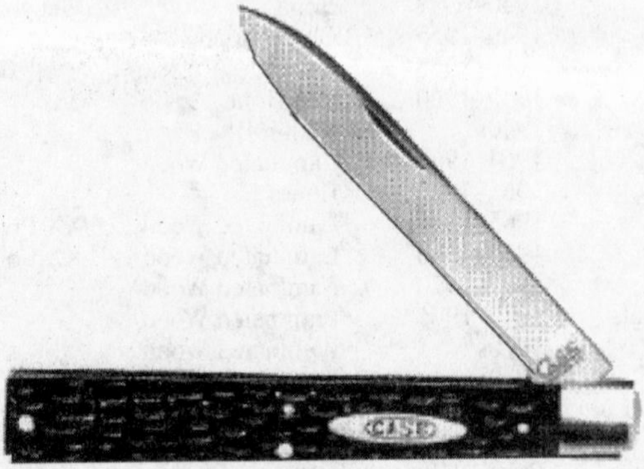

3⅝″ Doctor's Knife

3⅝″ Doctor's Knife

3185	Tested	Prior 1940	Yellow Composition		400
3185	XX	1940–1965	Yellow Composition		200
3185	USA	1965–1970	Yellow Composition		150
3185	10 Dot	1970–1971	Yellow Composition		200
3185	Dots	1971–1975	Yellow Composition		90
6185	Tested	Prior 1940	Green Bone		750
6185	Tested	Prior 1940	Red Bone		700
6185	XX	1940–1965	Red Bone		375
6185	XX	1940–1965	Bone		240
6185	USA	1965–1970	Bone		150
6185	10 Dots	1970–1971	Bone		175
6185	Dots	1971–1976	Bone		125
6185	Dots	1971–1976	Delrin		80

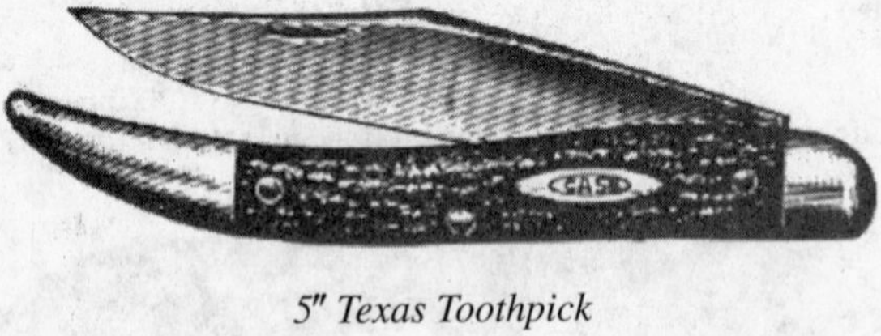

5″ Texas Toothpick

5″ Texas Toothpick

61093	Tested	Prior 1940	Green Bone		675
R1093	Tested	Prior 1940	Candy Strip Celluloid		650
61093	XX	1940s	Green Bone		600
61093	XX	1949–1953	Red Bone		375
61093	XX	1949–1965	Bone		250
31093	XX	1960–1965	Yellow Composition		175
61093	USA	1965–1970	Bone		150
61093	10 Dots	1970–1971	Bone		160
61093	Dots	1970–1975	Bone		90
61093	Dots	1973–1975	Delrin		60
61093	7 Dots	1973	Bone		110
31095	Tested	Prior 1940	Yellow Composition	high pull	425
R1095	Tested	Prior 1940	Red/White Celluloid	high pull	525

Pattern	*Stamping*	*Years Made*	*Handle*	*Variation/Blade*	*Mint Price*
HA1095	Tested	Prior 1940	Picture celluloid	high pull	550
61095	Tested	Prior 1940	Greenbone	high pull	675
5″ Leg Knife					
B1097	Tested	Prior 1940	Christmas Tree		575
RM1097	Tested	Prior 1940	Yellow Composition		475

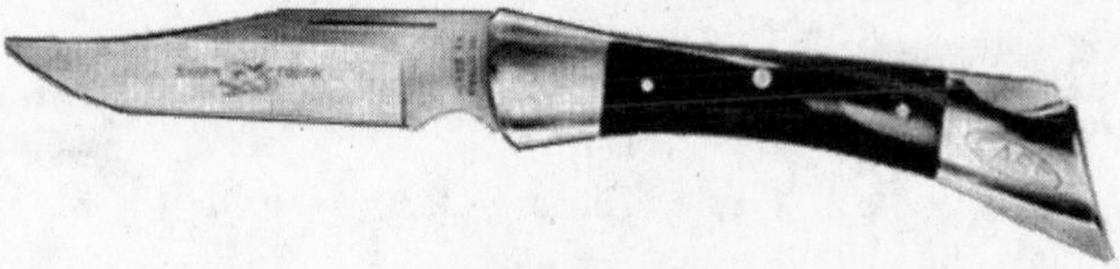

4¾″ Sharkstooth

4¾″ Sharkstooth				
P197LSS	Dots	1970s	Black Pakkawood	85
P197LSS	"S" 10 Dots	1980	Black Pakkawood	65
P197LSSP	"S" Dots	1980s		60
7197LSS	Dots	1976	Black Pakkawood	85
7197LSSP	8 Dots	Curly Maple		200
7197LSSP	7 Dots	Curly Maple		175
5197LSSP	1 Dot	Stag		120
5197LSSP	"S" Dots			85
5½″ Texas Toothpick				
61098	Tested	Prior 1940	Green Bone	775

4⅛″ Navy Knife

4⅛″ Navy Knife				
1199SHRSS	XX	1960–1965	Walnut	75
1199SHRSS	USA	1965–1970	Walnut	45
1199SHRSS	10 Dots	1970–1971	Walnut	45
1199SHRSS	Dots	1970s	Walnut	25
1199SHRSS	"S" Dots	1980	Walnut	20

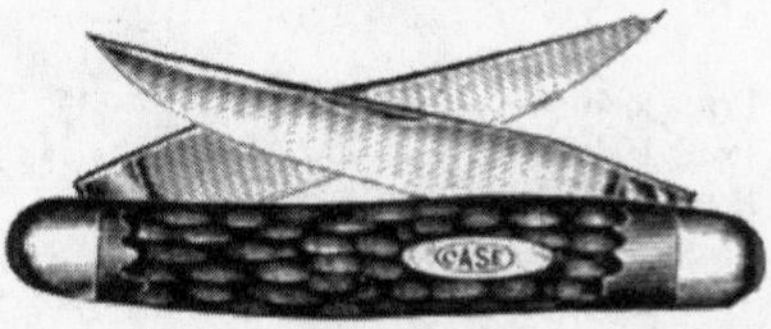

3⅞″ Muskrat

Pattern	Stamping	Years Made	Handle	Variation/Blade	Mint Price
3⅞″ Muskrat					
Muskrat	Tested	Prior 1940	Green Bone		2500
Muskrat	XX	1940s	Green Bone		1300
Muskrat	XX	1940s	Rough Black		1100
Muskrat	XX	1940s–1965	Red Bone		600
Muskrat	XX	1940s–1965	Bone		350
Muskrat	USA	1965–1970	Bone		200
Muskrat	10 Dots	1970–1971	Bone		250
Muskrat	Dots	1970s	Bone		125
Muskrat	2 Dots	1979	Stag	From collector set	135
Muskrat	"S" Dots	1980s	Bone		90
3⅞″ Muskrat Hawbaker Special					
Muskrat	XX	1940–1960s	Bone		1100
Muskrat	USA	1965–1970	Bone		1000
Muskrat	10 Dots	1970–1971	Bone		1050
Muskrat	Dots	1970	Bone		300
Muskrat	Dots	1970–1973	Delrin		175
Muskrat	2 to 3 Dots	1978	Bone	1000 made in 1978	175

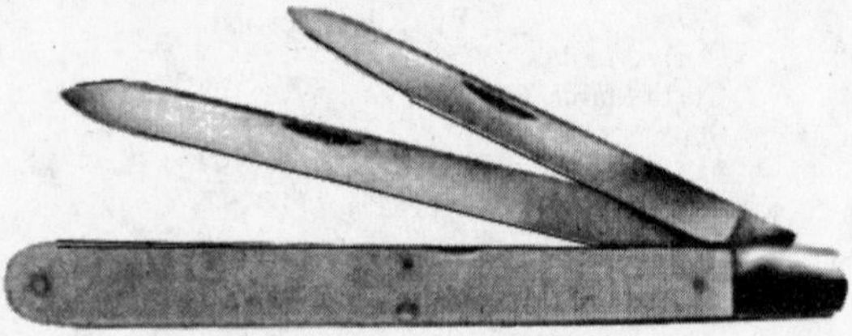

5½″ Melon Tester

5½″ Melon Tester					
4200SS	XX	1964–1965	White Composition		750
4200SS	USA	1965–1970	White Composition		250
4200SS	10 Dots	1970–1971	White Composition		250
4200SS	Dots	1971–1973	White Composition		110
5½″ Melon Tester Contract Knife					
4200SS	USA	1965	White Composition	Serrated blades	850

3¹⁵⁄₁₆″ Jumbo Jack

3¹⁵⁄₁₆″ Jumbo Jack					
3200	Tested	Prior 1940	Yellow Composition		850
5200	Tested	Prior 1940	Genuine Stag		1800
6200	Tested	Prior 1940	Green Bone		1700
9200	Tested	Prior 1940	Imitation Pearl		850
2⅝″ Senator Pen					
3201	Tested	Prior 1940	Yellow Composition		110
3201	XX	1940–1965	Yellow Composition		65
3201	USA	1965–1970	Yellow Composition		70

Pattern	Stamping	Years Made	Handle	Variation/Blade	Mint Price
3201	10 Dots	1970–1971	Yellow Composition		50
3201	Dots	1971–1975	Yellow Composition		30
6201	Tested	Prior 1940	Green Bone		185
6201	XX	1964–1965	Bone		100
6201	USA	1965–1970	Bone		65
6201	10 Dots	1970–1971	Bone		65
6201	Dots	1970s	Bone		30
6201	Dots	1970s	Delrin		25
9201	Tested	Prior 1940	Cracked Ice		110
9201	XX	1940–1965	Imitation Pearl		50
9201	XX	1940–1965	Cracked Ice		50

9201R	XX	1940–1965	Imitation Pearl	Bail in handle	60
9201R	XX	1940–1965	Cracked Ice	Bail in handle	60
9201	USA	1965–1970	Imitation Pearl		35
9201	10 Dots	1970–1971	Imitation Pearl		35
9201	Dots	1970–1975	Imitation Pearl		25

$2^{5}/_{8}$″ Senator Pen

$2^{5}/_{8}$″ Senator Pen					
22001R	Tested	Prior 1940	Black Composition		120
62001	Tested	Prior 1940	Green Bone		190
82001	Tested	Prior 1940	Pearl		225
82001R	Tested	Prior 1940	Pearl		220
$2^{1}/_{4}$″ Lobster Pen					
S2	Tested	Prior 1940	Sterling Silver		165
S2	XX	1963–1965	Sterling Silver	Long pull	135
S2	XX	1963–1965	Sterling Silver		140
S2	USA	1965–1968	Sterling Silver		175
$2^{1}/_{4}$″ Sleeveboard Pen					
82101R	Tested	Prior 1940	Pearl		185
92101R	Tested	Prior 1940	Imitation Pearl		130

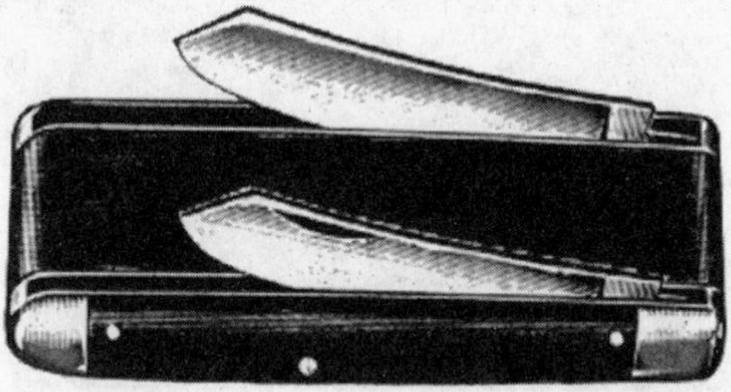

$3^{3}/_{8}$″ Grafting and Budding Knife

Pattern	*Stamping*	*Years Made*	*Handle*	*Variation/Blade*	*Mint Price*
3³/₈″ Grafting and Budding Knife					
1202D&B	Tested	Prior 1940	Cocobolo		575

3³/₈″ Jack

Pattern	*Stamping*	*Years Made*	*Handle*	*Variation/Blade*	*Mint Price*
3³/₈″ Jack					
5202RAZ	Tested	Prior 1940	Stag		500
5202	Tested	Prior 1940	Stag		375
5202¹/₂	Tested	Prior 1940	Stag		375
6202	Tested	Prior 1940	Green Bone		250
6202¹/₂	Tested	Prior 1940	Green Bone		250
	XX	1940–1965	Green Bone		200
2202¹/₂	XX	1940s	Black Composition		130
6202¹/₂	XX	1940–1955	Bone		95
	USA	1965–1970	Bone		50
	10 Dots	1970–1971	Bone		50
	10 Dots	1970–1971	Delrin		35
	Dots	1970s	Delrin		30
6202RAZ	Dots	1970s	Delrin		35

1³/₄″ Pen Knife

Pattern	*Stamping*	*Years Made*	*Handle*	*Variation/Blade*	*Mint Price*
1³/₄″ Pen Knife					
82103	Tested	Prior 1940	Pearl		225
82103R	Tested	Prior 1940	Pearl		250

3³/₄″ Barlow

Pattern	Stamping	Years Made	Handle	Variation/Blade	Mint Price
3³/₄″ Barlow					
6205	Tested	Prior 1940	Green Bone		800
6205¹/₂	Tested	Prior 1940	Green Bone		850
5205RAZ	Tested	Prior 1940	Stag		1100
6205RAZ	Tested	Prior 1940	Green Bone		875
6205	XX	1940s	Green Bone		325
6205	XX	1940s	Bone		250
6205RAZ	XX	1940s	Green Bone		550
6205RAZ	XX	1940–1965	Bone		325
6205RAZ	USA	1965–1970	Bone		130
6205RAZ	10 Dots	1970–1971	Bone		150
6205RAZ	Dots	1970s	Bone		100
2⁵/₈″ Jack					
5206¹/₂	Tested	Prior 1940	Stag		250
6206¹/₂	Tested	Prior 1940	Green Bone		225
6206¹/₂	Tested	1940s	Rough Black		200
6206¹/₂	XX	Early 1950s	Rough Black		135

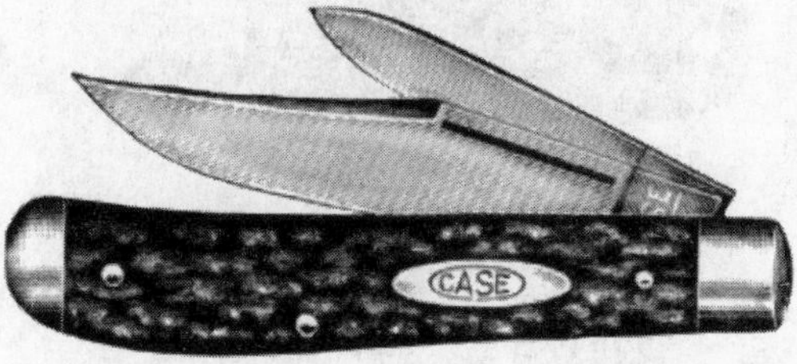

3¹/₂″ Serpentine Jack

3¹/₂″ Serpentine Jack					
3207	Tested	Prior 1940	Yellow Composition	Long pull	525
5207	Tested	Prior 1940	Stag	Long pull	900
6207	Tested	Prior 1940	Green Bone	Long pull	650
2207	XX	1940s	Black Composition		400
6207	XX	1940s	Green Bone		475
6207	XX	1940s	Rough Black		375
6207	XX	1940–1955	Red Bone		225
6207	XX	1940–1965	Bone		150
6207	USA	1965–1970	Bone		85
6207	10 Dots	1970–1971	Bone		85
6207	Dots	1970s	Bone		60
6207	Dots	1970s	Delrin		40
6207SSP	"S" Dots	1980s	Bone	Mini trapper	35

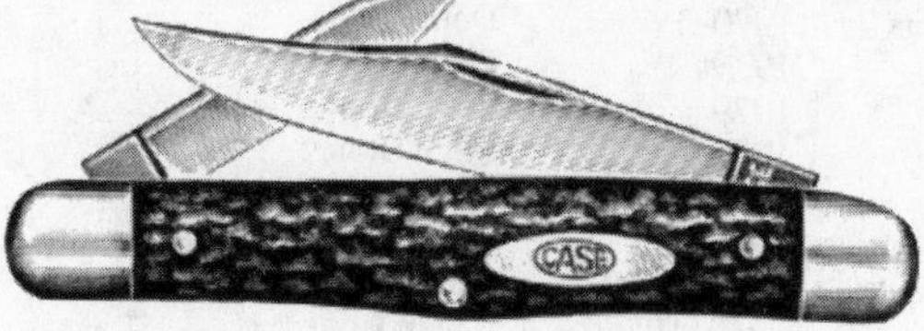

3¹/₄″ Half Whittler

3¹/₄″ Half Whittler					
5208	Tested	Prior 1940	Stag		425
6208	Tested	Prior 1940	Green Bone		375
6208	XX	1940–1953	Green Bone		275
6208	XX	1940–1955	Rough Black		140
6208	XX	1940–1965	Bone		125

Pattern	*Stamping*	*Years Made*	*Handle*	*Variation/Blade*	*Mint Price*
6208	USA	1965–1970	Bone		65
6208	10 Dots	1970–1971	Bone		70
6208	Dots	1970–1979	Bone		45
6208	Dots	1970–1979	Delrin		30
A6208	1 Dot	1979	Bone		40
A6208	"S" Dots	1980s	Bone		35

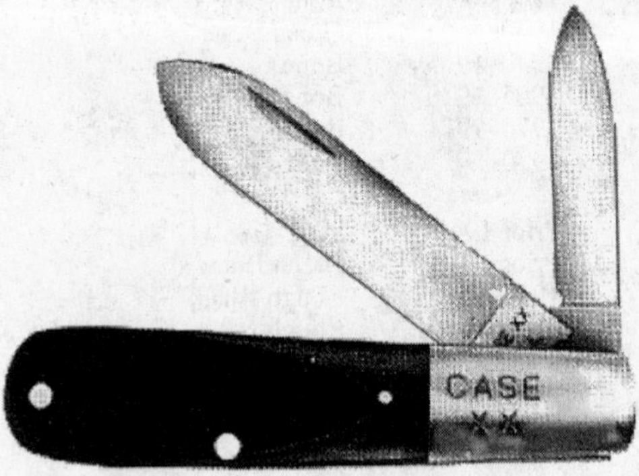

3 5/16″ Barlow

3 5/16″ Barlow

62009SH	Tested	Prior 1940	Brown Bone		425
	XX	1940–1945	Black Composition		175
62009SP	Tested	Prior 1940	Brown Bone		450
62009	Tested	Prior 1940	Brown Bone		400
62009	XX	1940–1945	Black Composition		135
62009	XX	Early 1950s	Green Bone		225
62009	XX	1940–1965	Red Bone		150
62009	XX	1940–1965	Bone		110
62009	USA	1965–1970	Bone	Master blade in front	75
62009	USA	1965–1970	Bone	Master blade in back	75
62009	10 Dots	1970–1971	Bone		75
62009	10 Dots	1970–1971	Delrin		50
62009	Dots	1970–1976	Delrin		35
62009½	Tested	Prior 1940	Green Bone		375
62009½	XX	1940s	Black Composition		150
62009½	XX	1940–1955	Green Bone		250
62009½	XX	1945–1955	Red Bone		150
62009½	XX	1940–1965	Bone		100
62009½	USA	1965–1970	Bone	Master blade in front	75
62009½	USA	1965–1970	Bone	Master blade in back	75
62009½	10 Dots	1970–1971	Bone		75
62009½	10 Dots	1970–1971	Delrin		95
62009½	Dots	1970s	Delrin		50
A62009½	1 Dot	1979	Slick Bone		60
A62009½	"S" 10 Dots	1980	Slick Bone		50
A62009½-SS	"S" Dots	1980s			50
62009RAZ	Tested	Prior 1940	Green Bone		525
62009RAZ	XX	1940–1955	Green Bone		325
62009RAZ	XX	1955–1965	Bone	Long pull	140
62009RAZ	XX	1955–1965	Bone		125
62009RAZ	USA	1965–1970	Bone	Master blade in front	100
62009RAZ	USA	1965–1970	Bone	Master blade in back	100
62009RAZ	10 Dots	1970–1971	Bone		95
62009RAZ	10 Dots	1970–1971	Delrin		60
62009RAZ	Dots	1970s	Delrin		25

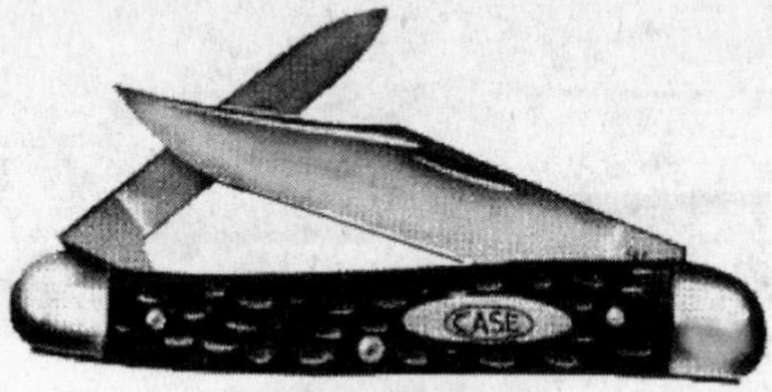

3 1/8″ Baby Copperhead

Pattern	*Stamping*	*Years Made*	*Handle*	*Variation/Blade*	*Mint Price*
3 1/8″ Baby Copperhead					
62109	Tested		Green Bone		750
62109X	XX	1940–1951	Rough Black		225
62109X	XX	1940–1965	Green Bone		425
62109X	XX	1940–1955	Bone		165
62109X	USA	1965–1970	Bone		95
62109X	10 Dots	1970	Bone		95
62109X	Dots	1971	Bone		45
62109X	Dots	1970s	Delrin		40
62109X	"S" Dots	1980	Bone		35

3 3/8″ Switchblade

3 3/8″ Switchblade

62210	Tested	Prior 1940	Green Bone		1600
92210	Tested	Prior 1940	Imitation Pearl		875
H2210	Tested	Prior 1940	Brn/Cream Composition		900
T2210	Tested	Prior 1940	Imit. Tortoise Shell		875

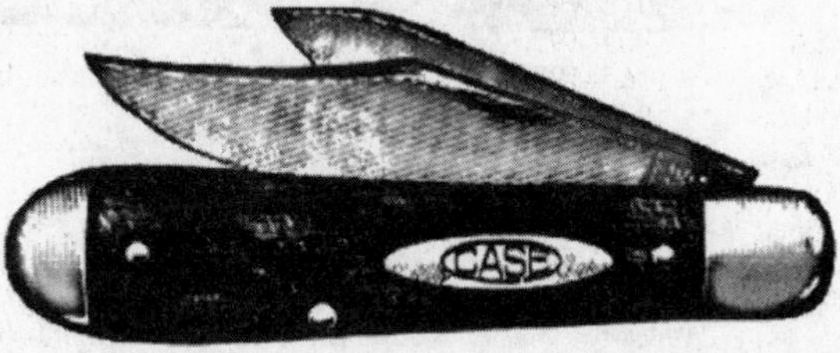

3 1/8″ Sleeveboard Jack

3 1/8″ Sleeveboard Jack

3210½	Tested	Prior 1940	Yellow Composition		325
5210½	Tested	Prior 1940	Stag		675
6210½	Tested	Prior 1940	Green Bone		600

4⅜″ Slim Jack

Pattern	*Stamping*	*Years Made*	*Handle*	*Variation/Blade*	*Mint Price*
4⅜″ Slim Jack					
6211	Tested	Prior 1940	Green Bone		1600
6211½	Tested	Prior 1940	Green Bone		1600
3⅝″ Electrician Knife					
2212L	Tested	Prior 1940	Walnut		170

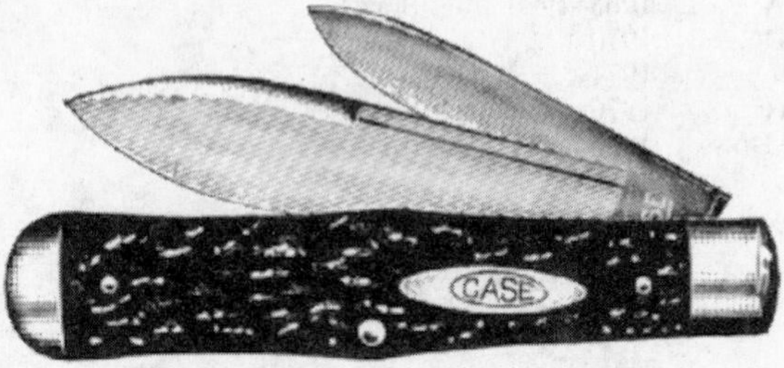

4″ Swell Center Jack

4″ Swell Center Jack					
6213	Tested	Prior 1940	Green Bone		1500

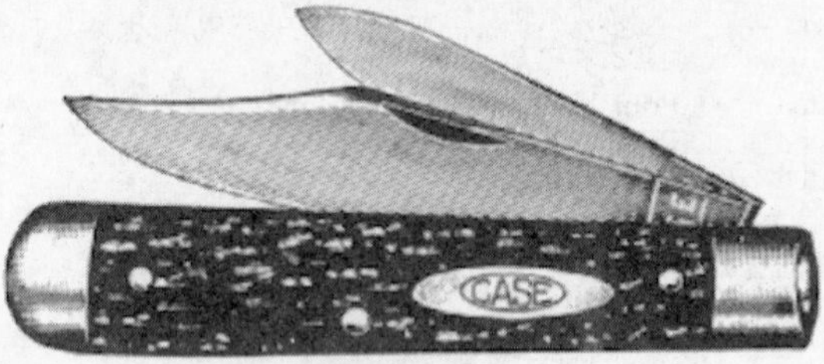

3⅜″ Jack

3⅜″ Jack					
6214	Tested	Prior 1940	Green Bone		275
6214	XX	1940–1955	Green Bone		235
6214	XX	1940s	Rough Black	With shield	120
6214	XX	1940s	Rough Black	Without shield	110
6214	XX	1940–1965	Bone		125
6214	USA	1965–1970	Bone		70
6214	10 Dots	1970–1971	Bone		65
6214	10 Dots	1970–1971	Delrin		45
6214	Dots	1970s	Delrin		30
5214½	Tested	Prior 1940	Stag		350
6214½	Tested	Prior 1940	Green Bone		300
6214½	XX	1940–1955	Green Bone		250
6214½	XX	1940s	Rough Black		125
6214½	XX	1955–1965	Bone		135
6214½	USA	1965–1970	Bone		65

Pattern	*Stamping*	*Years Made*	*Handle*	*Variation/Blade*	*Mint Price*
6214½	10 Dots	1970–1971	Bone		60
6214½	10 Dots	1970–1971	Delrin		40
6214½	Dots	1970s	Delrin		25

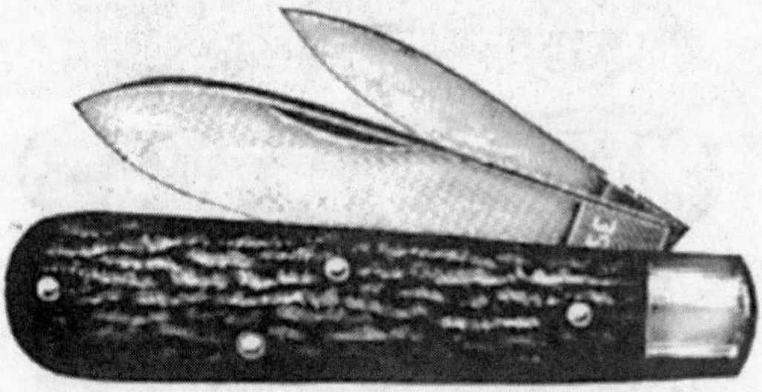

3⅜″ Jack

3⅜″ Jack

6216	Tested	Prior 1940	Green Bone	325
6216	XX	1964–1965	Bone	125
6216½	Tested	Prior 1940	Green Bone	300
6216½	XX	1964–1965	Bone	110
6216½	USA	1965–1967	Bone	65

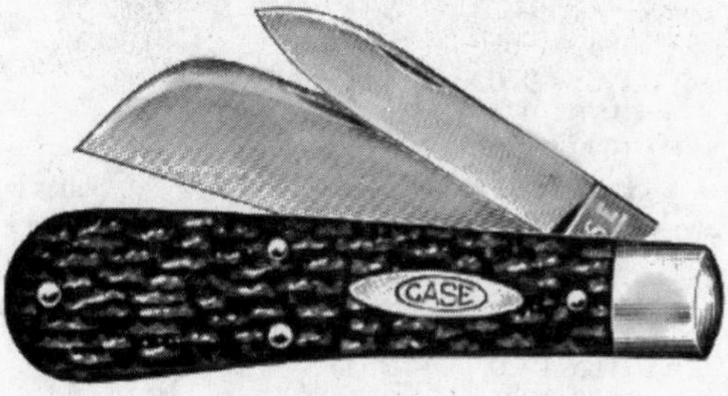

4″ Curved Jack

4″ Curved Jack

2217	Tested	Prior 1940	Black Composition	300
6217	Tested	Prior 1940	Green Bone	600
6217	XX	1940s	Black Composition	250
6217	XX	1940–1955	Green Bone	425
6217	XX	1940–1965	Red Bone	300
6217	XX	1940–1955	Bone	200
6217	USA	1965–1970	Bone	140
6217	USA	1965–1970	Wood	70
6217	10 Dots	1970–1971	Laminated Wood	70
6217	10 Dots	1970–1971	Bone	150
6217	Dots	1970s	Laminated Wood	40

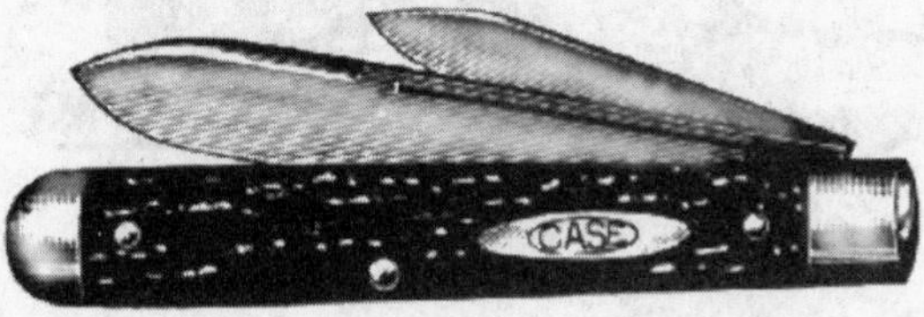

4⅛″ Slim Jack

Pattern	Stamping	Years Made	Handle	Variation/Blade	Mint Price
4 1/8″ Slim Jack					
62019	Tested	Prior 1940	Green Bone		1350

2 3/4″ Peanut

Pattern	Stamping	Years Made	Handle	Variation/Blade	Mint Price
2 3/4″ Peanut					
2220	Tested	Prior 1940	Black Composition		375
2220	XX	1940–1965	Black Composition		110
2220	USA	1965–1970	Black Composition		80
2220	10 Dots	1970–1971	Black Composition		75
2220	Dots	1970–1975	Black Composition		50
3220	Tested	Prior 1940	Yellow Composition		300
3220	XX	1940–1965	Yellow Composition		110
3220	USA	1965–1970	Yellow Composition		85
3220	10 Dots	1970–1971	Yellow Composition		85
3220	Dots	1971–1975	Yellow Composition		50
5220	Tested	Prior 1940	Stag		475
5220	XX	1940–1965	Stag		150
5220	USA	1965–1970	Stag		120
5220	10 Dots	1970–1971	Stag		100
5220	2 Dots	1979	Red Scroll		90
6220	Tested	Prior 1940	Green Bone	Saber ground	525
6220	XX	1940–1965	Green Bone		425
6220	XX	1940s	Rough Black		210
6220	XX	1940–1965	Red Bone		275
6220	XX	1940–1965	Bone		125
6220	USA	1965–1970	Bone		100
6220	10 Dots	1970–1971	Bone		90
6220	10 Dots	1970–1971	Delrin		225
6220	9 Dots	1971–1972	Bone	Limited number in bone	200
6220	Dots	1970s	Delrin		40
A6220	Dots	1979	Bone	"Appaloosa"	70
SR6220	1 Dot	1979	Red Bone	"Slick Bone"	70
SR6220	"S" Dots	1980s	Delrin		30
8220	Tested	Prior 1940	Pearl		550
9220	Tested	Prior 1940	Imitation Pearl		320
9220	XX	1940–1965	Cracked Ice		180
9220	XX	1940–1965	Imitation Pearl		180

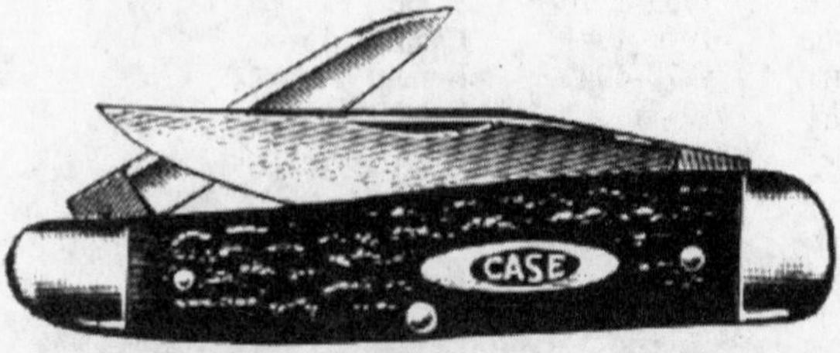

3 1/2″ Sleeveboard Pen

Pattern	Stamping	Years Made	Handle	Variation/Blade	Mint Price
3 1/2″ Sleeveboard Pen					
0221 1/2	Tested	Prior 1940	Black Composition		325

Pattern	*Stamping*	*Years Made*	*Handle*	*Variation/Blade*	*Mint Price*
06221½	Tested	Prior 1940	Green Bone		575
3″ Jack—"Little John Carver"					
220024SP	XX	1959–1960	Black Composition	With original box	1000
220024SP				Without box	325

3″ Jack

3″ Jack

2224SH	Tested	Prior 1940	Black Composition	275
2224RAZ	Tested	Prior 1940	Black Composition	300
2224SP	XX	1940s	Black Composition	200
2224SH	XX	1940s	Black Composition	195
2224RAZ	XX	1940s	Black Composition	225
3224	Tested	Prior 1940	Yellow Composition	210
3224½	Tested	Prior 1940	Yellow Composition	225
5224½	Tested	Prior 1940	Stag	350
32024½	XX	1957–1965	Yellow Composition	80
32024½	USA	1965–1968	Yellow Composition	80
52024½	Tested	Prior 1940	Stag	300
62024	Tested	Prior 1940	Green Bone	275
62024RAZ	Tested	Prior 1940	Green Bone	350
62024½	Tested	Prior 1940	Green Bone	275
62024½	XX	1940–1965	Green Bone	200
62024½	XX	1955–1965	Bone	100
62024½	USA	1965–1968	Bone	55

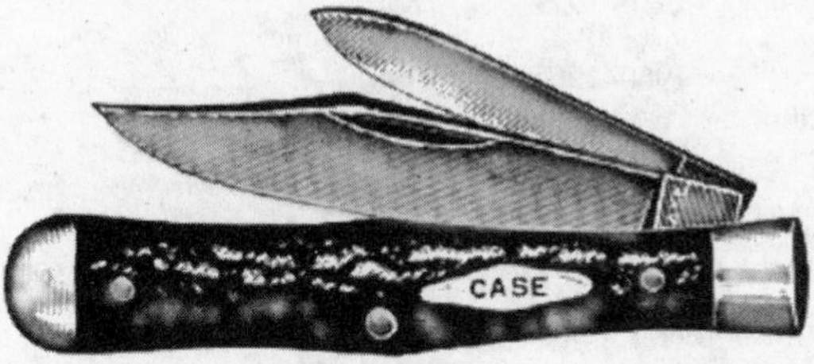

3″ Coke Bottle

3″ Coke Bottle

5225½	Tested	Prior 1940	Stag	600
6225½	Tested	Prior 1940	Green Bone	500
6225½	XX	1940–1955	Green Bone	400
6225½	XX	1942–1950	Rough Black	185
6225½	XX	1940–1965	Bone	125
6225½	USA	1965–1970	Bone	90
6225½	10 Dots	1970–1971	Bone	90
6225½	Dots	1970s	Bone	80
6225½	Dots	1970s	Delrin	45
SR6225½	1 Dot	1979	Smooth Bone	45
SR6225½	"S" Dots	1980s	Smooth Bone	30
32025½	Tested	Prior 1940	Yellow Composition	350
62025½	Tested	Prior 1940	Green Bone	550

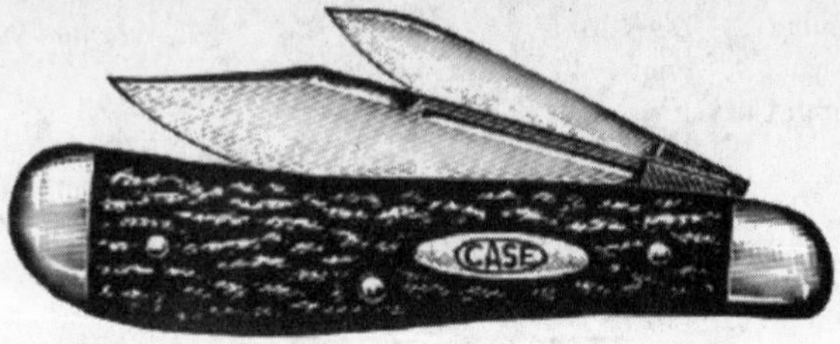

3" Dogleg Jack

Pattern	*Stamping*	*Years Made*	*Handle*	*Variation/Blade*	*Mint Price*
3" Dogleg Jack					
6226½	Tested	Prior 1940	Green Bone		700
3" Jack					
6227	Tested	Prior 1940	Bone		225
6227	XX	1955–1965	Bone		100
6227	USA	1965–1970	Bone		60
6227	10 Dots	1970–1971	Bone		60
6227	10 Dots	1970–1971	Delrin		55
6227	Dots	1970s	Delrin		30

2¾" Sleeveboard

2¾" Sleeveboard					
62027	Tested	Prior 1940	Green Bone		225
62027	Dots	1978–1979	Delrin		25
62027½	Tested	Prior 1940	Green Bone		230
62027½	XX	1960–1965	Bone		95
92027	Tested	Prior 1940	Imitation Pearl		165
92027½	Tested	Prior 1940	Imitation Pearl		160
92027½	XX	1940	Cracked Ice		90
SR62027	1 Dot	1979	Red Bone		55
SR62027	"S" 10 Dots	1980	Red Bone		35

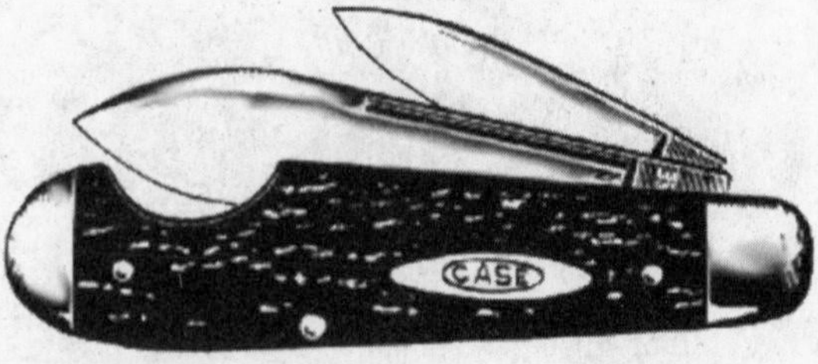

3½" Easy Open Jack

3½" Easy Open Jack					
6228EO	Tested	Prior 1940	Green Bone		450
2228EO	Tested	Prior 1940	Black Composition		300
6228EO	XX	Early 1950	Red Bone		185

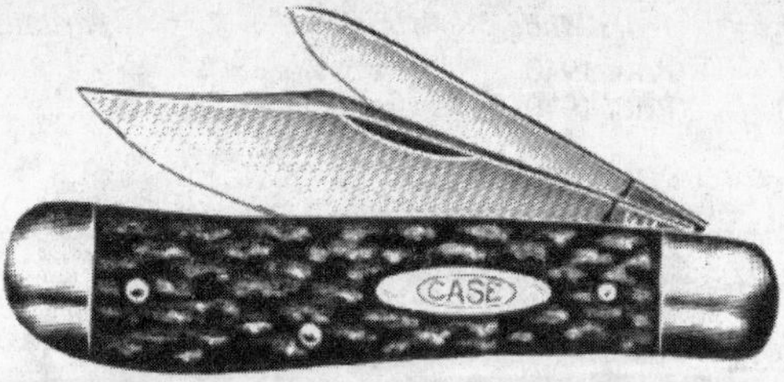

3½″ Serpentine Jack

Pattern	Stamping	Years Made	Handle	Variation/Blade	Mint Price
3½″ Serpentine Jack					
22028	Tested	Prior 1940	Black Composition		325
62028	Tested	Prior 1940	Green Bone		525
22028½	XX	1940–1965	Black Composition		125
62028½	Tested	Prior 1940	Green Bone		400
62028½	XX	1940s	Rough Black		185

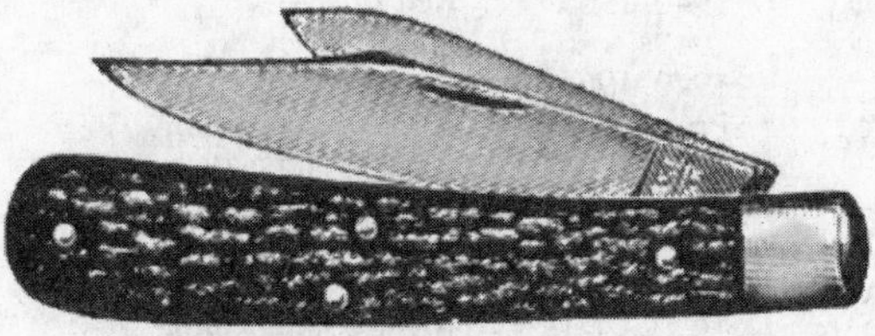

2½″ Curved Jack

2½″ Curved Jack					
B229½R	Tested	Prior 1940	Waterfall		265
2229½	XX	1958–1965	Black Composition		150
2229½	USA	1958–1965	Black Composition		185
6229½	Tested	Prior 1940	Green Bone		325
6229½	XX	1960–1965	Bone		135
6229½	USA	1965–1967	Bone		95
8229½	Tested	Prior 1940	Mother-of-Pearl		400
9229½	Tested	Prior 1940	Imitation Pearl		250
9229½	XX	1940–1955	Imitation Pearl		160

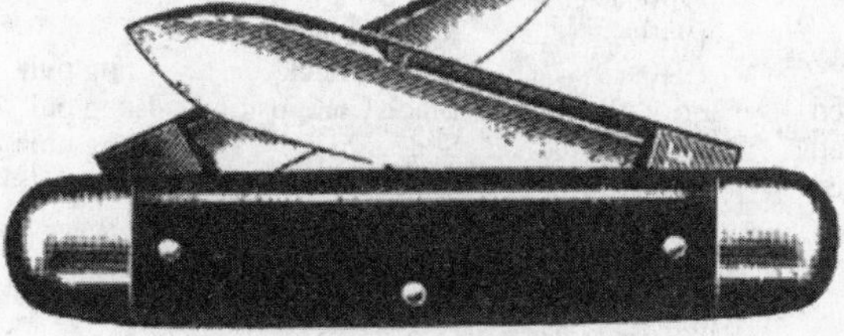

3¼″ Equal End

3¼″ Equal End					
02230	Tested	Prior 1940	Black Composition		200
02230½	Tested	Prior 1940	Black Composition		200
05230½	Tested	Prior 1940	Stag		450
06230	Tested	Prior 1940	Green Bone		400
06230½	Tested	Prior 1940	Green Bone		400
06230SP	Tested	Prior 1940	Green Bone		425

Pattern	Stamping	Years Made	Handle	Variation/Blade	Mint Price
06230SH	Tested	Prior 1940	Green Bone		425
09230	Tested	Prior 1940	Cracked Ice		225

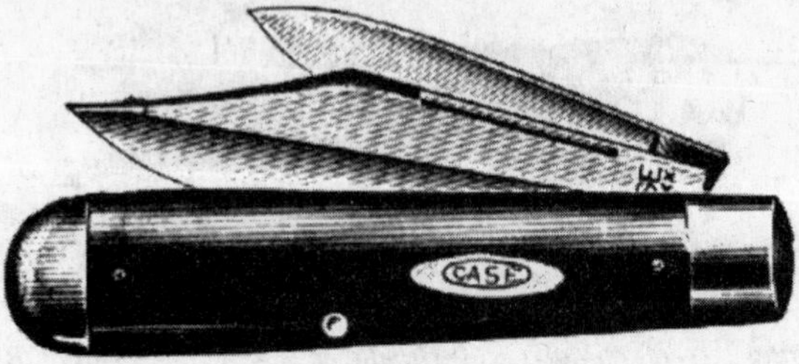

3³/4″ Jack

3³/4″ Jack

6231	Tested	Prior 1940	Green Bone	Long pull	375
6231	XX	1940–1955	Green Bone		300
6231	XX	1940s	Green Bone	Long pull	325
6231	XX	1940–1965	Red Bone		275
6231	XX	1940s	Rough Black		200
6231	XX	1940–1965	Bone		175
2231¹/2	Tested	Prior 1940	Black Composition		225
2231¹/2	XX	1940–1954	Black Composition		125
2231¹/2SAB	Tested	Prior 1940	Black Composition		200
2231¹/2SAB	XX	1940–1965	Black Composition		125
2231¹/2SAB	USA	1965–1970	Black Composition		50
2231¹/2SAB	10 Dots	1970–1971	Black Composition		50
2231¹/2SAB	Dots	1970s	Black Composition		40
4231¹/2	XX	1948–1949	White Composition		210
6231¹/2	XX	1940–1955	Green Bone		250
6231¹/2	XX	1940–1965	Red Bone		225
6231¹/2	XX	1940s	Rough Black		150
6231¹/2	XX	1940–1965	Bone		140
6231¹/2	USA	1965–1970	Bone		80
6231¹/2	10 Dots	1970–1971	Bone		80
6231¹/2	Dots	1970s	Bone		65
6231¹/2	"S" 10 Dots	1980	Bone		30
52031	Tested	Prior 1940	Stag	Long pull	500
62031	Tested	Prior 1940	Green Bone	Long pull	425
62031	XX	1940–1955	Green Bone	Long pull	325
62031	XX	1940s	Green Bone	Long pull	375
62031	XX	1940–1965	Red Bone		275
62031	XX	1940s	Rough Black		175
62031	XX	1940s	Rough Black	Long pull	250
22031¹/2	Tested	Prior 1940	Black Composition	Long pull	225
52031¹/2	Tested	Prior 1940	Stag	Long pull	450
62031¹/2	Tested	Prior 1940	Green Bone	Long pull	400
62031¹/2	XX	1940–1955	Green Bone		325
62031¹/2	XX	1940s	Rough Black		140
62031¹/2	XX	1940–1960	Bone		175

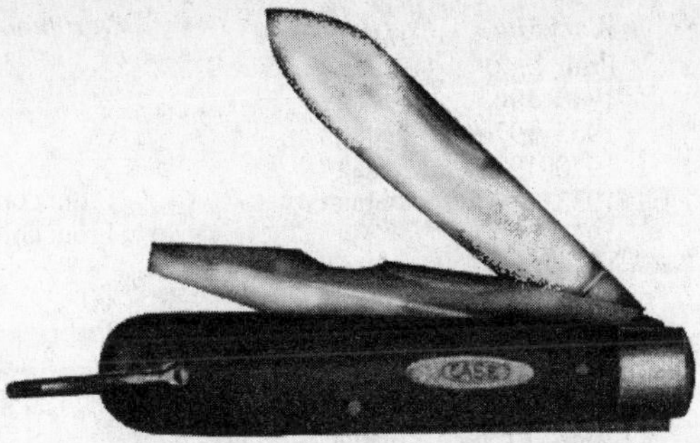

$3^{11}/_{16}$″ Electrician Knife

Pattern	*Stamping*	*Years Made*	*Handle*	*Variation/Blade*	*Mint Price*
$3^{11}/_{16}$″ Electrician Knife					
12031	Tested	Prior 1940	Walnut		125
12031	XX	1940–1965	Walnut		65
12031	USA	1965–1970			40
12031	10 Dots	1970–1971			45
12031	Dots	1970s			30
12031LHR	Dots	1978	Hawkbill blade		45

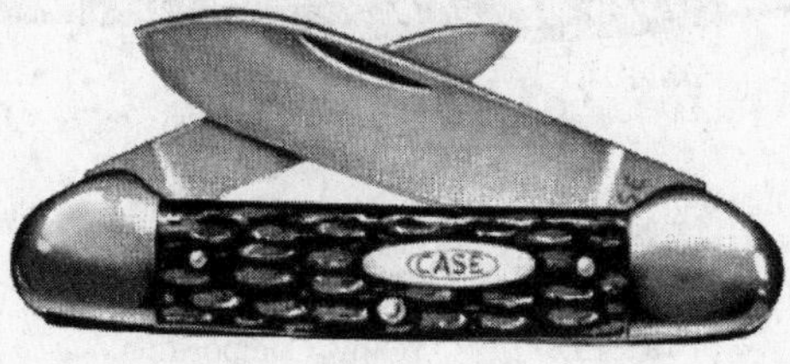

$3^{5}/_{8}$″ Canoe

$3^{5}/_{8}$″ Canoe					
52131	Tested	Prior 1940	Stag		1000
52131	XX	1940–1950	Stag	Long pull	800
52131	XX	1940–1965	Stag		525
52131	USA	1965–1970	Stag		325
52131	10 Dots	1970–1971	Stag	"Canoe" etching	300
52131SS	3 Dots	1978	Stag	Blue scroll	150
62131	XX	1966	Bone		650
62131	USA	1966–1970	Bone		140
62131	10 Dots	1970–1971	Bone		150
62131	Dots	1970s	Bone		70
62131	Dots	1970s	Bone	"Canoe" etching	95
62131	"S" Dots	1980s	Bone		50

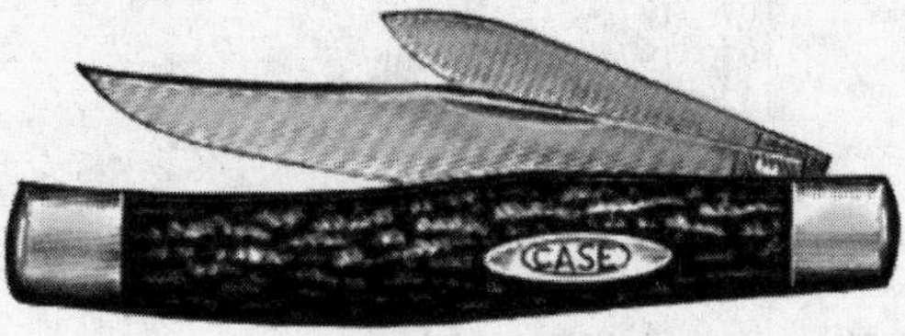

$3^{5}/_{8}$″ Premium Jack

$3^{5}/_{8}$″ Premium Jack					
3232	Tested	Prior 1940	Yellow Composition		165
3232	XX	1960–1965	Yellow Composition		90

Pattern	*Stamping*	*Years Made*	*Handle*	*Variation/Blade*	*Mint Price*
5232	Tested	Prior 1940	Stag		275
5232	XX	1940–1965	Stag		225
5232	USA	1965–1970	Stag		125
5232	10 Dots	1970–1971	Stag		125
5232	9 Dots	1973	Stag	From collector sets	150
5232	2 Dots	1979	Stag	From collector sets	100
6232	Tested	Prior 1940	Green Bone		275
6232	XX	1940–1955	Green Bone		250
6232	XX	1940–1965	Red Bone		200
6232	XX	1940s	Rough Black		155
6232	XX	1940–1965	Bone		125
6232	USA	1965–1970	Bone		60
6232	10 Dots	1970–1971	Bone		65
6232	Dots	1970s	Bone		50
6232	Dots	1970s	Delrin		30
6232	"S" 10 Dots	1980	Bone		25

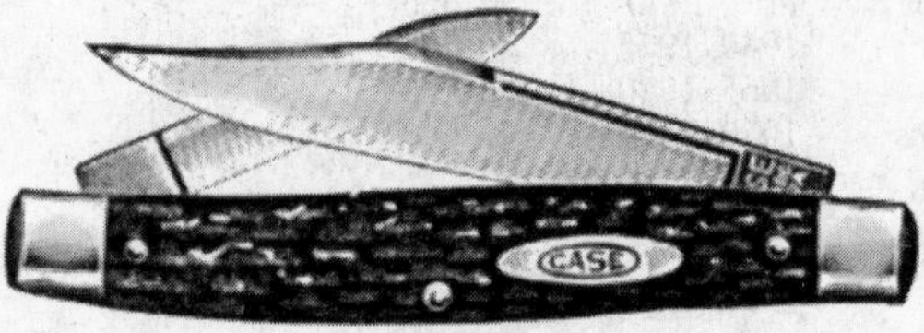

2⁵/₈″ Pen

2⁵/₈″ Pen					
GS233	Tested	Prior 1940	Gold Metal Flake		325
3233	Tested	Prior 1940	Yellow Composition		225
3233	XX	1940–1965	Yellow Composition		70
3233	USA	1965–1970	Yellow Composition		50
3233	10 Dots	1970–1971	Yellow Composition		55
3233	Dots	1971–1975	Yellow Composition		35
5233	XX	1960–1965	Stag		225
5233	USA	1965–1970	Stag		150
5233	10 Dots	1970–1971	Stag		175
5233SSP	4 Dots	1977	Stag		75
5233SSP	3 Dots	1978	Stag		75
52033SSP	3 Dots	1978	Stag		85
6233	Tested	Prior 1940	Rough Black		200
6233	XX	1940s	Rough Black		140
6233	XX	1940s	Rough Black	Long pull	250
6233	Tested	Prior 1940	Green Bone		300
6233	XX	1940–1955	Green Bone		200
6233	XX	1940–1955	Green Bone	Long pull	300
6233	XX	1940–1965	Bone		85
6233	USA	1965–1970	Bone		60
6233	10 Dots	1970–1971	Bone		60
6233	10 Dots	1970–1971	Delrin		60
6233	Dots	1970s	Delrin		35
62033	Dots	1976	Delrin		30
62033	Dots	1976–1979	Delrin		30
A62033	1 Dot	1979	Smooth Bone		35
A62033	"S" 10 Dots	1980	Smooth Bone		40
8233	Tested	Prior 1940	Pearl		350
8233	XX	1960–1965	Pearl		150
8233	USA	1965–1970	Pearl		95
8233	10 Dots	1970–1971	Pearl		100
8233	Dots	1970–1975	Pearl		70
9233	Tested	Prior 1940	Imitation Pearl		225

Pattern	*Stamping*	*Years Made*	*Handle*	*Variation/Blade*	*Mint Price*
9233	XX	1940–1965	Cracked Ice	Shad, no bolsters	225
9233	XX	1940–1965	Imitation Pearl		65
9233	XX	1940–1965	Cracked Ice		55
9233	XX	1940–1965	Cracked Ice	Long pull	95
9233	USA	1965–1970	Imitation Pearl		40
9233	10 Dots	1970–1971	Imitation Pearl		40
9233	Dots	1970s	Imitation Pearl		30
92033	Dots	1976	Cracked Ice		35
Doctor's Knife					
2234	Tested	Prior 1940	Slick Black		675
5234	Tested	Prior 1940	Stag		1250

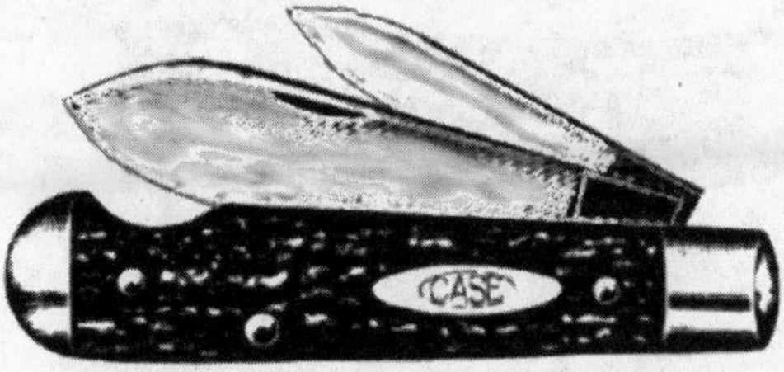

3¼″ Swell End Jack

3¼″ Swell End Jack					
6235EO	Tested	Prior 1940	Green Bone	Easy open	425
6235EO	XX	1940–1950	Bone	Easy open	250
6235EO	XX	1940s	Rough Black	Easy open	325
6235	Tested	Prior 1940	Green Bone		300
6235	XX	1940–1955	Green Bone		250
6235	XX	1940s	Rough Black	With shield	125
6235	XX	1940s	Rough Black	Without shield	110
6235	XX	1940–1965	Bone		125
6235SH	Tested	Prior 1940	Green Bone		400
3235½	Tested	Prior 1940	Yellow Composition		235
5235½	Tested	Prior 1940	Stag		450
6235½P	Tested	Prior 1940	Green Bone	punch	400
6235½	Tested	Prior 1940	Green Bone		300
6235½	XX	1940–1955	Green Bone		250
6235½	XX	1940s	Rough Black	With shield	125
6235½	XX	1940s	Rough Black	Without shield	125
6235½	USA	1965–1970	Bone		70
6235½	10 Dots	1970–1971	Bone		70
6235½	Dots	1970s	Bone		55
62035½	Tested	Prior 1940	Green Bone		500
A6235½	1 Dot	1979	Smooth Bone		70
A6235½	"S" 10 Dots	1980	Smooth Bone		55
A6235½SS	"S" 10 Dots	1980	Smooth Bone		55

3¼″ Jack

Pattern	*Stamping*	*Years Made*	*Handle*	*Variation/Blade*	*Mint Price*
3¼″ Jack					
620035	XX	1940–1960	Black Plastic	Standard long pull	55
620035½	XX	1940–1960	Black Plastic	Standard long pull	55
620035EO	XX	1945–1950	Black Plastic	Standard long pull	90
3½″ Jack					
6237½	Tested	Prior 1940	Green Bone		975

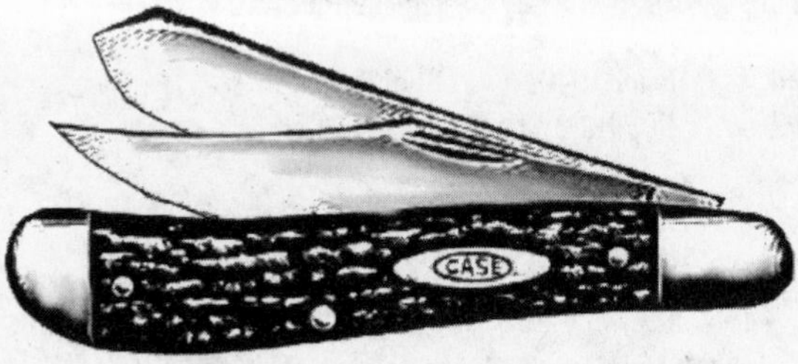

4 7/16″ Large Trapper

4 7/16″ Large Trapper					
6240	Tested	Prior 1940	Green Bone		1800
6240SP	Tested	Prior 1940	Green Bone		2000

3″ Pen

3″ Pen					
52042	Tested	Prior 1940	Stag		250
62042	Tested	Prior 1940	Green Bone		200
62042	XX	1940–1955	Green Bone		150
62042	XX	1940s	Rough Black		90
62042	XX	1940–1965	Bone		95
62042	USA	1965–1970	Bone		50
62042	10 Dots	1970–1971	Bone		50
62042	Dots	1970s	Bone		35
62042	Dots	1970s	Delrin		30
62042R	XX	1957–1965	Bone	Bail in handle	90
62042R	USA	1965–1970	Bone		60
62042R	10 Dots	1970	Bone		60
82042	Tested	Prior 1940	Pearl		275
92042	Tested	Prior 1940	Imitation Pearl		140
92042	XX	1940–1965	Imitation Pearl		55
92042	XX	1940–1965	Cracked Ice		55
92042	USA	1965–1970	Imitation Pearl		40
92042	10 Dots	1970–1971	Imitation Pearl		40
92042	Dots	1970s	Imitation Pearl		35
92042R	XX	1957–1965	Imitation Pearl	Bail in handle	60
92042R	XX	1957–1965	Cracked Ice	Bail in handle	60
92042R	USA	1965–1970	Imitation Pearl	Bail in handle	45
92042R	10 Dots	1970	Imitation Pearl		40
A62042	1 Dot	1979	Smooth Bone		40
A62042	"S" 10 Dots	1980	Smooth Bone		30
52042R	"S" Dots	1980s	Stag		50

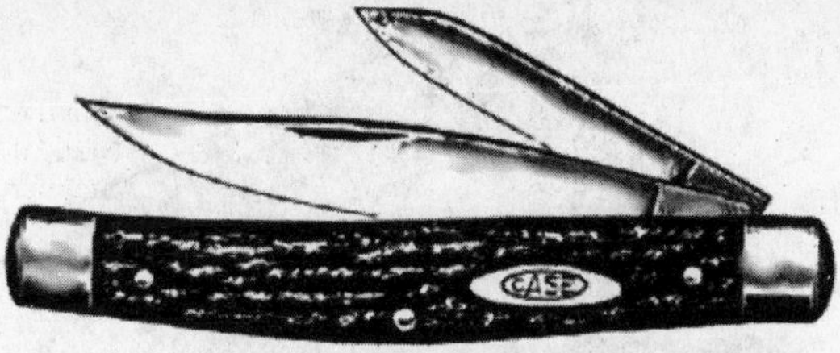

3¼″ Premium Jack

Pattern	*Stamping*	*Years Made*	*Handle*	*Variation/Blade*	*Mint Price*
3¼″ Premium Jack					
3244	Tested	Prior 1940	Yellow Composition		150
5244	Tested	Prior 1940	Stag		325
6244	Tested	Prior 1940	Green Bone		250
9244	Tested	Prior 1940	Imitation Pearl		150
6244	XX	1955–1965	Bone		95
6244	USA	1965–1970	Bone		60
6244	10 Dots	1970–1971	Bone		60
6244	10 Dots	1970–1971	Delrin		75
6244	Dots	1970s	Delrin		35
SR-6244	1 Dot	1979	Smooth Bone		35
SR-6244	"S" 10 Dots	1980	Smooth Bone		40
SR-6244SS	"S" Dots	1980s	Smooth Bone		35

3¼″ Pen

3¼″ Pen					
05244	Tested	Prior 1940	Stag		375
06244	Tested	Prior 1940	Green Bone		250
06244	XX	1940–1955	Green Bone		200
06244	XX	1940–1965	Red Bone		150
06244	XX	1940–1965	Bone		95
06244	USA	1965–1970	Bone		60
06244	10 Dots	1970–1971	Bone		65
06244	10 Dots	1970–1971	Delrin		40
06244	9 Dots	1971–1972	Bone		35
06244	Dots	1970s	Delrin		25
82044	Tested	Prior 1940	Pearl		300
3¼″ Grafting Knife					
2245SHSP	XX	1960–1965	Black Composition		160

$3\frac{5}{8}$″ Equal End

Pattern	*Stamping*	*Years Made*	*Handle*	*Variation/Blade*	*Mint Price*
$3\frac{5}{8}$″ Equal End					
06245DG	Tested	Prior 1940	Green Bone	Dog grooming knife	575
06245	Tested	Prior 1940	Green Bone	Long pull	350
06245	XX	Prior 1940	Green Bone	Long pull	325
06245$\frac{1}{2}$	Tested	Prior 1940	Green Bone	Long pull	475

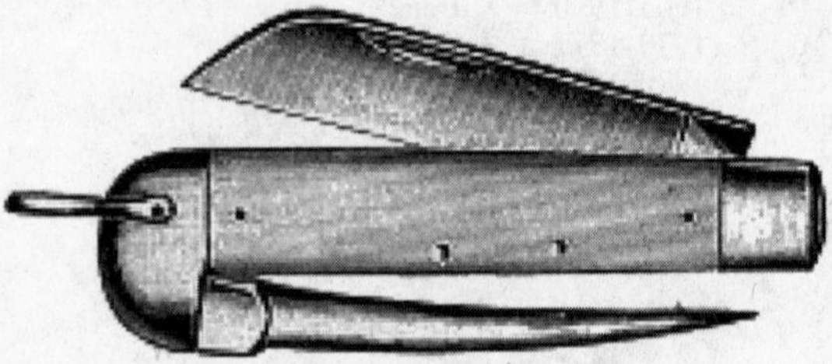

$4\frac{3}{8}$″ Rigger's Knife

$4\frac{3}{8}$″ Rigger's Knife					
3246	Tested	Prior 1940	Yellow Composition		400
3246R	XX	1940–1952	Yellow Composition		300
3246SS	XX	1940–1965	Yellow Composition		175
3246SS	USA	1965–1970	Yellow Composition		250
6246SS	Tested	Prior 1940	Green Bone		750
6246SS	XX	1963–1965	Bone		225
6246SS	USA	1965–1970	Bone		150
6246SS	10 Dots	1970–1971	Bone		150
6246SS	Dots	1970s	Bone		90
6246RSS	"S" Dots	Delrin			50
4″ Greenskeeper Knife					
4247K	XX	Prior 1965	White Composition		475
4247K	USA	1965–1970	White Composition		425
4247K	10 Dots	1970	White Composition		425
4247K	Dots	1970s	White Composition		375

$3\frac{7}{8}$″ Moose

Pattern	Stamping	Years Made	Handle	Variation/Blade	Mint Price
$3^7/_8$″ Moose					
5247J	Tested	Prior 1940	Stag		1500
6247J	Tested	Prior 1940	Green Bone		1100

$3^7/_8$″ Texas Jack

$3^7/_8$″ Texas Jack

04247SP	Tested	Prior 1940	White Composition		450
05247SP	Tested	Prior 1940	Stag		800
06247SP	Tested	Prior 1940	Green Bone		700
06247PEN	Tested	Prior 1940	Green Bone		700
04247SP	XX	1940–1965	White Composition		225
04247SP	USA	1965–1966	White Composition		150
05247SP	XX	1940–1965	Stag		400
05247SP	USA	1965–1966	Stag		325
06247PEN	XX	1940–1955	Green Bone		325
06247PENP	XX	1940s	Rough Black		275
06247PEN	XX	1940–1965	Bone		150
06247PEN	USA	1965–1970	Bone		85
06247PEN	10 Dots	1970–1971	Bone		90
06247PEN	Dots	1970s	Bone		50
06247PEN	Dots	1970s	Delrin		40
06247PEN	"S" 10 Dots	1980	Bone		35

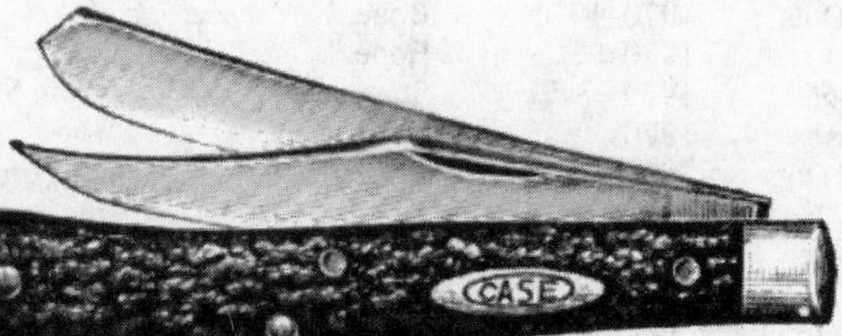

4″ Slim Serpentine Jack

4″ Slim Serpentine Jack

32048SP	XX	1949–1965	Yellow Composition		110
32048SP	USA	1965–1970	Yellow Composition		65
32048SP	10 Dots	1970–1971	Yellow Composition		70
32048SP	Dots	1970s	Yellow Composition		45
32048	"S" Dots	1980s	Yellow Composition		25
62048	Tested	Prior 1940	Green Bone		650
62048	"S" Dots	1980s	Delrin		30
62048	10 Dots	1970	Bone		250
62048SS	"S" Dots	1980s	Delrin		25
B2048SP	Tested	Prior 1940	Imitation Onyx		525
62048SP	Tested	Prior 1940	Green Bone		650
62048SP	XX	1940–1955	Green Bone		375
62048SP	XX	1940–1965	Bone		150
62048SP	USA	1965–1969	Bone		95

Pattern	*Stamping*	*Years Made*	*Handle*	*Variation/Blade*	*Mint Price*
62048SP	USA	1969–1970	Delrin		50
62048SP	10 Dots	1970–1971	Delrin		50
62048SP	Dots	1970s	Delrin		35
62048SP-SSP	USA	1966–1967	Bone	"Tested XX Stainless"	125
62048SP-SSP	USA	1967–1969	Bone	"Tested XX Razor Edge"	140
62048SP-SSP	USA	1966–1970	Delrin		50
62048SP-SSP	10 Dots	1970–1971	Delrin		50
62048SP-SSP	Dots	1970s	Delrin		35
62048SP-SSP	"S" 10 Dots	1980	Delrin		30

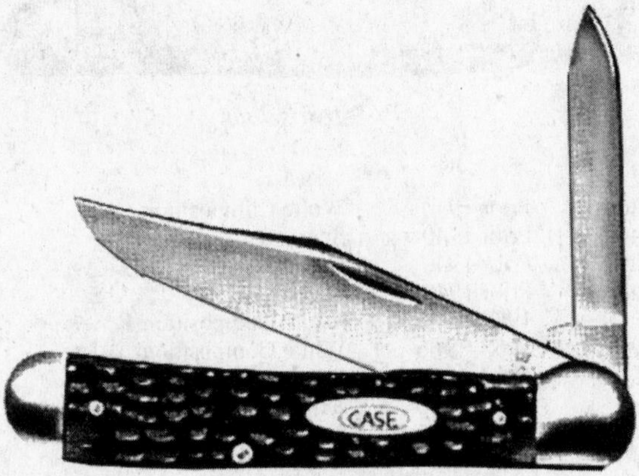

3 15/16" Copperhead

3 15/16" Copperhead					
6249	Tested	Prior 1940	Green Bone		1700
6249	XX	1940–1955	Green Bone		850
6249	XX	1940s–1965	Bone		300
6249	USA	1965–1970	Bone		175
6249	10 Dots	1970–1971	Bone		200
6249	Dots	1970s	Bone		70
5249	1 Dot	1979	Stag	From Stag set	125
6249	Dots	1970s	Delrin		45
6249	"S" Dots	1980s	Bone		50

4 3/8" Sunfish

4 3/8" Sunfish					
6250	Tested	Prior 1940	Green Bone		2300
6250	XX	1940–1955	Green Bone		1500

Pattern	Stamping	Years Made	Handle	Variation/Blade	Mint Price
6250	XX	1940–1965	Red Bone		700
6250	XX	1940–1965	Bone		450
6250	XX	1964–1965	Laminated Wood		225
6250	USA	1964–1965	Bone		500
6250	USA	1965–1970	Laminated Wood		150
6250	10 Dots	1970–1971	Laminated Wood		175
6250	Dots	1970s	Laminated Wood		100
6250	Dots	1970s	Laminated Wood	Elephant etching	150
6250	"S" 10 Dots	1980	Laminated Wood		75

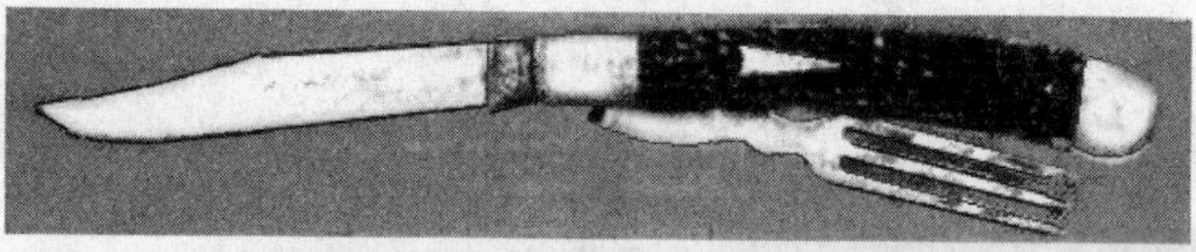

6¾″ Knife & Fork Combination

6¾″ Knife & Fork Combination

6251CLASP	Tested	Prior 1940	Green Bone	Knife/fork	1600
9251	Tested	Prior 1940	Imitation Pearl	Knife/fork	950

3¾″ Hobo—Knife & Fork Comb

6252	Tested	Prior 1940	Green Bone		800
3252	Tested	Prior 1940	Composition Ivory		600

3½″ Congress

3½″ Congress

62052	Tested	Prior 1940	Green Bone	750
62052	XX	1940–1956	Green Bone	425
62052	XX	1940–1965	Bone	225
62052	USA	1965–1970	Bone	125
62052	10 Dots	1970–1971	Bone	125
62052	Dots	1971–1976	Bone	90
62052	Dots	1971–1976	Delrin	50

3¼″ Equal End Pen

3¼″ Equal End Pen

5253	Tested	Prior 1940	Stag	275
5253	XX	1950	Stag	275
6253	Tested	Prior 1940	Green Bone	250
6253	XX	1940–1950	Green Bone	150
6253	XX	1950	Rough Black	120

Pattern	*Stamping*	*Years Made*	*Handle*	*Variation/Blade*	*Mint Price*
9253	Tested	Prior 1940	Imitation Pearl		140
9253	XX	1950	Imitation Pearl		100

2¹³/₁₆″ Equal End Pen

2¹³/₁₆″ Equal End Pen

62053SS	XX	1940–1965	Bone		125
62053SS	USA	1965–1969	Bone		190
82053SR	Tested	Prior 1940	Pearl		225
82053	XX	1940–1964	Pearl		100
82053SS	XX	1949–1964	Pearl	Bolsters	110
82053SRSS	XX	1949–1965	Pearl	Bail, no bolsters	90
82053SRSS	USA	1965–1970	Pearl		70
82053SRSS	Dots	1970s	Pearl		65

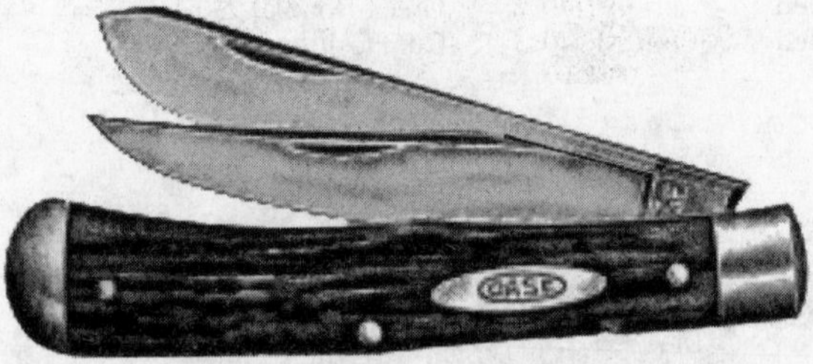

4¹/₈″ Trapper

4¹/₈″ Trapper

3254	Tested	Prior 1940	Yellow Composition		3000
3254	XX	1940–1965	Yellow Composition		350
3254	USA	1965–1970	Yellow Composition		150
3254	USA	1965–1967	Yellow Composition	Muskrat blade	500
3254	10 Dots	1970–1971	Yellow Composition		150
3254	Dots	1970s	Yellow Composition		110
3254	"S" Dots	1980s	Yellow Composition		35
5254	Tested	Prior 1940	Rogers Stag		5000
5254	Tested	Prior 1940	Stag		4000
5254	XX	1950	Stag	Tested frame	850
5254	XX	1940–1965	Stag		650
5254	USA	1965–1970	Stag		300
5254	USA	1965–1967	Stag	Muskrat blade	600
5254	USA	1965–1970	Second Cut Stag		850
5254	USA	1965–1967	Second Cut Stag	Muskrat blade	1000
5254	10 Dots	1970–1971	Stag		300
5254SS	4 Dots	1970–1971	Stag	Part of 1976 set	150
5254SS	3 Dots	1970–1971	Stag	Part of 1977 set	175
6254	Tested	Prior 1940	Green Bone		4200
6254	XX	1941–1953	Green Bone	1st model	1850
6254	XX	1958–1965	Bone		700
6254	USA	1965–1970	Second Cut Stag		775
6254	USA	1965–1967	Bone	Muskrat blade	600
6254	USA	1965–1970	Bone		250
6254	10 Dots	1970–1971	Bone		250

Pattern	*Stamping*	*Years Made*	*Handle*	*Variation/Blade*	*Mint Price*
6254	Dots	1970s	Bone		150
6254	Dots	1970s	Delrin		150
6254	"S" dots	1980s	Bone		45
6254SSP	USA	1965–1966	Bone	Polished blades	300
6254SSP	USA	1965–1967	Bone	Muskrat blade polished	500
6254SSP	USA	1965–1967	Bone	Blade edges polished	225
6254SSP	USA	1965–1970	Bone	Brush finish blades	275
6254SSP	10 Dots	1970–1971	Bone		225
6254SSP	Dots	1970s	Bone		150
6254SSP	Dots	1970s	Delrin		100
6254SSP	"S" Dots	1980s	Bone		50

3 1/2″ Equal End Jack

3 1/2″ Equal End Jack

22055	Tested	Prior 1940	Black Composition		275
32055	Tested	Prior 1940	Yellow Composition		325
92055	Tested	Prior 1940	Imitation Pearl		325
22055	XX	1940–1965	Black Composition		100
22055	XX	1940s	Black Composition	Long pull	190
22055	USA	1965–1967	Black Composition		175
62055	Tested	Prior 1940	Green Bone		475
62055	XX	1940–1955	Green Bone	Long pull	475
62055	XX	1940–1955	Green Bone		350
62055	XX	1940s	Rough Black	Long pull	325
62055	XX	1940s	Rough Black		250
62055	XX	1940–1965	Bone		150
62055	USA	1965–1970	Bone		125
62055	10 Dots	1970–1971	Bone		125
62055	Dots	1970s	Bone		70
62055	Dots	1970s	Delrin		40

3 5/16″ Office Knife

3 5/16″ Office Knife

4257	Tested	Prior 1940	Imitation Ivory		115
4257	XX	1940–1950	Imitation Ivory		125
4257	XX	1940–1960	Imitation Ivory	Handle not etched	70
42057	Tested	Prior 1940	Imitation Ivory		150

Pattern	Stamping	Years Made	Handle	Variation/Blade	Mint Price
42057	XX	1940–1950	Imitation Ivory		125
42057	XX	1940–1955	Imitation Ivory	Handle not etched	75
92057	Tested	Prior 1940	Imitation Pearl		115
3¼″ Equal End Pen					
92058	Tested	Prior 1940	Imitation Pearl		125

3¼″ Senator Pen

3¼″ Senator Pen					
62059	Tested	Prior 1940	Green Bone		225
62059SP	Tested	Prior 1940	Green Bone		225
3 7/16″ Senator Pen					
5260	Tested	Prior 1940	Stag		350
5260	XX	1940–1952	Stag		300

2 7/8″ Senator Pen

2 7/8″ Senator Pen					
2261	Tested	Prior 1940	Black Composition		150
6261F	Tested	Prior 1940	Green Bone		200
6261	Tested	Prior 1940	Green Bone		200
8261F	Tested	Prior 1940	Pearl		225
8261	Tested	Prior 1940	Pearl		225
8261	XX	1940–1965	Pearl		90
8261	USA	1965–1970	Pearl		90
8261	10 Dots	1970–1971	Pearl		90
8261	Dots	1970–1976	Pearl		65
9261F	Tested	Prior 1940	Imitation Pearl		125
9261	Tested	Prior 1940	Imitation Pearl		110
9261	XX	1940–1965	Imitation Pearl		50
9261	XX	1945–1950	Cracked Ice		50
9261	USA	1965–1970	Imitation Pearl		40
9261	10 Dots	1970–1971	Imitation Pearl		40
9261	Dots	1970–1975	Imitation Pearl		30

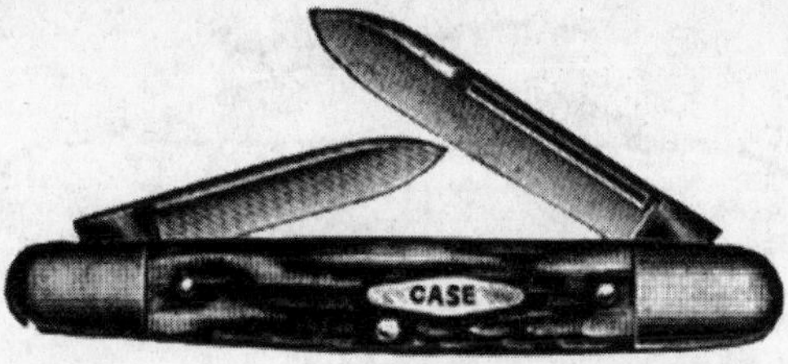

3¹/8″ Equal End Pen

Pattern	Stamping	Years Made	Handle	Variation/Blade	Mint Price
3¹/8″ Equal End Pen					
05263	Tested	Prior 1940	Stag		275
05263	XX	1940–1952	Stag		225
05263SS	XX	1940–1965	Stag		150
05263	USA	1965–1970	Stag		100
05263	10 Dots	1970–1971	Stag		100
06263	Tested	Prior 1940	Green Bone		200
06263	XX	1945–1950	Green Bone		210
06263SS	XX	1945–1955	Green Bone		185
06263	XX	1945–1955	Bone		100
06263SS	XX	1940–1965	Bone		100
06263SS	USA	1965–1970	Bone		50
06263SS	10 Dots	1970	Bone		55
06263F	XX	1940–1945	Bone		110
06263SS	XX	1940–1965	Bone		100
06263SSP	USA	1965–1966	Bone	"Tested XX Stainless"	65
06263SSP	USA	1965–1970	Delrin	"Tested XX Razor Edge"	50
06263SSP	10 Dots	1970–1971	Delrin		45
06263SSP	Dots	1970s	Bone		50
06263SSP	Dots	1970s	Delrin		30
06263SSP	"S" Dots	1980s	Delrin		25

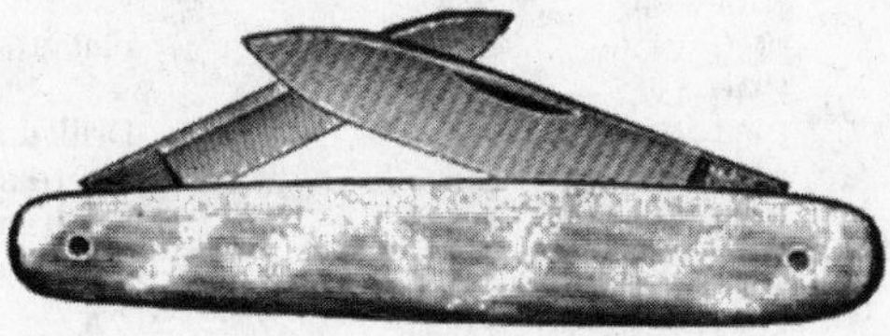

3¹/16″ Sleeveboard Pen

Pattern	Stamping	Years Made	Handle	Variation/Blade	Mint Price
3¹/16″ Sleeveboard Pen					
62063¹/2SS	XX	1940–1960	Bone		100
62063¹/2SS	XX	1940–1955	Green Bone		190
62063¹/2	Tested	Prior 1940	Green Bone		225
62063¹/2	XX	1940–1955	Green Bone		185
82063SHAD	Tested	Prior 1940	Pearl		200
82063¹/2	Tested	Prior 1940	Pearl		250
82063	Tested	Prior 1940	Pearl		200
82063SHAD	XX	1940–1955	Pearl		110
82063SHAD-SS	XX	1940–1965	Pearl		140
92063¹/2	Tested	Prior 1940	Imitation Pearl		140
92063¹/2	XX	1940–1942	Imitation Pearl		100

3¹/8″ Senator Pen

Pattern	Stamping	Years Made	Handle	Variation/Blade	Mint Price
3¹/8″ Senator Pen					
8264T	Tested	Prior 1940	Pearl		250
9264TF	Tested	Prior 1940	Imitation Pearl		150
6264TG	Tested	Prior 1940	Green Bone		225
6264T	Tested	Prior 1940	Green Bone		225

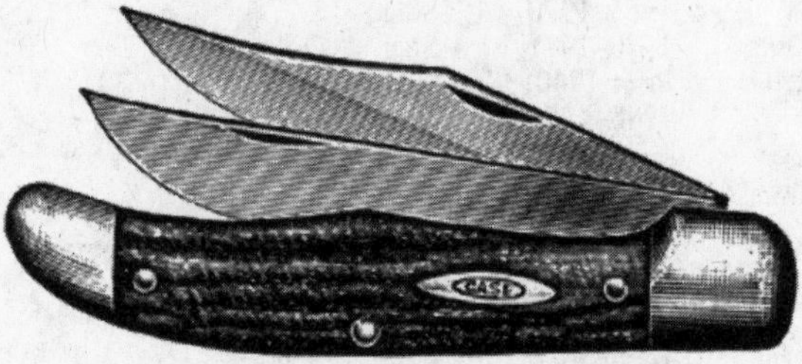

5¹/4″ Folding Hunter

5¹/4″ Folding Hunter					
3265SAB	Tested	Prior 1940	Yellow Composition		675
3265	Tested	Prior 1940	Yellow Composition		700
5265SAB	Tested	Prior 1940	Stag		1000
5265	XX	1940–1950	Stag	Flat ground blade	850
5265SAB	XX	1940–1965	Stag		500
5265SAB	XX	1964–1965	Stag	Drilled bolster	500
5265SAB	USA	1965–1966	Stag	XX frame, not drilled	350
5265SAB	USA	1965–1966	Stag	XX frame, drilled	325
5265SAB	USA	1965–1970	Stag	Drilled	275
5265SAB	10 Dots	1970–1971	Stag		275
5265SSP	3 Dots	1978	Stag		175
6265	Tested	Prior 1940	Green Bone		1100
6265	XX	1940–1955	Green Bone	Flat ground blade	1000
6265	XX	1940s	Green Bone		850
6265SAB	Tested	Prior 1940	Green Bone		950
6265SAB	XX	1940–1955	Green Bone		800
6265SAB	XX	1940s	Rough Black		450
6265SAB	XX	1940–1965	Red Bone		500
6265SAB	XX	1940–1965	Bone		350
6265SAB	USA	1965–1966	Bone	XX frame, not drilled	325
6265SAB	USA	1965–1966	Bone	XX frame drilled	340
6265SAB	USA	1965–1966	Laminated Wood	XX frame not drilled	100
6265SAB	USA	1965–1970	Laminated Wood		85
6265SAB	10 Dots	1960–1971	Laminated Wood		65
6265SAB	Dots	1970s	Laminated Wood		50
6265SAB-SS	"S" 10 Dots	1980	Laminated Wood		60
6265SAB	"S" Dots	1980	Laminated Wood		40
5¹/4″ Bill Boatman Special					
6265SAB	XX	1960–1965	Bone	Serrated skinner blade	500
6265SAB	XX	1964–1965	Laminated Wood	Serrated skinner blade	325
6265SAB	USA	1965–1966	Bone	Serrated skinner blade	500

Pattern	*Stamping*	*Years Made*	*Handle*	*Variation/Blade*	*Mint Price*
6265SAB	USA	1965–1970	Laminated Wood	Serrated skinner blade	225
6265SAB	10 Dots	1970	Laminated Wood	Serrated skinner blade	250
6265SAB	Dots	1970s	Laminated Wood	Serrated skinner blade	160

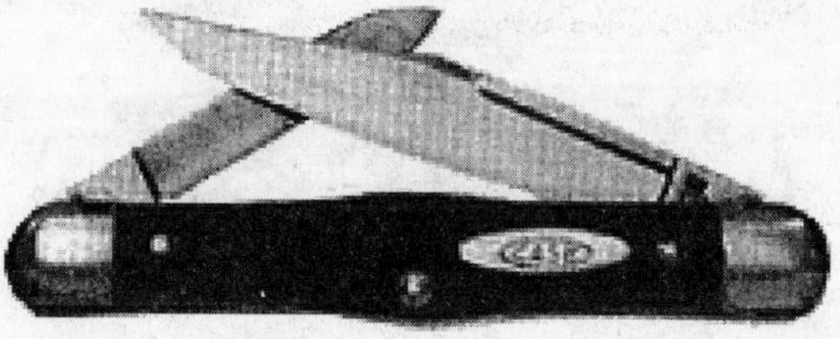

3¼″ Swell Center Pen

3¼″ Swell Center Pen

06267	Tested	Prior 1940	Green Bone		300
06267	XX	1940–1965	Bone	Long pull	180
06267	USA	1965–1970	Bone		165

3¼″ Congress

6268	Tested	Prior 1940	Green Bone		775

3″ Congress

3″ Congress

6269	Tested	Prior 1940	Green Bone		425
8269	Tested	Prior 1940	Pearl		500
9269	Tested	Prior 1940	Imitation Pearl		325
6269	XX	1940s	Rough Black		160
6269	XX	1940–1955	Green Bone		275
6269	XX	1940–1965	Red Bone		175
6269	XX	1940–1965	Bone		110
6269	USA	1965–1970	Bone		80
6269	10 Dots	1970–1971	Bone		95
6269	Dots	1970s	Bone		65
6269	Dots	1970s	Delrin		35

3¼″ Senator Pen

3¼″ Senator Pen

6271SS	XX	1963–1965	Bone		150
8271	Tested	Prior 1940	Pearl		375
8271	XX	1940–1958	Pearl	Long pull	265
8271F	Tested	Prior 1940	Pearl		375

Pattern	Stamping	Years Made	Handle	Variation/Blade	Mint Price
8271F	XX	1940–1958	Pearl		225
8271SS	XX	1940–1960	Pearl	Long pull	250
8271SS	XX	1940–1960	Pearl		225

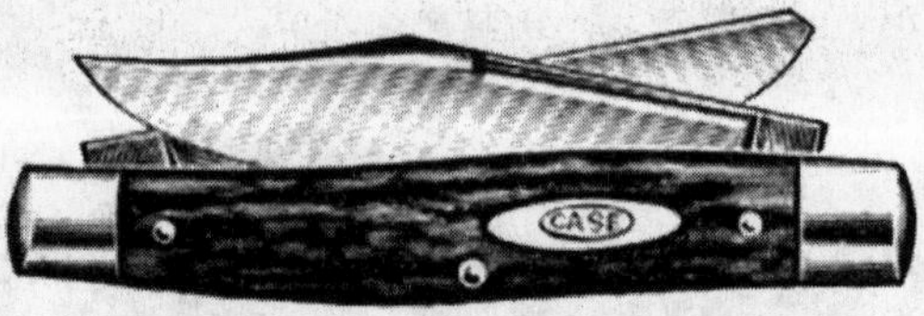

4¼″ Moose

Pattern	Stamping	Years Made	Handle	Variation/Blade	Mint Price
4¼″ Moose					
5275SP	Tested	Prior 1940	Stag		1400
6275SP	Tested	Prior 1940	Green Bone		1200
6275SP	XX	1940–1955	Green Bone	Long pull	800
6275SP	XX	1940s	Rough Black	Long pull	450
6275SP	XX	1940–1965	Red Bone	Long pull	575
6275SP	XX	1940–1965	Red Bone		400
6275SP	XX	1940–1965	Bone		225
6275SP	USA	1965–1971	Bone		150
6275SP	10 Dots	1970–1971	Bone		150
6275SP	Dots	1970s	Bone		100
6275SP	Dots	1970s	Delrin		75
5275SSP	1 Dot	1979	Stag	From Stag set	125
6275SP	"S" 10 Dots	1980	Bone		90
6275SP	"S" Dots	1980s	Bone		65
3⅝″ Sleeveboard Pen					
5276½	Tested	Prior 1940	Stag		475
6276½	Tested	Prior 1940	Green Bone		425

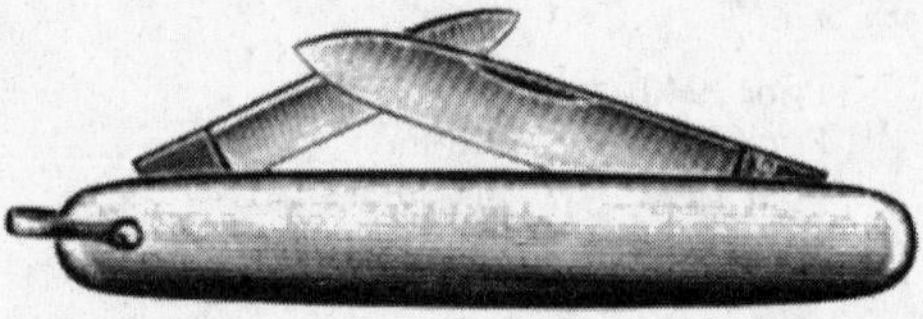

3⅛″ Senator Pen

Pattern	Stamping	Years Made	Handle	Variation/Blade	Mint Price
3⅛″ Senator Pen					
M279	Tested	Prior 1940	Metal		85
M279R	Tested	Prior 1940	Metal		80
GM279	Tested	Prior 1940	Gun Metal		110
M279SS	XX	1940–1965	Stainless Steel		35
M279SS	USA	1965–1970	Stainless Steel		30
M279SS	10 Dots	1970–1971	Stainless Steel		30
M279SS	Dots	1970s	Stainless Steel		25
M279SS	"S" 10 Dots	1980	Stainless Steel		20
M279FSS	XX	1962–1965	Stainless Steel		50
M279FSS	USA	1965–1970	Stainless Steel		30
M279FSS	10 Dots	1970–1971	Stainless Steel		30
M279FSS	Dots	1970s	Stainless Steel		20

3$^{1}/_{8}$" Senator Pen

Pattern	*Stamping*	*Years Made*	*Handle*	*Variation/Blade*	*Mint Price*
3$^{1}/_{8}$" Senator Pen					
R279	Tested	Prior 1940	Red Striped Celluloid		250
2279SHAD-SS	Tested	Prior 1940	Black Composition	No bolster	125
3279R	Tested	Prior 1940	Yellow Composition		115
3279	Tested	Prior 1940	Yellow Composition		110
5279	Tested	Prior 1940	Stag		225
5279	XX	1940–1950	Stag		240
5279SS	XX	1940–1965	Stag		150
5279SS	USA	1965–1966	Stag		260
5279SSP	2 Dots	1979	Stag		85
6279	Tested	Prior 1940	Green Bone		200
6279	XX	1940–1955	Green Bone		200
6279	XX	1940s	Rough Black		140
6279SS	XX	1940s	Rough Black		110
6279	XX	1940–1965	Bone		110
6279SS	USA	1965–1970	Bone		65
6279SS	10 Dots	1970–1971	Bone		65
6279SS	Dots	1970s	Bone		50
6279SS	Dots	1970s	Delrin		35
6279SS	"S" 10 Dots	1980	Delrin		25
8279	Tested	Prior 1940	Pearl		275
8279	XX	1940s	Pearl		120
8279SS	XX	1940–1960	Pearl		100
9279	XX	1945–1955	Imitation Pearl		95
9279SHAD-SS	XX	1962–1963	Cracked Ice	No bolster	45

3$^{1}/_{4}$" Sleeveboard Pen

3$^{1}/_{4}$" Sleeveboard Pen					
62079$^{1}/_{2}$F	Tested	Prior 1940	Green Bone		210
62079	Tested	Prior 1940	Green Bone		210
92079	Tested	Prior 1940	Imitation Pearl		150
92079$^{1}/_{2}$	XX	Late 1940	Imitation Pearl		110
82079	Tested	Prior 1940	Pearl		250
82079$^{1}/_{2}$	Tested	Prior 1940	Pearl		250
82079$^{1}/_{2}$	XX	1940–1965	Pearl		95
82079$^{1}/_{2}$SS	USA	1965–1970	Pearl		80
82079$^{1}/_{2}$SS	10 Dots	1970–1971	Pearl		95
82079$^{1}/_{2}$	Dots	1970–1971	Pearl		70

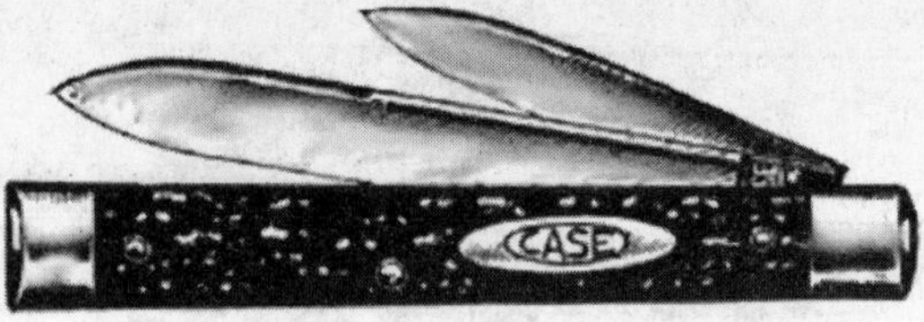

2³/₄″ Square End Jack

Pattern	Stamping	Years Made	Handle	Variation/Blade	Mint Price
2³/₄″ Square End Jack					
5282	Tested	Prior 1940	Stag		1100
6282	Tested	Prior 1940	Green Bone		875
8282	Tested	Prior 1940	Pearl		950

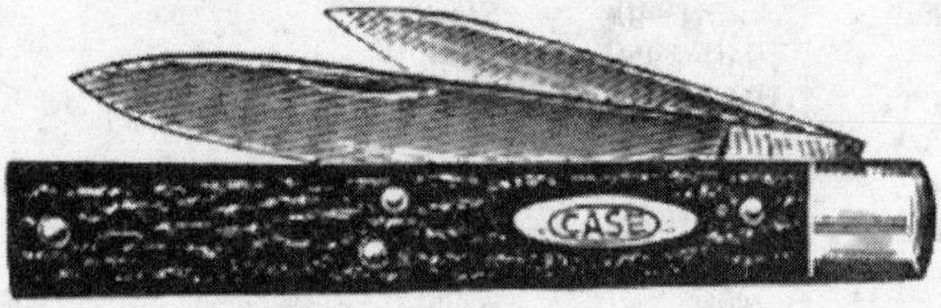

3⁵/₈″ Doctor's Knife

3⁵/₈″ Doctor's Knife					
3285	Tested	Prior 1940	Yellow Composition		675
5285	Tested	Prior 1940	Stag		1250
6285	Tested	Prior 1940	Green Bone		1150
7285	Tested	Prior 1940	Imitation Tortoise Shell		875
7285	Tested	Prior 1940	Christmas Tree		1100

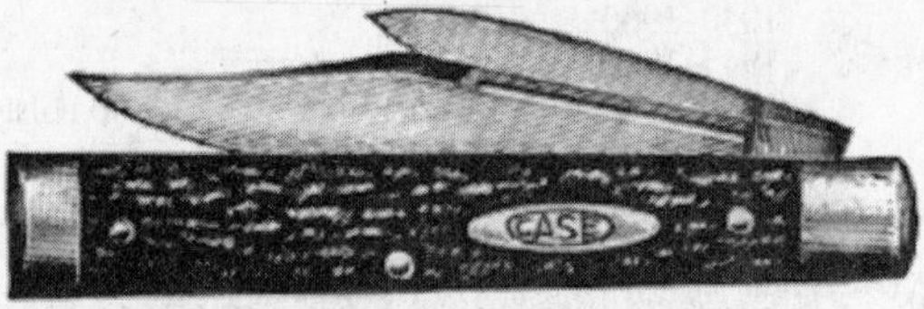

3¹/₄″ Doctors Knifek

3¹/₄″ Doctors Knifek					
52086	Tested	Prior 1940	Stag		1000
62086	Tested	Prior 1940	Green Bone		825
82086	Tested	Prior 1940	Pearl		1000
3¹/₂″ Gunstock					
5287	Tested	Prior 1940	Stag		975

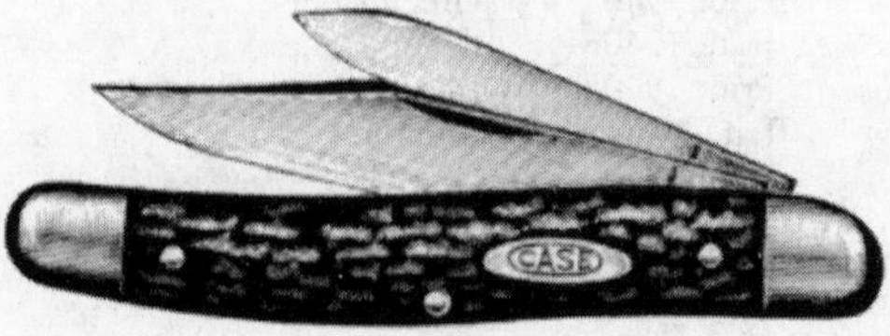

3³/₈″ Serpentine Jack

3³/₈″ Serpentine Jack					
22087	Tested	Prior 1940	Black Composition		140
22087	XX	1940–1955	Black Composition		50

Pattern	*Stamping*	*Years Made*	*Handle*	*Variation/Blade*	*Mint Price*
22087	USA	1965–1970	Black Composition		40
22087	10 Dots	1970–1971	Black Composition		40
22087	Dots	1970s	Black Composition		35
22087	"S" 10 Dots	1980	Black Composition		30
22087	"S" Dots	1984	Black Composition	Etched	30
42087	Tested	Prior 1940	White Composition		170
52087	XX	1955–1965	Stag		150
52087	USA	1965–1970	Stag		125
52087	10 Dots	1970	Stag		150
62087	Tested	Prior 1940	Green Bone		220
62087	XX	1940–1955	Green Bone		175
62087	XX	1940s	Rough Black		135
62087	XX	1940–1955	Red Bone		150
62087	XX	1940–1965	Bone		90
62087	USA	1965–1970	Bone		55
62087	10 Dots	1970–1971	Bone		55
62087	10 Dots	1970–1971	Delrin		40
62087	Dots	1970s	Delrin		30

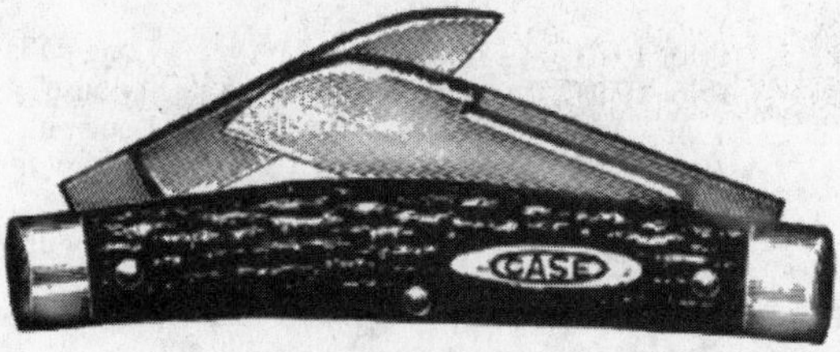

4¹/₈″ Congress

4¹/₈″ Congress

6288	Tested	Prior 1940	Green Bone		3000

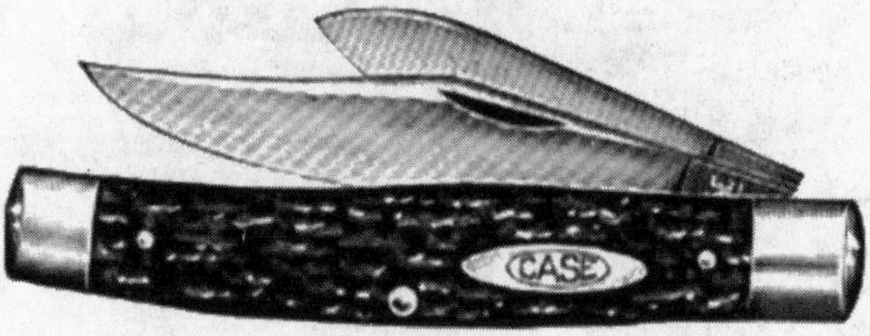

4″ Premium Jack

4″ Premium Jack

3292	Tested	Prior 1940	Yellow Composition		275
6292	Tested	Prior 1940	Green Bone		475
6292	XX	1940–1955	Green Bone		325
6292	XX	1940s	Rough Black		225
6292	XX	1940–1965	Red Bone		225
6292	XX	1940–1965	Bone		140
6292	USA	1965–1970	Bone		85
6292	10 Dots	1970–1971	Bone		100
6292	Dots	1970s	Bone		80
6292	"S" 10 Dots	1980	Bone		45
5292SSP	1 Dot	1979	Stag	From Stag set	125

5″ Texas Toothpick

32093F	Tested	Prior 1940	Yellow Composition		300
62093F	Tested	Prior 1940	Green Bone		475

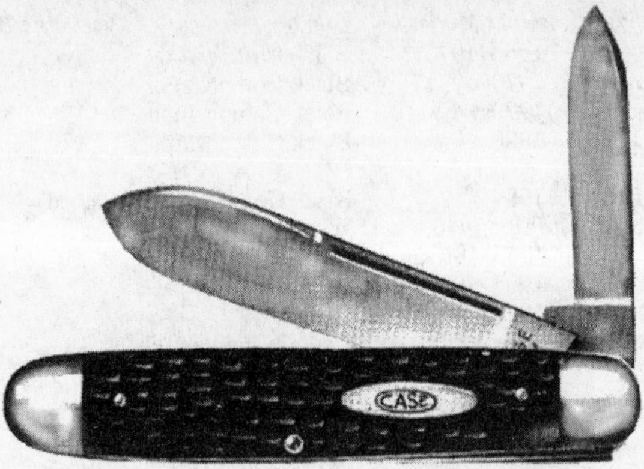

4¼″—Equal End Jack

Pattern	*Stamping*	*Years Made*	*Handle*	*Variation/Blade*	*Mint Price*
4¼″—Equal End Jack					
6294	Tested	Prior 1940	Green Bone	Long pull	1700
6294J	Tested	Prior 1940	Green Bone	"Moose"	3200
6294	XX	1940–1955	Green Bone	Long pull	1200
6294	XX	1940–1955	Red Bone	Long pull	800
6294	XX	1940–1965	Red Bone		600
6294	XX	1940–1965	Bone	Long pull	700
6294	XX	1940–1965	Bone		400

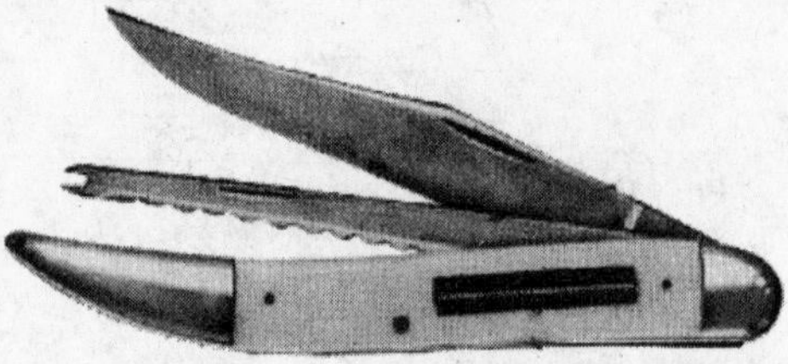

4⅞″ Fisherman Knife

4⅞″ Fisherman Knife					
32095FSS	Tested	Prior 1940	Yellow Composition		300
B2095FSS	Tested	Prior 1940	Imitation Onyx		325
32095FSS	XX	1940–1965	Yellow Composition		125
32095FSS	USA	1965–1970	Yellow Composition		85
32095FSS	10 Dots	1970–1971	Yellow Composition		90
32095FSS	Dots	1970s	Yellow Composition		65
32095FSS	"S" 10 Dots	1980	Yellow Composition		50

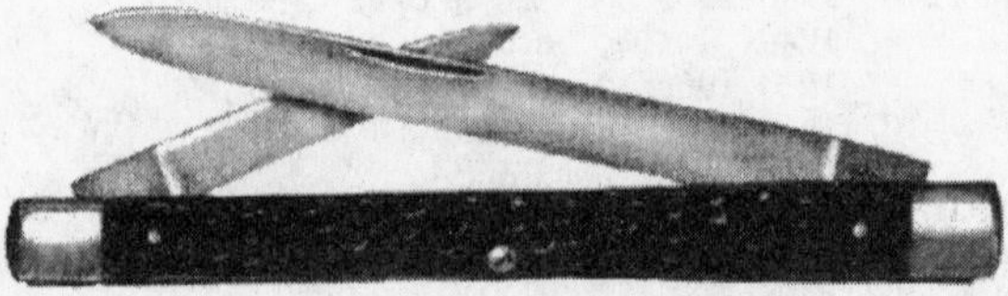

4¼″ Citrus Knife

4¼″ Citrus Knife					
6296X	Tested	Prior 1940	Green Bone		1800
6296XSS	XX	1940–1955	Green Bone		1200

Pattern	*Stamping*	*Years Made*	*Handle*	*Variation/Blade*	*Mint Price*
6296XSS	XX	1940–1965	Bone		550
6296XSS	USA	1965	Bone		600
4$^{1}/_{2}$″ Leg Knife					
3297	Tested	Prior 1940	Yellow Composition		350

5$^{1}/_{2}$″ Fish Knife

5$^{1}/_{2}$″ Fish Knife					
32098F	Tested	Prior 1940	Yellow Composition		350
62098F	Tested	Prior 1940	Green Bone		625
4$^{1}/_{8}$″ Swell End Jack					
6299SHOPR	Tested	Prior 1940	Green Bone		700
2$^{7}/_{8}$″ Oval Lobster					
82099R	Tested	Prior 1940	Pearl		215

4″ Jumbo Jack

4″ Jumbo Jack					
2299$^{1}/_{2}$	Tested	Prior 1940	Black Composition	“A” Blade	275
3299$^{1}/_{2}$	Tested	Prior 1940	Yellow Composition		300
3299$^{1}/_{2}$	XX	1940–1965	Yellow Composition	“A” Blade	150
3299$^{1}/_{2}$	XX	1940–1965	Yellow Composition		125
3299$^{1}/_{2}$	USA	1965–1970	Yellow Composition		110
3299$^{1}/_{2}$	10 Dots	1970–1971	Yellow Composition		95
3299$^{1}/_{2}$	Dots	1970s	Yellow Composition		60
5299$^{1}/_{2}$	Tested	Prior 1940	Stag		875
5299$^{1}/_{2}$	XX	1940–1965	Stag	“A” Blade	400
5299$^{1}/_{2}$	XX	1940–1965	Stag		250
5299$^{1}/_{2}$	USA	1965–1970	Stag		185
5299$^{1}/_{2}$	10 Dots	1970–1971	Stag		200
5299	Tested	Prior 1940	Stag		1100
6299$^{1}/_{2}$	Tested	Prior 1940	Green Bone		1000
6299	Tested	Prior 1940	Green Bone		575
6299	Tested		Rough Black		300
6299	XX	1940s	Rough Black		265
6299	XX	1940s	Green Bone		550

4⁵/₈″ Saddlehorn

Pattern	Stamping	Years Made	Handle	Variation/Blade	Mint Price
4⁵/₈″ Saddlehorn					
62100	Tested	Prior 1940	Green Bone		1850
32100	Tested	Prior 1940	Yellow Composition		1100
92100	Tested	Prior 1940	Imitation Pearl		1200

3¹/₄″ Swell Center Whittler

Pattern	Stamping	Years Made	Handle	Variation/Blade	Mint Price
3¹/₄″ Swell Center Whittler					
2308	Tested	Prior 1940	Black Composition		425
3308	Tested	Prior 1940	Yellow Composition		425
5308	Tested	Prior 1940	Stag		1000
6308	Tested	Prior 1940	Green Bone		850
6308	Tested	Prior 1940	Rough Black		500
6308	XX	1940s	Rough Black		325
6308	XX	1940–1955	Green Bone		600
6308	XX	1940–1955	Red Bone		300
6308	XX	1940–1965	Bone		200
6308	USA	1965–1970	Bone		150
6308	10 Dots	1970–1971	Bone		150
6308	Dots	1970s	Bone		85
6308	Dots	1970s	Delrin		50
6308	"S" Dots	1980s	Bone		45
8308	Tested	Prior 1940	Pearl		1000
3¹/₂″ Premium Stock Knife					
2318	"S" Dots	1984	Black Composition		35
3318SHSP	Tested	Prior 1940	Yellow Composition		300
3318SHPEN	Tested	Prior 1940	Yellow Composition		300

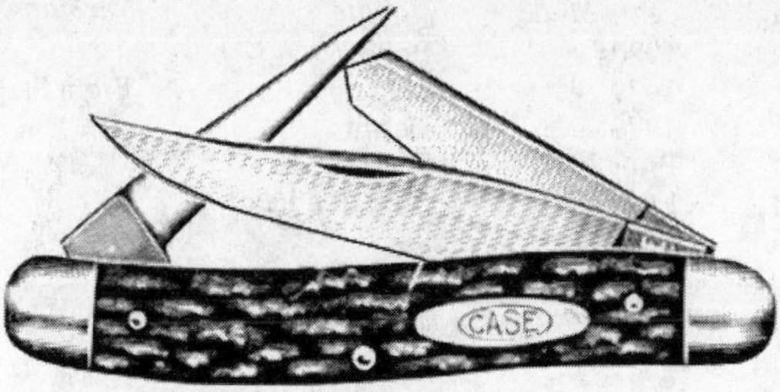

3½" Premium Stock Knife

Pattern	*Stamping*	*Years Made*	*Handle*	*Variation/Blade*	*Mint Price*
3318SHPEN	XX	1940–1965	Yellow Composition		90
3318SHPEN	USA	1965–1970			85
3318SHPEN	10 Dots	1970–1971			85
3318	"S" Dots	1980s			35
3318	Dots	1970s			35
4318PP	XX	1940–1957	White Composition		200
4318SHSP	XX	1957–1965			100
4318SHSP	XX	1957–1965		California clip blade	110
4318SHSP	USA	1965–1970			100
4318SHSP	10 Dots	1970–1971			110
4318SHSP	Dots	1970s			65
5318SHSP	Tested	Prior 1940	Stag		675
6318SHP	Tested	Prior 1940	Green Bone		475
6318SPP	Tested	Prior 1940	Green Bone		475
6318SPP	XX	1940–1955	Green Bone		350
6318SPP	XX	1940s	Rough Black		300
6318SPP	XX	1950–1955	Red Bone		300
6318SPP	XX	1962–1965	Bone		200
6318SPP	USA	1965–1970	Bone		100
6318SPP	10 Dots	1970–1971	Bone		125
6318SPP	Dots	1970s	Bone		75
6318SPP	"S" 10 Dots	1980	Bone		50
6318SPP	"S" Dots	1980s	Bone		40
6318SHSP	Tested	Prior 1940	Green Bone		475
6318SHSP	XX	1940–1955	Green Bone	Long pull	350
6318SHSP	XX	1940–1955	Green Bone		250
6318SHSP	XX	1940s	Rough Black		210
6318SHSP	XX	1940–1965	Red Bone		225
6318SHSP	XX	1940–1965	Bone		140
6318SHSP	USA	1965–1970	Bone		100
6318SHSP	10 Dots	1970–1971	Bone		100
6318SHSP	Dots	1970s	Bone		70
6318SHSP	Dots	1970s	Delrin		40
6318SHSP	"S" Dots	1980s	Bone		40
6318SPPEN	Tested	Prior 1940	Green Bone		475
6318SHPEN	XX	1940–1955	Green Bone		275
6318SHPEN	XX	1940s	Rough Black		225
6318SHPEN	XX	1940–1965	Red Bone		225
6318SHPEN	XX	1940–1965	Bone		125
6318SHPEN	USA	1965–1970	Bone		100
6318SHPEN	10 Dots	1970–1971	Bone		110
6318SHPEN	Dots	1970s	Bone		70
6318SHPE	Dots	1970s	Delrin		35
6318SHPE	"S" Dots	1980s	Bone		45
6318SHSPSSP	USA	1965–1966	Bone	Flat ground	150
6318SHSPSSP	USA	1965–1970	Bone	Concave ground	155
6318SHSPSSP	10 Dots	1970–1971	Bone		125
6318SHSPSSP	10 Dots	1970–1971	Bone	Entire blade polished	140
6318SHSPSSP	Dots	1970s	Bone		70

Pattern	*Stamping*	*Years Made*	*Handle*	*Variation/Blade*	*Mint Price*
6318SHSPSSP	"S" Dots	1980s	Bone		40
5318SSP	1 Dot	1979	Stag	From Stag set	130
5318SS	Dots	1979	Delrin		30
8318	Tested	Prior 1940	Pearl		775
9318SHPEN	Tested	Prior 1940	Imitation Pearl		375

2³/4″ Baby Premium Stock

2³/4″ Baby Premium Stock

6327SHSP	XX	1957–1965	Bone	120
6327SHSP	USA	1965–1970	Bone	90
6327SHSP	10 Dots	1970–1971	Bone	100
6327SHSP	10 Dots	1970–1971	Delrin	100
6327SHSP	Dots	1970s	Delrin	45
9327SHSP	XX	1957–1965	Imitation Pearl	95
6327SHSP	USA	1965–1970	Imitation Pearl	45
6327SHSP	10 Dots	1970–1971	Imitation Pearl	45
6327SHSP	Dots	1971–1974	Imitation Pearl	35
6327SHSP	"S" Dots	1980s	Delrin	25

3⁵/8″ Canoe

3⁵/8″ Canoe

53131	Tested	Prior 1940	Stag	2500

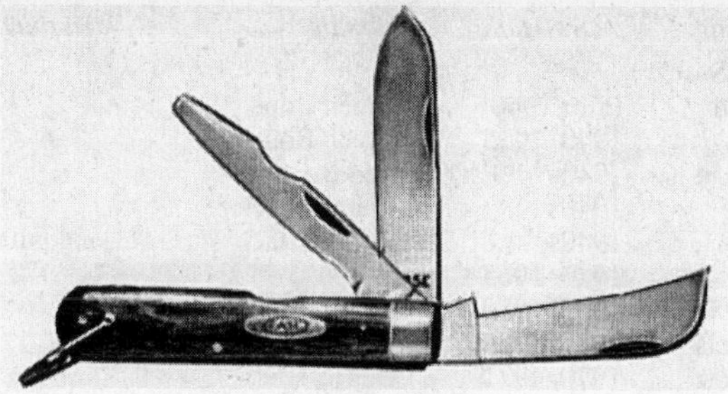

3¾″ Electrician Knife

Pattern	*Stamping*	*Years Made*	*Handle*	*Variation/Blade*	*Mint Price*
3¾″ Electrician Knife					
13031LR	XX	1964–1965	Walnut		85
13031LR	USA	1965–1970	Walnut		65
13031LR	10 Dots	1970	Walnut		70
13031LR	Dots	1970–1974	Walnut		40
13031LR	8 Dots	1970–1974	Walnut		40

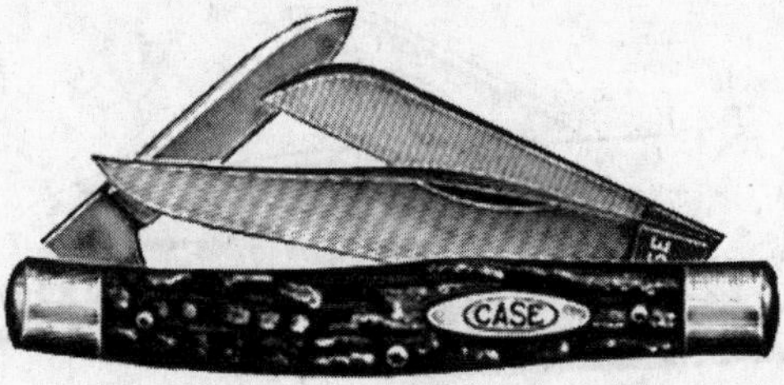

3⅝″ Gunstock Stockman

3⅝″ Gunstock Stockman					
5332	Tested	Prior 1940	Stag		650
5332	XX	1960–1965	Stag		250
5332	USA	1965–1970	Stag		200
5332	10 Dots	1970–1971	Stag		200
6332	Tested	Prior 1940	Green Bone		500
6332	XX	1940–1955	Green Bone		375
6332	XX	1940s	Rough Black		275
6332	XX	1940–1955	Red Bone		275
6332	XX	1940–1965	Bone		175
6332	USA	1965–1970	Bone		100
6332	Dots	1970s	Bone		80
6332	Dots	1970s	Delrin		45
63032	"S" Dots	1980s	Bone		40
63032	USA	1965–1970	Black Composition		85

2⅝″ Baby Premium Stock

Pattern	Stamping	Years Made	Handle	Variation/Blade	Mint Price
2⅝″ Baby Premium Stock					
6333	Tested	Prior 1940	Green Bone		350
6333	XX	1940–1955	Green Bone		250
6333	XX	1940s	Red Bone		150
6333	XX	1940s	Rough Black		125
6333	XX	1940s	Rough Black	Long pull	200
6333	XX	1940–1965	Bone		95
6333	USA	1965–1970	Bone		75
6333	10 Dots	1970–1971	Bone		75
6333	10 Dots	1970–1971	Delrin		45
6333	Dots	1970s	Delrin		30
9333	Tested	Prior 1940	Imitation Pearl		200
9333	XX	1940–1965	Imitation Pearl	Long pull	150
9333	XX	1940–1965	Imitation Pearl		60
9333	USA	1965–1970	Imitation Pearl		45
9333	10 Dots	1970–1971	Imitation Pearl		50
9333	Dots	1970–1974	Imitation Pearl		35
63033	1 Dot	1979	Delrin		30
93033	1 Dot	1979	Imitation Pearl		30
63033	"S" Dots	1980s	Delrin		25

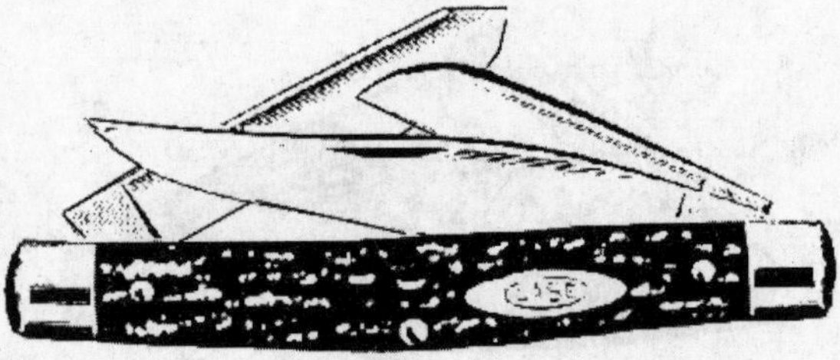

3¼″ Premium Stock

Pattern	Stamping	Years Made	Handle	Variation/Blade	Mint Price
3¼″ Premium Stock					
3344SPP	Tested	Prior 1940	Imitation Onyx		300
3344SHP	Tested	Prior 1940	Yellow Composition		200
3344SPP	Tested	Prior 1940	Yellow Composition		200
3344SHSP	Tested	Prior 1940	Yellow Composition		225
5344SHSP	Tested	Prior 1940	Stag		550
5344SHPEN	Tested	Prior 1940	Stag		500
6344SHP	Tested	Prior 1940	Green Bone		400
6344SSP	Tested	Prior 1940	Green Bone		400
6344SPPEN	Tested	Prior 1940	Green Bone		400
6344SHSP	Tested	Prior 1940	Green Bone		400
6344SHPEN	Tested	Prior 1940	Rough Black		325
6344SHSP	XX	1940–1955	Green Bone		300
6344SHSP	XX	1940–1965	Red Bone		200
6344SHSP	XX	1960–1965	Bone		125
6344SHSP	USA	1965–1970	Bone		85
6344SHSP	10 Dots	1970–1971	Bone		90
6344SHSP	10 Dots	1970–1971	Delrin		100
6344SHSP	9 Dots	1971–1972	Bone		90
6344SHSP	Dots	1970s	Delrin		40
6344SHSP	"S" 10 Dots	1980	Delrin		30
6344SHPEN	Tested	Prior 1940	Green Bone		425
6344SHPEN	XX	1940–1955	Green Bone	Long pull	325
6344SHPEN	XX	1940–1965	Red Bone	Long pull	225
6344SHPEN	XX	1940–1965	Bone	Long pull	125
6344SHPEN	USA	1965–1970	Bone		90
6344SHPEN	10 Dots	1970–1971	Bone	Long pull	90

Pattern	*Stamping*	*Years Made*	*Handle*	*Variation/Blade*	*Mint Price*
6344SHPEN	10 Dots	1970–1971	Delrin		85
6344SHPEN	Dots	1970s	Delrin		35
9344SHPEN	Tested	Prior 1940	Imitation Pearl		225
9344SHSP	Tested	Prior 1940	Imitation Pearl		200
6344SHPEN-SS	"S" Dots	1980s	Delrin		30

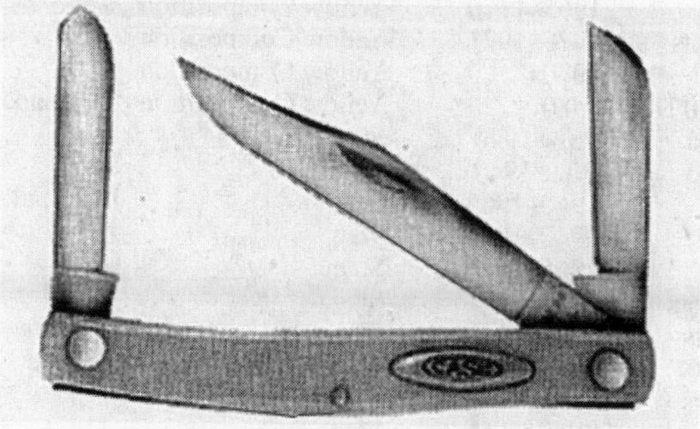

3¼″ Birdseye

3¼″ Birdseye

33044SHSP	XX	1964–1965	Yellow Composition		125
33044SHSP	USA	1965–1970	Yellow Composition		100
33044SHSP	10 Dots	1970–1971	Yellow Composition		90
33044SHSP	Dots	1970s	Yellow Composition		65

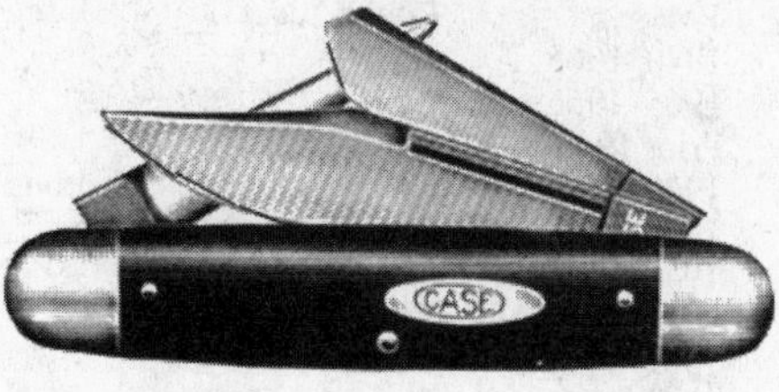

3⅝″ Equal End Cattle Knife

3⅝″ Equal End Cattle Knife

2345½SPPEN	Tested	Prior 1940	Black Composition		275
2345½P	Tested	Prior 1940	Black Composition		300
2345½P	Tested	1940s	Black Composition	Long pull	325
2345½SH	XX	1940–1965	Black Composition		120
2345½SH	USA	1965–1967	Black Composition		150
6345½PU	Tested	Prior 1940	Green Bone		550
6345½SH	Tested	Prior 1940	Green Bone		550
6345½SH	XX	1940–1955	Green Bone		425
6345½SH	XX	1940–1965	Red Bone		325
6345½SH	XX	1940–1965	Bone		225

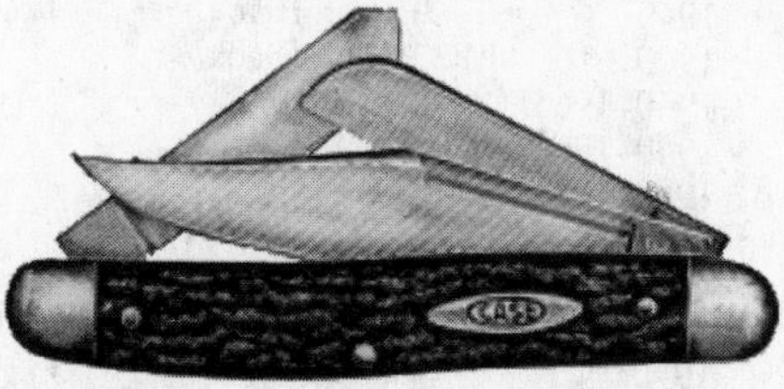

3⅞″ Premium Stock

Pattern	Stamping	Years Made	Handle	Variation/Blade	Mint Price
3⅞″ Premium Stock					
3347SHP	Tested	Prior 1940	Yellow Composition	"A" blade	500
3347SHSP	Tested	Prior 1940	Yellow Composition		500
3347SPPEN	Tested	Prior 1940	Yellow Composition	"A" blade	500
3347SHSP	XX	1940–1953	Yellow Composition	Long pull	325
3347SHSP	XX	1940–1965	Yellow Composition		125
3347SHSP	USA	1965–1970	Yellow Composition		90
3347SHSP	10 Dots	1970–1971	Yellow Composition		95
3347SHSP	Dots	1970s	Yellow Composition		60
3347SHSP	"S" 10 Dots	1980	Yellow Composition	"A" blade	40
5347SHPEN	Tested	Prior 1940	Stag		1200
5347SHSP	Tested	Prior 1940	Stag		1200
5347SHSP	XX	1940–1965	Stag	Long pull	750
5347SHSP	XX	1940–1965	Stag		350
5347SHSP	USA	1965–1970	Stag		200
5347SHSP	10 Dots	1970–1971	Stag		225
5347SSP	4 Dots	1977	Stag		100
5347SS	3 Dots	1978	Stag	1978 sets	125
5347SSP	2 Dots	1979	Stag		125
5347SHSP-SS	XX	1940–1965	Stag		425
5347SHSP-SS	USA	1965–1970	Stag		225
5347SHSP-SS	10 Dots	1970–1971	Stag		400
5347SHSP-SSP	9 Dots	1973	Stag	From collector set	175
6347J	Tested	Prior 1940	Green Bone		1000
6347PJ	Tested	Prior 1940	Green Bone		950
6347SHP	Tested	Prior 1940	Green Bone		700
6347SHP	XX	1940–1955	Green Bone	Long pull	600
6347SHP	XX	1940–1955	Green Bone		475
6347SHP	XX	1940s	Rough Black	Long pull	425
6347SHP	XX	1940–1965	Bone		250
6347SHP	USA	1965–1966	Bone		125
6347PP	Tested	Prior 1940	Green Bone		1000
6347PP	XX	1940–1955	Green Bone	Long pull	750
6347PP	XX	1940–1955	Green Bone		550
6347PP	XX	1940–1965	Red Bone		375
6347PP	XX	1940–1965	Bone		275
6347PP	USA	1965–1970	Bone		175
6347PP	10 Dots	1970–1971	Bone		150
6347PP	Dots	1970–1975	Bone		90
6347SPPEN	Tested	Prior 1940	Green Bone		950
6347SHPEN	Tested	Prior 1940	Green Bone		950
6347SHPEN	XX	1955–1965	Bone		120
6347SHPEN	XX	1940–1955	Green Bone		450
6347SHPEN	XX	1940s	Rough Black		350
6347SHPEN	XX	1940–1965	Red Bone		375
6347SHPEN	XX	1940–1965	Bone		225
6347SHPEN	USA	1965–1970	Bone		125
6347SHPEN	10 Dots	1970–1971	Bone		125
6347SHPEN	Dots	1970–1976	Bone		100
6347SHSP	Tested	Prior 1940	Green Bone		1000
6347SHSP	XX	Prior 1940	Green Bone	Long pull	650
6347SHSP	XX	1957–1965	Green Bone		475
6347SHSP	XX	1940s	Rough Black	Long pull	475
6347SHSP	XX	1940s	Rough Black		375
6347SHSP	XX	1940–1965	Red Bone		375
6347SHSP	XX	1940–1965	Bone		225
6347SHSP	USA	1965–1970	Bone		125
6347SHSP	"S" 10 Dots	1980	Bone		45
6347	"S" Dots	1980s	Bone		40
6347SHSP-SSP	10 Dots	1970–1971	Bone		125
6347SHSP-SSP	Dots	1970s	Bone		95
6347SHSP-SSP	Dots	1970s	Delrin		55
6347SHSP-SS	XX	1940–1955	Green Bone		675

Pattern	*Stamping*	*Years Made*	*Handle*	*Variation/Blade*	*Mint Price*
6347SHSP-SSP	XX	1940–1965	Bone		425
6347SHSP-SSP	XX	1955–1965	Red Bone		500
6347SHSP-SSP	USA	1965–1970	Bone		150
6347SHSP-SSP	"S" Dots	1980s	Bone		45
6347SHSP-SSP	USA	1965	Green Bone	"Tested XX Stainless"	225
6347SHSP-SSP	USA	1965–1970	Bone	Polished blade	375
6347SHSP-SSP	10 Dots	1970	Green Bone		150
53047	XX	1955–1965	Stag	California clip	350
53047	USA	1965–1970	Stag		250
53047	10 Dots	1970	Stag		250
63047	XX	1955–1965	Bone		250
63047	USA	1965–1970	Bone		150
63047	10 Dots	1970–1971	Bone		150
63047	Dots	1970s	Bone		85
63047	Dots	1970s	Delrin		50
SR63047	1 Dot	1980	Smooth Rose Bone		100
SR63047	1 Dot	1980	Smooth Green Bone		95
93047	XX	1940–1956	Imitation Pearl		350

4″ Premium Stock

4″ Premium Stock

630047	Tested	Prior 1940	Green Bone		750
630047P	Tested	Prior 1940	Green Bone		800
630047SHPEN	Tested	Prior 1940	Green Bone		725

3½″ Congress Whittler

3½″ Congress Whittler

63052	Tested	Prior 1940	Green Bone		3000

3½″ Whittler

33055P	Tested	Prior 1940	Yellow Composition		500
23055	XX	1942	Black Composition	Long pull	400
73055	Tested	Prior 1940	Imitation Tortoise	Whittler	550
5355	Tested	Prior 1940	Stag	Wharncliffe Whittler	750

3⁷⁄₁₆″ Senator Pen

8360SCI	Tested	Prior 1940	Pearl		275

3¹/8″ Senator Pen

Pattern	Stamping	Years Made	Handle	Variation/Blade	Mint Price
3¹/8″ Senator Pen					
5364T	Tested	Prior 1940	Stag		350
8364SCIS	Tested	Prior 1940	Pearl		325
8364T	Tested	Prior 1940	Pearl		325
8364TSS	XX	1940–1960	Pearl		140
8364SCIS SS	XX	1940–1965	Pearl		140
8364SCIS SS	USA	1965–1970	Pearl		130
8364SCIS SS	10 Dots	1970–1971	Pearl		130
8364SCIS SS	Dots	1971–1979			95
3¹/8″ Jr. Premium Stock					
6366	Tested	Prior 1940	Green Bone		575
6366PEN	Tested	Prior 1940	Green Bone		575

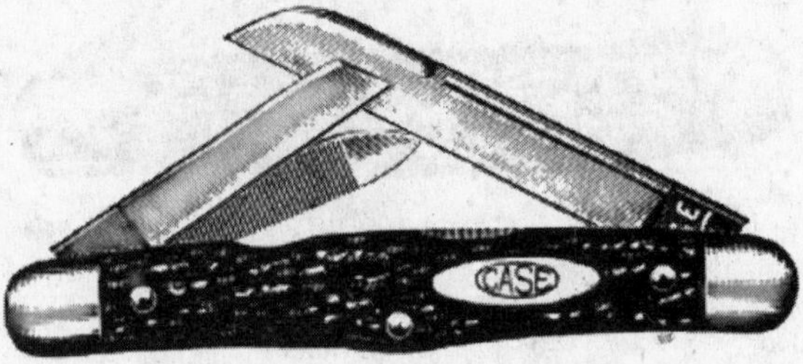

3¹/8″ Swell Center Whittler

3¹/8″ Swell Center Whittler					
6370	Tested	Prior 1940	Green Bone	Long pull	950
8370F	Tested	Prior 1940	Mother-of-Pearl	Long pull	1000

4⁵/16″ Stockman

4⁵/16″ Stockman					
5375	Tested	Prior 1940	Stag	Long pull	2300
5375	XX	1940–1954	Stag	Long pull	800
5375	XX	1940–1965	Stag		500
5375	XX	1960–1965	Second Cut Stag		1250
5375	USA	1965–1970	Second Cut Stag		1200
5375	USA	1965–1970	Stag		375
5375	10 Dots	1970s	Stag		350
6375	Tested	Prior 1940	Green Bone	Long pull	2300
6375	XX	1940–1955	Green Bone	Long pull	1300

Pattern	Stamping	Years Made	Handle	Variation/Blade	Mint Price
6375	XX	1940s	Rough Black	Long pull	700
6375	XX	1940–1955	Red Bone	Long pull	850
6375	XX	1940–1965	Red Bone		475
6375	XX	1940–1955	Bone	Long pull	575
6375	XX	1940–1965	Bone		375
6375	USA	1965–1970	Bone		250
6375	10 Dots	1970–1971	Bone		250
6375	Dots	1970s	Bone		125
6375	Dots	1970s	Delrin		70
6375	"S" Dots	1980s	Bone		65

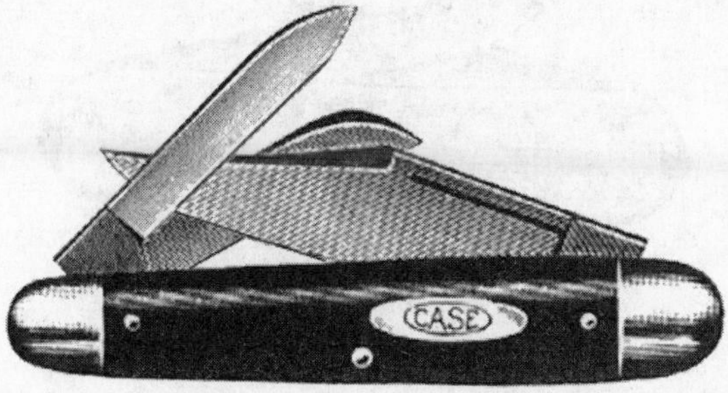

4″ Sleeveboard Whittler

4″ Sleeveboard Whittler				
2376	Tested	Prior 1940	Black Composition	625
3 5/8″ Sleeveboard Whittler				
2376 1/2	Tested	Prior 1940	Black Composition	625
5376 1/2	Tested	Prior 1940	Stag	1000
6376 1/2	Tested	Prior 1940	Green Bone	850

3 1/4″ Sleeveboard Pen

3 1/4″ Sleeveboard Pen				
63079 1/2F	Tested	Prior 1940	Green Bone	700

3 7/8″ Whittler

Pattern	*Stamping*	*Years Made*	*Handle*	*Variation/Blade*	*Mint Price*
3 7/8″ Whittler					
6380	Tested	Prior 1940	Green Bone		3200
6380	XX	1940–1955	Green Bone		1500
6380	XX	1940–1955	Red Bone		700
6380	XX	1955–1965	Bone		450
6380	USA	1965–1970	Bone		300
6380	10 Dots	1970–1971	Bone		300
6380	Dots	1970s	Bone		200
6380	Dots	1970s	Delrin		75

3″ Lobster Pen

3″ Lobster Pen					
83081	Tested	Prior 1940	Pearl		225
3 3/16″ Oval Lobster					
63083	Tested	Prior 1940	Green Bone		400
83083	Tested	Prior 1940	Pearl		325

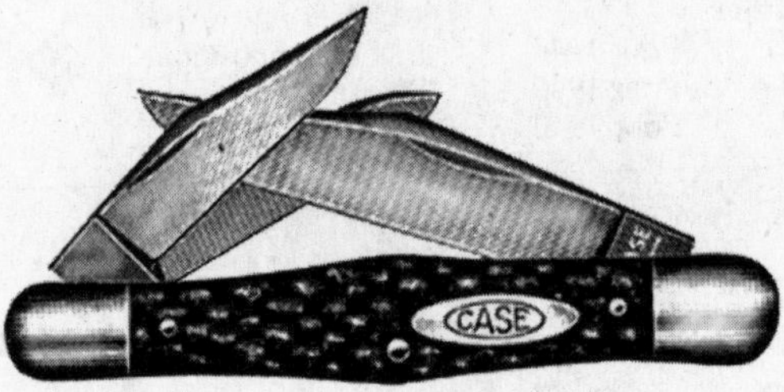

3 1/2″ Balloon Whittler

3 1/2″ Balloon Whittler					
2383	Tested	Prior 1940	Black Composition		600
2383SAB	XX	1940s	Rough Black		500
2383	XX	1940–1965	Black Composition		250
2383	USA	1965–1966	Black Composition		175
5383	Tested	Prior 1940	Stag		1100
5383	XX	1940–1965	Stag		500
5383	USA	1965–1970	Stag		350
5383	10 Dots	1970–1971	Stag		325
6383SAB	Tested	Prior 1940	Green Bone		1400
6383SAB	XX	1940–1942	Green Bone		1100
6383SAB	XX	1940s	Rough Black		600
6383	Tested	Prior 1940	Green Bone		1000
6383	XX	1940s	Rough Black		450
6383	XX	1940–1955	Red Bone		500
6383	XX	1955–1965	Bone		425
6383	USA	1965–1970	Bone		225
6383	10 Dots	1970–1971	Bone		225
6383	Dots	1970s	Bone		125
6383	Dots	1970s	Delrin		75
6383	"S" 10 Dots	1980	Bone		125

Pattern	*Stamping*	*Years Made*	*Handle*	*Variation/Blade*	*Mint Price*
9383SAB	Tested	Prior 1940	Imitation Pearl		750
9383SAB	XX	1955–1965	Imitation Pearl		500

3¹/4″ Premium Stock

3¹/4″ Premium Stock

23087SHPEN	Tested	Prior 1940	Black Composition		175
23087SHPEN	XX	1940–1965			70
23087SHPEN	USA	1965–1970			65
23087SHPEN	10 Dots	1970–1971			55
23087SHPEN	Dots	1970s			30
23087	"S" Dots	1980s	Black Composition		25
43087SHSP	Tested	Prior 1940	White Composition		210
43087SPPEN	Tested	Prior 1940	White Composition		210
53087SHPEN	XX	1940–1965	Stag		225
53087SHPEN	USA	1965–1970	Stag		150
53087SHPEN	10 Dots	1970–1971	Stag		150
63087SHPEN	XX	1940–1955	Green Bone		325
63087SHPEN	XX	1940s	Rough Black		200
63087SHPEN	XX	1940–1965	Red Bone		200
63087SHPEN	XX	1940–1965	Bone		125
63087SHPEN	USA	1965–1970	Bone		85
63087SHPEN	10 Dots	1970–1971	Bone		85
63087SHPEN	10 Dots	1970–1971	Delrin		50
63087SHPEN	Dots	1970s	Delrin		40
63087	"S" Dots	1980s	Delrin		30

3¹/8″ Lobster Pen

3¹/8″ Lobster Pen					
83088SS	Tested	Prior 1940	Pearl		240
83088SS	XX	1940–1964	Pearl		200
3¹/16″ Lobster Pen					
83089	Tested	Prior 1940	Pearl		240
83089SCFSS	XX	1940–1965	Pearl		180
83089SCFSS	USA	1965–1966	Pearl		250
2¹/4″ Lobster Pen					
83090SCRSS	Tested	Prior 1940	Pearl		210
83090SCRSS	XX	1940–1965	Pearl		180
83091	Tested	Prior 1940	Pearl		250

4½″ Whittler

Pattern	Stamping	Years Made	Handle	Variation/Blade	Mint Price
4½″ Whittler					
3391	Tested	Prior 1940	Yellow Composition		3000
5391	Tested	Prior 1940	Stag		3500
5391	Tested	Prior 1940	Second Cut Stag		3750
5391	XX	1940–1942	Red Stag		3000
6391	Tested	Prior 1940	Green Bone		5000

4″ Birdseye

4″ Birdseye					
33092	Tested	Prior 1940	Yellow Composition		300
33092	XX	1940–1965	Yellow Composition	Without shield	150
33092	XX	1940–1965	Yellow Composition	With shield	150
33092	USA	1965–1970	Yellow Composition		120
33092	10 Dots	1970–1971	Yellow Composition		100
33092	Dots	1970s	Yellow Composition		70

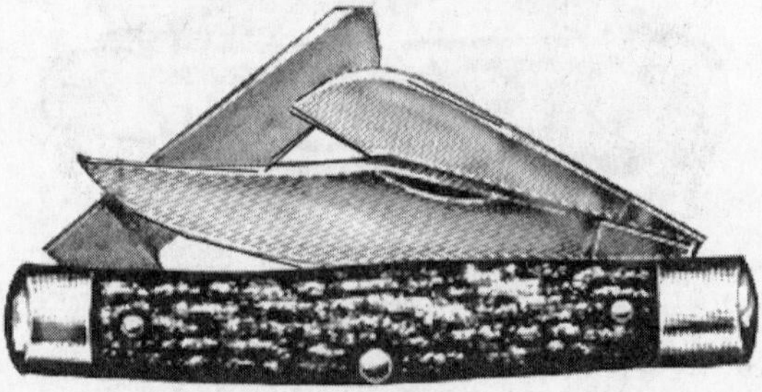

4″ Premium Stock

4″ Premium Stock				
630092	Tested	Prior 1940	Green Bone	625
630092P	Tested	Prior 1940	Green Bone	675
4″ Premium Stock				
5392	Tested	Prior 1940	Stag	900
5392	XX	1940–1965	Stag	375

Pattern	*Stamping*	*Years Made*	*Handle*	*Variation/Blade*	*Mint Price*
5392	USA	1965–1970	Stag		275
5392	10 Dots	1970	Stag		275
6392P	Tested	Prior 1940	Green Bone	Punch blade	900
6392	Tested	Prior 1940	Green Bone		750
6392	XX	1940s	Rough Black		325
6392	XX	1940–1950s	Green Bone		550
6392	XX	1940–1950s	Red Bone		350
6392	XX	1940–1965	Bone		250
6392	USA	1965–1970	Bone		150
6392	10 Dots	1970–1971	Bone		150
6392	Dots	1970s	Bone		100
6392	"S" Dots	1980s	Bone		45
3 15/16″ Premium Stock					
6393PEN	Tested	Prior 1940	Green Bone		900
6393	Tested	Prior 1940	Green Bone		900
5393	Tested	Prior 1940	Stag		1000
9393	Tested	Prior 1940	Imitation Pearl		575
4 1/4″ Cattle Knife					
5394 1/2	Tested	Prior 1940	Stag		5000
6394 1/2	Tested	Prior 1940	Green Bone		3750
6394 1/2	XX	1940s	Green Bone	Long pull	3000
6394 1/2	XX	1940s	Red Bone		2200

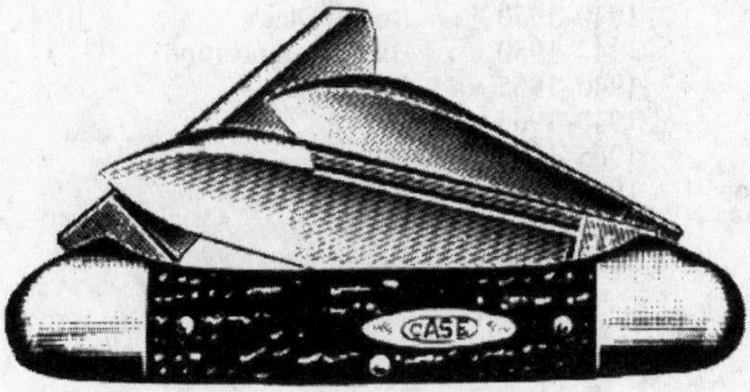

4 1/4″ Gunboat

4 1/4″ Gunboat

5394	Tested	Prior 1940	Stag		5000
6394	Tested	Prior 1940	Green Bone		4000

4 13/16″ Navy Knife

Pattern	*Stamping*	*Years Made*	*Handle*	*Variation/Blade*	*Mint Price*
4 13/16″ Navy Knife					
Case	XX	1942–1945	Metal		225
Case	XX	1942–1945	Metal	British Ordmarks	225

3 3/4″ Scout/Utility Knife

3 3/4″ Scout/Utility Knife

2445R	Tested	Prior 1940	Black Composition	300
6445R	Tested	Prior 1940	Green Bone	450
6445R	Tested	Prior 1940	Rough Black	300
6445R	XX	1940–1950	Rough Black	200
6445R	XX	1942–1950	Black Composition	110
6445R	XX	1940–1955	Red Bone	275
6445R	XX	1940–1965	Bone	175
6445R	USA	1965–1970	Bone	125
6445R	10 Dots	1970–1971	Bone	140
6445R	Dots	1970s	Bone	75
6445R	Dots	1970s	Delrin	80

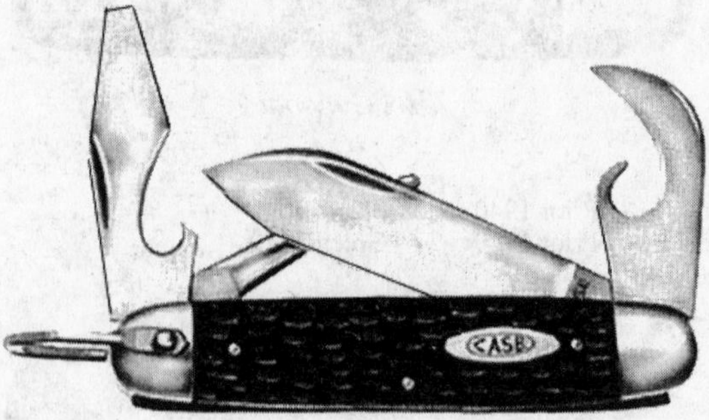

3 5/8″ Scout Knife

3 5/8″ Scout Knife

640045R	Tested	Prior 1940	Green Bone	375
640045R	XX	1940–1965	Black Composition	50
640045R	XX	1940–1965	Brown Composition	50
640045R	USA	1965–1970	Brown Composition	50
640045R	10 Dots	1970–1971	Brown Composition	40
640045R	Dots	1970s	Brown Composition	25

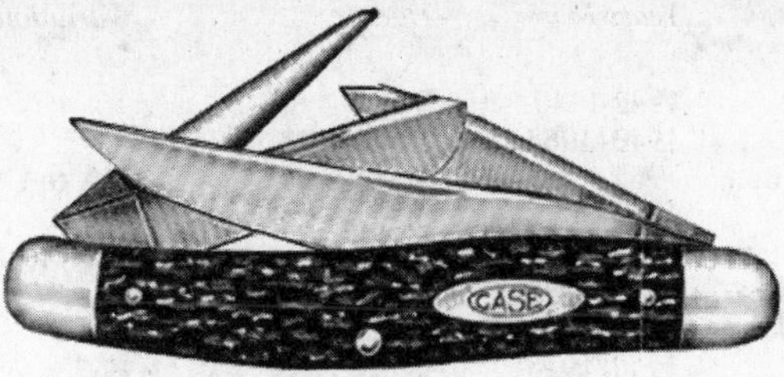

4″ Serpentine Stock

Pattern	*Stamping*	*Years Made*	*Handle*	*Variation/Blade*	*Mint Price*
4″ Serpentine Stock					
64047P	Tested	Prior 1940	Green Bone		1250
64047P	XX	1940–1955	Green Bone		900
64047P	XX	1942–1955	Rough Black		500
64047P	XX	1940–1965	Bone		350
64047P	USA	1965–1970	Bone		225
64047P	10 Dots	1970–1971	Bone		225
64047P	Dots	1970s	Bone		125
64047P	Dots	1970s	Delrin		75
64047P	Dots	1979	Bone		100
94047P	Tested	Prior 1940	Imitation Pearl		800

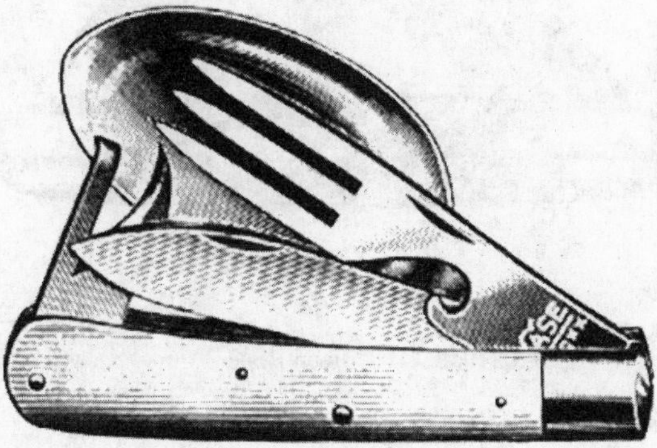

4″ Hobo

4″ Hobo					
3452	Tested	Prior 1940	Yellow Composition		500
6452	Tested	Prior 1940	Green Bone		750

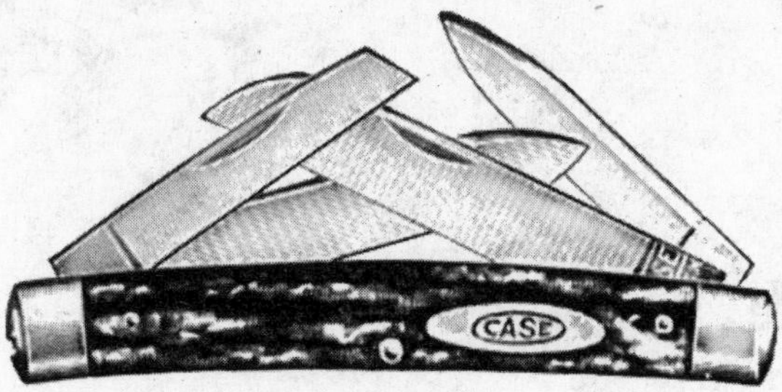

3½″ Congress

Pattern	Stamping	Years Made	Handle	Variation/Blade	Mint Price
3¹/₂″ Congress					
54052	Tested	Prior 1940	Stag		2500
54052	XX	1940–1965	Stag		750
54052	Transition	1964–1965	Stag	XX to USA	750
54052	USA	1965–1970	Stag		350
54052	Transition	1969–1970	Stag	USA to 10 Dot	400
54052	10 Dots	1970–1971	Stag		350
64052	Tested	Prior 1940	Green Bone		1800
64052	XX	1940–1955	Green Bone		700
64052	XX	1940–1955	Red Bone		450
64052	XX	1955–1965	Bone		400
64052	Transition	1964–1965	Bone	XX to USA	375
64052	USA	1965–1970	Bone		275
64052	Transition	1969–1970	Bone	USA to 10 Dots	300
64052	10 Dots	1970–1971	Bone		200
64052	Dots	1970s	Bone		100
64052	Dots	1970s	Delrin		65
64052	"S" 10 Dots	1980	Bone		70
94052	Tested	Prior 1940	Yellow Composition		650

3⁷/₁₆″ Cattle Knife

3⁷/₁₆″ Cattle Knife

64055P	Tested	1940–1942	Green Bone		1500

3³/₈″ Senator Pen

5460	Tested	Prior 1940	Stag		700

3⁵/₁₆″ Bartender's Knife

84062K	Tested	Prior 1940	Pearl		950
94062K	Tested	Prior 1940	Imitation Pearl	Cracked Ice	575

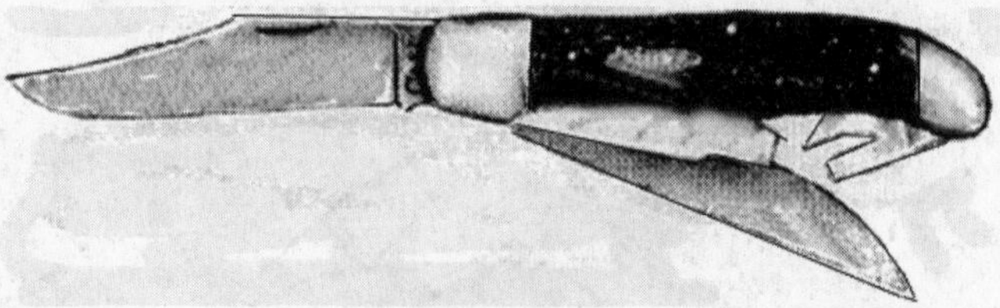

5¹/₄″ Folding Hunter

5¹/₄″ Folding Hunter

6465CLASP	Tested	Prior 1940	Green Bone		3250
9465CLASP	Tested	Prior 1940	Cracked Ice		2700

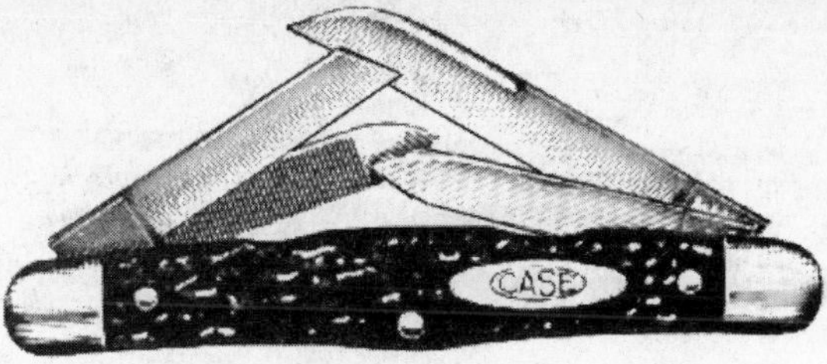

3 1/8" Swell Center

Pattern	*Stamping*	*Years Made*	*Handle*	*Variation/Blade*	*Mint Price*
3 1/8" Swell Center					
6470	Tested	Prior 1940	Green Bone		750

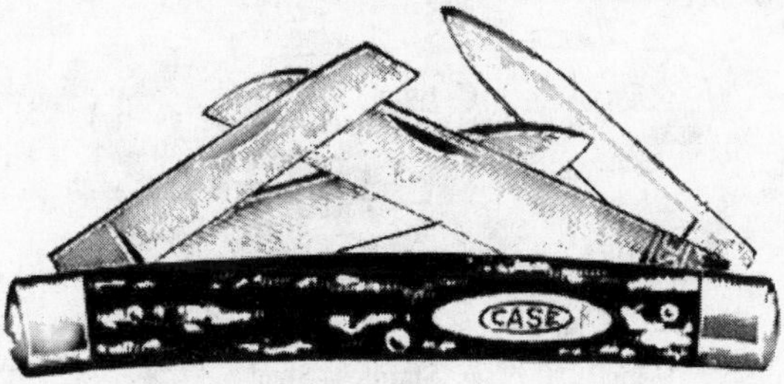

4 1/8" Congress

4 1/8" Congress					
5488	Tested	Prior 1940	Stag		5000
5488	Tested	Prior 1940	Stag	Long pull	6000
5488	XX	1940–1954	Stag	Long pull	2750
5488	XX	1940–1965	Stag		1000
5488	XX	1960–1965	Second Cut Stag		1200
5488	Transition	1964–1965	Stag	XX to USA	800
5488	Transition	1964–1965	Second Cut Stag	XX to USA	1100
5488	USA	1965–1970	Stag		500
5488	USA	1965–1970	Second Cut Stag		1000
5488	10 Dots	1970	Stag		550
6488	Tested	Prior 1940	Green Bone		6500
6488	Tested	Prior 1940	Green Bone	Long pull	4500
6488	XX	1940–1955	Rough Black	Long pull	1800
6488	XX	1940–1955	Red Bone	Long pull	2100
6488	XX	1940–1955	Red Bone		1200
6488	XX	1940–1955	Bone	Long pull	1600
6488	XX	1940–1955	Bone	Reg pull	600
6488	Transition	1964–1965	Bone	XX to USA	800
6488	USA	1965–1970	Bone		400
6488	USA	1965–1970	Second Cut Stag		1200
6488	Transition	1969–1970	Bone	USA to 10 Dots	450
6488	10 Dots	1970–1971	Bone		450
6488	Dots	1970s	Bone		275
6488	Dots	1970s	Delrin		100
6488	Transition	1970s	Bone	8 to 10 Dots	175

3³/₈″ Baby Scout Knife

Pattern	*Stamping*	*Years Made*	*Handle*	*Variation/Blade*	*Mint Price*
3³/₈″ Baby Scout Knife					
640090	Tested	Prior 1940	Green Bone		600

3⁷/₈″ Fly Fisherman

3⁷/₈″ Fly Fisherman					
Fly Fisherman	Tested	Prior 1940	Stainless Steel		800
	XX	1940–1955	Stainless Steel	Blades not stainless	350
	XX	1940–1955			250
	Transition	1964–1965			250
	USA	1965–1970			325
	Transition	1969–1970	USA to 10 Dots		325
	10 Dots	1970–1971			300
	Dots	1970s			250

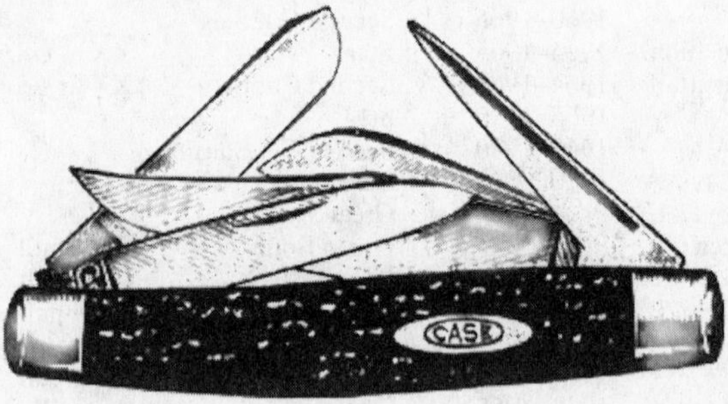

4″ Premium Stock

4″ Premium Stock					
6592	Tested	Prior 1940	Green Bone		4500

Older Case Knives

Older Case knives, those marked with stampings used prior to or near 1920, are included in the following listing. In this instance, the name "Case" does not necessarily mean a W. R. Case & Sons stamped knife. Knives made for or by Case Brothers, bearing marks of the several locations, are included since the patterns were usually very similar. The value estimates shown are for knives stamped "W. R. Case & Sons." Those with different Case family stampings are normally valued at an additional premium of 20–30%. The following listing is by number of blades and ascending pattern number order, as is the preceding pictorial listing.

Pattern	*Mint Price*
MAIZE 1	325
MAIZE 2	325
6103B&G	250
2104	250
6104BUD	325
6106	275
6106 25 cents	550
B1011	300
R111½	800
11011	150
3111½	1000
6111½	1300
6111½LP	1350
61011	250
61013	350
P125	225
6116	230
6116½	225
61016½	230
3124	150
3124½	125
6124	200
6124½	200
1131SH	150
1139	200
11040	175
6143	425
B1048	425
G1048	400
R1048	400
61048	775
R1049L	800
61049	650
61049L	700
B10050	1100
CB1050SAB	1200
C31050SAB	1000
310050	650
C51050SAB	1800
610050	1250
61050	1250
C61050	900
C61050SAB	1500
C61050L	5500
C91050SAB	1250
B1051	700
G1051	700
R1051	700
R1051L	850
6151	1100
6151L	1100
61051	650
61051L	700
81051	950
9151	1250
5161L	4100
6161L	3700
61063½	200
3165SAB	650
5165SAB	1250
6165SAB	1000
8165	3500
9165SAB	750

Pattern	*Mint Price*
5171L	4200
6172	5500
3185	400
6185	650
R185	750
B1093	900
G1093	600
R1093	600
61093	775
B1095	750
G1095	750
HA1095	750
R1095	750
31095	675
61095	700
B1097	750
G1097	850
GS1097	785
R1097	800
61098	800
6199	375
31100	1000
61100	1800
31113	550
61113	1000
MUSKRAT	1500
5200	1450
6200	1400
9200	1000
2201	125
3201	125
3201R	125
6201	170
62001	160
8201	220
82001	200
9201	110
9201R	110
P202	270
R202	225
1202D&B	500
5202RAZ	400
5202½	400
6202	350
6202½	275
6203	550
6204½	300
5205	700
5205RAZ	1100
5205½	950
6205	775
6205RAZ	1050
6205½	700
5206½	400
6206	250
6206½	325
62006½	215
7206	300
8206	875
3207	425
5207	800
6207	650
5208	575

Pattern	Mint Price
6208	650
6209	200
62009	325
62009RAZ	400
62009SH	375
62009SP	350
62009½	375
3210½	250
5210½	350
6210	250
6210S	250
62010	200
6210½	400
6211	1300
6211½	1300
1212L	170
62012	190
6213	700
5214½	400
6214	275
6214½	275
22016	175
22016½	175
6216	350
6216EO	350
62016	225
62016½	200
62016S	200
6216½	240
6216½L	250
2217	260
6217	400
6219	700
62019	750
Y220	450
3220	300
5220	575
6220	450
62020	300
62020S	325
62020½	325
8220	700
9220	425
B221	450
OB221	350
6221	400
62021	375
06221	400
06221½LP	450
08221	550
G222	500
6222	700
8222	775
P223	475
6223	425
9223	425
B224	260
3224	200
3224½	200
5224	500
52024	400
5224½	450
52024½	450
6224	200
62024	200
62024RAZ	325
62024SH	275
62024½	225
8224	525
32025½	325
5225½	700
6225	550
6225½	550
62025	500
62025½	500
8225	750
B226	300
6226	325
62026	325
6226½	375
82026	375
62027	250
62027½	250
82027	325
92027	200
92027½	200
P228EO	325
2228	225
2228EO	250
2228P	275
6228	375
6228EO	400
6228P	400
62028	350
82028	600
6229½	260
9229½	250
P0230	175
02230	175
02230½	175
05230½	500
06230	300
06230½	250
09230	250
09230½	200
6230SH	275
2231	275
22031	225
2231½	250
2231½SAB	275
22031½	200
52031	575
52031½	575
62031½	450
52131	1500
6231	475
62031	450
6231½	475
G232	275
3232	200
6232	275
3233	190
6233	275
62033	250
8233	375
9233	225

Pattern	*Mint Price*
5234	1000
G2035	250
3235½	210
5235½	475
6235	250
6235EO	375
62035	350
6235½	240
62035½	325
2237	475
2237½	475
6237	525
6237½	575
5238	475
B239	1850
G2039	2000
6239	1500
3240P	2000
6240	2200
6240SP	2250
6241	275
G242	250
52042	300
6242	250
62042	200
82042	325
92042	150
3244	200
5244	350
05244	250
6244	225
06244	225
62044	225
62044FILE	200
8244	350
82044	350
82044FILE	375
08244	350
9244	325
02245	225
02245½	225
04245B&G	375
05245	650
05245½	500
06245	425
06245½	400
G2046	425
3246	375
6246	450
62046	450
04247SP	375
5247J	1800
05247SP	850
6247J	1750
06247	400
06247PEN	400
06247SP	400
B2048	650
B2048SP	700
G2048	650
G2048S	625
R2048	650
R2048S	650

Pattern	*Mint Price*
62048	675
62048SP	800
P249	875
R2049	1000
6249	1250
62049	975
6250	3500
8250	4300
6251	1650
P2052	425
3252	575
32052	400
52052	850
6252	900
62052	500
GA253	200
5253	250
6253	175
62053	175
8253	200
82053	200
82053SR	180
9253	150
22055	200
32055	240
62055	350
82055	550
92055	225
62056	275
82056	375
4257	125
42057	125
8257	225
92057	125
32058	130
6258	300
8258	325
92058	150
P259	350
62059	175
62059SP	175
8259	325
5260	375
8260	275
B2063	275
P263	200
05263	225
62063	175
06263	175
82063	175
08263	200
82063½	200
92063½	150
82062K	500
6264	190
6264FILE	190
62064	175
8264T	250
8264TFILE	250
9264TFILE	225
G265	975
3265SAB	750
5265SAB	1500

Pattern	*Mint Price*
6265SAB	1100
8265	3800
9265SAB	1000
62067	200
06267	260
82067	250
08267	250
6268	325
8268	425
G2069	300
6269	300
8269	325
9269	200
8271	300
22074½P	250
62074½	275
5275SP	1300
6275SP	775
06275½	750
6276½	550
06276	550
06276½	575
4277	175
8277	200
6278T	200
GM279	150
M279R	175
3279	125
3279R	125
5279	175
6279	200
62079	190
62079½	190
8279	275
8279SHAD	275
82079	250
92079½	200
P280	600
6280	600
G281	500
6281	500
9281	175
6282	650
B285	1000
G285	1000
3285	600
6285	1100
G2086	650
52086	1000
82086	1050
5287	1500
6288	1300
M2090R	125
3292	260
5292	700
6292	550
32093F	300
6293	225
62093F	375
05294	875
6294	3500
6294J	4000
B2095F	300

Pattern	*Mint Price*
32095F	275
B296	550
6296	625
P297	400
R297	600
3297	500
8297	875
32098F	350
62098F	475
GM2099R	175
3299	325
3299½	300
5299½	775
6299	650
6299½	650
82099R	300
62100	2500
82101R	175
92101R	125
32113	750
62113	1250
B3102	250
63102	225
83102	250
3308	375
5308	850
6308	650
8308	1050
B3109-Christmas	900
63109	1500
83109	800
3318SHSP	400
3318SHPEN	400
5318SHSP	975
6318SHSP	600
6318SHP	600
6318SHPEN	625
8318SHSP	925
9318SPPEN	550
6321	700
53131	2500
53131PUNCH	2700
5332	825
6332	550
6333	275
9333	225
B339	2000
G3039	2500
6339	4100
63039	3650
63042	650
83042	800
93042	600
5343	3000
B334SHSP	225
3344SHSP	320
5344SHSP	675
6344SHSP	400
6344SHPEN	400
8344	625
9344SHPEN	300
2345½	875
5345	1500

Pattern	*Mint Price*
5345P	1675
5345½	1575
6345	1100
6345P	1200
6345-½	1050
6345½P	1100
6345½2SH	1500
2346	975
B346P	1700
G3046	1750
6346	1150
63046	700
B3047	1100
P347SHSP	1250
3347SHSP	775
3347SPPEN	775
43047	750
5347SHPEN	1750
53047	1800
6347SHPEN	1750
6347SHP	1750
6347PPEN	1700
6347PH	1800
6347SHSP	2000
63047	2000
630047	1200
630047P	1400
8347SHSP	4000
83047	4000
9347SHSP	1500
9347PJ	1750
93047	1600
63052	1800
6353	350
6353P	450
53053	400
63056	550
83056	700
8358	675
8360SCI	325
B3063	450
63063	450
83063	525
6366	425
6366PEN	425
8366PEN	475
B3067	375
6367	425
63067	425
8367	525
83067	575
9367	400
6369	850
8369	1050
6370FILE	825
8370FILE	1050
8371	1075
5372	700
B3074	550
B3074½	550
B3074½P	575
5374	850
63074	575
63074½	550
63074½P	650
83074	825
G375	1850
5375	3300
6375	2200
2376½	575
6376	1300
6376½	1400
B3079	700
63079	650
63079½FILE	650
73079	425
83079	575
83081	300
P383	875
2383	675
5383	1400
6383	1250
6383SAB	1500
8383	1600
9383	1000
63083	525
83083	300
5387	2000
6388	2200
83088	225
83089	250
83090SCI	250
GM3091	175
GM3091R	175
5391	5000
83091	250
63092	250
5392	1300
6392	850
6392P	1050
630092	525
63092LP	900
B393	650
H393	675
4393	600
5393	1400
6393	1000
6393S	1100
6393PEN	1050
9393	875
93093	825
5394	5000
6394	4500
B396	650
6396	750
8407	975
5438	1000
8438	1050
B445R	375
6445R	450
640045R	300
5447SHSP	1700
5447SPP	1700
64047P	1650
94047P	1650
3452	725

Pattern	*Mint Price*	*Pattern*	*Mint Price*
54052	2000	84081	2000
6452	950	5488	6000
64052	4000	6488	5000
64055P	1400	B490R	500
5460	725	6490R	850
8460	750	640090R	725
84062K	700	FLYFISHERMAN	1100
94062	600	1502SCOUT	900
6470FILE	975	1503JR SCOUT	750
64081	1800	6539	4500

CATTARAUGUS CUTLERY COMPANY

Cattaraugus founder John Brown Francis Champlin first became associated with cutlery at the age of twenty-five when he became a cutlery salesman for importers Friedman and Lauterjung. After working for about sixteen years, Champlin left his employer in 1882 to join with his son, Tint, in starting their own business. The cutlery jobbing firm was named J.B.F. Champlin & Son.

In 1886, four of the elder Champlin's brothers-in-law joined in the J.B.F. Champlin & Son business. The relatives were W. R., Jean, John and Andrew, sons of Job Russell Case and brothers of Champlin's wife, Theresa. When the Case brothers entered into the business, its name was changed to Cattaraugus Cutlery Company. Although the Case brothers soon dropped out the new business, it was the beginning of the longtime association of the Case family with cutlery.

In 1890, the Champlins purchased the knife making equipment owned by Beaver Falls Cutlery Company of Beaver Falls, Pennsylvania. With the purchase of this equipment and the building of their factory in Little Valley, New York, Cattaraugus had changed from a jobbing operation to a cutlery manufacturer.

Under the leadership of the Champlin family, Cattaraugus remained in business until 1963. During this time, the company name was a respected one within the industry as well as with consumers. Cattaraugus made knives for the U.S. Armed Forces and the Byrd Polar expedition and, in promotional efforts, sponsored whittling competitions, offering up to $50,000 in prizes.

In 1984, A. G. Russell revived the Cattaraugus brand name for special issue knives sold by the Knife Collectors Club and these should not be confused with knives made by the original company.

Cattaraugus seemed to favor bone handled, large pattern knives, but it also produced some knives with plastic handles. The company's knives were stamped "Whittle Craft," "3" and a "C" inside a circle and "Cattaraugus Cutlery Company, Little Valley, New York."

Most Cattaraugus knives were stamped with pattern numbers. The first digit indicates the number of blades (up to five blade knives were made by Cattaraugus), and the second digit indicates the type of bolsters as follows:

0—No bolsters
1—One bolster
2—Two bolsters
3—Tip bolsters
4—Unknown
5—Slant bolsters

The third and fourth digits are the factory handle frame pattern numbers. The last digit indicates the knife's handle material as follows:

0—White Fiberloid
2—Pearl (French)
3—Mother-of-Pearl
4—Fiberloid
5—Genuine Stag
6—Ebony
7—Cocobolo, Fancy Fiberloid, Burnt Bone
8—White bone
9—Stag bone

Unlike Case and some other manufacturers, the Cattaraugus numbers were not consistent to the point that they are a reliable reference. The 20224 pattern will be a different knife than a 22223 pattern, although both knives will be 22 patterns. And, the company made so many patterns—over 100—that few collectors, if any, have memorized them. We recommend that you learn the pattern number from the knife itself and, for pricing reference, find it on the following list which is arranged first by number of blades, next by pattern number and then by handle material code number.

Pattern		*Description*	*Handle*	*Mint Price*
P-1		Pencil Knife	Metal	170
1-W	4 1/2″	Wrench Knife	Bone	400

3-W	4 1/2″	Wrench Knife	Bone	400
One-Blade Knives				
1012	2 3/8″	Equal End Jack	Embossed Metal	90
10101	3 3/4″	Florist's Knife	White Composition	90
10484	4 1/2″	Budding Knife	Celluloid	175
10851	3 1/8″	Corn Knife	White Composition	150
11047	4 1/8″	Jumbo Jack	Cocobolo	200
11057	4 1/8″	Pruning knife	Cocobolo	200
11067-S	4 1/4″	Maize Knife	Cocobolo	225

11079	4 1/8″	Cotton Sampler	Bone	350
11099	3 5/16″	Slim Jack	Bone	175
1159-BW	3 3/8″	Barlow	Bone	125
11227	3 5/16″	Castrating Knife	Cocobolo	150
11247	3 1/2″	Regular Jack	Cocobolo	125
11339	3 7/8″	Pruning knife	Bone	165
11404	3 3/8″	Budding Knife	Celluloid	125
11486	4 1/2″	Budding Knife	Ebony	200
11704-L	4″	Lockback Hunter	Celluloid	300
11709	4″	Slim Lockback Hunter	Bone	300
11709-L	4″	Lockback Hunter	Bone	325
11804	3 1/8″	Cartoon Knife	Celluloid	135
11827	3 3/8″	Swell End Jack	Cocobolo	150
11837	3 3/8″	Open End Jack	Cocobolo	150
11839	3 3/8″	Regular Jack	Bone	135
11844	4 3/8″	Folding Hunter	Celluloid	450

Pattern		*Description*	*Handle*	*Mint Price*
11849	4 3/8″	Folding Hunter	Bone	500
12099	4 1/2″	Jumbo Jack	Bone	400
12099-L	4 1/2″	Lockback Folding Hunter	Bone	600
12109	4 1/2″	Jumbo Jack	Bone	400
12114	4 5/8″	Powderhorn Hunter	Celluloid	300

12134-Y	5″	Fishing Knife	Yellow Composition	150
12144	5″	Fishing Knife	Celluloid	175
12719	3 7/8″	Slim Jack	Bone	225
12719-CP	3 7/8″	Slim Jack	Bone	225
12819	5 3/8″	King of the Woods	Bone	1100
12829	5 3/8″	King of the Woods	Bone	1200
12829-L	5 3/8″	King of the Woods LB	Bone	1400

12839	5 3/8″	Folding Hunter	Bone	1200
12919	5 1/4″	Powderhorn Hunter	Bone	1100
12919-L	5 1/4″	Powderhorn Hunter LB	Bone	1250
Two-Blade Knives				
200-OP	2 1/2″	Lobster Pen	Opal Pearl	90
200-PP	2 1/2″	Lobster Pen	Abalone Pearl	100
2000	2 5/8″	Veterinary Knife	Metal	125
201-R	3″	Serpentine Lobster Pen	Composition	95
201-OP	3″	Serpentine Lobster Pen	Opal Pearl	120
201-B	3″	Serpentine Lobster Pen	Blue Celluloid	90
2013	3″	Lobster Pen	Genuine Pearl	140
2014	2 7/8″	Equal End Pen	Embossed Metal	150
203-G	2 5/8″	Oval Lobster Pen	Gambier Pearl	90
203-Ori	2 5/8″	Oval Lobster Pen	Oriental Pearl	90
203-O	2 5/8″	Oval Lobster Pen	Nickel Silver	80

203-OP	2 5/8″	Oval Lobster Pen	Opal Pearl	90
2059-Ori	3 1/4″	Senator Pen	Oriental Pearl	90
2059-OP	3 1/4″	Senator Pen	Opal Pearl	130
2059PP	3 1/4″	Senator Pen	Abalone Pearl	140

Pattern		*Description*	*Handle*	*Mint Price*
206-32nd	2 7/8″	Senator Pen/Emblem	Silver and Enamel	90
206-O	2 3/4″	Senator Pen/Emblem	Silver and Enamel	85
206-KofP	2 3/4″	Senator Pen/Emblem	Silver and Enamel	100
206-IOOF	2 3/4″	Senator Pen/Emblem	Silver and Enamel	95

206-Shrine	2 7/8″	Senator Pen/Emblem	Silver and Enamel	90
2066-Ori	2 3/4″	Senator Pen	Oriental Pearl	90
2066-G	2 3/4″	Senator Pen	Gambier Pearl	95
2066-OP	2 3/4″	Senator Pen	Opal Pearl	90
2066-O	2 3/4″	Senator Pen	Nickel Silver	85
2066-PP	2 3/4″	Senator Pen	Abalone Pearl	95
2073	3 1/2″	Equal End Pen	Genuine Pearl	140
2073	3″	Orange Blossom	Genuine Pearl	175
20090	3 5/16″	Boy's Knife	Embossed Metal	125
2022	2 1/2″	Crown Pen	Imitation Pearl	110
2022-OP	3 5/16″	Sleeveboard Pen	Opal Pearl	125
2022-PP	3 5/16″	Sleeveboard Pen	Abalone Pearl	120
20222	3 5/16″	Sleeveboard Pen	Imitation Tortoise	110
20223	3 5/16″	Sleeveboard Pen	Genuine Pearl	150
20224	3 5/16″	Sleeveboard Pen	Celluloid	90
20228	3 5/16″	Sleeveboard Pen	White Bone	120
20229	3 5/16″	Sleeveboard Pen	Bone	120
20232	2 7/8″	Sleeveboard Pen	Celluloid	100
20233	2 7/8″	Sleeveboard Pen	Genuine Pearl	135
20234	2 7/8″	Sleeveboard Pen	Celluloid	85
20371	3 1/4″	Office Knife	White Composition	90
2043	2 5/8″	Equal End Pen	Genuine Pearl	140
2046	3 9/16″	Lobster Pen	Celluloid	100
20594	3 1/4″	Office Knife	Celluloid	100
20603	3″	Senator Pen	Genuine Pearl	145
20663	2 3/4″	Senator Pen	Genuine Pearl	130
20664	2 3/4″	Senator Pen	Celluloid	75
20673	3″	Senator Pen	Genuine Pearl	140
20677	3″	Senator Pen	Cocobolo	95

20701	3 11/16″	Office Knife	White Composition	120
20706	3 11/16″	Office Knife	Ebony	130
20773	3″	Senator Pen	Genuine Pearl	145
20803	2 3/8″	Senator Pen	Genuine Pearl	130
20833	2 1/2″	Senator Pen	Genuine Pearl	125
20853	2 7/8″	Equal End Pen	Genuine Pearl	125
21019	3 1/8″	Open End Jack	Bone	160
21027	3 1/8″	Open End Jack	Cocobolo	125
21029	3 1/8″	Open End Jack	Bone	175
21039	3 1/8″	Open End Jack	Bone	150
21046	4 1/8″	Jumbo Jack	Ebony	225

Pattern		*Description*	*Handle*	*Mint Price*
21049	4 1/8″	Jumbo Jack	Bone	275
21087	3 1/4″	Electrician's Knife	Cocobolo	125
21089	3 1/4″	Electrician's Knife	Bone	150
B2109	3 7/8″	Dogleg Trapper	Bone	175
21129	3 3/8″	Open End Jack	Bone	140
2139-BW	3 3/8″	Barlow	Bone	150
21146	4 1/8″	Jumbo Jack	Ebony	250
21149	4 1/8″	Jumbo Jack	Bone	275
21166	3 5/8″	Harness Knife	Ebony	175

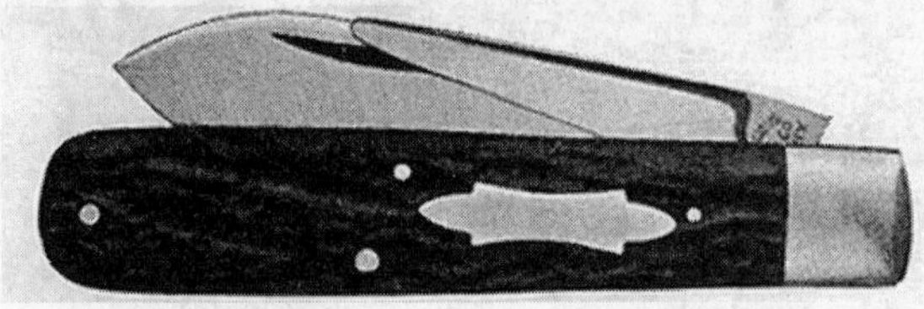

21169	3 5/8″	Open End Jack	Bone	140
21169-G	3 5/8″	Open End Jack	Bone	150
21177	3 11/16″	Swell Center Jack	Cocobolo	145
21229	3 5/16″	Speying Knife	Bone	200
21246	3 1/2″	Regular Jack	Ebony	130
21249	3 1/2″	Regular Jack	Bone	150
21259	3 1/2″	Regular Jack	Bone	150
21266	3 7/8″	Folding Hunter	Ebony	250
21269	3 7/8″	Folding Hunter	Bone	300
21269-C	3 7/8″	Folding Hunter	Bone	325
21269-CC	3 7/8″	Folding Hunter	Bone	350
2159-BW	3 3/8″	Barlow	Bone	175
21286	3 7/8″	Swell Center Jack	Ebony	275
21306	3 5/8″	Open End Jack	Ebony	160
21309	3 5/8″	Open End Jack	Bone	175
21316	3 7/16″	Open End Jack	Ebony	190
21319	3 7/16″	Open End Jack	Bone	225
21336	3 7/8″	Jumbo Curved Jack	Ebony	200
21339	3 7/8″	Jumbo Curved Jack	Bone	225
21346	3 7/8″	Open End Jack	Ebony	200
21349	3 3/4″	Open End Jack	Bone	220
21356	3 3/4″	Open End Jack	Ebony	150
21359	3 3/4″	Open End Jack	Bone	170
21396	3 9/16″	Teardrop Jack	Ebony	175
21399	3 9/16″	Teardrop Jack	Bone	200
21411	3 3/4″	Knife-Fork	White Composition	275

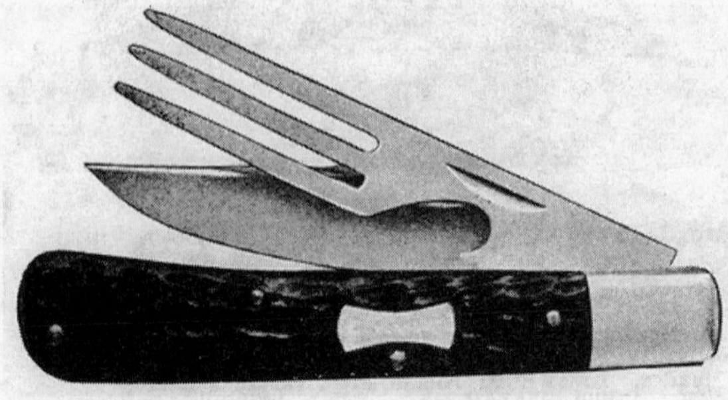

21419	3 3/4″	Knife-Fork	Bone	375
21476	3 3/8″	Regular Jack	Ebony	135
21479	3 3/8″	Regular Jack	Bone	165
21484	3 3/8″	Regular Jack	Celluloid	115
21486	3 3/8″	Regular Jack	Ebony	135

Pattern		*Description*	*Handle*	*Mint Price*
21489	3 3/8″	Regular Jack	Bone	160
21559	3 7/8″	Jumbo Jack	Bone	275
21709	4″	Slim Folding Hunter	Bone	375

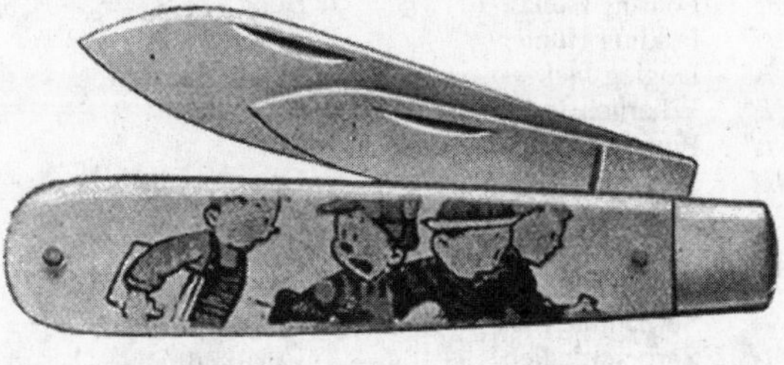

21804	3 1/8″	Cartoon Knife	Celluloid	175
21816	3 3/8″	Regular Jack	Ebony	150
21817	3 3/8″	Regular Jack	Cocobolo	140
21819	3 3/8″	Regular Jack	Bone	175
21826	3 3/8″	Regular Jack	Ebony	150
21829	3 3/8″	Regular Jack	Bone	175
21839	3 3/8″	Regular Jack	Bone	180
21847	3 1/4″	Open End Jack	Cocobolo	140
21899-C	3″	Regular Jack	Bone	150
21899-S	3″	Regular Jack	Bone	150
2227	3 5/8″	Swell Center Jack	Cocobolo	175
2239	4 1/2″	Gunstock Hunter	Bone	550
2249	4″	Slim Folding Hunter	Bone	350
2261-OP	2 3/4″	Senator Pen	Opal Pearl	130
2269	4″	Slim Gunstock Jack	Bone	425
2279	3 7/8″	Texas Jack	Bone	250
2279-P	3 7/8″	Texas Jack	Bone	275
2281-OP	3″	Swell Center Pen	Opal Pearl	130
2289-C	3″	Regular Jack	Candy Stripe	150
2289-G	3″	Regular Jack	Bone	150
2295-OP	3 3/8″	Swell Center Whittler	Opal Pearl	275
22029	3 1/4″	Serpentine Jack	Bone	300
22039	3 1/8″	Regular Jack	Bone	150
22053	3 1/4″	Congress Pen	Genuine Pearl	260
22059	3 1/4″	Congress Pen	Bone	200

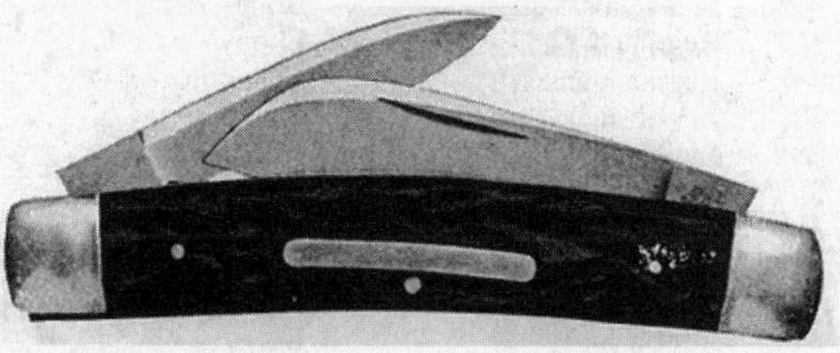

22069	3 3/4″	Congress Jack	Bone	275
22079	3″	Dogleg Jack	Bone	225
22083	2 3/4″	Dogleg Jack	Genuine Pearl	300
22084	3 1/8″	Dogleg Jack	Celluloid	190

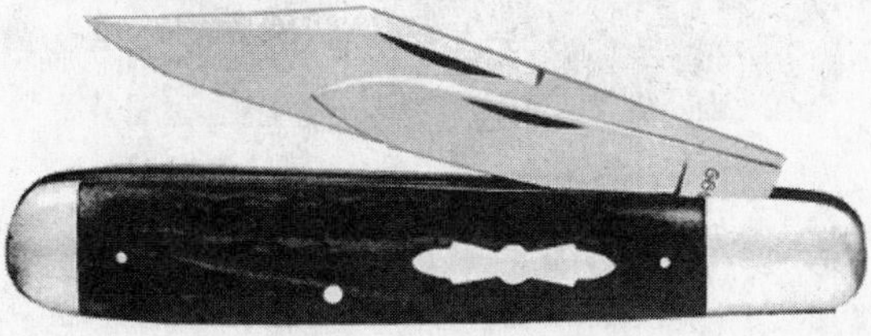

Pattern		*Description*	*Handle*	*Mint Price*
22099	4 1/2″	Folding Hunter	Bone	450
22099-F	4 1/2″	Folding Hunter	Bone	450
22104	4 1/2″	Folding Hunter	Celluloid	325
22109	4 1/2″	Folding Hunter	Bone	450
22109-F	4 1/2″	Folding Hunter	Bone	450
22119	3 3/8″	Dogleg Jack	Bone	220
22139	3 1/2″	Wharncliffe Pen	Bone	250
22149	3 7/8″	Premium Jack	Bone	200
22153	3 1/8″	Wharncliffe Pen	Genuine Pearl	300
22156	3″	Wharncliffe Pen	Ebony	195
22159	3 1/8″	Wharncliffe Pen	Bone	230
22162	3 1/4″	Serpentine Pen	Imitation Pearl	110
22163	3 1/4″	Serpentine Jack	Genuine Pearl	200
22167	3 1/4″	Serpentine Pen	Cocobolo	100
22169	3 1/4″	Serpentine Pen	Bone	155
22179	4″	Serpentine Jack	Bone	275
22182	3 3/4″	Serpentine Jack	Imitation Pearl	150
22182-SS	3 3/4″	Serpentine Jack	Imitation Pearl	150
22186	3 3/4″	Serpentine Jack	Ebony	165
22187	3 3/4″	Serpentine Jack	Cocobolo	160

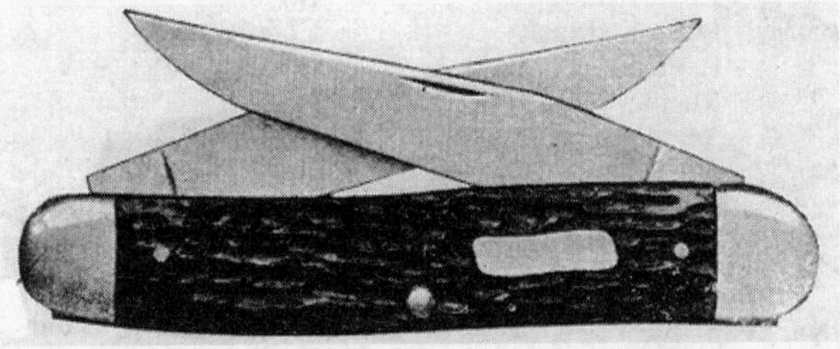

22199	3 1/2″	Muskrat	Bone	360
22213	3 5/8″	Sleeveboard Pen	Genuine Pearl	235
22219	3 5/8″	Sleeveboard Pen	Bone	190
22222	3 5/16″	Sleeveboard Pen	Imitation Pearl	175
22223	3 5/16″	Sleeveboard Pen	Genuine Pearl	250
22226	3 5/16″	Sleeveboard Pen	Ebony	180
22229	3 5/16″	Sleeveboard Pen	Bone	190
22233	2 7/8″	Sleeveboard Jack	Genuine Pearl	200
22239	2 7/8″	Sleeveboard Jack	Bone	175
22246	3 5/8″	Regular Jack	Ebony	135
22247	3 5/8″	Regular Jack	Cocobolo	150
22248	3 5/8″	Jumbo Jack	White Bone	150
22249	3 5/8″	Jumbo Jack	Bone	175
2224B	3 5/8″	Jumbo Jack	Burnt Bone	175
22256	3 5/8″	Jumbo Jack	Ebony	160
22257	3 5/8″	Jumbo Jack	Cocobolo	150
22258	3 5/8″	Jumbo Jack	White Bone	170
22259	3 5/8″	Jumbo Jack	Bone	220
22269	3 5/8″	Regular Jack	Bone	210

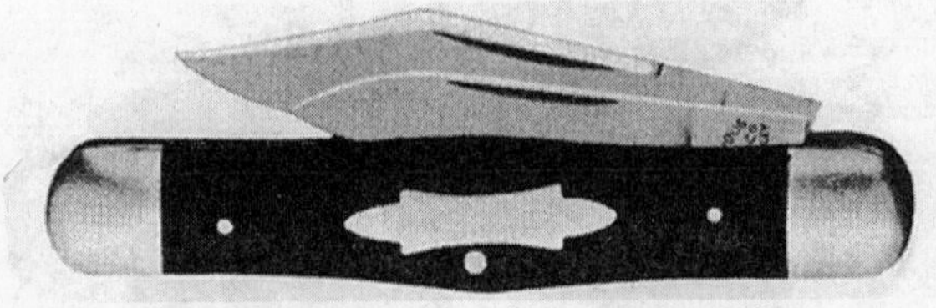

22276	3 3/8″	Swell Center Jack	Ebony	225
22278	3 3/8″	Swell Center Jack	White Bone	190
22279	3 3/8″	Swell Center Jack	Bone	225
22286	3 3/8″	Swell Center Jack	Ebony	200

Current production pocketknives by Case Cutlery, handled in bone and stag.
Photo courtesy of Case Cutlery.

Schatt & Morgan group—Queen Cutlery Company's finely made reproductions of Schatt & Morgan pocketknives made in the early twentieth century. Photo courtesy of Queen Cutlery Co.

WINCHESTER—Tooling and dies used to make Winchester knives in the early twentieth century are still used in making these Winchester reproduction pieces. Bone–handled trapper and hunters are joined by embossed metal handled penknives. Photo courtesy of Bluegrass Cutlery Co.

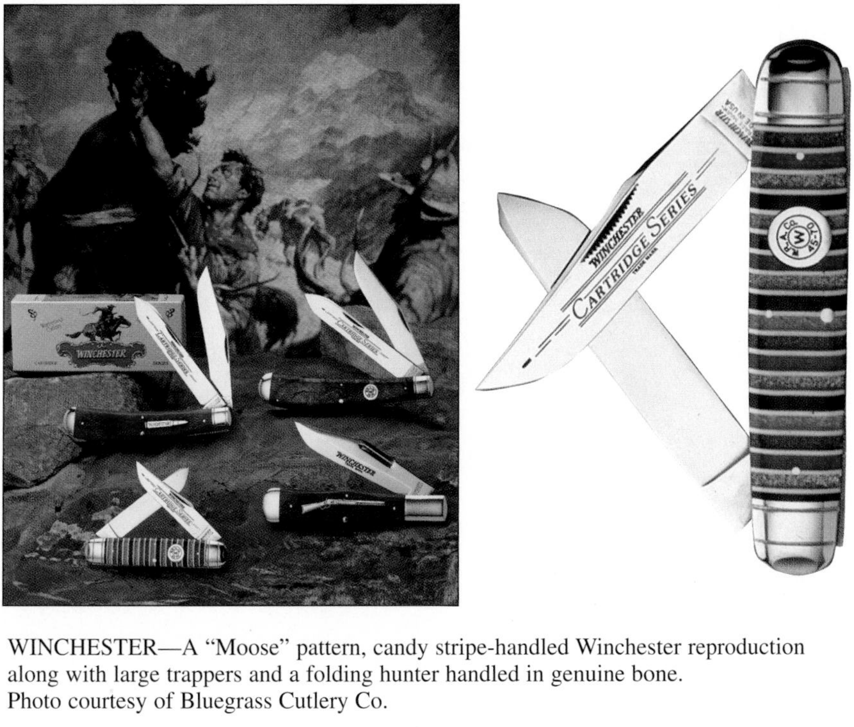

WINCHESTER—A "Moose" pattern, candy stripe-handled Winchester reproduction along with large trappers and a folding hunter handled in genuine bone.
Photo courtesy of Bluegrass Cutlery Co.

Current Marble knives—A Grandaddy Barlow and Dall DeWessse model hunter/skinner are two of Marble Safety Axe Company's current offerings. Photo by Mark Zalesky.

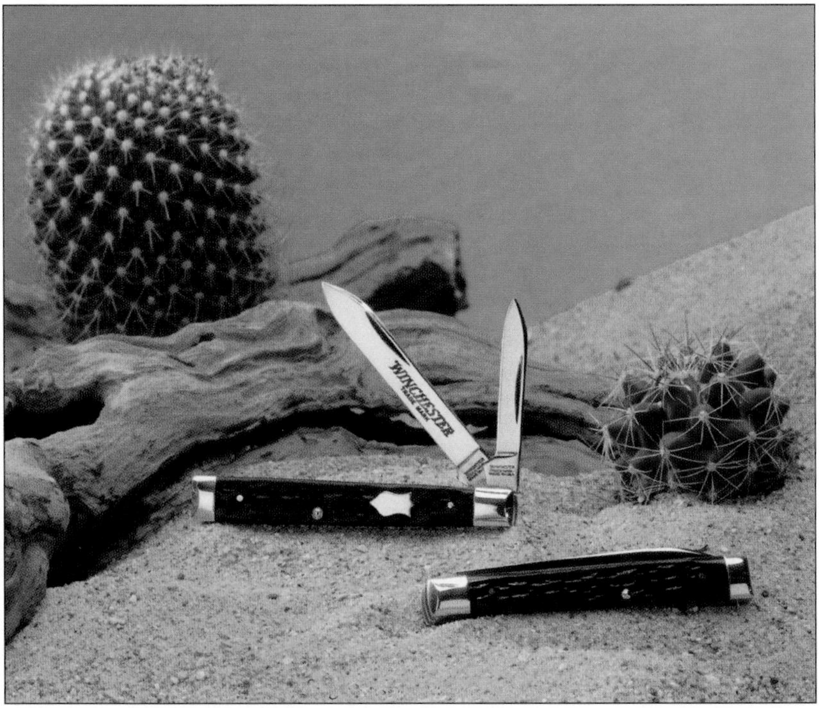

Winchester Slim Jack, a gentleman's knife in a using size. Photo courtesy of Bluegrass Cutlery Co.

Case Pearl—Current production Case pocketknives, handled in mother of pearl.
Photo courtesy of Case Cutlery.

Knives designed by Al Mar and transformed, through engraving and color scrimshaw, into a Limited Edition collection. Photo courtesy of Al Mar Knives.

WINCHESTER—Winchester "Bullet Reproductions" feature cartridge- and rifle-handle shields. Photo courtesy of Bluegrass Cutlery Co.

Very rare mid-nineteeth century bowie made by Samuel Bell. Engraved silver mounts and ivory handle are typical of this master's work. Its blade is held within a handmade and engraved silver sheath. Its value is in excess of $50,000. Photo by Mark Zalesky.

Pattern		*Description*	*Handle*	*Mint Price*
22287	3 3/8"	Swell Center Jack	Cocobolo	185
22289	3 3/8"	Swell Center Jack	Bone	220
22292	3"	Premium Pen	Imitation Pearl	110
22294	3"	Premium Pen	Composition	120
22299	3"	Premium Pen	Bone	135
22329-SS	3"	Swell Center Pen	Bone	190
22336	4 1/4"	Moose	Ebony	425
22339	4 1/4"	Moose	Bone	475
22346	3 3/4"	Regular Jack	Ebony	160
22347	3 3/4"	Regular Jack	Cocobolo	150

22349	3 3/4"	Regular Jack	Bone	180
22356	3 3/4"	Regular Jack	Ebony	155
22357	3 3/4"	Regular Jack	Cocobolo	145
22359	3 3/4"	Regular Jack	Bone	180
22366	3 3/8"	Swell Center Pen	Ebony	225
22369	3 3/8"	Swell Center Pen	Bone	250
22376	3 3/8"	Equal End Jack	Ebony	140
22378	3 3/8"	Equal End Jack	White Bone	190
22379	3 3/8"	Equal End Jack	Bone	200
22389	3 5/8"	Powderhorn	Bone	250
22389-SS	3 5/8"	Powderhorn	Bone	260
22396	3 5/8"	Teardrop Jack	Ebony	180
22399	3 5/8"	Teardrop Jack	Bone	220
22406	3 3/8"	Teardrop Jack	Ebony	190
22409	3 1/4"	Teardrop Jack	Bone	210
22416	3 1/16"	Teardrop Jack	Ebony	250

22419	3 1/8"	Gunstock Jack	Bone	300
22426	3 5/8"	Gunstock Jack	Ebony	275
22429	3 5/8"	Gunstock Jack	Bone	325
22436	3 5/8"	Dogleg Jack	Ebony	225
22439	3 5/8"	Dogleg Jack	Bone	250
22449	3 5/8"	Slim Jack	Bone	225
22459	3 5/16"	Slim Jack	Bone	200
22463	3"	Congress Pen	Genuine Pearl	285
22469	3"	Congress Pen	Bone	220
22474	3 1/4"	Regular Jack	Celluloid	100
22476	3 1/4"	Regular Jack	Ebony	120
22479	3 1/4"	Regular Jack	Bone	140

Pattern		*Description*	*Handle*	*Mint Price*
22486	3 3/8"	Regular Jack	Ebony	120
22489	3 3/8"	Regular Jack	Bone	150

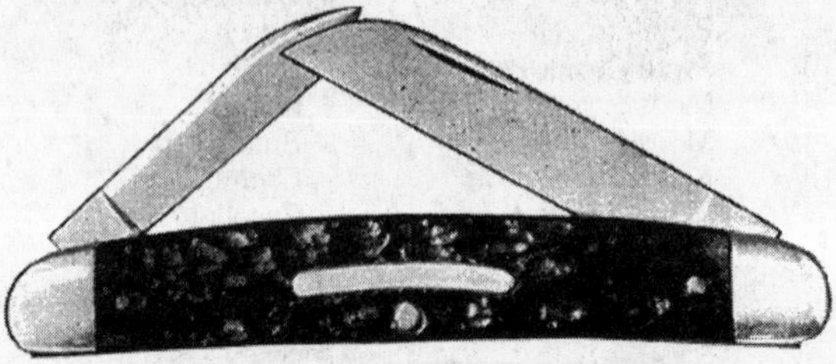

22509	3 1/2"	Congress Jack	Bone	200
22519	3 1/2"	Swayback Pen	Bone	250
22526	3 7/16"	Dogleg Jack	Ebony	250
22529	3 7/16"	Dogleg Jack	Bone	275
22536	3 7/16"	Dogleg Jack	Ebony	250
22539	3 7/16"	Dogleg Jack	Bone	275
22546	3 7/16"	Equal End Pen	Ebony	150
22549	3 7/16"	Equal End Pen	Bone	175
22551	3 3/8"	Equal End Pen	Composition	100
22554	3 3/8"	Equal End Pen	Celluloid	110
22557	3 3/8"	Equal End Pen	Cocobolo	100
22559	3 3/8"	Equal End Pen	Bone	125
22556	3 3/8"	Equal End Pen	Ebony	115
22569	3 3/4"	Balloon Pen	Bone	250
22576	3 3/8"	Equal End Pen	Ebony	150
22579	3 3/8"	Equal End Pen	Bone	165
22586	3 3/8"	Equal End Pen	Ebony	160
22589	3 3/8"	Equal End Pen	Bone	170
22594-SS	3"	Office Knife	Celluloid	95
22599-SS	3"	Swell Center Pen	Bone	175
22599	3"	Swell Center Pen	Bone	165
22603	3"	Senator Pen	Genuine Pearl	175
22609	3"	Senator Pen	Bone	120

22612	2 3/4"	Senator Pen	Imitation Pearl	100
22613	2 3/4"	Senator Pen	Genuine Pearl	165
22614	2 3/4"	Equal End Jack	Celluloid	100
22622	3"	Equal End Jack	Imitation Pearl	110
22624-Y	3"	Equal End Jack	Yellow Composition	110
22628-SS	3"	Equal End Jack	White Bone	135
22629-SS	3"	Equal End Jack	Bone	145
22629	3"	Equal End Jack	Bone	140
22633-SS	3"	Congress Pen	Genuine Pearl	225
22639	3"	Congress Pen	Bone	150
22642	3"	Equal End Jack	Imitation Pearl	100
22643-SS	3"	Equal End Jack	Genuine Pearl	225
22649	3"	Equal End Jack	Bone	145
22652	2 3/4"	Peanut	Imitation Pearl	125
22653	2 3/4"	Peanut	Genuine Pearl	250

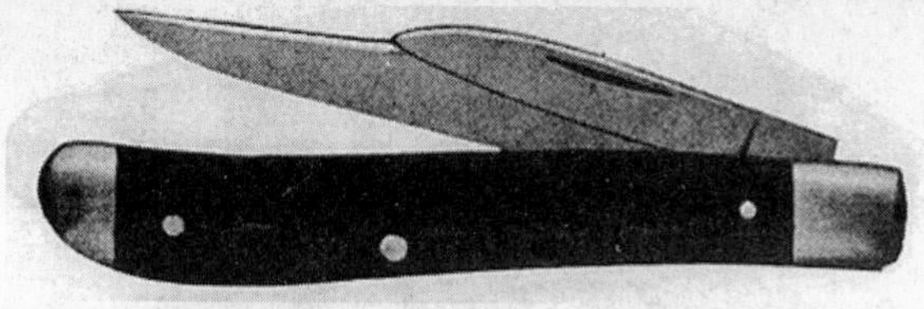

Pattern		*Description*	*Handle*	*Mint Price*
22654	2 3/4″	Peanut	Celluloid	120
22659-SS	2 3/4″	Peanut	Bone	165
22659	2 3/4″	Peanut	Bone	150
22663	2 3/4″	Senator Pen	Genuine Pearl	165
22664	2 3/4″	Senator Pen	Celluloid	100
22673	3″	Senator Pen	Genuine Pearl	175
22682-SS	3 1/4″	Equal End Pen	Imitation Pearl	130
22683	3 1/4″	Equal End Pen	Genuine Pearl	225
22684	3 1/4″	Equal End Pen	Celluloid	135
22686	3 1/4″	Equal End Pen	Ebony	150
22689	3 1/4″	Equal End Pen	Bone	170
22689-SS	3 1/4″	Equal End Pen	Bone	170
22716	3 7/8″	Slim Jack	Ebony	175
22719	3 7/8″	Slim Jack	Bone	250
22726	3 5/8″	Crown Jack	Ebony	250
22729	3 5/8″	Crown Jack	Bone	300
22736	3 9/16″	Gunstock Jack	Ebony	250
22739	3 5/8″	Gunstock Jack	Bone	275
22746	3 7/8″	Doctor's Knife	Ebony	375
22752	3″	Doctor's Knife	Imitation Pearl	275

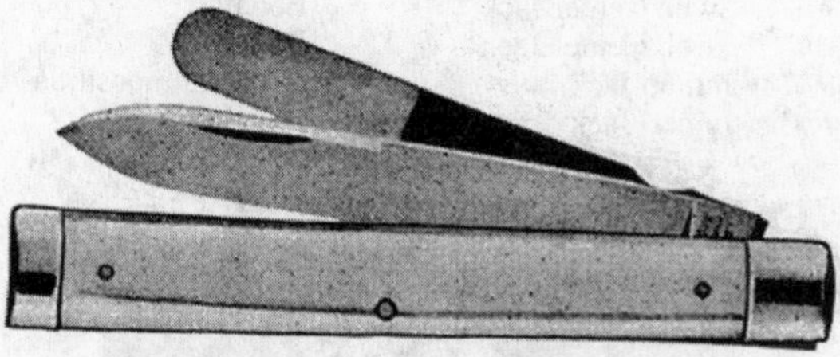

22753	3″	Doctor's Knife	Genuine Pearl	450
22754	3″	Doctor's Knife	Celluloid	300
22759	3″	Doctor's Knife	Bone	325
22761	3 7/16″	Equal End Pen	Composition	120
22762	3 7/16″	Equal End Pen	Imitation Pearl	120
22763	3 7/16″	Equal End Pen	Genuine Pearl	250
22766	3 7/16″	Equal End Pen	Ebony	150
22769	3 7/16″	Equal End Pen	Bone	160
22772	3 7/16″	Equal End Pen	Imitation Pearl	120
22773	3 7/16″	Equal End Pen	Genuine Pearl	250
22779	3 7/16″	Equal End Pen	Bone	160
22783	2 9/16″	Oval Pen	Genuine Pearl	240
22793	3″	Equal End Pen	Genuine Pearl	200
22793-SS	3″	Equal End Pen	Genuine Pearl	200
22794	3″	Equal End Pen	Celluloid	115
22796	3″	Equal End Pen	Ebony	135
22799	3″	Equal End Pen	Bone	160
22799-N	3″	Equal End Pen	Bone	150
22813	2 3/4″	Swell Center Pen	Genuine Pearl	200
22814	2 3/4″	Swell Center Pen	Celluloid	135
22819	2 3/4″	Swell Center Pen	Bone	145
22822	2 1/2″	Slim Pen	Imitation Pearl	115
22823	2 1/2″	Slim Pen	Genuine Pearl	165
22833	2 7/16″	Sleeveboard Pen	Genuine Pearl	170
22849	2 3/4″	Swell Center Pen	Bone	175

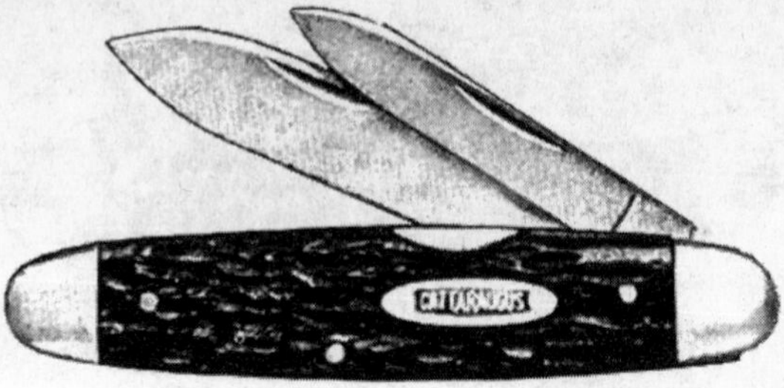

Pattern		*Description*	*Handle*	*Mint Price*
22859	3 1/4″	Easy Open Jack	Bone	175
22869	3 3/16″	Curved Jack	Bone	250
22874	3″	Premium Jack	Celluloid	120
22877	3″	Premium Jack	Cocobolo	110
22879	3″	Premium Jack	Bone	145
22879-SS	3″	Premium Jack	Bone	150
22882	2 3/4″	Equal End Jack	Imitation Pearl	115
22883	2 3/4″	Equal End Jack	Genuine Pearl	185
22884	2 3/4″	Equal End Jack	Celluloid	110
22886	2 3/4″	Equal End Jack	Ebony	130
22889	2 3/4″	Equal End Jack	Bone	140
22893	3 1/4″	Swell End Jack	Genuine Pearl	185
22894	3 1/4″	Swell End Jack	Celluloid	120
22896	3 1/4″	Swell End Jack	Ebony	140
22899	3 1/4″	Scout/Utility	Bone	240
22899-Jr.	3 1/4″	Scout/Utility Jr.	Bone	225
22906	3 9/16″	Swell Center Jack	Ebony	150
22909-SS	3 1/8″	Swell Center Jack	Bone	165
22911	4 1/4″	Jumbo Jack	White Composition	475
22916	4 1/4″	Jumbo Jack	Bone	500

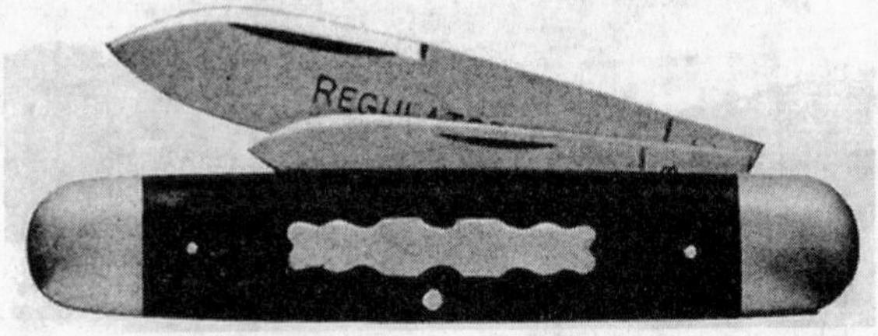

22919	4 1/4″	Jumbo Jack	Bone	575
22929	4″	Elephant's Toenail	Bone	850
22936	3 3/4″	Balloon Pen	Ebony	270
22939	3 3/4″	Balloon Pen	Bone	300
22949	4 1/4″	Moose	Bone	600
22952	3 1/2″	Sleeveboard Pen	Imitation Pearl	220
22959	3 1/2″	Sleeveboard Pen	Bone	265
22963	3 1/8″	Balloon Pen	Genuine Pearl	275
22964	3 1/8″	Balloon Pen	Celluloid	175
22967	3 1/8″	Balloon Pen	Cocobolo	175
22969	3 1/4″	Balloon Pen	Bone	200
22979	3 1/2″	Balloon Jack	Bone	240
2313	3″	Serpentine Lobster Pen	Genuine Pearl	230
2314	3″	Serpentine Lobster Pen	Composition	150
23156	3 1/8″	Wharncliffe Pen	Ebony	175
2319	3″	Lobster Pen	Bone	200
2342	2 3/4″	Equal End Pen	Imitation Pearl	100
2343	2 3/4″	Equal End Pen	Genuine Pearl	150
2344	2 3/4″	Equal End Pen	Celluloid	90
2349	2 3/4″	Equal End Pen	Bone	120
2379	3 3/8″	Texas Jack	Bone	200

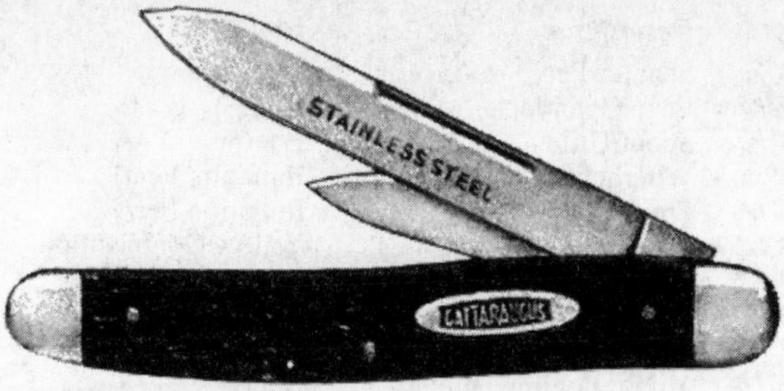

Pattern		*Description*	*Handle*	*Mint Price*
2389	3³/8″	Serpentine Jack	Bone	160
23224	3⁵/16″	Sleeveboard Pen	Celluloid	140
23229	3⁵/16″	Sleeveboard Pen	Bone	175

23234	2⁷/8″	Sleeveboard Jack	Celluloid	100
23236	2⁷/8″	Sleeveboard Jack	Ebony	130
23232	2⁷/8″	Sleeveboard Jack	Imitation Pearl	115
23232C-SS	2⁷/8″	Sleeveboard Jack	Imitation Pearl	115
23642-SS	3″	Senator Pen	Imitation Pearl	100
23649	3″	Senator Pen	Bone	125
23662	2³/4″	Senator Pen	Imitation Pearl	100
23663	2³/4″	Senator Pen	Genuine Pearl	150
23669	2³/4″	Senator Pen	Bone	110
23669-N	2³/4″	Senator Pen	Bone	125
23672	3″	Senator Pen	Imitation Pearl	100
23673	3″	Senator Pen	Genuine Pearl	165
23679	3″	Senator Pen	Bone	130
23689	3¹/4″	Senator Pen	Bone	150
23799	3″	Senator Pen	Bone	160
23966	3³/8″	Swell Center Pen	Ebony	175
24376	3³/8″	Easy Open Jack	Ebony	150
24379	3³/8″	Easy Open Jack	Bone	200
24396	3⁵/8″	Easy Open Jack	Ebony	200

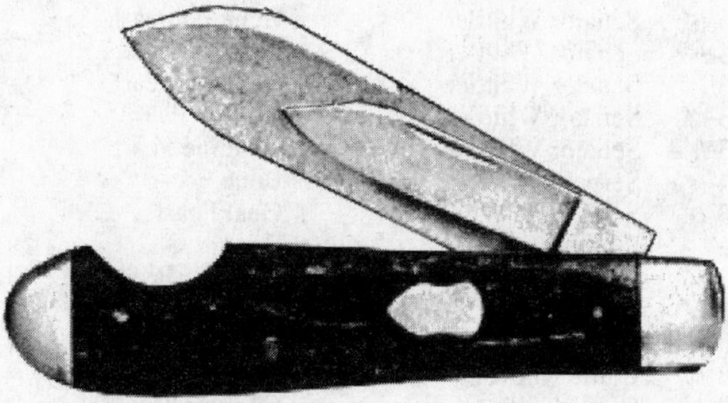

24397	3⁵/8″	Easy Open Jack	Cocobolo	180
24399	3⁵/8″	Easy Open Jack	Bone	220
24409	3³/8″	Easy Open Jack	Bone	200

Pattern		*Description*	*Handle*	*Mint Price*
24674	3″	Senator Pen	Celluloid	120
24889	2 3/4″	Easy Open Jack	Bone	120
2586	3 1/2″	Scout/Utility	Ebony	175
25152	3″	Wharncliffe Pen	Imitation Pearl	180
B2672	3 3/8″	Premium Jack	Imitation Pearl	110
B2874-Y	3 3/8″	Premium Jack	Yellow Composition	130
B2879	3 3/8″	Premium Jack	Bone	145
B2909	3″	Swell Center Pen	Bone	150
B2909-SS	3″	Swell Center Pen	Bone	160
2929	5 1/4″	Yukon Folding Hunter	Bone	900
B2919	3″	Swayback Pen	Bone	175
B2919-SS	3″	Swayback Pen	Bone	175

Three-Blade Knives

300-Ori	3″	Sleeveboard Lobster Pen	Oriental Pearl	150
300-G	3″	Sleeveboard Lobster Pen	Gambier Pearl	160
300-OP	3″	Sleeveboard Lobster Pen	Opal Pearl	150
301	2 7/8″	Sleeveboard Lobster Pen	Silver and Enamel	120
301-Ori	2 7/8″	Sleeveboard Lobster Pen	Oriental Pearl	150
303-G	2 5/8″	Equal End Lobster Pen	Gambier Pearl	155
303-D-Ori	2 5/8″	Equal End Lobster Pen	Oriental Pearl	145
304-Ori	2 5/8″	Oval Lobster Pen	Oriental Pearl	140
304-G	2 5/8″	Oval End Lobster Pen	Gambier Pearl	145
305	2 5/8″	Sleeveboard Lobster Pen	Silver/Emblem	100
309-Ori	3 1/4″	Equal End Lobster Pen	Oriental Pearl	140
309-OP	3 1/4″	Equal End Lobster Pen	Opal Pearl	140
3003	3″	Sleeveboard Pen	Genuine Pearl	165
3004	3″	Sleeveboard Lobster Pen	Composition	120
3009	3″	Sleeveboard Pen	Bone	145
3013	2 3/4″	Sleeveboard Lobster Pen	Genuine Pearl	175
3016	2 3/4″	Oval Lobster Pen	Metal	100
3093	3 1/4″	Equal End Lobster Pen	Genuine Pearl	200
3094	3 1/4″	Sleeveboard Lobster Pen	Composition	150
3099	3 1/4″	Equal End Lobster Pen	Bone	175
30663	2 3/4″	Senator Whittler Pen	Genuine Pearl	225
30669	2 3/4″	Senator Whittler Pen	Bone	160
30673	3″	Whittler Pen	Genuine Pearl	240
30679	3″	Senator Whittler	Bone	190
30683	3 3/8″	Senator Whittler	Genuine Pearl	250
30689	3 3/8″	Senator Whittler	Bone	200
30693	3 1/2″	Senator Whittler	Genuine Pearl	265
30699	3 1/2″	Senator Whittler	Bone	210
30773	3 3/8″	Senator Whittler	Genuine Pearl	260
32009	4″	Serpentine Stock	Bone	350
3216-OP	3 3/8″	Serpentine Whittler	Opal Pearl	300
3229	3″	Small Stockman	Bone	125
3233	3 1/4″	Bartender's Knife	Genuine Pearl	500
3239-H	3 1/4″	Bartender's Knife	Bone	350
3264-OP	3 7/16″	Senator Whittler	Opal Pearl	300
3289	3 1/4″	Cattle Knife	Bone	300
3293	3 1/4″	Cattle Knife	Genuine Pearl	550
3299	3 1/4″	Cattle Knife	Bone	285

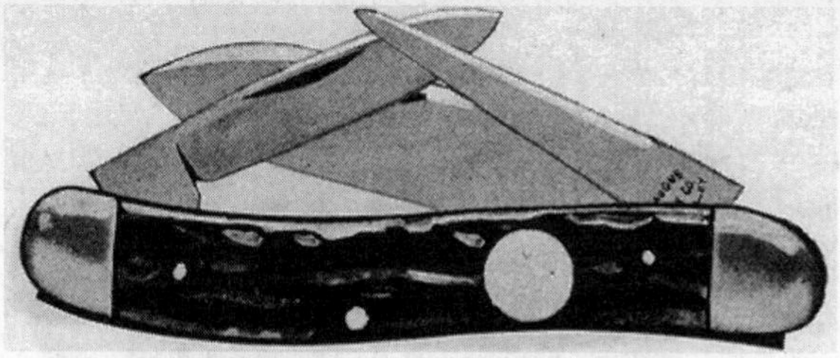

Pattern		*Description*	*Handle*	*Mint Price*
32019	3 3/8″	Serpentine Stock	Bone	300
32019-S	3 3/8″	Serpentine Stock	Bone	300
32019-G	3 3/8″	Serpentine Stock	Bone	325
32029	3 3/8″	Serpentine Stock	Bone	300
32039	3 3/4″	Serpentine Stock	Bone	400

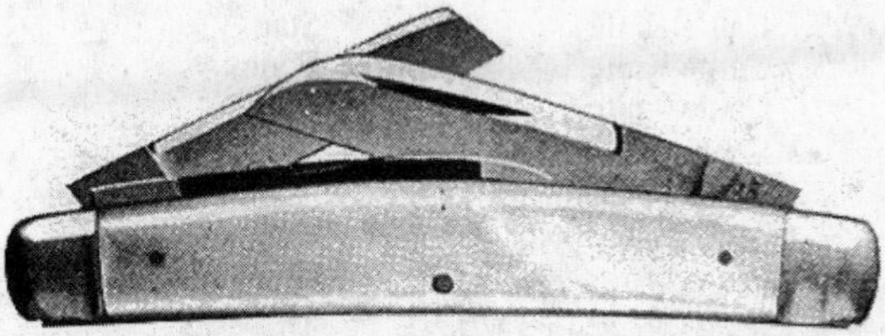

32053	3 1/4″	Congress Whittler	Genuine Pearl	375
32059	3 1/4″	Congress Whittler	Bone	300
32073	3″	Equal End Pen/Scissors	Genuine Pearl	250
32079	3″	Equal End Pen/Scissors	Bone	175
32093	3 3/8″	Swell Center Whittler	Genuine Pearl	350
32096	3 3/8″	Swell Center Whittler	Ebony	250
32099	3 3/8″	Premium Whittler	Bone	275
32109	3 3/8″	Cattle Knife	Bone	275
32125	3 9/16″	Wharncliffe Whittler	Stag	450
32126	3 9/16″	Wharncliffe Whittler	Ebony	350
32129	3 9/16″	Wharncliffe Whittler	Bone	500
32131	3 9/16″	Wharncliffe Whittler	Bone	450
32133	3 9/16″	Wharncliffe Whittler	Genuine Pearl	650
32136	3 9/16″	Wharncliffe Whittler	Ebony	375
32139	3 9/16″	Wharncliffe Whittler	Bone	425
32141	3 7/8″	Premium Stock	White Composition	200
32144	3 7/8″	Premium Stock	Celluloid	220
32145	3 7/8″	Premium Stock	Stag	325
32149	3 7/8″	Premium Stock	Bone	275
32153	3 1/8″	Wharncliffe Whittler	Genuine Pearl	500
32156	3 1/8″	Wharncliffe Whittler	Ebony	350
32159	3 1/8″	Wharncliffe Whittler	Bone	390
32163	3 1/4″	Serpentine Whittler	Genuine Pearl	375
32164	3 1/4″	Serpentine Whittler	Celluloid	225
32169	3 1/4″	Serpentine Whittler	Bone	275
32173	3 7/8″	Premium Stock	Genuine Pearl	375
32174	3 7/8″	Premium Stock	Celluloid	185
32175	3 7/8″	Serpentine Stock	Stag	375
32179	3 7/8″	Serpentine Stock	Bone	300
32183	3 7/16″	Cattle Knife	Genuine Pearl	500

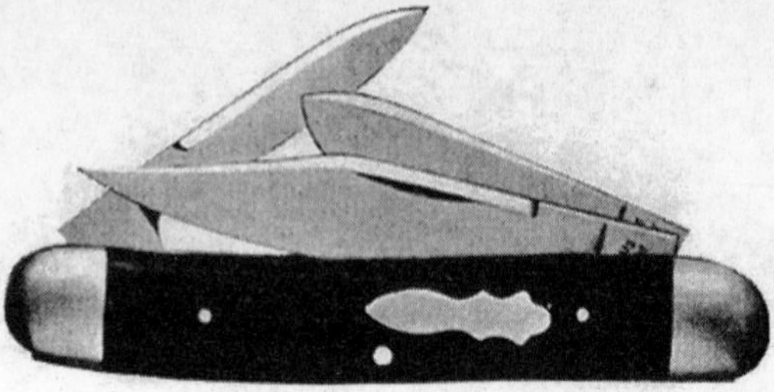

Pattern		*Description*	*Handle*	*Mint Price*
32184	3 7/16″	Cattle Knife	Celluloid	250
32189	3 7/16″	Cattle Knife	Bone	275
32199	3 3/8″	Cattle Knife	Bone	250
32203	3 5/8″	Cattle Knife	Genuine Pearl	450
32204	3 5/8″	Cattle Knife	Celluloid	265
32205	3 5/8″	Cattle Knife	Stag	350
32206	3 5/8″	Cattle Knife	Ebony	275
32209	3 5/8″	Cattle Knife	Bone	290

32223	2 7/8″	Sleeveboard Whittler	Genuine Pearl	300
32233	2 7/8″	Sleeveboard Whittler	Genuine Pearl	300
32243	3″	Premium Stock	Genuine Pearl	325
32244	3″	Premium Stock	Celluloid	140
32245	3″	Premium Pen	Stag	225
32249	3″	Premium Stock	Bone	150
32389	3 3/8″	Serpentine Stock	Bone	250
32401	3 3/8″	Sleeveboard Whittler	Composition	215
32403	3 3/8″	Sleeveboard Whittler	Genuine Pearl	400
32404	3 3/8″	Sleeveboard Whittler	Celluloid	225
32406	3 3/8″	Sleeveboard Whittler	Ebony	250
32409	3 3/8″	Sleeveboard Whittler	Bone	300

32443	3″	Congress Whittler	Genuine Pearl	475
32449	3″	Congress Whittler	Bone	350
32459	3 5/16″	Congress Whittler	Bone	350
32463	3″	Congress Whittler	Genuine Pearl	425
32469	3″	Congress Whittler	Bone	275
32566	3 3/4″	Swell Center Whittler	Ebony	300
32567	3 3/4″	Swell Center Whittler	Cocobolo	280
32569	3 3/4″	Swell Center Whittler	Bone	350
32575	3 7/16″	Equal End Whittler	Stag	375

Pattern		*Description*	*Handle*	*Mint Price*
32576	3 7/16"	Equal End Whittler	Ebony	300
32579	3 7/16"	Equal End Whittler	Bone	325
32586	3 7/16"	Equal End Whittler	Ebony	300
32589	3 7/16"	Equal End Whittler	Bone	320
32593	3"	Swell Center Whittler	Genuine Pearl	275
32599	3"	Swell Center Whittler	Bone	200
32603	3"	Senator Whittler	Genuine Pearl	250
32609	3"	Senator Whittler	Bone	180
32633	3"	Congress Whittler	Genuine Pearl	375
32639	3"	Congress Whittler	Bone	225
32643	3 5/16"	Sleeveboard Whittler	Genuine Pearl	400
32644	3 5/16"	Sleeveboard Whittler	Celluloid	225
32646	3 5/16"	Sleeveboard Whittler	Ebony	250
32649	3 5/16"	Sleeveboard Whittler	Bone	300
32653	3 1/2"	Balloon Whittler	Genuine Pearl	450
32656	3 1/2"	Balloon Whittler	Ebony	300
32657	3 5/8"	Swell Center Whittler	Cocobolo	300
32659	3 1/2"	Balloon Whittler	Bone	350
32683	3 1/4"	Equal End Whittler	Genuine Pearl	325
32689	3 1/4"	Equal End Whittler	Bone	225

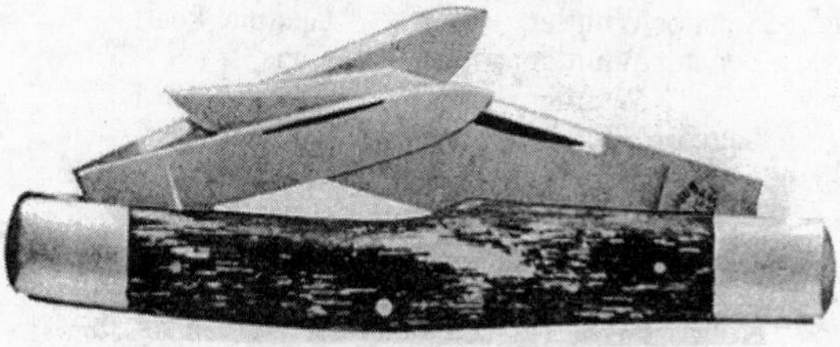

32733	3 3/8"	Gunstock Whittler	Genuine Pearl	500
32734	3 5/8"	Gunstock Whittler	Celluloid	350
32739	3 5/8"	Gunstock Whittler	Bone	375
32743	3 3/8"	Gunstock Whittler	Genuine Pearl	525
32749	3 5/8"	Gunstock Whittler	Bone	375
32775	3 3/8"	Equal End Whittler	Stag	375
32779	3 3/8"	Equal End Whittler	Bone	300
32793	3"	Equal End Whittler	Genuine Pearl	400
32794	3"	Equal End Whittler	Celluloid	225
32799	3"	Equal End Whittler	Bone	250
32866	3 5/8"	Sleeveboard Whittler	Ebony	320
32869	3 5/8"	Sleeveboard Whittler	Bone	350
32875	3 5/8"	Sleeveboard Whittler	Stag	425
32876	3 5/8"	Sleeveboard Whittler	Ebony	300
32879	3 5/8"	Sleeveboard Whittler	Bone	350
32889	4"	Sleeveboard Whittler	Bone	450

32916	4 3/8"	Balloon Whittler	Ebony	400
32919	4 3/8"	Balloon Whittler	Bone	450
32936	3 7/8"	Swell Center Whittler	Ebony	250
32937	3 7/8"	Swell Center Whittler	Cocobolo	230
32939	3 7/8"	Swell Center Whittler	Bone	325
32956	3 1/2"	Sleeveboard Whittler	Ebony	300

Pattern		*Description*	*Handle*	*Mint Price*
32959	3 1/2″	Sleeveboard Whittler	Bone	340
32963	3 1/4″	Swell Center Whittler	Genuine Pearl	400
32964	3 1/4″	Swell Center Whittler	Composition	270
32969	3 1/4″	Swell Center Whittler	Bone	300
32973	3 1/2″	Balloon Whittler	Genuine Pearl	550
32976	3 1/2″	Balloon Whittler	Ebony	300
32979	3 1/2″	Balloon Whittler	Bone	340
32989	3 9/16″	Swell Center Whittler	Bone	300
3343	2 3/4″	Bartender's Knife	Genuine Pearl	275
3349	2 3/4″	Bartender's Knife	Bone	200
3373	3″	Senator Pen w/Spatula	Genuine Pearl	275
3379	3″	Senator Pen w/Spatula	Bone	200
33073	3″	Senator Pen	Genuine Pearl	200
33079	3″	Senator Pen	Bone	150
33663	2 3/4″	Senator Whittler	Genuine Pearl	300
33669	2 3/4″	Senator Whittler	Bone	200
33673	3″	Senator Whittler	Genuine Pearl	300
33674	3″	Senator Whittler	Celluloid	175
33679	3″	Senator Whittler	Bone	225
33683	3 1/4″	Senator Whittler	Genuine Pearl	300
33689	3 1/4″	Senator Whittler	Bone	225
33693	3 1/2″	Senator Whittler	Genuine Pearl	325
33699	3 1/2″	Senator Whittler	Bone	265
33773	3 3/8″	Senator Whittler	Genuine Pearl	300
33793	3″	Senator Whittler	Genuine Pearl	325
33794	3″	Senator Whittler	Composition	225
33799	3″	Senator Whittler	Bone	250

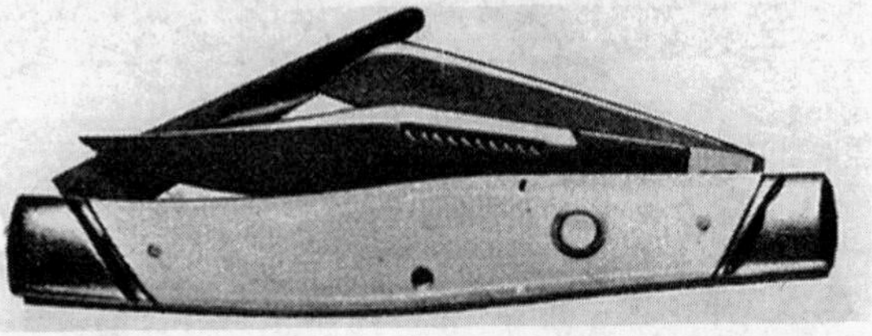

35141	3 7/8″	Premium Stock	White Composition	235
35144	3 7/8″	Premium Stock	Celluloid	235
35151	3 7/8″	Premium Stock	White Composition	230
Four-Blade Knives				
4003	3 3/4″	Lobster Pen w/scissors	Genuine Pearl	300
40503	3 1/4″	Swayback Pen	Genuine Pearl	350
4059-Ori	3 1/4″	Senator Pen	Oriental Pearl	300
4059-OP	3 1/4″	Senator Pen	Opal Pearl	250
40593	3 1/4″	Senator Pen	Genuine Pearl	275
40633	2 7/8″	Congress Pen	Genuine Pearl	300
40663	2 3/4″	Senator Pen	Genuine Pearl	275
40669	2 3/4″	Senator Pen	Bone	200
40673	3″	Senator Pen	Genuine Pearl	325
40679	3″	Senator Pen	Bone	200
40683	3 1/4″	Senator Pen	Genuine Pearl	350
40689	3 5/16″	Senator Pen	Bone	250
40773	3″	Senator Pen	Genuine Pearl	350
42049	3 5/8″	Congress	Bone	325
42049-N	3 5/8″	Congress	Bone	340
42053	3 1/4″	Congress	Genuine Pearl	450
42059	3 1/4″	Congress	Bone	375
42069	3 3/4″	Congress	Bone	400

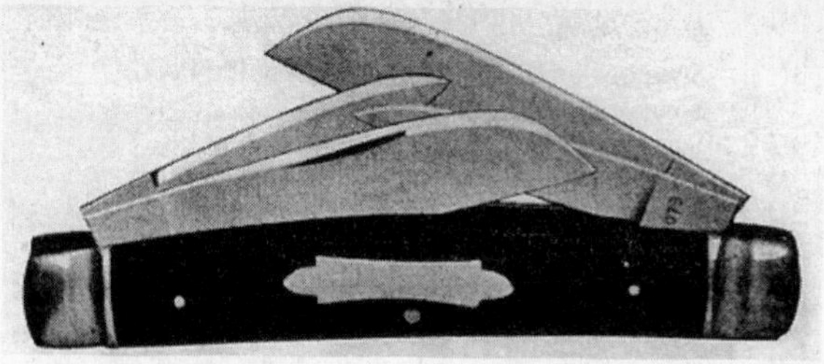

Pattern		*Description*	*Handle*	*Mint Price*
42079	4 1/8″	Large Congress	Bone	550
42093	3 3/8″	Swell Center Pen	Genuine Pearl	350
42099	3 3/8″	Premium Pen	Bone	300
42109	3 5/8″	Balloon Cattle Knife	Bone	375
42172	3 7/8″	Premium Stock	Imitation Pearl	300
42179	3 7/8″	Premium Stock	Bone	450
42209B	3 5/8″	Scout/Utility	Burnt Bone	300

42363	3 5/16″	Bartender's Knife	Genuine Pearl	450
42369	3 5/16″	Bartender's Knife	Bone	300
42453	3 1/8″	Congress	Genuine Pearl	350
42459	3 1/4″	Congress	Bone	250
42463	3″	Congress	Genuine Pearl	350
42469	3″	Congress Pen	Bone	290
42509	3 1/4″	Congress	Bone	300
42519	3 5/8″	Congress	Bone	400

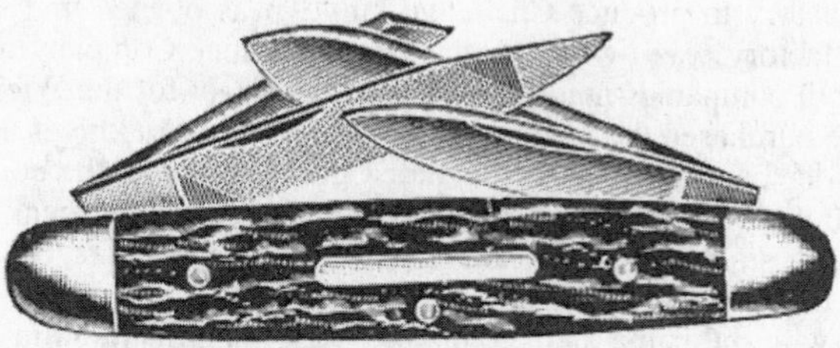

42559	3 3/8″	Equal End	Bone	250
42633	3″	Congress Pen	Genuine Pearl	375
42639	3″	Congress	Bone	240
42683	3 1/4″	Senator Pen	Genuine Pearl	325
42689	3 1/4″	Senator Pen	Bone	225
42793	3″	Senator Pen	Genuine Pearl	300
42795	3″	Senator Pen	Stag	250
42799	3″	Senator Pen	Bone	200
43073	3″	Equal End Pen	Genuine Pearl	325
43559	3 3/8″	Senator Pen	Bone	190
43593	3 1/4″	Senator Pen	Genuine Pearl	275
43663	2 3/4″	Senator Pen	Genuine Pearl	250
43669	2 3/4″	Senator Pen	Bone	200

Pattern		*Description*	*Handle*	*Mint Price*
43673	3″	Senator Pen	Genuine Pearl	300
43679	3″	Senator Pen	Bone	225
43683	3¼″	Senator Pen	Genuine Pearl	325
43689	3¼″	Senator Pen	Bone	240
43693	3½″	Senator Pen	Genuine Pearl	325
43699	3½″	Senator Pen	Bone	190
43773	3″	Senator Pen	Genuine Pearl	300

D2589	3½″	Scout Knife	Bone	300
C2589	3½″	Scout/Utility	Bone	275
4503	3⅛″	Orange Blossom	Genuine Pearl	450
4509	3⅛″	Orange Blossom	Bone	300
5003	3¼″	Equal End Lobster Pen	Genuine Pearl	325
5009	3¼″	Equal End Lobster Pen	Bone	250

CHALLENGE CUTLERY

Challenge knives were made in Sheffield by the B. J. Eyre Company as early as 1867. When the Frederick Wiebusch Company purchased the Eyre company in 1877, the tradename was a part of that purchase. After the 1893 death of Wiebusch, his company became the Wiebusch and Hilger Company of New York.

The first U.S. factory to produce Challenge knives was opened in 1891 in Bridgeport, Connecticut. The factory was owned by the Hatch Cutlery Company and, later, Griffon Cutlery Works. Both companies made knives under contract for the Wiebusch companies. In 1905, Challenge purchased the factory and continued to make knives until 1928.

About 1920, under license from the inventor George Schrade, the company introduced their Flylock knife in two sizes. The smaller size was a two-blade penknife handled with pearl, shell rosewood, smoked pearl, nickel silver with a beaded edge, or sterling silver. The larger pattern was the same pattern as the Schrade Hunters Pride.

Knives marked with the name and "company" were manufactured in Sheffield and imported by the Wiebusch company. Those made in the United States were marked with the brand name and "corporation." The various stampings used were:

1867–1914	Challenge Cutlery Co. New York
	Challenge Cutlery Co. Sheffield
1905–1928	Challenge Cut'l Co. Bridgeport
	Challenge Cut. Corp.
	Challenge Cut. Corp. B'port Conn.
	Challenge CC Bridgeport CT

CLAUSS CUTLERY COMPANY

Located in Fremont, Ohio, Clauss is a shear and scissors manufacturer that has been in business since 1887. For a short time during the mid-1920s, Clauss sold pocketknives made under contract by companies such as Schatt & Morgan Cutlery Company and W. R. Case & Sons. While facts are not known, it is possible that Clauss actually made some of their own knives. Clauss Cutlery Company knives were marketed in an assortment of patterns, using both bone and celluloid.

COLONEL COON KNIVES

Adrian Harris formed the Tennessee Knife Works in 1978 and operated the company in Columbia, Tennessee, until 1988. The shop hand assembled and finished knives made from parts stamped out by major knife manufacturers. The patterns made were primarily barlow, muskrat, stockman and congress. Although a few knives were handled in pearl, most Colonel Coon knives were handled in bone or genuine stag. The knives were well made and their quality was recognized in the southeastern United States where they were primarily marketed. They have become desirable collectibles in these states and their values are substantially higher than their original sales price.

Collector values for regularly produced knives range from $50 to $150. Limited editions such as those produced with "Tennessee River Pearl" (mussel shell) handles and serially numbered range from $100 to $200.

COLONIAL KNIFE COMPANY

Colonial knives and the several tradenames used on them have been a mainstay in the American cutlery industry since the company's beginning in 1926. Names such as Forest Master, Topper, Ranger, Old Cutler and Snappy are but a few that may be recalled from the collectors' memories.

The family that founded and still owns Colonial was experienced in cutlery manufacture prior to establishment of their Providence, Rhode Island, company. Frederick Paolantonio, the founder of Colonial, was first trained in the cutler's art in his home town of Frosolone, Italy. He arrived in the United States in 1903, worked briefly in a Rhode Island cutlery shop, and then went to work for Empire Knife Company, where he remained for five years.

He next went to work for Miller Brothers Cutlery Company and became production foreman there in 1914. While there, he met Edward Oefinger, and together they started their own company named Meriden to make skeleton knives for Miller Brothers. (These knives were not stamped "Meriden" and should not be confused with the older Meriden Cutlery Company knives.) In 1920, they started P. & S. Cutlery Company in Meriden, Connecticut, but sold it the following year to Imperial—a company also started by former Empire employees. Paolantonio's brothers, Dominick and Anthony, had immigrated in 1910 and worked for Empire until 1917. At that time they started the Providence Cutlery Company, making skeleton knives.

In 1920, Anthony formed the A. Paolantonio Cutlery Company in Providence, making gold and pearl handled knives. Dominick sold his Providence Cutlery Company in 1925 and joined Anthony in his business. By 1926, the three brothers joined together to form and organize the Colonial Knife Company. The Colonial organization had taken over the A. Paolantonio business and soon expanded the factory to manufacture a standard line of pocketknives.

Colonial Knife Company, under the leadership of the founding brothers' sons and grandsons, still operates today and manufactures large quantities of lower priced pocketknives.

COLT KNIVES

Like other major gun manufacturers, Colt made knives and most of them have become collectibles—a few were originally intended for the collector market. Unlike their firearms competitors, Remington and Winchester, Colt's entry into the knife market came in recent years and its tenure lasted only four years—from 1969 to 1973.

About fifteen different models, primarily fixed blade knives, were made. The most unique of Colt's knives and the one that is in greatest demand by collectors was designed by Barry Wood of Venice, California. Wood had been using the patented design since 1967 on his own handmade knives and was approached by Colt about making the knives for them in 1968. Production on the first knives was completed in October 1969 with Wood having the blades made by Russell Harrington Company and several other components made by different manufacturers. He then assembled and finished the knives in his own California shop.

During the next four years, 15,300 of the Colt folders were made in several variations. The first 500 knives, stamped with the Colt rearing horse trademark, have a handle shaped like a rectangle with rounded edges. These knives have canvas micarta handles and are probably the rarest of the Colt knife variations.

The second model is similar to the first with the same shape and handle, but is stamped with the Rampant Colt trademark and COLT, HARTFORD, CONN. in large letters. With the knife's blade at a half-open position, it is possible to see these markings and the Colt Serpentine trademark as well. Two thousand of these knives were made.

The most common Colt Woods Folder is the third model which features a change in shape and handle material on most of them. Its shape is slightly curved and, while a few knives used the canvas micarta handles, the majority had a burgundy micarta handle. This model did not have the Colt lettering stamp on the liner.

These knives were originally sold at prices in the $30 range. Those of the third variation are now valued in the $200 to $250 range with premiums paid for knives with original sheaths and boxes. The first and second variation models are valued more highly and may range up to $400, especially with the original sheath and box.

There were two other variations made but will rarely, if ever, be found in the collector market. Twelve knives were made with black micarta handles and used as salesman samples. Two knives handled with stag were made especially for Colt executives. If found, these knives would be quite expensive and a prospective buyer should expect to receive letters of verification to accompany the rare knife.

Although Wood terminated his agreement with Colt in 1978, he continued to make a similar knife using 154CM steel and a variety of handle materials. Prices for these handmade knives stamped with the maker's name range from $200 upward.

The Colt sheath knives were packaged in a wood grain paper box with the knife contained in a red velvet drawstring pouch, which is embossed with the Rampant Colt emblem. Sheath knives stamped "Sheffield" were made by J. and F. Hopkins & Sons of Sheffield, England. They were imported through Indian Ridge Traders in quantities of approximately 2,500 each. There were four variations of the Sheffield made knives, each with sweeping clip blades. The three larger patterns included a sheath with a snap that closes over the bottom of the guard. The smallest skinner came with a pouch sheath.

There were about 20,000 sheath knives made in this country by the Olsen Knife Company of Howard City, Michigan. They were stamped with the Cold Serpentine trademark and the words "Hartford Conn." Most of these knives were equipped with black leather sheaths while the Sheffield knives came with brown sheaths. Both included the red velvet pouches.

Retail prices of the fixed blade knives ranged from $29 to $49 in 1973. Current collector values are about $125 with large patterns valued slightly higher and smaller knives valued at slightly less.

In 1993, the Colt trademark for knives was acquired by the United Cutlery Company and a variety of fixed blade knives is currently being marketed.

CRANDALL CUTLERY COMPANY

This company was founded in 1902 by Herbert Crandall and located in Bradford, Pennsylvania. Cutlery historians may recall that Crandall was married to Theresa Case, the daughter of W. R. Case. Most of the company's knives were handled in bone and were stamped "Crandall, Bradford, PA." In 1912, Crandall merged his company with W. R. Case & Sons Cutlery Company. Knives made during the company's ten-year existence are rarely found and, when found, are desirable collectibles.

CRIPPLE CREEK CUTLERY

In 1981, Cripple Creek Cutlery was formed in Lockport, Illinois, by Bob Cargill. His goal was the revival of old-time patterns and production of them in limited numbers. Cargill had been involved in collecting antique factory-made knives for a number of years and had served several years as a factory authorized repairman for W. R. Case & Sons Cutlery. More recently, he had been a custom knife maker for a half dozen years and many of his custom knives were patterned after the antique favorites. Cripple Creek was the fruition of a dream to apply modern-day handcrafting methods with age-old favorite knives.

The first patterns to be produced were narrowed down to ten favorites designated LI-1 through LI-10 and referred to as the "ten little Indians" because of Cargill's devotion to American Indian lore. Distribution of the new brand was to be through a limited number of distributor/dealers and seven display sets containing one each of these ten knives were made. Those sets were valued at about $350 when produced in 1981 but will command prices of about $3,000 in today's collector market.

Identification of a Cripple Creek is made primarily by noting the shield and stamping. Except for knives made in 1981, all knives have the year of manufacture stamped on the master blade's reverse tang. The shield found on most Cripple Creek knives is an oval one embossed with a three-legged buffalo, modeled after the one on the 1937 "D" nickel. The very earliest knives produced, however, used an oval shield with "C.C.C." or "Cripple Creek" stamped onto it. These knives, which retailed in the $30 to $45 range, are now valued in the $400 to $500 range.

Production of the standard Cripple Creek patterns in 1981 was approximately 500 knives and approximately 250 in 1982. Shortly after introduction of the brand, Cripple Creek contracted to make a special knife for Knife World Publications. The 1st Edition Knife World knife was limited to 2,000 pieces but its production required most of Cargill's time during the latter portion of 1981 and much of 1982. Therein lies the reason for the very low production of regular Cripple Creek Little Indian series knives during this period.

Most Cripple Creek knives have been handled in bone and genuine stag; another favorite handle material used, although less frequently, is mother-of-pearl. While other patterns have been added to the line or substituted for the original ten, most follow the patterns of knives made during the earlier part of this century.

In 1986, Cripple Creek was relocated to Tennessee and, in 1987, the name "Old Fort, TN" was added to knife stampings.

A variety of handle materials has been used for Cripple Creek but the majority have been handled in bone. During the first three years, a light brown colored bone was used and referred to as "Honey Bone." It became a favorite for collectors of the brand. Other colors used have been brown bone, strawberry bone, green bone and white bone. Except for 1986, when Christmas celluloid and red-white-blue micarta was used on two special knives, natural handle materials have been used. Stag has been second in use to bone, followed by mother-of-pearl.

The following is a description of the original Little Indian patterns:

LI-1—Dog Leg Jack; clip and pen blades
LI-2—Canoe; spear and pen blades
LI-3—Peanut; clip and pen blades
LI-4—Coke Bottle; clip and pen blades
LI-5—Stockman; clip, spey and sheepfoot blades

LI-6—Whittler; clip, pen and coping blades
LI-7—Trapper; clip and spey blades
LI-8—Muskrat; two long clip or "California Clip" blades
LI-9—Barlow; variety of clip, spear, spey or razor master blades and pen blade
LI-10—Buffalo Skinner (Large Dog Leg Folding Hunter); one blade model with clip blade; two blade models also included skinner blade.

As with all knives, values of Cripple Creeks vary depending upon pattern, year made and handle material used. With this brand of knives, however, it is possible to offer some general value guidelines for mint condition knives that apply to all or most patterns:

Any knife bearing the "C.C.C." or "Cripple Creek" shields will have a minimum collector value of $300 and some will range up to $800.

Any knife made in 1981, regardless of shield type, will have a minimum collector value of $250, ranging upward to $400. With the limited production of regular patterns in 1982, any standard Cripple Creek pattern knife dated that year will be valued as highly as one produced in 1981.

Any knife bearing an "Oak Leaf" shield is an especially desirable collectible and these will vary in value from $175 for the LI-1 pattern one-blade "White Hawk," made in 1983, to $400 for the LI-4 made in 1981.

In 1984, Cripple Creek produced the five-blade sowbelly stockman in three handle materials. Those handled in stag have a collector value of $300, while the honey bone and strawberry bone models are valued at $250 to $300.

Finally, any mint condition Cripple Creek knife bearing a date stamp up to 1986 will have a minimum collector value of $125.

In 1993, Cripple Creek knives was sold to Blackjack Knives and production moved from Tennessee to Effingham, Illinois. A limited number of patterns were produced there prior to ownership of the brand returning to Cargill and to Tennessee. Production had ceased before the turn of the 21st century.

Pictured above is a sampling of early Cripple Creek knives, all with bone handles. They are now valued at three to ten times their original retail price.

EAGLE POCKETKNIFE COMPANY

This firm was founded in 1916 by the Hemming brothers, Otto, Frank and Carl, and operated in New Haven, Connecticut. Their primary product was the all-metal knife with wraparound handles. The brothers invented machinery which made it possible to manufacture knives of this type on an assembly line basis.

Markings used on this company's knives included EAGLE KNIFE CO. PAT PEND. MADE IN U.S.A. and EAGLE KNIFE CO. In addition to these all-metal knives, the company made knives handled with black fiber based materials. While the majority were of lesser quality, some of Eagle's knives were excellent quality in keeping with other brands made near that time. Knives made by this company should not be confused with those made by other companies but bearing similar marks such as EAGLE CUTLERY CO. (Eagle Pencil Company c.1883–1945), EAGLE, PHILA. (G. F. Creutzberg c.1875–1943) and EAGLE JAPAN (Parker Cutlery Company (1974–1992).

In 1919, the Winchester Arms Company purchased the Eagle firm, primarily for the Hemming designed and patented machinery for blade blanking and grinding. The Hemming automatic grinding machine would allow mechanization of Winchester's own cutlery manufacture. The machine became widely used among cutlery manufacturers and many of those manufactured during this era are still in use today.

ELECTRIC CUTLERY COMPANY

This was a trademark of Friedman and Lauterjung, a cutlery importing firm that was in business from 1866 to 1909. Knives stamped with Electric's brand were of excellent quality and were handled in bone, celluloid and rosewood. Made under contract in Walden, New York, by both New York Knife Company and Walden Knife Company, the knives were stamped ELECTRIC CUTLERY COMPANY, WALDEN, NEW YORK and ELECTRIC CUTLERY COMPANY, NEWARK, NEW JERSEY.

EYE BRAND—CARL SCHLIEPER

The best known trademark for knives manufactured by Carl Schlieper is popularly called "Eye Brand" or sometimes "German Eye." These names aptly describe the tang marking of this Solingen, Germany, company's logo—an eye plus the word GERMANY or the words C. SCHLIEPER or CARL SCHLIEPER plus the eye.

This company was established in 1898 as a branch of the Schlieper Tool and Cutlery Company by Carl Schlieper. It is now managed by a sixth-generation member of the family, Hanspeter Schlieper. Knives exported by the company to the United States include pocketknives, hunting knives, kitchen cutlery and scissors. The company's pocketknives have been handled in stag, bone, composition and genuine pearl.

Other lesser known trademarks for pocketknives made by Schlieper include JIM BOWIE/GERMANY and EL GALLO/GERMANY, but the "Eye Brand" line is best recognized for excellent quality and will be the brand most often found by collectors.

FIGHT'N ROOSTER

The Frank Buster Cutlery Company was formed in Lebanon, Tennessee, and the first knives stamped with the Fight'n Rooster brand were produced in 1976. Their blades' front or mark side tang was stamped with two fighting roosters and the words SOLINGEN or GERMANY underneath. The reverse side tang was stamped FRANK BUSTER CUTLERY CO./GERMANY. The logo introduced by these early knives has become recognized and respected by collectors from most parts of the country. In 1982, the rear tang stamping was changed to FRANK BUSTER CELEBRATED CUTLERY/GERMANY and the front tang stamping retained the logo with the name FIGHT'N ROOSTER above the two roosters. Although the mark side stamping remains the same, knives produced after 1994 are marked FRANK BUSTER & SON CELEBRATED CUTLERY/GERMANY.

The company has been very active in making special knives for a large number of regional knife collecting clubs and in supplying the regular Fight'n Rooster line to collectors through dealers who participate in knife show and mail order businesses. Most Fight'n Rooster knives have been made in traditional styles and a large variety of handle materials have been used. Especially significant have been those that have reintroduced colorful celluloid handles such as Christmas tree, waterfall and candy stripe. A number of limited issues have used old parts that have been found in European factories.

In consideration of the needs and desires of collectors, Buster has kept the quantity of his knives low and the quality high. Recognizing that statistics are important to collectors, the company has maintained records of the numbers of each knife produced and the year of production. Noteworthy among the company's other activities within the collector market has been encouragement and support of participation by ladies and youngsters in a hobby that has too often been considered one for men only. Visitors to knife shows, especially those held in the southeast, will find several elaborate and informative displays of Fight'n Rooster knives.

Limited production of each release has been the company's policy since its beginning.

The majority of the near 2,000 different knife variations released have been made in quite limited numbers. No small number have been limited to 100 or 150 knives and some have been produced in numbers up to 600; most are limited to 200 of each pattern/handle. The majority of Fight'n Rooster knives have etching on the master blade. Although some are etched in black with the brand and logo, finding a Buster-made knife with elaborate and multi-colored blade etching is not unusual. With so many variations of the theme of accepted old patterns, a complete listing here is not practical. The company has published two editions of a book listing Fight'n Rooster knives, describing them and stating their collector values. A recently published third book pictures and offers collector values of more than 1,500 Fight'n Rooster knives. Since values range from tens of dollars to thousands of dollars and the production listing is so extensive, these books are the collector's best source of exact pricing information.

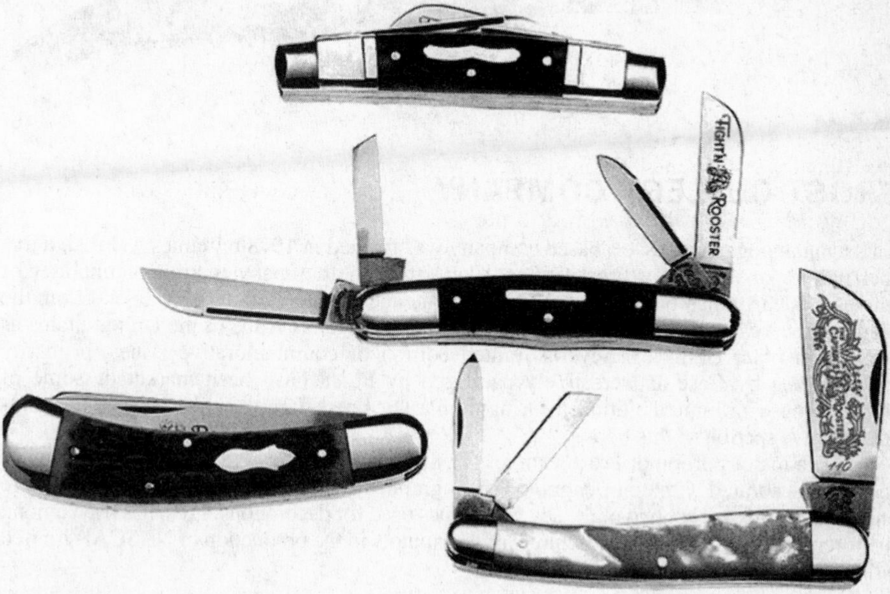

The knives pictured above illustrate the unusual combination of handle patterns, blade styles, handle materials and blade etchings that make Fight'n Rooster knives appealing to collectors.

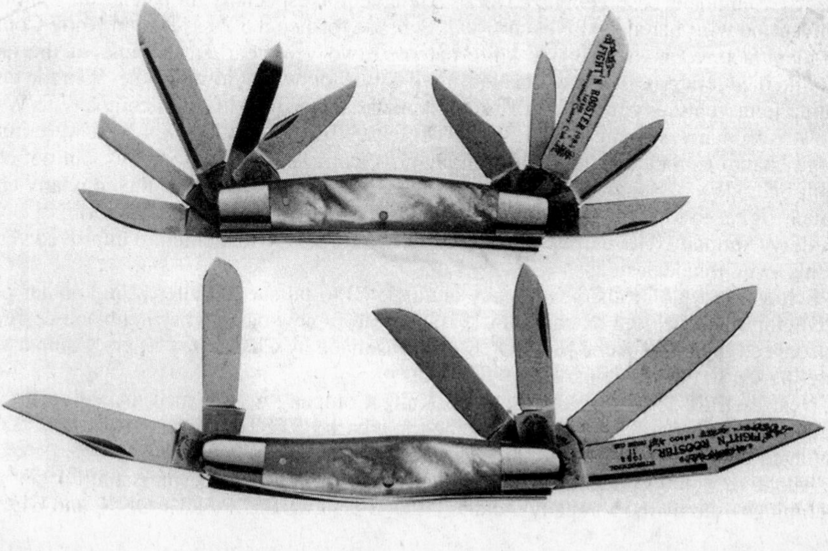

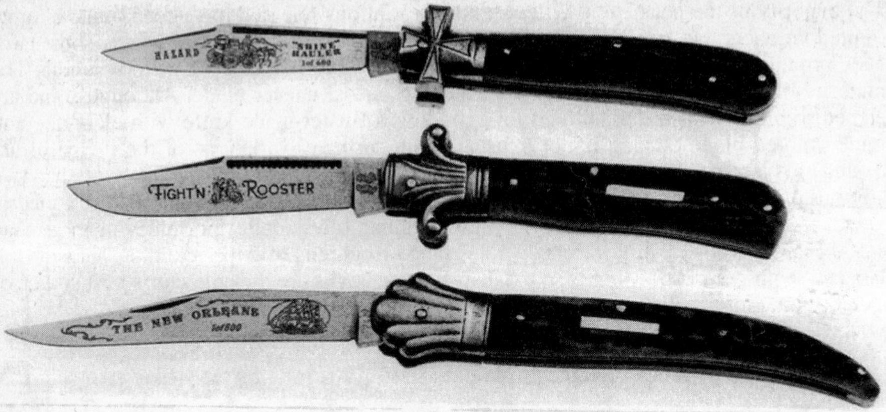

FROST CUTLERY COMPANY

This Chattanooga, Tennessee, based company was formed in 1978 by James A. Frost, a former partner of the Parker-Frost Cutlery Company. The company is a major importer of knives made in Japan but bearing the Frost name and "Falcon" trademark. In addition, the company serves as a distributor of several other knife brands made in the United States as well as in other countries. Several limited edition or commemorative issues, primarily knives made by Case and creatively packaged by Frost, have been marketed. Some of these, along with limited editions bearing the Parker-Frost stamping, are listed in the commemorative section of this book.

While a major portion of Frost's knives are made and sold for regular knife use, many of these are decorated with color engraved (panographed) handles and blade etching. Wildlife and sports teams are but two of the several themes used for decorations. Frost has been among the forerunners of cutlery manufacturers or distributors in the production of NASCAR limited edition series knives and knife sets.

GEORGE SCHRADE KNIFE COMPANY

George Schrade is best recognized as a knife inventor, especially for patents on push-button knives and wire-handled knives. In 1893, Schrade formed the Press Button Knife Company to manufacture his switchblade knife patented two years earlier. Because of the lack of qualified cutlers production at his New York City shop was at low volume, Schrade entered into a joint venture with Walden Knife Company and moved his own company to Walden, New York. Knives stamped PRESS BUTTON KNIFE CO. WALDEN N.Y. were made in large quantities and in at least a dozen patterns from 1893 until the 1920s, but not always with Schrade's personal involvement. In 1903, he sold his interest in the company and his patent rights to Walden Knife Company and joined with his brothers in forming Schrade Cutlery Company. The purpose of the new company was to manufacture improved versions of his switchblade designs.

Schrade left the brothers' company about 1910 to pursue his interest in another patent, the automatic shielding machine. In 1916, Schrade's new patented switchblade design was introduced under the name FLYLOCK and was made by Challenge Cutlery Company, who later purchased the trademark from Schrade.

Near the mid-1920s, George Schrade Knife Company was formed in Bridgeport, Connecticut, and the knife was made with the trademark PRESTO. In the early 1940s, Schrade patented his wire-handled jack knives and produced them in large quantities.

Although Schrade died in 1945, his company remained in business until 1958. Knife stampings used by the company include GEO. SCHRADE B'PORT CONN. and GEORGE

SCHRADE KNIFE CO. B'PORT CONN. Some stampings used during the company's later years included patent dates for wire jack knives.

GERBER LEGENDARY BLADES

The formation of this company began in 1939 when an advertising executive, Joseph R. Gerber, arranged for the production of a couple of dozen knives for use as Christmas gifts to his clients. The local craftsman who made the knives was David Z. Murphy, a knife maker who would soon be supplying a large number of Murphy Combat knives for use by servicemen fighting in World War II. When an executive of Abercrombie & Fitch offered to buy as many knives as could be produced, a business was started.

The earliest knives featured a cast aluminum handle and the design gained early recognition, especially as household cutlery. When Gerber branched out into sportsman's knives in 1950, a variation of the cast handle would be followed through in their Magnum series. Just as the earlier knives, these would earn recognition as well as respect for their high quality.

Gerber added folding knives to its line and became an innovator of new knife designs, some of which were produced in Japan as a supplement to those produced in the company's own Portland, Oregon, factory. In addition to its own designs, knives designed by Paul Poehlmann, Bob Loveless and "Blackie" Collins were produced bearing the stamping GERBER/PORTLAND, OR 97223/USA. A large number of the company's products were stamped with its trademark, the "Excalibur" sword embedded in a large rock.

Ownership of Gerber Legendary Blades remained with the Gerber family until 1987, when the company was sold to Fiskars.

HUMASON & BECKLEY

The Humason & Beckley Manufacturing Company was founded in 1853 by William L. Humason and F. W. Beckley. Along with several hardware items, the New Britain, Connecticut, company manufactured pocketknives of exceptionally good quality.

Handle materials used for its knives included buffalo horn, ebony, stag, bone, pearl and sterling silver. Trademark stamping was H&B MFG. CO./NEW BRITAIN/CONN and the initials "H. & B." were often stamped on the center of the knife's main blade as well.

H & B knives are rarely found in the collector market because the numbers made were never high, compared to knives of larger manufacturers such as this company's own successor. The company was purchased in 1912 by another New Britain cutlery firm, Landers, Frary & Clark. Although L. F. & C. was probably the world's top cutlery producer at the time, its line did not include pocketknives. The Humason & Beckley factory became its pocketknife division and continued to manufacture H & B knives until 1916.

J. A. HENCKELS

One of the best-known trademarks in imported knives is that of the J. A. Henckels company of Solingen, Germany, established in 1731. Henckels "Twinworks" knives are stamped with the name J. A. HENCKELS and the logo of two men in silhouette and joined at the arm and leg. Collectors normally refer to these high-quality pocketknives as "Twin Heckles".

Expansion of the brand began in its home country in the early 1800s when Johann Abraham Henckels established his second cutlery showroom in Berlin, a three-week journey from Solingen. The first American showroom was opened in New York City in 1883 when the brand became associated with the importing firm of Graef & Schmidt.

The Henckels factory continues to operate today and is an extremely large cutlery manufacturing complex. The company produces a wide line of products—over 2,000 different patterns of cutlery including pocketknives, kitchen cutlery and scissors.

HOLLEY MANUFACTURING COMPANY

Alexander H. Holley first entered the knife manufacturing business in 1844, after hearing of the efforts of a small group of English workmen to introduce "spring cutlery" (folding pocketknives) to the United States. Holley bought out their failing business, hired the former owners, and built a new building to house the manufacturing of pocketknives in Salisbury, Connecticut. He soon took in Nathan W. Merwin as a partner and, a little later, the two were joined by George P. Burrell. The partners made knives under the names Holley and Merwin, HOME and Holley & Company. The knife stamping used at that time (1844–1846) for company location was Salisbury. The area where the factory was located was reestablished in 1846 as being part of Salisbury's neighbor, Lakeville, and the stamping was changed to HOLLEY & CO. LAKEVILLE (1846–1854). A new stamping was introduced in 1854, when the partners incorporated their business under the name of Holley Manufacturing Company. From that year until the 1930s, their knives were marked HOLLEY LAKEVILLE CONN.

Holley made high-quality knives and, for a number of years, enjoyed good business. About the turn of the 20th century, Holley's market share began to dwindle as newer and more modernized manufacturers began to compete. The company delayed too long in updating manufacturing methods and had lost much of its national sales volume by 1904. The firm continued to make knives in a much smaller volume until 1930, when it ceased production.

The company handled its knives in horn, bone, ivory, metal and wood, always using brass liners. Due to the very low production during the company's latter years, Holley knives are difficult to find and are quite desirable in the collector market.

HONK FALLS KNIFE COMPANY

This firm was formed in Napanoch, New York, around 1921 by four former employees of the Napanoch Knife Company. When Winchester purchased the Napanoch business and moved production to Connecticut, one of the employees who moved was John J. Cushner. By 1920, Cushner had returned home to Napanoch and joined with Melvin Quick, Melvin Schoonmaker and George Brackley in buying the old knife company's factory from Winchester. They formed the Honk Falls Knife Company and employed their beginning workforce of ten men to produce their own brand of pocketknives.

Knives stamped HONK FALLS, NAPANOCH, NEW YORK, U.S.A. were produced until the factory burned in 1929. These knives were of high quality and, when found, are valuable collectibles.

HOWARD CUTLERY COMPANY

The C. B. Barker Co. of New York City, a sewing machine parts distributor, introduced the name "Howard" as a knife brand during the early 1880s. The brand was made until 1905. Barker contracted with Canastota Knife Company for knives to be made under the Howard name. In addition and since the Barker firm was an importer, some of its knives were made in Germany. Stampings used include HOWARD CUTLERY CO./GERMANY and HOWARD (with the logo of an owl on a limb and Howard Cutlery Co stamped on the reverse tang). While either is a desirable brand, those knives made by Canastota are of higher value than the those made in Germany.

HIBBARD, SPENCER AND BARTLETT

Founded in 1855, this company was a large wholesaler of hardware until 1960. The Chicago-based company's best known and most collectible pocketknife brand was OVB (Our Very Best). Other knives were marked TRUE VALUE, HIBBARD and HIBSPEBAR.

Hibbard, Spencer and Bartlett was not a cutlery manufacturer and knives were made for it under contract by manufacturers such as Camillus, Ulster and Schrade.

HENRY SEARS & SON

The firm of Henry Sears & Co. was started about 1865 as a Chicago-based manufacturer. It became Henry Sears & Son in 1883 with ownership by Henry Sears, E. B. Sears and E. W. Beattie Cutlery and was stamped H. SEARS MFG. CO. between 1865 and 1883. From 1883 until 1897, the stamping was HENRY SEARS & SON CHICAGO. During this latter period (about 1887), the business was sold to the Farwell-Ozmun-Kirk & Co. Hardware firm of St. Paul, Minnesota, but the stamping continued until 1897. From 1897 until 1959, the stamping HENRY SEARS & SON 1865 was used by the hardware distributor. Although the date "1865" was included in the stamping or as a blade etching, the knives do not date to that year of manufacture. Those knives sold by Farwell-Ozmun-Kirk using that date marking were made under contract by several prominent cutlery manufacturers.

GEORGE IBBERSON & COMPANY

This company was founded in Sheffield, England, in 1700 and the first knife marking used was an S over a T. The trademark that is most often associated with Ibberson knives is the violin logo, first used in 1880. During its long history, the company used thirty-three trademarks.

Although Ibberson includes table cutlery, letter openers and scissors, none of its products compare in terms of quality of workmanship and personal appeal with its pocketknives. Besides a regular line of pocketknives, Ibberson produced several patterns of "chased knives," those with their backsprings and liners filed with artistic designs; they are usually handled in mother-of-pearl. The company ceased its long history of knife manufacture in 1988.

IMPERIAL KNIFE COMPANY

In 1916, the brothers Michael and Felix Mirando arrived in Providence, Rhode Island, from Winsted, Connecticut, where they had worked for the Empire Knife Company. The Mirando family had made knives in Italy for several generations and the move from Empire was with the intent of starting their own cutlery business. Their first knives were made during 1917 in a small rented blacksmith shop and the Imperial Knife Company was formed. The company at first made only knife skeletons which were used by the area's jewelry trade in making watch chain knives and, within less than a year of the company's founding, Imperial was producing more than a thousand pieces per week.

Business grew and, in 1919, the Mirandos were joined in business by Domenic Fazzano, a boyhood friend from Italy's Frosilone cutlery center. By the early 1920s, wrist watches began replacing pocket watches and necessity became the mother of invention for Imperial. Its innovation of the shadow knife (skeletons with mounted plastic scales) was responsible for its continuing success. In fact, continued practical application of innovative ideas not only helped Imperial to weather the storm of the Great Depression, but also helped make the company into the giant it is today. During a time when knives were handled in bone, stag, cocobolo and horn, Imperial pioneered knives with colorful plastic handles. When the buying public was exceptionally cost-conscious, Imperial's sales of bumped tip bolstered knives and those of shell wrapped handle construction offered reasonable alternatives.

By 1940, Imperial was the world's largest cutlery manufacturer, producing as many as 100,000 knives per day. During World War II, production of knives for civilian use was restricted and Imperial converted to full wartime production. The company produced over half the trench knives used by the various branches of the U.S. Armed Forces. After playing the key role in designing the M-4 bayonet, Imperial produced the largest quantity of all bayonets purchased by the government. With wartime production priorities, Imperial began to work cooperatively with the Ulster Knife Company, owned by Albert and Henry Baer.

In 1947, the three established company names of Imperial, Schrade and Ulster came together under the leadership of the Mirandos, the Fazannos and the Baers in a company named the Imperial Knife Associated Companies. The Baer brothers bought out their partners in 1984 and the company name was changed to Imperial Schrade Corporation.

Some of the stampings used by Imperial included IMPERIAL KNIFE CO., IMPERIAL/ PROV. R. I., HAMMER BRAND, I.K.CO., JACK-MASTER, KAMP KING and FRONTIER, as well as several contract brands. While older knives were handled in traditional materials such as bone and celluloid, those using plastic, metal and delrin are more commonly found.

KA-BAR CUTLERY COMPANY, INC.

Originally named Union Razor Company, this cutlery firm was started about 1898 by Wallace R. Brown, a grandson of Job R. Case. Founded in Tidioute, Pennsylvania, the company specialized in straight razors but also made pocketknives and other lines of cutlery. After operating for fourteen years in Tidioute, the company relocated to the nearby town of Olean, New York.

Olean offered Union Razor Company several enticements to bring its industry to the small town. During the next two years the company moved and, by 1921, it was in full operation at the Olean facility. The knives made at this time were stamped "Union Cutlery Company, Olean New York" (the Razor Company trademark had been dropped on January 15, 1909).

Union was soon making an extensive line of pocketknives bearing such stampings as "Olcut," "Keenwell" and another trademark that was popular on their large folding hunter patters "Ka-bar."

According to legend, this latter trademark came from a testimonial letter. It was written by an old trapper whose life had allegedly been saved in a bear fight by a well-made Union Cutlery Company knife. Due to his lack of education, the written account of how he had been able to "kil a bar" was shortened and appeared as "KA-BAR."

A trademark was born and the Ka-bar name soon became more popular than the Union Cutlery name stamping. In 1951, the corporate name was changed to KA-BAR Cutlery Company, Inc. and the tang stamping was changed from KA-BAR to Kabar.

In the early 1950s, Ka-Bar attempted to move the production of its pocketknives to Dawsonville, Georgia, hoping to take advantage of the inexpensive labor supply in the North Georgia mountains. Ka-Bar management, however, failed to reckon with the area residents taking off work completely for much of the planting and harvest seasons. Then, too, although laborers were plentiful, there was a general lack of skilled workers in the area. Within a year, the company moved back to Olean.

After Danforth Brown's death, the company changed ownership several times and, for a brief time in the 1960s, completely stopped knife production. Then, in 1966, Cole National Corporation purchased the company and again started national distribution with emphasis upon marketing through several large discount stores.

By 1977, Ka-Bar had ceased all knife production by its own employees, but the old factory is still used for storage and shipping purposes. The company has recently moved more toward importation of knives made in Japan and other cutlery production-oriented countries. Special limited edition knives are made, many in U.S. factories, for sales to members of the company's Ka-Bar Collectors Club.

Unfortunately for collectors, the company failed to stamp pattern numbers on the majority of its knives. Once one becomes familiar with those that are stamped, the pattern numbers on Ka-Bar knives can tell quite a bit about them. The first number represents the handle material designated as follows:

1—Ebony	O—Pyraline Candy Stripe and Fancy Celluloid
2—Natural Stag	P—Imitation Pearl
3—Redwood	H—Horn

4—White Imitation Ivory
5—Black Celluloid
6—Bone Stag
7—Mother-of-Pearl
8—Unknown
9—Silver Pyraline
T—Fancy Pearl (early) Cream Celluloid (late)
R—Rainbow Celluloid
C—Unknown

The second digit in the pattern number signifies the number of blades. The company made knives with up to seven blades. Four-blade knives by Ka-Bar are not very commonplace but the seven-blade knife is a very rare find.

The remaining digits designate the factory pattern number, and knives listed in this guide are arranged by this pattern number.

Although a few early knives were made with iron liners, most Ka-Bars will be found with brass liners and nickel silver bolsters. Knives with every blade stamped will bring a 10–15% premium over those with just the master blade stamped. Of extra rarity and extra value is a "Ka-bar USA" stamped knife with bone handles. Rarer still is the "Ka-bar" stamped bone handle knife since, by the time this stamping was used, almost all the company's knives were made with plastic handles. Several Ka-Bar folding hunters featured a shield shaped like the silhouette of a dog's head. Popularly known as "dogs head Ka-Bars," these knives are quite desirable and are valued considerably higher than most other knives produced by the company.

Value estimates listed in this section are not for the extra rare Union Razor stamping. Knives with this stamping should be worth from one and a half to two times the value of the same pattern in a "Union Knife Co." or "Ka-Bar" stamping. Also of greater value are the knives stamped "KA-BAR Olean, New York." A knife with this stamping should be valued about 50% higher than one of like pattern but with the "Kabar, USA" stamping.

Ka-Bar Stampings

Ka-Bar has used numerous tang stampings during the several stages of its long tenure. Some that the collector may encounter are:

UNION RAZOR CO. Tidioute, PA
UNION CUTLERY CO. Tidioute, PA
UNION CUT. CO. Tidioute
Union (inside an American shield)
Union Cut. Co. Olean, N. Y.
Union Cut. Co.
Unionco
KA-BAR
KA-BAR Olean, N. Y.
Ka-Bar Olean, N. Y.
Ka-Bar Stainless
Kabar Stainless
Olcut
Kabar (pattern no #) USAKA-BAR-LO

Pattern	*Length*	*Stamping*	*Description*	*Handle*	*Mint Price*
Ka-Bar Knives with Dogs Head Shields					
22 Bullet	4½″	KA-BAR/UNION CUT.	Folding Hunter	Stag	850
62 Bullet	4½″	KA-BAR/UNION CUT.	Folding Hunter	Bone	650
6191LG	5¼″	KA-BAR/UNION CUT.	Lockback Hunter	Bone	775
P191LG	5¼″	KA-BAR/UNION CUT.	Lockback Hunter	Celluloid	700
6291	5¼″	UNION in a shield	Knife & Fork	Bone	600
6291	5¼″	UNION CUT. CO.	Knife & Fork	Bone	575
2291	5¼″	UNION CUT. CO.	Knife & Fork	Stag	700
6291	5¼″	KA-BAR/UNION CUT.	Knife & Fork	Bone	500
6391	5¼″	KA-BAR/UNION CUT.	Knife/Fork/Spoon	Bone	850
61106LG	5⅜″	UNION	Folding Hunter	Bone	900

Pattern	*Length*	*Stamping*	*Description*	*Handle*	*Mint Price*
61106LG	5 3/8″	UNION CUT. CO.	Folding Hunter	Bone	800
61106LG	5 3/8″	KA-BAR/UNION CUT.	Folding Hunter	Bone	700
61106	5 3/8″	UNION in a shield	Folding Hunter	Bone	750
61106	5 3/8″	UNION CUT. CO.	Folding Hunter	Bone	600
21106	5 3/8″	KA-BAR/UNION CUT.	Folding Hunter	Stag	800
61106	5 3/8″	KA-BAR/UNION CUT.	Folding Hunter	Bone	600
P1106	5 3/8″	KA-BAR/UNION CUT.	Folding Hunter	Celluloid	475
21107	5 1/4″	UNION CUT. CO.	Folding Hunter	Stag	600
21107	5 1/4″	KA-BAR/UNION CUT.	Folding Hunter	Stag	500
21107	5 1/4″	Current Model Dated	Folding Hunter	Stag	100
22107	5 1/4″	Ka-Bar Olean, N.Y.	Folding Hunter	Stag	350
22107	5 1/4″	Kabar (no #)	Folding Hunter	Stag	100

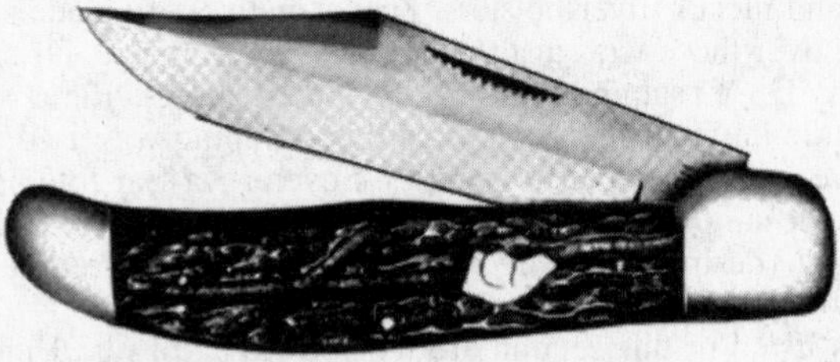

61107LG	5 1/4″	KA-BAR/UNION CUT.	Folding Hunter	Bone	850
22107LG	5 1/4″	KA-BAR/UNION CUT.	Folding Hunter	Stag	950
T1107LG	5 1/4″	KA-BAR/UNION CUT.	Folding Hunter	Celluloid	650
61107	5 1/4″	UNION in a shield	Folding Hunter	Bone	800
61107	5 1/4″	UNION CUT. CO.	Folding Hunter	Bone	550
61107	5 1/4″	KA-BAR/UNION CUT.	Folding Hunter	Bone	450
62107	5 1/4″	UNION CUT. CO.	Folding Hunter	Bone	475
62107	5 1/4″	KA-BAR/UNION CUT.	Folding Hunter	Bone	425
62107	5 1/4″	Ka-Bar Olean, N.Y.	Folding Hunter	Bone	300
61110	4 5/8″	UNION in a shield	Folding Hunter	Bone	550
02118	4″	Bicentennial Model	Trapper	Celluloid	125
61126L	4 5/8″	UNION CUT. CO.	Switchblade Hunter	Bone	2500
22156	5 1/4″	UNION in a shield	Hatchet Knife	Stag	800
22156	5 1/4″	UNION CUT. CO.	Hatchet Knife	Stag	725
62156	5 1/4″	UNION in a shield	Hatchet Knife	Bone	650
62156	5 1/4″	UNION CUT. CO.	Hatchet Knife	Bone	575
One-Blade Knives					
T-19	5″	KA-BAR Stainless	Fishing Knife	Celluloid	60

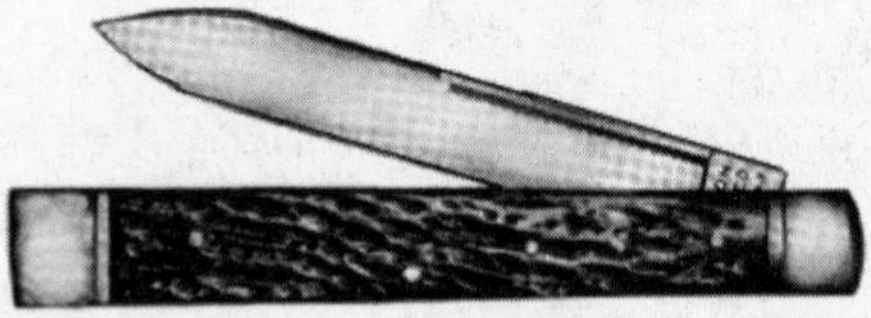

6111	3 7/8″	UNION CUT. CO.	Doctor Knife	Bone	275
0111	3 7/8″	UNION CUT. CO.	Doctor Knife	Pyraline	200
6112	4″	UNION CUT. CO.	Slim Jack	Bone	150
0112	4″	UNION CUT. CO.	Slim Jack	Pyraline	130
6112	4″	KA-BAR	Slim Jack	Bone	110
0112	4″	KA-BAR	Slim Jack	Pyraline	100
6112	4″	kabar	Slim Jack	Composition	50
T112	4″	kabar	Slim Jack	Celluloid	45
T118	3″	KA-BAR	Dogleg Pen	Celluloid	75
3163	3 1/2″	UNION CUT. CO.	Regular Jack	Redwood	60
6163	3 1/2″	UNION CUT. CO.	Regular Jack	Bone	75
6165	4 1/2″	UNION CUT. CO.	Folding Hunter	Bone	250
0165	4 1/2″	UNION CUT.	Folding Hunter	Celluloid	175
6165LG	4 3/8″	UNION CUT. CO.	Folding Hunter	Bone	275

Pattern	*Length*	*Stamping*	*Description*	*Handle*	*Mint Price*
6165LG	4 3/8"	KA-BAR	Folding Hunter	Bone	225
2165LG	4 3/8"	Kabar	Folding Hunter	Stag	150
6165LG	4 3/8"	Kabar	Folding Hunter	Composition	90
6165LG	4 3/8"	Kabar (no #) USA	Folding Hunter	Delrin	55
3170	4"	UNION CUT. CO.	Jumbo Jack	Redwood	200
3174	3 3/4"	UNION CUT. CO.	Pruner	Redwood	90
6174	3 3/4"	UNION CUT. CO.	Pruner	Bone	100
3174	3 3/4"	KA-BAR	Pruner	Redwood	65
6174	3 3/4"	KA-BAR	Pruner	Bone	80

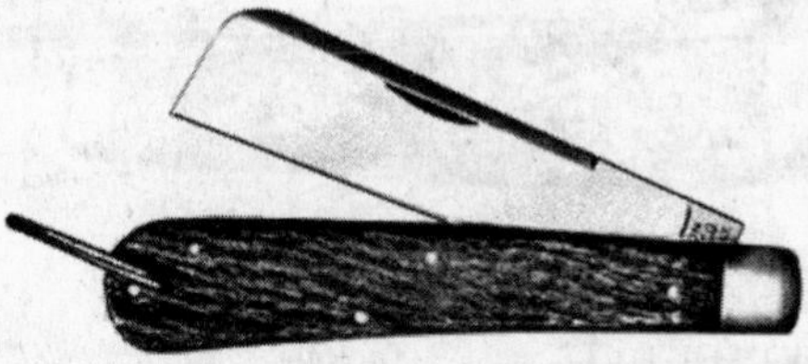

Pattern	*Length*	*Stamping*	*Description*	*Handle*	*Mint Price*
6175RG	4 1/2"	UNION CUT. CO.	Navy Knife	Bone	90
2179L	5 1/2"	KA-BAR	"Grizzly"	Stag	2500
T179	5 1/2"	KA-BAR	Folding Hunter	Celluloid	600
9179	5 1/2"	KA-BAR	Folding Hunter	Pyraline	675
6191L	5 1/2"	UNION CUT. CO.	Lockback Hunter	Bone	750
6191L	5 1/2"	UNION CUT. CO.	Lockback Hunter	Stag	900
61103	3 3/8"	UNION CUT. CO.	Bowtie	Bone	175
01103	3 3/8"	UNION CUT. CO.	Bowtie	Celluloid	150

Pattern	*Length*	*Stamping*	*Description*	*Handle*	*Mint Price*
71103	3 3/8"	UNION CUT. CO.	Bowtie	Pearl	275
61103	3 3/8"	KA-BAR	Bowtie	Bone	140
01103	3 3/8"	KA-BAR	Bowtie	Celluloid	100
21105	4 1/2"	UNION CUT. CO.	Switchblade	Stag	1800
21105	4 1/2"	KA-BAR	Switchblade	Stag	1000
61105	4 1/2"	KA-BAR	Switchblade	Bone	750
T1105	4 1/2"	KA-BAR	Switchblade	Celluloid	600
61106	5 3/8"	UNION CUT. CO.	Folding Hunter	Bone	500
66106	5 3/8"	KA-BAR	Folding Hunter	Bone	450
T1106	5 3/8"	KA-BAR	Folding Hunter	Celluloid	375
61106L	5 3/8"	UNION CUT. CO.	Folding Hunter	Bone	700
21107L	5 1/4"	KA-BAR	"Little Grizzly"	Stag	2200
61107	5 1/4"	UNION CUT. CO.	Folding Hunter	Bone	650
61107	5 1/4"	KA-BAR	Folding Hunter	Bone	550
61107	5 1/4"	KA-BAR	Folding Hunter	Composition	400
P-2207	5 1/4"	KA-BAR	Folding Hunter	Celluloid	375
61107	5 1/4"	Kabar	Folding Hunter	Composition	125
31108	5 1/4"	Kabar	Sodbuster	Redwood	50
31108	5 1/4"	Kabar (no #) USA	Sodbuster	Redwood	35
61110	4 1/2"	UNION CUT. CO.	Folding Hunter	Bone	275
61118	4 1/4"	UNION CUT. CO.	Trapper	Bone	325
01118	4 1/4"	UNION CUT. CO.	Trapper	Celluloid	275

Pattern	*Length*	*Stamping*	*Description*	*Handle*	*Mint Price*
61125L	4½″	UNION CUT. CO.	Folding Hunter	Bone	600

61126L	4½″	UNION CUT. CO.	Switchblade Hunter	Bone	2500
61129	5″	UNION CUT. CO.	Toothpick	Bone	275
G1129	5″	UNION CUT. CO.	Toothpick	Pyraline	225
61129	5″	KA-BAR	Toothpick	Bone	175
K1129	5″	KA-BAR	Toothpick	Celluloid	150
T1129	5″	KA-BAR	Toothpick	Celluloid	140
31130	4″	kabar	Grafting Knife	Redwood	45
31130	4″	kabar (no #) USA	Grafting Knife	Redwood	35
31131	4⅝″	UNION CUT. CO.	Pruner	Redwood	90
31131	4⅝″	KA-BAR	Pruner	Redwood	70
61132	5½″	UNION CUT. CO.	Swell Center Hunter	Bone	475
11132	5½″	UNION CUT. CO.	Swell Center Hunter	Ebony	400
91132	5½″	UNION CUT. CO.	Swell Center Hunter	Pyraline	375
61132	5½″	KA-BAR	Swell Center Hunter	Bone	325
P-1147	4½″	KA-BAR	Mellon Tester	Imit. Pearl	120
T-1147	4½″	KA-BAR	Mellon Tester	Celluloid	100
P-1154	4¾″	UNION CUT. CO.	Leg Knife	Celluloid	350
P-1154	4¾″	KA-BAR	Leg Knife	Celluloid	300
71155	1½″	UNION CUT. CO.	Fob Knife	Pearl	90
X-1157	5¾″	UNION CUT. CO.	Fish Knife	Metal	175
X-1157	5¾″	KA-BAR	Fish Knife	Metal	135
R-1160	4¼″	UNION CUT. CO.	Budding Knife	Celluloid	75
61161	4½″	UNION CUT. CO.	Safety Fold Hunter	Bone	350
61161-Bail	4½″	KA-BAR	Safety Fold Hunter	Bone	300
T-1161	4½″	KA-BAR	Safety Fold Hunter	Celluloid	300
61169	4½″	KA-BAR	Bowtie	Bone	250
T-1175	4½″	KA-BAR	Bowtie	Celluloid	150
21187	5¼″	KA-BAR	Swell Center Hunter	Stag	500
61187	5¼″	KA-BAR	Swell Center Hunter	Bone	400
31187	5¼″	KA-BAR	Swell Center Hunter	Redwood	325
61187	5¼″	UNION CUT. CO.	Swell Center Hunter	Bone	425
51187	5¼″	Kabar	Swell Center Hunter	Composition	100
51187	5¼″	Kabar (no #) USA	Swell Center Hunter	Celluloid	55
Two-Blade Knives					
42027S	3½″	UNION CUT. CO.	Office Knife	Imit. Ivory	110
42027S	3″	UNION CUT. CO.	Office Knife	Imit. Ivory	100
T-29	5″	KA-BAR	Fish Knife	Celluloid	125
T-29	5″	kabar	Fish Knife	Celluloid	60
T-29	5″	kabar (no #) USA	Fish Knife	Celluloid	40
6200	2½″	UNION CUT. CO.	Equal End Pen	Bone	85
T200	2½″	UNION CUT. CO.	Equal End Pen	Celluloid	65
T200RG	2½″	UNION CUT. CO.	Equal End Pen	Celluloid	60
T200RG	2½″	UNION CUT. CO.	Equal End Pen	Pearl	110
T200RG	2½″	KA-BAR	Equal End Pen	Celluloid	50
6200	2½″	KA-BAR	Equal End Pen	Bone	60
6201T	2⅞″	UNION CUT. CO.	Swell Center Pen	Bone	90
7201T	2⅞″	UNION CUT. CO.	Swell Center Pen	Pearl	130
6201	2⅞″	KA-BAR	Swell Center Pen	Bone	75

Pattern	Length	Stamping	Description	Handle	Mint Price
6202	3″	UNION CUT. CO.	Equal End Pen	Bone	90
7202	3″	UNION CUT. CO.	Equal End Pen	Pearl	150
6202	3″	KA-BAR	Equal End Pen	Bone	60
7202	3″	KA-BAR	Equal End Pen	Pearl	110

Pattern	Length	Stamping	Description	Handle	Mint Price
6203 1/2	3″	UNION CUT. CO.	Equal End Jack	Bone	85
0203 1/2	3″	UNION CUT. CO.	Equal End Jack	Pyraline	75
7203 1/2	3″	UNION CUT. CO.	Equal End Jack	Pearl	140
6204	3″	UNION CUT. CO.	Equal End Pen	Bone	90
7204	3″	UNION CUT. CO.	Equal End Pen	Pearl	150
6204	3″	KA-BAR	Equal End Pen	Bone	75
6204	3″	KA-BAR	Equal End Pen	Composition	55
6205	3 1/8″	UNION CUT. CO.	Equal End Pen	Bone	100
6205	3 1/8″	KA-BAR	Equal End Pen	Bone	75
1206	3 1/4″	UNION CUT. CO.	Equal End Jack	Ebony	75
2206	3 1/4″	UNION CUT. CO.	Equal End Jack	Stag	110
6206	3 1/4″	UNION CUT. CO.	Equal End Jack	Bone	85
7206	3 1/4″	UNION CUT. CO.	Equal End Jack	Pearl	150
9206	3 1/4″	UNION CUT.	Equal End Jack	Pyraline	70
2206	3 1/4″	KA-BAR	Equal End Jack	Stag	100
6206	3 1/4″	KA-BAR	Equal End Jack	Bone	75
P206	3 1/4″	KA-BAR	Equal End Jack	Celluloid	65
2206	3 1/4″	Kabar	Equal End Jack	Pearl	75
6206	3 1/4″	Kabar	Equal End Jack	Bone	45
P206	3 1/4″	Kabar	Equal End Jack	Celluloid	35
7206	3 1/4″	Kabar	Equal End Jack	Pearl	75
6206	3 1/4″	Kabar (no #) USA	Equal End Jack	Delrin	20
6209 1/2	3 1/4″	UNION CUT. CO.	Gardner's Knife	Bone	175
6210	3 1/2″	UNION CUT. CO.	Moose	Bone	200
6210	3 1/2″	KA-BAR	Moose	Bone	165
6212J	4 1/8″	UNION CUT. CO.	Trapper	Bone	225

Pattern	Length	Stamping	Description	Handle	Mint Price
0212J	4 1/8″	UNION CUT. CO.	Trapper	Pyraline	200
6212J	4 1/8″	KA-BAR	Trapper	Bone	150
6212J	4 1/8″	Kabar	Trapper	Bone	75
5212J	4 1/8″	Kabar	Trapper	Celluloid	65

Pattern	*Length*	*Stamping*	*Description*	*Handle*	*Mint Price*
6213J	3 7/8″	UNION CUT. CO.	Texas Jack	Bone	200
2213J	3 7/8″	KA-BAR	Texas Jack	Stag	250
6213J	3 7/8″	KA-BAR	Texas Jack	Bone	165
1215	3 5/8″	UNION CUT. CO.	Equal End Jack	Ebony	120
6215	3 5/8″	UNION CUT. CO.	Equal End Jack	Bone	160
6215PU	3 5/8″	UNION CUT. CO.	Equal End Jack	Bone	165
6215	3 5/8″	KA-BAR	Equal End Jack	Bone	140
6215 1/2	3 5/8″	KA-BAR	Equal End Jack	Bone	140
6215	3 5/8″	Kabar	Equal End Jack	Bone	100
6215	3 5/8″	Kabar	Equal End Jack	Composition	65
6215	3 5/8″	Kabar (no #) USA	Equal End Jack	Delrin	30
1218	3 1/4″	UNION CUT. CO.	Regular Jack	Ebony	85
2218	3 1/4″	UNION CUT. CO.	Regular Jack	Stag	125
6218	3 1/4″	UNION CUT. CO.	Regular Jack	Bone	100
7218	3 1/4″	UNION CUT. CO.	Regular Jack	Pearl	175
1218	3 1/4″	KA-BAR	Regular Jack	Ebony	65
6218	3 1/4″	KA-BAR	Regular Jack	Bone	75
6219 1/2	3 1/4″	UNION CUT. CO.	Slim Jack	Bone	125
6220J	3 1/2″	UNION CUT. CO.	Half Whittler	Bone	175
2220J	3 1/2″	KA-BAR	Half Whittler	Stag	150
6220J	3 1/2″	KA-BAR	Half Whittler	Bone	120
7220J	3 1/2″	KA-BAR	Half Whittler	Pearl	200
6221	3 1/4″	UNION CUT. CO.	Congress Pen	Bone	100
6221	3 1/4″	KA-BAR	Congress Pen	Bone	85
6221	3 1/4″	Kabar	Congress Pen	Composition	45
T221	3 1/4″	Kabar	Congress Pen	Composition	30
1222T	3 3/8″	UNION CUT. CO.	Sleeveboard Pen	Ebony	80
6222T	3 3/8″	UNION CUT. CO.	Sleeveboard Pen	Bone	90
7222T	3 3/8″	UNION CUT. CO.	Sleeveboard Pen	Pearl	150
9222T	3 3/8″	UNION CUT. CO.	Sleeveboard Pen	Pyraline	75
5223	3 1/4″	KA-BAR	Barlow	Composition	90
6223	3 1/4″	KA-BAR	Barlow	Bone	115
6223 1/2	3 1/4″	KA-BAR	Barlow	Bone	110
5223SH	3 1/4″	Kabar	Barlow	Composition	50
5223	3 1/4″	Kabar	Barlow	Composition	40
5223 1/2	3 1/4″	Kabar	Barlow	Composition	40
6223	3 1/4″	Kabar (no #) USA	Barlow	Delrin	25
6223 1/2	3 1/4″	Kabar (no #)	Barlow	Delrin	25
6224	2 3/4″	UNION CUT. CO.	Equal End Pen	Bone	85
6224	2 3/4″	KA-BAR	Equal End Pen	Bone	70
P225	3 3/4″	UNION CUT. CO.	Equal End Jack	Celluloid	100
6225 1/2	3 3/4″	KA-BAR	Equal End Jack	Bone	125
6225	3 3/4″	KA-BAR	Equal End Jack	Bone	125
5226	3″	UNION CUT. CO.	Emblem Knife	Pyraline	70
7226	3″	UNION CUT. CO.	Emblem Knife	Pearl	95
6226	3″	KA-BAR	Equal End Pen	Bone	70
7226	3″	KA-BAR	Equal End Pen	Pearl	100
1228	3 5/8″	UNION CUT. CO.	E.O. Jack	Ebony	95
2228	3 5/8″	UNION CUT. CO.	E.O. Jack	Stag	140
6228	3 5/8″	UNION CUT. CO.	E.O. Jack	Bone	125
9228	3 5/8″	UNION CUT. CO.	E.O. Jack	Pyraline	115
6229	3 1/4″	UNION CUT. CO.	Sleeveboard Jack	Bone	90
6229 1/2	3 1/4″	UNION CUT. CO.	Sleeveboard Jack	Bone	85
6229	3 1/4″	KA-BAR	Sleeveboard Jack	Bone	70
6229 1/2	3 1/4″	Kabar	Sleeveboard Jack	Composition	35
6229 1/2	3 1/4″	Kabar (no #) USA	Sleeveboard Jack	Delrin	20

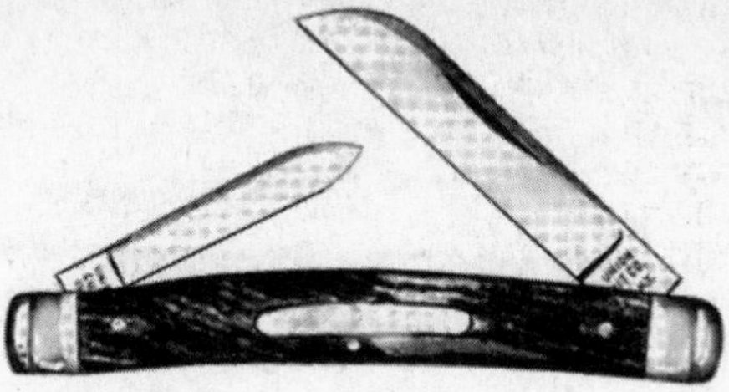

Pattern	*Length*	*Stamping*	*Description*	*Handle*	*Mint Price*
6230	3¼″	UNION CUT. CO.	Congress Pen	Bone	100
7230	3¼″	UNION CUT. CO.	Congress Pen	Pearl	150
1232	3⅜″	UNION CUT. CO.	Regular Jack	Ebony	85
6232	3⅜″	UNION CUT. CO.	Regular Jack	Bone	100
9232	3⅜″	UNION CUT. CO.	Regular Jack	Pyraline	80
1232	3⅜″	KA-BAR	Regular Jack	Ebony	65
6232	3⅜″	KA-BAR	Regular Jack	Bone	85
6232	3⅜″	Kabar	Regular Jack	Composition	40
6232½	3⅜″	Kabar (no #) USA	Regular Jack	Delrin	20
1233	3⅝″	UNION CUT. CO.	Crown End Jack	Ebony	140
2233	3⅝″	UNION CUT. CO.	Crown End Jack	Stag	200
6233	3⅝″	UNION CUT. CO.	Crown End Jack	Bone	175
9233	3⅝″	UNION CUT. CO.	Crown End Jack	Pyraline	160
2233	3⅝″	KA-BAR	Crown End Jack	Stag	165
6233	3⅝″	KA-BAR	Crown End Jack	Bone	130
6236LL	3⅜″	KA-BAR	Regular Jack	Bone	85
6236LL	3⅜″	Kabar	Regular Jack	Composition	45
6237	3⅛″	UNION CUT. CO.	Gunstock	Bone	185
P237	3⅛″	UNION CUT. CO.	Gunstock	Celluloid	160
6237	3⅛″	KA-BAR	Gunstock	Bone	135
2237	3⅛″	KA-BAR	Gunstock	Stag	165
7237	3⅛″	KA-BAR	Gunstock	Pearl	225
P237	3⅛″	KA-BAR	Gunstock	Celluloid	140
6239	3″	UNION CUT. CO.	Senator Pen	Bone	75
9239	3″	UNION CUT. CO.	Senator Pen	Celluloid	60

6240J	3¼″	UNION CUT. CO.	Dogleg Jack	Bone	175
6240J	3¼″	KA-BAR	Dogleg Jack	Bone	125
6241	2¾″	UNION CUT. CO.	Equal End Pen	Bone	65
7241	2¾″	UNION CUT. CO.	Equal End Pen	Pearl	90
P241	2¾″	KA-BAR	Equal End Pen	Celluloid	45
6241	2¾″	KA-BAR	Equal End Pen	Bone	50
7241G	2¾″	KA-BAR	Equal End Pen	Pearl	80
P241	2¾″	Kabar	Equal End Pen	Celluloid	25
2241	2¾″	Kabar	Equal End Pen	Stag	35
6242	3½″	UNION CUT. CO.	Regular Jack	Bone	85
6242	3⅛″	KA-BAR	Regular Jack	Bone	70
T242	3⅛″	KA-BAR	Regular Jack	Celluloid	60
6242	3⅛″	Kabar	Regular Jack	Bone	50

Pattern	Length	Stamping	Description	Handle	Mint Price
6244	3 5/8″	UNION CUT. CO.	Doctor Knife	Bone	225
7244	3 5/8″	UNION CUT. CO.	Doctor Knife	Pearl	300
1246	3 1/2″	UNION CUT. CO.	Serpentine Jack	Ebony	120
2246	3 1/2″	UNION CUT. CO.	Serpentine Jack	Stag	200
6246	3 1/2″	UNION CUT. CO.	Serpentine Jack	Bone	175
P246	3 1/2″	UNION CUT. CO.	Serpentine Jack	Celluloid	125
2246	3 1/2″	KA-BAR	Serpentine Jack	Pearl	170
6246	3 1/2″	KA-BAR	Serpentine Jack	Bone	140
6247	3 1/4″	UNION CUT. CO.	Regular Jack	Bone	95
6249	3 5/8″	UNION CUT. CO.	Sleeveboard Jack	Bone	135
6250	4 1/2″	UNION CUT. CO.	Sunfish	Bone	600
R250	4 1/2″	UNION CUT. CO.	Sunfish	Celluloid	475
6250	4 1/2″	KA-BAR	Sunfish	Bone	400
6251	4″	KA-BAR	Swell End Jack	Bone	150
6251 1/2	4″	KA-BAR	Swell End Jack	Bone	150
1252	3 3/4″	UNION CUT. CO.	Regular Jack	Ebony	95
2252 1/2	3 3/4″	UNION CUT. CO.	Regular Jack	Stag	150

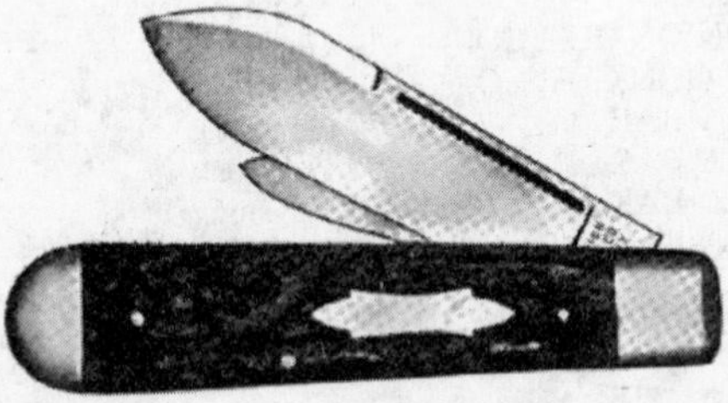

6252	3 3/4″	UNION CUT. CO.	Regular Jack	Bone	125
2253	3 1/8″	UNION CUT. CO.	Equal End Pen	Stag	110
7253	3 1/8″	UNION CUT. CO.	Equal End Pen	Pearl	130
2253	3 1/8″	KA-BAR	Equal End Pen	Stag	95
3253	3 1/8″	KA-BAR	Equal End Pen	Redwood	55
6253	3 1/8″	KA-BAR	Equal End Pen	Bone	65
7253	3 1/8″	KA-BAR	Equal End Pen	Pearl	100
T253	3 1/8″	KA-BAR	Equal End Pen	Celluloid	50
6253	3 1/8″	Kabar	Equal End Pen	Composition	35
T253	3 1/8″	Kabar	Equal End Pen	Celluloid	25
2255	3 1/8″	UNION CUT. CO.	Congress Pen	Stag	130
6255	3 1/8″	UNION CUT. CO.	Congress Pen	Bone	110
7255	3 1/8″	UNION CUT. CO.	Congress Pen	Pearl	150
9255	3 1/8″	UNION CUT. CO.	Congress Pen	Celluloid	85
6255	3 1/8″	KA-BAR	Congress Pen	Bone	80
7255	3 1/8″	KA-BAR	Congress Pen	Pearl	120
6255	3 1/8″	Kabar	Congress Pen	Composition	40
T255	3 1/8″	Kabar	Congress Pen	Celluloid	35
6256J	3 1/4″	UNION CUT. CO.	Premium Pen	Bone	95
7256J	3 1/4″	UNION CUT. CO.	Premium Pen	Pearl	135
R256J	3 1/4″	UNION CUT. CO.	Premium Pen	Celluloid	80
6256J	3 1/4″	KA-BAR	Premium Pen	Bone	80
2256J	3 1/4″	KA-BAR	Premium Pen	Stag	110
7256J	3 1/4″	KA-BAR	Premium Pen	Pearl	140
P256J	3 1/4″	KA-BAR	Premium Pen	Celluloid	70

Pattern	*Length*	*Stamping*	*Description*	*Handle*	*Mint Price*
6256J	3 1/4"	Kabar	Premium Pen	Bone	50
2256J	3 1/4"	Kabar	Premium Pen	Stag	60
T256J	3 1/4"	Kabar	Premium Pen	Celluloid	30
6256	3 1/4"	Kabar (no #) USA	Premium Pen	Delrin	20
6257	3 5/8"	KA-BAR	Muskrat	Bone	175
6257	3 5/8"	Kabar	Muskrat	Imit. Bone	65
2257	3 5/8"	Kabar	Muskrat	Stag	90

2260K&F	3 7/8"	UNION CUT. CO.	Knife & Fork	Stag	300
6260K&F	3 7/8"	UNION CUT. CO.	Knife & Fork	Bone	250
T260K&F	3 7/8"	KA-BAR	Knife & Fork	Celluloid	200
6261	4"	UNION CUT. CO.	Congress	Bone	250
6261	4"	KA-BAR	Congress	Bone	175
6261	4"	KA-BAR	Congress	Composition	140
6261	4"	kabar	Congress	Composition	50
6263	3 3/8"	UNION CUT. CO.	Regular Jack	Bone	90
6263PU	3 3/8"	UNION CUT. CO.	Regular Jack	Bone	95
6263	3 3/8"	KA-BAR	Regular Jack	Bone	70
6263	3 3/8"	Kabar	Regular Jack	Composition	35
6263	3 3/8"	Kabar (no #) USA	Regular Jack	Delrin	20
6265	4 1/2"	UNION CUT. CO.	Folding Hunter	Bone	350
0265	4 1/2"	UNION CUT. CO.	Folding Hunter	Celluloid	300
6265	4 1/2"	KA-BAR	Folding Hunter	Bone	250

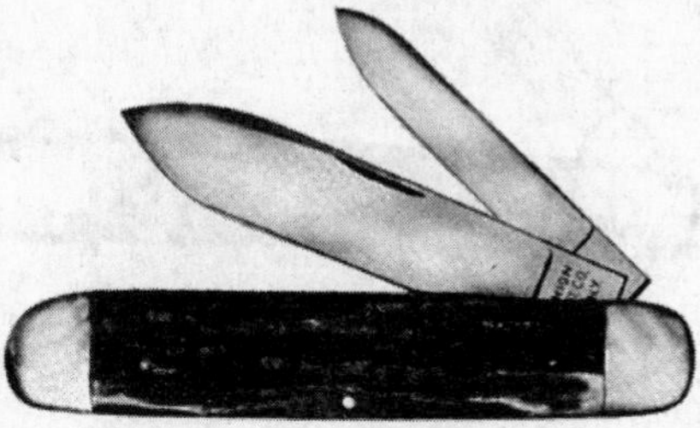

2266J	4 3/8"	UNION CUT. CO.	Jumbo Jack	Stag	400
6266J	4 3/8"	UNION CUT. CO.	Jumbo Jack	Bone	340
2266J	4 3/8"	KA-BAR	Jumbo Jack	Stag	350
6266J	4 3/8"	KA-BAR	Jumbo Jack	Bone	285
6267	4"	UNION CUT. CO.	Moose	Bone	350
6267	4"	KA-BAR	Moose	Bone	275
P269J	4"	UNION CUT. CO.	Texas Jack	Celluloid	175
2269J	4"	UNION CUT. CO.	Texas Jack	Stag	250
6269J	4"	UNION CUT. CO.	Texas Jack	Bone	200
P269J	4"	KA-BAR	Texas Jack	Celluloid	100
2269J	4"	KA-BAR	Texas Jack	Stag	160
6269J	4"	KA-BAR	Texas Jack	Bone	120
5269J	4"	KA-BAR	Texas Jack	Celluloid	75

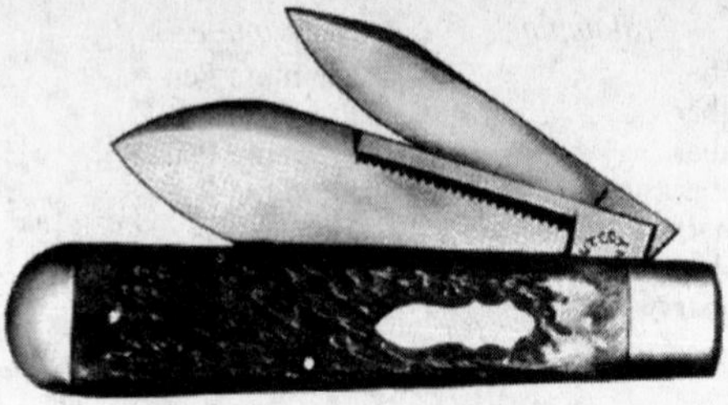

Pattern	Length	Stamping	Description	Handle	Mint Price
6270	4 1/2"	UNION CUT. CO.	Jumbo Jack	Bone	300
2270 1/2	4 1/2"	KA-BAR	Jumbo Jack	Stag	250
6270 1/2	4 1/2"	KA-BAR	Jumbo Jack	Bone	185
2270 1/2	4 1/2"	Kabar	Jumbo Jack	Stag	75
6270 1/2	4 1/2"	Kabar	Jumbo Jack	Delrin	40
6271J	4 1/4"	UNION CUT. CO.	Texas Jack	Bone	200
2271J	4 1/4"	UNION CUT. CO.	Texas Jack	Stag	275
6271	4 1/4"	UNION CUT. CO.	Texas Jack	Bone	200
6271J	4 1/4"	KA-BAR	Texas Jack	Bone	150
2271J	4 1/4"	KA-BAR	Texas Jack	Stag	190
3273	3 5/8"	UNION CUT. CO.	Electrician	Redwood	90
3273	3 5/8"	KA-BAR	Electrician	Redwood	70
TL-29	3 5/8"	KA-BAR	Electrician	Redwood	75
5273	3 5/8"	Kabar (no #) USA	Electrician	Celluloid	20
T275	4 1/4"	KA-BAR	Fishing Knife	Celluloid	90
T275	4 1/4"	Kabar	Fishing Knife	Celluloid	45
7285	2 5/8"	UNION CUT. CO.	Crown Pen	Pearl	175
7285	2 5/8"	UNION CUT. CO.	Crown Pen-Emblem	Pearl	140
7286RG	2 1/2"	UNION CUT. CO.	Crown Pen	Pearl	130
6288	4 1/4"	UNION CUT. CO.	Congress	Bone	275
6288	4 1/4"	KA-BAR	Congress	Bone	200
7289R	2 1/4"	KA-BAR	Lobster Pen	Pearl	135

6290	3 1/8"	UNION CUT. CO.	Sleeveboard Pen	Bone	110
2291K&F	5 1/4"	UNION CUT. CO.	Knife & Fork	Stag	475
6291K&F	5 1/4"	UNION CUT. CO.	Knife & Fork	Bone	425
7291K&F	5 1/4"	UNION CUT. CO.	Knife & Fork	Pearl	750
0291K&F	5 1/4"	UNION CUT. CO.	Knife & Fork	Celluloid	375
6291K&F	5 1/4"	KA-BAR	Knife & Fork	Bone	375
6295EX	3 1/2"	UNION CUT. CO.	Swell End Jack	Bone	125
9295EX	3 1/2"	UNION CUT. CO.	Swell End Jack	Pearl	175
6295EX	3 1/2"	UNION CUT. CO.	Swell End Jack	Stag	150
9295EX	3 1/2"	KA-BAR	Swell End Jack	Bone	100

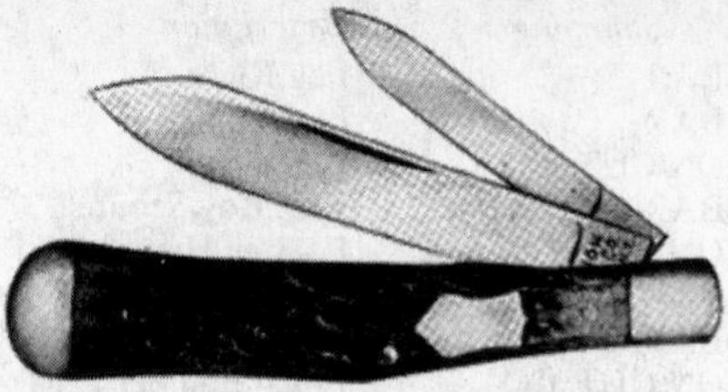

Pattern	*Length*	*Stamping*	*Description*	*Handle*	*Mint Price*
6299	2 7/8″	UNION CUT. CO.	Dogleg Jack	Bone	125
7299	2 7/8″	UNION CUT. CO.	Dogleg Jack	Pearl	200
22106	5 1/4″	KA-BAR	Cleaver	Stag	550
62107	5 1/4″	UNION CUT. CO.	Folding Hunter	Bone	400
62107	5 1/4″	KA-BAR	Folding Hunter	Bone	325
62107	5 1/4″	KA-BAR	Folding Hunter	Composition	250
P2107	5 1/4″	KA-BAR	Folding Hunter	Celluloid	250
22107	5 1/4″	Kabar	Folding Hunter	Stag	100
62107	5 1/4″	Kabar	Folding Hunter	Composition	60
22107	5 1/4″	Kabar (no #) USA	Folding Hunter	Imit. Stag	30
P2109	3 1/8″	UNION CUT. CO.	Equal End Pen	Celluloid	75
52109	3 1/8″	UNION CUT. CO.	Equal End Pen	Celluloid	75
72109	3 1/8″	UNION CUT. CO.	Equal End Pen	Pearl	150
52109	3 1/8″	KA-BAR	Equal End Pen	Celluloid	60
02109	3 1/8″	KA-BAR	Equal End Pen	Celluloid	80
22110	3 9/16″	UNION CUT. CO.	Lobster Pen	Stag	175
62110	3 9/16″	UNION CUT. CO.	Lobster Pen	Bone	150
62110	3 9/16″	KA-BAR	Lobster Pen	Bone	110
72110	2″	UNION CUT. CO.	Lobster Pen	Abalone	200
72111	2″	UNION CUT. CO.	Lobster Pen	Abalone	200
62118	4 1/4″	UNION CUT. CO.	Trapper	Bone	350
22118	4 1/4″	KA-BAR	Trapper	Stag	350
62118	4 1/4″	KA-BAR	Trapper	Bone	285
P2118	4 1/4″	KA-BAR	Trapper	Celluloid	250
R2118	4 1/4″	KA-BAR	Trapper	Celluloid	260
22118	4 1/4″	Kabar	Trapper	Stag	90
62118	4 1/4″	Kabar	Trapper	Bone	75
62118	4 1/4″	Kabar	Trapper	Composition	60
T2118	4 1/4″	Kabar	Trapper	Composition	55
62118	4 1/4″	Kabar (no #) USA	Trapper	Delrin	35
T2118	4 1/4″	Kabar (no #) USA	Trapper	Composition	35
72124RG	2 1/4″	UNION CUT. CO.	Lobster Pen	Pearl	110

P2127	3 1/4″	UNION CUT. CO.	Leg Knife	Celluloid	150
R2127	3 1/4″	UNION CUT. CO.	Leg Knife	Celluloid	150

Pattern	Length	Stamping	Description	Handle	Mint Price
52125	3¼″	KA-BAR	Leg Knife	Celluloid	125
P2127	3¼″	KA-BAR	Leg Knife	Celluloid	125
62128	3¼″	UNION CUT. CO.	E.O. Jack	Bone	100
62128	3¼″	KA-BAR	E.O. Boy Scout	Bone	150
62132	5¼″	UNION CUT. CO.	Folding Hunter	Bone	325
62132	5¼″	KA-BAR	Folding Hunter	Bone	250
T2132	5¼″	KA-BAR	Folding Hunter	Celluloid	220
62133	2¾″	UNION CUT. CO.	Equal End Pen	Bone	75
72133	2¾″	UNION CUT. CO.	Equal End Pen	Pearl	100
R2133	2¾″	UNION CUT. CO.	Equal End Pen	Celluloid	65
62133	2¾″	KA-BAR	Equal End Pen	Bone	55
72133	2¾″	KA-BAR	Equal End Pen	Pearl	85
62133	2¾″	Kabar	Equal End Pen	Bone	40
T2133	2¾″	Kabar	Equal End Pen	Composition	25
P2133	2¾″	Kabar	Equal End Pen	Celluloid	25
62134	3⅜″	UNION CUT. CO.	Dogleg Jack	Bone	250
62134	3⅜″	KA-BAR	Dogleg Jack	Bone	225
62135	3⅞″	UNION CUT. CO.	Equal End Jack	Bone	100
B2135	3⅞″	UNION CUT. CO.	Equal End Jack	Celluloid	85
72135	3⅞″	KA-BAR	Equal End Jack	Pearl	140
62140	3⅛″	UNION CUT. CO.	Serpentine Pen	Bone	120
72140	3⅛″	UNION CUT. CO.	Serpentine Pen	Pearl	165
H2140	3⅛″	UNION CUT. CO.	Serpentine Pen	Horn	125
62140	3⅛″	KA-BAR	Serpentine Pen	Bone	95

Pattern	Length	Stamping	Description	Handle	Mint Price
62141	3″	UNION CUT. CO.	Peanut	Bone	125
72141	3″	UNION CUT. CO.	Peanut	Pearl	175
62141	3″	KA-BAR	Peanut	Bone	100
T2141	3″	KA-BAR	Peanut	Celluloid	85
62141	3″	kabar	Peanut	Composition	45
T2141	3″	kabar	Peanut	Celluloid	45
62141	3″	kabar (no #) USA	Peanut	Delrin	25
62142	3″	UNION CUT. CO.	Balloon Pen	Bone	120
72142	3″	UNION CUT. CO.	Balloon Pen	Pearl	160
62142	3″	KA-BAR	Balloon Pen	Bone	100
72142	3″	KA-BAR	Balloon Pen	Pearl	140
62143	3″	UNION CUT. CO.	Serpentine Pen	Bone	120
72143	3″	UNION CUT. CO.	Serpentine Pen	Pearl	160
62143	3″	KA-BAR	Serpentine Pen	Bone	100
72143	3″	KA-BAR	Serpentine Pen	Pearl	130
92143	3″	KA-BAR	Serpentine Pen	Pyraline	95
22144	2⅞″	UNION CUT. CO.	Doctor Knife	Stag	240
62144	2⅞″	UNION CUT. CO.	Doctor Knife	Bone	220
72144	2⅞″	UNION CUT. CO.	Doctor Knife	Pearl	275
22144	2⅞″	KA-BAR	Doctor Knife	Stag	225
62144	2⅞″	KA-BAR	Doctor Knife	Bone	185
72144	2⅞″	KA-BAR	Doctor Knife	Pearl	240
62145	2⅝″	UNION CUT. CO.	Sleeveboard Pen	Bone	75
72145	2⅝″	UNION CUT. CO.	Sleeveboard Pen	Pearl	125
62145	2⅝″	KA-BAR	Sleeveboard Pen	Bone	70

Pattern	*Length*	*Stamping*	*Description*	*Handle*	*Mint Price*
72145	2 5/8″	KA-BAR	Sleeveboard Pen	Pearl	110
92145	2 5/8″	KA-BAR	Sleeveboard Pen	Celluloid	80
22146	3 1/4″	UNION CUT. CO.	Equal End Pen	Stag	120
62146	3 1/4″	UNION CUT. CO.	Equal End Pen	Bone	95
72146	3 1/4″	UNION CUT. CO.	Equal End Pen	Pearl	150
P2146EX	3 1/4″	UNION CUT. CO.	Equal End Pen	Celluloid	80
H2147	2 7/8″	UNION CUT. CO.	Mellon Knife	Celluloid	85
62147	2 7/8″	UNION CUT. CO.	Mellon Knife	Bone	100
72147	2 7/8″	UNION CUT. CO.	Mellon Knife	Pearl	150
62147	4 3/4″	KA-BAR	Mellon Knife	Bone	100
M2147	4 3/4″	KA-BAR	Mellon Knife	Metal	60
P2147	4 3/4″	Kabar	Mellon Knife	Celluloid	40
T2147	4 3/4″	Kabar	Mellon Knife	Celluloid	40
62148	3 1/4″	UNION CUT. CO.	Swell Center Pen	Bone	120
72148	3 1/4″	UNION CUT. CO.	Swell Center Pen	Pearl	160
62148	3 1/4″	KA-BAR	Swell Center Pen	Bone	110
72148	3 1/4″	KA-BAR	Swell Center Pen	Pearl	140
62149	3″	UNION CUT. CO.	Equal End Pen	Bone	95
72149	3″	UNION CUT. CO.	Equal End Pen	Pearl	125
P2149	3″	KA-BAR	Equal End Pen	Celluloid	70
22150	3 3/4″	UNION CUT. CO.	Barlow	Stag	190
22150R	3 3/4″	UNION CUT. CO.	Barlow	Stag	210
22150 1/2	3 3/4″	UNION CUT. CO.	Barlow	Stag	175
22150	3 3/4″	KA-BAR	Barlow	Stag	160
220151	3 1/4″	UNION CUT. CO.	Doctor Knife	Stag	235
620151	3 1/4″	UNION CUT. CO.	Doctor Knife	Bone	185
22151	3 1/4″	UNION CUT. CO.	Doctor Knife	Stag	240
62151	3 1/4″	UNION CUT. CO.	Doctor Knife	Bone	220
02151	3 1/4″	UNION CUT. CO.	Doctor Knife	Celluloid	185
22151	3 1/4″	KA-BAR	Doctor Knife	Stag	200
62151	3 1/4″	KA-BAR	Doctor Knife	Bone	175
72151	3 1/4″	KA-BAR	Doctor Knife	Pearl	300
62152	3 1/2″	UNION CUT. CO.	Muskrat	Bone	190
62152	3 1/2″	KA-BAR	Muskrat	Bone	165
62153	3 5/8″	UNION CUT. CO.	Curved Jack	Bone	190
62153	3 5/8″	KA-BAR	Curved Jack	Bone	175
62156	5″	UNION CUT. CO.	Hatchet Knife	Bone	325
62156	5″	KA-BAR	Hatchet Knife	Bone	250
62156	5″	KA-BAR	Boy Scout Model	Bone	275
52198	4″	KA-BAR	Swell End Jack	Celluloid	75
52198	4″	kabar	Swell End Jack	Celluloid	45
T2217	4 1/2″	KA-BAR	Sailor's Knife	Celluloid	95
T2217	4 1/2″	Kabar	Sailor's Knife	Celluloid	60
52217	4 1/2″	Kabar	Sailor's Knife	Composition	45
52217	4 1/2″	Kabar (no #) USA	Sailor's Knife	Composition	20
Three-Blade Knives					
Army	5″	UNION CUT. CO.	Mess Kit K/F/S	Ebony	185
T-33	5″	KA-BAR	Fishing Knife	Celluloid	125
T-33	5″	kabar	Fishing Knife	Celluloid	85
6306	3 1/4″	UNION CUT. CO.	Whittler	Bone	250
6306	3 1/4″	KA-BAR	Whittler	Bone	225
2307	3″	UNION CUT. CO.	Lobster Pen	Stag	95
7307	3″	UNION CUT. CO.	Lobster Pen	Pearl	130
7307	3″	UNION CUT. CO.	Lobster Pen	Abalone	185
1309 1/2	3 7/8″	UNION CUT. CO.	wharncliffe Pen	Ebony	260
6309	3 7/8″	UNION CUT. CO.	wharncliffe Pen	Bone	320
6313F	3 7/8″	UNION CUT. CO.	Premium Stock	Bone	190
9313F	3 7/8″	UNION CUT. CO.	Premium Stock	Pyraline	170
6314	3 5/8″	UNION CUT. CO.	Cattle Knife	Bone	250
6314	3 5/8″	KA-BAR	Cattle Knife	Bone	230
2314EX PU	3 5/8″	UNION CUT. CO.	Cattle Knife	Stag	750

Pattern	*Length*	*Stamping*	*Description*	*Handle*	*Mint Price*
6314EX	3 5/8″	UNION CUT. CO.	Cattle Knife	Bone	650
6314PU	3 5/8″	UNION CUT. CO.	Cattle Knife	Bone	325
6314PU	3 5/8″	KA-BAR	Cattle Knife	Bone	275
2320 1/2	3 1/2″	UNION CUT. CO.	Whittler	Stag	350
6320 1/2	3 1/2″	UNION CUT. CO.	Whittler	Bone	300
7320 1/2	3 1/2″	UNION CUT. CO.	Whittler	Pearl	475
2320 1/2	3 1/2″	KA-BAR	Whittler	Stag	300
6320 1/2	3 1/2″	KA-BAR	Whittler	Bone	275
7320 1/2	3 1/2″	KA-BAR	Whittler	Pearl	375
6322T	3 3/8″	UNION CUT. CO.	Whittler	Bone	300
6324RG	3 1/2″	KA-BAR	Utility Knife	Bone	100
6326	3″	KA-BAR	Utility Knife	Bone	210
P326	3″	kabar	Utility Knife	Celluloid	140

6331EX PU	3 1/4″	UNION CUT. CO.	Cattle Knife	Bone	650
7331EX PU	3 1/4″	UNION CUT. CO.	Cattle Knife	Pearl	900
6331EX PU	3 1/4″	KA-BAR	Cattle Knife	Bone	600
6340 1/2	3 1/4″	UNION CUT. CO.	Whittler	Bone	300
7340 1/2	3 1/4″	KA-BAR	Whittler	Pearl	400

2345	3 3/8″	UNION CUT. CO.	Lobster Pen	Stag	135
7345	3 3/8″	UNION CUT. CO.	Lobster Pen	Pearl	160
6349	3 5/8″	UNION CUT. CO.	Whittler	Bone	375
6349 1/2	3 5/8″	KA-BAR	Whittler	Bone	350
T3256CC	3 3/8″	KA-BAR	Premium Stock	Celluloid	110

Pattern	*Length*	*Stamping*	*Description*	*Handle*	*Mint Price*
T3256CC	3 3/8″	Kabar	Premium Stock	Celluloid	70
6356	3 1/4″	UNION CUT. CO.	Premium Stock	Bone	175
7356	3 1/4″	UNION CUT. CO.	Premium Stock	Pearl	250
6356	3 1/4″	KA-BAR	Premium Stock	Bone	140
2356	3 1/4″	Kabar	Premium Stock	Stag	80
6356	3 1/4″	Kabar	Premium Stock	Bone	65
P356	3 1/4″	Kabar	Premium Stock	Celluloid	50
6356	3 1/4″	Kabar (no #) USA	Premium Stock	Delrin	25

T3257CC	3 5/8″	KA-BAR	Serpentine Stock	Celluloid	125
T3257CC	3 5/8″	Kabar	Serpentine Stock	Celluloid	65
2357	3 5/8″	UNION CUT. CO.	Serpentine Stock	Stag	220
6357	3 5/8″	UNION CUT. CO.	Serpentine Stock	Bone	180
9357	3 5/8″	UNION CUT. CO.	Serpentine Stock	Celluloid	165
2357	3 5/8″	KA-BAR	Serpentine Stock	Stag	180
6357	3 5/8″	KA-BAR	Serpentine Stock	Bone	150
9357	3 5/8″	KA-BAR	Serpentine Stock	Celluloid	135
2357	3 5/8″	Kabar	Serpentine Stock	Stag	85
6357	3 5/8″	Kabar	Serpentine Stock	Composition	55
P357	3 5/8″	Kabar	Serpentine Stock	Celluloid	50
6357	3 5/8″	Kabar (no #) USA	Serpentine Stock	Delrin	25
6360	3 7/8″	UNION CUT. CO.	Knife/Fork/Spoon	Bone	260
9360	3 7/8″	UNION CUT. CO.	Knife/Fork/Spoon	Stag	300
6360	3 7/8″	KA-BAR	Knife/Fork/Spoon	Bone	210

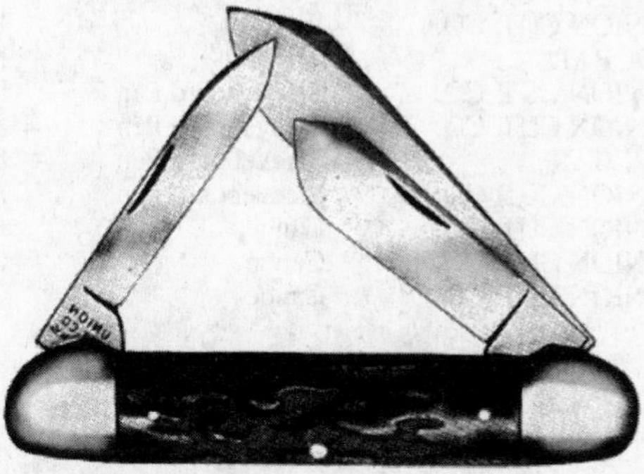

2366EX	4 1/2″	UNION CUT. CO.	Gunboat	Stag	850
6366EX	4 1/2″	UNION CUT. CO.	Gunboat	Bone	650
2366EX	4 1/2″	KA-BAR	Gunboat	Stag	700
6366EX	4 1/2″	KA-BAR	Gunboat	Bone	575
2367	4″	UNION CUT. CO.	Whittler	Stag	700
6367	4″	UNION CUT. CO.	Whittler	Bone	600
2369	3 7/8″	UNION CUT. CO.	Premium Stock	Stag	275
6369	3 7/8″	UNION CUT. CO.	Premium Stock	Bone	245
6369PU	3 7/8″	UNION CUT. CO.	Premium Stock	Bone	250
P369PU	3 7/8″	UNION CUT. CO.	Premium Stock	Celluloid	200
2369	3 7/8″	KA-BAR	Premium Stock	Stag	225

Pattern	*Length*	*Stamping*	*Description*	*Handle*	*Mint Price*
6369	3 7/8″	KA-BAR	Premium Stock	Bone	165
P369	3 7/8″	KA-BAR	Premium Stock	Celluloid	155
2369	3 7/8″	Kabar	Premium Stock	Stag	90
6369	3 7/8″	Kabar	Premium Stock	Bone	75
6369	3 7/8″	Kabar	Premium Stock	Composition	65
P369	3 7/8″	Kabar	Premium Stock	Celluloid	55
P369	3 7/8″	Kabar (no #) USA	Premium Stock	Delrin	25
2371	4 1/4″	UNION CUT. CO.	Premium Stock	Stag	325
6371	4 1/4″	UNION CUT. CO.	Premium Stock	Bone	275
2371	4 1/4″	KA-BAR	Premium Stock	Stag	275
6371	4 1/4″	KA-BAR	Premium Stock	Bone	250
9371	4 1/4″	KA-BAR	Premium Stock	Celluloid	215
T371	4 1/4″	Kabar	Premium Stock	Celluloid	65
2381	2 3/4″	UNION CUT. CO.	Lobster Pen	Stag	120
7381	2 3/4″	UNION CUT. CO.	Lobster Pen	Pearl	150
7381	2 3/4″	KA-BAR	Lobster Pen	Pearl	130
P381	2 3/4″	KA-BAR	Lobster Pen	Celluloid	85
6390	2 5/8″	KA-BAR	Stock Pen	Bone	90
6390	2 5/8″	KA-BAR	Stock Pen	Celluloid	75
6390	2 5/8″	Kabar	Stock Pen	Composition	40
P390	2 5/8″	Kabar	Stock Pen	Celluloid	40
6390	2 5/8″	Kabar (no #) USA	Stock Pen	Delrin	20

6397	3 5/8″	UNION CUT. CO.	Whittler	Bone	450
6397	3 5/8″	KA-BAR	Whittler	Bone	350
23101	2 5/8″	UNION CUT. CO.	Sleeveboard Pen	Stag	90
73101	2 5/8″	UNION CUT. CO.	Sleeveboard Pen	Pearl	140
73101	2 5/8″	KA-BAR	Sleeveboard Pen	Pearl	120
73101	3″	UNION CUT. CO.	Sleeveboard Pen	Abalone	235
63104	4 1/4″	UNION CUT. CO.	Canoe	Bone	800
73104	4 1/4″	UNION CUT. CO.	Canoe	Pearl	1200
P3104	4 1/4″	UNION CUT. CO.	Canoe	Celluloid	650

63111	4 1/4″	UNION CUT. CO.	Premium Stock	Bone	275
P3111	4 1/4″	UNION CUT. CO.	Premium Stock	Celluloid	225
P3111PU	4 1/4″	UNION CUT. CO.	Premium Stock	Celluloid	250

Pattern	*Length*	*Stamping*	*Description*	*Handle*	*Mint Price*
63111	4 1/4"	KA-BAR	Premium Stock	Bone	225
P3111	4 1/4"	KA-BAR	Premium Stock	Celluloid	180
P3111PU	4 1/4"	KA-BAR	Premium Stock	Celluloid	195
23116	4"	UNION CUT. CO.	Serpentine Stock	Stag	325
63116	4"	UNION CUT. CO.	Serpentine Stock	Bone	250
P3116	4"	UNION CUT. CO.	Serpentine Stock	Celluloid	195
23116	4"	KA-BAR	Serpentine Stock	Stag	250
63116	4"	KA-BAR	Serpentine Stock	Bone	200
P3116	4"	KA-BAR	Serpentine Stock	Celluloid	170
23116	4"	kabar	Serpentine Stock	Stag	90
63116	4"	kabar	Serpentine Stock	Composition	70
63116	4"	kabar (no #) USA	Serpentine Stock	Delrin	25
63118	4 1/4"	UNION CUT. CO.	Trapper	Bone	375
63152	3 1/2"	UNION CUT. CO.	Sowbelly Stock	Bone	275
W3152	3 1/2"	UNION CUT. CO.	Sowbelly Stock	Celluloid	250
63152	3 1/2"	KA-BAR	Sowbelly Stock	Bone	250
62163	3 1/4"	KA-BAR	Senator Pen	Bone	130
62195	4"	KA-BAR	Texas Jack	Bone	165
62195	4"	KA-BAR	Texas Jack	Composition	125
T2195	4"	KA-BAR	Texas Jack	Celluloid	110
62195	4"	kabar	Texas Jack	Composition	45
T2195	4"	kabar	Texas Jack	Celluloid	40
62195	4"	kabar (no #) USA	Texas Jack	Delrin	20
Four-Blade Knives					
6401T	2 7/8"	UNION CUT. CO.	Swell Center Pen	Bone	225
7401T	2 7/8"	UNION CUT. CO.	Swell Center Pen	Pearl	300
R466	4"	KA-BAR	Cattle Knife	Fiberoid	200
T4107	5 1/4"	KA-BAR	Utility Hunter	Celluloid	1200
64107	5 1/4"	KA-BAR	Utility Hunter	Green Bone	1800
24107	5 1/4"	KA-BAR	Utility Hunter	Stag	2400

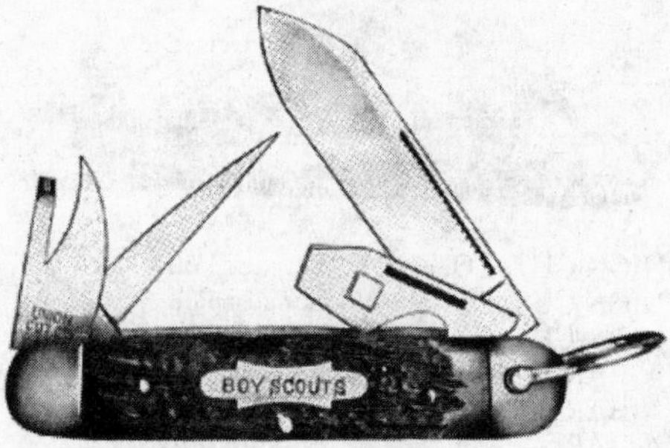

6415RG	3 5/8"	UNION CUT. CO.	Scout/Utility	Bone	250
6415RG	3 5/8"	KA-BAR	Scout/Utility	Bone	200
P415RG	3 5/8"	KA-BAR	Scout/Utility	Celluloid	165
6415RG	3 5/8"	Kabar	Scout/Utility	Composition	55
6415RG	3 5/8"	Kabar (no #) USA	Scout/Utility	Composition	35
6421	3 1/4"	UNION CUT. CO.	Congress	Bone	275
6421	3 1/4"	KA-BAR	Congress	Bone	255
6426	3"	UNION CUT. CO.	Equal End Pen	Bone	160
7426	3"	UNION CUT. CO.	Equal End Pen	Pearl	225
7426	3"	KA-BAR	Equal End Pen	Pearl	185
7455	3 1/8"	UNION CUT. CO.	Congress	Pearl	300
7455	3 1/8"	KA-BAR	Congress	Pearl	265
6460	3 7/8"	UNION CUT. CO.	Equal End Jack	Bone	190
6460	3 7/8"	KA-BAR	Equal End Jack	Bone	170
2461PU	4"	UNION CUT. CO.	Congress	Stag	350
6461PU	4"	UNION CUT. CO.	Congress	Bone	275
6461PU	4"	KA-BAR	Congress	Bone	250
2461	4"	kabar	Congress	Stag	140
6461	4"	kabar	Congress	Composition	100

Pattern	*Length*	*Stamping*	*Description*	*Handle*	*Mint Price*
2462	4 1/8"	UNION CUT. CO.	Moose	Stag	325
6766	4 1/8"	KA-BAR	Utility Knife	Bone	2800
T766	4 1/8"	Kabar	Utility Knife	Celluloid	2400
6469PU	4"	UNION CUT. CO.	Premium Stock	Bone	300
5480	3 1/8"	UNION CUT. CO.	Bartender	Celluloid	160
P480	3 1/8"	UNION CUT. CO.	Bartender	Celluloid	160
P480	3 1/8"	KA-BAR	Bartender	Celluloid	130
7487	3"	UNION CUT. CO.	Bartender	Pearl	260
T487	3"	UNION CUT. CO.	Bartender	Abalone	275

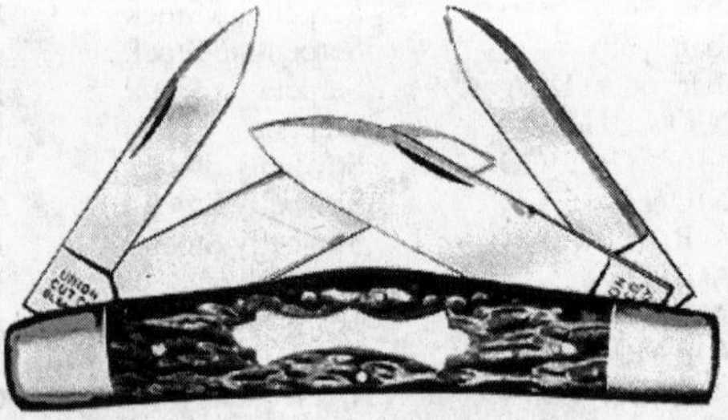

2488	4 1/4"	UNION CUT. CO.	Congress	Stag	400
6488	4 1/4"	UNION CUT. CO.	Congress	Bone	325
2488	4 1/4"	KA-BAR	Congress	Stag	325
6488	4 1/4"	KA-BAR	Congress	Bone	275
7489	3"	UNION CUT. CO.	Lobster Pen	Pearl	250
7489	3"	KA-BAR	Lobster Pen	Pearl	240
24100	3 1/2"	UNION CUT. CO.	Congress	Stag	325
64100	3 1/2"	UNION CUT. CO.	Congress	Bone	250

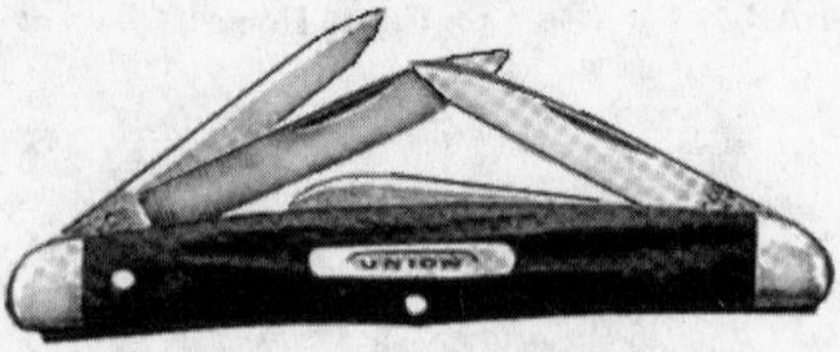

24163	3 1/4"	UNION CUT. CO.	Senator Pen	Stag	225
64163	3 1/4"	UNION CUT. CO.	Senator Pen	Bone	190
74163	3 1/4"	UNION CUT. CO.	Senator Pen	Pearl	275
64168	4"	KA-BAR	Scout/Utility	Bone	140
54202	4"	KA-BAR	Scout/Utility	Celluloid	120
T4202	4"	KA-BAR	Scout/Utility	Celluloid	130
M4202	4"	KA-BAR	Scout/Utility	Metal	125
54202	4"	kabar	Scout/Utility	Celluloid	90
T4202	4"	kabar	Scout/Utility	Celluloid	90
66158	3 1/4"	KA-BAR	Bartender Knife	Bone	200

KEEN KUTTER

The Keen Kutter brand was used for pocketknives as well as numerous tools and hardware items marketed during the late 19th and early 20th centuries. It was a brand stamping used by the E. C. Simmons Hardware Company of St. Louis, Missouri, beginning about 1870. Simmons Hardware owned controlling interest in Walden Knife Company and testimony to the quality of its products is evidenced by an award presented at the 1905 Lewis & Clark Exposition, held in Portland, Oregon, for the "superior excellence of quality and finish of their Walden and Keen Kutter pocketknives."

The 1923 merger of Simmons Hardware and Winchester resulted in the movement of Walden Knife Company equipment to New Haven, Connecticut. Walden had made Keen Kutter knives and, for the next ten years, they would be made by Winchester.

In 1940, the merged companies were again split when Shapleigh Hardware purchased the assets (including controlling interest in Walden Knife Company) of Simmons Hardware. The brand and knife patterns were continued by Shapleigh.

It is difficult to use Keen Kutter pattern numbers to determine knife description. The following listing, which includes knife style, closed length, handle material and number of blades, should permit one to find most Keen Kutter knives and determine their collector values.

Pattern	*Size*	*Handle*	*Style*	*Mint Price*
One-Blade Knives				

K01881	3 1/2″	Bone Stag	Barlow	120
K1734 1/2	3 1/2″	Bone Stag	Premium Jack	90
K1881	3 3/8″	Smooth Bone	Barlow	70
K1704 1/4	3 3/4″	Cocobolo	Regular Jack	60
K1695 3/4	4 3/8″	Red/Blk Celluloid	Texas Toothpick	100
K1698 3/4	4 3/8″	Bone Stag	Texas Toothpick	115
K1771 3/4	5″	Smooth Bone	Daddy Barlow	150
K1773 3/4	5″	Bone Stag	Daddy Barlow	160
K1895 3/4	5″	Gold Celluloid	Texas Toothpick	150

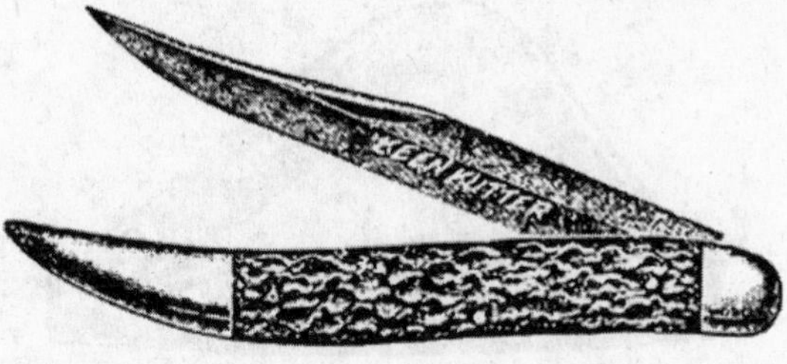

K1898 3/4	5″	Bone Stag	Texas Toothpick	185
K1920	5 1/4″	Bone Stag	Folding Hunter	275
Two-Blade Knives				
K013	2 1/4″	Pearl	Equal End Pen	70
K013/S	2 1/4″	Bone Stag	Equal End Pen	55
K02527	2 5/8″	Bone Stag	Equal End Pen	55
K27122	2 5/8″	Pearl Celluloid	Sleeveboard Pen	50
K27233 3/4	2 3/4″	Bone Stag	Peanut	70
K02529	2 3/4″	Pearl	Equal End Pen	75
K02529/S	2 3/4″	Pearl	Equal End Pen	75

Pattern	*Size*	*Handle*	*Style*	*Mint Price*
K711	2 3/4"	Pearl	Dogleg Pen	125
K711G	2 3/4"	Gold Celluloid	Dogleg Pen	70
K711/SC	2 3/4"	Silver Celluloid	Dogleg Pen	70
K713	2 3/4"	Bone Stag	Peanut	70
K0529	2 3/4"	Pearl	Balloon Pen	100
K0797	2 7/8"	Bone Stag	Sleeveboard Pen	75
K0798	2 7/8"	Pearl	Sleeveboard Pen	90
K0799	2 7/8"	Pearl Celluloid	Sleeveboard Pen	60
K0486	2 7/8"	Bone Stag	Senator Pen	55
K0488	2 7/8"	Pearl	Senator Pen	75
K713 3/4	2 7/8"	Bone Stag	Peanut	65
K23628 3/4	3"	Bone Stag	Curved Jack	80
K0151	3"	Bone Stag	Serpentine Lobster Pen	65
K0153	3"	Pearl	Serpentine Lobster Pen	90
K153	3"	Bone Stag	Serpentine Lobster Pen	80
K0207R	3"	Bone Stag	Equal End Pen	65
K0109R	3"	Pearl	Equal End Pen	90
K0214	3"	Bone	Square End Pen	70

K0214K	3"	Red/Blk Celluloid	Square End Pen	65
K0214TC	3"	Pearl Celluloid	Square End Pen	65
K0498	3"	Bone Stag	Congress Pen	85
K0499	3"	Pearl	Congress Pen	135
K0612R	3"	Pearl	Balloon Pen	125
K0814	3"	Nickel Silver	Senator Pen	55
K0815/S	3"	Nickel Silver	Senator Pen	55
K02070M	3"	Bone Stag	Equal End Pen	70
K02235N	3"	Silver Celluloid	Serpentine Pen	80
K02237	3"	Bone Stag	Serpentine Pen	90
K02239	3"	Pearl	Serpentine Pen	125
K02463	3"	Pearl	Serpentine Pen	125
K2720	3"	Cocobolo	Regular Jack	55
K2723	3"	Bone Stag	Regular Jack	65
K02736	3"	Fibre	Serpentine Pen	55
K5328	3"	Bone Stag	Gunstock Pen	160
K7WCCEE	3 1/8"	Green Celluloid	Regular Jack	65
K7WCS	3 1/8"	Bone Stag	Regular Jack	75

Pattern	*Size*	*Handle*	*Style*	*Mint Price*
K7WPC	3⅛″	Pearl	Regular Jack	150
K080	3⅛″	Pearl Celluloid	Senator Pen	65
K083T	3⅛″	Pearl	Sleeveboard Pen	145
K0883	3⅛″	Pearl	Equal End Pen	125
K0188A	3⅛″	Abalone Celluloid	Senator Pen	65
K0188OR	3⅛″	Iridescent Celluloid	Senator Pen	70
K01884	3⅛″	Bone Stag	Equal End	110
K7733	3⅛″	Bone Stag	Teardrop Jack	110
K7733¾	3⅛″	Bone Stag	Teardrop Jack	110

K094T	3¼″	Pearl	Sleeveboard Pen	140
K0256	3¼″	Bone Stag	Equal End Pen	90
K0258	3¼″	Pearl	Senator Pen	110
K264	3¼″	Bone Stag	Regular Jack	75
K264¾	3¼″	Bone Stag	Regular Jack	80
K03342J	3¼″	Grn/Blk Celluloid	Equal End Pen	65
K03342K	3¼″	Red/Blk Celluloid	Equal End Pen	65
K03344/S	3¼″	Fancy Nickel Silver	Senator Pen	60
K03706	3¼″	Bone Stag	Muskrat	100
K03706¼	3¼″	Bone Stag	Muskrat	100
K03707	3¼″	Ebony	Muskrat	85
K04527	3¼″	Bone Stag	Congress Pen	125
K04529	3¼″	Pearl	Congress Pen	160
K06256F	3¼″	Bone Stag	Equal End Pen	75
K72423	3¼″	Fibre	Equal End Jack	65
K0333	3¼″	Bone Stag	Congress Pen	115
K50	3⅜″	Cocobolo	Regular Jack	65
K51¾	3⅜″	Ebony	Regular Jack	70
K53	3⅜″	Bone Stag	Regular Jack	70
K099T	3⅜″	Pearl	Sleeveboard Pen	150
K0195¾K	3⅜″	Blue Celluloid	Muskrat	85
K0195¾P	3⅜″	Red/Blk Celluloid	Muskrat	85
K0196	3⅜″	Ebony	Equal End Jack	65
K0197¾K	3⅜″	Red/Blk Celluloid	Equal End Jack	70
K0198	3⅜″	Bone Stag	Muskrat	100
K0198¾	3⅜″	Bone Stag	Muskrat	100
K0281T	3⅜″	Bone Stag	Sleeveboard Pen	75
K02071	3⅜″	Bone Stag	Equal End Pen	70
K02074	3⅜″	Bone Stag	Equal End	75
K02074L	3⅜″	Varicolor Celluloid	Equal End	65
K02120	3⅜″	White Celluloid	Office Knife	75
K02220	3⅜″	White Celluloid	Office Knife	75
K2881	3⅜″	Smooth Bone	Barlow	80
K02436¾	3⅜″	Black Celluloid	Serpentine Jack	75
K02437¾	3⅜″	Bone Stag	Serpentine Jack	85
K03471	3⅜″	Bone Stag	Equal End Pen	70
K50K	3½″	Red/Blk Celluloid	Regular Jack	80
K50¾K	3½″	Red/Blk Celluloid	Regular Jack	80
K72783	3½″	Bone Stag	Regular Jack	70
K0348	3½″	Bone Stag	Texas Jack	135
K0698	3½″	Bone Stag	Texas Jack	145
K02238	3½″	Pearl Celluloid	Serpentine Pen	95

Pattern	*Size*	*Handle*	*Style*	*Mint Price*
K95J	3½″	Varicolored Celluloid	Easy Open Jack	90
K7725C	3½″	Cocobolo	Dogleg Jack	95

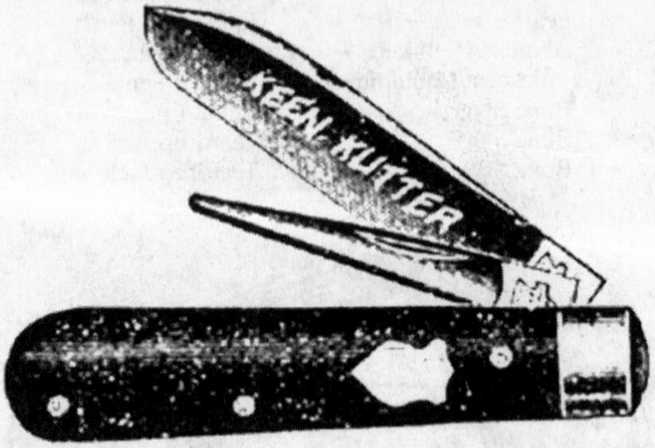

K72286	3½″	Ebony	Regular Jack	70
K72288	3½″	Bone Stag	Regular Jack	75
K72783¾	3½″	Bone Stag	Regular Jack	70
K713¾A	3⅝″	Abalone Celluloid	Peanut	90
K2765	3⅝″	Cocobolo	Easy Open Jack	65
K02878	3⅝″	Bone Stag	Texas Jack	120
K2878¾	3⅝″	Bone Stag	Texas Jack	115
K03311	3⅝″	Bone Stag	Swell Center Pen	90
K0878	3¾″	Bone Stag	Congress Pen	90
K02423	3¾″	Bone Stag	Equal End Jack	65
K07243	3¾″	Bone Stag	Texas Jack	135
K0247	3⅞″	Bone Stag	Texas Jack	135
K0147¾	4″	Bone Stag	Muskrat	225
K03433	4″	Bone Stag	Texas Jack	175
Three-Blade Knives				
K0388/S	2⅞″	Pearl	Senator Pen	125
K3908/S	2⅞″	Pearl	Senator Whittler	150
K0643	2¾″	Pearl	Sleeveboard Lobster Pen	130
K309R	3″	Pearl	Lobster Pen	125
K3036T	3″	Bone Stag	Sleeveboard Lobster Pen	100
K3037T	3″	Pearl	Sleeveboard Lobster Pen	125
K3305RJ	3″	Grn/Blk Celluloid	Equal End Whittler	90
K3307R	3″	Bone Stag	Equal End Whittler	140
K73625G	3″	Gold Celluloid	Cattle Knife	130
K73628	3″	Bone Stag	Cattle Knife	140
K357	3⅛″	Pearl	Gunstock Lobster Pen	200

K3483	3⅛″	Pearl	Sleeveboard Whittler	160
K341	3¼″	Bone Stag	Equal End Whittler	110
K343	3¼″	Pearl	Equal End Whittler	150
K3073	3¼″	Pearl	Equal End Whittler	175
K0334	3¼″	Bone Stag	Equal End Pen	90

Pattern	*Size*	*Handle*	*Style*	*Mint Price*
K3527	3 1/4"	Bone Stag	Congress Whittler	200
K3706 1/4D	3 1/4"	Red Celluloid	Premium Whittler	150
K3708 1/4	3 1/4"	Pearl	Serpentine Whittler	220

K7530J	3 1/4"	Grn/Blk Celluloid	Serpentine Whittler	150
K33251	3 1/4"	Bone Stag	Bartender's Knife	95
K33253	3 1/4"	Pearl	Bartender's Knife	200
K33720R	3 1/4"	Iridescent Celluloid	Serpentine Stock	100
K33721	3 1/4"	Bone Stag	Serpentine Stock	125
K73706	3 1/4"	Bone Stag	Premium Stock	120
K3070J	3 3/8"	Grn/Blk Celluloid	Equal End Whittler	145
K3070FK	3 3/8"	Red/Blk Celluloid	Equal End Whittler	140
K3070FL	3 3/8"	Red/Grn Celluloid	Equal End Whittler	140
K3071F	3 3/8"	Bone Stag	Equal End Whittler	170
K3071 1/4	3 3/8"	Bone Stag	Equal End Whittler	165
K3071 1/2	3 3/8"	Bone Stag	Equal End Whittler	155
K3215 3/4G	3 3/8"	Gold Celluloid	Cattle Knife	160
K3218 3/4	3 3/8"	Bone Stag	Cattle Knife	175
K3553	3 3/8"	Bone Stag	Cattle Knife	170
K3599T	3 3/8"	Pearl	Sleeveboard Whittler	200
K3619	3 3/8"	Pearl	Cattle Knife	260
K3681T	3 3/8"	Bone Stag	Sleeveboard Whittler	165
K32436 3/4	3 3/8"	Black Celluloid	Serpentine Whittler	130
K32437	3 3/8"	Bone Stag	Sleeveboard Whittler	150
K73845 1/4L	3 3/8"	Varicolor Celluloid	Serpentine Cattle Knife	175
K73845 1/4D	3 3/8"	Red Celluloid	Serpentine Cattle Knife	175
K73878 1/4	3 3/8"	Bone Stag	Cattle Knife	185
K73878 3/4	3 3/8"	Bone Stag	Cattle Knife	175
K3472	3 3/8"	Bone Stag	Whittler	175
K73553 3/4	3 3/8"	Bone Stag	Cattle Knife	175
K3698 3/4	3 1/2"	Bone Stag	Balloon Whittler	200
K3705 1/2	3 1/2"	Bone Stag	Premium Stock	125
K3732	3 1/2"	Gold Celluloid	Premium Stock	120
K3733	3 1/2"	Bone Stag	Premium Stock	125
K33732K	3 1/2"	Red/Blk Celluloid	Serpentine Stock	120
K37334	3 1/2"	Bone Stag	Serpentine Stock	135
K73733	3 1/2"	Bone Stag	Cattle Knife	170
K73848	3 1/2"	Bone Stag	Serpentine Cattle Knife	175
K73848 1/4	3 1/2"	Bone Stag	Serpentine Cattle Knife	175
K3878 3/4"	3 5/8"	Bone Stag	Cattle Knife	160
K735 3/4A	3 5/8"	Abalone Celluloid	Serpentine Stock	135
K735 3/4	3 5/8"	Red Celluloid	Serpentine Stock	135

Pattern	*Size*	*Handle*	*Style*	*Mint Price*
K737$\frac{3}{4}$	$3\frac{5}{8}''$	Red/White Celluloid	Serpentine Stock	170
K3278	$3\frac{5}{8}''$	Bone Stag	Cattle Knife	175
K3310	$3\frac{5}{8}''$	Black Celluloid	Balloon Whittler	175
K3311$\frac{1}{4}$	$3\frac{5}{8}''$	Bone Stag	Swell Center Whittler	190
K3316	$3\frac{5}{8}''$	Bone Stag	Balloon Whittler	210
K3317	$3\frac{5}{8}''$	Golden Celluloid	Balloon Whittler	190
K8464$\frac{1}{4}$	$3\frac{5}{8}''$	Ivory Celluloid	Cattle Knife	175
K73310$\frac{1}{4}$R	$3\frac{5}{8}''$	Iridescent Celluloid	Swell Center Cattle Knife	175
K73311$\frac{1}{2}$	$3\frac{5}{8}''$	Bone Stag	Swell Center Cattle Knife	190

K73477$\frac{3}{4}$	$3\frac{5}{8}''$	White Celluloid	Cattle Knife	165
K38$\frac{3}{4}$	$3\frac{3}{4}''$	Bone Stag	Swell Center Whittler	225
K738$\frac{3}{4}$	$3\frac{3}{4}''$	Bone Stag	Premium Stock	180
K78433	$3\frac{3}{4}''$	Bone Stag	Premium Stock	150
K73875$\frac{3}{4}$P	$3\frac{5}{8}''$	Blue Celluloid	Cattle Knife	155
K3430	$4''$	Buffalo Horn	Premium Stock	190
K3433	$4''$	Bone Stag	Premium Stock	180
K343	$3\frac{1}{4}''$	Bone Stag	Premium Stock	140
K3825	$4''$	Blk Celluloid	Premium Stock	140
K3825H	$4''$	Pearl Celluloid	Premium Stock	130
K3826	$4''$	Red/White Celluloid	Premium Stock	155
K3828	$4''$	Bone Stag	Premium Stock	175
K33433	$4''$	Bone Stag	Premium Stock	160
K73433$\frac{1}{4}$	$4''$	Bone Stag	Cattle Knife	185
K73828	$4''$	Bone Stag	Premium Stock	165
Four-Blade Knives				
K4843	$2\frac{3}{4}''$	Pearl	Sleeveboard Lobster Pen	165
K356	$3\frac{1}{8}''$	Bone Stag	Sleeveboard Lobster Pen	150
K4738/S	$3\frac{1}{8}''$	Pearl	Senator Pen	140

Pattern	*Size*	*Handle*	*Style*	*Mint Price*
K443	3 1/4″	Pearl	Senator Pen	140
K4208	3 1/4″	Pearl	Equal End Pen	135
K6353	3 1/2″	Bone Stag	Scout Knife	200
K6559	3 5/8″	Bone Stag	Scout Knife	225

K4527	3 3/4″	Bone Stag	Congress	225
K4428	4″	Bone Stag	Premium Stock	185
K74825E	4″	Pearl Celluloid	Premium Stock	165
K74828	4″	Bone Stag	Premium Stock	175

KINFOLKS, INC.

The brand name "Kinfolks" was derived from the fact that the company's founders were cousins. The company was formed in Little Valley, New York, in 1927 by J. Russell Case, Dean J. Case and Tint Champlin. Champlin served as the company's first president and was succeeded in that office by Dean J. Case in 1929.

The firm produced sheath knives, household knives, razors, hatchets and pocketknives. The majority of its knife production was in sheath knives and a large number was made for World War II military use. In addition to knives stamped KINFOLKS USA, the factory also produced knives marked JEAN CASE or J. CASE until it ceased operation in 1948.

When Emerson Case went to work for Robeson in the 1950s, he had somehow obtained rights to the Kinfolks trademark. Robeson made a line of approximately ten knives bearing that brand and with the Kinfolks brand and marketed them through the Robeson dealers. These knives usually had green bone handles and, when Robeson changed to the traditional strawberry bone, the Kinfolks stamping was dropped.

ROBERT KLAAS COMPANY—KISSING CRANE

This company's story began when a scissors maker named Peter Daniel Pauls married Johanne Amalie Storsberg, whose father was a maker of pen knives. Shortly thereafter, in 1834, he began his own production of pen knives. In 1850, when the first shipment of Pauls knives to the United States was made, the high quality of his three- and four-blade knives was recognized and appreciated. Pauls daughter had married a young scissors maker named Frederich Robert Klass and, after Pauls's death, the old company was merged with the Robert Klaas Company in 1869. The Klass business grew in reputation and sales under Robert Klass leadership and, in 1895, he registered the "Kissing Crane" logo as its trademark.

Ownership and management of the Klass firm has been passed through several generations succeeding Robert Klass. Although the owners' names changed through marriage of Klass daughters, the company still carries the Robert Klass name and the trademark he designed. Hugo Schiesen, Klass's great-grandson of Robert Klass, began work with the company in 1930. Presently, leadership of the company rests with the brothers, Hans-Gerd and Ernst-Jorgen Schiesen, sixth-generation descendants of the company's founder.

For several years afterwards, Kissing Crane knives were distributed exclusively by Star Sales of Knoxville, Tennessee. U.S. distribution rights were purchased in 1987 by a group of leading knife distributors.

In 1972, Klaas began to use a dating system on its knives. The first two numbers indicate the pattern number, the third number indicates the number of blades, and the fourth number indicates handle material as follows:

1—Imitation Ivory
2—Black Composition
3—Imitation Bone
4—Imitation Pearl
5—Genuine Deer Stag
6—Yellow Composition
7—Mother-of-Pearl
8—Wood
9—Genuine Bone
0—Red Composition

Following those numbers are Roman numeral keys beginning with "XI" signifying the year of manufacture as 1972 and incrementing one numeral for each year thereafter. For example, the number 2929XII would indicate a small canoe pattern with two blades, handled in bone, and made in 1973.

LACKAWANNA CUTLERY COMPANY

This firm was originally started in Nicholson, Pennsylvania, in 1911 as the Eureka Cutlery Company. Its owner was unable to build a successful business and the factory was sold to some local businessmen who re-opened it as the Lackawanna Cutlery Company. The company manufactured knives at that factory from about 1917 until the factory burned in 1923. From 1923 until 1930, the company owners purchased parts from other manufacturers and assembled them under their company's name. Knives from the latter era were primarily celluloid and picture handled knives. Stampings used included LACKAWANNA (curved) and L. C. CO./NICHOLSON PA.

LANDERS, FRARY AND CLARK

This firm was first organized in 1865 with its major production focused on tableware and kitchen knives. James Frary, the company's president, patented a hollow handle for table cutlery in 1869. In 1871, his patent for making knife bolsters from sheet metal as well as other innovations for pocketknife making led Frary to resign and open his own company, the Frary Cutlery Company, in Bridgeport, Connecticut. His company lasted from 1876 to 1884.

Landers, Frary & Clark had, in the meantime, grown into a major cutlery producer and the company name was shortened to L. F. & C. in 1898. Using the trade name UNIVERSAL (purchased from the Universal Knife Company), L. F. & C. entered into pocketknife manufacture in 1912. During that same year, the company purchased the Humason & Beckley Manufacturing Company and used that company's knife patterns along with new ones of its own. Another major acquisition was made in 1918 when the company purchased the Meriden Cutlery Company. In 1950, L. F. & C. of New Britain, Connecticut, discontinued its cutlery division.

MAHER AND GROSH

Established by two dentists in 1877, the Maher and Grosh firm is probably the oldest mail-order knife businesses in the United States. Located in Toledo, Ohio, during its earlier years, the company manufactured none of the numerous knives stamped with its name. Knives were made under contract by companies such as Schrade, Queen and Miller Brothers and were stamped MAHER & GROSH TOLEDO OHIO (or the city name followed by O.).

The company actively pursued the agricultural trade with horticultural knives as well as the quality line of pocketknives. A late 1880s catalog listed over 125 knives; some Maher & Grosh knives bore a pattern while others were given colorful names such as "The Indian Trapper" or "Old Dixie Knife" and "Kattle King" etched on the master blades.

The firm was moved to Clyde, Ohio, in 1963 and continues to offer knives of other brand stampings as well as other supplies.

AL MAR KNIVES

Al Mar, the founder of this company, was employed as a knife designer by Gerber Legendary Blades and is credited with many of the successful Gerber designs of the 1970s. In 1979, he determined to have knives of his design produced with his own trademark and the company Al Mar Knives was formed.

Not unlike most of the knives that are collected today, Mar knives were made for using and not necessarily for collecting. Before long, his products earned an excellent reputation for quality of design, materials and workmanship. Each knife was designed by Mar and manufactured to his rigid specifications by Sakai Cutlery, a respected knife maker of Japan's Seki City cutlery center. Several of the earlier Mar series were manufactured in relatively low quantities and are becoming of increasing interest to collectors. More recent additions to the AMK line, such as the earlier S.E.R.E. knives, are of significance as trend-setting examples of modern cutlery.

For dating information, the first 5,000 of each utility series knife was marked with the Al Mar name and logo and the blade tangs were stamped USA/SEKI, JAPAN. The stamping was later changed to SEKI JAPAN. A fixed-blade model, the Fang I, was first produced (3,000 knives) with tapered tangs. Knives of all models made afterwards have nontapered tangs.

MARBLE ARMS AND MANUFACTURING COMPANY

Born in 1854, Webster L. Marble grew up learning hunting, fishing and trapping skills. During his early adult life, Marble worked as a timber surveyor and cruiser. These experiences may not have been important except for the effect they would have upon the knives we used and trusted years ago, knives that have become highly regarded collectibles today. Marble recognized certain needs and used his talents to fill them. His earliest contributions were the waterproof match box and safety pocket axe. Marble made these items part-time until 1898, when he built a sixty-four square-foot building for his growing business.

Operating as W. L. Marble, Gladstone, Michigan, he started full-time manufacturing and national advertising in 1899. That year, he was joined in the business by a partner, Frank H. Van Cleve. A move was made into a 9,000-square-foot building and, in 1902, the company name was changed to The Marble Safety Axe Company.

Marble's first knife was introduced in 1900. Named "The Ideal," this knife became the basic model from which later models were developed. Other sheath knives, such as the "Dall DeWeese" and "Woodcraft" models, furthered a quality image for the company. The Marble's Safety Hunting Knife, patented in 1902 and introduced in 1903, was deserving of the success it achieved. Combining features of the safety axe with a quality hunting or sporting blade, this knife is one of today's choice collectibles. For about a five-year period, beginning in 1903, the company marketed a line of contract-made pocketknives marked "M.S.A. Co./Gladstone/Mich USA." These knives, also of high quality, were made for Marbles by Case Brothers and some advertisements show knives with "XX" on the blade. Possibly a few models were of German manufacture. All are extremely rare, and counterfeits far outnumber originals. Beware!

In 1911, the company name changed again, this time to The Marble Arms and Manufacturing Company, and another move was made into even larger quarters. Marble's knives were so respected that they were used by Teddy Roosevelt, the Perry Arctic Expedition and the Smithsonian Institute expeditions. It was about this time that the knife tang stamping changed to "Marbles/Gladstone/Mich USA."

Many of Marble's patents expired during the 1920s and other manufacturers began to capitalize upon his designs. Their quality was usually lower, but so were their prices and the competition began to take its toll on the Marble's company. His company's business was still quite good when Webster Marble died in 1930. By the end of World War II, however, Marble's sales volume and profits were declining. The axe and folding knife line was dropped during the war and sheath knife patterns were cut to four models. Manufacture of the axe line was revived in 1954 and remained in production for a few years. The company began adding new sheath knife patterns, such as the "Sportsman," in 1954 and the number of models or variations grew to ten during the mid-1960s. The year 1979 saw the end of the company's knife manufacturing.

Marble sheath and folding knives are listed by model, stampings and handle variations. Several are unique and rare and a good example of a highly prized Marble product is the Coquina Outfit sold during the company's early days. Named in honor of editor G. O. Shields (Coquina), the outfit's unique feature is its fancy sheath that holds two knives and a sharpening steel. The purchaser could choose the handle variations of an Ideal at a regular price ranging from $2.25 to $3.50, a Skinning model knife at $1.50 and a stag or leather handled steel at $1. With these purchases, the sheath was free; it was for sale without knives or steel at $1. Today, a Coquina Outfit in near-mint condition is valued over $5,000.

The astute collector should beware of fakes and be aware that some commemoratives or reproduction Marble knives have been made. In 1973, 500 pieces of a commemorative "Trailmaker" were made. During the 1980s and 1990s, a variety of knives manufactured by other firms were stamped with the Marble trademark. These included folding and fixed-blade knives in both modern and reproduction patterns. In 1997, the company, under new ownership, began offering some of the popular old-pattern knives.

Safety Hunting Knife

Designed in 1902, Marble's Safety Hunting Knife was the brainchild of a leatherworker at the Marble plant, Milton H. Rowland. Its long blade—relative to the shorter handle—made it an ideal sporting and using knife. The blade guard that extends over the blade's tip when closed serves as a safety lock when the blade is opened. Initially offered in three blade lengths (4$\frac{1}{2}$″, 5″ and 6″) and four handle materials ("engraved" hard rubber, stag, ivory and pearl), the knife was redesigned in 1913 and thenceforth available only with stag handles in two blade lengths. It was finally dropped from the line in 1941, as war began to loom. This knife is one of today's choice collectibles. There are approximately forty variations known to exist, many of which are extremely rare, and the astute collector should beware of fakes.

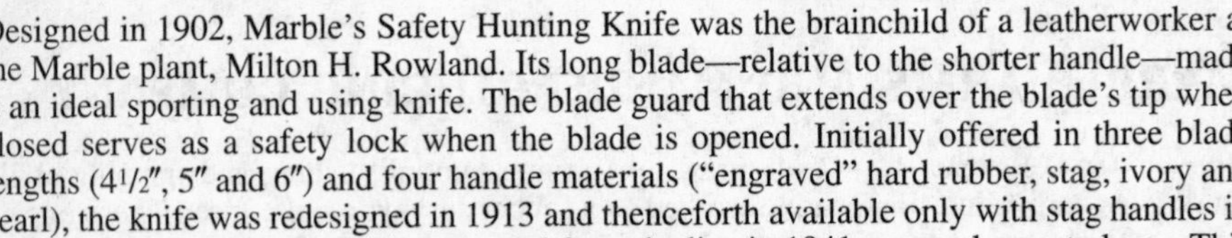

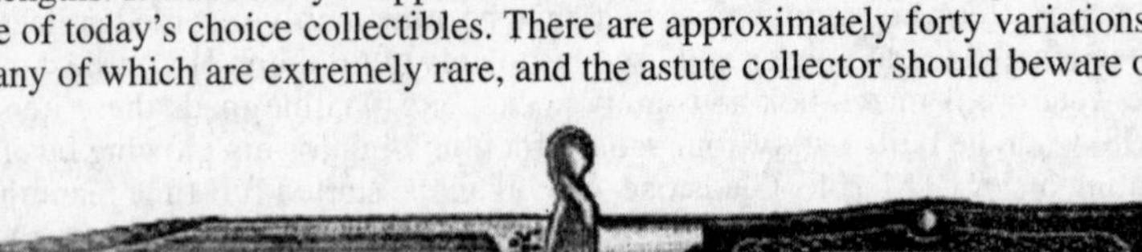

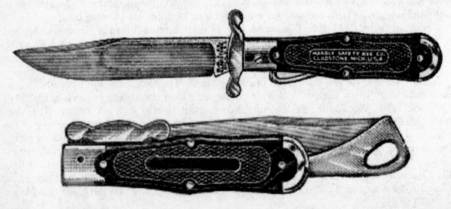

Stamping	Handle	Mint Price 4½"	5"	6"
MSA	Hard Rubber, "U" Bolster	1100	1500	2500
MSA	Stag, "U" Bolster	1600	2500	3500
MSA	Hard Rubber, Solid Bolster	1000	1400	2250
MSA	Stag, Solid Bolster	1600	2500	3500
MSA	Pearl or Ivory	2200	3000	5000
MARBLES	Stag, No Bottom Bolster	1100	1250	n/a
MARBLES	Stag	800	900	n/a

Ideal Hunting Knife

The first of Marble's sheath knife models, the Ideal was produced from 1900 to 1977. During this period, the knife was manufactured in five blade sizes, two guard types (full- and half-guard) and four handle types. Since guard types make little or no difference in value, they are not indicated in the listing below.

Stamping	Handle	Mint Price 4½", 5" or 6"	7"	8"
W.L. MARBLE	Leather/Stag butt	3000	n/a	n/a
MSA	Leather/Stag butt (5" & 6" only)	500	900	1200
MSA	Leather/Wood butt (5" & 6" only)	500	850	1100
MSA	Stag/Stag butt (5" & 6" only)	700	1600	2500
MSA	Hard Rubber (6" only)	2500	n/a	n/a
MARBLES	Leather/Stag butt	350	600	750
MARBLES	Leather/Aluminum butt	135	325	425
MARBLES	Leather/Bakelite butt	150	350	450
MARBLES	Stag/Stag butt (4-pin)	400	1000	1500
MARBLES	Stag/Stag butt (no pin)	350	850	1350
MARBLES	Stag/Aluminum butt (4-pin)	300	850	1200
MARBLES	Round Stag/Aluminum butt	225	400	n/a
MARBLES	Wood/Aluminum butt	150	250	n/a
MARBLES	Leather/Hex butt (Longhorn)	250	375	n/a
MARBLES	Round Stag/Hex butt (Longhorn)	350	450	n/a

Canoe Knife

Similar to the 4½" blade Ideal, the Canoe Knife was made from 1904 to 1923. Described in Marble's catalog as "short and stout," the blade has a dropped point and is 4" to 4½" in length. It was only available with the brass half-guard but in both leather and stag handle styles. Because many knives presented as Canoes are actually shortened 5" Ideals, beginning collectors are advised to have any Canoe verified by a Marble knives expert.

Stamping	Handle	Mint Price
MSA	Leather/Stag butt	1500
MSA	Leather/Wood butt	1400
MSA	Stag/Stag butt	2200
MARBLES	Leather/Stag butt	800
MARBLES	Leather/Aluminum butt	550

Stamping	*Handle*	*Mint Price*
MARBLES	Stag/Stag butt	1250
MARBLES	Stag/Aluminum butt	1100

Yacht Knife

Another variation or the Ideal model, the Yacht Knife featured a 5½″ spear point blade that was thinner and lighter than the Ideal blade. Both handle styles were available in this Marble's product manufactured circa 1904. The Yacht model is extremely rare, so verification by a Marble knives expert is recommended.

Stamping	*Handle*	*Mint Price*
MSA	Leather/Stag butt	2200
MSA	Stag/Stag butt	3000

Expert Hunting Knife

Made in two blade lengths, the Expert was designed for the professional hunter and trapper. The clip type blade has a thin, keen edge and a false edge on the clip. Introduced about 1906, the pre-1915 models have no guard; knives made after have a half-guard.

Stamping	*Handle*	*Mint Price* 5″	6″
MSA	Wood/Wood butt	800	1500
MSA	Wood/Stag butt	850	1600
MARBLES	Wood/Stag butt	600	n/a
MARBLES	Leather/Aluminum butt	130	n/a
MARBLES	Leather/Bakelite butt	130	n/a
MARBLES	Wood/Aluminum butt	140	n/a
MARBLES	Round Stag/Aluminum butt	275	n/a
MARBLES	Leather/Hex butt	175	n/a
MARBLES	Round Stag/Hex butt	300	n/a

Woodcraft

A very popular sheath knife, this model was introduced in 1915 and continued in production until 1975. Its 4½″ blade is its distinctive feature. Upswept with a thick back and tapering cutting edge, the design gives the blade more width and strength and makes it an all-purpose knife. The blade back is knurled for thumb grip.

Stamping	*Handle*	*Mint Price*
MARBLES	Leather/Stag butt, "Pat. Pend"	550
MARBLES	Stag/Stag "Pat. Pend"	1000

Stamping	*Handle*	*Mint Price*
MARBLES	Leather/Stag butt, "Pat'd 1916"	350
MARBLES	Leather/Aluminum butt	140
MARBLES	Leather/Bakelite butt	150
MARBLES	Stag/Stag butt (4-pin)	400
MARBLES	Stag/Stag butt (no pin)	350
MARBLES	Stag/Aluminum butt (4-pin)	350
MARBLES	Round Stag/Aluminum butt	260
MARBLES	Leather/Aluminum butt, "Official Boy Scout"	550
MARBLES	Leather/Aluminum butt, "Buster Brown"	425
MARBLES	Leather/Hex butt (Maverick)	210
MARBLES	Stag/Hex butt (Maverick)	350

Haines Hunting Knife

The Haines Model Hunting Knife was designed by Ashley A. Haines as a skinning, hunting and camping knife. A full tang design, the knife has bone stag handle scales and was made with and without guard. The thick and heavy 6″ blade has a "bowie hunter" pronounced clip point. Made from about 1909 to 1916.

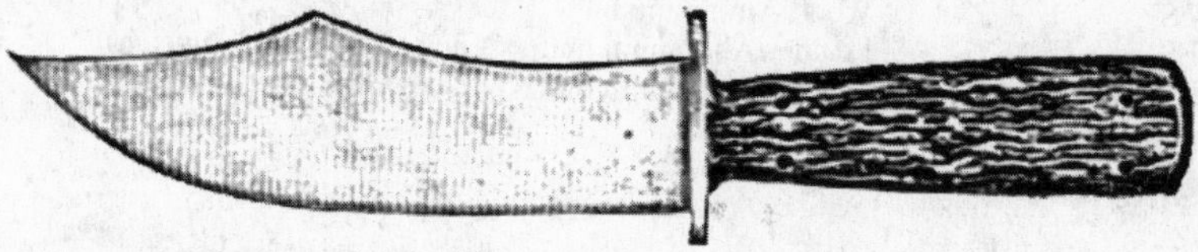

Stamping	*Handle*	*Mint Price*
MSA	Stag	2250

Dall DeWeese Model

Designed by Dall DeWeese, a widely known game hunter during the early part of the 20th century, the knife is short but sturdily constructed. The 4″-long blade is wide and its top edge has dull saw-type notches for placement of the thumb during heavy-duty skinning use. The knife is a full tang design, with handle scales of stag or wood, and has no guard. Made from 1902 to 1929.

Stamping	*Handle*	*Mint Price*
MSA	Stag	2000
MSA	Wood	2200
MARBLES	Stag	850

Special Hunting Knife

This early model, cataloged as No. 57, has a 5″ blade and a full tang design. Its handle is guardless but designed to allow a firm grip. Handle slabs are of stag. Made from around 1904 to 1915.

Stamping	Handle	Mint Price
MSA	Stag	3000

Sport Knife

Introduced in 1929, this knife was much like the Expert but with a 4″ blade. During the 1930s, the Sport was used as the official Boy Scout and Girl Scout Knives, with these special production knives marked with the appropriate emblem on both the blade and the sheath. Production continued until 1977.

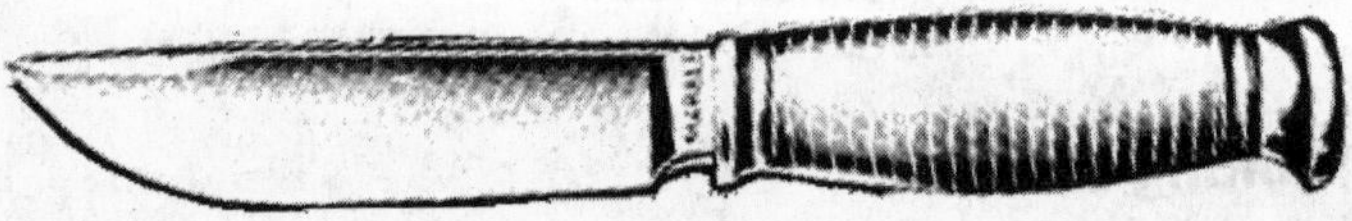

Stamping	Handle	Mint Price
MARBLES	Leather/Bakelite butt	145
MARBLES	Leather/Aluminum butt	130
MARBLES	Stag/Stag butt	450
MARBLES	Wood/Aluminum butt	110
MARBLES	Leather/Aluminum butt, "Official Boy Scout" (w/etch)	650
MARBLES	Leather/Aluminum butt, "Official Girl Scout" (w/etch)	550

Sportsman

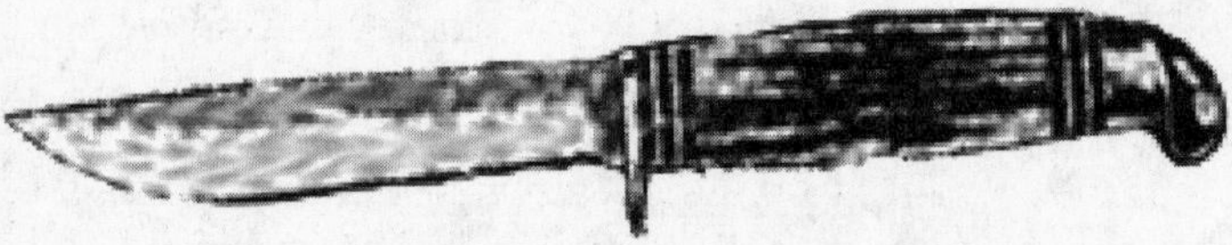

Stamping	Handle	Mint Price
MARBLES	Leather/Aluminum butt	100
MARBLES	Wood/Aluminum butt	90
MARBLES	Stag/Aluminum butt	250

Skinning Knife

Early knife featuring a thin blade varying from 4½″ to 5″ with upswept blunted point. Full tang design without guard but with notch for index finger grip. Made from 1904 to 1909.

Stamping	Handle	Mint Price
MSA	Stag	1500
MSA	Wood	1600

Trailmaker

The largest of Marble's sheath knives, the Trailmaker featured a 10″ clip blade and half-guard. The bowie-type knife was made from 1909 until 1959 and is today a collector's prize.

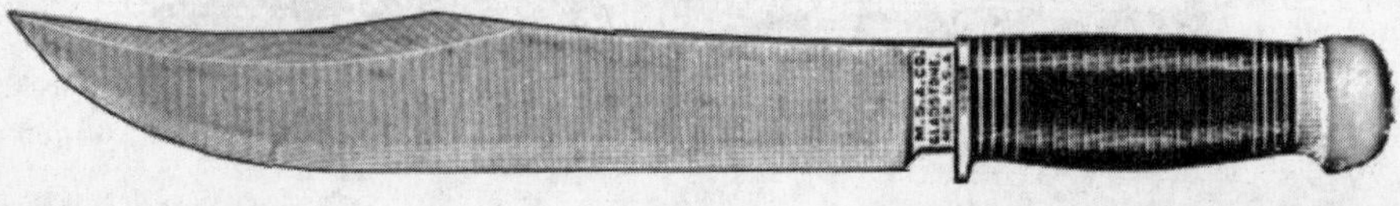

Stamping	*Handle*	*Mint Price*
MSA	Leather/Stag butt	3000
MARBLES	Leather/Stag butt	1100
MARBLES	Leather/Aluminum butt	800
MARBLES	Stag/Stag butt (beware of fakes)	1500

Safety Folding Fish Knife

Unlike the other Marble's knives called a "safety" knife, this model has its 4″ blade completely contained within the nickel silver handle when closed. The blade has an upswept clip point that is sharpened on top and scaler-type knurling on the blade back. Made from 1906 to 1942.

Stamping	*Handle*	*Mint Price*
MSA (marked on blade)	Embossed nickel silver	450
MARBLES (marked on blade)	Embossed nickel silver	250

Camp Carver

This kitchen-type knife was produced from 1904 until 1909. It was a large knife with an 8″ blade but so light in weight that it was not well accepted. Handles were full tang design with either stag or wood slabs attached with pins.

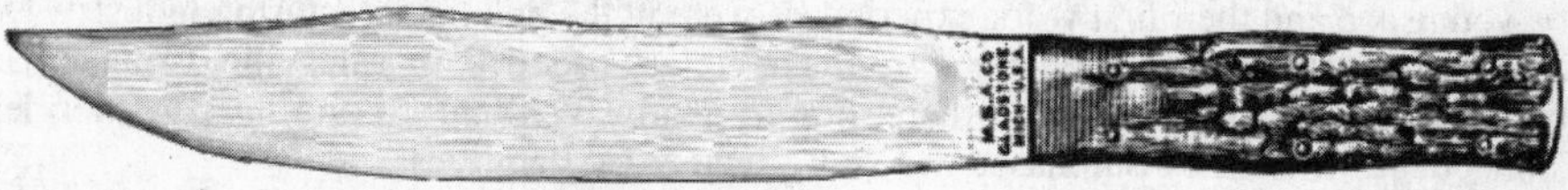

Stamping	*Handle*	*Mint Price*
MSA	Stag	2500
MSA	Wood	2500

Safety Carver

This unique folding knife has a blade 8″ long but the folded knife measures only a fraction of an inch more than that. One-half of the two-section nickel silver handle folds within the other half when the blade is opened, making it as strong and rigid as a regular fixed blade knife. Made from 1906 to 1914.

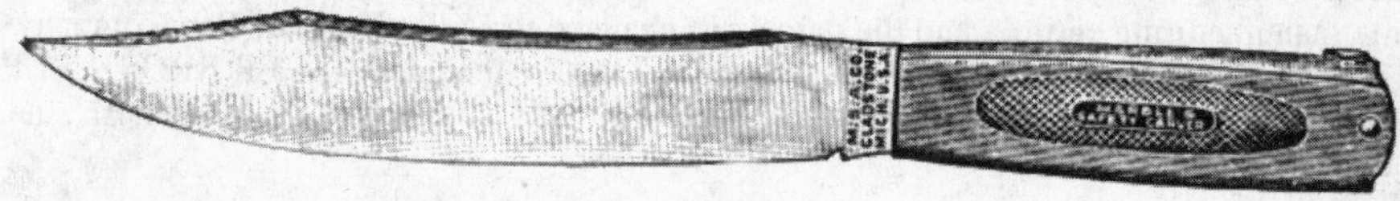

Stamping	*Handle*	*Mint Price*
MSA	Embossed nickel silver	900

Pilot's Survival Knifer

This knife, which was called the Survival model in its commercial version, was first developed in 1959 as the U.S. Navy Jet Pilot's Knife. It has a 6″ blade and is based on the Ideal blade design except that it also has a saw-tooth back. The military-issue version has blued blade and steel guard. The commercial version has a polished blade and a brass guard. Stamping is "Marbles/Gladstone/Mich/USA."

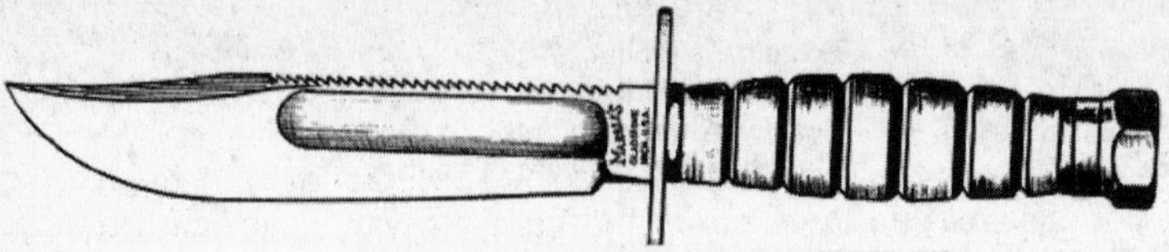

Stamping	*Handle*	*Mint Price*
Military	Leather washer w/hex steel butt	1000
Commercial	Leather washer w/hex steel butt	350

MERIDEN CUTLERY COMPANY

The origin of this Meriden, Connecticut, company can be traced to a table cutlery manufacturing company started in 1832 by David Ropes. When Ropes was joined by new business partners, the company became Platt, Ropes, Webb and Company. In 1855, the company was incorporated as the Meriden Cutlery Company. Although primary manufacture was in table cutlery, some smaller knife patterns such as lobster penknives and watch fob knives can be found with the company's stamping. Meriden Cutlery became a part of Landers, Frary & Clark in 1918.

MILLER BROTHERS CUTLERY COMPANY

The Miller brothers, William H. and George W., were toolmaker and gunsmith apprentices at a young age and their first work experiences were in the gun manufacturing industry. Desiring their own business, they began to make cutlery products in Yalesville, Connecticut, about 1863. They soon relocated their shop to nearby Wallingford and later to Meriden, Connecticut, where they purchased the Pratt, Read & Co. facilities.

The larger factory enabled the Miller Brothers' company to expand its knife line and to make knives under contract for a number of other firms as well as the government. Its knives were of very high quality and a good number of its patterns featured handles attached with small brass screws rather than pins—a feature unique to Miller Brothers manufacture. The brothers and their employees were indeed innovative and their contributions to the knife industry include methods and machinery to stamp knife parts and methods to manufacture bolsters.

In spite of the high quality of its knives and its innovative methods, the company failed in 1878. It was reorganized with William Rockwell serving as general manager and continued to use the Miller Brothers company name. The firm sold its cutlery division in 1917 to Meriden Knife Company, favoring the business of steel pen manufacture. In 1926, it ceased knife manufacturing entirely and the name was changed to Miller Brothers Pen Company.

Stampings used during the years of cutlery manufacture include MILLER BROS. CELEBRATED CUTLERY, MILLER BROS., MILLER BROS. CUT. CO. MERIDEN, and MILLER BROS. U.S.A.

NAPANOCH KNIFE COMPANY

A knife manufacturing company was formed in 1900 when the brothers Irving and William Carmen joined with William Hoornbeek in leasing the DuVall Rake Manufactory in Napanoch, New York. Using water as a power source and employing between fifteen and twenty-five craftsmen, the factory produced knives of exceptionally good quality. The company was renamed to Napanoch Knife Company in 1905 and was incorporated in 1909.

In addition to knives branded "Napanoch," the company made knives on contract for other companies such as Wilbert Cutlery Co., Ulery, Keene Cutlery Co. and Hibbard, Spencer & Bartlett.

The corporation was sold to Winchester Repeating Arms Company in 1919, about the same time that Winchester acquired the Eagle knife manufacturing facilities. Some of the skilled craftsmen were transferred by Winchester to the Eagle factory and the brand Napanoch was continued for two or three years on knives produced in that factory.

The factory in Napanoch was purchased from Winchester in 1921 by four former employees and it again manufactured knives, this time stamped "Honk Falls Knife Company," from 1921 until it burned in 1929.

In 1931, the Napanoch trademark was revived when John Cushner converted an old barn into a knife shop near his Napanoch, New York, home. These knives, stamped "Napanoch Knife Co., Napanoch, New York U.S.A." were made until his death in 1938.

NEW YORK KNIFE COMPANY

This manufacturer of some of the finest quality pocketknives ever made in America was founded in 1852. The New York Knife Company was started by a group of English cutlers who had previously worked for the Waterville Company in Waterbury, Connecticut. It began making knives in the town of Matteawan and operated there until 1856, using the stamping "New York Knife Co. Matteawan."

The town of Walden, New York, was just across the Hudson River and Walden's town fathers offered factory facilities as inducement for the company to move there. The company's management accepted the offer and, when the move was made, the entire populace of Walden reportedly turned out with their wagons and horses to assist. The company's president at the time of this move was Thomas W. Bradley and, under his management, the New York Knife Company had become the nation's largest knife manufacturer by the time of his death in 1879.

In 1878, the company adopted as a trademark the picture of a muscular arm with sleeves rolled up and the hand holding a hammer. Four years later, the words "Hammer Brand" were added to the pictorial logo. From that time, most of the company's pocketknives had the trademark etched on the blades and some knives will be found with tangs stamped with both the company name and the trademark. In addition to the high-quality knives marketed with the "New York Knife Co. Walden N.Y." stamping and the Hammer Brand trademark, the company made a less expensive and lower quality knife under the name of Walkill River Works, beginning about 1928. In 1931, New York Knife Company went out of business.

Collectors should be aware that the Hammer Brand trademark was purchased in 1936 by Imperial Knife Company for use on its shell handled type knives. These knives will normally have patent numbers on a second blade, crimped bolsters and no "New York Knife Co." stamping. While the New York Knife Company's Hammer Brand knives are choice collectibles, these inexpensive knives are not as desirable to collectors.

NORTHFIELD KNIFE COMPANY

This company was formed when Samuel Mason, who had learned the cutlery trade working in the Sheffield factory of Joseph Mappin & Son, joined with several businessmen and lured a group of former Sheffield cutlers from their jobs in Waterville to Northfield, Connecticut, for the purpose of establishing a knife manufactory. The Northfield Knife Company was established in 1858 and made the first cast iron handled knives, patented by Mason in 1862.

Although the business prospered, Mason left the company in 1865 when ownership control passed to Franklin H. and John H. Catlin. Mason joined with Edward Binns in making knives at Rochester, Pennsylvania, in a company that would later become Beaver Falls Cutlery Company.

Northfield's success led the Catlin brothers to expand through the purchase of several of the area's smaller knife companies. American Knife Company of Plymouth Hollow (Thomaston), Connecticut, was purchased in 1865 and the Excelsior Knife Company of Torrington, Connecticut, was purchased in 1884.

In 1872, Charles N. Platts (see Cattaraugus) became plant superintendent and continued in that capacity until 1896. Platts's sons worked at the Northfield company and gained there the early cutlery experiences that would influence much of America's cutlery industry. Platts and other Sheffield-trained cutlery provided the leadership and expertise for the company to produce an excellent grade of knives. The trademark UN-X-LD, meaning unexcelled, was adopted in 1876. The company's exhibit at the 1901 Pan American Exposition displayed over a thousand different knife styles.

The Northfield Knife Company was sold to Clark Brothers Cutlery of St. Louis, Missouri, in 1919. The new owner dropped the Northfield name and stamped the knives made in the Northfield factory with their own logo. The company was declared bankrupt in 1929.

PAL CUTLERY COMPANY

Pal was first a trademark of Utica Knife and Razor Company of Utica, New York, for knives made in Germany. Stampings used during the 1924–1939 period were PAL and PAL BRAND, and both included "Germany." The Pal Blade Company of Chicago, Illinois, was started in 1934 by Otto E. Kraus. The two firms joined together in 1935 as Pal Blade Company and opened manufacturing facilities in Plattsburg, New York. The company's knife stampings during the 1934–1953 period were PAL BLADE CO. MADE IN USA and PAL CUTLERY CO. MADE IN USA.

Near 1940, Pal purchased the cutlery division of Remington Arms Co. and its purchase included Remington's stock of knives and knife parts as well as the factory in Holyoak, Massachusetts. Some knives made by Pal near this time may have blades stamped with both Pal and Remington markings. One may find a "Pal" knife with at least one Remington blade or a "Remington" knife with one or more Pal blades. These transition knives represented expediency and production economy and should not be considered counterfeits.

Pal's knife production, prior to the Remington purchase, had been primarily pocketknives. Afterwards, the company was a prolific manufacturer of fixed blade or hunting knives, made in styles identical to the Remingtons of earlier years. The company produced these knives under several government contracts during World War II. In 1953, Pal ceased production of knives.

PARKER CUTLERY COMPANY

Several company and brand names have been initiate by and associated with James F. Parker, the founder of this company. During the 1960s when his primary employment was as a sales representative for a major paint manufacturer, Parker conducted a sideline business of buying and selling knives. In addition to his activity within the gun and knife show circuit, Parker was one of the first to effectively utilize direct mail for selling and buying antique or collectible knives. In 1970, Parker Distributing Company was formed with headquarters in Chattanooga, Tennessee.

Parker began to import knives from Japan using the company name as well as EAGLE BRAND or the logo of an eagle with wide-spread wings for tang stampings. In 1976, the Parker-Frost Cutlery Company was formed as a partnership with James F. Frost and the PARKER-FROST CUTLERY CO. (Eagle logo) brand stamp was used. In addition to knives made in Japan, the company marketed several commemorative issues and individual knives made by manufacturers such as Schrade and Rodgers-Wostenholm. The partnership was dissolved in 1978, but some knives that had already been ordered prior to that time were marketed for a short while afterwards. Parker Cutlery Company concentrated its efforts upon promotion of the EAGLE BRAND knives, stamped with the Parker company name and logo.

In addition to the above named companies and stampings, Parker has been responsible for the formation of several other companies and brand stampings. In 1978, PARKER BROTHERS (Eagle logo) CHATTANOOGA, TN knives were introduced and about three dozen different models were sold for a short while under the partnership of the brothers James and

Mack Parker. PARKER & SON (Eagle logo) CHATTANOOGA, TN was used on a limited number of knives handled in stag and second-cut stag from 1982 to about 1985.

In 1982, Parker invested in the Japanese cutlery manufacturer Imai. The Imai factory was enlarged and new quality control measures were instituted, giving birth to the PARKER-IMAI stamping which replaced the Parker Brother's stamping on most patterns. This stamping was discontinued in 1984 when most of the stag handled knives were no longer manufactured.

In 1984, Parker Cutlery purchased Rodgers Wostenholm USA Ltd., including its inventory and the right to use the IX*L Trademark for a period of twelve years. Subsequently, high-quality benchmade pocket folders with the I*XL trademark were produced. Knives of this special series were handled in mother-of-pearl, black pearl, abalone, buffalo horn and stag. Except for 1,200 butterfly knives, these patterns were limited to 300 knives each.

In 1984, Parker Cutlery contracted with Fain Edwards Ironworks to produce Damascus steel for 30,000 folders handled in stag. Edwards, a bladesmith and knife maker, had begun producing Damascus steel in sufficient quantities to commercially make Damascus knives. Edwards and Parker formed a corporation, the Parker-Edwards Cutlery Co. Inc., in 1985. The company, located in Jacksonville, Alabama, was formed to manufacture Damascus folders and hunting knives, as well as pocketknives and sporting knives made from 440C steel. In 1986, Parker became the sole owner of the company through the purchase of Edwards's stock. Because a supply of knife blades had already been produced, the PARKER-EDWARDS stamp was used on some knives made during the next two years. These knives, along with those from earlier years stamped PARKER-FROST, are becoming of greater interest to collectors.

With total ownership of the Jacksonville factory, manufacture of a number of Parker Cutlery Company knives was moved to that location and the stamping, PARKER U.S.A., had been used.

During recent years, James F. Parker and the companies which he has started or acquired have had a significant impact upon the cutlery industry. In 1987, Parker purchased Cutlery World, the nation's largest retail cutlery chain. With stores located in major shopping malls in most parts of the country, Cutlery World offered a wide line of both using and collectible knives. Perhaps the most significant of Parker's acquisitions was accomplished in January 1989 with the purchase of W. R. Case & Sons Cutlery Company.

Parker Cutlery Company and other of Parker's knife-related companies or holdings were affected by the March 1990 bankruptcy of James Parker and his knife companies.

PLATTS

C. Platts & Sons Cutlery Company

Charles Platts began his apprenticeship as a cutler in Sheffield, England, in 1854 when he was fourteen years old. Before immigrating to the United States in 1864, he worked at both Joseph Rodgers and George Wostenholm cutlery factories. Shortly after his arrival, he began working for the American Cutlery Company in Reynolds Bridge, Connecticut.

Platts became plant superintendent for Northfield Knife Company in 1872 and remained in that capacity until 1893, when he was hired as superintendent of Cattaraugus Cutlery Company. Charles Platts's son, Harlow Nixon (H. N.), was already employed by Cattaraugus and his other four sons joined him in the move to that company.

With five trained cutlers as sons, Platts conceived the idea of a family-owned business and, in 1896, they started the C. Platts & Sons Cutlery Company. Its first factory was in the Gowanda, New York, building that had been vacated when Schatt and Morgan had moved to Titusville, Pennsylvania. Knife stamping during this 1896–1897 period was C. PLATTS & SONS GOWANDA N.Y.

The company's business was very good and the manufacturing was moved to Eldred, Pennsylvania. In addition to knives stamped C. PLATTS & SONS ELDRED PA., the firm made knives on contract for other companies such as Case Brothers and W. R. Case & Son.

When Charles Platts died in 1900, his sons renamed the company C. Platts' Sons Cutlery Company and operated it until 1905.

Platts Brothers Cutlery Company

The Platts brothers, Charlie, Ray, Joe and Frank, had been employees and shareholders in the cutlery company started by their father in 1897. After their father's death in 1900, they had continued ownership along with their brother, H. N. Platts. After H. N. purchased his brothers' shares in the old company in 1905, and it was merged with W. R. Case & Son Cutlery, the other brothers began plans for their own cutlery company.

The stamping PLATTS BROS. UNION N.Y. likely dates from 1905 to 1907 and indicates that the brothers' began as a jobbing firm. Their own factory in Andover, New York, was started in 1907 and lasted only a few years. The stamping PLATTS BROS. ANDOVER N.Y. was used from around 1907 to 1909.

After the demise of the company, each of the brothers worked with a variety of cutlery companies, including Thomaston, Eureka, W. R. Case & Sons and Remington.

PUMA

Puma-Werk Lauterjung & Sohn of Solingen, Germany, is a cutlery manufacturer with a tenure of more than 200 years. In 1769, Johann Wilhelm Lauterjung received his first trademark from the Solingen Master Cutlers Guild. Along with his son, Johann Wilhelm II, a knife works was established on the bank of the Wupper River near Solingen. The shop produced knives, razors, tableware and shears, along with swords and daggers for military use. Ownership of the business was passed through several generations of the founder's descendants. In the mid-1800s, Nathanael Lauterjung, the founder's great-grandson, relocated the cutlery shop to Solingen, where it continued to prosper. In the early part of the 1900s, the succeeding generation of Eugen and Franz Lauterjung led the company in its boldest move: building a complete production factory and major expansion into the export market.

The Lauterjung business, which had become known as the Puma Werks, began to change after World War II. Renate Lauterjung von Frankenberg's husband, Baron Oswald von Frankenberg, became the first company chief executive not born in the Lauterjung family. His decision to concentrate in sporting knives brought a number of new products into production. Most noteworthy, at least in terms of the company's recognition in the United States, was the introduction of a knife of his design known as the Puma White Hunter. His experience as a hunter of all types of game, as well as his association with Germany's Forest Rangers, allowed for testing and evaluation of each product. The White Hunter was first imported into the United States by Kurt Gutmann, founder of Gutmann Cutlery, and it led the way for Puma's knives to become known for their quality and performance in the field.

Many other types of knives for the sportsman were developed. Herr von Frankenberg's experience as a renowned hunter along with his close association with the chief Forest Ranger of Germany assured the most severe and rugged testing for each product.

The Puma name and logo have been associated with not only fixed blade hunting knives, but quality pocketknives as well. The Puma line today consists of more than seventy-five regular models. In addition to older knives such as early White Hunters and Scale Knives (for fishermen), the company has produced several fine commemorative or limited edition series that attract serious collectors.

Dating the manufacture of Puma knives is no easy task, especially for those not intended for the export market. Puma did develop a control number coding system in 1964 that indicated not only the year, but also the quarter during which a knife was manufactured. Had the system not changed four times since, explanation may have been possible. The collector interested in Puma knives should not be discouraged, however, because information can be found. The company produced a chart in 1985 which explained the coding system as well as listed the years that Puma knife models had been exported to this country. The older knives in good condition have appreciated in value as have most of the special issues. If found, one of the 1985 charts will be extremely helpful and it may well be a collectible in itself.

QUEEN CUTLERY COMPANY

This well-known company was started shortly after World War I as a "moonlighting operation" of six foremen of the Schatt & Morgan factory. The story is that each foreman made and stole a few extra knife parts before ending his day's work. They then used the parts to assemble their own knives and sold them under the brand QUEEN CITY CUTLERY COMPANY. The operation of the six foremen officially became Queen City Cutlery about 1920 or 1921.

Schatt & Morgan's sales were depressed and management recognized that part of their problem was that the competing sales of Queen City's knives were made at their own expense. The disloyal foremen were fired but the loss of experienced supervisors added other problems. Schatt & Morgan went out of business around 1931 and the six Queen City founders pooled their savings to buy the old factory. They moved into it in 1932 and Queen knives are still made in that same factory today.

As members of the original six died, those remaining bought out their interests. Eventually, only two of the original families were in the business, the Mathews and the Ericsons. Soon after, Will Mathews and Ericson decided to make knife blades of 440C steel. At first, their knives were stamped QUEEN CITY until 1945, when it changed to "Q" or "Q" with a crown on top. Some of these knives were also stamped STAINLESS on the tang, but many consumers would not buy them because they considered stainless steel an inferior product for pocketknife blades. Consequently, the company discontinued use of the STAINLESS stamping and adopted QUEEN STEEL instead—the steel did not change.

QUEEN CITY
ABOUT 1922 TO 1945

Queen City
ABOUT 1935 TO 1945

QUEEN CUT. CO.
ABOUT 1945 TO 1948

QUEENCUTLERYCO TITUSVILLE, PA.
ABOUT 1945 TO 1948

ABOUT 1946 TO 1955

QUEEN
ABOUT 1946 TO 1950

QUEEN STAINLESS
ABOUT 1946 TO 1950

STAINLESS
ABOUT 1946 TO 1948

STAINLESS
ABOUT 1947 TO 1948

STAINLESS
ABOUT 1946 TO 1948

STAINLESS
ABOUT 1946 TO 1948

Queen STAINLESS
ABOUT 1946 TO 1949

STEEL
ABOUT 1948 TO 1955

Queen STEEL
ABOUT 1949 TO 1955

1922 1972
USED 1972 ONLY

Queen
ABOUT 1973 TO 1975

76
USED 1976 ONLY

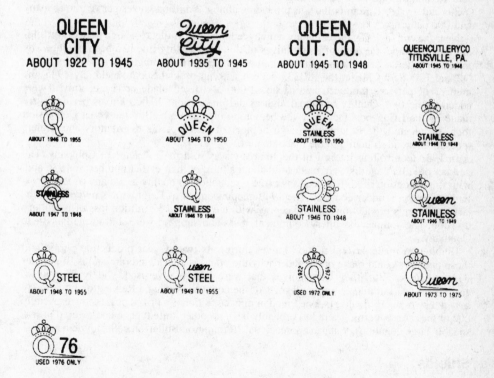

During the early 1960s, the company discontinued stamping of blade tangs in favor of etching QUEEN STEEL on the master blade. In 1971, using old dies, the company again began stamping its knives on the tang and a new stamping was used: a crown and the word QUEEN (with the long pointed tail of the "Q" extending the length of the word). In 1976 and 1977, the stamping became a large "Q" with a crown on top, the long tail, and the numbers 76 or 77 over the tail. Queen Cutlery was sold to Servotronics, Inc., in 1969 and continues to make knives.

REMINGTON

The company that began manufacturing knives branded "Remington" in 1920 started about a century before when Eliphalet Remington forged his first gun barrel. Shortly thereafter, Union Metallic Cartridge Company was founded by Marcellus Hartley. After the death of Remington, the two businesses came together through Hartley's purchase of the firearm company. Years later, Marcellus Hartley Dodge became chief executive of the two companies and consolidated them under the name of the Remington Union Metallic Cartridge Company. The cartridge company was the smaller of the two entities and the Remington trademark had far greater recognition, so the UMCC portion of the name was dropped. But, it was not forgotten. Knife collectors today will find the initials "UMC" stamped along with the name "Remington" on knives and sportsmen will find the "U" stamped on rim fire cartridges made by the company.

Remington prospered during the early part of the 20th century but, at the end of World War I, found itself with extensive manufacturing facilities and without government contracts to keep busy. The relatively new Bridgeport, Connecticut, factory was near idle and management knew that cutlery manufacture was not an entirely new endeavor since Remington had made a large number of bayonets, beginning about 1915. A decision was made to enter the cutlery field and Remington's first pocketknives (R-103) were made in February 1920.

The manufacture of pocketknives got quickly underway and, by 1921, over 2,000 dealers sold Remington knives in most parts of the country. Further expansion came during the 1920s and, by 1931, Remington was producing almost 3 million knives per year in as many as 1,000 patterns.

Near the end of 1922, the company announced the first "Bullets"—large trappers or folding hunters—and a dozen different knives of this high-quality line had been produced by the end of the decade. Further success came in 1923 with Remington's production of the Official Boy Scout Knife, the R-3333 pattern with an official Scout shield. By 1925, the number of patterns produced approached 1,000 and fixed blade or sheath knives were added to the line. Quality remained high as did production; 10,000 knives per day were made by the Bridgeport factory at the beginning of the 1930s. But, the Great Depression took its toll and the failure of a large number of Remington's distributors and dealers brought financial difficulty to the manufacturer.

In 1933, controlling interest in the company was sold to E. I. DuPont Company. The number of knife patterns were reduced to about a third of their earlier number by 1936 and, with this reduction in knife selections came a reduction in quality and many of those patterns were made under contract. The 1940 announcement of Remington's revival of military small arms production was in keeping with the rumored $2 million loss of its cutlery division. The company's cutlery equipment, parts and supplies were sold to the Pal Blade Company.

Remington made several million knives during its twenty-year production period and those numbers could make one wonder why the brand is considered rare and is so popular with collectors. But, they were knives that were highly advertised, widely distributed, easily sold and faithfully used in all parts of the country. Finding a Remington knife today may not be really difficult; but, one found in mint condition is a prized possession, especially one of the rarer patterns. There has probably been no other knife type, manufactured in reasonably large quantities, that can approach the "Remington Bullet" in collector demand.

Shields

Remington used a variety of handle shields, but the most recognized and desirable are knives with the replicated cartridge ("Bullet") or the acorn shield. Knives bearing the bullet shield are normally the larger folding hunter patterns and are recognized, respected and highly valued by collectors. The acorn shield was used by Remington on knives with a leather punch blade. A good rule of thumb in evaluating these knives is that a Remington knife with an acorn shield and without a punch blade should be subject to suspicion.

Pattern Numbers

Collectors are fortunate in that Remington stamped pattern numbers on most knives produced and several of the company's catalogs have been reprinted for reference use. The letter "R" before the pattern number indicates a pocketknife and the last digit indicates its handle material as follows:

1 = Redwood	6 = Genuine Stag
2 = Black Composition	7 = Imitation Ivory or White Bone
3 = Bone	8 = Cocobolo
4 = Pearl	9 = Metal
5 = Pyremite	0 = Buffalo Horn

Ch = after the numbers means a chain attached

Pattern numbers R1 through R2999 are jack knives; R3000 through R5999 are cattle, premium stock, farmers, mechanics and scout knives; and R6000 through R9000 are pen knives.

Stamping

Most Remington knife stampings are either the "Circle Remington" stamping or the "Straight line" stamping. As a general rule, the company's higher quality pocketknives will have the circle stamping and the straight line stamp will be found on those of lesser quality.

A variety of stampings were used by Remington but, primarily, they were REMINGTON in straight line script stamped horizontally on the tang or REMINGTON inside a circle in several variations as shown below.

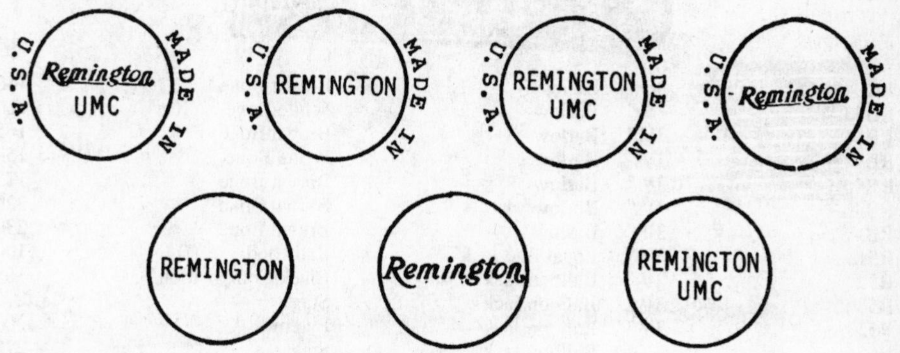

Pattern No.		*Description*	*Handle*	*Mint Price*
R1	3 3/8″	Speying Knife	Redwood	120
R2	3 3/8″	Regular Jack	Black Composition	125
R3	3 3/8″	Regular Jack	Bone	125
RA1	3 3/8″	Regular Jack	Redwood	115
RC5	3 3/8″	Regular Jack	Pyremite	110

Pattern No.	*Description*		*Handle*	*Mint Price*
RC6	$3^{3}/_{8}''$	Regular Jack	Genuine Stag	125
RC7	$3^{3}/_{8}''$	Regular Jack	Imitation Ivory	120
RC8	$3^{3}/_{8}''$	Regular Jack	Cocobolo	100
RC9	$3^{3}/_{8}''$	Regular Jack	Metal	95
R15	$3^{1}/_{4}''$	Leg Knife	Pyremite	350
R015	$3^{1}/_{4}''$	Leg Knife	Pyremite	250
R17	$2^{3}/_{4}''$	Ball Pull Opener	White Composition	175
R21	$3^{3}/_{8}''$	Regular Jack	Redwood	110
R21-CH	$3^{3}/_{8}''$	Boy's Jack	Redwood	150
R22	$3^{3}/_{8}''$	Regular Jack	Black Composition	120
R23	$3^{3}/_{8}''$	Regular Jack	Bone	125
R23-CH	$3^{3}/_{8}''$	Boy's Jack	Bone	150
R25	$3^{3}/_{8}''$	Regular Jack	White Pyremite	125
R31	$3^{3}/_{8}''$	Regular Jack	Redwood	120
R32	$3^{3}/_{8}''$	Regular Jack	Black Composition	110
R33-CH	$3^{3}/_{8}''$	Regular Jack	Bone	125
R35	$3^{3}/_{8}''$	Regular Jack	Pyremite	135
RB040	$3^{3}/_{8}''$	Barlow	Brown Bone	140

RB041	$3^{3}/_{8}''$	Barlow	Brown Bone	140
RB43-W	$3^{3}/_{8}''$	Barlow	White Bone	160
RB44	$3^{3}/_{8}''$	Barlow	Brown Bone	165
RB44-W	$3^{3}/_{8}''$	Barlow	White Bone	150
RB45	$3^{3}/_{8}''$	Barlow	Brown Bone	175
RB46	$3^{3}/_{8}''$	Barlow	Brown Bone	220
RB47	$3^{3}/_{8}''$	Barlow	Brown Bone	230
R51	$3^{1}/_{2}''$	Equal End Jack	Redwood	100
R52	$3^{3}/_{4}''$	Balloon Jack	Black Composition	165
R53	$3^{3}/_{4}''$	Balloon Jack	Stag	275
R55	$3^{3}/_{4}''$	Balloon Jack	Pyremite	200
R63	$3^{3}/_{4}''$	Balloon Jack	Stag	275
R65	$3^{3}/_{4}''$	Balloon Jack	Pyremite	200
R71	$3^{1}/_{8}''$	Regular Jack	Redwood	130
R72	$3^{1}/_{8}''$	Regular Jack	Black Composition	120
R73	$3^{1}/_{8}''$	Regular Jack	Bone	165
R75	$3^{1}/_{8}''$	Regular Jack	Pyremite	150
R81	$3^{1}/_{2}''$	Regular Jack	Redwood	110
R82	$3^{1}/_{2}''$	Regular Jack	Black Composition	110
R83	$3^{1}/_{2}''$	Regular Jack	Bone	140
R85	$3^{1}/_{2}''$	Regular Jack	Pyremite	125
RCO90	$3^{3}/_{8}''$	Barlow	Black Bone	135
RCO91	$3^{3}/_{8}''$	Barlow	Black Bone	135
R91	$3^{3}/_{8}''$	Regular Jack	Redwood	140
R92	$3^{3}/_{8}''$	Regular Jack	Black Composition	145
R93	$3^{3}/_{8}''$	Regular Jack	Stag	250
R95	$3^{3}/_{8}''$	Regular Jack	Pyremite	180
R103	$3^{1}/_{2}''$	Regular Jack	Bone	155
R103-CH	$3^{1}/_{2}''$	Boy's Jack	Bone	165
R105	$3^{3}/_{8}''$	Regular Jack	Black Composition	175
R105-A	$3^{3}/_{8}''$	Premium Stock	Onyx	180
R105-B	$3^{3}/_{8}''$	Premium Stock	Pyremite	165

Pattern No.		Description	Handle	Mint Price
R108-CH	3 3/8"	Boy's Jack	Cocobolo	140
R111	3 1/2"	Regular Jack	Redwood	120
R112	3 1/2"	Regular Jack	Black Composition	120
R113	3 1/2"	Regular Jack	Bone	160
R115	3 1/2"	Regular Jack	Pyremite	135
R122	3 1/2"	Regular Jack	Black Composition	140
R123	3 1/2"	Regular Jack	Bone	180
R125	3 1/2"	Regular Jack	Pyremite	160
R131	3 1/2"	Regular Jack	Redwood	140
R132	3 1/2"	Regular Jack	Black Composition	145
R133	3 1/2"	Regular Jack	Stag	250
R135	3 1/2"	Regular Jack	Pyremite	190
R141	3 1/4"	Regular Jack	Redwood	150
R142	3 1/4"	Regular Jack	Black Composition	135
R143	3 1/4"	Regular Jack	Bone	185
R145	3 1/4"	Regular Jack	Pyremite	175
R151	3 1/2"	Regular Jack	Redwood	185
R152	3 1/2"	Regular Jack	Black Composition	165
R153	3 1/2"	Regular Jack	Bone	215

R155	3 1/2"	Sleeveboard Jack	Pyremite	200
R161	3 1/2"	Regular Jack	Redwood	175
R162	3 1/2"	Regular Jack	Black Composition	180
R163	3 1/2"	Regular Jack	Bone	210
R165	3 1/2"	Regular Jack	Pyremite	200
R171	3 3/4"	Teardrop Jack	Redwood	175
R172	3 3/4"	Teardrop Jack	Black Composition	190
R173	3 3/4"	Teardrop Jack	Brown Bone	240
R175	3 3/4"	Teardrop Jack	Pyremite	200

R181	3 5/8"	Teardrop Jack	Redwood	175
R182	3 5/8"	Teardrop Jack	Black Composition	175
R183	3 5/8"	Teardrop Jack	Bone	250
R185	3 5/8"	Teardrop Jack	Pyremite	210
R191	3 5/8"	Teardrop Jack	Redwood	200
R192	3 5/8"	Teardrop Jack	Black Composition	200
R193	3 5/8"	Teardrop Jack	Bone	275
R195	3 5/8"	Teardrop Jack	Pyremite	210
R201	3 5/8"	Easy Open Teardrop Jack	Redwood	200
R202	3 5/8"	Easy Open Teardrop Jack	Black Composition	210
R203	3 5/8"	Easy Open Teardrop Jack	Brown Bone	270

Pattern No.		Description	Handle	Mint Price
R205	3 5/8"	Easy Open Teardrop Jack	Pyremite	240

R211	3 5/8"	Easy Open Teardrop Jack	Redwood	175
R212	3 5/8"	Easy Open Jack	Black Composition	185
R213	3 5/8"	Easy Open Jack	Bone	225
R219	3 5/8"	Easy Open	Brass	190
R222	3 5/8"	Teardrop Jack	Black Composition	175
R223	3 5/8"	Teardrop Jack	Bone	220
R225	3 5/8"	Teardrop Jack	Pyremite	180
R228	3 5/8"	Teardrop Jack	Cocobolo	175
R232	3 5/8"	Teardrop Jack	Black Composition	160
R233	3 5/8"	Teardrop Jack	Bone	225
R235	3 5/8"	Teardrop Jack	Pyremite	180
R238	3 5/8"	Teardrop Jack	Cocobolo	160
R242	3 5/8"	Easy Open Jack	Black Composition	190
R243	3 5/8"	Easy Open Jack	Bone	225
R245	3 5/8"	Easy Open Jack	Pyremite	210
R248	3 5/8"	Easy Open Jack	Cocobolo	185
R252	3 5/8"	Teardrop Jack	Black Composition	180
R253	3 5/8"	Teardrop Jack	Bone	220
R255	3 5/8"	Teardrop Jack	Pyremite	210
R258	3 5/8"	Teardrop Jack	Cocobolo	180
R262	4"	Texas Jack	Black Composition	220
R263	4"	Texas Jack	Bone	250
R265	4"	Texas Jack	Pyremite	225
R272	4"	Texas Jack	Black Composition	200
R273	4"	Texas Jack	Brown Bone	270
R275	4"	Texas Jack	Pyremite	250
R282	3 3/4"	Serpentine Jack	Black Composition	210
R283	3 3/4"	Serpentine Jack	Bone	240
R293	5 1/4"	"Hunter-Trader-Trapper"	Brown Bone	4250
R303	3 3/4"	Slim Trapper	Bone	300

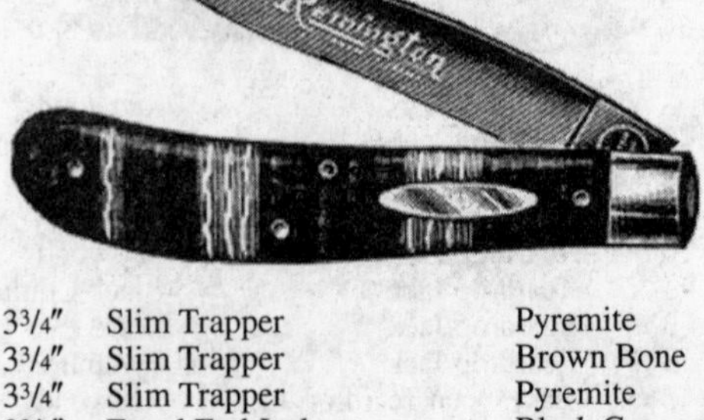

R305	3 3/4"	Slim Trapper	Pyremite	265
R313	3 3/4"	Slim Trapper	Brown Bone	350
R315	3 3/4"	Slim Trapper	Pyremite	325
R322	3 3/4"	Equal End Jack	Black Composition	210
R323	3 3/4"	Equal End Jack	Bone	275

Pattern No.		*Description*	*Handle*	*Mint Price*
R325	3 3/4″	Equal End Jack	Pyremite	225
R328	3 3/4″	Equal End Jack	Cocobolo	210
R333	3 3/4″	Equal End Jack	Bone	250
R341	3 3/4″	Equal End Jack	Redwood	225
R342	3 3/4″	Equal End Jack	Black Composition	225
R343	3 3/4″	Equal End Jack	Bone	325
R352	3 3/4″	Equal End Jack	Black Composition	225
R353	3 3/4″	Equal End Jack	Bone	275
R355	3 3/4″	Equal End Jack	Pyremite	235
R358	3 3/4″	Equal End Jack	Cocobolo	210
R363	3 3/4″	Equal End Jack	Bone	270
R365-G	3 3/4″	Equal End Jack	Pyremite	235
R372	3 3/4″	Equal End Jack	Black Composition	220
R373	3 3/4″	Equal End Jack	Bone	270
R375	3 3/4″	Equal End Jack	Pyremite	235
R378	3 3/4″	Equal End Jack	Cocobolo	240
R383	3 3/4″	Equal End Jack	Bone	270
R391	3 3/8″	Teardrop Jack	Redwood	225
R392	3 3/8″	Teardrop Jack	Black Composition	225
R393	3 3/8″	Teardrop Jack	Bone	275
R395	3 1/2″	Teardrop Jack	Pyremite	250
R402	3 1/2″	Teardrop Jack	Black Composition	200
R403	3 1/2″	Teardrop Jack	Bone	275
R405	3 1/2″	Teardrop Jack	Pyremite	210
R410	3 1/2″	Teardrop Jack	Buffalo Horn	300
R412	3 1/2″	Easy Open Jack	Black Composition	185
R413	3 1/2″	Easy Open Jack	Bone	225
R415	3 1/2″	Easy Open Jack	Pyremite	215
R423	3 3/4″	Congress	Bone	325
R432	3 1/2″	Doctor's Knife	Black Composition	400

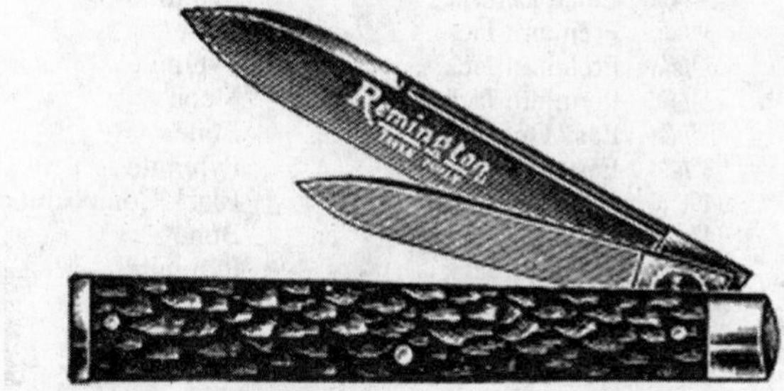

R433	3 1/2″	Doctor's Knife	Bone	600
R435	3 1/2″	Doctor's Knife	Pyremite	500
R443	3 1/2″	Doctor's Knife	Bone	600
R444	3 1/2″	Doctor's Knife	Pearl	850
R453	3 3/4″	Doctor's Knife	Bone	600
R455	3 3/4″	Doctor's Knife	Pyremite	575
R463	3 1/4″	Equal End Jack	Bone	220
R465	3 1/4″	Equal End Jack	Pyremite	220
R473	3 1/4″	Equal End Jack	Bone	275
R475	3 1/4″	Equal End Jack	Pyremite	250
R482	3 1/2″	Equal End Jack	Black Composition	190
R483	3 1/2″	Equal End Jack	Bone	240
R485	3 1/2″	Equal End Jack	Pyremite	220
R488	3 1/2″	Equal End Jack	Cocobolo	200
R493	3 1/2″	Equal End Jack	Bone	275
R495	3 1/2″	Equal End Jack	Pyremite	240
R503	3 1/2″	Equal End Jack	Bone	265
R505	3 1/2″	Equal End Jack	Pyremite	220
R512	3 1/2″	Equal End Jack	Black Composition	210
R513	3 1/2″	Equal End Jack	Bone	265

Pattern No.	Description		Handle	Mint Price
R515	3 1/2″	Equal End Jack	Pyremite	225
R523	3 1/2″	Equal End Jack	Bone	250
R525	3 3/4″	Equal End Jack	Pyremite	230
R551	3 1/4″	Equal End Jack	Redwood	160
R552	3 1/4″	Equal End Jack	Black Composition	155
R553	3 1/4″	Equal End Jack	Brown Bone	200
R555	3 1/4″	Equal End Jack	Candy Stripe	240
R563	3 1/4″	Easy Open Jack	Brown Bone	210
R565	3 3/8″	Easy Open Jack	R/W/B Composition	325
R572	3 1/4″	Equal End Jack	Black Composition	165
R573	3 1/4″	Equal End Jack	Stag	225
R575	3 1/4″	Equal End Jack	Pyremite	200
R583	3 1/4″	Equal End Jack	Bone	220
R585	3 1/4″	Equal End Jack	Pyremite	185
R590	3 1/4″	Equal End Jack	Buffalo Horn	275
R593	3 1/4″	Equal End Jack	Bone	265
R595	3 1/4″	Equal End Jack	Pyremite	260
R603	3 3/8″	Premium Jack	Bone	225
R605	3 3/8″	Premium Jack	Pyremite	200
R609	3 3/8″	Premium Jack	Metal	175
R613	3 5/8″	Easy Open Jack	Bone	235
R615	3 5/8″	Easy Open Jack	Pyremite	210
R622	4″	Premium Jack	Black Composition	220
R623	4″	Premium Jack	Bone	260
R625	4″	Premium Jack	Pyremite	250
R633	4″	Premium Jack	Bone	260
R635	4″	Premium Jack	Pyremite	225
R643	4″	Bowtie	Bone	325
R645	4″	Bowtie	Pyremite	275
R645-F2	4″	Bowtie Switch	Candy Stripe	1100
R653	4″	Bowtie	Black Composition	425

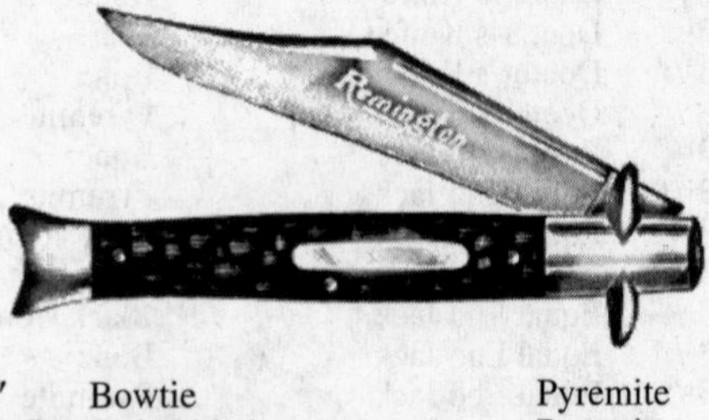

R655	4″	Bowtie	Pyremite	600
R655	3 7/8″	Switchblade	Pyremite	900
R662	3 5/8″	Jumbo Jack	Black Composition	325
R663	3 5/8″	Jumbo Jack	Bone	375
R668	3 5/8″	Jumbo Jack	Cocobolo	300
R672	3″	Dogleg Jack	Black Composition	175
R673	3″	Dogleg Jack	Bone	175
R674	3″	Dogleg Jack	Pearl	350

Pattern No.		*Description*	*Handle*	*Mint Price*
R675	3″	Dogleg Jack	Pyremite	190
R677	3″	Dogleg Jack	Imitation Ivory	220
R679	3″	Dogleg Jack	Metal	175
R682	3″	Gunstock Jack	Black Composition	350
R683	3″	Gunstock Jack	Brown Bone	425
R684	3″	Gunstock Jack	Pearl	575
R685	3″	Gunstock Jack	Pyremite	425
R693	4″	Pruning Knife	Bone	200
R698	4″	Pruning Knife	Cocobolo	150
R703	3$^5/_8$″	Pruning Knife	Bone	170
R706	3$^5/_8$″	Pruning Knife	Genuine Stag	200
R708	3$^5/_8$″	Pruning Knife	Cocobolo	150
R713	3$^3/_4$″	Pruning Knife	Bone	195
R718	3$^3/_4$″	Pruning Knife	Cocobolo	210

R723	4$^1/_2$″	Pruning Knife	Bone	300
R728	4$^1/_2$″	Pruning Knife	Cocobolo	200
R732	3$^1/_2$″	Regular Jack	Black Composition	175
R733	3$^1/_2$″	Regular Jack	Bone	225
R735	3$^1/_2$″	Regular Jack	Pyremite	200
R738	3$^1/_2$″	Regular Jack	Cocobolo	175
R743	3$^1/_2$″	Regular Jack	Bone	220
R745	3$^1/_2$″	Regular Jack	Pyremite	170
R753	3$^1/_2$″	Regular Jack	Bone	250
R755	3$^1/_2$″	Regular Jack	Pyremite	325
R756	3$^1/_2$″	Regular Jack	Genuine Stag	375
R763	3$^1/_2$″	Regular Jack	Bone	250
R772	3$^1/_2$″	Teardrop Jack	Black Composition	220
R773	3$^1/_2$″	Teardrop Jack	Bone	250
R775	3$^1/_2$″	Teardrop Jack	Pyremite	255
R783	3$^1/_2$″	Teardrop Jack	Bone	240
R793	3$^7/_8$″	Regular Jack	Bone	285
R803	3″	Premium Jack	Bone	200
R805	3$^7/_8$″	Premium Jack	Pyremite	175
R813	3$^1/_2$″	Regular Jack	Bone	325
R823	3$^5/_8$″	Premium Jack	Bone	240
R825	3$^5/_8$″	Premium Jack	Pyremite	220
R833	3$^5/_8$″	Premium Jack	Bone	375
R835	3$^5/_8$″	Premium Jack	Pyremite	350
R843	3$^5/_8$″	Premium Jack	Bone	240
R845	3$^5/_8$″	Premium Jack	Pyremite	240
R853	3$^5/_8$″	Premium Jack	Bone	240
R855	3$^5/_8$″	Premium Jack	Pyremite	220
R863	3$^7/_8$″	Equal End Jack	Bone	260
R865	3$^7/_8$″	Equal End Jack	Pyremite	240
R873	3$^1/_8$″	Sleeveboard Pen	Bone	180
R874	3$^1/_8$″	Sleeveboard Pen	Pearl	300
R875	3$^1/_8$″	Sleeveboard Pen	Pyremite	160
R881	3$^1/_2$″	Regular Jack	Redwood	200
R882	3$^1/_2$″	Regular Jack	Black Composition	240
R883	3$^1/_2$″	Regular Jack	Bone	260
R892	3$^1/_2$″	Easy Open Jack	Black Composition	230
R893	3$^1/_2$″	Easy Open Jack	Bone	240

Pattern No.		*Description*	*Handle*	*Mint Price*
R895	3 1/2"	Easy Open Jack	Pyremite	225
R901	3 1/2"	Regular Jack	Redwood	185
R913	3 3/4"	Equal End Jack	Bone	240
R921	4 1/8"	Maize Knife	Redwood	250
R932	5"	Toothpick	Black Composition	320
R933	5"	Toothpick	Bone	425
R935	5"	Toothpick	Pyremite	360
R942	5"	Toothpick	Black Composition	400
R943	5"	Toothpick	Bone	475
R945	5"	Toothpick	Pyremite	465
RC953	5"	Toothpick	Bone	425

R953	5"	Bullet Toothpick	Bone	850
R955	5"	Toothpick	Pyremite	350
R962	4 1/4"	Easy Open	Black Composition	270
R963	4 1/4"	Easy Open Scout	Imitation Bone	650
R965	4 1/4"	Easy Open	Pyremite	325
R971	4 1/8"	Cotton Sampler	Redwood	550
R982	2 7/8"	Dogleg Jack	Black Composition	210
R983	2 7/8"	Dogleg Jack	Bone	250
R985	2 7/8"	Dogleg Jack	Pyremite	225
R992	3 1/4"	Equal End Jack	Black Composition	150
R993	3 1/4"	Equal End Jack	Bone	175
R995	3 1/4"	Sleeveboard Jack	Blu/Wh Composition	185
R1002	3 5/8"	Regular Jack	Black Composition	210
R1003	3 5/8"	Regular Jack	Bone	240
R1005	3 5/8"	Regular Jack	Pyremite	220
R1012	3 5/8"	Equal End Jack	Black Composition	220
R1013	3 5/8"	Equal End Jack	Bone	240
R1022	4 1/4"	Equal End Jack	Black Composition	475
R1023	4 1/4"	Equal End Jack	Bone	550
R1032	3 3/8"	Equal End Jack	Black Composition	150
R1033	3 3/8"	Equal End Jack	Bone	175
R1035	3 3/8"	Equal End Jack	Pyremite	140
R1042	3 3/8"	Equal End Jack	Black Composition	175
R1043	3 3/8"	Equal End Jack	Bone	225
R1045	3 3/8"	Equal End Jack	Pyremite	200
R1051	3 1/2"	Regular Jack	Redwood	150
R1053	3 1/2"	Regular Jack	Bone	200
R1055	3 3/8"	Regular Jack	Pyremite	175
R1061	3 3/8"	Regular Jack	Redwood	125
R1062	3 3/8"	Regular Jack	Black Composition	140
R1063	3 3/8"	Regular Jack	Bone	175
R1065-W	3 3/8"	Regular Jack	Pyremite	160
R1071	3 3/8"	Regular Jack	Cocobolo	140
R1072	3 3/8"	Regular Jack	Black Composition	150
R1073	3 3/8"	Regular Jack	Bone	175
R1075	3 3/8"	Regular Jack	Pyremite	165

Pattern No.		*Description*	*Handle*	*Mint Price*
R1082	3 3/8″	Regular Jack	Black Composition	125
R1083	3 3/8″	Regular Jack	Bone	155
R1085	3 3/8″	Regular Jack	Pyremite	120
R1092	3 3/8″	Regular Jack	Black Composition	120
R1093	3 3/8″	Regular Jack	Bone	135
R1102	3 3/8″	Regular Jack	Black Composition	125
R1103	3 3/8″	Regular Jack	Brown Bone	200
R1112	3 3/8″	Regular Jack	Black Composition	125
R1113	3 3/8″	Regular Jack	Bone	170

R1123	4 1/2″	Bullet Trapper	Bone	2200
R1128	4 1/2″	Bullet Trapper	Cocobolo	3000
R1133	4 3/8″	Folding Hunter	Bone	300
R1143	4 3/8″	Folding Hunter	Bone	300
R1153	4 1/2″	Folding Hunter	Bone	650
R1163	4 1/2″	Folding Hunter	Bone	550
R1173	3 1/2″	Baby Bullet	Brown Bone	5500
R1182	3 1/2″	Swell Center Jack	Black Composition	345
R1183	3 1/2″	Swell Center Jack	Bone	325
R1192	3 1/2″	Swell Center Jack	Black Composition	250
R1193	3 1/2″	Swell Center Jack	Bone	300
R1202	3 5/8″	Swell Center Jack	Black Composition	325
R1203	3 1/2″	Swell Center Jack	Bone	300
R1212	4 1/4″	Jumbo Jack	Black Composition	375
R1213	4 1/4″	Jumbo Jack	Bone	450
R1222	4 1/4″	Jumbo Jack	Black Composition	350
R1223	4 1/4″	Jumbo Jack	Bone	450
R1225-W	4 1/4″	Jumbo Jack	White Composition	425

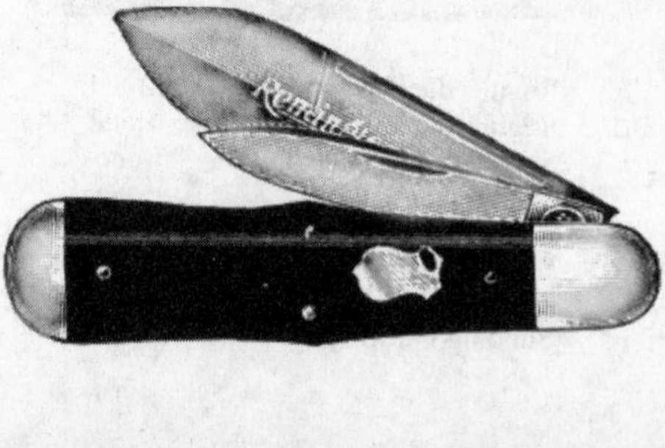

Pattern No.		*Description*	*Handle*	*Mint Price*
R1232	3 1/2″	Swell Center Jack	Black Composition	220
R1233	3 1/2″	Swell Center Jack	Bone	300
R1240	5″	Daddy Barlow	Brown Bone	475
R1241	5″	Daddy Barlow	Redwood	400
R1242	5″	Daddy Barlow	Black Composition	425
R1243	5″	Daddy Barlow	Bone	500
R1253	5 1/4″	Bullet Trapper	Brown Bone	2300
R1263	5 1/4″	Bullet Trapper	Brown Bone	3000
R1273	5 1/4″	Bullet Trapper	Brown Bone	3400
R1283	3″	Balloon Jack	Bone	200
R1284	3″	Balloon Jack	Pearl	300
R1285	3″	Balloon Jack	Tortoise Shell	250
R1293	4 1/4″	Toothpick	Bone	425
R1295	4 1/4″	Toothpick	Pyremite	400
R1303	4 1/2″	Bullet Lockback	Brown Bone	3200

R1306	4 1/2″	Bullet Lockback	Genuine Stag	3500
R1315	3″	Serpentine Jack	Pyremite	250
R1323	3″	Dogleg Jack	Bone	180
R1324	3″	Dogleg Jack	Pearl	350
R1325	3″	Dogleg Jack	Pyremite	200
R1333	3 1/4″	Equal End Jack	Bone	200
R1343	4″	Folding Hunter	Bone	400
R1353	3 1/2″	Dogleg Jack	Bone	300
R1363	3 1/2″	Dogleg Jack	Bone	300
R1373	3 1/2″	Dogleg Jack	Bone	325
R1379	3 1/4″	Regular Jack	Metal	200
R1383	4 1/4″	Bowtie	Bone	550
R1383-L	4 1/4″	Bowtie Lock	Pyremite	500
R1389	3 1/2″	Regular Jack	Metal	200

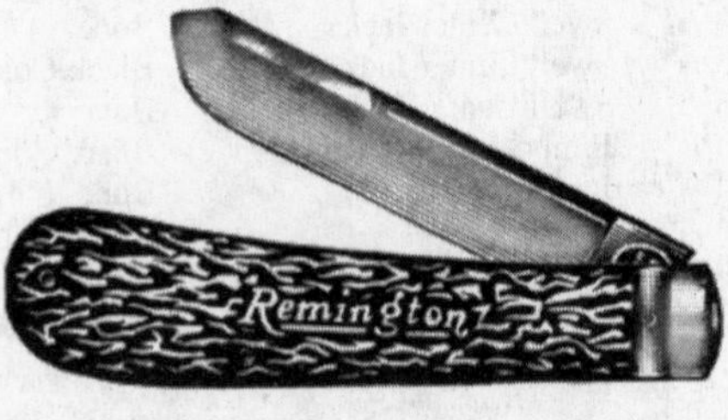

R1399	3 1/2″	Regular Jack	Metal	140
R1409	3 1/2″	Regular Jack	Metal	150
R1413	3 3/8″	Serpentine Jack	Bone	175
R1423	3 3/8″	Serpentine Jack	Bone	175
R1437	4″	Budding Knife	Imitation Ivory	175
R1447	4″	Budding Knife	Imitation Ivory	175
R1457	4″	Budding Knife	Imitation Ivory	200
R1465	3 5/8″	Budding/Grafting	Pyremite	220

Pattern No.		*Description*	*Handle*	*Mint Price*
R1477	4″	Budding Knife	Imitation Ivory	175
R1483	3 1/8″	Wharncliffe Pen	Bone	200
R1485	3 1/8″	Wharncliffe Pen	Pyremite	180
R1493	3 1/8″	Serpentine Pen	Bone	200
R1495	3 1/8″	Serpentine Pen	Pyremite	190
R1535	3 3/4″	Florist's Knife	Imitation Ivory	150
R1537-CH	3″	Boy's Knife	Imitation Bone	175
R1545	3 3/4″	Florist's Knife	Imitation Ivory	150
R1555-W	3 1/2″	Budding/Grafting	Pyremite	225
R1568	4″	Maize Knife	Cocobolo	175
R1572	3″	Equal End Jack	Black Composition	140
R1573	3″	Equal End Jack	Bone	150
R1582	3″	Equal End Jack	Slick Black	165
R1592	3 1/8″	Equal End Jack	Black Composition	175
R1593	3 1/8″	Equal End Jack	Bone	200
R1595	3 1/8″	Equal End Jack	Pyremite	175
R1608	4″	Pruning Knife	Cocobolo	125
R1613	5″	Toothpick Cartridge Shield	Bone	3000

R1613	5″	Toothpick Round Shield	Bone	2500
R1615	5″	Fishing Knife	Pyremite	400
R1622	3″	Equal End Jack	Black Composition	135
R1623	3″	Equal End Jack	Bone	145
R1623-CH	3″	Boy's Knife	Imitation Bone	170
R1630	5″	Daddy Barlow	Bone	700
R1643	2 7/8″	Serpentine Pen	Bone	175
R1644	2 7/8″	Serpentine Pen	Pearl	300
R1645	2 7/8″	Serpentine Pen	Pyremite	175
R1653	2 7/8″	Serpentine Pen	Bone	175
R1655	2 7/8″	Serpentine Pen	Pyremite	185
R1668	4″	Jumbo Jack	Cocobolo	175
R1671	3 3/8″	Easy Open	Redwood	165
R1673	3 3/8″	Easy Open	Bone	225
R1685	3 3/4″	Budding Knife	Pyremite	170
R1687	3 3/4″	Budding Knife	Imitation Ivory	275
R1688	3 3/4″	Budding Knife	Cocobolo	150
R1697	4″	Budding Knife	Imitation Ivory	275
R1707	5″	Budding Knife	Imitation Ivory	350
R1715	4 1/4″	Budding Knife	Pyremite	200
R1717	4 1/4″	Budding Knife	Imitation Ivory	265

R1723	3 1/2″	Regular Jack	Bone	220
R1751	3 1/2″	Teardrop Jack	Redwood	175

Pattern No.		*Description*	*Handle*	*Mint Price*
R1752	3 1/2″	Teardrop Jack	Black Composition	200
R1753	3 1/2″	Teardrop Jack	Bone	225
R1755	3 1/2″	Teardrop Jack	Pyremite	200
R1763	3 1/2″	Teardrop Jack	Bone	225
R1772	3 1/2″	Easy Open	Black Composition	200
R1782	3 1/2″	Teardrop Jack	Black Composition	200
R1783	3 1/2″	Teardrop Jack	Bone	225
R1785	3 1/2″	Teardrop Jack	Pyremite	200
R1803	3 3/8″	Regular Jack	Bone	225
R1823	3 5/8″	Serpentine Jack	Brown Bone	210
R1825	3 5/8″	Serpentine Jack	Imitation Tortoise	185
R1833	3 5/8″	Sleeveboard Jack	Bone	240
R1853	3 3/8″	Equal End Jack	Bone	210
R1855-M	3 3/8″	Equal End Jack	Pyremite	200
R1863	3 3/8″	Equal End Jack	Bone	200
R1873	3 5/8″	Serpentine Jack	Bone	225
R1882-B	3″	Razor "One Arm Man" Jack	Black Composition	250
R1903	3″	Sleeveboard Jack	Bone	190

R1905	3″	Sleeveboard Jack	Pyremite	180
R1913	3 3/8″	Serpentine Jack	Bone	225
R1915	3 3/8″	Serpentine Jack	Candy Stripe	210
R1962	3 5/8″	Regular Jack	Black Composition	220
R1973	3 3/4″	Electrician Knife	Bone	300
R1995	4 1/4″	Budding/Grafting	Pyremite	200
R2043	3 1/4″	Sleeveboard Jack	Bone	160
R2045	3 1/4″	Sleeveboard Jack	Pyremite	150
R2053	3 1/4″	Sleeveboard Jack	Bone	160
R2055	3 1/4″	Sleeveboard Jack	Pyremite	150
R2063	3 1/8″	Sleeveboard Jack	Bone	160
R2065	3 1/8″	Sleeveboard Jack	Pyremite	140
R2073	3 1/8″	Sleeveboard Jack	Bone	125
R2075	3 1/8″	Sleeveboard Jack	Pyremite	170
R2083	3 1/4″	Sleeveboard Jack	Bone	150
R2085	3 1/4″	Sleeveboard Jack	Pyremite	120
R2093	3 1/8″	Sleeveboard Jack	Bone	110
R2095	3 1/8″	Sleeveboard Jack	Blk/Wh Composition	175
R2103	3 1/8″	Sleeveboard Jack	Bone	160
R2105-MW	3 1/8″	Sleeveboard Jack	Pyremite	150
R2111	3 3/8″	Electrician Knife	Redwood	200
R2203	3 3/8″	Sleeveboard Jack	Bone	210
R2205D	3 3/8″	Sleeveboard Jack	Pyremite	185
R2213	3 3/8″	Sleeveboard Jack	Bone	210
R2215-M	3 3/8″	Sleeveboard Jack	Red/Black	225
R2223	3 3/8″	Sleeveboard Jack	Bone	165
R2303	4 1/8″	Switchblade	Bone	700
R2403	5″	Switchblade	Bone	850
R2503	3 3/8″	Equal End Jack	Bone	225
R2505	3 3/8″	Equal End Jack	Pyremite	225
R2603	3 3/8″	Serpentine Jack	Bone	200
R2605-B	3 3/8″	Serpentine Jack	Red Composition	170
R3003	3 3/4″	Balloon Stock	Bone	475

Pattern No.		*Description*	*Handle*	*Mint Price*
R3005	3¾″	Balloon Stock	Pyremite	450
R3013	3¾″	Balloon Stock	Bone	475
R3015	3¾″	Balloon Stock	Pyremite	450
R3033	3¾″	Cattle Knife	Bone	600
R3035	3¾″	Cattle Knife	Pyremite	575
R3050	4″	Premium Stock	Buffalo Horn	500
R3053	4″	Premium Stock	Bone	550

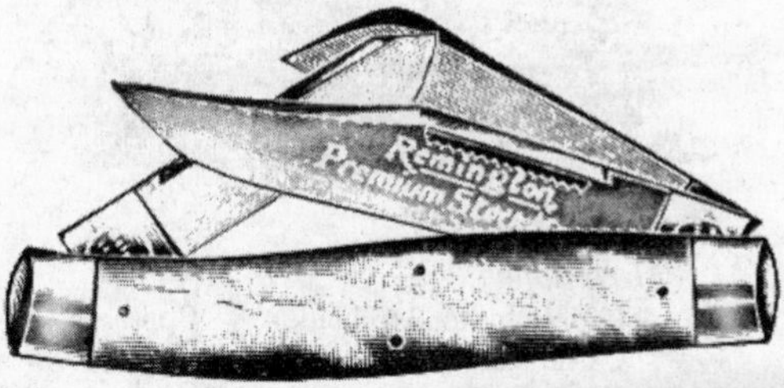

R3054	4″	Premium Stock	Pearl	900
R3055	4″	Premium Stock	Pyremite	500
R3056	4″	Premium Stock	Genuine Stag	750
R3059	4″	Premium Stock	Metal	375
R3062	4″	Premium Stock	Black Composition	400
R3063	4″	Premium Stock	Bone	550
R3064	4″	Premium Stock	Pearl	900
R3065-A	4″	Premium Stock	Pyremite	500
R3065-W	4″	Premium Stock	Pyremite	500
R3065-L	4″	Premium Stock	Yellow Composition	425
R3070	3⅞″	Premium Stock	Buffalo Horn	575
R3073	3⅞″	Premium Stock	Bone	625
R3075	3⅞″	Premium Stock	Pyremite	475
R3083	3⅞″	Premium Stock	Bone	600
R3085	3⅞″	Premium Stock	Pyremite	475
R3093	3⅞″	Premium Stock	Bone	600
R3095	3⅞″	Premium Stock	Pyremite	450
R3103	3⅞″	Premium Stock	Bone	525
R3105	3⅞″	Premium Stock	Pyremite	475
R3113	4″	Texas Jack	Bone	400

R3115-G	4″	Texas Jack	Pyremite	375
R3115-W	4″	Texas Jack	Pyremite	375
R3123	3⅞″	Texas Jack	Bone	425
R3133	4″	Premium Stock (4 blade)	Bone	850

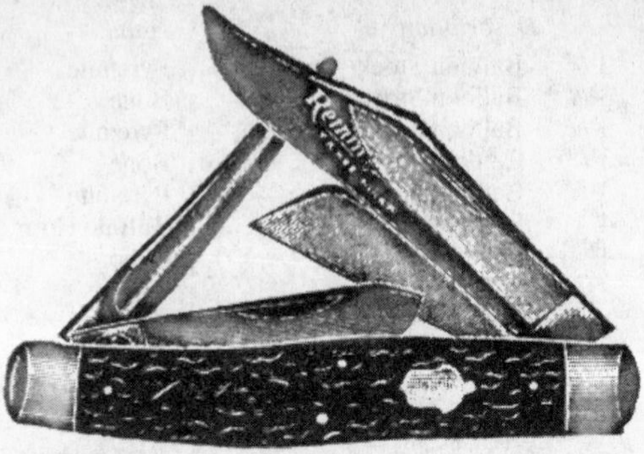

Pattern No.		*Description*	*Handle*	*Mint Price*
R3143	4″	Premium Stock (5 blade)	Bone	2500
R3153	3 1/2″	Cattle Knife	Brown Bone	425
R3154-T	3 1/2″	Cattle Knife	Pyremite	375
R3155	3 1/2″	Cattle Knife	Pyremite	385
R3163	3 1/2″	Cattle Knife	Bone	375
R3173	4 1/4″	Cattle Knife	Bone	450
R3183	3 1/2″	Cattle Knife	Bone	375
R3185	3 1/2″	Cattle Knife	Pyremite	350
R3193	3 1/2″	Cattle Knife	Bone	400
R3202	3 1/2″	Cattle Knife	Black Composition	350
R3203	3 1/2″	Cattle Knife	Bone	375
R3212	3 3/4″	Cattle Knife	Black Composition	400
R3213	3 3/4″	Cattle Knife	Bone	400
R3215	3 3/4″	Cattle Knife	Pyremite	375
R3222	3 3/4″	Cattle Knife	Black Composition	375
R3223	3 3/4″	Cattle Knife	Bone	400
R3225	3 3/4″	Cattle Knife	Pyremite	390
R3232	3 3/4″	Cattle Knife	Black Composition	365
R3233	3 3/4″	Cattle Knife	Bone	400
R3235	3 3/4″	Cattle Knife	Pyremite	385
R3242	3 3/4″	Cattle Knife	Black Composition	450
R3243	3 3/4″	Cattle Knife	Bone	465
R3245	3 3/4″	Cattle Knife	Pyremite	500
R3253	3 3/4″	Cattle Knife	Bone	450
R3255	3 3/4″	Cattle Knife	Pyremite	425
R3263	3 3/4″	Cattle Knife	Bone	450
R3265	3 3/4″	Cattle Knife	Pyremite	400
R3273	3 3/4″	Cattle Knife	Brown Bone	435
R3274	3 3/4″	Cattle Knife	Pearl	750
R3275	3 3/4″	Cattle Knife	Pyremite	425
R3283	3 3/4″	Cattle Knife	Bone	450
R3285	3 3/4″	Cattle Knife	Pyremite	425
R3293	3 3/4″	Cattle Knife	Bone	475
R3295	3 3/4″	Cattle Knife	Pyremite	425
R3302	3 3/4″	Cattle Knife	Black Composition	525

Pattern No.		*Description*	*Handle*	*Mint Price*
R3303	3 3/4"	Cattle Knife	Bone	625
R3305-D	3 3/4"	Cattle Knife	Pyremite	600
R3312	3 3/4"	Cattle Knife	Black Composition	500
R3313	3 3/4"	Cattle Knife	Bone	650
R3315-B	3 3/4"	Cattle Knife	Pyremite	575
R3322	3 3/4"	Scout/Utility	Black Composition	300
R3333	3 3/4"	Scout/Utility	Brown Bone	375
R3335	3 3/4"	Scout/Utility	Red/White/Blue	525
R3352	3 3/4"	Equal End Jack	Black Composition	360
R3353	3 3/4"	Equal End Jack	Bone	425
R3363	3 3/4"	Equal End Jack	Brown Bone	400
R3372	3 3/4"	Equal End Jack	Black Composition	265
R3373	3 3/4"	Equal End Jack	Bone	300
R3375	3 3/4"	Equal End Jack	Pyremite	275
R3382	3 3/4"	Equal End Jack	Black Composition	265
R3383	3 3/4"	Equal End Jack	Bone	300
R3385-S	3 3/4"	Equal End Jack	Pyremite	265
R3393	3 3/4"	Cattle Knife	Bone	290
R3395-T	3 3/4"	Cattle Knife	Pyremite	275
R3403	3 3/4"	Cattle Knife	Bone	325
R3405-J	3 3/4"	Cattle Knife	Pyremite	325
R3413	3 3/8"	Cattle Knife	Brown Bone	300
R3414	3 3/8"	Cattle Knife	Pearl	550

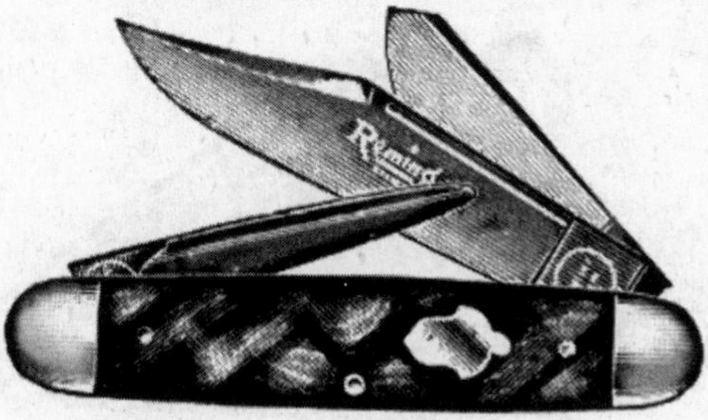

Pattern No.		*Description*	*Handle*	*Mint Price*
R3415	3 3/8"	Cattle Knife	Pyremite	300
R3423	3 1/4"	Whittler	Bone	325
R3424	3 3/8"	Whittler	Pearl	475
R3425-P	3 3/8"	Whittler	Pyremite	325
R3432	3 1/4"	Equal End Jack	Black Composition	190
R3433	3 1/4"	Equal End Jack	Bone	225
R3435	3 1/4"	Equal End Jack	Pyremite	190
R3442	3 1/4"	Equal End Jack	Black Composition	190
R3443	3 1/4"	Equal End Jack	Bone	250
R3445-B	3 1/4"	Equal End Jack	Pyremite	240
R3453	3 1/4"	Whittler	Bone	450
R3455	3 1/4"	Whittler	Pyremite	425
R3463	3 1/4"	Whittler	Bone	375
R3465-B	3 1/4"	Cattle Knife	Pyremite	375
R3475	3 1/4"	Cattle Knife	Pyremite	350
R3480	3 3/8"	Premium Stock	Buffalo Horn	300
R3483	3 3/8"	Premium Stock	Bone	325
R3484	3 3/8"	Premium Stock	Pearl	425
R3485-J	3 3/8"	Premium Stock	Gold Pyremite	250
R3489	3 3/8"	Premium Stock	Metal	225
R3494	3 3/8"	Premium Stock	Pearl	450
R3495-M	3 3/8"	Premium Stock	Pyremite	275
R3499	3 3/8"	Premium Stock	Metal	300
R3500	3 3/8"	Premium Stock	Buffalo Horn	300
R3503	3 3/8"	Premium Stock	Bone	300
R3504	3 3/8"	Premium Stock	Pearl	450
R3505	3 3/8"	Premium Stock	Pyremite	300

Pattern No.	Description		Handle	Mint Price
R3513	3³/₈″	Premium Stock	Brown Bone	325
R3514	3³/₈″	Premium Stock	Pearl	500
R3515	3³/₈″	Premium Stock	Pyremite	325
R3520	3³/₈″	Whittler	Buffalo Horn	325
R3523	3³/₈″	Whittler	Bone	350
R3524	3³/₈″	Whittler	Pearl	500
R3525	3³/₈″	Whittler	Pyremite	325
R3533	3³/₈″	Texas Jack	Bone	250
R3535	3³/₈″	Texas Jack	Pyremite	220
R3545	3³/₈″	Premium Stock	Pyremite	200
R3553	4″	Premium Stock	Brown Bone	450
R3554	4″	Premium Stock	Pearl	600

R3555-G	4″	Premium Stock	Pyremite	450
R3555-IW	4″	Premium Stock	Red Composition	400
R3563	4″	Premium Stock	Bone	475
R3565-D	3⁷/₈″	Premium Stock	Pyremite	425
R3573	3⁷/₈″	Premium Stock	Bone	500
R3575	3⁷/₈″	Premium Stock	Pyremite	425
R3580	4″	Whittlerk	Buffalo Horn	550
R3583	4″	Whittler	Bone	550
R3585	4″	Premium Stock	Pyremite	450
R3593	3⁷/₈″	Premium Stock	Bone	500
R3595	3⁷/₈″	Premium Stock	Pyremite	475
R3596	3⁷/₈″	Premium Stock	Genuine Stag	650
R3600	3⁷/₈″	Premium Stock	Buffalo Horn	400
R3603	3⁷/₈″	Premium Stock	Bone	450
R3604	3⁷/₈″	Premium Stock	Pearl	675
R3605	3⁷/₈″	Premium Stock	Pyremite	425
R3613	3⁷/₈″	Premium Stock	Bone	450
R3615	3⁷/₈″	Premium Stock	Pyremite	400
R3620	3⁷/₈″	Premium Stock	Buffalo Horn	375
R3623	3⁷/₈″	Premium Stock	Bone	450
R3625	3⁷/₈″	Premium Stock	Pyremite	425
R3633	3⁷/₈″	Premium Stock	Bone	475
R3635	3⁷/₈″	Premium Stock	Pyremite	400
R3643	3⁷/₈″	Premium Stock	Bone	450
R3644	4″	Premium Stock	Pearl	800
R3645	4″	Premium Stock	Pyremite	475

Pattern No.		Description	Handle	Mint Price
R3653	3⅞″	Premium Stock	Bone	500
R3655	3⅞″	Premium Stock	Pyremite	450
R3665	3⅞″	Premium Stock	Pyremite	650
R3675	3⅞″	Premium Stock	Pyremite	650
R3683	3½″	Cattle Knife	Bone	425
R3685	3½″	Cattle Knife	Pyremite	400
R3693	3½″	Cattle Knife	Brown Bone	575
R3695-G	3½″	Cattle Knife	Pyremite	550
R3700	4″	Premium Stock	Buffalo Horn	500
R3703	4″	Premium Stock	Bone	600
R3704	4″	Premium Stock	Pearl	850
R3705	4″	Premium Stock	Pyremite	500
R3710	3⅞″	Premium Stock	Buffalo Horn	500

R3713	3⅞″	Premium Stock	Bone	550
R3714	3⅞″	Premium Stock	Genuine Pearl	875
R3715-F	3⅞″	Premium Stock	Pyremite	575
R3722	3⅝″	Jumbo Punch	Black Composition	875
R3723	3⅝″	Sleeveboard Whittler	Bone	1250
R3725	3⅝″	Sleeveboard Whittler	Pyremite	1000
R3732	3⅝″	Jumbo Punch	Black Composition	875
R3733	3⅝″	Jumbo Punch	Bone	1250
R3735	3⅝″	Jumbo Punch	Pyremite	1000
R3843	3⅝″	Scout/Utility	Brown Bone	550
R3853	4″	Pruner	Bone	425
R3855	4″	Pruner	Imitation Ivory	375
R3858	4″	Pruner	Cocobolo	325
R3863	3¾″	Scout/Utility	Brown Bone	375
R3870	4″	Premium Stock	Buffalo Horn	425
R3873	4″	Premium Stock	Bone	475
R3874	4″	Premium Stock	Genuine Pearl	700
R3875-A	4″	Premium Stock	Pyremite	425
R3883	4″	Premium Stock	Bone	550
R3885	4″	Premium Stock	Pyremite	525
R3893	3⅞″	Premium Jack	Bone	240
R3895	3⅞″	Premium Jack	Pyremite	225

R3903	3⅞″	Premium Jack	Bone	375
R3926	3⅞″	Premium Jack	Genuine Stag	600
R3932	3⅝″	Sleeveboard Whittler	Black Composition	800
R3933	3⅝″	Sleeveboard Whittler	Bone	1250
R3935	3⅝″	Sleeveboard Whittler	Pyremite	1000

Pattern No.		*Description*	*Handle*	*Mint Price*
R3942	3 5/8"	Sleeveboard Half Whittler	Black Composition	600
R3952	3 3/4"	Equal End Jack	Black Composition	325
R3953	3 3/4"	Equal End Jack	Bone	300
R3955	3 3/4"	Equal End Jack	Pyremite	275
R3962	3 3/4"	Premium Stock	Black Composition	375
R3963	3 5/8"	Premium Stock	Bone	400
R3965	3 5/8"	Premium Stock	Pyremite	400
R3973	3 5/8"	Premium Stock	Bone	450
R3975	3 5/8"	Premium Stock	Pyremite	425
R3983	3 3/8"	Premium Stock	Bone	475
R3985	3 3/8"	Premium Stock	Pyremite	425
R3993	3 5/8"	Premium Stock	Bone	450
R3995	3 5/8"	Premium Stock	Pyremite	400
R4003	3 5/8"	Texas Jack	Bone	250
R4005	3 5/8"	Texas Jack	Pyremite	225
R4013	3 5/8"	Texas Jack	Bone	350
R4015	3 5/8"	Texas Jack	Pyremite	300
R4023	3 5/8"	Premium Stock	Bone	500
R4025	3 5/8"	Premium Stock	Pyremite	475
R4033	3 5/8"	Premium Stock	Bone	500
R4035	3 5/8"	Premium Stock	Pyremite	425
R4043	3 5/8"	Premium Stock	Bone	450
R4045	3 5/8"	Premium Stock	Pyremite	425
R4053	3 5/8"	Premium Stock	Bone	500
R4055	3 5/8"	Premium Stock	Pyremite	450
R4063	3 5/8"	Premium Stock	Bone	600
R4065	3 5/8"	Premium Stock	Pyremite	550
R4073	4"	Premium Stock	Brown Bone	500
R4075	4"	Premium Stock	Pyremite	450
R4083	3 7/8"	Premium Stock	Bone	475
R4085	3 7/8"	Premium Stock	Pyremite	450
R4093	3 7/8"	Premium Stock	Bone	500

R4095	3 7/8"	Premium Stock	Pyremite	450
R4103	3 3/8"	Texas Jack	Bone	250
R4105	3 3/8"	Texas Jack	Pyremite	225
R4113	3 7/8"	Premium Stock	Bone	500
R4114	3 7/8"	Premium Stock	Pearl	825
R4123	3 7/8"	Premium Stock	Bone	500
R4124	3 7/8"	Premium Stock	Pearl	850
R4133	3 3/8"	Premium Stock	Bone	450
R4134	3 3/8"	Premium Stock	Pearl	700
R4135	3 3/8"	Premium Stock	Pyremite	400
R4143	3 3/8"	Premium Pen	Bone	225
R4144	3 3/8"	Premium Pen	Pearl	375
R4145	3 3/8"	Premium Pen	Pyremite	225
R4163	3 3/8"	Premium Stock	Bone	300
R4173	3 3/8"	Premium Stock	Bone	325
R4175	3 3/8"	Premium Stock	Pyremite	300
R4200	4"	Premium Stock	Buffalo Horn	400
R4203	4"	Premium Stock	Bone	375
R4213	4"	Premium Stock	Bone	500
R4223	3 1/4"	Cattle Knife	Bone	300

Pattern No.		*Description*	*Handle*	*Mint Price*
R4225	3 1/4″	Cattle Knife	Pyremite	285
RS4233	3 3/8″	Scout Knife (Jr.)	Brown Bone	300
R4234	3 3/8″	Scout/Utility	Pearl	575

R4235	3 3/8″	Scout/Utility	Red/White/Blue Pyremite	375
R4243	4 3/4″	Bullet Scout	Brown Bone	2750
R4253	3 3/4″	Sowbelly Stock	Bone	1750
R4263	3 3/4″	Sowbelly Stock	Bone	2200
R4273	3 3/4″	Sowbelly Stock	Bone	2500
R4274	3 3/4″	Sowbelly Stock	Pearl	4000
R4283	3 3/4″	Sowbelly Stock (5 blade)	Bone	5500
R4293	3 5/8″	Premium Stock	Bone	450
R4303	3 5/8″	Premium Stock	Bone	400
R4313	3 7/8″	Premium Stock	Bone	400
R4323	3 7/8″	Premium Stock	Bone	400
R4334	3 1/2″	Bartender Knife	Pearl	450
R4336	3 1/2″	Bartender Knife	Genuine Stag	400
R4343	4 1/4″	Jumbo Jack	Bone	400
R4345	4 1/4″	Jumbo Jack	Pyremite	325

R4353	4 1/4″	Bullet Moose	Bone	3200
R4363	3 5/8″	Premium Stock	Bone	500
R4365	3 5/8″	Premium Stock	Pyremite	475
R4373	3 3/8″	Girl Scout Knife	Bone	325
R4375	3 3/8″	Scout/Utility	Pyremite	250
R4383	3 3/8″	Scout/Utility	Bone	275
R4384	3 3/8″	Scout/Utility	Pearl	550
R4394	3 5/8″	Scout/Utility	Pearl	575
R4403	3 3/8″	Premium Stock	Bone	325
R4405	3 3/8″	Premium Stock	Christmas Tree	300
R4413	3 3/8″	Cattle Knife	Bone	325
R4423	3 3/8″	Cattle Knife	Bone	250
R4425	3 3/8″	Cattle Knife	Pyremite	300
R4433	3 1/4″	Whittler	Bone	425
R4443	3 3/8″	Premium Stock	Bone	250
R4466	3 3/4″	Bullet Muskrat	Genuine Stag	5500
R4473	3 1/4″	Equal End Jack	Bone	250

Pattern No.	*Description*		*Handle*	*Mint Price*
R4483	3 1/2″	Cattle Knife	Bone	300
R4493	3 3/4″	Cattle Knife	Bone	225
R4495	3 3/4″	Florist's Knife	Pyremite	200
R4505	3 7/8″	Premium Stock	Pyremite	400
R4506	3 7/8″	Premium Stock	Genuine Stag	500
R4513	4″	Premium Stock	Bone	850
RC4523	3 3/4″	Scout Knife	Bone	500
R4533	3 1/4″	Scout Knife Jr.	Bone	475
R4548	3 3/4″	Electrician Knife	Cocobolo	325
R4555	4″	Serpentine Stock	Pyremite	375
R4563	4 1/4″	Premium Stock	Bone	525
R4573	3 1/2″	Cattle Knife	Bone	300
R4583	3 7/8″	Texas Jack	Bone	275
R4593	4″	Muskrat	Brown Bone	325
R4603	3 1/4″	Cattle Knife	Brown Bone	275
R4605	3 1/4″	Cattle Knife	Pyremite	250
R4613	3 1/4″	Cattle Knife	Bone	250
R4623	3 3/8″	Whittler	Brown Bone	325
R4625	3 3/8″	Whittler	Pyremite	275
R4633	3 3/8″	Cattle Knife	Bone	250
R4635-G	3 3/8″	Cattle Knife	Pyremite	220
R4643	3 3/8″	Serpentine Stock	Bone	275
R4679	3 3/8″	Serpentine Stock	Metal	200
R4683	3 1/4″	Cattle Knife	Bone	275

R4685	3 1/4″	Cattle Knife	Pyremite	250
R4695	3 7/8″	Cattle Knife	Pyremite	140
R4702	4 1/4″	Moose	Black Composition	375
R4703	4 1/4″	Moose	Brown Bone	450
R4713	3 3/4″	Electrician Knife	Bone	325
R4723	3 3/4″	Girl Scout Knife	Bone	375
R4733	3 3/4″	Dog Groomer	Bone	375
R4783	3 1/2″	Scout Knife	Bone	300
R4813	3 3/4″	Cattle Knife	Bone	250
R4815	3 3/4″	Cattle Knife	Pyremite	250
R4823	3 3/8″	Cattle Knife	Bone	270
R4825	3 3/8″	Cattle Knife	Pyremite	255
R4833	3 3/8″	Cattle Knife	Bone	260
R4835	3 3/8″	Cattle Knife	Pyremite	265
R4843	3 3/8″	Serpentine Stock	Imitation Bone	250
R4845	3 3/8″	Serpentine Stock	Black Composition	225
R4853	3 3/8″	Serpentine Stock	Bone	275
R4855	3 3/8″	Serpentine Stock	Pyremite	250
R4863	3 3/8″	Serpentine Stock	Bone	275
R4865	3 3/8″	Serpentine Stock	Pyremite	245
R6013	3 1/4″	Swayback Pen	Bone	400
R6014	3 1/4″	Swayback Pen	Pearl	500
R6015	3 1/4″	Swayback Pen	Pyremite	375
R6023	3 1/4″	Balloon Pen	Bone	450

Pattern No.		*Description*	*Handle*	*Mint Price*
R6024	3 1/4″	Balloon Pen	Pearl	600
R6025	3 1/4″	Balloon Pen	Bone	425
R6032	3 1/2″	Congress	Black Composition	450

R6033	3 1/2″	Congress	Bone	475
R6034	3 1/2″	Congress	Pearl	700
R6043	4 1/8″	Congress	Bone	750
R6053	4 1/8″	Congress	Bone	700
R6063	4 1/4″	Congress	Brown Bone	475
R6073	3 3/4″	Congress	Brown Bone	550
R6083	3 3/4″	Congress	Bone	475
R6093	3 3/4″	Congress	Bone	325
R6103	3″	Congress Pen	Bone	250
R6104	3″	Congress Pen	Pearl	375
R6105	3″	Congress Pen	Pyremite	250
R6113	3 1/2″	Congress Pen	Bone	325
R6123	3 1/2″	Congress Pen	Brown Bone	450
R6133	3 1/2″	Congress Pen	Brown Bone	475
R6143	3 1/2″	Congress Pen	Bone	240
R6145	3 1/2″	Congress Pen	Pyremite	225
R6153	3 1/2″	Congress Pen	Bone	300
R6155	3 1/2″	Congress Pen	Pyremite	250
R6163	4″	Congress Pen	Bone	400
R6175-W	3 3/4″	Office Knife	Pyremite	175
R6182	3 1/4″	Senator Pen	Black Composition	110
R6183	3 1/4″	Senator Pen	Bone	150
R6184	3 1/4″	Senator Pen	Pearl	225
R6185	3 1/4″	Senator Pen	Pyremite	150
R6192	3 3/8″	Equal End Pen	Black Composition	130
R6193	3 3/8″	Equal End Pen	Bone	175
R6194	3 3/8″	Equal End Pen	Pearl	200
R6195	3 1/4″	Equal End Pen	Brown Composition	150
R6203	3 1/4″	Senator Pen	Bone	160
R6204	3 1/4″	Senator Pen	Pearl	200
R6205	3 1/4″	Senator Pen	Pyremite	160
R6213	3 1/4″	Whittler Pen	Bone	325
R6214	3 1/4″	Whittler Pen	Pearl	425
R6215	3 1/4″	Whittler Pen	Pyremite	300
R6223	3 1/4″	Whittler Pen	Bone	325
R6224	3 1/4″	Whittler Pen	Pearl	425
R6225	3 1/4″	Whittler Pen	Pyremite	310
R6233	3 1/4″	Whittler Pen	Bone	350
R6234	3 1/4″	Whittler Pen	Pearl	425
R6235	3 1/4″	Whittler Pen	Pyremite	325
R6243	3 1/4″	Lobster Pen	Bone	140
R6244	3 1/8″	Lobster Pen	Pearl	165
R6245	3″	Lobster Pen	Pyremite	110
R6249	3″	Lobster Pen	Metal	95
R6255	3 1/8″	Lobster Pen	Pyremite	90
R6259	3 1/8″	Lobster Pen	Metal	95
R6265	3 1/4″	Half Whittler	Pyremite	225

Pattern No.		Description	Handle	Mint Price
R6275	3 1/4"	Whittler	Pyremite	425
R6285	3 1/4"	Whittler	Pyremite	425
R6295	3 1/4"	Whittler	Pyremite	500
R6303	3 1/4"	Half Whittler	Bone	190
R6313	3 1/4"	Whittler	Bone	450
R6323	3 1/4"	Whittler	Bone	450
R6325	3 1/4"	Whittler	Pyremite	400
R6330	3 1/8"	Sleeveboard Whittler	Buffalo Horn	325
R6333	3 1/8"	Sleeveboard Whittler	Bone	320
R6334	3 1/8"	Sleeveboard Whittler	Pearl	475
R6335	3 1/8"	Sleeveboard Whittler	Pyremite	300
R6340	3 1/2"	Whittler	Buffalo Horn	450
R6343	3 1/2"	Whittler	Bone	425
R6344	3 1/2"	Whittler	Pearl	600
R6345-T	3 1/2"	Whittler	Pyremite	425
R6350	3 1/2"	Whittler	Buffalo Horn	400
R6353	3 1/2"	Whittler	Bone	400
R6355G	3 1/2"	Whittler	Pyremite	375
R6363	3 1/2"	Half Whittler	Bone	250
R6365-A	3 1/2"	Half Whittler	Pyremite	220
R6390	3 3/8"	Whittler	Buffalo Horn	420
R6393	3 3/8"	Sleeveboard Whittler	Brown Bone	575
R6394	3 3/8"	Sleeveboard Whittler	Pearl	800
R6394-G	3 3/8"	Sleeveboard Whittler	Pyremite	475
R6400	3 3/8"	Whittler	Buffalo Horn	325
R6403	3 3/8"	Whittler	Bone	350
R6404	3 3/8"	Whittler	Pearl	475
R6405	3 3/8"	Whittler	Pyremite	375
R6423	2 3/4"	Lobster Pen	Bone	150
R6424	2 3/4"	Lobster Pen	Pearl	225
R6429	2 3/4"	Lobster Pen	Metal	120
R6433	2 3/4"	Lobster Pen	Bone	140
R6434	2 3/4"	Lobster Pen	Pearl	175
R6439	2 3/4"	Lobster Pen	Metal	125
R6443	2 3/4"	Lobster Pen	Bone	160
R6444	2 3/4"	Lobster Pen	Pearl	225
R6445	2 3/4"	Lobster Pen	Pyremite	150
R6448	2 3/4"	Lobster Pen	Cocobolo	125
R6454	3 1/8"	Lobster Whittler Pen	Pearl	450

Pattern No.		Description	Handle	Mint Price
R6456	3″	Lobster Pen	Genuine Stag	425
R6463	3″	Equal End Pen	Bone	110
R6464	3″	Equal End Pen	Pearl	135
R6465	3″	Equal End Pen	Onyx	110
R6473	3″	Equal End Pen	Bone	120
R6474	3″	Equal End Pen	Pearl	140
R6483	3″	Senator Pen	Bone	125
R6484	3″	Senator Pen	Pearl	175
R6494	3″	Senator Pen	Pearl	140
R6495	3″	Senator Pen	Pyremite	110
R6499	3″	Senator Pen	Metal	95
R6504	3″	Senator Pen	Pearl	150
R6505	3″	Senator Pen	Pyremite	125
R6513	3 1/8″	Lobster Pen	Bone	160
R6514	3 1/8″	Lobster Pen	Pearl	250
R6519	3″	Senator Pen	Metal	130
R6520	3″	Whittler Pen	Buffalo Horn	250
R6523	3″	Whittler Pen	Bone	250
R6524	3″	Whittler Pen	Pearl	325
R6533	3″	Whittler Pen	Brown Bone	290
R6534	3″	Whittler Pen	Pearl	325
R6535	3″	Whittler Pen	Pyremite	250
R6542	3 3/8″	Whittler	Black Composition	300
R6543	3 3/8″	Whittler	Bone	325
R6545	3 3/8″	Whittler	Pyremite	300
R6554	3″	Lobster Pen	Pearl	175
R6559	3″	Lobster Pen	Metal	140
R6563	3 5/8″	Sleeveboard Pen	Brown Bone	175
R6565	3 5/8″	Sleeveboard Pen	Pyremite	175
R6573	3 1/2″	Sleeveboard Pen	Bone	160
R6575	3 1/2″	Sleeveboard Pen	Pyremite	160
R6583	3 1/2″	Sleeveboard Jack	Bone	170
R6585	3 1/2″	Sleeveboard Jack	Pyremite	150
R6593	3 3/8″	Sleeveboard Pen	Bone	300
R6595	3 3/8″	Sleeveboard Pen	Pyremite	275
R6603	3 1/2″	Sleeveboard Pen	Bone	300
R6604	3 1/2″	Sleeveboard Pen	Pearl	375
R6605	3 1/2″	Sleeveboard Pen	Pyremite	275
R6613	3 3/8″	Whittler	Bone	275
R6615	3 3/8″	Whittler	Pyremite	300
R6623	3 1/8″	Sleeveboard Pen	Bone	175
R6624	3 1/8″	Sleeveboard Pen	Pearl	200
R6625	3 1/2″	Sleeveboard Pen	Cracked Ice	150
R6633	3 1/8″	Sleeveboard Pen	Bone	170
R6634	3 1/8″	Sleeveboard Pen	Pearl	175
R6635	3 1/8″	Sleeveboard Pen	Pyremite	150
R6643	3 1/8″	Sleeveboard Pen	Bone	140
R6644	3 1/8″	Sleeveboard Pen	Pearl	185
R6645	3 1/8″	Sleeveboard Pen	Cracked Ice	140

Pattern No.		*Description*	*Handle*	*Mint Price*
R6653	3 1/8″	Sleeveboard Pen	Bone	300
R6654	3 1/8″	Sleeveboard Pen	Pearl	375
R6655	3 1/8″	Sleeveboard Pen	Pyremite	300
R6664	3 1/8″	Congress Pen	Pearl	325
R6673	3 1/8″	Congress Pen	Bone	325
R6674	3 1/8″	Congress Pen	Pearl	425
R6683	3 1/8″	Congress Pen	Bone	325
R6693	3 1/8″	Congress Pen	Bone	375
R6694	3 1/8″	Congress Pen	Pearl	500
R6695	3 1/8″	Congress Pen	Pyremite	350
R6703	3″	Equal End Pen	Bone	275
R6704	3″	Equal End Pen	Pearl	350
R6705-Q	3″	Equal End Pen	Pyremite	275
R6713	3″	Senator Pen	Bone	275
R6714	3″	Senator Pen	Pearl	350
R6723	3 1/8″	Sleeveboard Pen	Bone	325
R6724	3 1/8″	Sleeveboard Pen	Pearl	400
R6725-F	3 1/8″	Sleeveboard Pen	Pyremite	300
R6733	3 1/4″	Senator Pen	Bone	150
R6735	3 1/4″	Senator Pen	Pyremite	140
R6744	3 1/8″	Sleeveboard Pen	Pearl	160
R6745-F	3 1/8″	Sleeveboard Pen	Pyremite	120
R6754	3 1/8″	Sleeveboard Pen	Pearl	225
R6755-A	3 1/8″	Sleeveboard Pen	Pyremite	250
R6763	3″	Congress Pen	Bone	350
R6764	3″	Congress Pen	Pearl	450
R6765-A	3″	Congress Pen	Pyremite	300
R6773	3 1/2″	Congress Pen	Bone	425
R6775	3 1/2″	Congress Pen	Pyremite	400
R6785-W	3 3/8″	Office Knife	Imitation Ivory	140
R6793	3 3/8″	Senator Pen	Bone	220
R6795	3 3/8″	Senator Pen	Pyremite	200
R6803	3 3/8″	Whittler	Bone	325
R6805	3 3/8″	Whittler	Pyremite	300

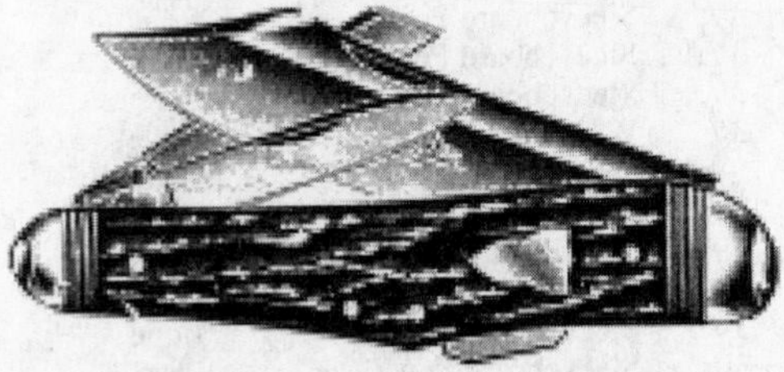

R6816	3 5/8″	Lockback Whittler	Genuine Stag	2700
R6823	3 5/8″	Humpback Whittler	Bone	1500
R6825	3 5/8″	Humpback Whittler	Pyremite	1100
R6834	3 1/8″	Humpback Whittler	Pearl	900
R6835	3 1/8″	Humpback Whittler	Pyremite	575
R6836	3 1/8″	Humpback Whittler	Genuine Stag	800
R6843	2 7/8″	Senator Pen	Bone	140
R6844	2 7/8″	Senator Pen	Pearl	175
R6845	2 7/8″	Senator Pen	Pyremite	110
R6854	2 7/8″	Senator Pen	Pearl	150
R6859	2 7/8″	Senator Pen	Metal	110
R6863	2 5/8″	Sleeveboard Pen	Bone	120
R6864	2 5/8″	Sleeveboard Pen	Pearl	140
R6865	2 5/8″	Sleeveboard Pen	Pyremite	115
R6872	3 1/8″	Equal End Pen	Black Composition	95
R6873	3 1/8″	Equal End Pen	Bone	125
R6874	3 1/8″	Equal End Pen	Pearl	175

Pattern No.		*Description*	*Handle*	*Mint Price*
R6875	3 1/8"	Equal End Pen	Pyremite	100
R6883	3"	Wharncliffe Pen	Bone	220
R6885	3"	Wharncliffe Pen	Pyremite	185
R6893	3 1/8"	Wharncliffe Whittler	Bone	500
R6894	3 1/8"	Wharncliffe Whittler	Pearl	750
R6895	3 1/8"	Wharncliffe Whittler	Pyremite	500
R6903	2 1/2"	Senator Pen	Bone	120
R6904	2 1/2"	Senator Pen	Pearl	150
R6905	2 1/2"	Senator Pen	Onyx	100
R6914	2 1/2"	Senator Pen	Pearl	150
R6919	3"	Senator Pen	Metal	100
R6923	3"	Congress Pen	Bone	190
R6924	3"	Congress Pen	Pearl	250
R6925	3"	Congress Pen	Imitation Ivory	165
R6933	3"	Congress Whittler	Bone	300
R6934	3"	Congress Whittler	Pearl	375
R6949	3"	Congress Whittler	Metal	175
R6954	3 5/8"	Whittler	Pearl	475
R6956	3 5/8"	Whittler	Genuine Stag	425
R6964	3 5/8"	Whittler	Pearl	450
R6966	3 5/8"	Whittler	Genuine Stag	425

R6973	3 1/4"	Balloon Whittler	Bone	375
R6974	3 1/4"	Balloon Whittler	Pearl	525
R6984	3 1/4"	Balloon Whittler	Pearl	875
R6993	3 1/4"	Balloon Pen	Bone	225
R6994	3 1/4"	Balloon Pen	Pearl	325
R6995	3 1/4"	Balloon Pen	Pyremite	260
R7003	3 1/4"	Balloon Whittler	Bone	500
R7004	3 1/4"	Balloon Whittler	Pearl	750

R7005	3 1/4"	Balloon Whittler	Pyremite	475
R7023	3 1/4"	Slim Whittler	Bone	325
R7024	3 1/4"	Slim Whittler	Pearl	425
R7026	3 1/4"	Slim Whittler	Genuine Stag	400
R7034	2 1/8"	Lobster Pen	Pearl	175
R7039/5 through /8	2 1/8"	Emblem Knife	Metal	150
R7044	2 9/16"	Fob Pen	Pearl	200
R7045	2 9/16"	Lobster Pen	Pyremite	165
R7049/21 through /24	2 1/4"	Emblem Knife	Metal	150
R7054	2 1/2"	Senator Pen	Pearl	190
RG7059/17 through /20	2 1/2"	Emblem Knife	Metal	150
RG7059/39 through /40	2 1/2"	Emblem Knife	Metal	150

Pattern No.		*Description*	*Handle*	*Mint Price*
R7064	2 9/16″	Fob Pen	Pearl	125
R7069/25 through /28	2 1/2″	Emblem Knife	Metal	150
R7074	2 5/16″	Lobster Pen	Pearl	190
RG7079/10 through /12	2 1/4″	Emblem Knife	Metal	150
GR7079/36 through /37	2 1/4″	Emblem Knife	Metal	150
R7084	2 3/8″	Lobster Pen	Pearl	175
RG7089/13 through /16	2 1/4″	Emblem Knife	Metal	125
RG7089/32 through /34	2 1/4″	Emblem Knife	Metal	110
R7090	2 5/8″	Lobster Pen	Buffalo Horn	150
R7091	2 5/8″	Lobster Pen	Redwood	110
R7094	2 5/8″	Lobster Pen	Pearl	200
RG7099/1 through /4	2 3/4″	Emblem Knife	Metal	200
RG7099/29 through /31	2 3/4″	Emblem Knife	Metal	200
RT7099	2 3/4″	Emblem Knife	Metal	200
R7103	3 1/4″	Senator Pen	Bone	200

R7104	3 1/4″	Senator Pen	Pearl	225
R7114	3 1/4″	Sleeveboard Pen	Pearl	225
R7116	3 1/4″	Sleeveboard Pen	Genuine Stag	200
R7120	3 1/4″	Sleeveboard Pen	Buffalo Horn	200
R7124	3 1/4″	Sleeveboard Pen	Pearl	375
R7126	3 1/4″	Sleeveboard Pen	Genuine Stag	350
R7134	3 1/4″	Sleeveboard Pen	Pearl	300
R7144	3 5/8″	Sleeveboard Pen	Pearl	350
R7146	3 5/8″	Sleeveboard Pen	Genuine Stag	375
R7153	3 3/8″	Swell Center Pen	Bone	250
R7163	3 3/8″	Swell Center Pen	Bone	225
R7176	3 3/8″	Swell Center Pen	Genuine Stag	325
R7183	3 3/8″	Swell Center Whittler	Bone	400
R7196	3 3/8″	Swell Center Whittler	Genuine Stag	450
R7203	3 3/8″	Swell Center Whittler	Bone	400
R7216	3 3/8″	Swell Center Whittler	Genuine Stag	450
R7223	3″	Swell Center Pen	Bone	150
R7224	3″	Swell Center Pen	Pearl	200
R7225	3″	Swell Center Pen	Pyremite	160
R7233	3″	Swell Center Pen	Bone	190
R7234	3″	Swell Center Pen	Pearl	200
R7236	3″	Swell Center Pen	Genuine Stag	225
R7243	3″	Swell Center Whittler	Bone	300
R7244	3″	Swell Center Whittler	Pearl	400
R7246	3″	Swell Center Whittler	Genuine Stag	350
R7254	2 1/2″	Senator Pen	Pearl	150
R7264	2 3/8″	Lobster Pen	Pearl	150
R7274	2 1/2″	Lobster Pen	Pearl	150
R7284	3″	Lobster Pen	Pearl	150
R7284/5	3″	Lobster Pen	Pearl	150
R7284/6	3″	Lobster Pen	Pearl	150
R7293	3 3/8″	Whittler	Bone	550
R7309	3 1/8″	Sleeveboard Pen	Metal	175
R7319	3 1/8″	Sleeveboard Pen	Metal	175
R7324	3″	Lobster Pen	Pearl	225

Pattern No.		Description	Handle	Mint Price
R7329	3″	Lobster Pen	Metal	100
R7335	3″	Watch Fob	Pyremite	100
R7339	3″	Watch Fob	Metal	95
R7343	3 1/8″	Sleeveboard Pen	Bone	190
R7344	3 1/8″	Sleeveboard Pen	Pearl	220
R7353	3 1/8″	Equal End Pen	Bone	275
R7363	2 5/8″	Lobster Pen	Bone	225
R7364	2 5/8″	Lobster Pen	Pearl	250
R7366	2 5/8″	Lobster Pen	Genuine Stag	225
R7374	2 5/8″	Lobster Pen	Pearl	225
R7375	2 5/8″	Lobster Pen	Pyremite	125
R7384	2 5/8″	Lobster Pen	Pearl	200

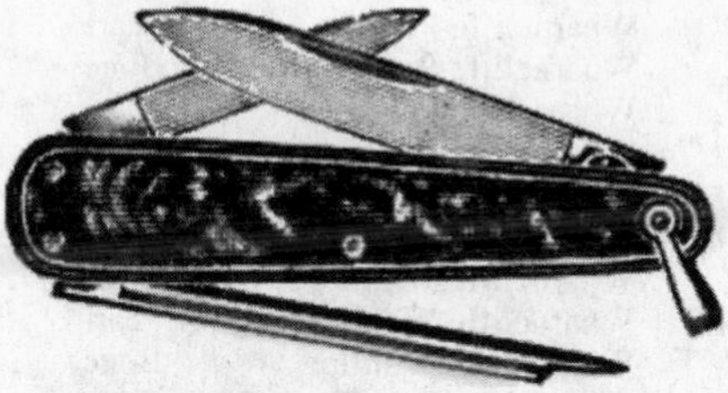

R7385	2 5/8″	Lobster Pen	Bone	150
R7394	2 5/8″	Lobster Pen	Pearl	225
R7396	2 5/8″	Lobster Pen	Genuine Stag	200
R7403	3 3/8″	Equal End Pen	Bone	240
R7404	3 3/8″	Equal End Pen	Pearl	300
R7414	3 1/4″	Equal End Pen	Pearl	275
R7423	3 1/8″	Sleeveboard Pen	Bone	160
R7425	3 1/8″	Sleeveboard Pen	Onyx	140
R7433	3 1/2″	Sleeveboard Whittler	Bone	375
R7443	3 1/4″	Sleeveboard Pen	Bone	275
R7453	3 3/8″	Sleeveboard Pen	Bone	225
R7463	3 3/8″	Serpentine Pen	Bone	225
R7465	3 3/8″	Serpentine Pen	Pyremite	120
R7473	3 3/8″	Serpentine Pen	Bone	240
R7475	3 3/8″	Serpentine Pen	Pyremite	110
R7483	3 3/8″	Whittler	Bone	375
R7485	3 3/8″	Whittler	Pyremite	350
R7493	3 3/8″	Whittler	Bone	375
R7495	3 3/8″	Whittler	Pyremite	350
R7500	3 3/8″	Whittler	Buffalo Horn	375

R7503	3 3/8″	Whittler	Bone	350
R7513	3 3/8″	Whittler	Bone	350
R7526	3 3/8″	Whittler	Genuine Stag	400
R7536	3 3/8″	Whittler	Genuine Stag	425
R7543	3 1/4″	Serpentine Pen	Bone	175
R7544	3 1/4″	Serpentine Pen	Pearl	225
R7546	3 1/4″	Serpentine Pen	Genuine Stag	225
R7554	3 1/4″	Serpentine Pen	Pearl	200
R7564	3 3/8″	Serpentine Pen	Pearl	250

Pattern No.		Description	Handle	Mint Price
R7566	3³/8″	Serpentine Pen	Genuine Stag	250
R7573	3¹/4″	Serpentine Pen	Bone	175
R7574	3¹/4″	Wharncliffe Pen	Pearl	225
R7576	3¹/4″	Wharncliffe Pen	Genuine Stag	250
R7584	3³/8″	Serpentine Whittler	Pearl	350
R7586	3³/8″	Serpentine Whittler	Genuine Stag	350
R7593	3¹/4″	Serpentine Whittler	Bone	300
R7594	3¹/4″	Serpentine Whittler	Pearl	350
R7596	3¹/4″	Serpentine Whittler	Genuine Stag	350
R7603	3¹/4″	Serpentine Pen	Bone	300
R7604	3¹/4″	Serpentine Whittler	Pearl	350
R7606	3¹/4″	Serpentine Whittler	Genuine Stag	375
R7613	3¹/8″	Wharncliffe Pen	Bone	140
R7614	3″	Wharncliffe Pen	Pearl	200
R7623	3″	Wharncliffe Pen	Bone	150
R7624	3″	Wharncliffe Pen	Pearl	200
R7633	3¹/8″	Wharncliffe Whittler	Bone	300
R7643	3¹/8″	Wharncliffe Pen	Bone	150
R7645	3¹/8″	Wharncliffe Pen	Pyremite	150
R7653	3″	Wharncliffe Whittler	Bone	325
R7654	3¹/8″	Wharncliffe Whittler	Pearl	400
R7663	3″	Wharncliffe Whittler	Bone	325
R7664	3″	Wharncliffe Whittler	Bone	325
R7674	2⁵/8″	Wharncliffe Pen	Pearl	160
R7683	2³/4″	Lobster Pen	Bone	140
R7684	2³/4″	Lobster Pen	Pearl	200
R7696	3⁵/8″	Whittler	Genuine Stag	450
R7706	3⁵/8″	Whittler	Genuine Stag	225
R7713	2¹/2″	Equal End Pen	Bone	125
R7725	3¹/4″	Budding Knife	Pyremite	125
R7734	3³/4″	Fob Pen	Pearl	225
R7744	2³/4″	Fob Pen	Pearl	225
R7756	4¹/4″	Whittler	Genuine Stag	1400

R7766	4¹/2″	Jumbo Whittler	Genuine Stag	1500
R7772	3¹/8″	Sleeveboard Pen	Black Composition	160
R7773	3¹/8″	Sleeveboard Pen	Bone	175
R7775	3¹/8″	Sleeveboard Pen	Pyremite	165
R7783	3¹/8″	Sleeveboard Pen	Bone	275
R7785	3¹/8″	Sleeveboard Pen	Pyremite	275
R7793	3¹/8″	Sleeveboard Pen	Bone	175
R7795	3¹/8″	Sleeveboard Pen	Pyremite	175
R7803	3¹/8″	Sleeveboard Pen	Bone	275
R7805	3¹/8″	Sleeveboard Pen	Pyremite	300
R7813	3¹/8″	Equal End Pen	Bone	175
R7814	3¹/8″	Equal End Pen	Pearl	275
R7823	3³/8″	Wharncliffe Jack	Bone	175

Pattern No.		*Description*	*Handle*	*Mint Price*
R7825	3 3/8"	Wharncliffe Cattle Knife	Pyremite	175
R7833	4 1/2"	Jumbo Sleeveboard	Bone	950
R7853	3"	Equal End Pen	Bone	160
RC7853	3"	Equal End Pen	Bone	140
R7854	3"	Equal End Pen	Pearl	225
R7857	3"	Equal End Pen	Imitation Ivory	175
R7863	3 1/8"	Equal End Pen	Bone	150
R7873	3 1/8"	Equal End Pen	Bone	150
R7895	3"	Emblem Pen	Pyremite	140
R7925	2 7/8"	Equal End Pen	Pyremite	125
R7985	3 1/8"	Novelty Bottle Knife	Pyremite	200
R7993	3 3/8"	Bartender Knife	Bone	250
R7995	3 3/8"	Bartender Knife	Pyremite	225
R8003	3"	Equal End Pen	Bone	140
R8004	3"	Equal End Pen	Pearl	200
R8013	3 3/8"	Equal End Pen	Bone	140
R8023	3 3/8"	Whittler	Bone	325
R8039	2 7/8"	Bartender Knife	Metal	225
R8044	2 3/4"	Lobster Pen	Pearl	300
R8055	3 3/8"	Switchblade	Pyremite	500
R8059	3 1/2"	Bartender Knife	Metal	200
R8063	3 1/4"	Switchblade	Bone	475
R8065	3 1/2"	Switchblade	Pyremite	450
R8069	3 1/2"	Switchblade	Metal	425
R9003-SS	3"	Sleeveboard Pen	Bone	175

Remington Sheath Knives

The success of Remington's pocketknife line, coupled with demand from dedicated users of its cutlery products, prompted the company to begin manufacture of sheath knives in 1925. Their production continued until the company ceased its cutlery manufacturing in 1940. Collectors recognize two eras of Remington sheath knives, the UMC era prior to 1933 and the DuPont ownership afterward until 1940. Fixed blade knives made during either era by Remington are of increasing interest to collectors. Remington's sheath knife pattern numbers are preceded by the designation RH and the majority of knives have the number marked on the blade tang.

The following listing indicates a variety of handle materials. Knives with handles called "leather" are made of leather washers compressed with fiber and metal spacers. The term "rubber" is used to indicate handles made of hard, black rubber embossed with checkering and "Remington." Handles described as "wood" are made of various woods that have been jigged (in a pattern similar to bone jigging) or checkered. Handles with wood types named are smooth wood. Several knives were handled with man-made plastic type materials combined with metal and fiber washers. These materials, which the knife manufacturer called "Pyremite," "DuRemite" or "Plastacele," are included in the listing below as "pyremite."

Prices shown are values for knives in excellent unworn condition and with original sheath. Remington's sheaths were sewn leather with a strap/snap for holding the knife. Most were embossed with the Remington circle logo or, for Official Boy Scout models, the scout emblem. The collector value of a knife without a sheath should be reduced by approximately 20%.

Model	*Length*	*Blade Length*	*Handle*	*Comment*	*Mint Price*

RH-4	7½″	4½″	Bone	No guard—UMC	125
RH-4	7½″	4½″	Bone	Full guard—DuPont	125
RH-6	9¼″	5¼″	Rosewood	"Campmaster"—DuPont	140
RH-14	7¾″	4″	Leather	DuPont	180
RH-22	6¼″	2″	Wood	Fish Scaler—DuPont	135
RH-24	7½″	4″	Leather	Basket weave sheath—DuPont	150

RH-28	8½″	4½″	Embossed Hard Rubber	UMC and DuPont	220

RH-29	9″	5″	Embossed Hard Rubber	UMC	225

RH-30	10″	5¾″	Bone	Full Guard—UMC and DuPont	650

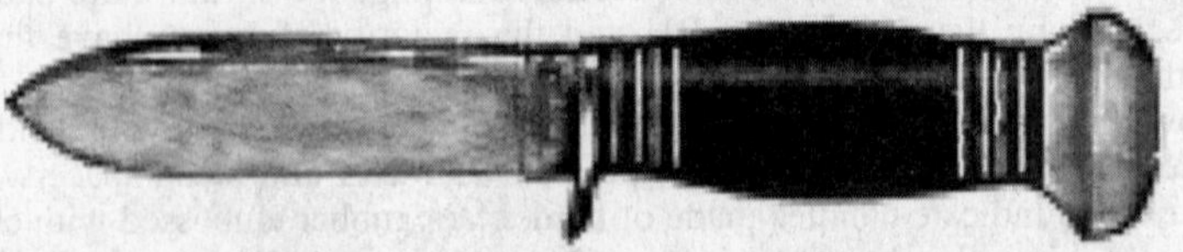

RH-31	7¾″	3⅞″	Leather	UMC	750

RH-32	8½″	4½″	Leather	UMC and DuPont	225

Model	*Length*	*Blade Length*	*Handle*	*Comment*	*Mint Price*
RH-33	9″	4 1/2″	Leather	UMC and DuPont	375

RH-34	9 3/8″	5″	Leather	UMC and DuPont	325

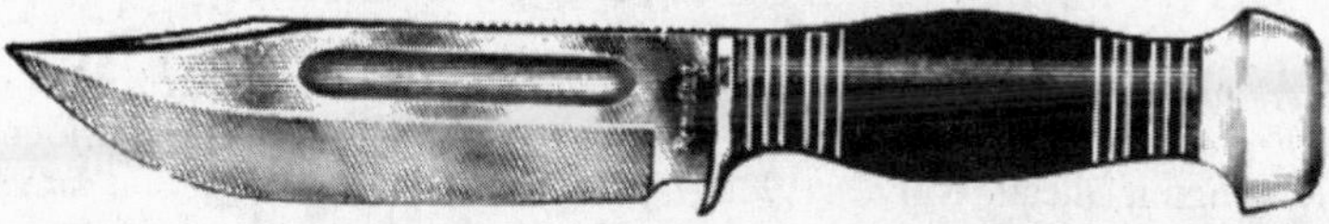

RH-35	9 3/4″	5 1/4″	Leather	UMC	450

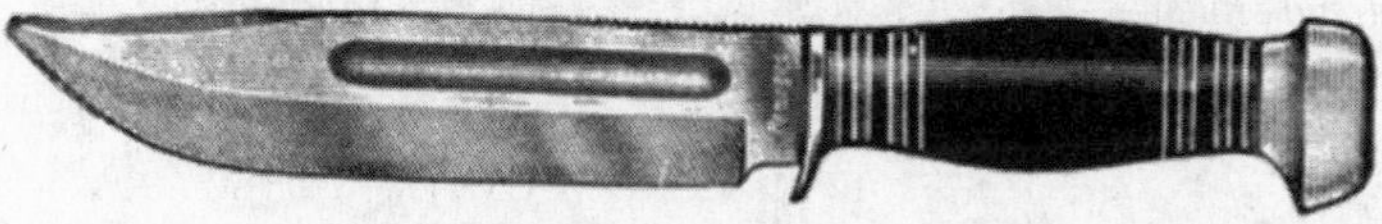

RH-36	10 3/4″	6 1/4″	Leather	UMC and DuPont	475
RH-38	12 1/2″	8″	Leather	UMC	1000

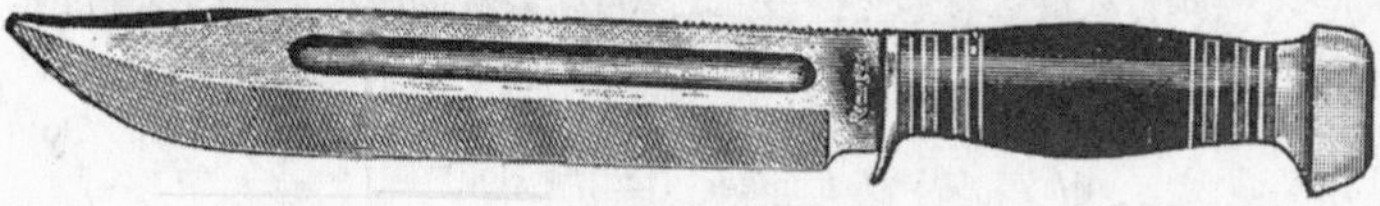

RH-40	14 1/2″	10″	Leather	UMC	2500
RH-42	8 1/2″	4 1/2″	Embossed Hard Rubber	DuPont	375

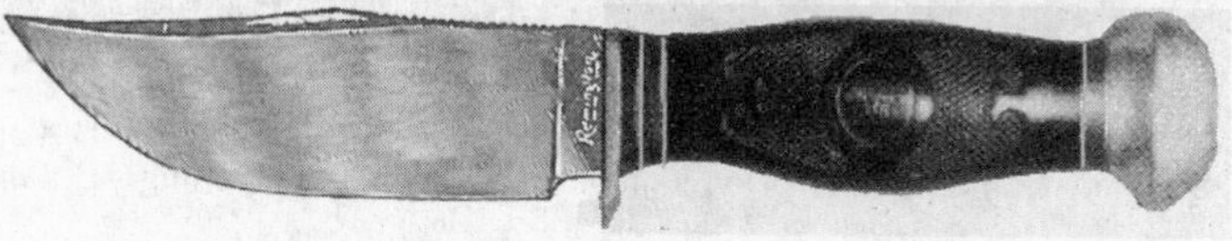

RH-43	9″	4 1/2″	Embossed Hard Rubber	DuPont	600

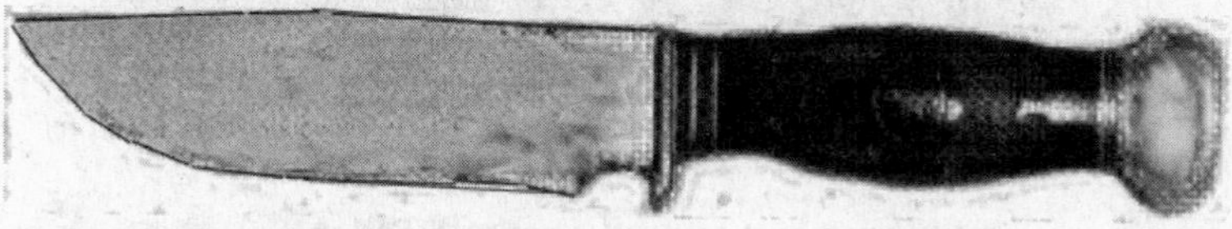

RH-44	9 3/8″	5″	Embossed Hard Rubber	DuPont	800
RH-45	9 3/4″	5 1/4″	Wood	Fish Knife—DuPont	175

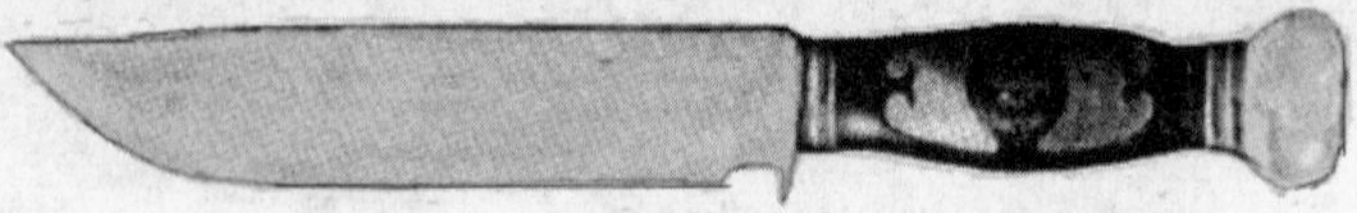

Model	*Length*	*Blade Length*	*Handle*	*Comment*	*Mint Price*
RH-46	10″	6¼″	Embossed Hard Rubber	Handle spacers—DuPont	1100

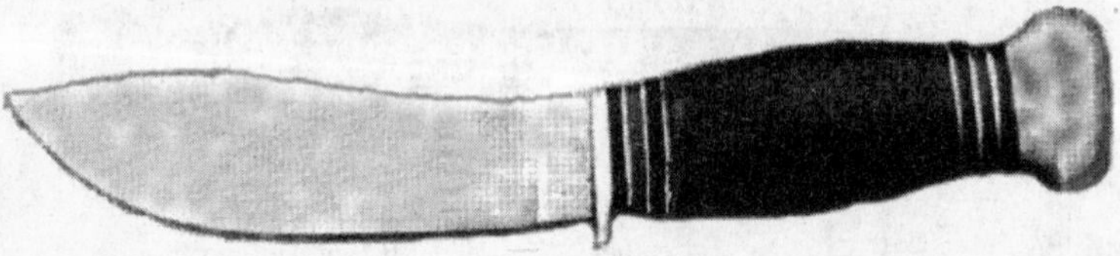

RH-50	8½″	4½″	Leather	UMC and DuPont	325

Note: There are several variations of the Remington RH-50 Boy Scout Knife, with scout insignia etched on the blade. D. Y. Grimm, in his excellent reference entitled Identification Guide to Remington Sheath Knives, 1925–1940, *describes seven different knives of this model and believes there may be others not yet identified. Variations are primarily in blade types (straight and curved), handle (with and without finger grooves) and butt caps (pinned and countersunk nuts).*

RH-51	8″	4″	Leather	Boy Scout Insignia—DuPont	250
RH-55	9″	4½″	Wood	"Fisherman"—DuPont	200

RH-65	8″	4½″	Cocobolo	Fish Knife—UMC and DuPont	175
RH-70	8″	4½″	Leather	DuPont	200

RH-71	8″	4½″	Leather	Deer Scene Etching—DuPont	250
RH-72	8″	4½″	Pyremite	Deer Scene Etching—DuPont	225

RH-73	8″	4½″	Genuine Stag	Deer Scene Etching—DuPont	375

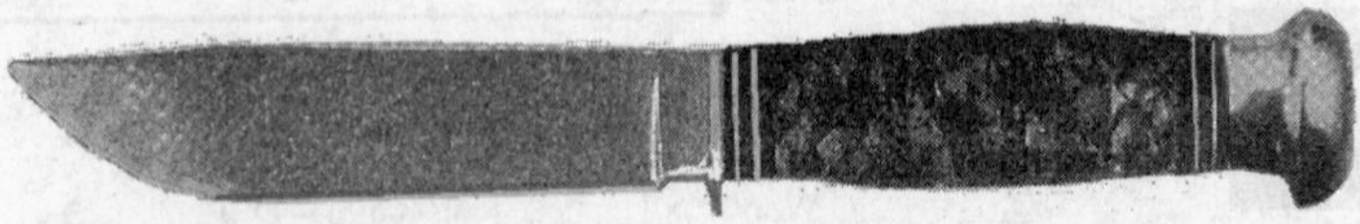

RH-74	8″	4″	Pyremite	DuPont	175

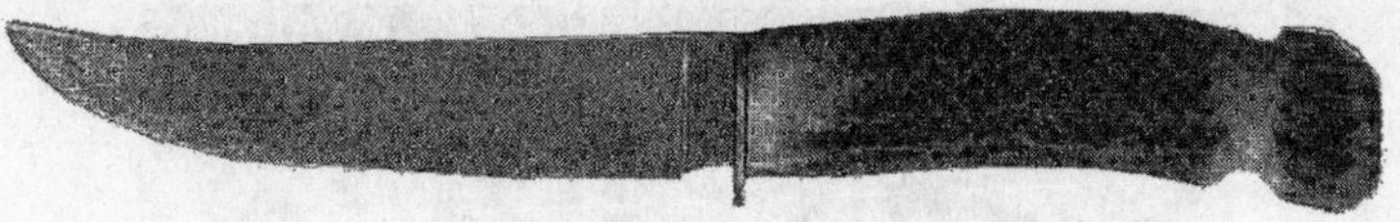

Model	*Length*	*Blade Length*	*Handle*	*Comment*	*Mint Price*
RH-75	8″	4″	Genuine Stag	DuPont	275

RH-84	8″	4″	Leather	Ring on pommel—DuPont	200

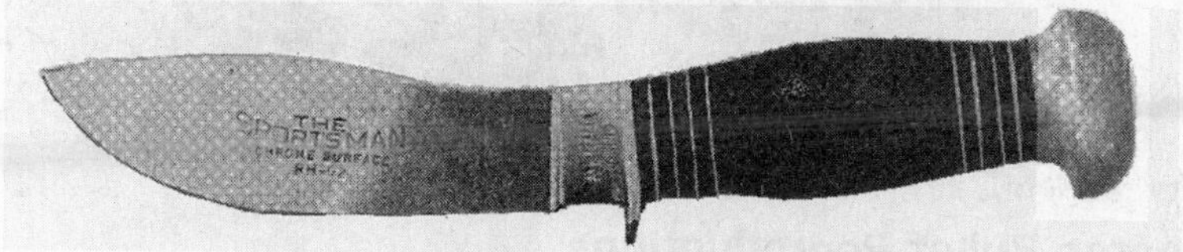

RH-92	8 1/2″	4 1/2″	Leather	Etch "Sportsman"—DuPont	425
RH-104	7 1/2″	3 3/4″	Red Pyremite	DuPont	250

RH-134	9 3/8″	5″	Leather	"Stainless Steel"—UMC	800
RH-204	7 1/2″	3 3/4″	Colored Plastic	Full guard—DuPont	300
RH-251	8″	4″	Leather	Girl Scout Knife—DuPont	275

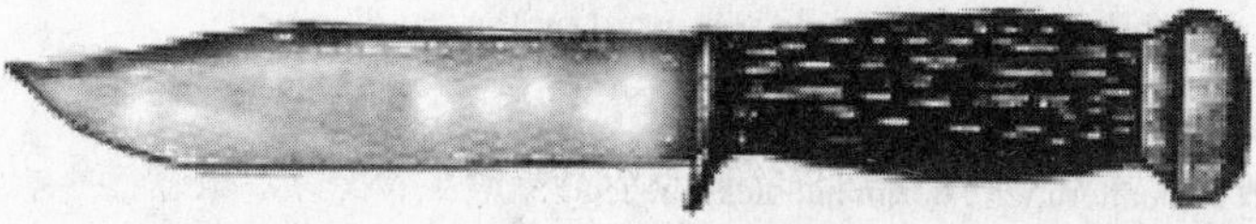

RH-290	9″	5″	Imitation Stag	UMC	275

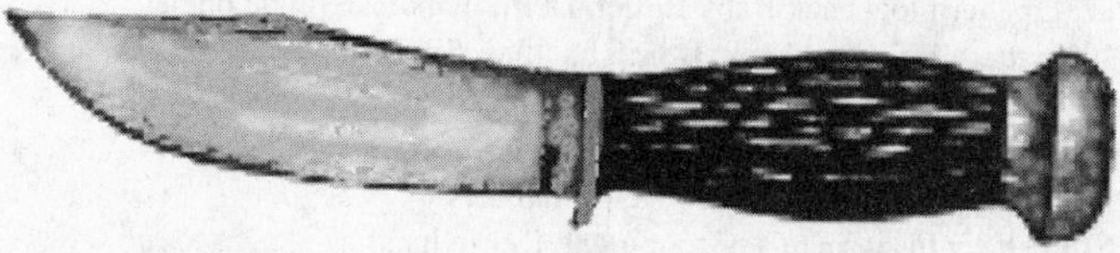

RH-320	8 1/2″	4 1/2″	Imitation Stag	UMC	325
RH-320	8 1/2″	4 1/2″	Genuine Stag	DuPont	400

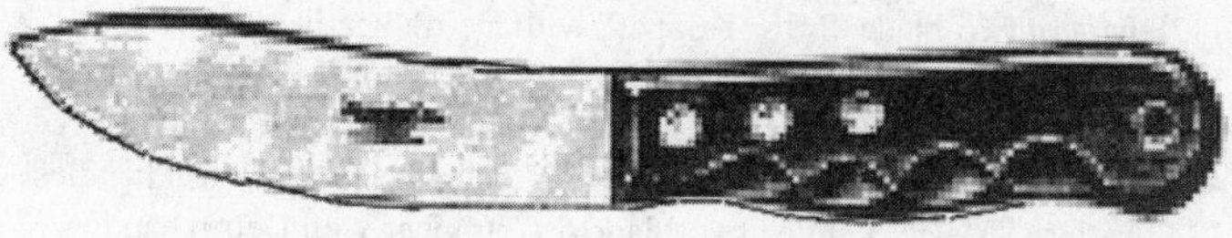

RH-405	10″	5″	Walnut	UMC and DuPont	175

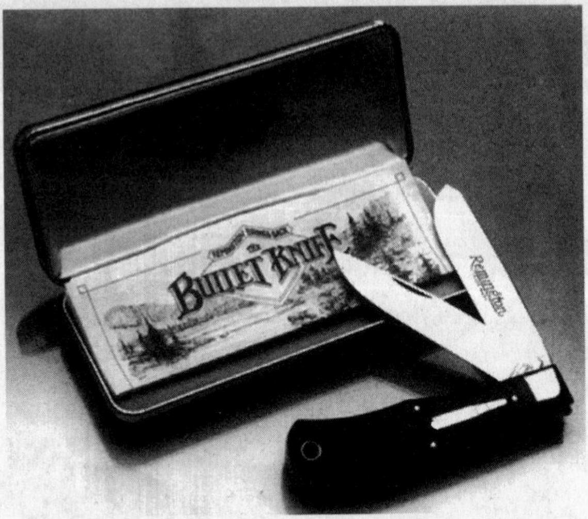

Remington Bullet Reproductions

In 1982, Remington Arms began a series of knives to be issued annually as reproductions of the famed Remington "Bullet" knives of a half-century ago. The knives are made for Remington by other manufacturers, such as Camillus, but are distributed through Remington's dealer network.

The success of Remington's program and the value increases of most of these reproductions has been quite good. The earlier releases are in growing demand and so are the companion posters, issued concurrently with the knives and reproducing posters of some fifty years ago. The first knife retailed at $39.95 and now commands prices of more than ten times that amount when accompanied by the original box and papers.

Remington Bullet reproduction knives are etched "Remington/Trade Mark" on their master blades and tang brand stampings are the circle Remington marking used years ago. Except for the first knife, issued in 1982, the reproduction series knives are also stamped with the year of their release. Bullet shields are used on the handles.

Year	*Model*	*Mint Price*
1982	R1123 pattern with delrin handles	$625
1983	R1173 pattern Baby Bullet. Remington blade etch. Delrin handles. Stamped "1983"on reverse blade tang	$285
1984	R1173L pattern lockback Baby Bullet. Delrin handles. Single blade	$175
1984	R1303 pattern large lockback. Delrin handles. Single blade	$210
1985	R4353 pattern "Woodsman." Two-blade Moose. Delrin handles. Stainless steel long clip and spey blades	$110
1986	R1263 pattern two-blade hunter. Delrin handles	$250
1987	R1613 pattern Fisherman's 5″ toothpick. Delrin handles	$175
1988	R4466 pattern Muskrat with delrin handles	$120
1989	R1128 pattern large two-blade trapper with cocobolo handles	$95
1990	R1306 pattern "The Tracker" lockback with Staglon (imitation stag) handles	$70
1991	R1178 pattern two-blade "Mini Trapper" with Delrin handles	$70
1992	R1253 pattern "Guide" one-blade lockback trapper with Delrin handles	$65
1993	R4356 pattern "Bush Pilot," two-blade "Muskrat" with Delrin handles	$80
1994	R4243 pattern "Camp Knife" four-blade 4 3/4″ equal end with Delrin handles	$95
1995	R1273 pattern "Master Guide" two-blade 5 1/4″ trapper with Delrin handles	$65
1996	R3843 pattern "Scout" with cartridge shield inset into Delrin handles	$60
1997	R4468 pattern "Lumber Jack″	$60
1998	R293 pattern "Big Banana" 5 1/4″ trapper with Delrin handles	$65

1999	R103 pattern "Ranch Hand" jack knife with Delrin handles	$65
2000	R1123 pattern "Navigator" bullet	$60
2001	R1613 pattern "Mariner" 5″ toothpick. Tortoise celluloid handles	$60
2002	"Apprentice" 4 1/8″ celluloid handled trapper	$65
2003	R1173 pattern "Pioneer" 3 1/2″ Baby Bullet. Cocobolo handled trapper.	$60
2003	20th Anniversary Bullet Knife gold gilded. Bullet shield on red/yellow delrin handles based on 4 1/2″ R1123 pattern	$55

ROBESON CUTLERY COMPANY

Millard F. Robeson founded the company which bore his name in 1879 as a cutlery jobbing firm, operating from his home in Elmira, New York. Selling knives was, at first, a side-line but business grew. Robeson's first storage area was his dresser drawers but, as additional space was needed, it overflowed into the closet and underneath the bed. Upon returning from a business trip and finding his cutlery inventory moved to the porch, he agreed with Mrs. Robeson that larger facilities were needed. They first came in the form of a new room added to the house, next a new building adjacent to the home and finally a move to the New York town of Camillus.

After leasing the cutlery works in Camillus, Robeson employed about three dozen workers making knives. Their tenure at this factory lasted about four years, until 1898. Robeson had purchased an interest in Rochester Stamping Works and it became Robeson Rochester Corporation. A move of the Robeson Cutlery Company's headquarters and manufacturing was made to Rochester and, about two years later, to an additional location in Perry, New York.

In 1901, the trade name SHUREDGE was adopted for Robeson's quality line of cutlery. After Robeson's death in 1903, his company remained although business declined. In 1940, the then bankrupt company was purchased by Saul Frankel, a Rochester businessman. Frankel was not like Robeson, who had the knowledge and expertise for manufacturing high-quality knives. But, he was an excellent businessman and recognized his shortcomings. In order to seek success for his company, Frankel sought out and hired Emerson Case to serve as Robeson's vice president and general manager. Case reorganized the company and became its president in 1948. Robeson continued to make knives until 1965 when Case retired.

The company had been purchased by Federal Cutlery Inc. in 1964 and from 1965 to 1977 sold knives marked with the Robeson stamping but manufactured by other companies. For about six years, Robeson knives were made by Camillus Cutlery Co. but were shipped from the Perry headquarters. In 1971, the Ontario Knife Company bought Robeson and made Robeson brand knives until 1977, when the trademark was dropped.

Robeson knives were stamped ROBESON CUTLERY CO. from 1894 to 1922. From 1922 to 1977, the well-known stampings of ROBESON SHUREDGE ROCHESTER and ROBESON SHUREDGE USA were used. A few Robeson knives will be found with a German stamping, indicating their country of manufacture.

A trademark popular with collectors is the line of Robeson knives named POCKETEZE and identified by the shield name. Registered in 1914, the trademark meant that the blade backs were recessed below the knife handles, reducing their wear on pant pockets. MASTERCRAFT, another Robeson trademark, was used and these knives were also identified by shield marking. Etched on the blades of some Robeson knives are the words "Frozen Heat," indicating a tempering process developed in 1950 by Emerson Case.

Older Robeson knives are handled in green bone, brown bone and a unique red bone referred to as strawberry bone. Of the bone handles used, strawberry bone was used later in the company's manufacturing years. It was dropped from the line in the 1950s in favor of plastic or composition handles of a similar color. The last Robeson knives made had a darker delrin handle.

Although Robeson bone was and is quite popular, Robeson also handled knives in mother-of-pearl, genuine stag and the various composition handle materials. The shortage of bone during World War II forced the company to use rough black composition handle materials.

With the exception of a very few German-made models, which use a four-digit number, the Robeson line used a six-digit pattern number.

The first number signifies handle material as follows:

0—Metal—Aluminum or Stainless Steel
1—Black Composition
2—Rosewood or Walnut
3—Black Pyraline
4—White Composition or Ivory Celluloid
5—Saw-Cut Bone, Stag or Delrin
6—Jigged Bone or Delrin
7—Pearl or Abalone
8—Swirl Composition or Celluloid
9—Gunmetal or Pearl Celluloid

The second number signifies the number of blades, while the third number indicates the liner and bolster materials as follows:

0—Combination handle-liner-bolster
1—Steel liners and bolsters
2—Brass liners, nickel silver bolsters
3—Nickel silver liners and bolsters
6—Iron liners and bolsters
8—Steel liners and bolsters
9—Stainless steel or chrome plated

The remaining three numbers are the factory pattern numbers.

Robeson knives listed below with six-digit numbers are listed first by number of blades, then in ascending order by handle material code number and finally, each blade/handle group is listed in order of the factory pattern number.

Model	*Size*	*Pattern*	*Handle*	*Mint Price*
One-Blade Knives				
116118	5 1/2"	Folding Hunter	Black Composition	450
211007	4"	Pruning Knife	Rosewood	75
211008	4"	Maize Knife	Rosewood	80

Model	*Size*	*Pattern*	*Handle*	*Mint Price*
211035	3 3/8"	Speying Knife	Rosewood	75
211908	3 3/8"	Maize Knife	Rosewood	75
212807	3 3/8"	Pruning Knife	Rosewood	75
511168	3 3/8"	Barlow	Stag	115
511178	3 3/8"	Barlow	Stag	115
511179	3 3/8"	Barlow	Stag	115
511224	5"	Daddy Barlow	Stag	300
512224	5"	Daddy Barlow	Stag	300
512872	4 1/2"	Folding Hunter	Stag	400
513872	4 1/2"	Folding Hunter w/guard	Stag	425
521179	3 3/8"	Barlow	Bone	100
612060	4 1/8"	Folding Hunter	Bone	325

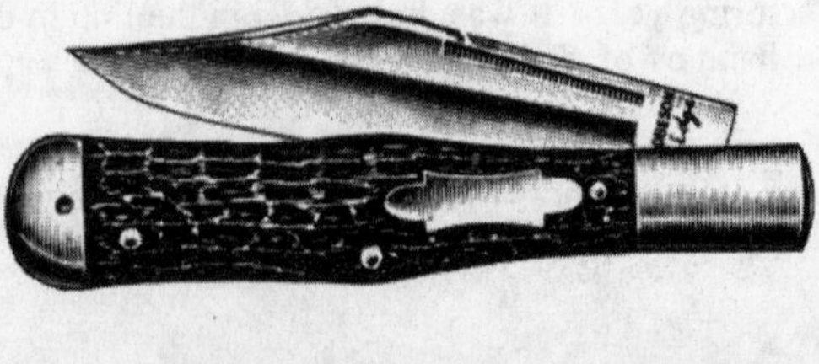

Model	*Size*	*Pattern*	*Handle*	*Mint Price*
612118	5 1/2"	Folding Hunter	Bone	500
612246	5 1/4"	Lockback Hunter	Bone	575
612407	5"	Powderhorn	Bone	275
612610	5"	Lockback Hunter	Bone	500
616118	5 1/2"	Folding Hunter	Bone	500
616407	5"	Powderhorn	Bone	290
619872	4 1/2"	Folding Hunter w/guard	Bone	400
812118	5 1/4"	Folding Hunter	Maize Pyraline	450
812872	4 1/2"	Folding Hunter	Maize Composition	300

816407	5"	Powderhorn	Red/White Pyraline	250
Two-Blade Knives				
026319		Father & Son Set	Bone	425
126056	3 3/4"	Regular Jack	Black Composition	110
126240	3 5/8"	Open End Jack	Black Composition	90
126636	3 3/8"	Sleeveboard Jack	Black Composition	95
128105	3"	Equal End Pen	Black Composition	60
222030	3 1/2"	Electrician Knife	Walnut	95
222050	3 7/8"	Bulldog Jack	Rosewood	200
322013	3 5/8"	Equal End Jack	Black Pyraline	100

322027	3 3/4"	Easy Open Jack	Black Pyraline	150
322286	3 3/8"	Regular Jack	Black Pyraline	85
323404	2 3/4"	Serpentine Pen	Black Pyraline	75
323480	3 3/8"	Serpentine Jack	Black Pyraline	95
323617	2 7/8"	Sleeveboard Pen	Black Pyraline	60
323646	3"	Dogleg Jack	Black Pyraline	120
323657	3 3/8"	Serpentine Jack	Black Pyraline	85
323669	3 1/2"	Dogleg Jack	Black Pyraline	120
323675	3"	Equal End Pen	Black Pyraline	80
323676	3"	Equal End Pen	Black Pyraline	80
323817	2 7/8"	Sleeveboard Pen	Black Pyraline	85

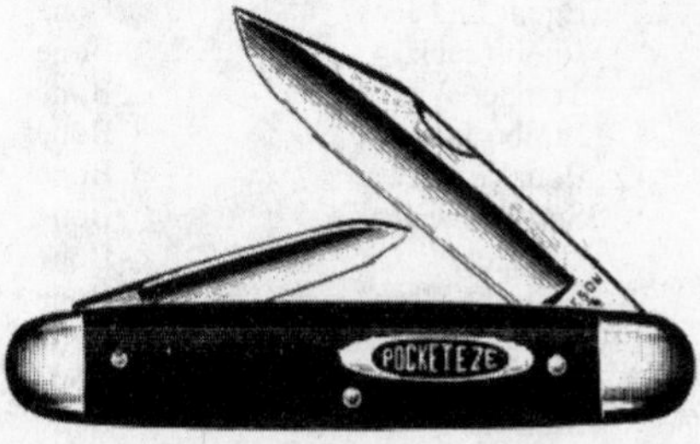

Model	Size	Pattern	Handle	Mint Price
323826	3⅝″	Equal End Pen	Black Pyraline	95
323865	3⅜″	Regular Jack	Black Pyraline	85
326011	3″	Equal End Jack	Black Pyraline	75
326015	3″	Equal End Jack	Black Pyraline	75
326242	3⅜″	Open End Jack	Black Pyraline	80
421179	3⅜″	Barlow	White Composition	135
421200	3⅜″	Barlow	White Composition	130
422064	2¾″	Equal End Pen	White Composition	75
422174	3¾″	Office Knife	White Composition	75
422274	3¼″	Office Knife	White Composition	75
423405	3¼″	Serpentine Pen	White Composition	95
423430	3⅜″	Barlow	White Composition	95

521168	3⅜″	Barlow	Stag	150
521178	3⅜″	Barlow	Stag	150
521179	3⅜″	Barlow	Stag	160
521199	3⅜″	Barlow	Stag	150
522482	4½″	Dogleg Trapper	Stag	350
523858	2⅞″	Sleeveboard Pen	Stag	120
529003	2¾″	Equal End Pen	Metal	55
529007	2¾″	Equal End Pen	Metal	55
529404	2¾″	Equal End Pen	Metal	55
529735	2½″	Lobster Pen	Metal	70
529740	2¾″	Lobster Pen	Metal	60
621105	3″	Equal End Pen	Bone	75
621177	3″	Congress Pen	Bone	120
622001	3¼″	Equal End Jack	Bone	95
622003	2¾″	Senator Pen	Bone	85
622013	3⅝″	Equal End Jack	Bone	120
622020	3⅝″	Slim Jack	Bone	140

622022	3⅝″	Sleeveboard Pen	Bone	125
622026	3″	Regular Jack	Bone	95
622027	3¾″	Easy Open Jack	Bone	150
622037	4″	Jumbo Jack	Bone	225
622048	1⅞″	Equal End Jack	Bone	55
622056	3¾″	Jumbo Jack	Bone	150
622061	4⅛″	Trapper	Bone	180
622062	4⅛″	Jumbo Jack	Bone	275
622064	2¾″	Equal End Pen	Bone	85
622083	2¾″	Serpentine Jack	Bone	120
622088	3¾″	Congress	Bone	150
622100	3¼″	"Jimmy Allen" Jack	Bone	300
622102	3¾″	Sleeveboard Pen	Bone	100
622105	3″	Equal End Pen	Bone	85
622119	4½″	Slim Jack	Bone	250

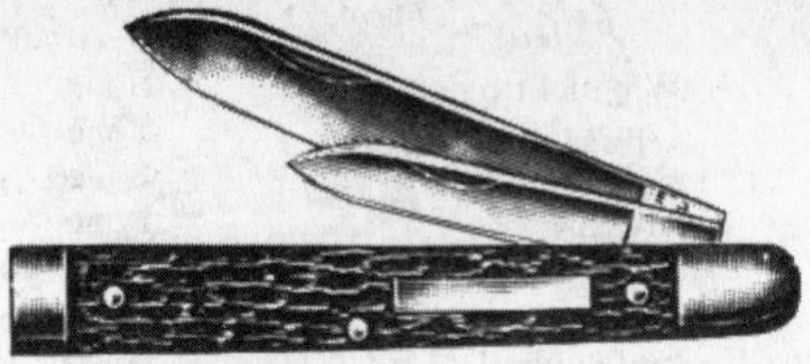

Model	*Size*	*Pattern*	*Handle*	*Mint Price*
622138	3 3/4″	Doctor's Knife	Bone	275
622151	4 1/2″	Jumbo Jack	Bone	275
622167	3″	Equal End Pen	Bone	100
622177	3″	Congress Pen	Bone	125
622183	2 3/4″	Serpentine Jack	Bone	95
622187	4″	Texas Jack	Bone	300
622193	3 3/4″	Congress Jack	Bone	190
622195	3″	Doctor's Knife	Bone	250
622225	3 5/8″	Half Whittler	Bone	145
622229	2 5/8″	Sleeveboard Pen	Bone	70

622253	3 5/8″	Equal End Pen	Bone	100
622295	3 3/8″	Premium Jack	Bone	90
622319	3″	Equal End Pen	Bone	80
622331	2 5/8″	Equal End Pen	Bone	75

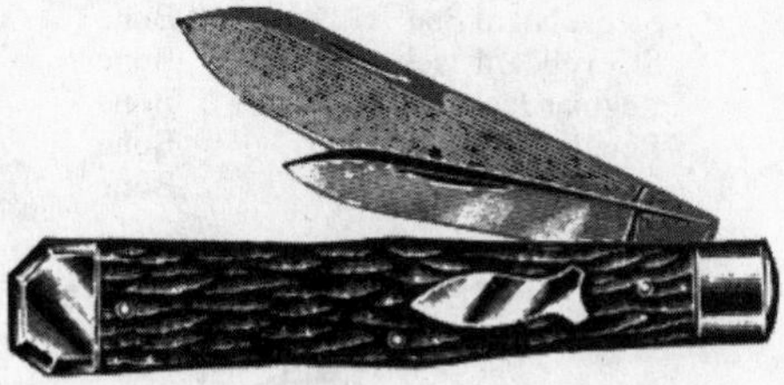

622358	3 1/2″	Crown Jack	Bone	275
622382	4 1/8″	Trapper	Bone	325
622393	2 3/4″	Peanut	Bone	100
622457	4 1/8″	Slim Jack	Bone	225
622597	3 7/8″	Premium Jack	Bone	140
622636	3 1/2″	Regular Jack	Bone	90
622841	3 3/8″	Sleeveboard Pen	Bone	135
623177	3″	Congress Pen	Bone	130
623191	3 1/4″	Equal End Pen	Bone	85
623405	3 1/4″	Serpentine Pen	Bone	95
623422	3 5/8″	Equal End Pen	Bone	110
623480	3 3/8″	Serpentine Jack	Bone	125

Model	*Size*	*Pattern*	*Handle*	*Mint Price*
623500	3 3/8″	Wharncliffe Pen	Bone	165
623501	3″	Equal End Pen	Bone	95
623505	3 1/4″	Equal End Pen	Bone	95
623595	3 7/8″	Muskrat	Bone	250
623603	2 3/4″	Equal End Pen	Bone	85
623662	3 1/4″	Equal End Pen	Bone	90
623667	3 7/8″	Serpentine Jack	Bone	110
623671	3″	Equal End Jack	Bone	90
623681	3″	Equal End Pen	Bone	85
623698	3 5/8″	Equal End Jack	Bone	100
623777	3 5/8″	Congress	Bone	175
623851	2 11/16″	Equal End Pen	Bone	80

623858	2 7/8″	Sleeveboard Pen	Bone	100
623875	3 5/8″	"Woodcraft" Knife	Bone	200
626041	3 3/8″	Regular Jack	Bone	90
626052	3 3/4″	Regular Jack	Bone	100
626054	3 3/4″	Regular Jack	Bone	100
626056	3 3/4″	Regular Jack	Bone	110
626094	3 3/8″	Open End Jack	Bone	85
626104	3 3/8″	Boy's Knife w/chain	Bone	110
626204	3 3/8″	Open End Jack	Bone	90
626240	3 3/8″	Open End Jack	Bone	95
626241	3 3/8″	Open End Jack	Bone	120
626242	3 3/8″	Regular Jack	Bone	120
626331	2 5/8″	Sleeveboard Pen	Bone	85
626636	3 3/8″	Sleeveboard Jack	Bone	110
626637	3 3/8″	Regular Jack	Bone	90
626765	3 3/8″	Regular Jack	Bone	95
626766	3 3/8″	Easy Open Jack	Bone	95

629005	3 1/4″	Senator Pen	Bone	85
629675	3″	Equal End Pen	Bone	85
722007	2 3/4″	Equal End Pen	Pearl	100
722110	2 3/4″	Swell Center Pen	Pearl	135
722120	2 1/2″	Sleeveboard Pen	Pearl	110
722159	2 3/8″	Senator Pen	Pearl	100
723167	3″	Equal End Pen	Pearl	120
722236	2 1/2″	Sleeveboard Pen	Pearl	110
722237	2 3/8″	Senator Pen	Pearl	100
722273	3″	Lobster Pen	Pearl	145
723317	2 3/4″	Sleeveboard Pen	Pearl	110
722319	3″	Equal End Pen	Pearl	100
722320	3″	Equal End Pen	Pearl	100
722380	2 1/2″	Senator Pen	Pearl	100
722381	3″	Senator Pen	Pearl	110

Model	*Size*	*Pattern*	*Handle*	*Mint Price*
723442	2 3/4″	Senator Pen	Pearl	100
723681	3″	Equal End Pen	Pearl	110
727304	3 1/8″	Office Knife	Pearl	140

822023	3 1/4″	Regular Jack	Horn Pyraline	95
822048	2 7/8″	Sleeveboard Pen	Gold Pyraline	90
822061	4 1/8″	Trapper	Maize Composition	250
822064	2 3/4″	Senator Pen	Black Pyraline	85
822094	3 3/8″	Open End Jack	Maize Pyraline	90
822183	2 3/4″	Serpentine Pen	Gold Pyraline	90

822253	3 5/8″	Equal End Jack	Maize Pyraline	90
822295	3 5/8″	Premium Jack	Horn Pyraline	90
822319	3″	Equal End Pen	Red Pyraline	85
822355	3 3/8″	Slim Jack	Imitation Pearl	100
822393	2 13/16″	Peanut	Maize Composition	120
822482	4 1/2″	Dogleg Trapper	Maize Composition	275
822497	5″	Fishing Knife	Maize Pyraline	175
822728	3 3/8″	Serpentine Pen	Maize Pyraline	110
822850	2 3/4″	Premium Jack	Gold Pyraline	80
823505	3 1/4″	Equal End Pen	Gray Pyraline	90
823724	3 1/2″	Dogleg Jack	Black Pyraline	150
823851	3 11/16″	Equal End Pen	Maize Composition	90

823881	3 5/8″	Texas Jack	Maize Pyraline	140
922253	3 3/8″	Equal End Jack	"Shur Wood"	95
922295	3 3/8″	Premium Pen	"Shur Wood"	95
922296	3 3/8″	Open End Pen	"Shur Wood"	85
922497	5″	Powderhorn	"Shur Wood"	150
929004	2 3/4″	Equal End Pen	Gunmetal	55
929007	2 3/4″	Equal End Pen	Gunmetal	55
929404	2 3/4″	Equal End Pen	Gunmetal	55
929735	2 1/2″	Lobster Pen	Gunmetal	70
929740	2 3/4″	Lobster Pen	Gunmetal	75

Model	*Size*	*Pattern*	*Handle*	*Mint Price*

Three-Blade Knives

033750	4″	Premium Stock	Metal	175
132433	3⅝″	Cattle Knife	Black Composition	175
333633	3⅝″	Cattle Knife	Black Pyraline	140
432868	3⅜″	Cattle Knife	White Composition	130
433594	3⅞″	Premium Stock	White Composition	120
433595	3⅞″	Premium Stock	White Composition	115
433727	3⅝″	Serpentine Stock	White Composition	110
533167	3″	Equal End Whittler	Stag	140
533728	3⅜″	Serpentine Stock	Nickel silver	95
533729	3⅜″	Serpentine Stock	Nickel silver	90
533750	4″	Premium Stock	Nickel silver	140
539445	2¾″	Lobster Pen	Metal	55
632102	3⅝″	Sleeveboard Whittler	Bone	250
632167	3″	Senator Whittler	Bone	175

632225	3⅝″	Balloon Whittler	Bone	275
632295	3⅝″	Premium Stock	Bone	150
632319	3″	Whittler Pen	Bone	160

632596	3⅞″	Premium Stock	Bone	140
632750	4″	Premium Stock	Bone	265
632751	4″	Premium Stock	Bone	230
632768	3⅝″	Cattle Knife	Bone	165
632800	3⅜″	Wrench Knife	Bone	500
632831	3⅜″	Premium Stock	Bone	135
632838	3⅜″	Premium Stock	Horn Pyraline	125
632868	3⅜″	Cattle Knife	Bone	135

Model	*Size*	*Pattern*	*Handle*	*Mint Price*
632882	3⁵/₈″	Premium Stock	Bone	125
633295	3³/₈″	Premium Stock	Bone	125
633295TC	3³/₈″	Premium Stock	Bone	130
633593	3⁷/₈″	Premium Stock	Bone	125
633594	3⁷/₈″	Premium Stock	Bone	150
633595	3⁷/₈″	Premium Stock	Red Pyraline	165
633596	3⁷/₈″	Premium Stock	Bone	150
633662	3¹/₄″	Senator Whittler	Bone	120
633670	3³/₈″	Serpentine Stock	Bone	175
633681	3″	Senator Whittler	Bone	120
633727	3⁵/₈″	Serpentine Stock	Bone	145
633728	3³/₈″	Serpentine Stock	Bone	130
633750	4″	Premium Stock	Bone	200
633830	3³/₈″	Serpentine Stock	Bone	160
633850	2⁵/₈″	Serpentine Pen	Bone	90
633865	3³/₈″	Cattle Knife	Bone	150
633866	3³/₈″	Cattle Knife	Bone	150

633875	3⁵/₈″	"Woodcraft" knife	Bone	275
633880	3⁵/₈″	Premium Stock	Bone	140
633881	3⁵/₈″	Premium Stock	Bone	150
633884	3⁵/₈″	Premium Stock	Bone	150
633885	3⁵/₈″	Premium Stock	Bone	150
633886	3⁵/₈″	Premium Stock	Bone	140
732118	3″	Premium Jack	Pearl	165
732167	3″	Whittler Pen	Pearl	175
732200	3¹/₄″	Barlow	Pearl	175
733505	3¹/₄″	Whittler Pen	Pearl	180
832597	3⁷/₈″	Premium Stock	Maize Composition	120
832726	3³/₈″	Serpentine Stock	Maize Pyraline	115
832838	3³/₈″	Premium Stock	Horn Pyraline	125
832883	3⁵/₈″	Premium Stock	Horn Pyraline	120
833295	3³/₈″	Premium Stock	Maize Composition	110
833595	3⁷/₈″	Premium Stock	Red Pyraline	115
833850	2⁵/₈″	Premium Stock	Imitation Pearl	115
833865	3³/₈″	Cattle Knife	Maize Pyraline	125
833867	3³/₈″	Cattle Knife	Maize Pyraline	125

Model	*Size*	*Pattern*	*Handle*	*Mint Price*
833880	3⅝″	Serpentine Stock	Maize Pyraline	130
833881	3⅝″	Cattle Knife	Maize Pyraline	150
833887	3⅝″	Premium Stock	Red Pyraline	135
939445	2¾″	Lobster Pen	Gunmetal	75
Four-Blade Knives				
642088	4⅛″	Congress	Bone	300
642208	4⅛″	Congress	Bone	350
642214	3⅝″	Scout/Utility	Bone	325

643453	3½″	Congress	Bone	275
643645	3⅝″	Scout/Utility	Bone	300
643777	3⅜″	Congress	Bone	270
742198	3¼″	Senator Pen	Pearl	175
742282	3⅜″	Lobster Pen	Pearl	175

J. RUSSELL & COMPANY

Although John Russell entered into the cutlery manufacturing business in 1834, it was forty-one years later that the company began to make pocketknives. His first factory was located in Greenfield, Massachusetts, where it sat on the banks of the Green River. Russell's first products were cast steel socket chisels and axe heads followed, shortly thereafter, by the addition of butcher knives and an assortment of kitchen knives.

Even though the company's products were well accepted for their high quality, its own fortunes were not so good. The first facility was destroyed by fire and its replacement, Russell's second shop, was severely damaged by a flood some two years after the company's founding.

In 1836, Russell was joined in business by his brother, Francis, and an investor named Henry Clapp. The new factory they built was christened the "Green River Works," a tradename that would soon be carried on knives across America. The Russells developed several labor-saving devices and introduced a steam engine to power much of their equipment. Their innovative ideas also included setting wages at a rate that lured skilled cutlery workers from the Sheffield, England, factories. The net result was a reputation for quality and a profitable business.

In the late 1830s, Russell began to make what was called "An American Hunting Knife" and stamped it with the company name and trademark. The knives were such a success that, during the next couple of decades, well over a half-million knives marked "J. Russell & Co., Green River Works" were sold to the western trade. The fame of these butcher and skinning-style knives was such that Sheffield capitalized upon it by flooding the American market with their own "Green River" knives.

In 1868, a fire destroyed much of the Greenfield factory and a new one was built in Turner Falls, Massachusetts. The John Russell Manufacturing Company's new cutlery factory was the largest in the world and featured many conveniences not found in the company's previous facilities. Nearly 500 employees worked there, but it was reported that the factory was large enough to employ over a thousand workmen. Although business was good, with sales volume near $750,000, the new factory had drained the company's financial resources. The company went bankrupt in 1873 and reorganization took place soon thereafter, with no members of the John Russell family remaining as investors.

Manufacture of pocketknives began in 1875 and, by 1877, Russell made over 400 different patterns and had sold over a half-million pieces. Similar to the fame earned by Russell's

Green River knives, another knife pattern's name would become synonymous with that of its manufacture. The first "Barlow" had been invented about 1667 by a Sheffield cutler, Obadiah Barlow, but it was Russell who would make it America's favorite for several decades. It became famous by selling for 15¢ and 25¢ for the one-blade and two-blade models, respectively. When the post–World War I steel price increases dictated a price increase on Russell's barlows, consumers were unhappy and the company discontinued its manufacture in the early 1930s.

In 1933, the John Russell Manufacturing Company merged with the Harrington Cutlery Company to become the Russell-Harrington Company and was moved to Southbridge, Massachusetts. When a popular *Louisville Courier Journal* columnist, Allen Trout, founded the Barlow Bobcats Club in the early 1950s (a requirement was to own an original Russell Barlow), the company participated for a while in the knife's renewed popularity by restoring Russell barlows for $1. Knife production today is primarily in kitchen cutlery, and pocketknives have not been made since about 1930. The 12,000 Russell Barlow Commemorative knives introduced by the company in 1974 were manufactured by another company, probably Schrade.

SCHATT & MORGAN

This company, at one time one of the largest cutlery manufacturers in the United States, was originated when J. W. Schatt and C. B. Morgan formed the New York Cutlery Company about 1890. Both men had considerable previous experience within the cutlery industry. Schatt had worked with the J. R. Torrey Razor Company and Morgan had sold knives manufactured by the Canastota Knife Company as well as his brother's Bayonne Knife Company.

Their business was at first a cutlery importing firm, but the partners soon opened their own factory in Gowanda, New York, and named it Schatt & Morgan Cutlery Company. Knives sold during the 1890–1895 period were stamped S & M NEW YORK and S & M GOWANDA N.Y., crossed with an elongated "X." When this facility was sold in 1895 to the Platts family, the partners' business was moved to nearby Titusville, Pennsylvania, and incorporated there.

Although the business headquarters had moved, Schatt continued to reside in Gowanda and work out of his hometown. In 1911, Morgan purchased Schatt's interest but continued the company under the dual name.

The demise of this producer of fine knives began about 1922 and was heralded with the announcement by American Cutler that "the Queen City Cutlery Company of Titusville, Pa., manufacturers of pocketknives, has been incorporated with a capital stock of $25,000." Another announcement that year reported that Schatt & Morgan's staff was 60 men, about one-third of its usual work force. The new company had been started at the expense of Schatt & Morgan by five of the factory foremen producing extra parts after the shift, then assembling them into knives marked with the QUEEN CITY brand. The company fired these employees but found it difficult to continue to operate efficiently with inadequate supervisory personnel and with the former employees now devoting full time to making the competitive brand. Schatt & Morgan Cutlery Company was forced to close its doors in 1930. The irony of this saga was Queen City Cutlery's 1932 purchase of the building, machinery, and stock of parts owned by the old company and subsequent move into the S & M factory.

Schatt & Morgan produced a large variety of knives in considerable quantities—near 600 different patterns were offered in 1911 and several million knives were sold. Still, when compared to several other brands, Schatt & Morgan knives are not easy to find. When found, they are not easy to identify because few were stamped with standardized pattern numbers offering information about number of blades, handle material, or bolster type. A large variety of bolster and liner materials were used including brass, nickel silver, steel, and Norway iron. Shield variety was also plentiful with most common styles of the period being used.

Knives marked SCHATT & MORGAN KNIVES GOWANDA N.Y. and S & M NEW YORK are the rarest since most will be found bearing an S & M TITUSVILLE PA. or

SCHATT & MORGAN, TITUSVILLE, PA. stamp. In addition to its own high quality knife line, the company also produced knives under contract for other marketing firms.

SCHRADE CUTLERY

Schrade Cutlery Company was incorporated in 1904 by the Schrade brothers, Louis, William and George. As former employees of Walden Knife Company, the brothers were well indoctrinated in the cutlery business and began their own in a building about 2,000 square feet in size. The primary goal was, at first, to produce and market the Push Button Knife that had been invented by George a dozen years earlier. Their business grew and, in 1915, Schrade purchased the Walden Cutlery Handle Company. This company had been formed by the Schrade brothers' company in cooperation with two other New York cutlery firms, New York Knife Company and Walden Knife Company.

About this time, George Schrade left the company and formed his own, the George Schrade Cutlery Company, in Bridgeport, Connecticut, in his own enterprising effort to manufacture the switchblade knife which he had invented. Upon his departure, Louis Schrade filled the office of president, left vacant by George. The new leader took immediate steps to revolutionized his factory into mass production. A second factory in Middletown, New York, was established in 1918 and managed by Joseph Schrade, another brother. This branch was closed in 1932 as a result of the Great Depression.

But the parent company would continue to survive and produce quality knives. In addition to its own extensive line, Schrade Cutlery Company made knives under contract for several major hardware distributing firms. Its capacity for producing large quantities of quality knives would stand in good stead for the business brought on during World War II through government contracts.

Schrade Cutlery Company remained under the ownership and leadership of the Schrade family until 1947. At that time, the brothers Henry and Albert Baer of Ulster Knife Company bought Schrade. The company name and knife stamping was changed at that time to Schrade-Walden. Ten years later, production of the company's knives was moved to Ellenville, New York. Although the Walden factory was closed, most of the employees remained with the company and many of them were transported daily by bus from Walden to Ellenville.

Schrade's earliest knife stamping is the rarest to be found. Used at the time of the company's founding, it is SCHRADE CUT CO. WALDEN, N.Y. GERMANY and it dates to about 1904. The next marking was SCHRADE CUT CO. in a half-circle over WALDEN, NY in a straight line. Although no records can be found showing how long this marking was used, it is believed to have been up until the World War I era. The straight line "Schrade Cut Co." marking was adopted after World War I and was used until World War II or shortly afterward when the company was sold. Even then, the USA stamping was not used until the early or mid-1950s when it was changed to SCHRADE WALDEN NY USA. This tang stamp was used until the change, in 1973, to SCHRADE NY USA. Beginning in the early 1970s, knives made by the company on contract and for special limited editions sold by Schrade were often stamped SW. CUT USA. on the blade's rear tang.

Through the years, Schrade has used practically every popular handle material on its knives. The favorite for collectors, however, has been bone and other natural materials. Bone handled knives made during the 1920–1955 era and commonly referred to as a peach tree seed bone or peach seed bone, due to the material's resemblance to a dried and cut peach seed, are especially favored. This bone, dyed to a medium tan to brown color, was made for Schrade by the Rogers Bone Company until its factory burned in 1956. The company made very few genuine bone handled knives after that. Even though peach seed bone has a distinctive appeal all its own, knives made by Schrade and handled in red bone and smooth tan bone are considered by collectors to be much rarer. From 1960 to 1978, Schrade did not produce any bone handle knives but used delrin or man-made materials instead. In 1978, several different bone handled knives were produced on contract for Parker-Frost Cutlery Company. Approximately 6,000 knives were produced in each of green, red and brown bone and these knives were stamped "Schrade" on the rear tang. In 1983, Schrade's own knives handled in genuine bone were reintroduced in the company's "Heritage" series. By the mid-1980s, these knives were dropped from the Schrade line.

During its ninety-year existence, Schrade has manufactured knives for a large number of other companies including Shapleigh Hardware, Hibbard, Spencer and Bartlett, L.L. Bean and Buck, as well as the above-mentioned Parker-Frost company.

Schrade has also been a major producer of commemorative knives and played a major role in building the popularity of commemoratives during the "early days" of the 1970s. They were produced in the thousands, but special issues such as Minuteman, Paul Revere, Liberty Bell, Jim Bowie, Will Rogers, Service Series, Buffalo Bill and Custer's Last Fight found homes with many would-be knife collectors. While the company's aim was profitable sales and collectors were a means to that end, its activities proved a benefit to the collector movement as the general public was made aware of limited edition knives as collectibles. Because of the numbers produced (18,000 to 24,000), most of those knives sold over thirty years ago are valued in the collector market at prices only slightly higher than their retail price at issue.

This book's listing of Schrade knives consists of those produced from 1904 to 1947, stamped "Schrade Cutlery Co., Walden N.Y." Many hundreds of patterns were produced from this large pocketknife manufacturer. The serious collector of Schrade Cutlery knives will find the reprinted *Catalog E and Supplements*, which pictures and describes knives made during the late 1920s to the mid-1930s, of great benefit. Even though a large quantity of this 108-page catalog reprint was produced a number of years ago, it is still available. During the era of the Schrade-Walden stamping—1948 to 1973—a good share of knives produced were patterned and produced as were their predecessors. Although a three-digit numbering system was adapted, the numbers of many of those early knives were adapted from the Schrade Cut era. Knives produced during the first ten years of this period are becoming as popular with collectors as the "Schrade Cuts" and, in general, their values are at least 80% of those of the older knives.

When Schrade's knife production moved in 1957 from the Walden factory to the Ulster factory in Ellenville, construction changes included a switch from bone to delrin and to different blade finishes. Knives produced during this latter portion of the Schrade-Walden era are generally less than half that of knives from the early Schrade-Walden era.

Key to Schrade Cutlery Company (1904–1946) Numbering System

The number of blades is denoted by the first number as follows:

1—represents a one-blade knife
2—represents a two-blade knife with both blades in one end
3—represents a three-blade knife with all blades in one end
7—represents a two-blade knife with a blade in each end
8—represents a three-blade knife with two blades in one end and 1 blade in the other end
9—represents a four-blade knife with two blades in each end

The second and third digits of the knife number indicate the handle die pattern. An example would be the 2013 with the second 01 indicating the Easy Open pattern.

The fourth digit indicates the kind of handle material used as follows:

1—Cocobolo
2—Ebony
3—Bone Stag
4—Celluloid
5—White Bone
6—Mother of Pearl
7—Stained or Dyed Bone
8—Buffalo Horn
9—Miscellaneous

The type or color of celluloid handles is indicated by a letter or letters after the fourth digit (always "4") as follows:

AC—Assorted Colors
AP—Abalone Pearl
B—Black
BLUE—Blue Pearl
BP—Black Pearl
BRNZ—Bronze
C—Cocobolo
GL—Goldaleur
GP—Golden Pearl
G—Green Pearl
H—Black and White Stripe
HORN—Horn
J—Red, White and Amber striped
K—Brown Lined Cream
M—Marine Pearl
MB—Mottled Blue
MR—Mottled Red
O—Onyx
P—Smoked Pearl
PP—Persian Pearl
S—Tortoise Shell
US—Red, White and Blue striped
W—(White) Imitation Ivory
X—Mottled Green

Miscellaneous handles are indicated by a letter or letters after the figure "9" as follows:

BR—Solid Brass
GM—Gunmetal
GOLD—Twelve-Karat Gold Plate
GS—Genuine Stag
GSIL—Nickel Silver
SS—Sterling Silver

A fraction at the end of a number indicates the kind of blade substituted for a spear blade as follows:

1/4—Spey
1/2—Sheepfoot
3/4—Clip
7/8—Razor Point

Other designations included:

T—After the pattern number indicates tip bolsters
S—Before the pattern number indicates a special combination or finish
SS—Before the pattern number indicates stainless steel blades and backsprings
B—Before the pattern number indicates a knife with brass liners that was usually made with steel liners
F—Before the pattern number indicates a knife with nail file blade that was usually made with cutting blades
LB—After the pattern number indicates the substitution of a punch blade
Ch—After the pattern number indicates a knife with chain
Sha—After the pattern number indicates a shackle on knife end
Emb—After the pattern number indicates an emblem on handle

Schrade Cutlery Company, Walden, N.Y.

Pattern	*Handle*	*Mint Price*
One-Blade Knives		
5″ Fisherman's Barlow		
SSC114$^{3}/_{4}$S	Bone Stag	350
4$^{5}/_{16}$″ Hawkbill Pruner		
123EW	Walnut	125
4″ Maize Knife		
M1001	Cocobolo	125
4″ Pruning Knife		
1003	Bone Stag	150
1001	Cocobolo	100

5″ Toothpick

5″ Toothpick		
1083	Bone Stag	225
1083$^{3}/_{4}$	Bone Stag	200
1084J	Pyralin	150
3$^{5}/_{8}$″ Open End Jack		
1091	Cocobolo	75
5$^{1}/_{4}$″ Folding Hunter		
1104$^{3}/_{4}$Stg	Celluloid Stag	220
1104$^{3}/_{8}$Mc	Pearl Pyralin	225
1104$^{3}/_{8}$PO	Onyx Celluloid	230
3$^{5}/_{8}$″ Florist's Knife		
11034$^{5}/_{8}$W	Ivory Celluloid	80
11034$^{1}/_{2}$W	Ivory Celluloid	80
3$^{1}/_{2}$″ Jack Knife		
1131	Cocobolo	80
1131$^{3}/_{4}$	Cocobolo	80
1133	Bone Stag	100

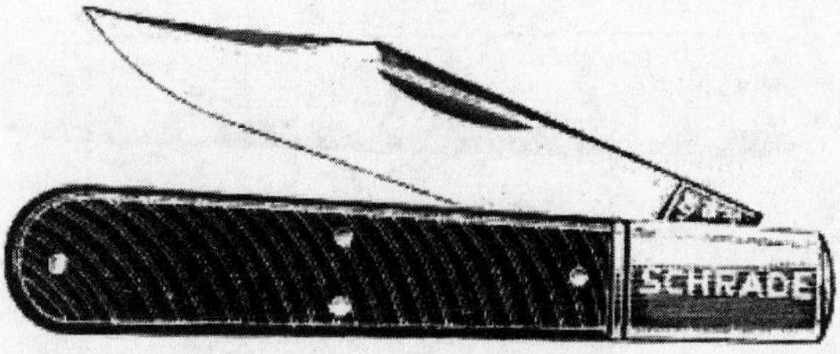

5″ Daddy Barlow

5″ Daddy Barlow		
1147$^{3}/_{4}$	Bone	275

Pattern	*Handle*	*Mint Price*
3 3/8" Barlow		
115S	Bone Stag	125
1151	Cocobolo	90
1152	Ebony	100
1153	Bone Stag	120
1153 3/4	Bone Stag	120
L1153	Bone Stag	130
1157	Bone	115
1157 1/4	Bone	120
1157 1/2	Bone	120
1157 3/4	Bone	120
3 1/4" Open End Jack		
1251	Cocobolo	85
1251-Ch	Cocobolo	95
1253-Ch	Bone Stag	110
1253	Bone Stag	100

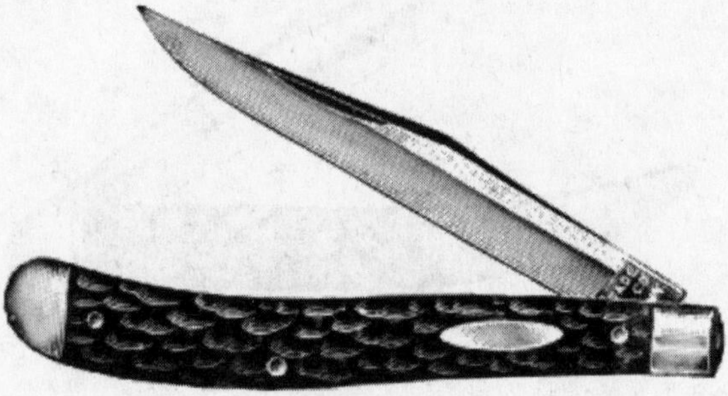

4 1/8" Slim Trapper

4 1/8" Slim Trapper		
1293 3/8	Bone Stag	200
1294 3/8J	Striped Pyralin	185
1294 3/8K	Cream Pyralin	160
3 1/8" Senator Pen		
1309GSIL	Nickel Silver	50

4" Budding Knife

4" Budding Knife		
1354 1/4W	White Celluloid	100
1354 1/4B	Black Celluloid	85
1354 1/2B	Black Celluloid	85
S1354 1/4B	Black Celluloid	85
4 7/16" Pruning Knife		
1361	Cocobolo	110

Pattern	Handle	Mint Price
4 7/16" Linemen's Knife		
1361 Sha	Cocobolo	125
4 7/16" Sailor's Knife		
N1361	Cocobolo	100
SN1364Stg Sha	Fibestos	100
3 9/16" Pruning Knife		
1391	Cocobolo	85
3 9/16" New England Whaler		
1392 1/2	Ebony	95

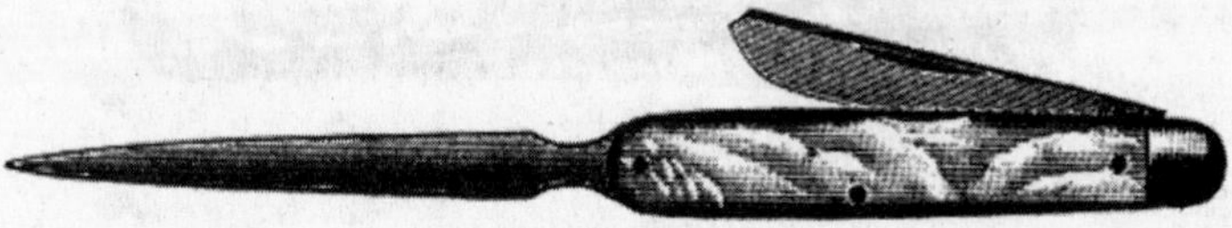

8 7/8" Letter Opener/Knife

Pattern	Handle	Mint Price
8 7/8" Letter Opener/Knife		
L1404W	White Celluloid	275
3 1/8" Ring Opener Pen		
LR1429GSIL	Nickel Silver	175
3 5/16" Senator Pen		
L1784M	Pearl Pyralin	125
3 3/8" Equal End Jack		
SS1564W	Ivory Celluloid	65
4 5/8" Budding Knife		
1694B	Black Celluloid	95
1693	Bone Stag	130
3 1/8" Corn Knife		
C1824W	Ivory Celluloid	95
6" Letter Opener/Knife		
L1824M	Pearl Pyralin	220
4 1/2" Folding Hunter		
1863 3/4	Bone Stag	250
1864 3/4J	Striped Pyralin	230
3 7/8" Serpentine Jack		
1943 3/4	Bone Stag	185
3 7/8" Florist's Knife		
S1944W (Pruning)	Ivory Celluloid	80
S1944W (Grafting)	Ivory Celluloid	80
S1944W (Budding)	Ivory Celluloid	80
C1944W (Budding)	Ivory Celluloid	80
4 1/4" Florist's Knife		
1974 1/2W	White Celluloid	100
Two-Blade Knives		
3 5/8" Easy Open Jack		
2013	Bone Stag	135
2011	Cocobolo	110
2012	Ebony	120
2014	Assorted Celluloid	120
2019BR	Solid Brass	100
2014X	Green Celluloid	120
SS2013	Bone Stag	150
3 5/8" Easy Open Jack		
2022	Ebony	120
2021	Cocobolo	100
2023	Bone Stag	150
2023Ch	Bone Stag	160

$3^3/_8$" Swell End Jack

Pattern	Handle	Mint Price
$3^3/_8$" Swell End Jack		
2033	Bone Stag	150
2034K	Cream Pyralin	135
2033¾	Bone Stag	150
$3^3/_4$" Open End Jack		
C2041SD	Cocobolo	95
C2041SD Sha	Cocobolo	95
2042	Ebony	100
2042SD	Ebony	100
2042SD Sha	Ebony	100
2043	Bone Stag	120
2043¾	Bone Stag	115
C2043¾	Bone Stag	140
2043SD Sha	Bone Stag	150

$3^1/_{16}$" Dogleg Jack

Pattern	Handle	Mint Price
$3^1/_{16}$" Dogleg Jack		
2054K	Cream Pyralin	115
2053	Bone Stag	125
2054M	Pearl Pyralin	110
S2053	Bone Stag	130
2053½	Bone Stag	150
$3^5/_8$" Teardrop Jack		
2063	Bone Stag	135
2061	Cocobolo	110
2062	Ebony	125
2064	Assorted Celluloid	120
2063½	Bone Stag	135
2061¾	Cocobolo	120
2062¾	Ebony	125
2063¾	Bone Stag	130
2069BR	Solid Brass	120
2069¾BR	Solid Brass	125
$3^5/_8$" Swell End Jack		
2072	Ebony	110

Pattern	*Handle*	*Mint Price*
2071	Cocobolo	100
2073	Bone Stag	140
2073¾	Bone Stag	140
2071¾	Cocobolo	110
2072¾	Ebony	115
3" Equal End Jack		
2083B	Bone Stag	110
2084	Assorted Celluloid	90
5" Fisherman's Knife		
SSD2084PO	Onyx Celluloid	200

3⅝" Swell End Jack

3⅝" Swell End Jack		
2091	Cocobolo	120
2092	Ebony	125
2093	Bone Stag	140
5¼" Trapper		
2102⅜	Bone Stag	300
2104⅜M	Pearl Pyralin	275
2104⅜PO	Onyx Celluloid	325
2109⅜GS	Genuine Stag	425
3½" Open End Jack		
2121	Cocobolo	95
2121¾	Cocobolo	95
2122	Ebony	95
2123	Bone Stag	120
2123¾	Bone Stag	125
2131	Cocobolo	90
2132	Ebony	95
2133	Bone Stag	115
2133-Ch	Bone Stag	125

3¼" Eureka Jack

3¼" Eureka Jack		
2134¾GP	Pearl Pyralin	140
2133¾	Bone Stag	160
2134¾M	Pearl Pyralin	135

Pattern	*Handle*	*Mint Price*
3³/₈″ Barlow		
215S	Bone Stag	135
215³/₄S	Bone Stag	175
215³/₄M	Pearl Pyralin	115
2155	White Bone	150
2157	Bone	135
2157¹/₄	Bone	135
2157¹/₂	Bone	135
2157³/₄	Bone	130
2157⁷/₈	Bone	130
3³/₈″ Regular Jack		
2151	Cocobolo	95
2151-Ch	Cocobolo	100
2151³/₄	Cocobolo	85
2151SD	Cocobolo	90
B2151	Cocobolo	80
B2151³/₄	Cocobolo	85
C2151	Cocobolo	85
C2151³/₄	Cocobolo	90
C2151LB	Cocobolo	120
S2151	Cocobolo	80
S2151LB	Cocobolo	120

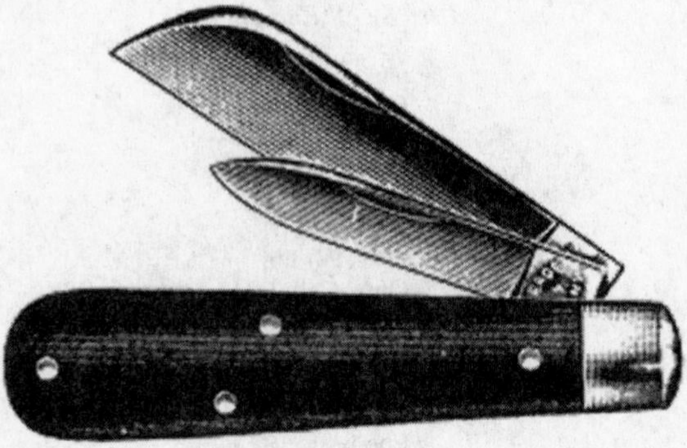

2152	Ebony	85
2152¹/₂	Ebony	90
2152³/₄	Ebony	85
B2152	Ebony	85
B2152¹/₂	Ebony	90
B2152³/₄	Ebony	85
C2152	Ebony	90
C2152³/₄	Ebony	95
C2152³/₄LB	Ebony	110
S2152	Ebony	85
S2152³/₄	Ebony	85
2153	Bone Stag	110
2153¹/₂	Bone Stag	110
2153³/₄	Bone Stag	95
2153-Ch	Bone Stag	125
B2153	Bone Stag	95
B2153¹/₂	Bone Stag	100
B2153³/₄	Bone Stag	95
C2153	Bone Stag	110
C2153¹/₂	Bone Stag	110
C2153³/₄	Bone Stag	115

3 3/8" Easy Open Jack

Pattern	*Handle*	*Mint Price*
3 3/8" Easy Open Jack		
C2153EO	Bone Stag	120
C2153SD	Bone Stag	125
L2153	Bone Stag	110
L2153 3/4	Bone Stag	100
S2153	Bone Stag	95
S2153 3/4	Bone Stag	100
S2153EO	Bone Stag	110
S2153LB	Bone Stag	115
2154 3/4M	Pearl Pyralin	125
C2154	Assorted Celluloid	100
C2154G	Pearl Pyralin	110
C2154 3/4KLB	Cream Pyralin	115
C2154 3/4APLB	Pearl Pyralin	115
C2154 3/4	Assorted Celluloid	100

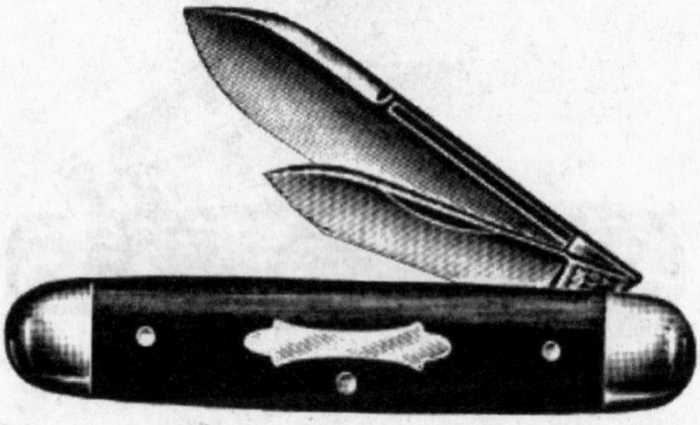

3 5/8" Equal End Jack

3 5/8" Equal End Jack		
2171	Cocobolo	100
2171 3/4	Cocobolo	95
2172	Ebony	110
2172 3/8	Ebony	120
2172 3/4	Ebony	115
2173	Bone Stag	125
2173 3/4	Bone Stag	120
2174W	Ivory Celluloid	115
2174 3/4W	Ivory Celluloid	110
2176	Genuine Pearl	275
2179GS	Genuine Stag	220

Pattern	*Handle*	*Mint Price*
3 5/8" Equal End Jack		
2193 3/4	Bone Stag	150
3 1/2" Regular Jack		
2202	Ebony	140
2203	Bone Stag	155
2203 3/4	Bone Stag	160
2211	Cocobolo	90
2211 3/4	Cocobolo	95
2212	Ebony	100
2212 3/4	Ebony	110
2213	Bone Stag	120
2213 1/2	Bone Stag	130
2213 3/4	Bone Stag	130
SS2213	Bone Stag	140
2214	Assorted Celluloid	110
2214 3/4W	Ivory Celluloid	100
2214 3/4	Assorted Celluloid	105
2219GS	Genuine Stag	175
2219 1/2GS	Genuine Stag	180
3 1/2" Serpentine Jack		
2221	Cocobolo	110
2222	Ebony	120
2223	Bone Stag	140
2223 1/2	Bone Stag	150
2223 3/4	Bone Stag	140
2224GP	Pearl Pyralin	120
2224	Assorted Celluloid	115
2226	Genuine Pearl	235

3 1/4" Open End Jack

3 1/4" Open End Jack		
2251	Cocobolo	90
2251-Ch	Cocobolo	90
2251 3/4	Cocobolo	85
B2251	Cocobolo	85
B2251 3/4	Cocobolo	85
2252	Ebony	90
2252 1/2	Ebony	90
2252 7/8	Ebony	90
2253	Bone Stag	100
2253-Ch	Bone Stag	115
2253 1/2	Bone Stag	115
2253 3/4	Bone Stag	100
B2253	Bone Stag	100
B2253 1/2	Bone Stag	100
S2253EO	Bone Stag	120

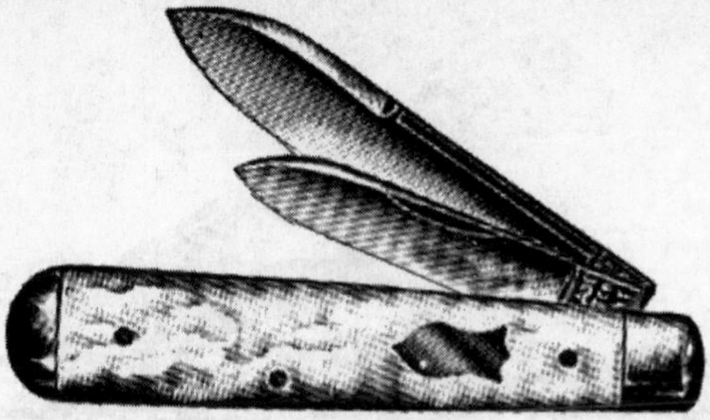

3¼″ Regular Jack

Pattern	*Handle*	*Mint Price*
3¼″ Regular Jack		
2261	Cocobolo	90
2262	Ebony	95
2263	Bone Stag	110
2264	Assorted Celluloid	95
2263½	Bone Stag	100
2263¾	Bone Stag	100
2266	Genuine Pearl	235
2269BR	Solid Brass	125
4⅛″ Slim Jack		
2273	Bone Stag	230
3½″ Jack Knife		
2271	Cocobolo	85
2281	Cocobolo	90
2283	Bone Stag	110
2283¾	Bone Stag	110
2283-Ch	Bone Stag	125
3½″ Easy Open Scout Knife		
S2282½	Ebony	160
S2283½	Bone Stag	180
3½″ Carpenter's Knife		
2293	Bone Stag	220
3⅛″ Senator Pen		
M2309GSIL	Nickel Silver	70
3⅝″ Electrician's Knife		
2311SD	Cocobolo	90
2314BSD	Black Celluloid	95
3⅜″ Serpentine Jack		
2331	Cocobolo	110
2332	Ebony	115
2333	Bone Stag	145
2334	Assorted Celluloid	120
2334K	Cream Pyralin	125
2333½	Bone Stag	140
2333¾	Bone Stag	145
3 5/16″ Serpentine Jack		
2343	Bone Stag	110
2344	Assorted Celluloid	95

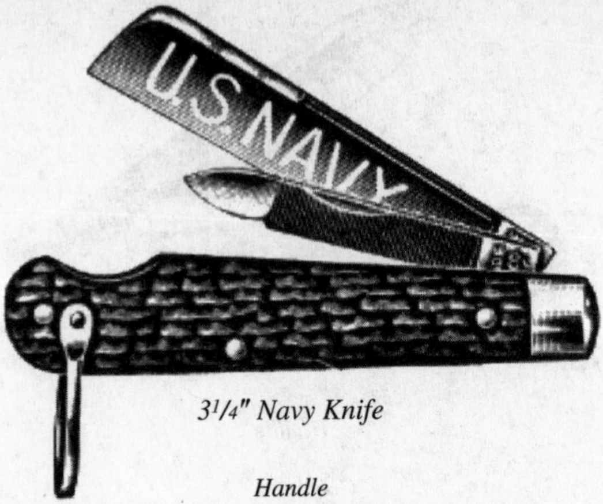

3¹/₄″ Navy Knife

Pattern	Handle	Mint Price
3¹/₄″ Navy Knife		
2353	Bone Stag	160
3¹/₂″ Jack		
2363	Bone Stag	135
2364³/₄B	Black Celluloid	85
2364³/₈B	Black Celluloid	90
3¹/₂″ Regular Jack		
2392	Ebony	130
2393	Bone Stag	150
2393³/₄	Bone Stag	150
S2393	Bone Stag	160
3⁹/₁₆″ New England Whaler		
2394¹/₂B	Black Celluloid	110
1394¹/₂B	Black Celluloid	100

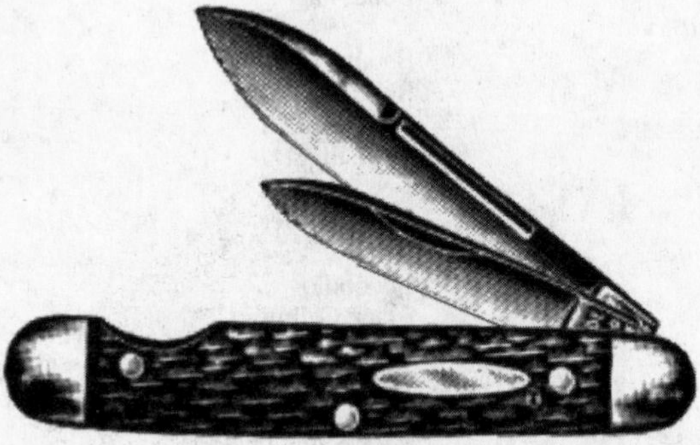

3¹/₈″ Equal End Jack

3¹/₈″ Equal End Jack		
2423	Bone Stag	95
2423³/₄	Bone Stag	100
SS2423	Bone Stag	120
2423EO	Bone Stag	100
2424	Assorted Celluloid	90
2424³/₄J	Striped Pyralin	110
2424³/₄	Assorted Celluloid	90
2424³/₄K	Cream Pyralin	90
SS2424	Assorted Celluloid	95
2426	Genuine Pearl	200
SS2426	Genuine Pearl	200
3¹/₁₆″ Equal End Jack		
C2534M	Pearl Pyralin	85
C2533	Bone Stag	95

Pattern	*Handle*	*Mint Price*
C2534K	Cream Pyralin	80
C2534¾E	Black/Pearl Celluloid	90
C2534¾Q	Blue/White Celluloid	85
C2533¾SQ	Bone Stag	110
3⅜" Equal End Jack		
2563	Bone Stag	100
2563¾	Bone Stag	100
SS2563	Bone Stag	125
2564	Assorted Celluloid	95
2564K	Cream Pyralin	95
SS2564	Assorted Celluloid	100
2566	Genuine Pearl	190
3½" Balloon Jack		
2623	Bone Stag	175
2623¾	Bone Stag	180

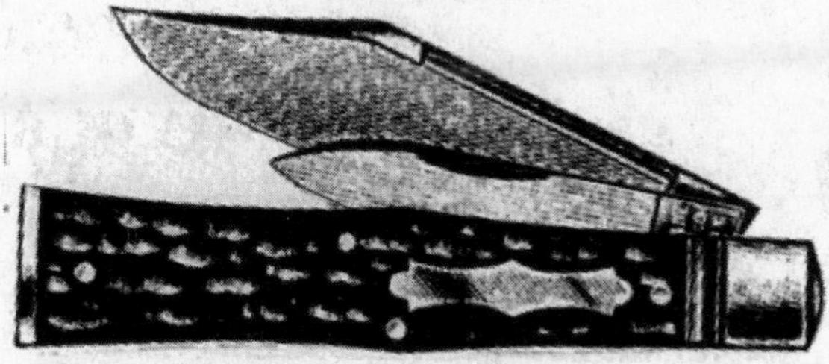

4" Balloon Pillbuster Jack

4" Balloon Pillbuster Jack		
2643¾	Bone Stag	600
2646	Genuine Pearl	850

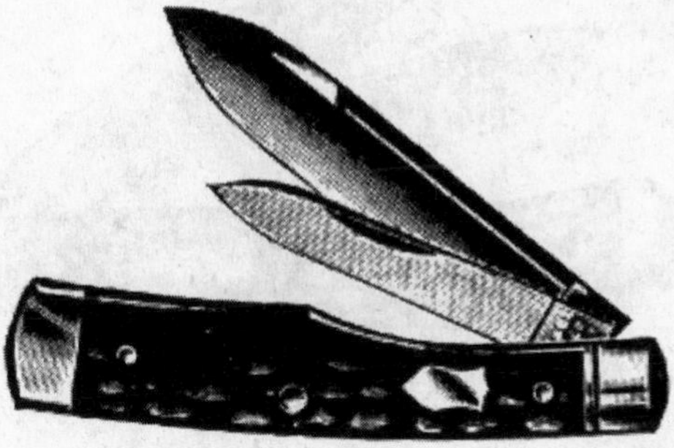

3" Gunstock Jack

3" Gunstock Jack		
2693	Bone Stag	325
2694	Assorted Celluloid	300
2⅞" Serpentine Jack		
2724⅜M	Pearl Pyralin	80
2723⅜	Bone Stag	95
2724⅜K	Cream Pyralin	85
2723	Bone Stag	100
2723¾	Bone Stag	100

$3^3/_4$" Doctor's Knife

Pattern	Handle	Mint Price
$3^3/_4$" Doctor's Knife		
2733	Bone Stag	275
4" Texas Jack		
$2813^3/_4$	Bone Stag	200
$2814^3/_4$	Assorted Celluloid	175
2813	Bone Stag	200
$4^1/_2$" Slim Jack		
2863	Bone Stag	275
$2863^3/_4$	Bone Stag	275
$L2863^3/_4$	Bone Stag	275
$3^1/_2$" Premium Jack		
2903	Bone Stag	100
$2903^3/_4$	Bone Stag	100
$2904^3/_4$	Assorted Celluloid	90

$3^7/_8$" Trapper

$3^7/_8$" Trapper		
$2943^3/_4$	Bone Stag	290
$2944^3/_4$J	Striped Pyralin	275
$S2943^3/_4$	Bone Stag	275
3" Serpentine Jack		
$2953^3/_4$	Bone Stag	110
$2954^3/_4$M	Pearl Pyralin	100
$2954^3/_4$	Assorted Celluloid	95
$2956^3/_4$	Genuine Pearl	175
2953	Bone Stag	110
2954	Assorted Celluloid	90

4 1/4" Jumbo Jack

Pattern	*Handle*	*Mint Price*
4 1/4" Jumbo Jack		
R2973	Bone Stag	275
2973 3/4	Bone Stag	275
2974 3/4W	Ivory Celluloid	250
R2974W	Ivory Celluloid	250
2 5/16" Sleeveboard Lobster Pen		
7076Sha	Genuine Pearl	100
7079GSIL Sha	Nickel Silver	70
3" Senator Pen		
7083B	Bone Stag	75
7086B	Genuine Pearl	100
7089GM	Gun Metal	70
SS7089GSIL	Nickel Silver	60
3 1/16" Senator Pen		
7099GM Sha	Gun Metal	70
7099GM	Gun Metal	65
M7099GSIL Sha	Nickel Silver	55
M7099GSIL	Nickel Silver	55
RM7099GSIL	Nickel Silver	55
7099GSIL	Nickel Silver	55
SS7099-I Sha	Stainless Steel	60
SSF7099SI Sha	Stainless Steel	60
SSM7099SI Sha	Stainless Steel	60
SS7099SI Sha	Stainless Steel	55
SS7099I	Stainless Steel	55
4 5/16" Texas Jack		
71043	Bone Stag	350
3 3/8" Sleeveboard Pen		
7113	Bone Stag	90
7113T	Bone Stag	90
7113B	Bone Stag	90
SS7113T	Bone Stag	95
7113SqB	Bone Stag	90
SS7114	Assorted Celluloid	80
7114HornB	Horn Pyralin	85

Pattern	*Handle*	*Mint Price*
7114	Assorted Celluloid	75
7114 Horn	Horn Pyralin	80
7114HornT	Horn Pyralin	80
7114SqMB	Pearl Celluloid	75
7116	Genuine Pearl	175
7116T	Genuine Pearl	175
7116B	Genuine Pearl	175
7118	Buffalo Horn	130
7118T	Buffalo Horn	125
7118B	Buffalo Horn	125
3" Corkscrew Knife		
7129GSIL	Nickel Silver	80
7129GSIL Sha	Nickel Silver	80
3¼" Wharncliffe Pen		
7133	Bone Stag	160
3⅛" Senator Pen		
7143T	Bone Stag	85
7143B	Bone Stag	85
7146T	Genuine Pearl	160
7149GST	Genuine Stag	125
3⅝" Equal End Jack		
7163	Bone Stag	120
7164½W	Ivory Celluloid	95
7171	Cocobolo	95
7172	Ebony	110
7173	Bone Stag	125
7173¾	Bone Stag	130
7174S	Tortoise Celluloid	125

3⅝" Equal End Jack

Pattern	*Handle*	*Mint Price*
3⅝" Equal End Jack		
7193	Bone Stag	150
7233	Bone Stag	180
3⅜" Sleeveboard Pen		
7243B	Bone Stag	90
7243¾B	Bone Stag	100
7243T	Bone Stag	95
7244HT	Black/White Pyralin	85
3⅛" Senator Pen		
7309GSIL Sha	Nickel Silver	60
7309GSIL	Nickel Silver	60
7309SS Sha	Sterling Silver	80
7309GM	Gun Metal	70

4 1/8" Budding and Pruning Knife

Pattern	Handle	Mint Price
4 1/8" Budding and Pruning Knife		
7303	Bone Stag	325
S7303	Bone Stag	300
RS7304W	Ivory Celluloid	250
S7309F	Fibestos	250
S7309GSIL	Nickel Silver	200
3 3/8" Sleeveboard		
7326	Genuine Pearl	175

4" Gardener's Knife

4" Gardener's Knife		
7324W	Ivory Celluloid	175
G7324W	Ivory Celluloid	175
G7324 1/2W	Ivory Celluloid	175
3 5/16" Serpentine Jack		
7344M	Pearl Celluloid	90
7343	Bone Stag	100
7344K	Cream Pyralin	90
7344	Assorted Celluloid	85
4 1/8" Marlin Spike Knife		
7353	Bone Stag	190
SS7359GSIL	Solid Nickel Silver	225
7359GSIL	Solid Nickel Silver	215
3 9/16" Serpentine Knife		
7364 3/4B	Black Celluloid	120

3 1/8" Senator Pen

Pattern	Handle	Mint Price
3 1/8" Senator Pen		
7423T	Bone Stag	80
7423B	Bone Stag	80
7423 3/4B	Bone Stag	80
7423SqB	Bone Stag	80
F7423T	Bone Stag	80
M7423TSha	Bone Stag	75
M7423T	Bone Stag	75
SS7423T	Bone Stag	95
SS7423B	Bone Stag	100
7424	Assorted Celluloid	75
7424GPT	Pearl Pyralin	75
7424MB	Pearl Pyralin	80
7424SqMB	Pearl Celluloid	75
SS7424	Assorted Celluloid	80
SS7424KT	Cream Pyralin	85
7426	Genuine Pearl	150
F7426	Genuine Pearl	150
F7426T	Genuine Pearl	150
7426T	Genuine Pearl	150
7426B	Genuine Pearl	150
SS7426T	Genuine Pearl	165
SS7426B	Genuine Pearl	165
7429GST	Genuine Stag	125
7429GSIL	Nickel Silver	60

3 1/8" Ring Opening Knife

Pattern	Handle	Mint Price
3 1/8" Ring Opening Knife		
R7429GM	Gun Metal	120
R7429GSIL	Nickel Silver	100
R7429SS	Sterling Silver	140
SSR7429GSIL	Nickel Silver	100
3 1/8" Senator Pen		
7433	Bone Stag	85
S7433	Assorted Celluloid	75
7434	Assorted Celluloid	70
7434C	Cocobolo Celluloid	65
7434G	Pearl Pyralin	70
7434MB	Blue Pyralin	65
7434MR	Red Pyralin	65
S7434M	Pearl Pyralin	60
S7434G	Pearl Pyralin	65
7439GSIL	Gun Metal	60
7439GM	Gun Metal	60
7479GSIL	Nickel Silver	55
7479GSIL Sha	Nickel Silver	55
3 1/4" Senator Pen		
7483T	Bone Stag	85
7484	Assorted Celluloid	75
7486	Genuine Pearl	150
O7484W	Ivory Celluloid	75
SS7486	Genuine Pearl	160

3⁷/16" Senator Pen

Pattern	*Handle*	*Mint Price*
3 7/16" Senator Pen		
7494W	Ivory Celluloid	65
O7494W (Office)	Ivory Celluloid	75
3 1/4" Serpentine Balloon Pen		
7554 3/4B	Black Celluloid	85
3 3/8" Equal End Jack		
7563	Bone Stag	100
7564B	Black Celluloid	85
7564 3/4S	Tortoise Celluloid	95
7563 3/4	Bone Stag	100
O7564W (Office)	Ivory Celluloid	85
7573	Bone Stag	150

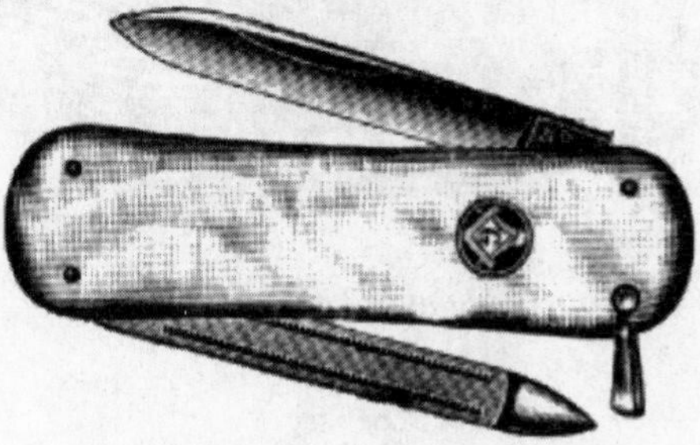

2 1/4" Lobster Pen

2 1/4" Lobster Pen		
7604W	Ivory Celluloid	70
7604	Assorted Celluloid	65
7604 Sha	Assorted Celluloid	65
7606	Genuine Pearl	140
7606 Sha	Genuine Pearl	140
7606 Sha Emb	Genuine Pearl	145
7609 GOLD Sha	Gold Plated	95
7609SS Sha	Sterling Silver	85
7609GSIL Sha	Nickel Silver	70
C7609SS Sha	Sterling Silver	80
7609GM Sha	Gun Metal	75
7609GM	Gun Metal	75
E7609GOLD Sha	Gold Filled	85

3½" Balloon Jack

Pattern	*Handle*	*Mint Price*
3½" Balloon Jack		
7623¾	Bone Stag	150
7624¾K	Cream Pyralin	120
3⅝" Balloon Jack		
7633	Bone Stag	165

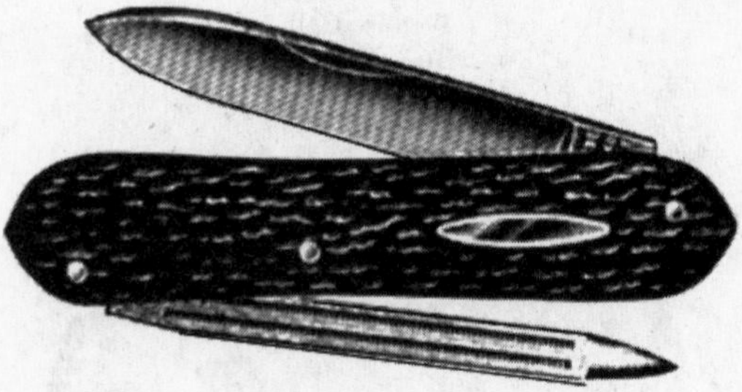

3" Sunfish Lobster Pen

3" Sunfish Lobster Pen		
7653	Bone Stag	80
7653T	Bone Stag	80
7654	Assorted Celluloid	70
7654W	Ivory Celluloid	70
7654Horn	Horn Celluloid	75
7654ACT	Assorted Celluloid	70
7656	Genuine Pearl	140
7656T Sha	Genuine Pearl	140
3 1/16" Wharncliffe Pen		
7663	Bone Stag	125
R7663	Bone Stag	125
7664M	Pearl Pyralin	95
R7664E	Black/Pearl Celluloid	90
R7663⅛	Bone Stag	120
R7663¾	Bone Stag	120
R7664¾B	Black Celluloid	90

2⅞" Senator Pen

Pattern	*Handle*	*Mint Price*
2 7/8" Senator Pen		
7703	Bone Stag	75
7703B	Bone Stag	80
7703T	Bone Stag	70
F7703T	Bone Stag	70
M7703T	Bone Stag	70
S7703B	Bone Stag	70
M7703T Sha	Bone Stag	70
7704WT	Ivory Celluloid	60
7704T	Assorted Celluloid	60
7704LT Sha	Pearl Celluloid	60
7704MT	Pearl Pyralin	60
7704MT Sha	Pearl Pyralin	60
7704NT	Striped Celluloid	65
7704ST Sha	Tortoise Celluloid	75
M7704GT	Jade Celluloid	75
M7704MT	Pearl Celluloid	65
M7704GT Sha	Jade Celluloid	70
M7704NT Sha	Striped Celluloid	65
M7704NT	Striped Celluloid	65
M7704MT Sha	Pearl Pyralin	60
M7704BT	Black Celluloid	60
SS7704LT	Pearl Celluloid	65
SS7704LT Sha	Pearl Celluloid	60
7706	Genuine Pearl	130
7706B	Genuine Pearl	130
7706T	Genuine Pearl	125
7706 Sha	Genuine Pearl	125
7706T Sha	Genuine Pearl	125
F7706T	Genuine Pearl	120
F7706	Genuine Pearl	120
M7706B	Genuine Pearl	125
SS7706T	Genuine Pearl	120
S7706B	Genuine Pearl	125
7709GSIL	Nickel silver	55
7709GOLD Sha	Gold Filled	65
7709GSIL Sha	Nickel Silver	55
M7709GOLD Sha	Gold Filled	75
M7709GOLD	Gold Filled	75
2 7/8" Senator Pen		
7719SS Sha	Sterling Silver	60
7719GSIL Sha	Nickel Silver	55
M7719GM	Gun Metal	60
M7719GM Sha	Gun Metal	60
3" Congress Pen		
7743	Bone Stag	125
7744M	Pearl Celluloid	100
7744K	Cream Pyralin	100
7746	Genuine Pearl	175
7749GS	Genuine Stag	160

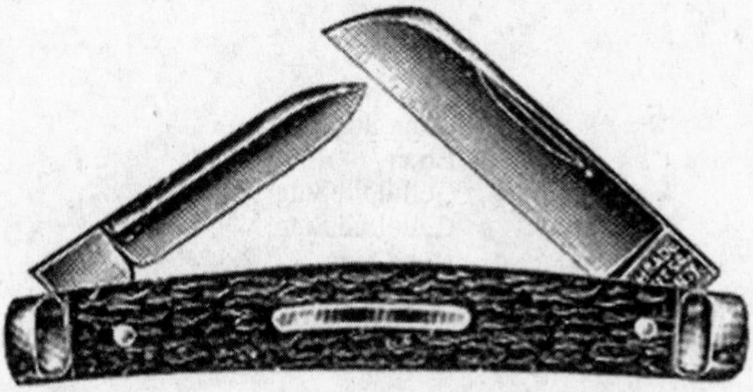

3 1/2" Congress

Pattern	Handle	Mint Price
3½" Congress		
7753	Bone Stag	130
SS7753	Bone Stag	140
3⅞" Congress		
7763	Bone Stag	175
3 5/16" Senator Pen		
7783B	Bone Stag	90
7783¾B	Bone Stag	95
7783T	Bone Stag	85
SS7783B	Bone Stag	100
7784	Assorted Celluloid	80
7784B	Assorted Celluloid	80
7784PT	Pearl Celluloid	80
7784MT	Pearl Pyralin	90
SS7784B	Assorted Celluloid	85
7786	Genuine Pearl	155
7786T	Genuine Pearl	150
7786B	Genuine Pearl	150
SS7786B	Genuine Pearl	165

3¼" Sleeveboard Jack

Pattern	Handle	Mint Price
3¼" Sleeveboard Jack		
7793T	Bone Stag	125
7793¾B	Bone Stag	125
7794¾MT	Pearl Pyralin	110

4" Muskrat

Pattern	Handle	Mint Price
4" Muskrat		
7803¾	Bone Stag	250
7813	Bone Stag	250
7812	Ebony	230
S7814Stg	Celluloid Stag	300
S7814¾Stg	Celluloid Stag	290
7843	Bone Stag	250
3¾" Equal End Jack		
O7894W (Office)	Ivory Celluloid	90
78942W (Florist)	Ivory Celluloid	95

Pattern	*Handle*	*Mint Price*
3½" Texas Jack		
7903	Bone Stag	150
7904	Assorted Celluloid	125
7913	Bone Stag	140
7923	Bone Stag	125
7924G	Pearl Pyralin	100
7924	Assorted Celluloid	100
2½" Senator Pen		
7933T	Bone Stag	70
7933T Sha	Assorted Celluloid	65
M7933T Sha	Bone Stag	75
7934BT	Black Celluloid	60
7934WT	Ivory Celluloid	60
7934BT Sha	Black Celluloid	65
7934WT Sha	Ivory Celluloid	65
7936	Genuine Pearl	120
7936T	Genuine Pearl	120
7936T Sha	Genuine Pearl	125
M7936	Genuine Pearl	120
M7936 Sha	Genuine Pearl	125
M7936T Sha	Genuine Pearl	125
7939GSIL	Nickel Silver	65
4¼" Moose		
9939R7973	Bone Stag	400

Three-Blade Knives

3⅝" Electrician's Knife

3⅝" Electrician's Knife		
3053½	Bone Stag	300
2½" Sleeveboard Lobster Pen		
81016 Sha	Genuine Pearl	120
3" Senator Pen		
C8083B	Bone Stag	100
8089GSB	Genuine Stag	140
8083B	Bone Stag	95
S8083B	Bone Stag	95
FS8086B	Genuine Pearl	165
3¹⁄₁₆" Senator Pen		
8099GSIL	Nickel Silver	65

4 5/16" Premium Stock

Pattern	*Handle*	*Mint Price*
4 5/16" Premium Stock		
81043	Bone Stag	350
3 1/8" Cattle Knife		
S8103	Bone Stag	140
8103 1/4LB	Bone Stag	140
S8104	Assorted Celluloid	125
8104 1/4LB	Assorted Celluloid	125

3 7/8" Carpenter's Knife

3 7/8" Carpenter's Knife		
81004 3/8	Fibestos	250
3 3/8" Sleeveboard Whittler		
8113T	Bone Stag	125
8113B	Bone Stag	125
8114W	Ivory Celluloid	110
8114SB	Tortoise Celluloid	125
8114PB	Pearl Celluloid	115
8114PT	Pearl Celluloid	110
8114ST	Tortoise Celluloid	120
8116	Genuine Pearl	200
8116T	Genuine Pearl	200
8116B	Genuine Pearl	200
8118B	Buffalo Horn	170
8118T	Buffalo Horn	160
3 1/4" Wharncliffe Cattle Knife		
8133 3/4	Bone Stag	225
8134 3/4KLB	Cream Pyralin	200

3¹/8″ Senator Pen

Pattern	*Handle*	*Mint Price*
3¹/8″ Senator Pen		
8103	Bone Stag	100
8104P	Pearl Celluloid	90
8143B	Bone Stag	100
8143T	Bone Stag	115
8146T	Genuine Pearl	175
SL8146B	Genuine Pearl	175
8149GST	Genuine Stag	150
8149GSB	Genuine Stag	155

3⁵/8″ Cattle Knife

3⁵/8″ Cattle Knife		
8163	Bone Stag	175
8172	Ebony	160
8173	Bone Stag	175
8173¹/4	Bone Stag	185
8173³/4	Bone Stag	185
SS8173	Bone Stag	210
S8173¹/4	Bone Stag	220
8174GP	Golden Pyralin	175
8174W	Ivory Celluloid	160
8174³/4G	Pearl Pyralin	155
8174³/4W	Ivory Celluloid	150
8176	Genuine Pearl	375
8179GS	Genuine Stag	300
S8174¹/4K	Cream Pyralin	220
8174³/4X	Green Celluloid	165
8182	Ebony	160
8183	Bone Stag	165
4″ Equal End Whittler		
8323B	Bone Stag	225

Pattern	*Handle*	*Mint Price*
3³/8" Sleeveboard Whittler		
8313T	Bone Stag	150
8313B	Bone Stag	150
8316B	Genuine Pearl	250
8323	Bone Stag	155
8324S	Tortoise Celluloid	140
3⁵/16" Serpentine Jack		
8344K	Cream Pyralin	120
8343	Bone Stag	140
3⁹/16" Serpentine Whittler		
S8363³/8	Bone Stag	250
8364³/8B	Black Celluloid	210
SC8364³/8B	Black Celluloid	200
S8364³/8B	Black Celluloid	210

3⁵/8" Cattle Knife

3⁵/8" Cattle Knife		
S8373	Bone Stag	200
S8373³/8	Bone Stag	200
S8373³/4	Bone Stag	210
S8374	Assorted Celluloid	160
S8374G	Pearl Celluloid	160
S8374³/8R	Red Celluloid	175
S8374³/4K	Cream Pyralin	160
S8374³/4	Assorted Celluloid	155
8383	Bone Stag	200
8383³/4	Bone Stag	195
8384	Assorted Celluloid	170
8384G	Pearl Pyralin	160
8384GP	Pearl Pyralin	165
3¹/8" Senator Whittler Pen		
8423B	Bone Stag	100
8423³/4B	Bone Stag	120
M8423B	Bone Stag	95
8423T	Bone Stag	100
L8423B	Bone Stag	100
M8423T	Bone Stag	90
8424³/4MB	Pearl Pyralin	90
8424SqMB	Pearl Celluloid	85
8424PB	Pearl Celluloid	90
L8424PB	Pearl Celluloid	90
M8424PT	Pearl Celluloid	80
8426B	Genuine Pearl	165
8426T	Genuine Pearl	170
M8426T	Genuine Pearl	150
M8426	Genuine Pearl	145
M8426B	Genuine Pearl	145

Pattern	Handle	Mint Price
$3^{1}/_{8}$" Scissors Knife		
8453T	Bone Stag	100
8456	Genuine Pearl	150
8456T	Genuine Pearl	155
8456B	Genuine Pearl	170

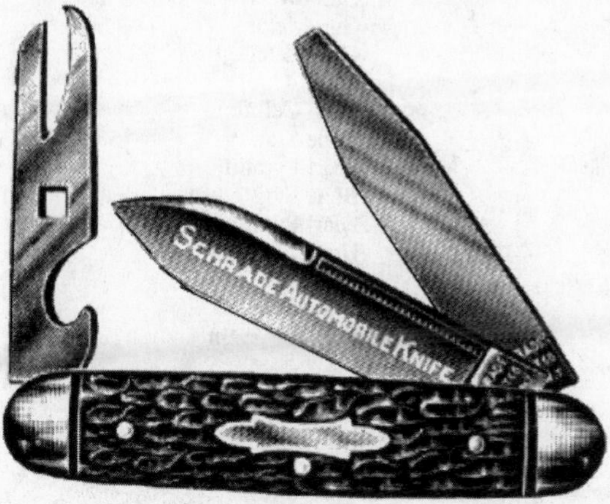

$3^{5}/_{8}$" Automobile/Camper Knife

$3^{5}/_{8}$" Automobile/Camper Knife		
8443	Bone Stag	400
8463	Bone Stag	375
$2^{3}/_{4}$" Sleeveboard Lobster Pen		
8476 Sha	Genuine Pearl	125
8476	Genuine Pearl	130
8479GSIL Sha	Nickel Silver	70
8479GM Sha	Gun Metal	65
8479GM	Gun Metal	65
8479GSIL	Nickel Silver	60
$3^{1}/_{4}$" Serpentine Balloon Whittler		
8554$^{3}/_{8}$B	Black Celluloid	150
$3^{3}/_{8}$" Cattle Knife		
8563	Bone Stag	180
8563$^{3}/_{4}$	Bone Stag	185
8564	Assorted Pyralin	160
8564$^{3}/_{4}$	Assorted Pyralin	165
8566	Genuine Pearl	325
8573$^{3}/_{4}$	Bone Stag	180
8574$^{3}/_{4}$AP	Pearl Pyralin	165
8583	Bone Stag	175
8584 Horn	Horn Pyralin	155
8584	Assorted Celluloid	140
8584$^{3}/_{4}$GP	Pearl Pyralin	150
8584$^{3}/_{4}$K	Cream Pyralin	140
8584$^{3}/_{4}$	Assorted Celluloid	150
8584K	Cream Pyralin	145
8584M	Pearl Celluloid	140
S8583	Bone Stag	175
8593	Bone Stag	165
8594G	Pearl Pyralin	160
8594$^{3}/_{4}$X	Green Celluloid	150
$2^{1}/_{4}$" Lobster Pen		
8604	Assorted Celluloid	60
8604W Sha	Ivory Celluloid	55
8604 Sha	Assorted Celluloid	60

Pattern	Handle	Mint Price
8606	Genuine Pearl	135
8606 Sha	Genuine Pearl	165
8606 Sha Emb	Genuine Pearl	120
8609 Gold Sha	Gold Plate	75
8609SS Sha	Sterling Silver	75
S8606 Sha	Genuine Pearl	125
8609GM Sha	Gun Metal	65
8609GM	Gun Metal	65
S8609GM Sha	Gun Metal	65
4" Serpentine Stock		
8614Y	Horn Celluloid	190
8613	Bone Stag	190
8614M	Pearl Pyralin	165
8613LB	Bone Stag	225
8614MLB	Pearl Pyralin	195
8614YLB	Horn Celluloid	195
3½" Balloon Cattle Knife		
8623¾LB	Bone Stag	200
8624¾KLB	Cream Pyralin	180
3⅝" Balloon Whittler		
C8633¾	Bone Stag	235
SC8633¾	Bone Stag	215

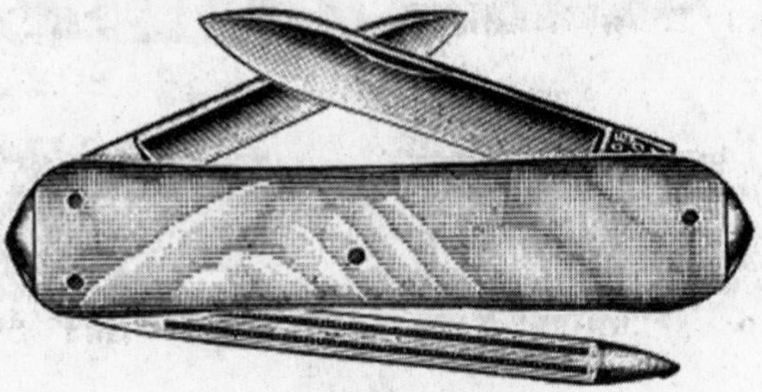

3" Sunfish Lobster Pen

Pattern	Handle	Mint Price
3" Sunfish Lobster Pen		
8653	Bone Stag	85
8653T	Bone Stag	90
8654	Assorted Celluloid	65
8654T	Assorted Celluloid	65
8654W	Ivory Celluloid	65
8654SqW	Ivory Celluloid	60
8654Sq	Assorted Celluloid	60
8654MT	Pearl Pyralin	70
8654MT Sha	Pearl Pyralin	70
8656	Genuine Pearl	120
8656 Emb	Genuine Pearl	135
8656T	Genuine Pearl	130
8656T Sha	Genuine Pearl	120
8656T Sha Emb	Genuine Pearl	135
8666T	Genuine Pearl	130
8666	Genuine Pearl	120

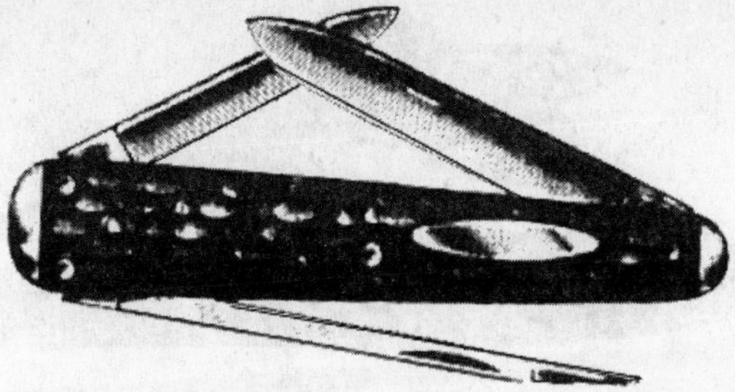

3″ Sleeveboard Lobster Pen

Pattern	*Handle*	*Mint Price*
3″ Sleeveboard Lobster Pen		
8673T	Bone Stag	95
8673T Sha	Bone Stag	100
8674GL Sha	Gold Celluloid	75
8676	Genuine Pearl	150
8676T	Genuine Pearl	155
8676T Sha	Genuine Pearl	160
8676 Sha	Genuine Pearl	150
8679GSil Sha	Nickel Silver	65
8679GM Sha	Gun Metal	60
8679GM	Gun Metal	60
3″ Sleeveboard Lobster Pen		
8683	Bone Stag	90
8683T	Bone Stag	90
8686	Genuine Pearl	150
2 7/8″ Senator Pen		
8704MT	Pearl Celluloid	60
8704 3/4BT	Black Celluloid	70
8706T	Genuine Pearl	120
8706B	Genuine Pearl	120
2 9/16″ Oval Lobster Pen		
8729GSIL	Nickel Silver	45
8729GSIL Sha	Nickel Silver	45
SS8729I	Stainless Steel	45
SS8729I Sha	Stainless Steel	45
SS8729ET Sha	Stainless Steel	45
8729GM Sha	Gun Metal	60
8729GM	Gun Metal	60
8729GOLD Sha	Gold Filled	65
8729GOLD	Gold Filled	70
2 7/8″ Scissors Knife		
8776	Bone Stag	110
8779GM	Gun Metal	70
8779GM Sha	Gun Metal	70
8779GSIL	Nickel Silver	75
3 5/16″ Senator Pen		
8783B	Bone Stag	125
8786B	Genuine Pearl	170

3¼″ Wharncliffe Whittler

Pattern	*Handle*	*Mint Price*
3¼″ Wharncliffe Whittler		
8793⅛B	Bone Stag	185
8794KT	Cream Pyralin	165
8793T	Bone Stag	185
4″ Serpentine Stock		
8803	Bone Stag	195
M8806	Genuine Pearl	325
8823	Bone Stag	200
8873	Bone Stag	190
8874	Assorted Celluloid	170
8876	Genuine Pearl	325

4″ Premium Stock

4″ Premium Stock		
8813	Bone Stag	195
SS8813	Bone Stag	250
8814P	Pearl Celluloid	185
8814G	Pearl Celluloid	185
8814GP	Pearl Pyralin	185
8814X	Green Celluloid	195
SO8814NP	Opal Celluloid	200
8833	Bone Stag	215
8834K	Cream Pyralin	190
8834AP	Pearl Pyralin	195
8834HORN	Horn Pyralin	210
O8834AP	Pearl Pyralin	200
O8833	Bone Stag	235
O8834	Assorted Celluloid	195
O8883	Bone Stag	230
3⁵⁄₁₆″ Serpentine Cattle Knife		
8853	Bone Stag	175
8853¼	Bone Stag	175
8854K	Cream Pyralin	160
8854¼K	Cream Pyralin	150

Pattern	*Handle*	*Mint Price*
8854¼	Assorted Celluloid	150
3½" Premium Stock		
8903	Bone Stag	110
8904K	Cream Pyralin	90
8904	Assorted Celluloid	80
8913	Bone Stag	105
8914HORN	Horn Pyralin	95
8914AP	Pearl Pyralin	95
8914G	Pearl Pyralin	95
8914K	Cream Pyralin	95
8914	Assorted Pyralin	95
8924GP	Pearl Pyralin	90
8923	Bone Stag	105
8924	Assorted Pyralin	90

3⁹⁄₁₆" Slim Premium Stock

3⁹⁄₁₆" Slim Premium Stock		
8964K	Cream Pyralin	150
8963	Bone Stag	160
8964GP	Pearl Pyralin	150
8964M	Pearl Celluloid	140
8983	Bone Stag	160
8983¼	Bone Stag	155
8984GP	Pearl Pyralin	140
8984K	Cream Pyralin	145
8984M	Pearl Celluloid	140
8984¼GP	Pearl Pyralin	135
8984¼K	Cream Pyralin	140
8984¼M	Pearl Celluloid	145
8993	Bone Stag	160
8993¼	Bone Stag	155
8994M	Pearl Celluloid	145
8994GP	Pearl Pyralin	140
8994K	Cream Pyralin	140
8994¼GP	Pearl Pyralin	140
8994¼K	Cream Pyralin	135
8994¼M	Pearl Celluloid	140
Four-Blade Knives		
3⅝" Automobile Knife		
9033	Bone Stag	300
9039GSIL	Solid Nickel Silver	235
3⅜" Sleeveboard Pen		
9113B	Bone Stag	130
9116B	Genuine Pearl	175
3¼" Bartender Knife		
9124M	Pearl Pyralin	160
9124B	Black Celluloid	165
9129GSIL	Nickel Silver	150

$3^1/_8$" Senator Pen

Pattern	*Handle*	*Mint Price*
$3^1/_8$" Senator Pen		
9143B	Bone Stag	110
9143T	Bone Stag	120
9144GLT	Gold Celluloid	100
9144WB	Ivory Celluloid	95
9144WT	Ivory Celluloid	95
9146	Genuine Pearl	170
9146T	Genuine Pearl	165
9149GST	Genuine Stag	150
$3^5/_8$" Cattle Knife		
9173	Bone Stag	250
$3^1/_8$" Senator Pen		
9423B	Bone Stag	95
9423T	Bone Stag	90
9424PB	Pearl Celluloid	90
9426	Genuine Pearl	140
9426T	Genuine Pearl	140
9426B	Genuine Pearl	150
$3^1/_8$" Scissors Knife		
M9456T	Genuine Pearl	165
$3^5/_8$" Scout/Utility Knife		
9463	Bone Stag	200
C9463$^3/_4$	Bone Stag	190
D9463	Bone Stag	225
S9463	Bone Stag	195
SD9463	Bone Stag	185
9464US	Red/White/Blue Celluloid	275
M9466	Genuine Pearl	450
$3^3/_8$" Cattle Knife		
9563	Bone Stag	300
$3^3/_8$" Junior or Girl Scout Knife		
9593	Bone Stag	240
G9593	Bone Stag	250
9594US	Red/White/Blue Celluloid	275
G9594US	Red/White/Blue Celluloid	275
G9594M	Pearl Pyralin	225
G9596	Genuine Pearl	425

$3^3/_8''$ *Cattle Knife*

Pattern	*Handle*	*Mint Price*
$3^3/_8''$ Cattle Knife		
9583	Bone Stag	300
$2^1/_4''$ Lobster Pen		
9604	Assorted Celluloid	70
9604W Sha	Ivory Celluloid	70
9604 Sha	Assorted Celluloid	70
9606	Genuine Pearl	150
9606 Sha	Genuine Pearl	150
9609GOLD Sha	Gold Plate	100
3″ Sleeveboard Lobster Pen		
9676T	Genuine Pearl	200
9679SS	Sterling Silver	100
$2^7/_8''$ Senator Pen		
9703B	Bone Stag	90
9704GT	Jade Celluloid	90
9704MT	Pearl Celluloid	75
9706T	Genuine Pearl	120
9706B	Genuine Pearl	125
9709GST	Genuine Stag	100
$2^5/_8''$ Lobster Scissors Knife		
9736 Sha	Genuine Pearl	140
9736	Genuine Pearl	120
9739GM Sha	Gun Metal	90
9739GM	Gun Metal	90
3″ Congress Pen		
9743	Bone Stag	165
9746	Genuine Pearl	225

$3^1/_2''$ *Congress*

Pattern	*Handle*	*Mint Price*
3$^{1}/_{2}$" Congress		
9753	Bone Stag	225
F9753	Bone Stag	225
3$^{7}/_{8}$" Congress		
9763	Bone Stag	300
3$^{5}/_{16}$" Senator Pen		
9783B	Bone Stag	125
9783T	Bone Stag	125
9786T	Genuine Pearl	200
9786B	Genuine Pearl	200
4" Serpentine Stock		
9803LB	Bone Stag	300
M9806	Genuine Pearl	550
M9803	Bone Stag	325

Schrade Safety Push-Button Pocket Knives

While a few of these knives were large hunting-type knives, most were gentlemen's pocketknives and office-type knives. The double-locked safety feature was as unique as was the easy "No Breaking of Finger Nails" opening. Since 1957, federal law has prohibited interstate sales or transportation of switchblade knives. Most, but not all, state and local laws prohibit possession or owning automatic opening knives. The collector would be well advised to understand ordinances specific to his or her location.

Pattern	*Handle*	*Mint Price*
3$^{3}/_{8}$" Equal End		
1404$^{3}/_{4}$W	Ivory Celluloid	225
1404$^{3}/_{4}$K	Cream Pyralin	225
1404$^{3}/_{4}$	Assorted Celluloid	200

4" Bowtie

4" Bowtie		
1514J	Striped Pyralin	300
1514	Assorted Celluloid	290
G1514K	Cream Pyralin	290
G1514	Assorted Celluloid	270

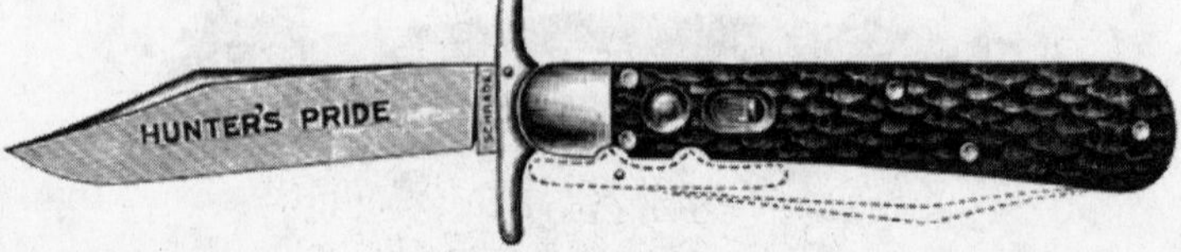

4$^{7}/_{8}$" Folding Hunter

Pattern	*Handle*	*Mint Price*
4 7/8″ Folding Hunter		
1543 3/4	Bone Stag	475
G1543 3/4	Bone Stag	500
1544BM	Assorted Celluloid	425
G1544 3/4M	Pearl Pyralin	440
G1544 3/4	Assorted Celluloid	430
B1544 3/4	Assorted Celluloid	430
1613 3/4	Bone Stag	430
4 1/4″ Folding Hunter		
1553 3/4	Bone Stag	360
1553	Bone Stag	360
1554 3/4M	Pearl Pyralin	310

3 3/8″ Equal End

3 3/8″ Equal End		
740SSD	Sterling Silver	280
740GOLD	Gold Plate	290
740SSET	Sterling Silver	270
740SSS	Sterling Silver	275
7403	Bone Stag	285
7403T	Bone Stag	285
7404	Assorted Celluloid	245
7404BLUE	Pearl Celluloid	240
7404 3/4	Assorted Celluloid	240
7404 3/4K	Cream Pyralin	230
7404 3/4E	Black/Pearl Celluloid	250
7404T	Assorted Celluloid	230
7404K	Cream Pyralin	220
SS7404	Black/Pearl Celluloid	200
7406	Genuine Pearl	400
7406T	Genuine Pearl	420
7409GSIL	Nickel Silver	235

3 3/8″ Office Knife

3 3/8″ Office Knife		
O7404W	Ivory Celluloid	250
NO7404W	Ivory Celluloid	250

3 3/8″ Equal End

Pattern	*Handle*	*Mint Price*
3³/₈″ Equal End		
741SSS	Scroll Sterling Silver	300
741SSD	Sterling Silver	275
7413	Bone Stag	235
7413T	Bone Stag	235
7414	Assorted Celluloid	220
7414BT	Black Celluloid	220
7414ST	Tortoise Celluloid	240
7414WT	Ivory Celluloid	230

7416	Genuine Pearl	375
7416T	Genuine Pearl	400
2⁷/₈″ Senator		
7444E	Black/Pearl Celluloid	200
7444	Assorted Celluloid	200
744SS	Sterling Silver	275
744GG	Gold Plate	300
744SS Sha	Sterling Silver	300
7444STG	Celluloid Stag	200
F7444B	Black Celluloid	205
F7444S	Shell Celluloid	210
F7449GSIL	Nickel Silver	210
F7444E	Black/Pearl Celluloid	195
F744SS	Sterling Silver	225
F7444 Sha	Assorted Celluloid	200
F744GG Sha	Gold Plate	275
F744SS Sha	Sterling Silver	225
F7444GG Sha	Gold Plate	275
F7444D Sha	Black/Green Celluloid	220
7449GSil	Nickel Silver	200

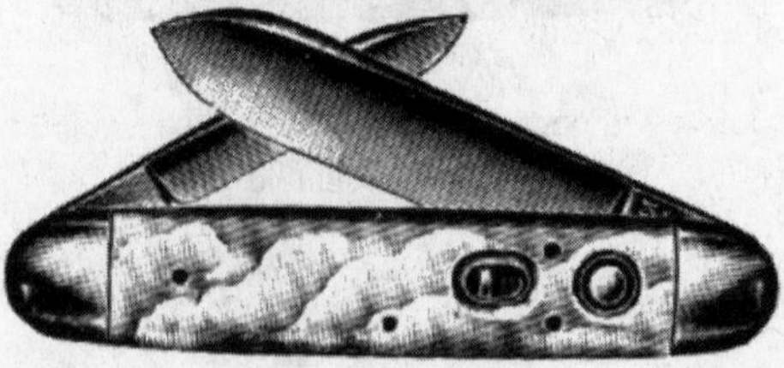

3³/₄″ Equal End

3³/₄″ Equal End		
7503	Bone Stag	275
7503³/₄	Bone Stag	275
7503B	Bone Stag	285
7503T	Bone Stag	275
7503³/₄T	Bone Stag	265

Pattern	*Handle*	*Mint Price*
7504	Assorted Celluloid	250
7504B	Assorted Celluloid	250
7504T	Assorted Celluloid	250
7504¾	Assorted Celluloid	240
7504¾G	Pearl Celluloid	235
7504¾K	Cream Pyralin	235
7504¾PT	Pearl Celluloid	245
7504¾T	Assorted Celluloid	230
7506B	Genuine Pearl	450
7506¾B	Genuine Pearl	400
3¾″ Equal End		
7523B	Bone Stag	420
7523¼B	Bone Stag	420
7534¾C	Cocobolo Celluloid	350
7534C	Cocobolo Celluloid	350
7533B	Bone Stag	400
7533¼B	Bone Stag	400
7533¾B	Bone Stag	400

SHAPLEIGH HARDWARE

Shapleigh Hardware Company of St. Louis, Missouri, was established in 1843 by A. F. Shapleigh. Although the company was a general line hardware distributor, it distributed a number of collectible pocketknife brands produced under contract by manufacturers such as Camillus and Schrade.

Perhaps its best-known trademark was DIAMOND EDGE, a name adopted in 1864 and used until 1960. The trademark is now used by Imperial and those knives of recent manufacture should not be confused with the older Shapleigh knives, which are of much greater value. Other brands include BRIDGE CUTLERY COMPANY (1902–1931), as well as stampings of the company's name such as SHAPLEIGH HDWE. CO. and SHAPLEIGH HDWE. CO. ST. LOUIS MO.

Shapleigh's knife line included over 600 patterns of quality pocketknives. The company went out of business in 1960, having been in the cutlery business for a century.

UTICA CUTLERY COMPANY

This Utica, New York, company was founded in 1910 by former Camillus employees and other investors. Utica knives were of high quality and are not often found in the collector market. Brands such as UTK SUPREME were joined by POCKET PARD and SENECA about 1930 and by KUTMASTER in 1937. That trademark, the company's best known, is still used today.

The company made knives under contract for several hardware distributors and other knife brand owners. During World War II, Utica made trench knives, bayonets and other items for military use. The stamping of most Utica knives is UTICA CUTLERY CO UTICA NY. The company remains in business today as a prominent manufacturer of knives and other cutlery products.

VALLEY FORGE

Valley Forge began cutlery production in Newark, New Jersey, in about 1892 and was acquired by Hermann Boker and Company in 1916. The factory made knives under the names of both Boker, USA and Valley Forge. Earliest knives were stamped VALLEY FORGE CUTLERY CO. NEWARK N.J. and knives dating from 1916 were stamped with the same name in both straight line and curved configurations. Those made during the 1916–1950 period have the letters "VF" inside a circle on the rear tang. The company went out of business in 1950.

One of the company's most desirable knives is a bone handled utility-type knife with a plier that folds into the handle. Mint or excellent knives of this type are valued in the $200 to $300 range.

VAN CAMP HARDWARE

In 1876, Cortland Van Camp and David C. Bergundthal founded Van Camp Hardware & Iron Company. The Indianapolis, Indiana, based company became a major supplier of hardware, implements and supplies within the Midwest. During the early years, the company purchased knives on contract from manufacturers such as Boker, Camillus and Imperial. From about 1904 to 1908, Van Camp operated its own cutlery factory, Capitol Cutlery Company. The factory made knives stamped with both the Van Camp and Capitol markings.

Among the stampings used from 1888 to 1960 were VAN CAMP HARDWARE INDPLS, VAN CAMP INDIANAPOLIS inside a circle, VANCO INDIANAPOLIS and VAN CAMP H. & I. MADE IN USA. Although still in the hardware wholesale business, the company no longer sells its own brand pocketknives.

WALDEN KNIFE COMPANY

The company was first formed as the Walden Cooperative Knife Company about 1870. As strange as it may seem, the eighteen original workers were members of competitive baseball teams. Employees of New York Knife Company would play baseball during their lunch period and Col. Tom Bradley, the company president, disapproved. A management-employee argument ensued, resulting in the employees being fired. The fired craftsmen rented some space in the Rider-Ericsson Engine Company's factory and began to make their own knives in a cooperative venture.

In 1874, the company incorporated as the Walden Knife Company and purchased a factory of its own. The company's products were of high quality, which resulted in excellent sales and profits. The number of employees grew to 125 by 1881 and nearly doubled by 1891.

The company's president persuaded George Schrade to move his Press Button Knife Company to Walden in 1893 and Walden Knife Company bought an interest in Schrade's firm. With Walden's support and Schrade's management, the firm had produced well over a million Press Button knives within a ten-year period. In 1903, Schrade sold his patents and interest in the company to Walden Knife Company.

By 1911, the Walden Knife Company factory had been expanded and over 600 workers were making more than 2,500 different patterns of pocketknives. These knives were marketed through the E. C. Simmons Hardware Company in St. Louis, Missouri.

When George Weller, the company's principal stockholder retired, Simmons purchased his stock. With it, Simmons gained control of the company and made Walden Knife Company the home of Keen Kutter knives. Simmons added several new buildings to the manufacturing complex and, during World War I, the company operated at full capacity making large knives for the U.S. Navy. At the war's end, Simmons merged with Winchester Repeating Arms Company and Winchester assumed responsibility for knife manufacturing. The Walden Knife Company ceased to make knives in the mid-1920s. A few years later, the old Walden factory was purchased by Schrade Cutlery Company.

Walden made high-quality knives handled in bone, celluloid, pearl and other materials popularly used at the time. Most were stamped WALDEN KNIFE CO., WALDEN, N.Y. or WALDEN KNIFE CO. MADE IN USA. Keen Kutter brand knives, made by Walden, and those made later by Winchester are practically indistinguishable one from another since Winchester duplicated many of Walden's patterns.

WESTER BROTHERS

Knives with the stampings WESTER & BUTZ/SOLINGEN (1832–1966), JACOBY & WESTER (1891–1904), WESTER BROS./GERMANY (1904–1967) and WESTER BROS. CUTLERY CO. (1904–1967) have a common ancestry. As early as 1832, Herr Butz was making pocketknives in Solingen, Germany, and he took in an apprentice named August Wester. Wester not only became a master cutler, but Butz's son-in-law as well. Together, they established the firm of Wester and Butz and made knives primarily for the European market.

In the 1880s, August Wester decided to establish a cutlery outlet in the United States in preference to paying an importer. Two of Wester's sons, Max and Charles, came to the United States and joined with a Mr. Jacoby in establishing the firm Jacoby and Wester in New York in 1891. Knives made in Germany by Wester and Butz for the American market were marked JACOBY & WESTER on one side of the blade tang; the other side was marked with the Wester & Butz company trademark of an anchor, star and arrow. Max and Charles Wester bought out Jacoby's interest in 1904 and changed the company name to Wester Brothers. Their knives, stamped WESTER BROS. CUTLERY CO. or WESTER BROS. NEW YORK, also used the previously described logo on the blade reverse tang. About 1915, the stamping WESTER-STONE INC. was used on a few large jack knife patterns made for them by New England area manufacturers.

Wester Brothers served as exclusive importers of knives and other cutlery products made by the Wester and Butz Solingen factory. Its knives were handled with materials such as genuine pearl, stag, bone stag, buffalo horn, gunmetal, nickel silver, celluloid and special alloys (used on bartender's knives).

Many of the advertising knives found in the collector market were made by Wester and Butz and imported by Wester Brothers. Those made for beer companies such as Anheuser-Busch are favorites of collectors. An excellent article, "Busch Knives by Wester," was written by Bernard Levine and published in the July 1990 issue of *Knife World.*

WESTERN CUTLERY COMPANY

The Western Cutlery Company story and that of several other manufacturers could begin in 1864, the year that Charles W. Platts emigrated from Sheffield, England. Platts was descended from a long line of knife makers and, in turn, his descendants were to have a significant impact upon a number of U.S cutlery businesses.

Platts's first employment in this country was the American Knife Company in Reynolds Bridge, Connecticut. A few years later, he became superintendent of the factory belonging to the Northfield Knife Company in the nearby town from which the company took its name. Charles and his wife, Sarah, reared five sons and each learned the cutlery craft at the Northfield cutlery firm. Although other sons and their descendants remained active in the cutlery industry, the focus here is on Harvey Nixon (H. N.) Platts.

H. N. Platts left Northfield in 1891 and moved west to Little Valley, in Cattaraugus County, New York. His experience led him to work in the blade grinding and finishing department of a new knife factory operated by Cattaraugus Cutlery Company. The company's early owners, J.B.F. Champlin and his son Tint, were joined temporarily in the business by four brothers of Mrs. Champlin (formerly Theresa Case). These Champlin brothers-in-law were W. R., Jean, John and Andrew Case.

Also working in the Cattaraugus office was Debbie Case, who lived with her brother, Russ, and their father, W. R. Case. In 1892, H. N. Platts and Debbie Case were married and, within a couple of years, they had become parents to two sons, Harlow and Reginald.

Charles Platts, still a respected cutlery leader, and his other sons reentered the picture when they moved from Northfield to Little Valley in 1893 and began work with Cattaraugus. Practically every department of the Cattaraugus factory now had a Platts family member at work and the result would be near inevitable—they decided to start their own cutlery business. In 1896, Charles Platts was joined by his five sons in forming the C. Platts & Sons Cutlery Company in nearby Gowanda, New York, and later moved to new and larger facilities in Eldred, Pennsylvania.

In 1900, when Charles Platts died, it was H. N. who assumed leadership of the family business. In addition to managerial responsibilities, H. N. served as the key salesman of Platts cutlery products. Ever expanding to new territories, his sales trips took him farther west through several states and into the midwestern plains states. More than a few of Platts's sales trips were made in the company of another cutlery salesman, brother-in-law Russ Case—Platts would sell knives on one side of the town street while Case sold on the other side, each selling knives branded with their own name.

A new company, with J. Russell Case and H. N. Platts as organizers and major stockholders, was to merge from this family and working relationship. The early days of the business would see the company selling knives branded both "Platts" and "Case," so choosing one family name seemed logical. Because Russ Case would have sales responsibility while Platts would oversee manufacturing, the name Case was selected. Sometime earlier, Russ had begun a jobbing company known as "W. R. Case and Son." The new company, incorporated in 1904 in Little Valley, would have a similar name except that an "s" would be added to the word "Son," thereby recognizing Platts family membership as the W. R. Case son-in-law. Debbie Case Platts supervised the office and summer school vacations saw the two young Platts boys working in the factory.

H. N. Platts's health began to decline due to "grinders consumption," a disease of the lungs caused from years of work with the sandstone grinding wheels. Although the business was doing very well and the now teenage Platts sons were becoming increasingly active in the business, the father's health hinged upon a move to a drier climate. In 1911, he sold his interest in the company to Russ Case and moved his family to Boulder, Colorado. But going with Platts and his family to the new home was his determination to continue his lifetime work in the cutlery industry.

A developing West proved to be fertile ground for knife sales since the cowboys, farmers, miners and other workers needed quality cutlery to use many times every day. Platts knew the business and he certainly had experience in starting a cutlery factory but, he also recognized the need to establish a base of business if he was to be successful in starting all over again. His connections with the eastern cutlery manufacturers were important as he sought sources of product. Before the year 1911 was over, orders were being sold and knives were arriving from the East to fill them. The new business was named "Western States Cutlery and Manufacturing Company." That name was selected instead of the founder's name because "Platts" had been used as a brand for the old company mentioned earlier and had very recently been used by Platts Brothers Cutlery Company, operated by H. N Platts's brothers. The geographical name was given to establish an identity separate from that of the Case and Platts businesses back East, and the "States" extension of the name signified the company's sales territory.

Early Western States knives were manufactured by Challenge, New York Knife Company, Valley Forge, Utica and Case Cutlery companies among others. Although the business was prospering and a manufacturing facility would have been in order, it would be several years coming. World War I had begun and had brought shortages of materials and labor. It had also required the services of the older son, Harlow, whose aid would have been needed for factory startup. Platts's dream was realized, however, with the opening of his new factory in 1920.

In the early 1940s, H. N. retired from active management of Western States Cutlery and those responsibilities were passed on to his sons, Reginald and Harlow, who continued in partnership until Reginald left the cutlery business in 1950. A new name, Western Cutlery Company was given the business in 1953 when Harlow Platts and his son, Harvey, reincorporated the company. Western remained in Boulder until its 1977 relocation to nearby Longmont, Colorado.

Harvey Platts had become company president and continued in that capacity until 1984, when Western was purchased by the Crossman Airgun division of Coleman Corporation, thus ending the more than 100-year involvement of the Platts family in the U.S. cutlery industry. The association with Coleman lasted until 1990, when the knife factory and trademarks were purchased by an investor group. Unable to obtain satisfactory profit performance, the company's assets and equipment were auctioned off in 1992. The Western trademarks and name are now owned by Camillus Cutlery and a number of the popular Western designs have been reintroduced.

Stampings and Trademarks

Early Western States knives had tangs stamped with the words "Western States" in a curve and "Boulder, Colorado" in a straight line below, similar to the stamp used by C. Platts and Sons. Pocketknife tangs were stamped with the curved "Western States" until about 1950, when a straight "Western" over a parallel "Boulder, Colorado" was adopted.

When the company began the manufacture of sheath knives in 1928, the tangs were stamped "Western." In 1931, when the double-tang knives went into production, the words "Pat. Pend.," "Patented" or "Pat. No. 1,967,479" were added. Most sheath knife stamps noted the patent until about 1950.

In addition to stamped tangs, many early knives had trademark etching on the blade. The company's best-known mark was a tic-tac-toe pattern, and the words "Sharp-Tested Temper" were used beginning in 1911. In 1928, the Buffalo trademark consisting of an old buffalo skull framed with "Western States" and "Sharp Cutlery" was adopted and gradually replaced the tic-tac-toe marking.

Tang stamps on pocketknives as well as sheath knives were gradually changed to "Western USA" during the 1960s. Beginning in 1978 and continuing until the mid-1980s, the stamp "Western USA" was used with a letter added beneath the "USA" to indicate the production year (A=1977, B=1978, etc.). Later stampings were WESTERN/model number/USA.

Identifying Western States Knives

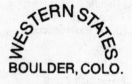

WESTERN STATES
BOULDER, COLO.

1911 - 1950

W | TESTED | S
TRADE | SHARP | MARK
© | TEMPER | ©

1911 - 1928

WESTERN STATES
SHARP CUTLERY

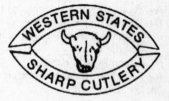

1928 - 1942

WESTERN
BOULDER, COLO.

1928 - 1931
1950 - 1961

WESTERN
BOULDER, COLO.
PAT.NO.1,967,479

1931 - 1950

WESTERN
U.S.A.

1961 - present

The company began stamping stock numbers on knives in 1954. Identification of Western States' early knives follows the traditional numbering system of a pattern number, along with letters and other numbers that described the knife's features. Unfortunately, the numbering system was an internal protocol for employees and not for marking the company's products. Collectors today must identify knives from catalogs and application of the numbering system. Most of the old stock numbers can be deciphered by using the numbering key explained below. Some older pocketknife numbers have a zero inserted just before the pattern number to signify a modification, usually in materials or finish (e.g. 9393 and 93093). The number "1" added at the beginning of the stock number was used when bolsters were on both ends of a knife that normally was a "bare headed" pattern.

NUMBERING SYSTEM

The first digit signifies handle material as follows:

2—Imitation Pearl Handle
3—Brown or Golden Shell Composition Handle
4—White or Ivory Handle
5—Genuine Stag Handle

6—Bone Stag Handle
7—Ivory or Agate Composition Handle
8—Genuine Pearl Handle

The second digit indicates the number of blades, while the next two or three digits indicate the pattern numbers.

PREFIX/SUFFIX ABBREVIATIONS:
These abbreviations follow the pattern number figures and indicate:

1/2—Clip Blade
B—Bale or Ring
BB—Black Border
BH—Barehead (bolster at one end)
CH—Chain
KFS—Knife, Fork and Spoon
GS—Goldstone Handle
T—Tip Bolstered Knife
TB—Tip Bolstered with Bale
CSP—Calif. Clip Pocket, Sheep and Pen Blades
P—Punch Blade
F—Nail File Blade, Florest and Stamp
D—Hook Disgorger
S—Long Special Spay Blade
SP—Spey and Pen Blades
PCS—Punch-Calif. Clip Pocket and Long Spey
E—Emblem in Handle
C—Calif. Clip Pocket Blade

These abbreviations precede the figure and indicate:

A—Agate (Butter and molasses) Handle
B—Black Composition Handle
C—Cornelia Red or Candy Colored Handle
G—Green Pyralin Handle
RP—Abalone (Rainbow Pearl) Handle
Nickel Silver Lining
Y—Yellow Composition Handle
X—"Westaco" Brand or Cheaper Brand of Knife
AG—Knife was Handmade by Experienced Cutler
J or P—Pearl Pyralin
R—Rainbow Celluloid
0—Blade in Each End of 2-Bladed Knife—Otherwise Jack

Pattern	*Handle*	*Blades*	*Description*	*Mint Price*
One-Blade Knives				
3 3/8" Boy's Knife				
1000	Steel	Spear		45

5 1/4" Folding Hunter

Pattern	*Handle*	*Blades*	*Description*	*Mint Price*
5 1/4" Folding Hunter				
2100	Imit. Pearl	Sabre Clip		300
2100V	Imit. Pearl	Clip		275
3100	Assorted Celluloids	Clip		260
6100	Bone	Sabre Clip		375
6100L	Bone	Locking Sabre Clip		425
A100BH	Imit. Pearl	Clip		200
2100BH	Imit. Pearl	Clip		225

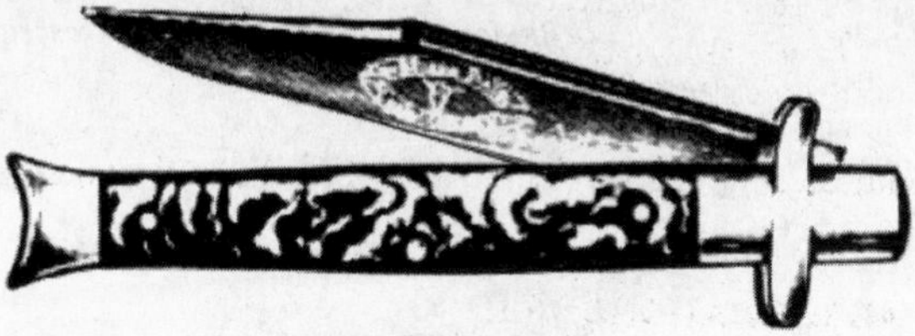

$3^{7}/_{8}$" Bow-Tie

Pattern	*Handle*	*Blades*	*Description*	*Mint Price*
$3^{7}/_{8}$" Bow-Tie				
R105	Rainbow Celluloid	Long Clip		200
2105	Assorted Celluloids	Long Clip		175
$5^{1}/_{4}$" Slender Clasp Knife				
2106	Imit. Pearl	Long Clip		150
2106V	Imit. Pearl	Long Clip		150
5106	Genuine Stag	Long Clip		250
3106	Assorted Celluloids	Long Clip		150
2106BH	Yellow Composition	Long Clip		175
5" Daddy Barlow				
6111	Saw-cut Bone	Long Clip		275
$3^{3}/_{8}$" Regular Jack				
$1113^{1}/_{2}$	Rosewood	Clip		50
1113S	Rosewood	Spey		55
$3^{3}/_{8}$" Regular Jack				
1116E	Rosewood	Sheepfoot		55
1116EB	Rosewood	Sheepfoot		55
5" Coke Bottle Hunter				
2121BH	Imit. Pearl	Clip		200
$5^{1}/_{2}$" Clasp Knife				
A125	Yellow Composition	Skinning Clip		450
2125	Imit. Pearl	Skinning Clip		400
$5^{1}/_{4}$"Clasp Knife				
A127	Yellow Composition	Clip		200
2127	Imit. Pearl	Clip		175
$4^{1}/_{2}$" Gunstock Hunter				
3130	Agate Celluloid	Sabre Clip, Skinning Blade		350
6130	Bone	Sabre Clip		400
$3^{1}/_{4}$" Maize Knife				
6148	Bone	Spey		45

$3^{3}/_{4}$" Jack

$3^{3}/_{4}$" Jack				
4149	Ivory Celluloid	Sheepfoot	Florist's Knife	50
16149	Bone	Sabre Clip	Serpentine Jack	85
$2^{1}/_{2}$" Watch Fob				
819R	Rainbow Celluloid	Small Wharncliffe, File		35
819G	Green Pyralin	Small Wharncliffe, File		35
919	Celluloid	Small Wharncliffe, File		35
819J	Genuine Pearl	Small Wharncliffe, File		125
819RP	Genuine Abalone	Small Wharncliffe, File		125
819P	Genuine Pearl	Small Wharncliffe, File		125

Pattern	Handle	Blades	Description	Mint Price
4 1/2" English Jack				
16153 1/2	Bone	Clip		300
16153 1/2L	Bone	Clip-Blade Locks		350

5 1/8" Powderhorn

5 1/8" Powderhorn				
2175V	Imit. Pearl	Long Clip		150
3175	Assorted Pyralines	Long Clip		150
6175	Bone	Long Clip		275
8175	Genuine Pearl	Long Clip		400
61751	Bone	Long Clip		275
61075	Bone	Long Clip		290
71075	Agate Pyralin	Long Clip		150
Two-Blade Knives				
2 1/2" Ladies Knife				
R201	Rainbow Celluloid	Spear, Pen		45
2201	Imit. Pearl	Spear, Pen		40
3201	Gold Shell Pyralin	Spear, Pen		40
8201	Genuine Pearl	Spear, Pen		75
3" Equal End Pen				
6202	Bone	Spear, Pen		75
7202	Ivory Composition	Spear, Pen		60
2 7/8" Oval Pen				
R203	Rainbow Celluloid	Spear, Pen		55
4" Pruning Knife				
1204	Rosewood	Pruning, Budding		75
6204	Bone	Pruning, Budding		125

5 1/4" Slender Clasp Knife

5 1/4" Slender Clasp Knife				
2206	Imit. Pearl	Clip, Skinning Blade		200
5206	Genuine Stag	Clip, Skinning Blade		400
6206	Imit. Pearl	Clip, Skinning Blade		275
3 3/8" Dogleg Jack				
R207	Rainbow Celluloids	Spear, Pen		175
16207	Bone	Spear, Pen		200
18207	Genuine Pearl	Spear, Pen		275
3 1/4" Regular Jack				
16208	Bone	Spear, Pen		75

Pattern	Handle	Blades	Description	Mint Price
16208½	Bone	Clip, Pen		80
13208	Gold Shell Pyralin	Spear, Pen		65
13208½	Gold Shell Pyralin	Clip, Pen		65
2⁷⁄₈″ Regular Jack				
16209	Bone	Spear, Pen		70

17209	Horn Pyralin	Spear, Pen		60
18209	Genuine Pearl	Spear, Pen		150
3¹⁄₄″ Leg Knife				
9210	Assorted Celluloids	Clip, Pen		150
3¹⁄₄″ Barlow				
6211	Saw-Cut Bone	Spear, Pen		150
6211½	Saw-Cut Bone	Clip, Pen		150
3¹⁄₄″ Regular Jack				
6212	Bone	Spear, Pen		90
6212½	Bone	Clip, Pen		90
62012	Bone	Spear, Pen		85
62012½	Bone	Clip, Pen		80
3³⁄₈″ Regular Jack				
6213	Bone	Spear, Pen		85
3¹⁄₈″ Swayback Jack				
16217	Bone	Spear, Pen		100
18217	Genuine Pearl	Spear, Pen		165
19217	Imit. Pearl	Spear, Pen		85

5″ Hatchet Knife

5″ Hatchet Knife				
2219	Imit. Pearl	Long Clip, Axe		225
3″ Balloon Jack				
16220	Bone	Spear, Pen		90
17220	Horn Pyralin	Spear, Pen		70
18220	Genuine Pearl	Spear, Pen		150
4″ Clasp Knife				
16221	Bone	Spear, Pen		250

Pattern	Handle	Blades	Description	Mint Price
3" Gunstock Jack				
16224	Bone	Spear, Pen		275
16224½	Bone	Clip, Pen		285
17224	Horn Pyralin	Spear, Pen		200
17224½	Horn Pyralin	Clip, Pen		200
3⅝" English Jack				
13226	Red Striped Pyralin	Long Spear, Pen		120
16226	Bone	Long Spear, Pen		165

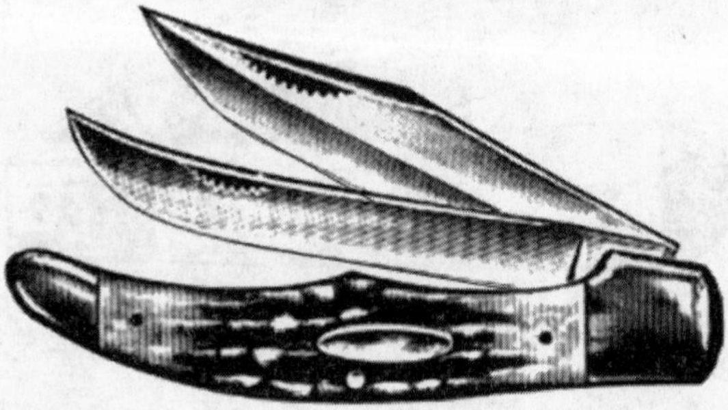

5¼" Clasp Knife

Pattern	Handle	Blades	Description	Mint Price
5¼" Clasp Knife				
2227	Imit. Pearl	Clip, Skinning Blade		200
5227	Genuine Stag	Clip, Skinning Blade		375
6227	Bone	Clip, Skinning Blade		225
3⅜" Serpentine Jack				
16228	Bone	Spear, Pen		120
16228½	Bone	Wide Clip, Pen		125
17228	Horn Pyralin	Spear, Pen		85
17228½	Horn Pyralin	Wide Clip, Pen		90
18228	Genuine Pearl	Spear, Pen		200

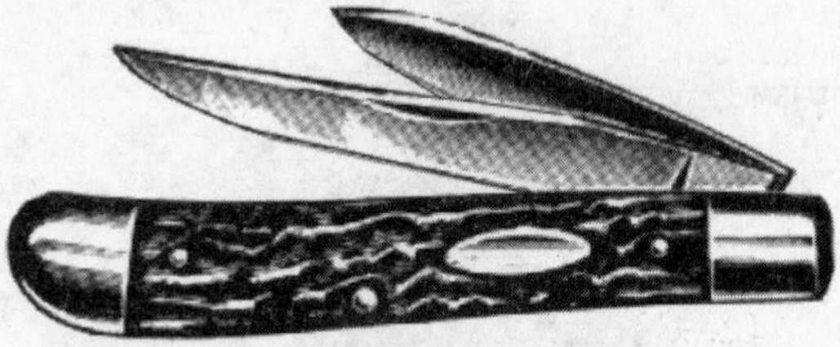

2¾" Serpentine Jack

Pattern	Handle	Blades	Description	Mint Price
2¾" Serpentine Jack				
15229C	Genuine Stag	California Clip, Pen		200
13229	Assorted Celluloids	Sabre Clip, Pen		100
16229C	Bone	California Clip, Pen		150
18229C	Genuine Pearl	California Clip, Pen		225

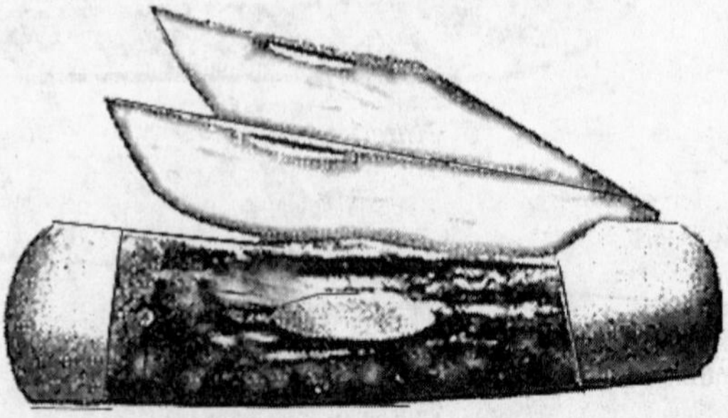

4½" Gunstock Hunter

Pattern	*Handle*	*Blades*	*Description*	*Mint Price*
4½″ Gunstock Hunter				
2230	Imit. Pearl	Sabre Clip, Skinning Blade		450
5230	Genuine Stag	Sabre Clip, Skinning Blade		650
3″ Senator Pen				
2232T	Imit. Pearl	Spear, Pen		50
3¾″ Balloon Jack				
16232	Bone	Spear, Pen		175
3⅜″ Teardrop Jack				
G2033	Green Pyralin	Spear, Pen		75
92033	Imit. Pearl	Spear, Pen		70
16233	Bone	Spear, Pen		120
16233E	Bone	Spear, Pen		100
16233P	Bone	Spear, Punch		125
16233½	Bone	Clip, Pen		100
17233E	Horn Pyralin	Clip, Pen		80
17233P	Horn Pyralin	Spear, Punch		90
3⅝″ Teardrop Jack				
6234	Bone	Spear, Pen	Easy Open	125
1234E	Rosewood	Spear, Pen		65
16234	Bone	Spear, Pen		125
16234E	Bone	Clip, Pen	Easy Open	140
16234½	Bone	Clip, Pen		80
3½″ Regular Jack				
P235	Smoked Pearl Pyralin	Spear, Pen		75
6235P	Bone	Spear, Punch		100
13235½	Gold Shell Pyralin	Clip, Pen		75
16235	Bone	Spear, Pen		90
16235P	Bone	Spear, Punch		100
16235½	Bone	Clip, Pen		85
3½″ Curved Jack				
6240½	Bone	Clip, Pen		90
6240½P	Bone	Clip, Punch		120
13240½	Assorted Celluloids	Clip, Pen		85
16240½	Bone	Clip, Pen		90

3¼″ Equal End Pen

3¼″ Equal End Pen				
R243	Red Striped Pyralin	Spear, Pen		75
6243	Bone	Spear, Pen		90
6243P	Bone	Clip, Punch		110
6243½	Bone	Clip, Pen		85
7243P	Gold Shell Pyralin	Spear, Punch		90
9243P	Imit. Pearl	Clip, Punch		75
02243T	Imit. Pearl	Spear, Pen		70
06243	Bone	Spear, Pen		85
06243½	Bone	Clip, Pen		85
2⅞″ Small Premium Jack				
6244	Bone	Clip, Pen		50
05244	Stag	Clip, Pen		80

$3^5/_8$″ Equal End Pen

Pattern	Handle	Blades	Description	Mint Price
$3^5/_8$″ Equal End Pen				
6245	Bone	Spear, Pen		90
6245½	Bone	Clip, Pen		90
6245J	Bone	Clip, Spear	Moose	250
06245½	Bone	Wide Clip, Pen		150
$3^5/_8$″ Eureka Jack				
A246	Imit. Abalone	Clip, Pen	Half Whittler	175
A246½	Imit. Pearl	Clip, Pen		150
9246½	Imit. Pearl	Clip, Pen		140
6246½	Bone	Clip, Pen		200
$3^1/_2$″ Serpentine Jack				
S247½	Horn Pyralin	Clip, Pen		90
R247P	Rainbow Celluloid	Clip, Punch		90
62047	Bone	Clip, Pen		110
C2047	Striped Pyralin	Clip, Pen		80
4″ Jumbo Jack				
6248	Bone	Spear, Pen		165
6248½	Bone	Clip, Pen		175
$3^7/_8$″ Hobo				
A249K&F	Yellow Composition	Knife, Fork		250
$3^3/_4$″ Trapper				
B249S	Black Composition	Clip, Long Spey		100
16249	Bone	Sabre Clip, Pen	Jack	200
16249S	Bone	Sabre Clip, Long Spey		300
15249S	Genuine Stag	Clip, Long Spey		400

$3^1/_8$″ Slant Bolster Pen

$3^1/_8$″ Slant Bolster Pen			
03250	Assorted Celluloids	Clip, Pen	75
06250	Bone	Clip, Pen	100
$4^1/_2$″ English Jack			
6253½	Bone	Clip, Pen	275
16253	Bone	Spear, Pen	250
3″ Ladies Knife			
7255	Horn Pyralin	Small Spear, Pen	55
8255	Genuine Pearl	Small Spear, Pen	90

3″ Balloon Pen

Pattern	*Handle*	*Blades*	*Description*	*Mint Price*
3″ Balloon Pen				
26256	Imit. Pearl	Spear, Pen		85
6256	Bone	Spear, Pen		125
06256	Bone	Spear, Pen		125
7256	Horn Pyralin	Spear, Pen		90
07256	Horn Pyralin	Spear, Pen		90
8256	Genuine Pearl	Spear, Pen		175
08256	Genuine Pearl	Spear, Pen		175
3⁵/₈″ Equal End Pen				
4257	Ivory Composition	Spear, Pen		60

3³/₄″ Office Knife

3³/₄″ Office Knife				
7258	Ivory Composition	Spear, Spey		70
3¹/₄″ Office Knife				
7259	Ivory Composition	Spear, Spey		70
3¹/₈″ Equal End Pen				
9262	Imit. Pearl	Spear, Pen		60
3262	Imit. Tortoise	Spear, Pen		65
8262	Genuine Pearl	Spear, Pen		135
6262	Bone	Spear, Pen		90

3¹/₈″ Oval Pen

3¹/₈″ Oval Pen				
P263	Smoked Pearl Pyralin	Spear, Pen		60
2263	Black Composition	Spear, Pen		50
2263T	Imit. Pearl	Spear, Pen		50

Pattern	*Handle*	*Blades*	*Description*	*Mint Price*
6263	Bone	Spear, Pen		80
6263T	Bone	Spear, Pen		80
3 1/4" Balloon Half Whittler				
R264	Rainbow Celluloid	Clip, Small Clip		90
6264	Bone	Clip, Small Clip		120
8264	Genuine Pearl	Clip, Small Clip		200
3 3/8" Premium Jack				
22066C	Imit. Pearl	California Clip, Pen		70
6266	Bone	Clip, Pen		90
P266	Imit. Smoked Pearl	Clip, Pen		75
R266	Green Pyralin	Clip, Pen		70
8266	Genuine Pearl	Clip, Pen		150
4 1/8" Congress				
6268	Bone	Sheepfoot, Pen		225
3 3/4" Doctor's Knife				
6270	Bone	Spear, Pen		325
9270	Imit. Pearl	Spear, Pen		175
3" Wharncliffe Pen				
G271	Green Pyralin	Spear, Pen		120
3 1/4" Wharncliffe Jack				
A272	Imit. Pearl	Clip, Pen		85
R272	Rainbow Celluloid	Clip, Pen		90
6272	Bone	Sheepfoot, Pen		120
7272	Assorted Celluloids	Wide Clip, Pen		100

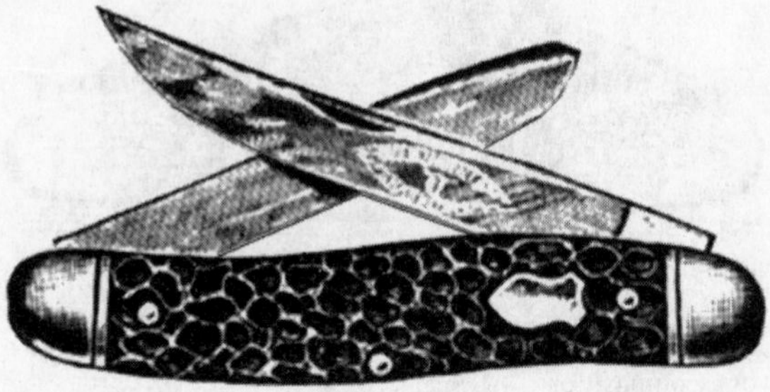

3 7/8" Texas Jack

3 7/8" Texas Jack				
3274	Gold Shell Pyralin	Clip, Pen		125
3274J	Gold Shell Pyralin	California Clip, Long Spey	Muskrat	275
6274	Bone	Clip, Pen		140
6274C	Bone	California Clip, California Clip	Muskrat	300
6274J	Bone	California Clip, Long Spey	Muskrat	325
6274S	Bone	Clip, Spey	Texas Jack	175
02274C	Imit. Pearl	California Clip, California Clip	Muskrat	240
5" Fishing Knife				
A275D	Yellow Composition	Long Clip, Scaler/ Hook Disgorger		90
2275D	Imit. Pearl	Long Clip, Scaler/ Hook Disgorger		85
4 1/4" Fishing Knife				
A2075D	Yellow Composition	Long Clip, Scaler/ Hook Disgorger		85
22075D	Imit. Pearl	Long Clip, Scaler/ Hook Disgorger		80
5 1/2" Fishing Knife				
A276	Yellow Composition	Long Clip, Scaler/ Hook Disgorger	"Sea Beast"	100

Pattern	Handle	Blades	Description	Mint Price
3³/8″ Sleeveboard Pen				
R277	Rainbow Celluloid	Spear, Pen		75
S277	Horn Pyralin	Spear, Pen		80

3¹/8″ Sleeveboard Pen

3¹/8″ Sleeveboard Pen				
G278	Green Pyralin	Spear, Pen		65
G278T	Green Pyralin	Spear, Pen		65
G278Emb	Green Pyralin	Spear, Pen		55
4278	Ivory Composition	Spear, Pen		55
6278	Bone	Spear, Pen		90
8278	Genuine Pearl	Spear, Pen		140
9278	Imit. Pearl	Spear, Pen		55
9278Emb	Imit. Pearl	Spear, Pen		55
9278T	Imit. Pearl	Spear, Pen		55

3″ Serpentine Lobster Pen

3″ Serpentine Lobster Pen				
G283	Green Pyralin	Spear, File		70
2283	Assorted Celluloids	Pen, File		65
8283	Genuine Pearl	Spear, File		125
9283	Imit. Pearl	Spear, File		55
2³/4″ Equal End Pen				
8287	Genuine Pearl	Spear, Pen		100
9287	Gold Shell Pyralin	Spear, Pen		60
3⁷/8″ Texas Jack				
3293	Gold Shell Pyralin	Clip, Pen	Premium Jack	125
03293	Gold Shell Pyralin	Clip, Pen		120
6293	Bone	Clip, Pen	Premium Jack	150
06293	Bone	Clip, Pen		150
6293J	Bone	Clip, Spey		170
4¹/4″ Jumbo Jack				
6294	Bone	Clip, Pen		275

4³/₈" Trapper

Pattern	*Handle*	*Blades*	*Description*	*Mint Price*
4³/₈" Trapper				
22094C	Imit. Pearl	Skinning Blade, Long Spey		225
52094C	Genuine Stag	Skinning Blade, Long Spey		375
3¹/₂" Balloon Pen				
6295	Bone	Spear, Pen		100
8295	Genuine Pearl	Spear, Pen		175
3⁵/₈" Balloon Pen				
6296¹/₂	Bone	Spear, Pen		110
R296¹/₂	Rainbow Celluloid	Spear, Pen		90
3¹/₄" Congress Pen				
6297	Bone	Sheepfoot, Pen		85

Three-Blade Knives

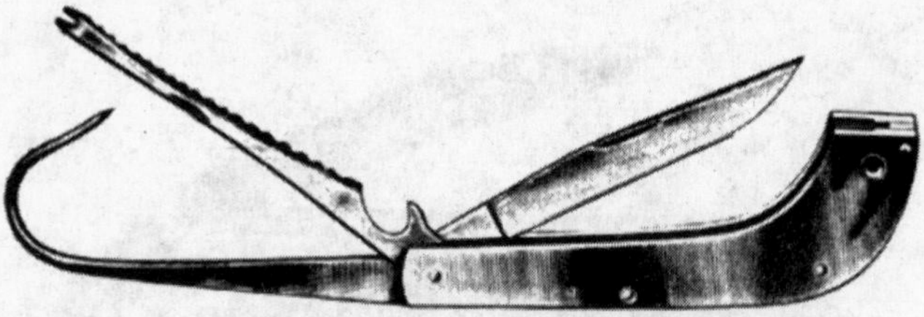

5" Fisherman's Knife

5" Fisherman's Knife				
A319	Yellow Composition	Long Clip, Gaff, Scaler		125
P319	Horn Pyralin	Long Clip, Gaff, Scaler		140
S319	Aluminum	Long Clip, Gaff, Scaler		80
3¹/₂" Serpentine Cattle Knife				
3331P	Gold Shell Pyralin	Clip, Spey, Punch		125
7331P	Horn Pyralin	Clip, Spey, Punch		125
3⁵/₈" Swell Center Surveyor				
3336	Gold Shell Pyralin	Clip, Spey, Sheepfoot		260
9336P	Imit. Pearl	Clip, Spey, Punch		240
3⁵/₈" Slant Bolster Surveyor				
7337	Horn Pyralin	Clip, Spey, Sheepfoot		250
9337	Imit. Pearl	Clip, Spey, Sheepfoot		225
3¹/₂" Rnd Bolster Premium Stock				
2342PCS	Imit. Pearl	Clip, Spey, Punch		85
6342C	Bone	Long Clip, Spey, Sheepfoot		120
6342CSP	Bone	Clip, Spey, Pen		100
6342P	Bone	Clip, Spey, Punch		120
6342SS	Bone	California Clip, Spey, Sheepfoot		125
7342	Brown Stripe Pyralin	Clip, Spey, Sheepfoot		75

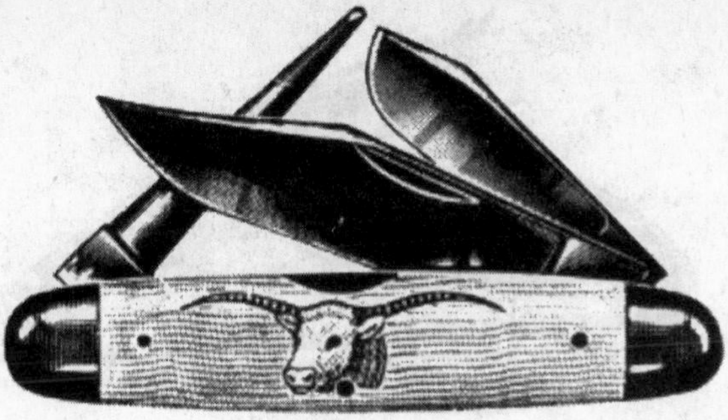

3⅝″ Cattle Knife

Pattern	*Handle*	*Blades*	*Description*	*Mint Price*
3¼″ Cattle Knife				
9343P	Imit. Pearl	Clip, Spey, Punch		90
2⅞″ Small Stock				
R344	Brown Celluloid	Clip, Spey, Sheepfoot		65
3⅝″ Cattle Knife				
S345	Horn Pyralin	Spear, Spey, Pen		165
33045P	Gold Shell Pyralin	Spear, Spey, Punch		190
4345½	Ivory Celluloid	Clip, Spey, Punch		175
6345	Bone	Spear, Spey, Pen		200
6345P	Bone	Spear, Spey, Punch		225
6345½	Bone	Clip, Spey, Pen		200
6345½P	Bone	Wide Clip, Spey, Punch		250
63045P	Bone	Spear, Spey, Punch		225
3⅝″ Balloon Whittler				
2346	Imit. Pearl	Clip, Spey, Pen		200
6346P	Bone	Clip, Spey, Punch		275
9346P	Imit. Pearl	Clip, Spey, Punch		220
6346½P	Bone	Clip, Spey, Punch	Eureka Pattern	300
9346½P	Waterfall	Clip, Spey, Punch	Eureka Pattern	350

3½″ Slant Bolster Premium Stock

3½″ Slant Bolster Premium Stock				
C347	Striped Pyralin	Clip, Spey, Pen		120
R347P	Rainbow Celluloid	Clip, Spey, Punch		130
R347P	Rainbow Celluloid	Clip, Spey, Punch		130
6347	Bone	Clip, Spey, Sheepfoot		140
6347	Bone	Clip, Spey, Pen		140
6347LP	Bone	Spear, Pen, Locking Punch		300
6347LP	Bone	Clip, Spey, Punch	Locking Blade	300
9347LP	Imit. Pearl	Clip, Spey, Punch	Locking Blade	200
9347LP	Imit. Pearl	Spear, Pen, Locking Punch		200
23047P	Imit. Pearl	Clip, Spey, Punch	Slant Bolsters	175

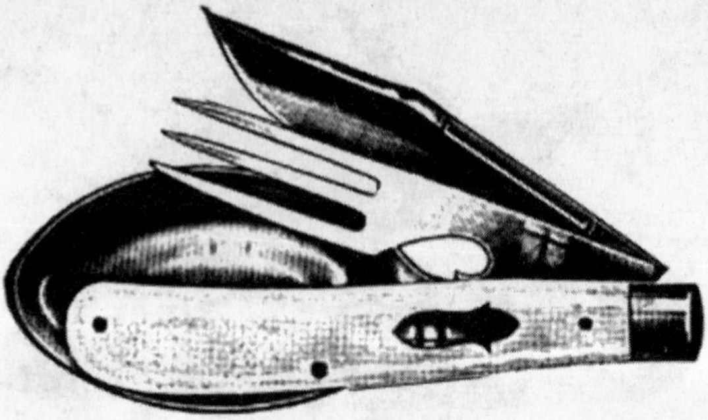

3 7/8" Hobo

Pattern	Handle	Blades	Description	Mint Price
3 7/8" Hobo				
Y349KFS	Yellow Composition	Knife, Fork, Spoon		225
3 1/8" Jr. Stock				
6351	Bone	Clip, Spey, Pen		85

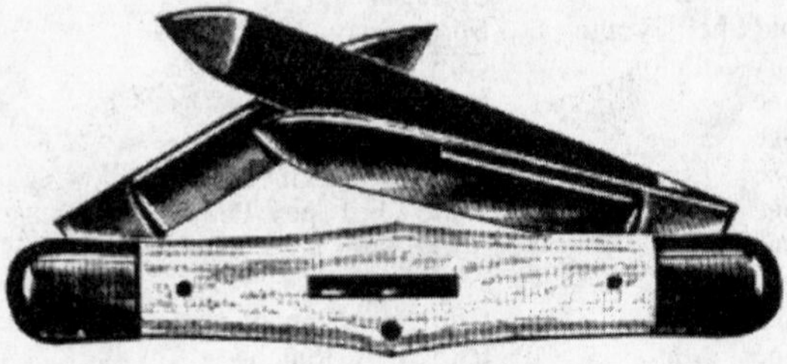

3" Balloon Pen

3" Balloon Pen				
2356F	Imit. Pearl	Pen, File, Pen		100
6356	Bone	Spear, Pen, File		125
9356	Imit. Pearl	Spear, Pen, File		100
8356	Genuine Pearl	Spear, Pen, File		225
3 1/8" Senator Pen				
6360T	Bone	Spear, Pen, File		80
8360T	Genuine Pearl	Spear, Pen, File		125

3" Equal End Whittler

3" Equal End Whittler				
2363	Imit. Pearl	Clip, Small Clip, Spey		100
6363	Bone	Clip, Small Clip, Spey		150
3 1/4" Balloon Whittler				
R364	Rainbow Celluloid	Clip, Small Clip, Spey		175
R364P	Rainbow Celluloid	Clip, Small Clip, Punch		200

Pattern	*Handle*	*Blades*	*Description*	*Mint Price*
6364	Bone	Clip, Small Clip, Spey		200
8364	Genuine Pearl	Clip, Small Clip, Spey		300
3 3/8" Square Bolster Premium Stock				
2366C	Imit. Pearl	California Clip, Spey, Sheepfoot		95
2366CSP	Imit. Pearl	California Clip, Spey, Pen		95
6366	Bone	Clip, Spey, Sheepfoot		120
8366	Genuine Pearl	Clip, Spey, Sheepfoot		200
9366	Imit. Pearl	Clip, Spey, Sheepfoot		75
3 1/4" Oval Whittler				
9367	Imit. Pearl	Spear, Pen, Coping		95
3 1/4" Wharncliffe Frame				
G372 1/2	Genuine Pearl	Clip, Spey, Pen		300
G372 1/2	Green Pyralin	Clip, Spey, Pen	Whittler	200
6372	Bone	Clip, Pen, Pen	Whittler	225
7372P	Imit. Tortoise	Clip, Spey, Punch		150
7372P	Horn Pyralin	Clip, Spey, Pen	Whittler	150
9372 1/2	Imit. Pearl	Clip, Spey, Pen		110
9372 1/2	Imit. Pearl	Clip, Spey, Pen	Whittler	140

3 7/8" Stockman

Pattern	*Handle*	*Blades*	*Description*	*Mint Price*
3 7/8" Stockman				
374	Imitation Horn	Clip, Spey, Sheepfoot	Round Bolsters	120
R474P	Rainbow Celluloid	California Clip, Punch, Spey	Round Bolsters	175
2374P	Imit. Pearl	Clip, Spey, Punch	Premium Stock	125
A3374PCS	Agate Celluloid	Clip, Spey, Punch	Premium Stock	175
5374	Genuine Stag	Clip, Spey, Sheepfoot	Round Bolsters	200
6374	Bone	Clip, Spey, Sheepfoot	Round Bolsters	200
6374P	Bone	Clip, Spey, Punch	Round Bolsters	210
6374PS	Bone	Clip, Spey, Pen	Round Bolsters	200
6374PP	Bone	Clip, Punch, Pen	Round Bolsters	225
6374S	Bone	Clip, Spey, Sheepfoot	Round Bolsters	220
6374C	Bone	California Clip, Sheepfoot, Spey	Round Bolsters	275
7374	Horn Pyralin	Clip, Spey, Sheepfoot	Premium Stock	170
7374P	Imitation Horn	Clip, Spey, Punch	Round Bolsters	150
8374	Genuine Pearl	Clip, Spey, Sheepfoot	Round Bolsters	450
8374C	Genuine Pearl	California Clip, Sheepfoot, Spey	Round Bolsters	500
9374C	Imit. Pearl	California Clip, Sheepfoot, Spey	Round Bolsters	175
3 5/8" Sleeveboard				
A376P	Imit. Pearl	Clip, Spey, Punch	Stockman	120
3376 1/2	Gold Shell Pyralin	Clip, Sheepfoot, Pen	Whittler	200
6376 1/2	Bone	Clip, Sheepfoot, Pen	Whittler	225
6376 1/2 P	Bone	Clip, Spey, Punch	Stockman	240
8376 1/2	Genuine Pearl	Clip, Sheepfoot, Pen	Whittler	350
3 1/8" Sleeveboard Whittler				
P378	Imit. Pearl	Spear, Small Clip, Pen		85
S378	Imit. Horn	Spear, Small Clip, Pen		85
6378	Bone	Spear, Pen, Pen		130

Pattern	Handle	Blades	Description	Mint Price
6378T	Bone	Spear, Pen, Pen		120
378	Bone	Spear, Pen, File		150
4" Jumbo Whittler				
6379	Bone	Wide Spear, Coping, Pen		500
6379P	Bone	Wide Spear, Coping, Punch		600
3" Serpentine Lobster Pen				
8381	Genuine Pearl	Spear, Pen, File		125
2 3/4" Lobster Pen				
R385	Rainbow Celluloid	Small Spear, Pen, File		70
9385	Imit. Pearl	Small Spear, Pen, File		60
3 1/8" Bartender's Knife				
2387	Imit. Pearl	Spear, Opener, Corkscrew		90
3 5/8" Balloon Stock				
A391	Imit. Pearl	Clip, Spey, Coping		100
A391P	Imit. Pearl	Clip, Spey, Punch		110
R391P	Imit. Pearl	Clip, Spey, Punch		110
7391	Imit. Tortoise	Clip, Spey, Coping		120
8391	Genuine Pearl	Clip, Spey, Coping		275

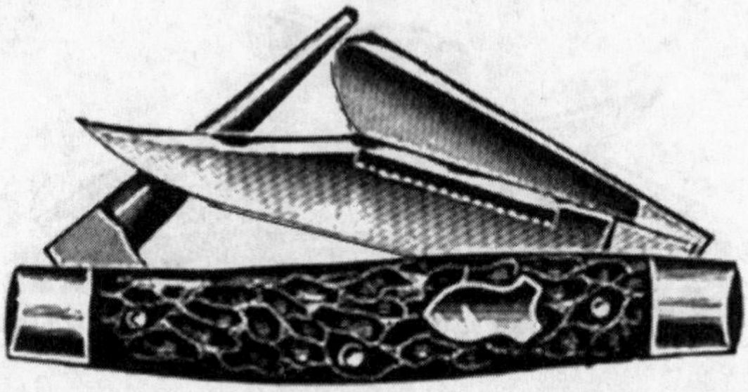

3 7/8" Square Bolster Premium Stock

Pattern	Handle	Blades	Description	Mint Price
3 7/8" Square Bolster Premium Stock				
2393	Imit. Pearl	Clip, Spey, Sheepfoot		120
3393	Gold Shell Pyralin	Clip, Spey, Sheepfoot		170
6393	Bone	Clip, Spey, Sheepfoot		220
9393	Imit. Pearl	Clip, Spey, Sheepfoot		75
33093	Gold Shell Pyralin	Clip, Spey, Sheepfoot	Gunstock	200
33093P	Gold Shell Pyralin	Clip, Spey, Punch		200
63093	Bone	Clip, Spey, Sheepfoot	Gunstock	275
63093P	Bone	Clip, Spey, Punch		250
4 1/4" Square Bolster Premium Stock				
5394	Genuine Stag	Clip, Spey, Sheepfoot		400
6394	Bone	Clip, Spey, Sheepfoot		300

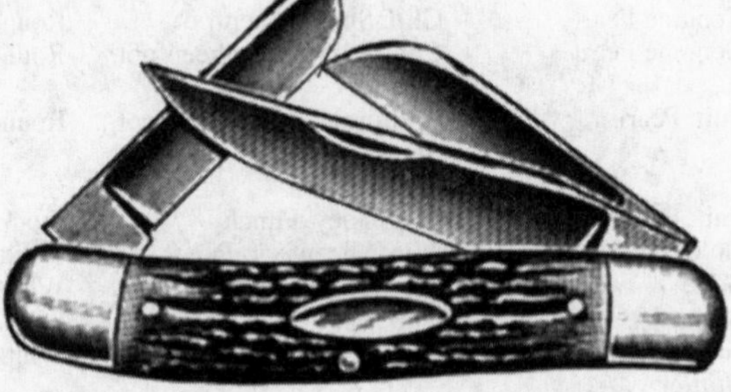

4 3/8" Jumbo Stock

Pattern	*Handle*	*Blades*	*Description*	*Mint Price*
4³/8″ Jumbo Stock				
23094	Imit. Pearl	Clip, Spey, Sheepfoot		275
53094C	Genuine Stag	California Clip, Spey, Sheepfoot		500
3⁵/8″ Balloon Whittler				
A396¹/2P	Agate Celluloid	Clip, Spey, Punch		150
2396¹/2P	Brown Composition	Clip, Spey, Punch		125
6396¹/2	Bone	Clip, Small Clip, Pen		250
9396¹/2	Imit. Pearl	Clip, Small Clip, Pen		125
8396¹/2	Genuine Pearl	Clip, Small Clip, Pen		350
93096¹/2	Imit. Pearl	Clip, Small Clip, Pen		150
3¹/4″ Congress Whittler				
6397	Bone	Wharncliffe, Pen, File		175
3¹/4″ Swayback Whittler				
9399	Horn Pyralin	Wharncliffe, Pen, File		150
4⁵/8″ Jumbo Whittler				
53103	Genuine Stag	Spear, Spey, Pen		600

Four-Blade Knives

4³/4″ Bull Head Utility

4³/4″ Bull Head Utility				
6400	Bone	Clip, Spey, Punch, Opener		550
7400	Imit. Pearl	Clip, Spey, Punch, Opener		450
3¹/8″ Senator Pen				
6460T	Bone	Spear, Pen, Pen, File		120
8460T	Genuine Pearl	Spear, Pen, Pen, File		160
3¹/4″ Swayback Pen				
8480	Genuine Pearl	Sheepfoot, Spear, Pen, File		200

3⁵/8″ Scout Knife

Pattern	Handle	Blades	Description	Mint Price
3⅝" Scout Knife				
6490	Bone	Spear, Punch 2 Openers		220

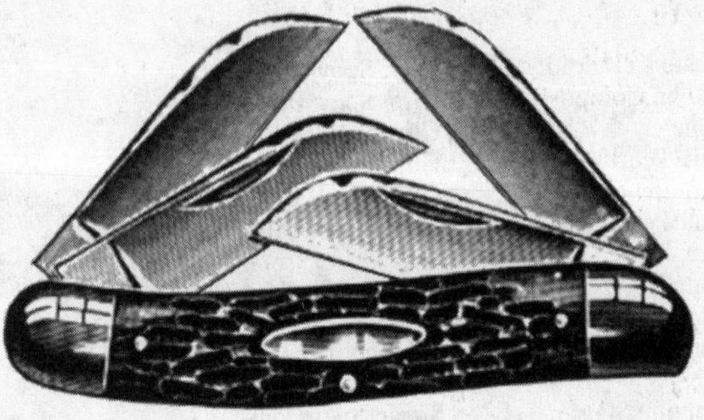

4⅛" Jumbo Jack

Pattern	Handle	Blades	Description	Mint Price
4⅛" Jumbo Jack				
6494	Bone	Four Sheepfoot Blades		500

WINCHESTER

When the Winchester Arms Company decided to expand into the cutlery field, shortly after World War I, it did so through acquisition. In 1919, Winchester purchased two very reputable knife manufacturers, the Eagle Knife Company of New Haven, Connecticut, and the Napanoch Knife Company of Napanoch, New York. For Winchester, these purchases were well founded in its entry into the knife market. Eagle had developed machinery and methods, such as blade blanking and automatic blade grinding, which would be so important to assembly line production. Napanoch had made a very high quality knife and the skill of Napanoch cutlers would compliment the modern production methods designed by Eagle. A large percentage of the employees of the two purchased companies became employees of Winchester in the New Haven, Connecticut, factory. By combining technology, skill and cutlery experience so acquired, Winchester was able to soon mass-produce a high-quality knife marked with its own brand. Convinced that it was solidly entrenched within the market, Winchester adopted the motto describing its knives "As good as the gun."

In 1922, Winchester and the E. C. Simmons Hardware Company of St. Louis, Missouri, merged to form the Winchester-Simmons Company. Winchester was to have production responsibility and Simmons was to be responsible for marketing. At the time of the merger, Simmons owned controlling interest in the Walden Knife Company. In 1923, production of Walden knives ended and all of Walden's equipment was moved to the Winchester site. In addition to knives marked with the Winchester trademark, the factory also made knives branded KEEN KUTTER for sale by Simmons.

The firm of Winchester-Simmons was dissolved, with Winchester retaining the manufacturing facilities and Simmons the marketing business. Up until the 1930s, Winchester knives were of excellent quality. Increasing competition from manufacturers of low-priced cutlery motivated the company to begin selling dealer assortments of lesser quality knives. The advent of World War II offered Winchester other manufacturing alternatives and cutlery production was ceased by early 1942.

Although a few German-made knives marked with the Winchester name appeared in the market during the late 1970s and early 1980s, these were cheap knives not authorized by the company. In the late 1980s, however, Winchester licensed the manufacture and distribution of a quality line of reproduction-type knives to Blue Grass Cutlery.

The pattern numbers used by Winchester can be used to identify knives as follows:

The first digit signifies the number of blades, while the second digit signifies the following handle material:

0—Celluloid
1—Fancy Celluloid
2—Nickel Silver
3—Genuine Pearl
6—Cocobolo or Other Wood
7—Bone
8—Bone Stag
9—Sometimes Used for Bone or Stag

The third and fourth digits signify factory pattern.

There were two distinct lines of Winchester knives. Those of higher quality (earlier manufacture) are stamped WINCHESTER/TRADEMARK/MADE IN USA on all blades; the lesser quality line knives are stamped on only one blade. While these stamping differences did exist on most of Winchester's production, the collector should be aware that there are some exceptions.

Pattern	*Size*	*Handle*	*Description*	*Mint Price*
1050	5″	Celluloid	Toothpick	400
1051	4 3/8″	Celluloid	Toothpick	375

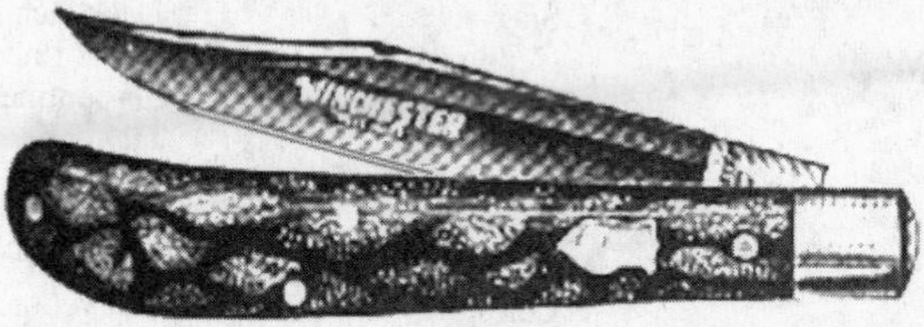

1060	4 1/8″	Celluloid	Folding Hunter	400
1201	3 1/4″	Nickel Silver	Easy Open Jack	175
1605	3 1/2″	Cocobolo	Jack	125
1608	3 1/2″	Cocobolo	Jack	135
1610	4″	Cocobolo	Pruner	135
1611	3 1/4″	Cocobolo	Jack	110
1613	3 3/8″	Cocobolo	Jack	135
1614	4 1/8″	Cocobolo	Maize Jack	190
1621	4 3/4″	Ebony	Budding Knife	200
1624	4″	Cocobolo	Maize Jack	175
1632	3 1/2″	Cocobolo	Regular Jack	125
1633	3 1/2″	Cocobolo	Pruner	130
1701	3 1/2″	Bone	Barlow	250
1703	5″	Bone	Daddy Barlow	600
1704	5″	Bone	Daddy Barlow	625
1785	3 1/2″	Bone	Barlow	250
1905	4 1/4″	Stag	Texas Jack	500

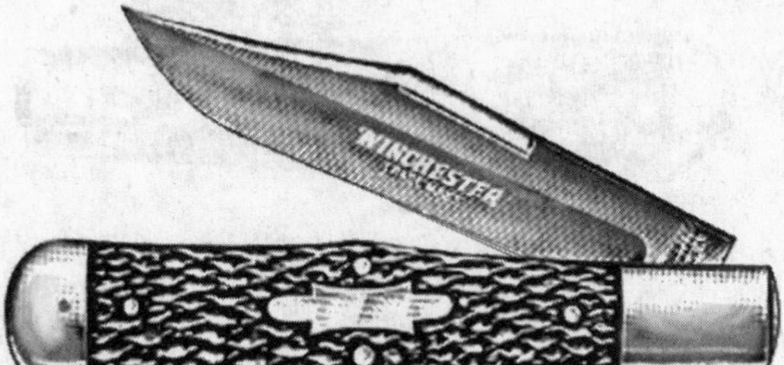

1920	5 1/4″	Bone	Folding Hunter	2000
1921	3 1/2″	Bone	Jack	200
1922	3 3/8″	Bone	Jack	200
1923	4 1/8″	Bone	Texas Jack	375
1924	4 1/4″	Bone	Toothpick	400
1925	3 1/2″	Bone	Jack	325
1936	5″	Bone	Toothpick	500

Pattern	*Size*	*Handle*	*Description*	*Mint Price*
1937	3 7/8″	Bone	Serpentine Jack	250
1938	3 1/2″	Bone	Jack	175

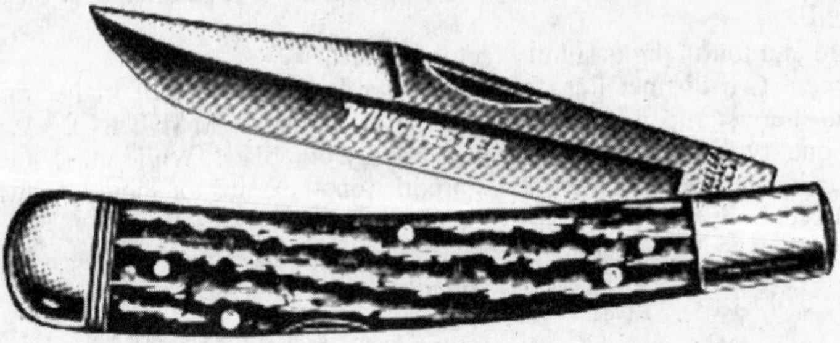

1950	5 1/4″	Stag	Lockback Hunter	2400
2028	3 3/8″	Celluloid	Equal End Jack	200
2037	3″	Celluloid	Serpentine Jack	165
2038	3″	Celluloid	Jack	185
2039	3″	Celluloid	Jack	140
2047	4 1/4″	Celluloid	Slim Jack	425
2051	3 1/4″	Bone	Senator Pen	175
2052	2 5/8″	Celluloid	Sleeveboard Pen	130
2053	2 5/8″	Celluloid	Senator Pen	140
2054	3 1/4″	Celluloid	Senator Pen	125
2055	3 1/4″	Celluloid	Senator Pen	125
2057	3 3/8″	Celluloid	Senator Pen	150
2058	3 1/8″	Celluloid	Senator Pen	150
2059	3 1/8″	Celluloid	Senator Pen	140
2067	3 3/8″	Celluloid	Wharncliffe Pen	240
2068	3 3/8″	Celluloid	Sleeveboard	225
2069	3 3/8″	Celluloid	Equal End Jack	250

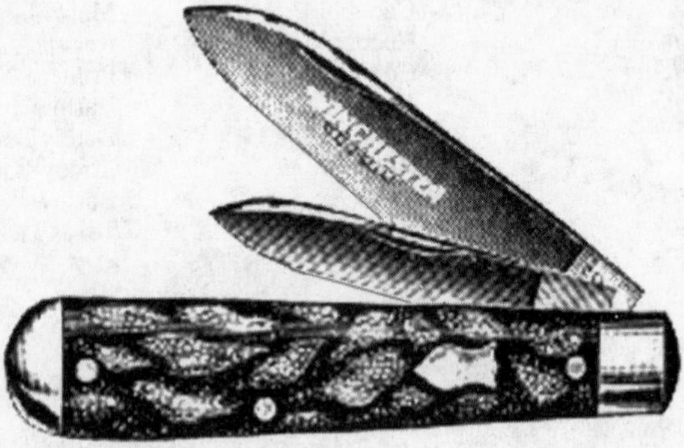

2070	3 1/2″	Celluloid	Equal End Jack	250
2078	3 3/8″	Celluloid	Wharncliffe Pen	225
2079	3 3/8″	Celluloid	Office Knife	200
2082	3 1/8″	Celluloid	Sleeveboard	175
2083	3 1/8″	Celluloid	Jack	185
2084	3 1/4″	Celluloid	Sleeveboard	200
2085	3″	Celluloid	Dogleg Jack	225
2086	2 7/8″	Celluloid	Dogleg Jack	200
2087	3″	Celluloid	Dogleg Jack	225
2088	3 3/8″	Celluloid	Wharncliffe Pen	225
2089	3 3/4″	Celluloid	Office Knife	190
2090	3″	Celluloid	Wharncliffe Pen	225
2094	3 1/2″	Celluloid	Teardrop Jack	275

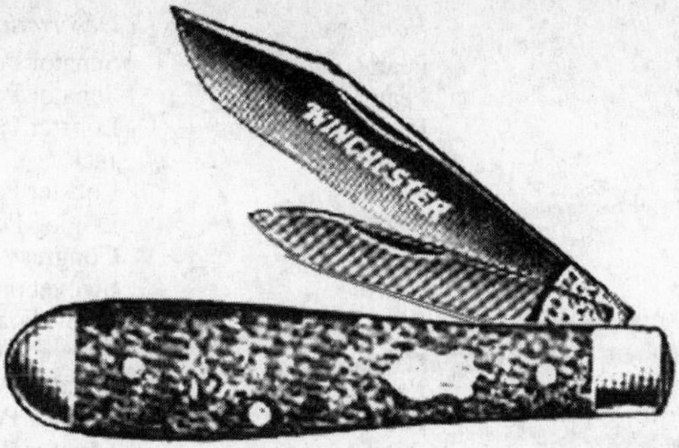

Pattern	*Size*	*Handle*	*Description*	*Mint Price*
2098	3 3/8″	Celluloid	Teardrop Jack	300
2099	3 3/4″	Celluloid	Slim Jack	225
2106	3 1/4″	Celluloid	Jack	200
2107	2 3/4″	Celluloid	Dogleg	190
2109	2 7/8″	Celluloid	Sleeveboard	150
2110	3 1/2″	Celluloid	Teardrop Jack	220
2111	3 1/2″	Celluloid	Jack	195
2112	3 1/2″	Celluloid	Jack	195
2113	2 3/4″	Celluloid	Serpentine Pen	160
2114	3″	Celluloid	Serpentine Jack	200
2115	2 7/8″	Celluloid	Sleeveboard Pen	175
2116	3 3/8″	Celluloid	Sleeveboard Pen	160
2117	3 1/8″	Celluloid	Serpentine Jack	225
2201	3 1/4″	Nickel Silver	Senator Pen	125
2202	3″	Fiber	Wharncliffe Pen	120
2204	3 1/8″	Nickel Silver	Senator Pen	110
2205	3 1/2″	Nickel Silver	Senator Pen	140
2207	3 3/8″	Nickel Silver	Easy Open Jack	175
2208	3 3/8″	Nickel Silver	Jack	165
2215	3 1/2″	Nickel Silver	Senator Pen	110
2301	2 1/4″	Pearl	Senator Pen	160
2302	2 1/4″	Pearl	Senator Pen	170
2303	2 5/8″	Pearl	Senator Pen	185

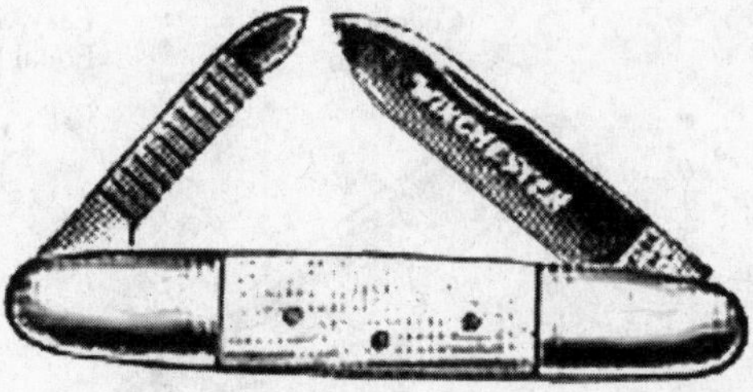

2306	2 5/8″	Pearl	Senator Pen	180
2307	2 7/8″	Pearl	Senator Pen	175
2308	2 7/8″	Pearl	Senator Pen	175
2309	3″	Pearl	Senator Pen	225
2314	3″	Pearl	Serpentine Jack	270
2316	3″	Pearl	Serpentine Jack	270
2317	3″	Pearl	Serpentine Jack	240
2320	2 7/8″	Pearl	Sleeveboard Pen	175
2324	3″	Pearl	Senator Pen	250
2331	3 1/4″	Pearl	Congress Pen	300
2335	3 1/4″	Pearl	Sleeveboard Pen	325
2337	3 1/4″	Pearl	Senator Pen	275
2338	3 1/4″	Pearl	Senator Pen	250

Pattern	*Size*	*Handle*	*Description*	*Mint Price*
2344	3 1/4"	Pearl	Senator Pen	260
2345	3 1/4"	Pearl	Senator Pen	270
2346	3"	Pearl	Lobster Pen	225
2352	3 1/8"	Pearl	Jack	300
2356	3"	Pearl	Lobster Pen	240
2361	2 7/8"	Pearl	Dogleg Pen	250
2363	3"	Pearl	Congress	300
2366	3 3/8"	Pearl	Sleeveboard Pen	280
2367	3"	Pearl	Sleeveboard Pen	250
2368	3"	Pearl	Sleeveboard Pen	250
2369	2 5/8"	Pearl	Senator Pen	225
2374	2 7/8"	Pearl	Senator Pen	225
2375	2 5/8"	Pearl	Senator Pen	210
2376	3"	Pearl	Senator Pen	250
2377	2 5/8"	Pearl	Senator Pen	225

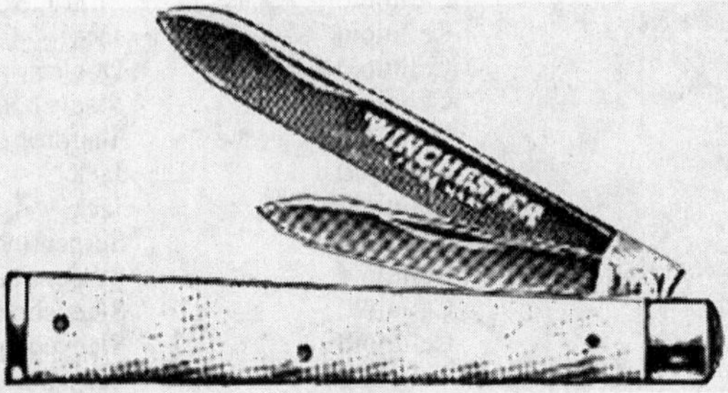

2380	3 1/4"	Pearl	Physician's Knife	700
2603	3 1/2"	Cocobolo	Jack	200
2604	3 3/8"	Cocobolo	Jack	200
2605	3 3/8"	Cocobolo	Easy Open Jack	225
2606	3 1/2"	Cocobolo	Jack	200
2608	3 1/2"	Cocobolo	Boy's Jack	225
2610	3 3/8"	Cocobolo	Jack	220
2611	3"	Cocobolo	Serpentine Jack	190
2612	3 5/8"	Cocobolo	Teardrop Jack	250
2613	3 5/8"	Cocobolo	Easy Open Jack	240
2614	3 5/8"	Cocobolo	Equal End Jack	240

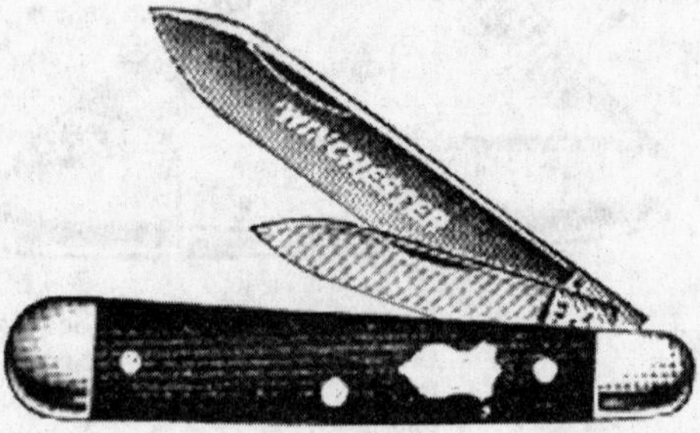

2627	3 1/4"	Cocobolo	Slim Jack	220
2629	3 1/2"	Ebony	Jack	225
2630	3 5/8"	Ebony	Teardrop Jack	240
2631	3 1/4"	Ebony	Sleeveboard	175
2632	3 3/8"	Cocobolo	Premium Stock	190
2633	3 1/4"	Ebony	Premium Stock	190
2635	3 1/2"	Cocobolo	Jack	175
2636	3 1/2"	Ebony	Jack	200

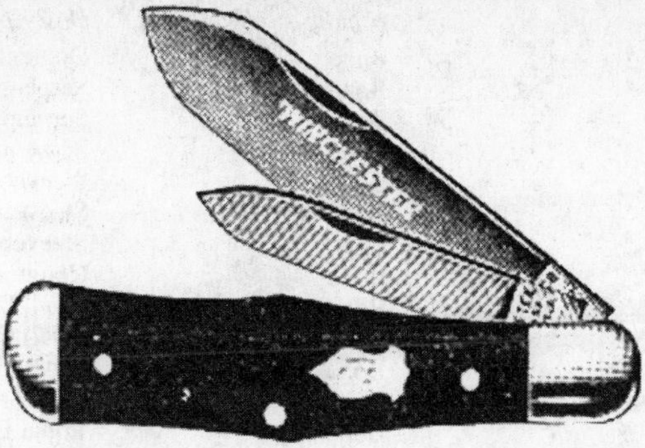

Pattern	*Size*	*Handle*	*Description*	*Mint Price*
2637	3 1/2″	Ebony	Balloon Jack	250
2638	3 1/2″	Ebony	Serpentine Jack	220
2640	3 3/4″	Ebony	Coke Bottle	275
2641	3 7/8″	Cocobolo	Trapper	425
2649	3 3/4″	Ebony	Jack	290
2660	3 1/2″	Ebony	Regular Jack	225
2661	3 1/2″	Cocobolo	Jack	225
2662	3 1/2″	Ebony	Jack	240
2665	3 3/8″	Ebony	Equal End Jack	220
2666	3 3/8″	Ebony	Jack	220
2681	3 3/4″	Ebony	Electrician	185
2690	4 1/2″	Ebony	Texas Jack	575
2701	3 1/2″	Bone	Barlow	325

2702	3 1/2″	Bone	Barlow	325
2703	3 1/2″	Bone	Barlow	320
2820	3 3/8″	Bone	Jack	270
2830	3 1/4″	Bone	Senator Pen	180
2840	2″	Bone	Senator Pen	190
2841	3″	Bone	Senator Pen	190
2842	3 1/4″	Bone	Senator Pen	200
2843	3 3/8″	Bone	Equal End Jack	225
2844	3 3/4″	Bone	Equal End Jack	285
2845	3 3/4″	Bone	Sleeveboard Jack	300
2846	3 1/4″	Bone	Premium Stock	210
2847	3 1/4″	Bone	Pen	210
2848	3 1/2″	Bone	Boy's Jack	225
2849	3 1/4″	Bone	Equal End Pen	250
2850	3 3/4″	Bone	Balloon Jack	475
2851	3″	Bone	Gunstock Jack	500
2852	3″	Bone	Cattle Knife	375
2853	3 3/8″	Stag	Gunstock	400
2854	3 1/4″	Bone	Jack	250
2855	3 1/4″	Bone	Equal End Jack	240

Pattern	*Size*	*Handle*	*Description*	*Mint Price*
2856	2 7/8"	Bone	Dogleg	225
2857	3 1/8"	Bone	Serpentine Jack	250
2858	3"	Bone	Serpentine Jack	210
2859	2 7/8"	Bone	Serpentine Jack	210
2860	3 1/4"	Bone	Sleeveboard	240
2861	3 1/4"	Bone	Sleeveboard	240
2862	3 3/8"	Bone	Sleeveboard	250
2863	3 1/4"	Bone	Congress	300
2864	3 3/8"	Bone	Swell Center	325
2865	3 1/2"	Bone	Swell Center	350
2866	2 7/8"	Bone	Senator Pen	190
2867	3 3/8"	Bone	Senator Pen	190
2868	3 1/4"	Bone	Equal End Pen	180
2869	3 3/4"	Bone	Gunstock	400
2870	3 3/4"	Bone	Gunstock	400
2871	3 3/4"	Bone	Gunstock	400
2872	3 1/4"	Bone	Gunstock	375
2873	3 1/2"	Bone	Barlow	290
2874	3 1/2"	Bone	Jack	275
2875	3 1/4"	Stag	Premium Stock	270
2876	3 1/4"	Bone	Muskrat	425
2878	4 1/4"	Bone	Texas Jack	500
2879	4 1/2"	Stag	Sleeveboard	800
2880	4 1/2"	Bone	Texas Jack	600
2881	4 1/2"	Bone	Texas Jack	600
2901	3 1/2"	Bone	Jack	225
2902	2 5/8"	Bone	Senator Pen	150
2903	3 1/2"	Bone	Swell Center	350

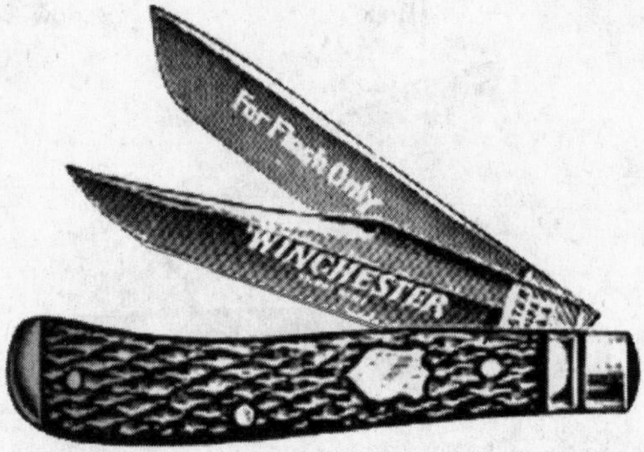

Pattern	*Size*	*Handle*	*Description*	*Mint Price*
2904	3 7/8"	Bone	Trapper	650
2905	4 1/4"	Bone	Texas Jack	600
2906	4 1/4"	Bone	Slim Jack	575
2907	4 1/4"	Bone	Texas Jack	600
2908	3 5/8"	Bone	Balloon Whittler	300
2910	3"	Bone	Lobster Pen	190
2911	3 1/2"	Bone	Jack	225

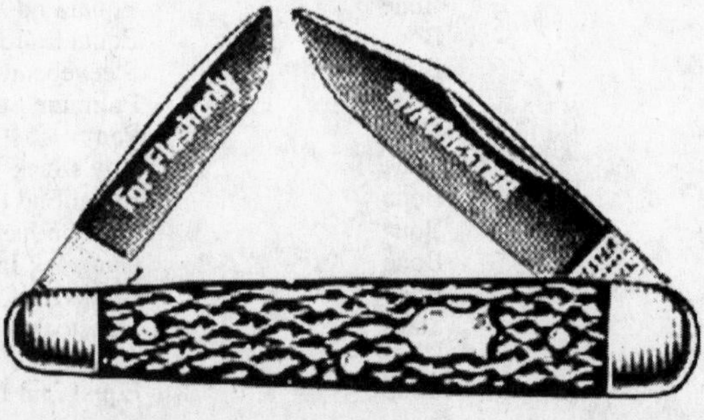

Pattern	*Size*	*Handle*	*Description*	*Mint Price*
2914	3 1/4″	Bone	Sleeveboard	225
2917	3″	Bone	Dogleg Jack	290
2918	3 3/8″	Bone	Wharncliffe Pen	275
2921	3 1/2″	Bone	Gunstock Jack	500
2923	4″	Bone	Premium Stock	325
2924	3″	Bone	Congress	250
2925	3 1/8″	Bone	Jack	225
2928	4″	Bone	Texas Jack	375
2930	3 5/8″	Bone	Easy Open Jack	275
2931	3 3/8″	Bone	Slim Jack	200
2932	3 1/4″	Bone	Congress	275

2933	3″	Bone	Sleeveboard Pen	200
2934	3 3/8″	Bone	Senator Pen	175
2938	3 1/4″	Bone	Sleeveboard	210
2940	3 3/8″	Bone	Teardrop Jack	275
2943	3 3/4″	Bone	Sleeveboard	250
2945	3 1/4″	Bone	Senator Pen	220
2948	3 3/8″	Bone	Slim Pen	225

2949	3 1/2″	Bone	Jack	250
2950	3 1/2″	Bone	Jack	225
2951	3 1/2″	Bone	Jack	250
2952	3 1/2″	Bone	Jack	250
2954	3 1/2″	Bone	Jack	250
2956	3 1/2″	Bone	Serpentine Jack	275
2958	3 1/2″	Bone	Jack	270
2959	3 3/8″	Bone	Easy Open Jack	285
2961	3 3/8″	Bone	Jack	225
2962	2 7/8″	Bone	Dogleg Jack	185
2963	3″	Bone	Senator Pen	175
2964	3 5/8″	Bone	Slim Jack	290
2966	3 5/8″	Bone	Equal End Jack	325
2967	3 7/8″	Bone	Swell Center	525

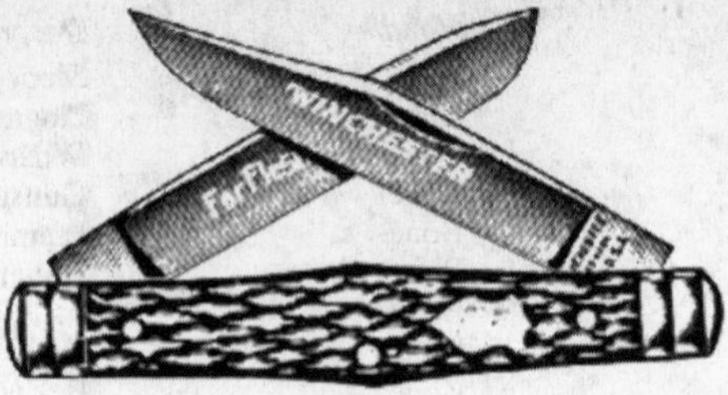

Pattern	*Size*	*Handle*	*Description*	*Mint Price*
2969	3 7/8″	Bone	Swell Center	500
2973	3 5/8	Bone	Equal End Jack	250
2974	3 1/2″	Bone	Serpentine Jack	270
2976	4″	Stag	Texas Jack	400
2978	3 1/2″	Stag	Physician	600
2980	3 5/8″	Bone	Equal End Jack	300
2981	3 1/4″	Bone	Senator Pen	220
2982	4″	Bone	Texas Jack	375
2983	3 1/2″	Bone	Boy's Jack	225
2988	4″	Bone	Texas Jack	400

2990	2 7/8″	Bone	Serpentine Jack	200
2991	3 5/8″	Stag	Equal End Jack	325
2992	3 5/8″	Bone	Serpentine Jack	275
2993	3 7/8″	Bone	Trapper	475
2994	3 5/8″	Bone	Easy Open Jack	275
2995	3 5/8″	Bone	Teardrop Jack	325
2996	3 3/4″	Bone	Congress	400
2997	3 3/8″	Bone	Wharncliffe Pen	275
2998	3 1/2″	Bone	Jack	240
2999	3 1/8″	Bone	Serpentine Jack	275
3001	3 1/2″	Celluloid	Cattle Knife	450
3002	3 5/8″	Celluloid	Balloon Whittler	425
3003	3 1/2″	Celluloid	Premium Stock	375
3005	3 5/8″	Celluloid	Balloon Whittler	450
3006	3 3/8″	Celluloid	Whittler	425

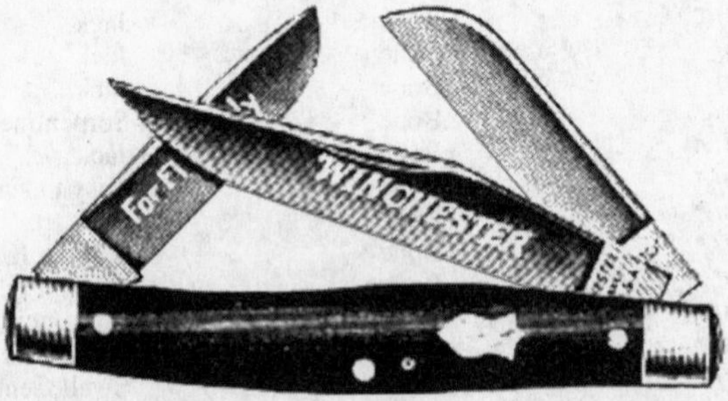

Pattern	*Size*	*Handle*	*Description*	*Mint Price*
3007	4″	Celluloid	Premium Stock	500
3008	3 5/8″	Celluloid	Cattle Knife	500
3009	3 5/8″	Celluloid	Cattle Knife	525
3010	3 3/4″	Celluloid	Cattle Knife	550
3014	4″	Celluloid	Premium Stock	550
3015	3 5/8″	Celluloid	Cattle Knife	425
3016	3 5/8″	Celluloid	Cattle Knife	450
3017	4″	Celluloid	Premium Stock	475
3018	4″	Celluloid	Premium Stock	475
3019	3 1/2″	Celluloid	Whittler	425
3020	3 1/2″	Celluloid	Whittler	425

3022	3 1/4″	Tortoise	Senator Pen	375
3023	3 5/8″	Celluloid	Whittler	475
3024	3 5/8″	Celluloid	Whittler	475
3025	3 1/2″	Celluloid	Premium Stock	350
3026	3 1/4″	Celluloid	Premium Stock	375
3027	3 1/4″	Celluloid	Premium Stock	350
3028	3 1/4″	Celluloid	Premium Stock	350
3029	3 1/4″	Celluloid	Premium Stock	325
3030	3 3/8″	Celluloid	Senator	300
3031	3 3/8″	Celluloid	Senator	350
3033	3″	Celluloid	Cattle Knife	325
3034	3″	Celluloid	Cattle Knife	325
3035	3 3/8″	Celluloid	Senator Pen	300
3036	3 3/8″	Celluloid	Cattle Knife	325
3040	3″	Celluloid	Whittler	325

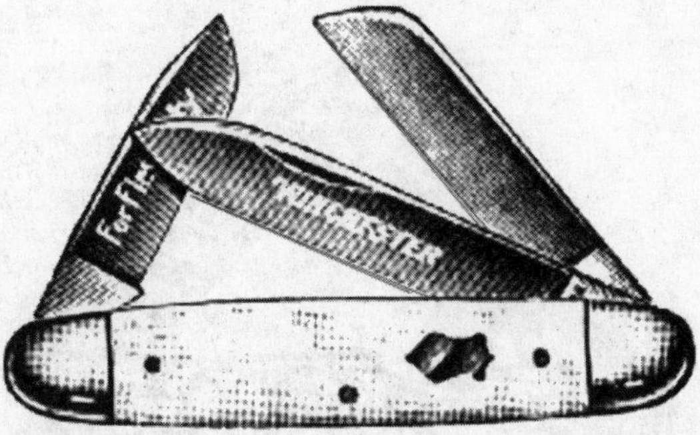

3041	3″	Celluloid	Senator	325
3042	3 3/8″	Celluloid	Senator	325
3043	3 3/8″	Celluloid	Senator	310
3044	3 3/8″	Celluloid	Senator	320
3045	3 1/4″	Celluloid	Senator Pen	275
3046	3 1/4″	Celluloid	Whittler	300
3047	3 1/2″	Celluloid	Premium Stock	300
3048	4″	Celluloid	Premium Stock	500
3049	3 5/8″	Imitation Bone	Cattle Knife	425

Pattern	*Size*	*Handle*	*Description*	*Mint Price*
3331	3 1/4″	Pearl	Lobster Pen	275
3338	3″	Pearl	Sleeveboard	290
3341	3 3/8″	Pearl	Cattle Knife	550
3345	3 1/4″	Pearl	Whittler	525
3347	3 1/4″	Pearl	Whittler	525
3348	3 1/4″	Pearl	Premium Stock	500
3349	3″	Pearl	Sleeveboard Pen	350
3350	3 1/4″	Pearl	Senator Whittler	350
3352	3 1/2″	Pearl	Senator Pen	300
3353	2 5/8″	Pearl	Senator Pen	250
3357	3 1/4″	Pearl	Whittler	425
3360	3 1/4″	Pearl	Bartender's Knife	450
3366	3 3/8″	Pearl	Senator Whittler	425
3370	3″	Pearl	Lobster Pen	275
3371	3″	Pearl	Lobster Pen	275
3373	2 7/8″	Pearl	Senator Whittler	275
3376	4″	Pearl	Premium Stock	700
3377	3 1/4″	Pearl	Whittler	350

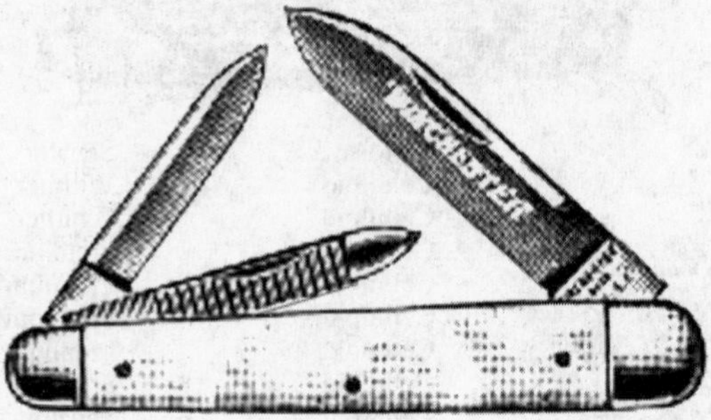

3378	3″	Pearl	Whittler	350
3379	3″	Pearl	Senator Whittler	325
3380	2 3/4	Pearl	Sleeveboard	275
3381	3 1/8″	Pearl	Lobster Pen	300
3382	3″	Pearl	Lobster Pen	275
3625	3 5/8″	Ebony	Cattle Knife	350

3902	3 1/2″	Bone	Swell Center	450
3903	3 3/4″	Stag	Cattle Knife	700
3904	3 3/4″	Stag	Whittler	800
3905	3 1/2″	Stag	Cattle Knife	475
3906	4″	Bone	Premium Stock	550
3907	4″	Stag	Premium Stock	675
3908	3 3/4″	Bone	Balloon Whittler	475
3909	3 3/8″	Bone	Equal End Jack	375

Pattern	*Size*	*Handle*	*Description*	*Mint Price*
3911	3″	Celluloid	Senator Whittler	300
3914	2 3/4″	Bone	Senator Pen	225
3915	3 1/2″	Bone	Cattle Knife	350
3916	3 1/2″	Bone	Premium Stock	350
3917	3 1/2″	Bone	Premium Stock	325
3924	3″	Bone	Senator	275
3925	3 5/8″	Bone	Balloon Whittler	550
3927	3 3/8″	Bone	Wharncliffe Pen	375
3928	4″	Bone	Premium Stock	500

3929	3 1/4″	Stag	Congress Pen	400
3931	3 1/8″	Stag	Sleeveboard Pen	275
3932	3 3/8″	Bone	Equal End Jack	300
3933	3 3/8″	Bone	Equal End Jack	300
3936	3 5/8″	Bone	Cattle Knife	450
3938	3 3/8″	Bone	Equal End Jack	300
3939	3 3/8″	Bone	Equal End Jack	325
3942	3 3/8″	Bone	Cattle Knife	375
3944	3 1/4″	Bone	Senator Pen	275
3948	3 3/4″	Bone	Reverse Gunstock	600
3949	3″	Bone	Cattle Knife	325
3950	3 5/8″	Bone	Cattle Knife	425
3951	3 5/8″	Bone	Cattle Knife	425
3952	3 5/8″	Bone	Cattle Knife	425
3953	3 1/4″	Bone	Bartender's Knife	325
3959	4″	Bone	Serpentine Stock	450
3960	4″	Bone	Premium Stock	450
3961	4″	Bone	Premium Stock	450
3962	4″	Horn	Premium Stock	450
3963	4″	Bone	Serpentine Stock	450
3964	4″	Bone	Premium Stock	450
3965	3 1/4″	Bone	Premium Stock	300
3966	3 1/4″	Bone	Premium Stock	320
3967	3 1/4″	Bone	Premium Stock	325
3968	3 1/4″	Bone	Premium Stock	350
3969	3 1/4″	Bone	Premium Stock	350
3971	3 5/8″	Bone	Whittler	475
3972	3 5/8″	Bone	Whittler	500
3973	3 1/2″	Bone	Cattle Knife	350
3975	3 3/8″	Bone	Cattle Knife	375
3977	3 3/8″	Bone	Cattle Knife	350
3978	3 1/4″	Bone	Serpentine Stock	350
3979	3 5/8″	Bone	Cattle Knife	450
3980	3″	Bone	Cattle Knife	325

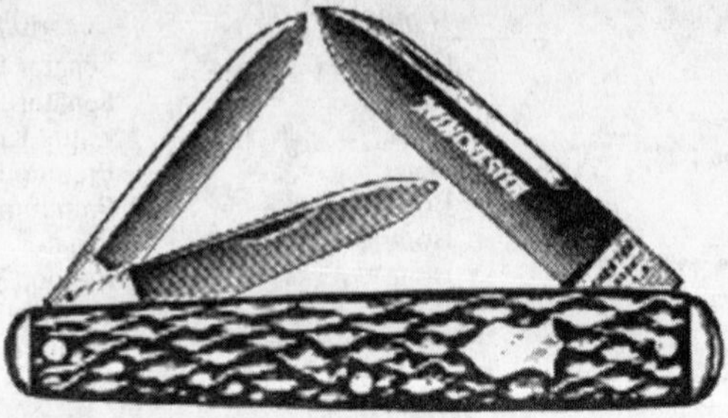

Pattern	Size	Handle	Description	Mint Price
3991	3 1/4″	Bone	Sleeveboard	350
3992	3 3/8	Bone	Slim Whittler	375
3993	4″	Bone	Premium Stock	450
4001	4″	Celluloid	Premium Stock	500
4301	2 3/4″	Pearl	Lobster Pen	275
4313	3″	Pearl	Senator Pen	375

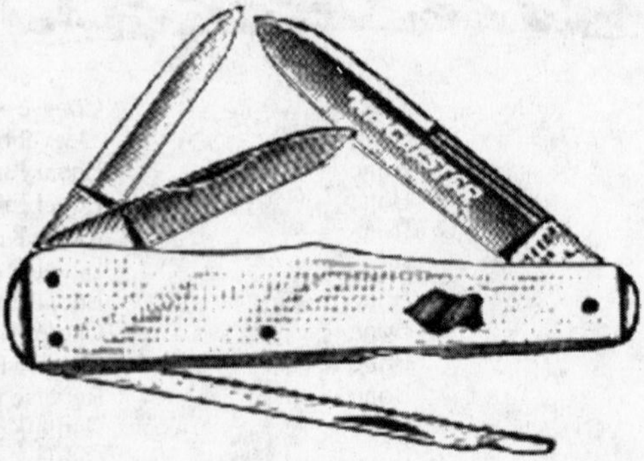

4320	3 1/4″	Pearl	Lobster Whittler	450
4340	3 1/4″	Pearl	Senator Pen	400
4341	3 1/4″	Pearl	Senator Pen	400
4901	3 3/8″	Bone	Scout/Utility	450
4910	4″	Bone	Premium Stock	650
4918	3″	Bone	Congress	375
4920	3 1/4″	Bone	Lobster	300
4930	3 1/4″	Bone	Congress	350
4931	3 1/2″	Bone	Congress	375
4950	3 3/4″	Bone	Scout/Utility	550
4951	3 5/8″	Bone	Scout/Utility	525

4961	4″	Bone	Premium Stock	550
4962	4″	Bone	Premium Stock	575

Pattern	*Size*	*Handle*	*Description*	*Mint Price*
4963	4″	Bone	Premium Stock	550
4975	3¼″	Bone	Bartender's Knife	500
4990	3⅝″	Bone	Scout/Utility	500
4991	3½″	Bone	Scout/Utility	475

Winchester Reproductions

New Winchester knives have been made by Blue Grass Cutlery Corporation of Manchester, Ohio, since 1987. These knives are reproductions of old Winchester knives and their manufacture is licensed and authorized by Olin Corporation, the owner of the Winchester trademark. They are made in the United States using old original dies from Winchester's factory of about a half-century ago. The knives are of high quality, most with old-style bone handles, pinned handle shields and hand-hammered rivets. The original Winchester trademark is used for blade etching and tang stamps. The pattern number and year of manufacture are stamped on the reverse tangs. Values shown are for knives made during the first five years of the new era of Winchester knives.

Year	*No. Made*	*Handles*	*Shield*	*Blade Etch*	*Mint Price*
W15 1036½—5″ Toothpick					
1992	250	Christmas Tree	Oval	Winchester	100
1992	250	Christmas Tree	Oval	Fancy Winchester	115
1992	250	Waterfall	Oval	Winchester	100
1992	250	Waterfall	Oval	Fancy Winchester	110
1992	250	Goldstone	Oval	Winchester	100
1992	250	Goldstone	Oval	Fancy Winchester	115
1992	250	Candy Stripe	Oval	Winchester	110
1992	250	Candy Stripe	Oval	Fancy Winchester	120
1992	250	Brown Bone	Oval	Winchester	115
1992	250	Brown Bone	Oval	Fancy Winchester	120
W15 1901—3⅞″ Bow Tie					
1987	3,308	Rogers Bone	Heraldic	Winchester	100
1987	841	Rogers Bone	Heraldic	Winchester	170
1992	502	Goldstone	Oval	Winchester	95
1992	317	Pearl	Heraldic	Winchester	175
W15 1920—5¼″ Folding Hunter					
1990	1,594	Peachseed Bone	Large Boat	Winchester	140
1990	55	Peachseed Bone	Large Boat	Southern California Club	175
1991	969	Stag	Large Boat	Winchester	200

W15 1924—4⅜″ Toothpick

W15 1924—4⅜″ Toothpick					
1987	4,173	Rogers Bone	Heraldic	Winchester	115
1987	100	Pearl	Heraldic	Mason-Dixon Club	200
1987	160	Pearl	Heraldic	Fort City Club	240
1992	544	Goldstone	Oval	Winchester	110

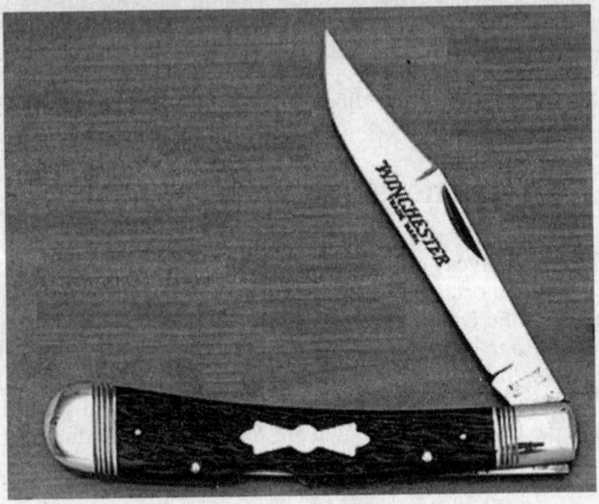

W15 1927—5³/₈″ Lockback Hunter

Year	No. Made	Handles	Shield	Blade Etch	Mint Price
W15 1927—5³/₈″ Lockback Hunter					
1988	3,248	Peach Seed Bone	Propeller	Winchester	140
1988	889	Peach Seed Bone	Propeller	Winchester	225
W15 1936—5″ Toothpick					
1990	1,566	Brown Bone	Heraldic	Winchester	150

W15 1950—5³/₈″ Lockback Hunter

Year	No. Made	Handles	Shield	Blade Etch	Mint Price
W15 1950—5³/₈″ Lockback Hunter					
1989	2,511	Genuine Stag	Propeller	Winchester	150
1989	110	Genuine Stag	Propeller	Mason-Dixon Club	190
1991	980	Stag	Rifle	Winchester	175
W15 1989-1—3″ Lockback Pen					
1989	980	Cast Bronze	None	Winchester	40
W15 1987-1—3¹/₂″ Equal End Pen					
1987	10,640	Cast bronze	None	Winchester	40
1988 (error)	553	Cast bronze	None	Winchester	85
W15 1988-1—3″ Lockback Pen					
1988	6,921	Cast Bronze	None	Winchester	40
W15 1990-1—3″ Lockback					
1990	2,315	Cast Bronze	None	Winchester	40
W15 1991-1—3¹/₂″ Pen					
1991	2,690	Cast Bronze	None	Winchester	40
1991	2,650	Cast Bronze	None	125th Anniversary	40
1991	454	Sterling Silver	None	125th Anniversary	135

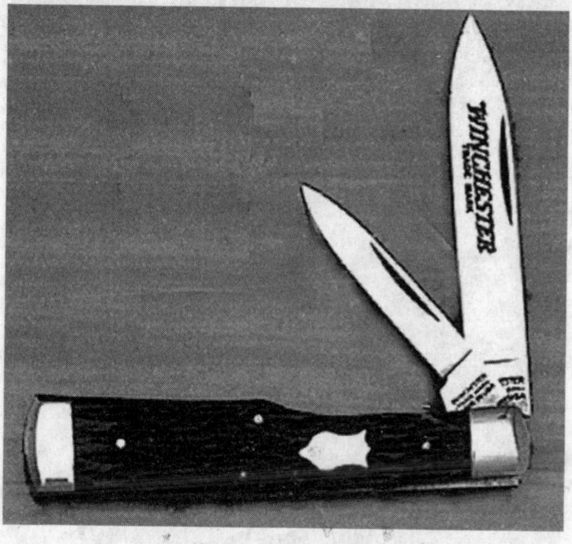

W15 2851—3″ Gunstock Jack

Year	*No. Made*	*Handles*	*Shield*	*Blade Etch*	*Mint Price*
W15 2851—3″ Gunstock Jack					
1988	3,234	Rogers Bone	Heraldic	Winchester	85
1991	511	Stag	Heraldic	Winchester	150
1991	317	Pearl	Heraldic	Winchester	175
1992	504	Goldstone	Heraldic	Winchester	80
W15 2857—3 7/8″ Teardrop Jack					
1987	3,070	Rogers Bone	Heraldic	Winchester	85
W15 2880 1/2—3 7/8″ Swell Center Pen					
1988	2,468	Peach Seed Bone	Balloon	Winchester	85
W15 2903—3 1/2″ Swell Center					
1990	1,186	Brown Bone	Heraldic	Winchester	75
W15 2904—4 1/8″ Trapper					
1987	3,387	Rogers Bone	Heraldic	Winchester	115

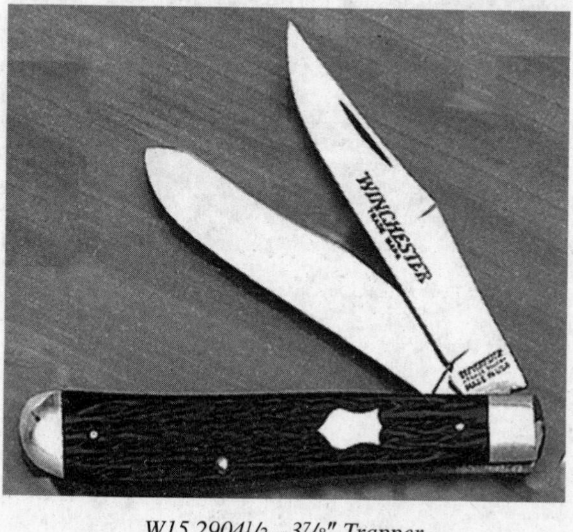

W15 2904 1/2—3 7/8″ Trapper

Year	No. Made	Handles	Shield	Blade Etch	Mint Price
W15 $2904\frac{1}{2}$—$3\frac{7}{8}$″ Trapper					
1989	2,639	Peach Seed Bone	Heraldic	Winchester	85
1989	147	Light Rogers Bone	Heraldic	Winchester	275
1989	71	Light Peach Seed Bone	Heraldic	Winchester	400
1992	730	Stag	Heraldic	Winchester	150

W15 $2913\frac{1}{2}$—$4\frac{1}{4}$″ Moose

W15 $2913\frac{1}{2}$—$4\frac{1}{4}$″ Moose					
1988	2,410	Peach Seed Bone	Heraldic	Winchester	100
W15 2921—$3\frac{1}{2}$″ Gunstock Jack					
1987	3,272	Rogers Bone	Heraldic	Winchester	100
1992	542	Goldstone	Oval	Winchester	95
1992	296	Pearl	Heraldic	Winchester	275

W15 2935—$3\frac{5}{8}$″ Congress Pen

W15 2935—$3\frac{5}{8}$″ Congress Pen					
1988	2,782	Rogers Bone	Curved bar	Winchester	80
1991	332	Pearl	Curved bar	Winchester	240
1991	529	Stag	Curved bar	Winchester	150

W15 2967—Texas Jack

Year	No. Made	Handles	Shield	Blade Etch	Mint Price
W15 2967—Texas Jack					
1988	2,587	Peach Seed Bone	Heraldic	Winchester	110
1992	488	Goldstone	Oval	Winchester	95
1992	280	Pearl	Heraldic	Winchester	225

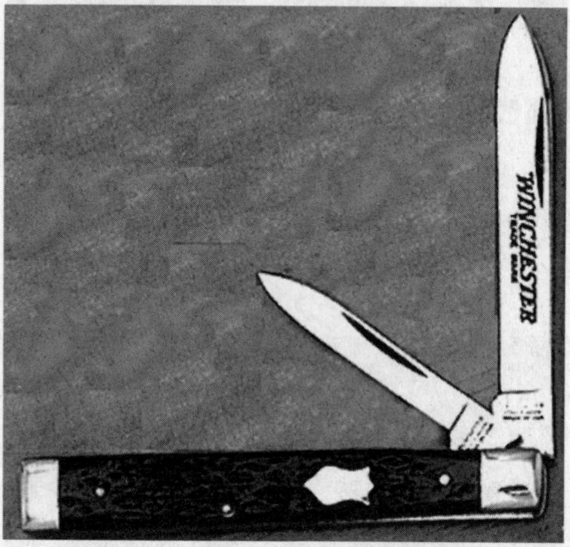

W15 2978—3¹/₈″ Doctor's Knife

W15 2978—3¹/₈″ Doctor's Knife					
1989	2,457	Rogers Bone	Heraldic	Winchester	75
1989	75	Rogers Bone	Heraldic	Forkland Festival	95
1992	524	Goldstone	Oval	Winchester	85
1992	581	Stag	Heraldic	Winchester	150
1992	250	Pearl	Heraldic	Winchester	225
W15 2991—3⁵/₈″ Equal End Pen					
1988	2,439	Rogers Bone	Propeller	Winchester	85
1992	287	Pearl	Heraldic	Winchester	225
W15 3049¹/₂—3³/₄″ Sowbelly Stock					
1992	250	Christmas Tree	Oval	Winchester	90
1992	250	Christmas Tree	Oval	Fancy Winchester	100

Year	*No. Made*	*Handles*	*Shield*	*Blade Etch*	*Mint Price*
1992	250	Goldstone	Oval	Winchester	85
1992	250	Goldstone	Oval	Fancy Winchester	95
1992	250	Waterfall	Oval	Winchester	85
1992	250	Waterfall	Oval	Fancy Winchester	95
1992	250	Candy Stripe	Oval	Winchester	85
1992	250	Candy Stripe	Oval	Fancy Winchester	95

W15 3902—3½″ Swell Center Whittler

W15 3902—3½″ Swell Center Whittler

1990	1,392	Rogers Bone	Heraldic	Winchester	80
1990	125	Rogers Bone	Heraldic	Forkland Festival	90
1991	894	Stag	Heraldic	Winchester	125

W15 3904—3⅝″ Whittler

1988	2,964	Rogers Bone	Heraldic	Winchester	115
1991	296	Pearl	Heraldic	Winchester	240
1991	580	Stag	Heraldic	Winchester	150

W15 3907—4″ Premium Stock

W15 3907—4″ Premium Stock

1991	966	Peach Seed Bone	Heraldic	Winchester	85

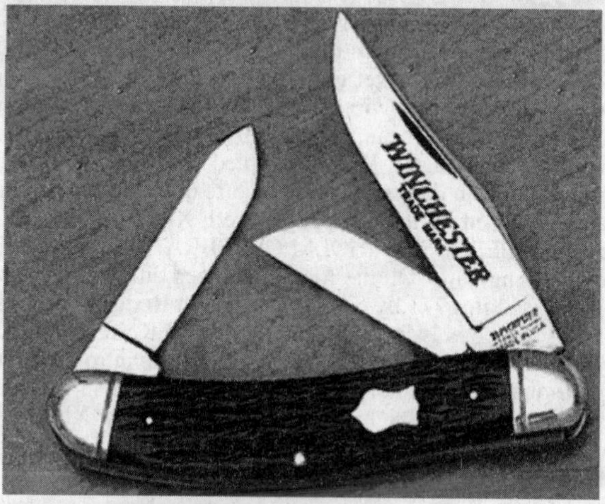

W15 3949—3³/4″ Sowbelly Stock

Year	*No. Made*	*Handles*	*Shield*	*Blade Etch*	*Mint Price*
W15 3949—3³/4″ Sowbelly Stock					
1989	2,185	Peach Seed Bone	Heraldic	Winchester	85
1991	982	Stag	Heraldic	Winchester	140
1991	482	Goldstone	Oval	Rifle & Yellow Boy	110
W15 3964—3⁵/8″ Stockman					
1987	2,578	Rogers Bone	Heraldic	Polished Winchester	90
1987	800	Rogers Bone	Small Heraldic	Satin Winchester	225
1987	600	Rogers Bone	Large Heraldic	Satin Winchester	320
1987	150	Rogers Bone	Small Heraldic	Polished Winchester	500
W15 3971—3⁵/8″ Whittler					
1989	2,409	Rogers Bone	Heraldic	Winchester	80
1992	561	Goldstone	Oval	Winchester	90
1992	254	Pearl	Heraldic	Winchester	240
W15 3995—4″ Whittler					
1991	1,440	Peachseed Bone	Heraldic	Winchester	100
W15 4935—3³/8″ Congress					
1991	1,380	Brown Bone	Bar	Winchester	95
1992	486	Stag	Bar	Winchester	150
1992	360	Pearl	Bar	Winchester	225

GEORGE WOSTENHOLM & SON CUTLERY COMPANY (I*XL)

The Wolstenholme family's involvement in cutlery dates back to 1745, when George Wolstenholme and his son Henry operated a small cutlery business in Stannington, England. Henry was one of the first cutlers to use springs for pocketknives and, in 1757, was granted the SPRING trademark. I*XL, the company's most famous trademark, was first used in 1787.

Henry Wolstenholme and his sons, Martin and George, continued the business. Upon Henry's death, George took over the business and moved it to nearby Sheffield. The name was changed at that time from "Wolstenholme" to "Wostenholm" so it would be easier to stamp on a blade tang. In 1832, the firm moved to the Rockingham Works. Wostenholm was one of the first to concentrate cutlers in a factory, as opposed to the cottage industry that had existed earlier. His son, another George and the third Wostenholme of that name to be involved in the business, expanded the firm into the world market and became sole owner of the company.

In 1848, Wolstenholm purchased the Washington Works and moved into that building, becoming a major factor in the world cutlery market. Wostenholm's primary customer became the United States and that market greatly influenced the patterns or types of knives made. A large percentage of the bowie knives sold and used in the United States were marked with the famed "I*XL" (meaning "I excel") stamping. The location markings of Rockingham Works and Washington Works, coupled with markings of the English monarchs, are of great assistance in dating the manufacture of Wostenholm knives.

Among the stampings used by the company were I*XL GEORGE WOSTENHOLM & SON LTD, I*XL GEORGE WOSTENHOLM CELEBRATED, SHEFFIELD, ENGLAND and the last named marking with "Oil the Joints" stamped on the reverse of the tang.

The firm was purchased in 1971 by Sheffield's Joseph Rodgers & Sons Cutlery to form Rodgers-Wostenholm, which was in turn sold to Imperial Knife Associated Companies in 1977. In the early 1980s, a line of Schrade-I*XL knives were introduced and, although they were knives of good quality, was short lived. A group of English investors purchased the firm in 1984 and U.S. distribution rights to both Rodgers and I*XL knives were sold to a new company called Rodgers-Wostenholm, USA Ltd.

LIMITED EDITION AND COMMEMORATIVE KNIVES

AFRICAN SAFARI SET

500 limited edition two-knife sets made for Remington Cutlery Stores. Includes two stag handled fixed blade knives housed in a green leather sheath and mounted on a wall plaque. Collector Value $275

AMERICAN ARMED FORCES SERIES

Produced by United/Boker in 1988. Six knives in the series, one for each branch of service plus "Vietnam Veterans" and American combat veterans. Bone handles. Special blade etching on both blades of each knife in the series. Display boxed. Collector Value $40 each.

AMERICAN BICENTENNIAL SERIES

Made by Alcas Cutlery for Parker-Frost Cutlery. 1,500 sets produced. Two 5½″ clasp knives, one each with wood and genuine stag handles; matching serial numbers. Blades etched with both the 1776 and 1976 U.S. flags. Housed in a walnut box. Collector Value $200

AMERICAN EAGLE BICENTENNIAL SERIES

Commemorative set of five knives honoring Patrick Henry, Nathan Hale, John Adams, Thomas Jefferson and George Washington. 12,000 sets produced. Matching serial numbers. Deluxe gift boxed with registration papers. Collector Value $150 set

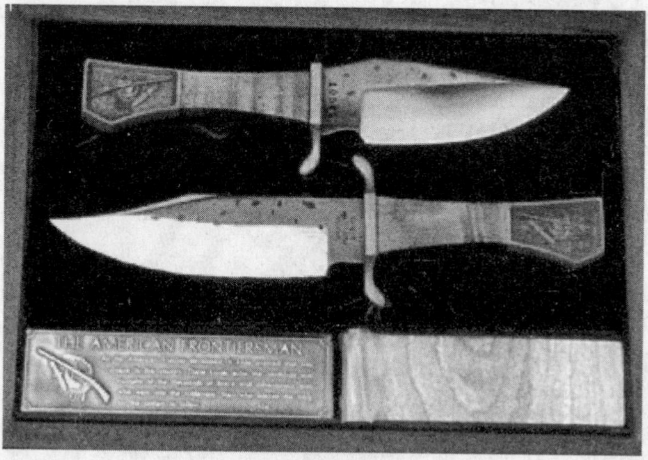

AMERICAN FRONTIERSMAN COLLECTOR KNIVES

The first of three issues made for the collector market by Alcas was produced from 1973 to 1975. This two-knife set, along with a sharpening stone and plaque, was housed in a walnut chest. Both fixed blade knives were handled in curly maple and had zinc die-cast guards and butts. Except for the bright finished grind, blades were distress finished and tangs were stamped "American Frontiersman." 2,500 of the sets were marketed through the company's consumer products sales. Collector Value $250

Production on the next American Frontiersman knife began in 1978. Called "The Tecumseh" and with its glaze finished blade etched accordingly, the fixed blade knife was handled in micarta and had die-cast and polished guard and butt. Housed with a plaque in an oak display chest. 5,000 of the sets were planned but a somewhat smaller number was marketed. Collector Value $150

The third and last American Frontiersman knife was planned by Alcas as part of "The Remington Art" series. In 1983, "The Longhunter" was introduced in the limited production of 500 pieces. Its blade is high-carbon stainless deep etched and gold filled with a Remington art scene. The handle is crown stag with a powder horn butt decoration. The guard is die-cast aluminum which has been 24k gold plated. Collector Value $300

BERETTA

In 1984, Beretta issued a boot knife in a special limited edition of 500 serial numbered knives. It has a 5¹/4″ blade and came complete with a sheath and presentation case. Collector Value $100

BOKER BONE HANDLED SET

5,000 sets containing five different patterns made by Boker, Solingen, in 1977. Total of 25,000 knives made. Collector Value $125 set

BOKER COAL MINERS SERIES

Set of three knives made by Boker. Medallion set into the handles. Housed in special wood box. Collector Value $100

BOKER SPIRIT OF AMERICA SERIES

Series of twenty-four knives introduced in 1974 with a different knife issued every three months until 1978. The original retail price was $12 each. The knives were as follows:

"Sweet Land of Liberty" Stockman knife issued May 1974. Collector Value $40
"American Eagle" Stockman knife issued July 1974. Collector Value $40
"The Alamo" Texas Jack issued September 1974. Collector Value $45
"Prairie Schooner" Equal End Jack issued December 1974. Collector Value $35
"Statue of Liberty" large Stockman issued February 1975. Collector Value $35

"Dixie" Congress pattern issued April 1975. Collector Value $50
"Last Frontier" Stockman knife issued July 1975. Collector Value $35
"Old Wild West" Trapper issued September 1975. Collector Value $35
"Rise to World Power" Swell End Jack issued November 1975. Collector Value $30
"War to End all Wars" Serpentine Jack issued February 1976. Collector Value $35
"Dawn of the Atomic Age" Stockman knife issued April 1976. Collector Value $30
"200 Years of Freedom" Stockman Knife issued July 1976. Collector Value $40
"Birth of Southern Industry" Congress pattern issued August 1976. Collector Value $35
"Westward Expansion" Trapper issued October 1976. Collector Value $35
"Blazing the Trail" Premium Stockman knife issued December 1976. Collector Value $30
"American Proclamation" Texas Jack issued February 1977. Collector Value $30
"California Gold Rush" Premium Stockman knife issued April 1977. Collector Value $35
"Bridging the Continent" Premium Stockman knife issued June 1977. Collector Value $35
"Modern Fuel" Jack Knife issued September 1977. Collector Value $30
"Continental Mail Service" Congress knife issued November 1977. Collector Value $40
"Modern Energy" Whittler issued December 1977. Collector Value $35
"On to Oklahoma" Dogleg Jack issued February 1978. Collector Value $35
"Revolution in Transportation" Stockman issued April 1978. Collector Value $30
"200 Million Americans" Premium Stockman issued June 1978. Collector Value $30

BOKER STORY TELLER SET

8,000 sets produced by Boker in 1983 consisting of a stockman "Jesse Chisholm" with green bone handles; a four-blade congress "Davy Crockett" with rosewood handles; and a trapper "Jim Bridger" with bone handles. Redwood box. Collector Value $150 set

BOKER-WISS COMMEMORATIVES

In 1971, Boker, Germany began to produce an annual series commemorating Boker U.S.A. and Wiss anniversaries. The knives were handled in various materials with two shields inlaid into the handles of earlier knives. One shield was the usual "Tree Brand" and the other was stamped "Wiss" and the issue year. Beginning in the late 1980's, the Wiss shield was discontinued and only the Boker shield was used.

1971—15,000 produced, not serial numbered. Premium stock pattern. Black composition handles with two shields. Collector Value $35

1972—20,000 nonserial numbered knives produced. Small stockman with black handles inlaid with two gold shields. Collector Value $35

1973—18,000 serial numbered knives produced. Four-blade congress pattern. Black handles with two red shields. Collector Value $45

1974—18,000 serial numbered knives produced. 4″ stock pattern with square bolsters. Black handles with two gold shields. Blades etched. Collector Value $40

1975—"The Sternwheeler" penknife pattern with simulated pearl handle. 20,000 produced, etched master blade. Collector Value $40

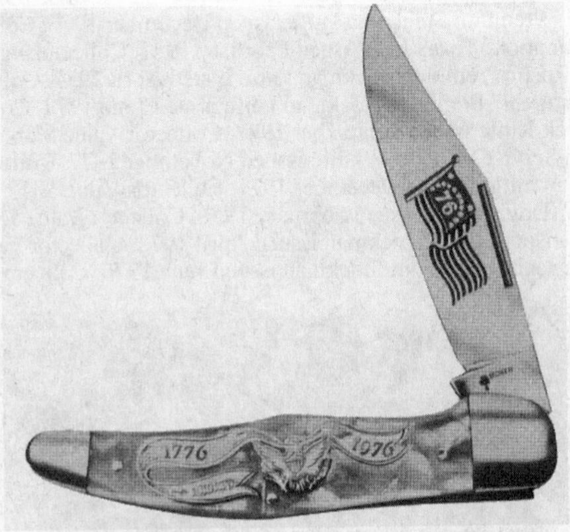

1976—"Heritage of Freedom" folding hunter bicentennial knife. 24,000 produced. Collector Value $55

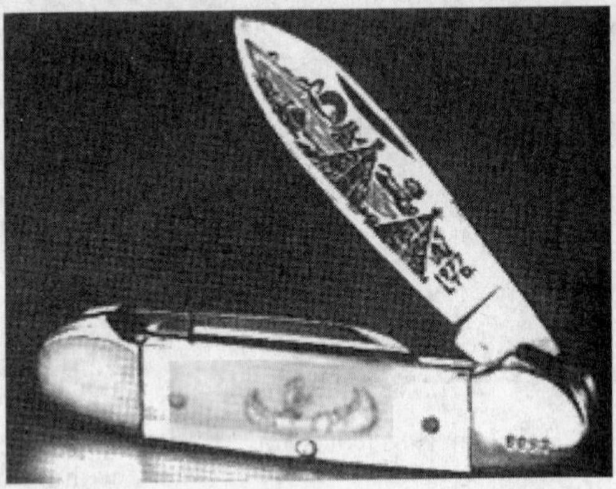

1977—Two-blade canoe with cracked ice handles. 12,000 produced. Collector Value $45

1978—Two-blade bone handled Trapper pattern honoring the southern mountaineer. Named the "Hill-billy." 12,000 produced. Collector Value $50

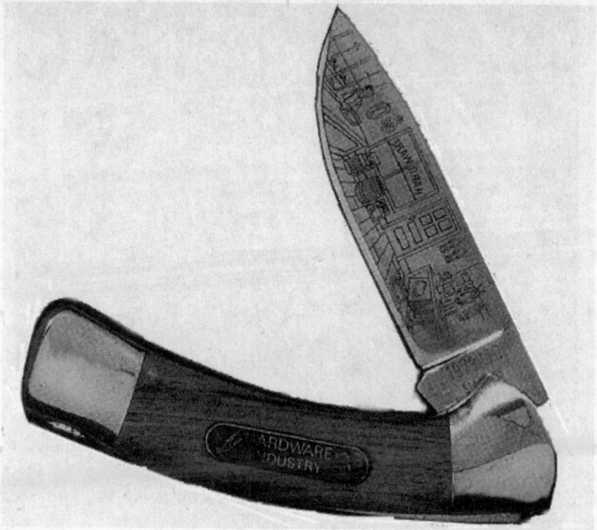

1979—Lockback folding hunter with wood handles and etched blades honoring the hardware industry. 20,000 produced. Collector Value $40

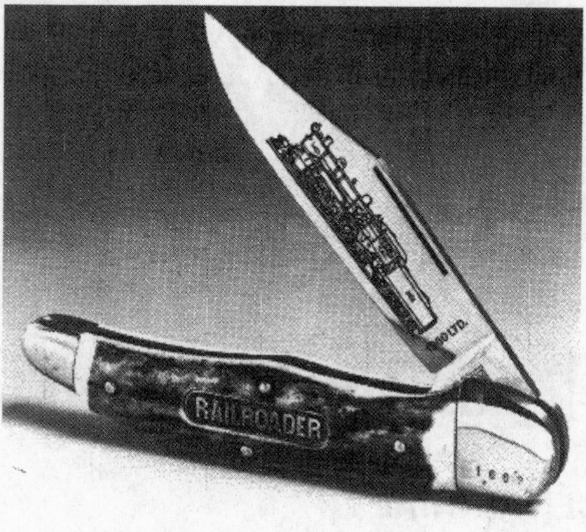

1980—"The Railroader" is a stag handled 5″ folding hunter with etched blade. 8,000 produced. Collector Value $80

1980—"White Lightning." 10,000 produced in limited edition. Collector Value $50

1981—"The Appalachian Trail" is a canoe with jigged rosewood handles. Blade etching. 10,000 knives were made. Collector Value $50

1981—"The Collector." Three-blade stockman. 10,000 produced. Collector Value $50

1982—"The Whittler." 10,000 produced. Collector Value $45

1983—"The Farm Boy." 8,000 produced. Collector Value $40

1984—"Old Tom." One-blade folding hunter. 8,200 produced. Collector Value $40

1985—"Blackbeard." Limited edition of 4,100 produced. Collector Value $100

1986—"The Forty-Niner" salute to Gold Rush. 5,000 produced. Collector Value $60

1987—"The Constitution." Four-blade congress pattern. Two sheepfoot blades deep etched. 8,000 produced. Collector Value $70

1988—"The Titanic." Lockback folding hunter with ivory composition handle scrimshawed. 3,000 produced. Collector Value $85

1989—"Spring Gobbler." Two-blade trapper with laser-engraved oak handles. 3,000 produced. Collector Value $55

1989—"The Graf Zeppelin." Two-blade trapper with blades etched. Black composition handles. 3,000 produced. Collector Value $60

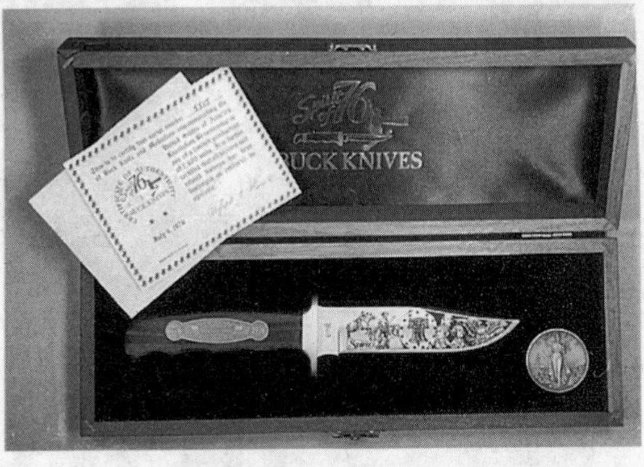

BUCK BICENTENNIAL

This Buck knife was a cased sheath knife with etched blade and a medallion. Collector Value $225

BUCK BUGLING ELKS

2,000 serial numbered Model 110 folding hunter limited edition knives produced by Buck. Dark mahogany wood handles. Collector Value $85

BUCK COMMEMORATIVE BOWIE

Produced by Buck Knives to honor Hoyt Buck. A 15″ bowie knife with gold-filled etching on blade reproducing a painting depicting Buck in his Kansas blacksmith shop at the turn of the 20th century. Birchwood handle, brass guard and rivets. Gift boxed. Collector Value $350

BUCK CUTLERY WORLD KNIFE

In 1981, Buck's custom shop issued a limited edition bowie exclusively for the Cutlery World retail chain. Most of the stores were allowed only one knife. Collector Value $500

BUCK—DUCKS UNLIMITED FIFTIETH ANNIVERSARY

Produced by Buck in the Ranger model lock back knife. Layered birch handle with brass anniversary symbol shield. Handle of U.S. knife is golden brown and Canadian knife is rich green. Blade of each has gold-filled etched design by Aurum. Collector Value $90

BUCK FREEDOM TRAPPER

5,000 knife limited edition made by Buck. Yellow celluloid handles with American flag engraving and Buck's "Knife, Bolt and Hammer" shield. Blades etched. Boxed with "Right to Bear Arms" belt buckle. Collector Value $45

BUCK GOLDEN EAGLE

1,500 serial numbered Model 110 folding hunter limited edition knives produced by Buck. Birchwood handle. Collector Value $90

BUCK GRAND SLAM SET

2,500 sets produced by Buck in 1982. Set consists of four model 501 knives with four different wood handles. Blades etched by Aurum featuring "Sheep of the Great West." Housed in wood case with special brass belt buckle. Collector Value $225

BUCK REDBONE SET

500 serialized sets made by Buck Knives in 1989 for Smoky Mountain Knifeworks. Includes 301 Stockman, 305 Lancer, 303 Cadet and 309 Companion. Original "Hammer, Bolt and Bolt" shield inlaid into jigged red bone handles. Engraved nickel silver bolsters. Collector Value $145 set

BUCK SILVER ANNIVERSARY COMMEMORATIVE

2,500 produced by Buck to honor its twenty-fifth anniversary. Model 110 with gold-filled blade etching by Aurum. Collector Value $100

BUCK STATUE OF LIBERTY COMMEMORATIVES

Buck Knives produced two limited edition knives in 1986 honoring the Statue of Liberty. 2,500 Model 500 folders were produced with walnut handles and etched blade and Statue of Liberty shield. With plaque. Collector Value $90

15,000 Model 525 knives were produced with cast pewter handled. Collector Value $25

BUCK YELLOWHORSE KNIVES

Knives by Buck with special channel inlay on handles blending turquoise, other stones, woods and metals. Hand-tooled bolsters. Decorative work is individually done by Navajo artisan David Yellowhorse, and no two knives are exactly alike. Knives used for these special series are Buck's Woodsman, Maverick and Ranger. Two series produced are "Buffalo" and "Running Horse." Collector Value $225 each

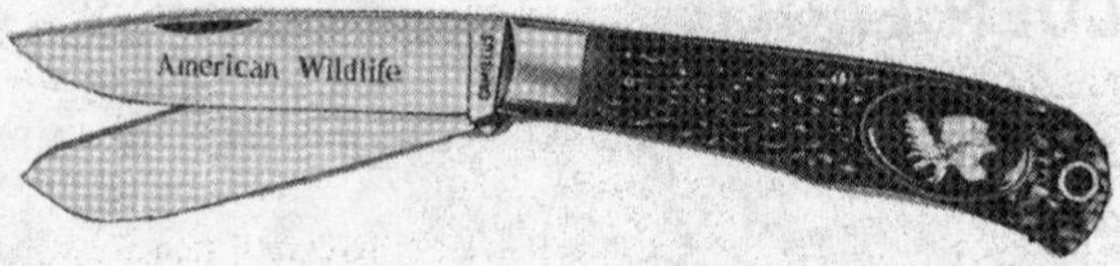

CAMILLUS WILDLIFE SERIES

Series of four knives produced by Camillus for Smoky Mountain Knifeworks. Delrin handles are inlaid with a cast pewter wildlife engraving from originals by Sid Bell. Each knife is 4 3/8″ trapper pattern with master blade etched "American Wildlife." Inlays include charging bear, running deer, razorback hog and american eagle. Collector Value $55

CASE ALAMO BOWIE

3,000 produced by Case in 1985. Bowie knife with black walnut handle and nickel silver guard. Blade color etched with The Alamo and Texas state outline. Serial numbered and housed in an oak case with story of the Alamo and its heroes inside. Collector Value $240

CASE 75TH ANNIVERSARY CANOE SET

5,000 matching serial number sets issued in commemoration of Case's 75th year of business. Consists of stag handled canoes with bolsters engraved and gold plated. Collector Value $500

CASE 75TH ANNIVERSARY SET

Produced in 1980. Consists of seven stag handled 10 dot knives, patterns: 5318, 5244, 5275, 5207, 52109X, 5208, and 52351/2 in wood box. Bolsters engraved. Collector Value $625

CASE 80TH ANNIVERSARY LIMITED EDITION

5,000 produced in 1985. Folding hunter 5165SS handled in bone. Blade is etched "W. R. Case & Sons 1905–1985 Anniversary." Wood display box. Collector Value $150

CASE 125TH ANNIVERSARY CIVIL WAR COMMEMORATIVE

Two-knife, matching serial numbered set produced by Case. Knives are a No. GR199½ "Battle of Bull Run" and a No. BL199½ "Fort Sumter, 1861" with blade etching. Smooth gray and blue synthetic handles with raised-letter shield. Housed in a presentation box. Collector Value $125

CASE APACHE AND ARAPAHO STAGS

2,000 each of the fixed blade patterns, 5300 and 5400, were handled in stag and pattern numbers engraved on the blade rather than stamped. Serial numbered and included leather basket-weave sheath. Collector Value $90 each

CASE ASTRONAUT'S KNIFE

2,494 made in 1972. This model knife was carried in 1965 by Major Virgil Grissom and Commander John Young and has been carried on all NASA flights since that time. The 11″ blade is 13-gauge high-carbon stainless steel and handle is polypropylene, attached by round brass rods and drilled for a lanyard. Housed in a display box. Collector Values $400 to $700 (depending on serial number)

In the mid-1980s, Case again made a limited number of these knives and called them "the NASA knife." Collector Value $250

CASE BICENTENNIAL KNIVES

Case made two different knives in 1976 to commemorate America's Bicentennial. Each was housed in a special wood box. The 5165 folding hunter with stag handles, engraved bolsters and a deep etched blade was produced in a quantity of 10,000 pieces. Collector Value $175

The 523-7SS stag handled bowie with eagle head pommel and etched blade was produced in a quantity of 2,500 pieces. Collector Value $325

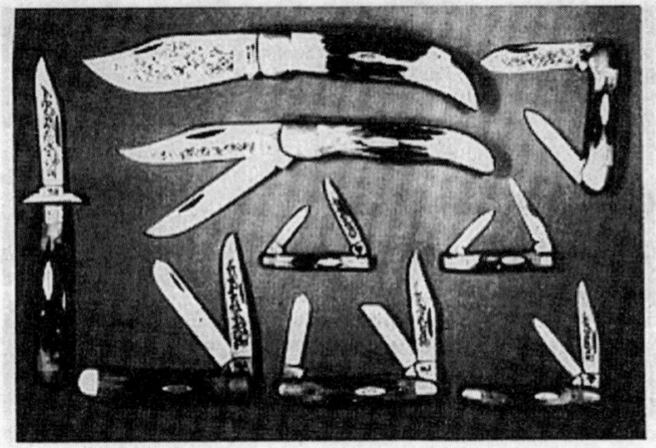

CASE BLUE SCROLL SET

In 1978, another set was issued which contained eight pocketknives, the seven patterns from the 1977 set plus a canoe. Patterns are 5347, 5254, 5111½L, 5233, 52131, 5265, 5172 and 52087 with blue scroll etching on blades and engraved bolsters. Housed in wood display box. 15,000 sets were produced. Collector Value $800

CASE BRADFORD CENTENNIAL SET

Produced in 1979. Consists of six stag handled knives, patterns: 52027, 5275, 5249, 5292, 5207 and 5318 in wood box. Bolsters engraved and blades etched "1879 Bradford Centennial 1979." Collector Value $500

CASE—CHIEF CRAZY HORSE

5,000 produced by Case in 1981 for exclusive distribution by Davidson's Inc. Stag handled "Kodiak" with blued blade photo etched on both sides. With leather sheath. Collector Value $400

CASE CHRISTMAS TREE SET

500 serialized mint sets were produced in 1989 by Case for Smoky Mountain Knifeworks. Knives include CT220SS Peanut, CT215SS Gunstock, CT225½SS Swell Center, CT1048SS Trapper, CT318SHSPSS Stockman, CT2131SS Canoe and CT254SS Trapper. Christmas tree celluloid handles with Case round 100 Years shield. Engraved bolsters. Housed in custom knife pack. Collector Value $400

In addition to the above engraved and serialized set, Case made 3,000 each of the knives without engraved bolsters and serial numbering. Collector Value $40 to $80, depending upon pattern.

CASE V-42 COMBAT STILETTO

1,500 knives made in 1984 for the American Historical Foundation. Reproduction of the famous V-42 World War II combat knife. One knife, with mirror polished blade, was designated the American Commemorative. The other, with blued blade, was designated the Canadian Commemorative. Collector Value $350 set

CASE CONGRESS SET

2,500 sets produced by Case. Includes pattern numbers 52052, 53052 and 54052 handled in genuine stag. Coffin-shaped bolsters. Master blades color etched. 500 sets made with engraved bolsters and housed in oak display box, 2,000 sets without bolster engraving and in cherry display box. Collector Value $350 (regular set) $475 (engraved set)

CASE DAMASCUS RAINBOW SET

500 sets produced by Case in 1989 for Cutlery World and Smoky Mountain Knifeworks. Includes five one-blade trappers, patterns: R6154D-red, Y6154D-yellow, G6154D-green, B6154D-blue and W6154D-white. Blades are 512 layer Damascus. Gold-colored raised-letter shield. Matching serial numbers. Wood display box with special color rainbow set label. Collector Value $950

ELVIS PRESLEY COMMEMORATIVE KNIVES

3,000 each of two No. 6240 trappers were produced by Case in 1989. Both clip and spey blades are etched. Each knife has the Case raised-letter shield inlaid into handle. The "Blue Elvis" has blue jigged bone handles. Collector Value $140

The "Music Box Elvis" has white bone handles and is housed in special wood music box display. Collector Value $175

CASE FAMILY TREE SET

550 sets made by Case consisting of six knives, patterns: G62087, G6215, G63033, G6199½, G6225½ and G6120. Green bone handles. Housed in display box that has Job Case family tree illustration in box top. Master blade of each knife is etched with the name of one of his children. Collector Value $325

CASE FOUNDERS KNIFE

20,000 produced by Case in 1980. Stag handled 5143SSP in special wood box. Blade etched with pictures of W. R., Job and J. Russell Case. Collector Value $120

CASE GATOR SET

2,750 sets containing two serial numbered Texas Toothpicks made by Case for Parker Cutlery in 1979. One handled in stag, the other in bone. Collector Value $200

CASE GREEN BONE SET

500 serial numbered sets produced by Case in 1988 consisting of six knives, patterns: G62087, G6215, G6120, G6199½, G6225½ and G63033. With display box. Collector Value $350

In addition to the matching serial numbered set, Case made 2,500 knives of each pattern that were not serial numbered nor sold in sets. Collector Value $45-$75, depending upon pattern.

CASE GUNBOAT SET

2,500 sets produced in 1985. Consists of three canoe-pattern knives handled in burned white bone. Patterns are 6194SS, 6294SS and 6394SS. Blades etched with warship names. Housed in wood case. Collector Value $400

CASE GUNSTOCK SET

3,000 sets called "The Guns That Tamed the Wild West" were produced in 1989 by Case. Includes patterns 5215SS (3″) and 5230SS (4″) gunstocks handled in India stag. Gold Case raised-letter shield. Master blades photo etched. Collector Value $275

CASE IVORY TRAPPERS

Produced by Case in 1989, these limited edition knives are considered transition knives designed to recognize an important period of change and progress for W. R. Case & Sons Cutlery. Handles are of mastodon ivory and blades combine Damascus steel with modern surgical steel. Display boxes are special-made cultured marble with special commemorative engraving.

500 knives were produced as "The Job Case-Jim Parker Commemorative Trappers." Has a 512-layer Damascus spey blade and surgical steel clip blade with illustration of Job Case and Jim Parker. Collector Value $600

200 knives were produced exclusively for Cutlery World stores as "The Cutlery World Ivory Trapper." Has a Damascus clip blade and etched surgical steel spey blade. Collector Value $550

CASE JACK DANIELS OLD NO. 7 SET

5,000 sets produced by Case in 1987. Consists of three whittler knives displayed on a wood whiskey barrel plaque. Knives are a No. B6108 one blade, a No. B6208 two blade and a No. B6308 three blade. All have genuine charcoal bone handles and special tang stampings. Collector Value $260

JOHNNY CASH COMMEMORATIVE

Commemorative Case Muskrat pattern with honeycomb bone handles. Raised-letter inlaid shield. Blades etched. Collector Value $100

CASE KENTUCKY BICENTENNIAL SERIES

30,000 each of three knives were produced in 1974. All knives were the Case 2137SS pattern, but with a variety of handles. One knife, stamped with the pattern number G137, had green delrin handles. A total of 35,299 of these knives were made with the Case five-dot stamping. The serial numbers used were: 0000001–00150000, 0001–9999, J0001–J9999, and the most collectible of the green handled knives, S0001–S2001. Collector Value $45

A very few of the knives were stamped and given out when Case's South Bradford plant opened in 1975. Heat stamped into the handle were the words "Grand Opening: South Bradford Plant," and on the reverse side, "April 1975." A few of these have made their way into the collector's market and are now valued at $125

The second of the series had wood handles. Collector Value $40

The third knife of the series was handled in stag and stamped with a large serial number. Most were stamped "Case XX U.S.A.," but a rarer version of 2,000 pieces was stamped "Case XX Stainless."

Collector Value (regular version) $60 (rarer version) $85

CASE LITTLE CONGRESS SET

Walnut box with etched lid houses three Case $3\frac{1}{2}$″ congress-pattern knives. Set includes one each 64052GSC, 64052BSC and 64052PS. Collector Value $190

LOU GEHRIG—THE IRON HORSE

Produced by Frost Cutlery Co. using the Case 6240 $4\frac{1}{2}$″ dogleg trapper pattern with green pickbone handles. Special blade etching and display box. Collector Value $90

CASE MOBY DICK

10,000 produced in 1978. 65 pattern with whaling scene scrimshaw on smooth white bone handles. Bolsters engraved. Housed in wood display box. Collector Value $180

CASE NANTUCKET SLEIGHRIDE

7,500 produced in 1979. 65 pattern with sleigh ride scrimshaw on smooth white bone handles. Bolsters engraved. Housed in wood display box. Collector Value $155

CASE NINE-DOT SET

Six stag handled pocketknives without blade etching. Blade stamping is nine dot "Lightning S" and knife patterns are: 52027, $5235\frac{1}{2}$, 5149, 5254, 52131 and Muskrat. Some of these sets have engraved bolsters and are valued higher than those with plain bolsters. Collector Value $500

CASE/PARKER COMMEMORATIVE

3,000 trapper pattern ROG6254SSD knives produced by Case in 1989. Rogers bone handle is inlaid with both a Case raised-letter shield and a Parker USA shield. Spey blade is Damascus steel. Clip blade is etched with likeness of Job Case and Jim Parker. Deluxe wood display case with sliding etched marble lid. Collector Value $200

CASE PEARL SET

1,000 sets produced in 1982. Consists of three pearl handled knives, patterns: 8207SP SSP, 8249SSP and 8254SSP with file-worked backsprings and housed in hardwood frame case. Collector Value $750

CASE PURE GOLD MINT SET

500 serialized sets made by Case in 1989 for exclusive distribution by Smoky Mountain Knifeworks. Includes patterns: 3347SS, 3249SS, 31048SS, 3207SS, 3220SS, 3225SS and 33033SS with brushed stainless steel blades. Golden celluloid handles with old-style Case logo shield. Engraved nickel silver bolsters. Collector Value $375

In addition to the set described above, Case made 3,000 each of the knives without engraved bolsters and serial numbering. Collector values range from $30 to $70, depending upon pattern.

CASE RED SCROLL SET

In 1979, 25,000 Red Scroll sets were made containing seven stag handled pocketknives, all with stainless steel blades. Collector Value $700

A companion set of four stag handled sheath knives was marketed in late 1979. Collector Value $300

CASE REDBONE MINT SET

100 limited edition serialized sets made exclusively for Smoky Mountain Knifeworks in 1987. Set includes R63052, R6205, R62109X, R6215, R6220 and R06263. Hand-engraved nickel silver bolsters, stainless steel blades and raised-letter fancy shield. Custom-made display. Collector Value $375

SECOND CUT SETS

A five-knife set made by Case and marketed in 1984 by Second Cut, Inc. Consists of patterns 5220, 5254, 52131, 5383 and Muskrat. Master blades etched "Case XX Second Cut Series." Collector Value $475

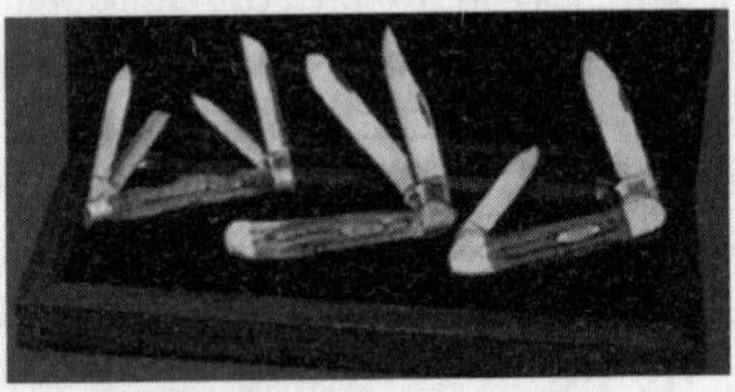

1993 CASE SECOND CUT STAG SET

Three Case knives with matching serial numbers and contained in a walnut display case. Knives are: 64052SC four-blade congress, 6249SC copperhead and 62131 canoe—each handled in second cut bone stag. Limited edition of 500 sets Collector Value $200

CASE SIGNATURE KNIFE

1,250 four-blade congress pattern G64088 knives produced in 1986. Special jigged green bone handles. Signatures of W. R. & J. Russell Case etched on both main blades. Golden, low-relief Case shield with long-tail "C" surrounding the serial number. Collector Value $200

CASE SMOKY MOUNTAIN TRAPPER SERIES

600 serial numbered sets produced by Case in 1980 exclusively for Smoky Mountain Knifeworks to commemorate the heritage of the Great Smoky Mountains. Consists of patterns 6254, 3254 and 6254SSP. Blades etched. Housed in presentation case with the Case logo. Collector Value $250

CASE STAG BARLOW SET

5,000 serial numbered stag handle barlows, patterns: 52009, 52009 RAZ and 52009½. In glass-front wood case. Collector Value $325

CASE STAG BOWIES

Three different limited editions bowies were produced by Case in 1985 for Smoky Mountain Knifeworks.

"Great Smoky Mountain 50th Anniversary" bowie was limited in production to 1,000. Genuine stag handle bowie with deep colored blade etching. On solid cherry plaque. Collector Value $200

Mason-Dixon Series consisted of two stag handled bowies, "Confederacy" and "Union." Each was limited in production to 750 knives. Housed in deluxe gift box. Collector Value $225 each.

CASE 1973 STAG SET

In 1970, concurrent with the stamping change, Case discontinued the use of stag for handles. In order to use the factory inventory of this handle material, the first Case collector's set of assorted stag handled knives was issued in 1973. The set consisted of eighteen pocketknives and five sheath knives and produced in a quantity of 2,000 sets. Knives contained in the sets varied in their date stamping and included "U.S.A.," ten dots, nine dots and eight dots. Two knives made especially for the set were the Cheetah (5111½) and the 5375. Collector Value $3500 set

CASE 1976 STAG SET

In 1976, 700 stag handled collector sets were issued by Case. 600 of the sets included two cheetahs and one bulldog. A canoe replaced one of the cheetahs in the other 100 sets. Collector Value $1500 set

CASE 1977 STAG SET

Set made by Case in 1977 containing seven pocketknives and five sheath knives. Approximately 10,000 sets were made. Several of the knives were made for the first time with stainless steel blades and were etched "Case XX Razor Edge." Collector Value $700

CASE STAG WHITTLER SET

In 1983, a set of three stag handled whittlers, with patterns 5383, 5308 and 5380, were made in a quantity of 2,500 sets. Blades are stainless steel; bolsters are engraved and gold plated. Collector Value $550

STAR SPANGLED BANNER COMMEMORATIVE BOWIE

A total of 2,000 stag handled bowie knives were produced by Case. Fully deep etched 9½″ blades. Each knife housed in wood music box. Etching on 1,500 is black filled and is gold filled on the remaining 500.
Collector Value (black filled) $270 (gold filled) $300

CASE TESTED XX LIMITED EDITION SET

3,000 produced in 1989. Raised gold-letter shields. Case Tested XX etched on blades R6111½SS with red bone handle and G6111½SS green bone handle. Housed in replica of old-style Case stock box.
Collector Value $160

CASE TEXAS'S SESQUICENTENNIAL 1836–1986

Produced by Case in 1986. Green bone Texas jack with blades etched in two colors. Includes display box. Collector Value $125

CASE TEXAS SPECIAL

A Case 4165 pattern with white composition handles designed by Bill and Buck Overall of Texas to commemorate the Lone Star State. The flat ground stainless steel blade is etched with a longhorn steer, map of Texas and the year of the Alamo battle. Collector Value $170

CASE TEXAS TOOTHPICK SET

2,000 sets produced by Case. Consists of patterns: 810096SS, 510094SS and G610098SS—small pearl, medium genuine stag and large green bone handled toothpicks. Each knife is serial numbered and master blades are color etched. Housed in a walnut display case. Collector Value $325

CASE TRANSITION MINT CANOE SET

W. R. Case & Sons Cutlery produced 300 sets of five canoe pattern knives, mounted on wood canoe-shaped plaque, as a 1989–1990 stamping transition special. The master blades of each of these two-blade knives were polished and etched with the canoe logo. One blade was tang stamped "1989," the other "1990." Bolsters are etched and handles are five different colors of "Corn Cob" jigged bone. Collector Value $375

CASE TRAPPER SET

2,500 matching serial number sets issued in 1983. Consists of patterns: 6254, 6207 and 6249 with a long spey blade. Blades etched with picture of a trapper. Collector Value $225

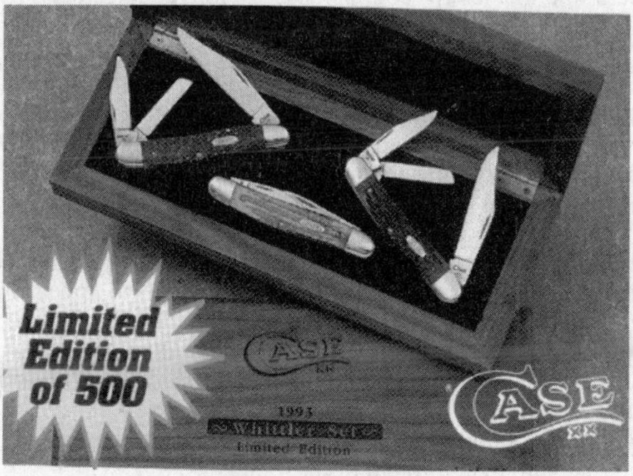

1993 CASE WHITTLER SET

Limited edition of 500 three-knife whittler sets, serially numbered and housed in laser-engraved walnut display box. Set consists of 06347RPB, 06347SC and 06347PSB patterns. Collector Value $275

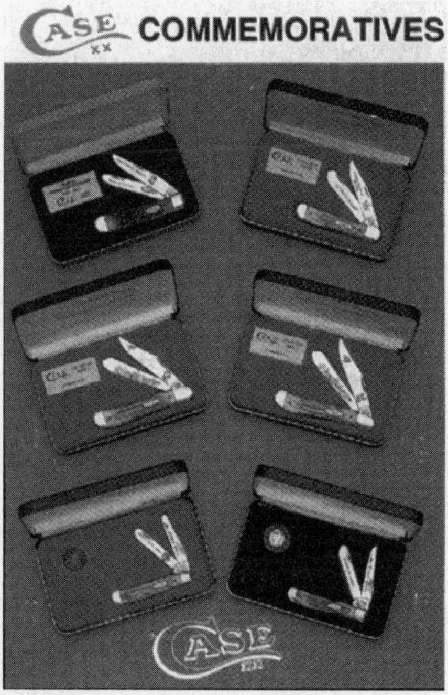

MISCELLANEOUS CASE TRAPPER COMMEMORATIVES

During recent years, the themes for commemorative knives have been limited only by the imagination—and that seems limitless. The majority of these have been based upon the popular Case trapper patterns. Many of these are not produced and marketed directly by Case. Instead, knives are purchased from the manufacturer by distributors, dealers or individual entrepreneurs and are then decorated in any or several manners such as blade etching, handle engraving and special boxing. The issues may be limited to a predetermined number or may be limited only by the number that can be sold.

The proliferation of these "special" knives has been largely due to two factors: first is the growing interest in knives as collectibles and second is the modern technology used for attractive and high-quality blade etching and handle engraving. Some have been and will continue to be desirable collectibles; others have their greatest appeal in the themes they follow—these, too, seem to be endless.

In considering these special knives, the collector should be aware that they can usually be purchased via mail order for near one-half their suggested retail price, and their collector values are normally within those ranges. The values of some will reach or exceed their suggested retail prices within a relatively short period. Others, however, may have more value through pride of ownership than through resale value.

The following are but a few examples of the many themes and variations of etching, engraving and creative packaging available on the Case trapper. Retail prices were approximately $80; collector value varies according to theme, but most are in the $50–$75 range.

Apache War Chief, Geronimo
Atlantic Coast Conference Teams
Babe Ruth
Chief Crazy Horse
Coal Miners of America "Black Gold"
Cochise, Apache War Chief
Davy Crockett
Gen. Ulysses S. Grant
Gen. Dwight D. Eisenhower
Gen. Douglas MacArthur
Gen. Robert E. Lee
George A. Custer, "Custer's Last Stand"
Iwo Jima
One Small Step—Astronaut Commemorative
Paul "Bear" Bryant
Southeastern Conference Teams
Statue of Liberty, 100th Anniversary
The Titanic
U.S. Constitution 200th Anniversary

COLEMAN/WESTERN TEXAS BOWIE

Less than 1,000 knives were made, although original plans were for 15,000. Genuine slab cut stag handled bowie. Both sides of the blade feature gold and black Aurum etch scenes from Texas. Collector Value $200

COLEMAN/WESTERN COMMEMORATIVE

2,000 knives were made in 1985 to recognize the joining together of Coleman and Western. Based upon Western's model 701, the knife has a stag handle and a 5½″ fully etched stainless steel blade. A hardwood presentation case with glass top, as well as a leather sheath, came with each knife.

The first 250 knives were etched on both sides of the blade, one side featuring Sheldon Coleman and Harvey Platts and the other side depicting a camping scene and the new company slogan "Two Great Names, One Great Knife." The remaining 1,750 knives were etched one side with the camping scene and slogan. Collector Value (both sides etched) $275 (one side etched) $140

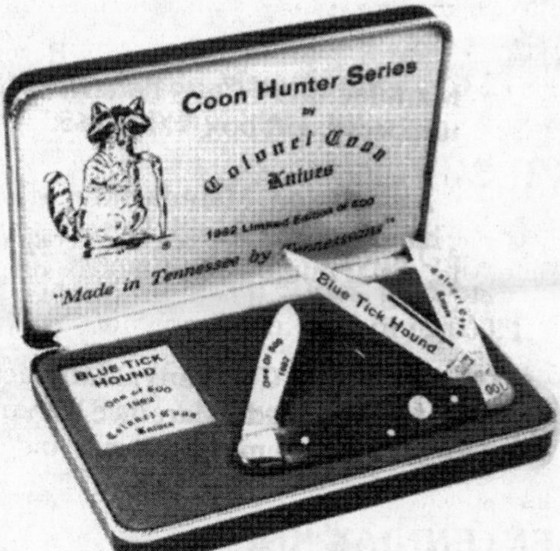

COLONEL COON BLUETICK HOUND

500 three-blade stock knives with blue jigged bone handles produced in 1983 by Tennessee Knife Works. Blade etched and serial numbered. Collector Value $135

COLONEL COON REDBONE HOUND

500 three-blade stock knives produced by Tennessee Knife Works in 1983. Red bone handles. Collector Value $120

COLONEL COON TENNESSEE RIVER PEARL

100 three-blade stock knives produced in 1983 by Tennessee Knife Works. Handled in unique pearl from Tennessee River mussels. All blades deep etched with gold filling. Hardshell display case. Collector Value $200

COURTHOUSE WHITTLER SERIES

600 two-knife sets made by Frank Buster Cutlery in 1977 for Parker-Frost Cutlery. The set consists of two three-blade whittlers with gold-etched blades. Handles are red and blue antique celluloid. Housed in simulated alligator box. Collector Value $165

COVERED BRIDGE

Made by Alcas in a limited edition for Mrs. Dewey Ferguson. Similar to the Case M1051L. Picture of a covered bridge is on the handle. It is tang stamped "Lavonna's Cutlery." Collector Value $60

THE GENERAL

1,200 3³/₈″ three-blade knives made by Bowen Knife Company. Honors the train "The General" that participated in the Civil War's great train chase. Collector Value $55

GERBER MK II SURVIVAL KNIFE

5,000 knives made by Gerber Legendary Blades to commemorate the twentieth anniversary of the Mark II knife. These are exact reproductions of the original model. Collector Value $175

KA-BAR BICENTENNIAL KNIFE

Two-blade dogshead trapper wtih red, white and blue celluloid handles. Issued in 1996 by Cole National (Ka-Bar) with Union Cut and Ka-Bar stampings on blades. Collector Value $80

KA-BAR D DAY COMMEMORATIVE FIGHTING KNIFE

To commemorate the fiftieth anniversary of the Normandy invasion, the company that produced the famed fighting knife used original World War II blueprints to reproduce this special issue. Gold-blade etching decorates the blackened blade. Leather washer handles are as used in the knives made fifty years before. Housed in a walnut display with gold lettering on the cover. Collector Value $75

KA-BAR PERSIAN GULF—DESERT STORM FIGHTING KNIFE

With its tang stamped "USMC," this Ka-Bar fighting knife salutes the Desert Storm conquest and victory of 1991. Gold-blade etching decorates the blackened blade and the walnut display housing the knife is imprinted with gold lettering as well. Collector Value $90

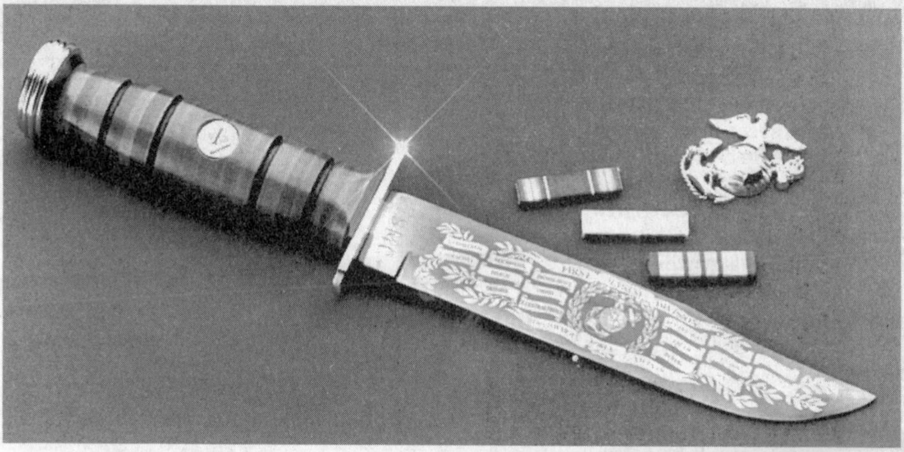

KA-BAR WORLD WAR II USMC FIGHTING KNIFE—KA-BAR FIRST MARINE DIVISION COMMEMORATIVE

To commemorate the fiftieth anniversary of World War II, Ka-Bar produced a reproduction of the famed U.S. Marine Corps fighting/utility knife. On the plexiglass cover of the walnut box that houses the knife is the U.S. Marine Corps emblem and appropriate commemorative wording. In gold lettering on the knife's black blade is an inscription and stamped into the tang is the "USMC" stamp as used on many of the originals. Collector Value $100

KISSING CRANE 150TH ANNIVERSARY KNIVES

Two knives were produced by Robert Klaas in 1984. Each is handled in red bone, inlaid with a special anniversary shield. Blade etched in two colors. Gift boxed with registration certificate. 1,000 three-blade 4″ whittlers. Collector Value $70. 1,200 one-blade 2⁷/₈″ barlow. Collector Value $40

R. KLAAS 155TH ANNIVERSARY

In 1989, Robert Klaas produced two lockback knives to commemorate the 155th anniversary of the company. One knife was handled in stag and the other in red bone. Blades of each knife are etched and tangs are stamped with the original "R. Klaas Prussia" stamping. Collector Value (stag) $75 (bone) $55

KISSING CRANE POWDERHORNS

Limited edition of 600 sets produced by Robert Klaas. Consists of two 5″ powderhorn pattern knives, one handled in stag and one in red bone. Each knife is serial numbered and boxed. Collector Value $110

KISSING CRANE REPRODUCTION SERIES

600 each of twelve knives were made by Robert Klaas. Each knife was a reproduction of some of the classic Kissing Crane patterns dating back for nearly a century. The following is a list of the knives and their values. The number preceding the description represents the year that the classic pattern was used.

(1891) Stag four-blade congress $65
(1892) Pearl four-blade congress $85
(1893) Pearl swell center whittler $70
(1894) Stag serpentine whittler $55
(1895) Stag sheepsfoot whittler $55
(1896) Pearl three-blade whittler $70
(1896) Stag four-blade congress $60
(1897) Stag four-blade congress $65
(1899) Stag whittler $60
(1900) Pearl senator whittler $65
(1901) Two-blade stag handled penknife $50
(1902) Stag gunstock $50

KLAAS GEORGE WASHINGTON VALLEY FORGE WHITTLER

1,200 serial numbered knives made by Robert Klaas—Kissing Crane for J. Nielsen-Meyer. A stag handled whittler in a pattern discontinued by Klaas prior to 1940. Blade etched. Collector Value $85

KNIFE COLLECTORS CLUB SERIES

The Knife Collectors Club was established by A. G. Russell in 1970 and issued its first knife in 1971. Since that time, a number of limited edition knives, made in varying quantities, have been offered to the membership. Earlier issues were offered in three grades: premier grade with exquisite blade engraving and 14K gold-engraved bolsters, excelsior grade with blade etching and engraved nickel silver bolsters, and collector grade with blade etching. All knives are serial numbered with the lowest numbers used for premier and excelsior grades. Descriptions and collector values shown are for collector-grade knives. Depending upon the knife model, values of higher-grade issues will range from five to twenty times that of the collector grade.

Shown above is CM-1 Premier Grade

CM-1—12,048 made by Schrade-Walden in 1971. Due to numbered blades rejection at the factory, some may be found with serial numbers up to 15,000. Known as the "Kentucky Rifle," the knife is a three-blade stockman pattern handled in ivory micarta with rifle shield inlay. Collector Value $100

CM-2—12,000 "Grandaddy Barlow" made by Camillus in 1973. One-blade 5½″ barlow pattern is handled with delrin. Special barlow knife shield inlay. Collector Value $75

CM-3—2,650 "Luger Pistol" made in 1974 by Puma-Werk honoring the seventy-fifth anniversary of the Luger pistol. One-blade knife handled in genuine stag with pistol on shield. Blade etched "Luger 1900–1974." 5,000 of the knives were made in three grades. Collector Value $95

CM-3—350 "Luger Cartridge." Same as above except with cartridge shield. Collector Value $150

CM-4—1,800 "Baby Barlow" made in 1975 by C. Bertram—Hen & Rooster. The 2 1/2″ barlow is handled in genuine ivory. Nickel silver bolsters and cartridge shield inlay. Collector Value $250

CM-5—1,200 ".44 Magnum Whittler" made in 1975 by C. Bertram—Hen & Rooster. Ebony handled 3 1/2″ whittler with cartridge shield. Nickel silver liners and bolsters. Collector Value $175

CM-6—2,400 "Straight Arrow" made in 1976 by C. Bertram—Hen & Rooster. 2 7/8″ Coffin-handle pattern with one saber ground blade. Handled in India stag. Collector Value $165

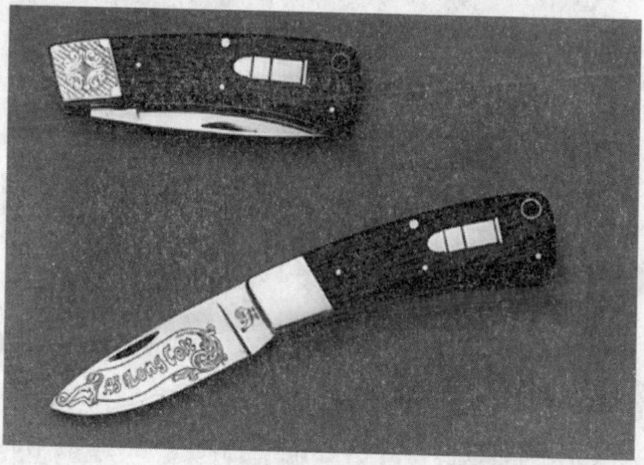

CM-7—2,800 "Long Colt" made in 1977 by C. Bertram—Hen & Rooster. 3 7/16″ vest pocket skinner with one blade. Cocobolo handles with cartridge shield. Collector Value $135

CM-8—2,200 ".219 Zipper" made in 1978 by C. Bertram—Hen & Rooster. 2 7/8″ barlow handled in ebony with .219 cartridge shield. Collector Value $150

CM-9—".300 Savage Canoe" made in 1979 by C. Bertram—Hen & Rooster. 3 1/4″ all stainless steel canoe pattern with nickel silver cartridge shield inlay. Collector Value $110

CM-10—3,600 "20th Century Barlow" made in 1984 and marked "Cattaraugus." Lockback barlow pattern handled in bone with cartridge shield. Collector Value $45

CM-11—3,000 "Pocket Barlow" made in 1986 and marked "Cattaraugus." 2 5/8″ lockback barlow pattern handled in bone with cartridge shield. Collector Value $40

CM-12—"Split Bolster Jack" single-blade liner-lock knife marked "Cattaraugus." Bone handles with nickel silver cartridge shield. Collector Value $40

KNIFE WORLD 1ST EDITION

2,000 made in 1982 by Cripple Creek Cutlery for Knife World Publications and issued to commemorate its fifth anniversary. Designed from a mid-1920s era Union Cutlery (KA-

BAR) pattern, the knife became known as a dogleg trapper. Master clip blade is etched "Knife World First Edition" and "1 of 2000." Serial numbers are stamped on the secondary spey blade. Bone handles inset with special shield. 1982 issue price was $45. Very low serial numbered knives are valued up to $300. Collector Value $140

KNIFE WORLD 2ND EDITION

500 limited edition knives made in 1987 by Cripple Creek Cutlery for Knife World Publications' tenth anniversary. The knife is a large two-blade equal end "cigar" jack handled in bone. The master clip blade is saber ground and frosted etched. Issue price was $65. Very low serial numbers currently valued up to $250. Collector Value $175

KNIFE WORLD 3RD EDITION

500 limited edition knives made in 1992 by Frank Buster Cutlery Co.—Fight'n Rooster for Knife World Publications' fifteenth anniversary commemorative. A single-blade powderhorn or Texas toothpick pattern, the knife is handled in genuine buffalo horn and has a gold gilded blade. Blade etching indicates the occasion and is serially numbered. Issue price was $65. Collector Value $85

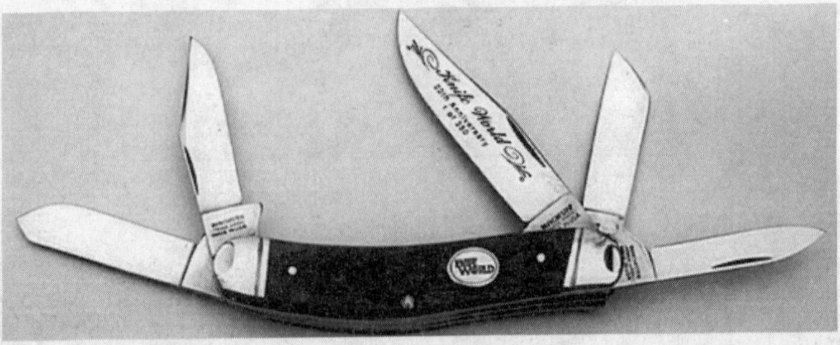

KNIFE WORLD 4TH EDITION

350 limited edition knives Winchester made in 1997 by Blue Grass Cutlery Co. for Knife World Publications' twentieth anniversary commemorative. A five-blade "sowbelly" stockman pattern, the knife is handled in honey bone and has special commemorative blade etching and serial number. Secondary blade has special Knife World stamping—first time ever used. Issue price was $95. Collector Value $125

1ST KNIFE WORLD AMBASSADOR KNIFE

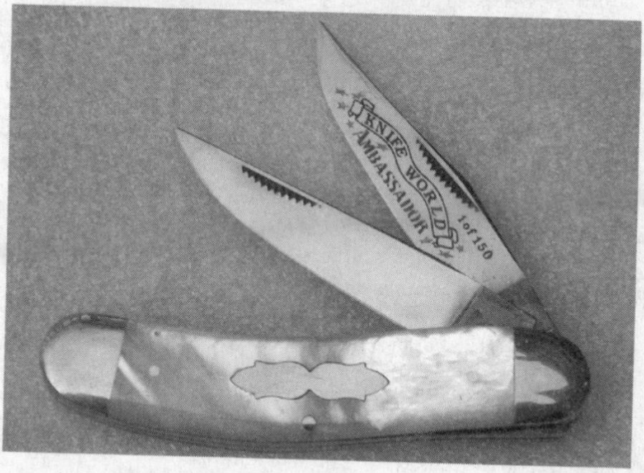

150 limited issue knives made in 1989 by Frank Buster Cutlery Co.—Fight'n Rooster for Knife World Publications. Sold only to lifetime subscribers ("Ambassador Club" members), issue price was $85. The knife is a two-blade sowbelly pattern with copperhead-type blades. The master blade is three-color etched and serial numbered. Handle is mother-of-pearl with inset shield. Collector Value $225

2ND KNIFE WORLD AMBASSADOR KNIFE

150 limited issue knives made in 1992 and 1993 by Bob Cargill and stamped "Cripple Creek." Made as they were ordered by lifetime subscribers ("Ambassador Club" members), each knife was accompanied by its special certificate of authenticity personalized for the ambassador for whom it was made. Issue price for the stag handled, three-blade, three backspring whittler was $120. Collector Value $160

MAC TOOLS KNIFE

Mac Tools, Inc., has contracted the production of several limited edition knives. The first, with 12,000 produced in 1979, was a three-blade stock knife with antique brass cast handles commemorating the fortieth anniversary of the company. Collector Value $40

In 1979, 3,600 serial numbered canoe-pattern knives were made by George Wostenholm I*XL. Handles are white bone handles. Collector Value $70

NKCA CLUB KNIVES

Beginning in 1975, the National Knife Collectors Association (NKCA) contracted for the manufacture of an annual club knife that would be available to its members. The rather remarkable value appreciation of that first knife was a motivating influence for newcomers to the knife collecting hobby. All subsequently issued NKCA club knives have appreciated in value, some dramatically and others only slightly. Each knife has been serial numbered, master blades have been etched, and the club's special shield has been inlaid into the handles. In 1989 and 1990, members were offered both a pocketknife and a sheath knife alternative. The following is a list of the knives issued since 1975.

1975—"Kissing Crane" three-blade whittler made by Robert Klaas in a limited number of 1,200 knives. Stag handles. Original cost was $12. Collector Value $650

1976—Case three-blade whittler made in a limited number of 3,000 knives. White composition handle. Original cost was $15. Collector Value $250

1977—"Kissing Crane" three-blade canoe made by Robert Klaas in a limited number of 5,000 knives. Stag handles. Original cost was $17.50. Collector Value $125

1978—Three-blade canoe made by Rodgers-Wostenholm division of Schrade in a limited number of 6,000 knives. Green bone handles. Original cost was $18.25. Collector Value $100

1979—One-blade trapper made by Case in a limited number of 12,000 knives. Stag handles. Original cost was $22. Collector Value $75

1980—"Kissing Crane" gunstock whittler made by Robert Klaas in a limited number of 12,000 knives. Stag handles. Original cost was $21.75. Collector Value $70

1981—Two-blade equal end "cigar" pattern made by Queen in a limited number of 12,000 knives. Stag handle. Original cost was $24.50. Collector Value $70

1982—Two-blade trapper made by Schrade in a limited number of 10,000 knives. Stag handles. Original cost was $24.50. Collector Value $70

1983—One-blade lockback folding hunter made by Case in a limited number of 7,000 knives. Green bone handles. Original cost was $45. Collector Value $140

1984—One-blade lockback "Hen & Rooster" made by Bertram, USA in a limited number of 7,000 knives. Bone handles. Original cost was $38. Collector Value $75

1985—Two-blade dogleg trapper made by Case in a limited number of 7,000 knives. Green bone handles. Original cost was $40. Collector Value $75

1986—One-blade lockback-type made by Gerber in a limited number of 6,200 knives. Bone handles. Shield is on bolster. Original cost was $39. Collector Value $120

1987—Three-blade cattleman's knife made by Case in a limited number of 7,000 knives. Green bone handles. Original cost was $43.95. Collector Value $80

1988—Two-blade bullet pattern made by Camillus in a limited number of 6,500 knives. Jigged bone handles. Original cost was $41.95. Collector Value $150

1989—Beginning with this year, the club began selecting two knives, a folder and a fixed blade, for member purchases. Either or both could be purchased by club members, with no limit to the number purchased.

Folder—Two-blade modified sunfish pattern made by Case in a limited number of 6,500. Green bone handles. Original cost was $50. Collector Value $70

Fixed blade—Wood handled skinning knife made by Buck in a limited number of 1,700 knives. Original cost was $80. Collector Value $85

1990—Folder—Three-blade stockman made by Robert Klaas in a limited number of 5,000. Stag handle. All blades etched. Original cost was $60. Collector Value $90

Fixed blade—Stag handled bowie made by Hen & Rooster in a limited number of 1,500. Original cost was $80. Collector Value $90

1991—Folder—4″, one-blade trapper made W. R. Case & Sons in a limited number of 4,000. Brown jigged bone handle. Master blade etched. Original cost was $69. Collector Value $70

Fixed blade—Stag handled bowie made by Hen & Rooster in a limited number of 1,500. Original cost was $80. Collector Value $90

1992—Folder—4″, two-blade trapper made for Sarco by Queen Cutlery in a limited number of 3,500. Brown jigged bone handle. Both blades etched. Original cost was $69. Collector Value $70

Fixed blade—Stag handled skinning knife made by Bear MGC in a limited number of 1,000. Original cost of $50 included leather sheath. Collector Value $55

1993—Folder—Bear MGC. 2,653 made. Original cost was $49. Collector Value $55

Fixed Blade—Bear MGC. 1,370 made. Original cost was $49. Collector Value $65

1994—Folder—$4^1/_2$″, two-blade trapper, model ROG6211½. 2,058 made by W. R. Case & Sons Cutlery. Handles are of jigged honey brown bone inset with NKCA shield as well as a Case shield. Master blade is etched and serial numbered. Original cost was $69. Collector Value $80

Fixed blade—$6^1/_2$″ drop-point hunter. 1,131 made by Bear MGC. Handle is genuine stag inset with NKCA shield. Each knife's blade is etched and serial numbered. Includes leather sheath. Original cost was $39. Collector Value $65

1995—Folder $5^1/_4$″, two-blade trapper handled in genuine stag. 1,850 made by W. R. Case & Sons Cutlery. Handles are inset with NKCA shield as well as a Case shield. Master blade is etched and serial numbered. Original cost was $65. Collector Value $65

1995—Folder $3^3/_4$″ "German Eye" brand muskrat pattern. 1,500 made by Carl Schliepper. Genuine stag handle inset with NKCA shield. Both blades have matchstriker pulls and are master blade etched and serial numbered. Original cost was $64. Collector Value $75

1996—Two folding knives, each a stag handled whittler pattern, were selected for this year. 1,550 German-made Eye Brand swell center balloon whittlers measuring $3^1/_2$″ closed and featuring full polish on their stainless steel blades. Collector Value $95

1996—1,675 Winchester $4^1/_2$″ cigar whittlers featuring full polish on spring and blades. Master blades of both knives are etched with the NKCS year-knife designation. Collector Value $90

1997—1,720 $4^1/_4$″ sunfish or elephant toenail by Smith & Wesson. With two shields (S & W and NKCA) inlayed onto the jigged brown bone handle. The two-blade knife has NKCA club knife etching on the master blade. Collector Value $90

1998—A large two-blade trapper by Camillus. 1,500 made. NKCA shield inlayed onto the jigged brown bone handle. The knife has NKCA club knife etching on the master blade. Collector Value $75

1999—A $4^5/_8$″ two-blade Saddlehorn with deep red bone handles inlaid with the NKCA shield. 1,535 made by W. R. Case & Sons Cutlery. Collector Value $75

2000—A doctor's knife made by Queen Cutlery. The dark brown smooth bone handles are inlaid with the NKCA shield. The two-blade knife (one blade plus spatula) has NKCA club knife etching on the master blade. Collector Value $100

2001—A Model 110 folding lockback, with walnut handle and brass bolsters, made especially for NKCA by Buck Knife Company. The blade is serially numbered and has a special NKCA cutout. Each knife included a brown leather sheath. Collector Value $90

2002—A four-blade congress pattern, with two sheepfoot and two coping blades and featuring the Schatt & Morgan brand. 1,200 knives were made by Queen Cutlery, featuring worm-grooved bone handles and the NKCA shield. Collector Value $90

2003—A Wharncliffe whittler made by Case. The "Chestnut Bone" handles are inlaid with the NKCA shield. The three-blade knife has NKCA club knife etching on the master blade and is serially numbered. Collector Value $75

NKCA 20TH ANNIVERSARY

To commemorate the organization's twentieth anniversary, a special custom-made knife was offered to the membership. A two-blade moose pattern, the knife was handled in pearl inset with two shields—one the NKCA shield, the other the maker's buffalo shield. Stainless steel blades have match striker pulls and are stamped "Cripple Creek USA." Nickel silver bolsters are engine-turned and the knife is polished throughout. Knife maker Bob Cargill made 475 pieces to fill orders placed by members. Issue price was $180. Collector Value $375

NASCAR KNIVES

Dale Earnhardt—Five-Time Winston Cup Champion Set

Limited edition of 1,000 walnut wall hanging displays consisting of a Case kodiak bowie and five Case trappers, handled in various materials. All knife blades are color etched with Dale Earnhardt's signature and commemorative notations of each of his Winston Cup wins. Also included in the display are three crafted marble inlays. Collector Value $750

Dale Earnhardt "#3" Signature Collection

Ten knives by Frost Cutlery housed in a large walnut wall hanging display case with a walnut signature centerpiece. 500 serialized sets made with each knife numbered, blades etched with Dale Earnhardt's signature and handles of black pakkawood. Collector Value $500

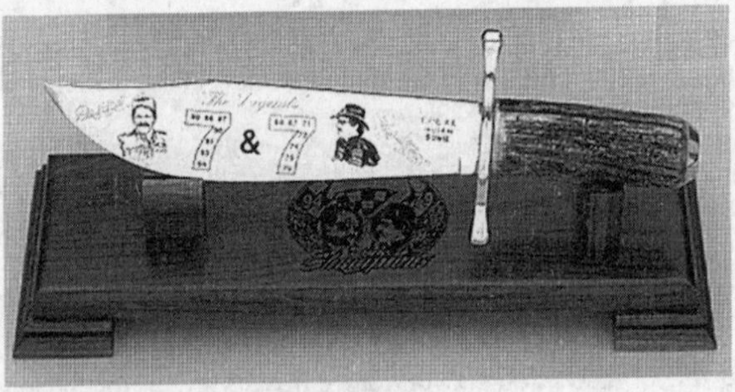

Dale Earnhardt "Seven-Time Champion Set"

A limited edition set (1,000 made) consisting of a Case #286 bowie and four serialized Case pocketknives. The different-pattern pocketknives are handled in red bone and each has full-color blade etching. The bowie has special color etching and a special "7 Time" shield. Housed in a large walnut wall hanging display case, with a full color Cloisonne medallion, a lithograph of a Sam Bass original painting, and a certificate of authenticity. Collector Value $750

Dale Earnhardt—Six-Time Winston Cup Champion Set

Frost Cutlery issued a limited edition of 750 special displays consisting of a stag handled Case kodiak hunter and six Case pocketknives of various patterns. The set is housed in a large walnut display case. Pocketknives are handled in second cut stag and all knife blades are color etched with Dale Earnhardt's signature and commemorative notations of each of his Winston Cup wins. Also included in the display are three crafted marble inlays. Collector Value $750

Dale Earnhardt "The Winston Winner"

A serially numbered (limit 1,000) Case 6254 trapper pattern knife with deep color etched blades. Housed in a walnut display case, with a marble inlay and certificate of authenticity. Collector Value $150

Davey Allison "1992 Hard Charger"

Limited edition of 2,000 Case imitation ivory handled two-blade trapper with deep etched stainless steel blades. In hard-shell display box. Collector Value $90

Glen "Fireball" Roberts

A Case 6254ROG trapper with Rogers bone handles and deep blade etching. Limited edition of 1,000 serialized knives housed in hard-shell display box. Collector Value $100

Handsome Harry Farewell Tour

Limited edition knife issued by Imperial-Schrade to commemorate Harry Gant's 1994 retirement from the NASCAR circuit. Produced in quantities of 2,500 and housed in a walnut presentation box, the knife is a 4″ stockman pattern handled in smooth green colored wood. Etched blades and a special shield decorate the knife, while the box contains a miniature #33 racing car and is covered by a license plate–style Gant and his racing car. Collector Value $65

Harry Gant Trapper

Limited edition of 5,000 pieces issued by Schrade and Smoky Mountain Knifeworks. The knife is housed in a walnut presentation box that is laser engraved with Gant's #33 Oldsmobile. The trapper is handled in green delrin and both blades are etched. Collector Value $45

The Intimidator Rolls a "7"

Large (14″ overall) stag handled Case bowie with three-color blade etching saluting Dale Earnhardt's 1994 seventh win of the Winston Cup Championship. Packaged in a walnut display case with a plexiglass cover and black velour interior. 1,000 knives made and serialized. Collector Value $450

Other "The Intimidator Rolls a 7" special knives include:

Frost 11½″ bowie limited to 5,000 pieces with imprinted wood display stand. Blade and handle are imprinted. Collector Value $100

Frost two-knife set limited to 2,500 sets with hard-shell display box. Blade and stainless steel handle of each knife etched. Matching serial numbers. Collector Value $90

Miscellaneous NASCAR Commemoratives

A series of commemorative knives based upon regular production knives made by Case and other manufacturers. Each of these knives are embellished with signature blade etching, custom display boxes or wall plaques and certificates of authenticity.

"Bobby Allison—1988 Daytona Winner"—1,000 produced. Case trapper. Collector Value $125

"Cale Yarborough—Tribute to a Legend"—2,000 produced. Hen & Rooster 4⅛″ with scrimshawed white smoothbone handles. Collector Value $100

"Cale Yarborough"—2,000 produced. 4⅛″ Case trapper with white pickbone handles. Collector Value $125

"Dale Earnhardt"—2,000 produced. Case 4⅛″ trapper with scrimshawed white smoothbone handles. Collector Value $130

"Dale Earnhardt"—2,000 produced. Case 5¼″ folding hunter with red pickbone handles. Collector Value $160

"Dale Earnhardt"—2,000 produced. Hen & Rooster 4⅛″ trapper with white smoothbone handles. Collector Value $100

"Dale Earnhardt—Five-Time Winston Cup Champion"—Case hunter produced in quantity of 1,500 with special engraved marble covering on walnut presentation box. Collector Value $190

"Dale Earnhardt—Six-Time Winner"—Two-knife set of Frost knives produced in quantity of 2,500 sets. Collector Value $110

"Dale Earnhardt—Winston Cup '86, '87"—2,000 Hen & Rooster knives produced. Collector Value $90

"Dale Earnhardt—#3 Signature Knives"—Frost Cutlery knives made in ten different patterns. Each knife's blade has Dale Earnhardt's signature and "3" etched on blade. Wood handles. Collector Value $45 for 5″ lockback, $25 for other patterns.

"Harry Gant—Handsome Harry"—1,000 Case trappers produced. Collector Value $100

"Harry Gant—Retirement"—Frost lockback with wood handles. Collector Value $45

"Junior Johnson—Last American Hero"—Case trapper produced in quantity of 2,000. Collector Value $125

"Lee Petty"—2,000 produced. Hen & Rooster $4\frac{1}{8}$″ trapper with full-color scrimshawed white smoothbone handles. Collector Value $100

"Lee Petty—Stock Car Legend"—500 produced. Case $5\frac{1}{4}$″ folding hunter with red pickbone handles. Collector Value $160

"Lee Petty—Stock Car Legend"—2,000 produced. Case trapper with scrimshaw on white smoothbone handles. Collector Value $120

"Petty/Earnhardt—7 Time"—Bowie by Frost saluting the seven wins of Petty and Earnhardt. Collector Value $120

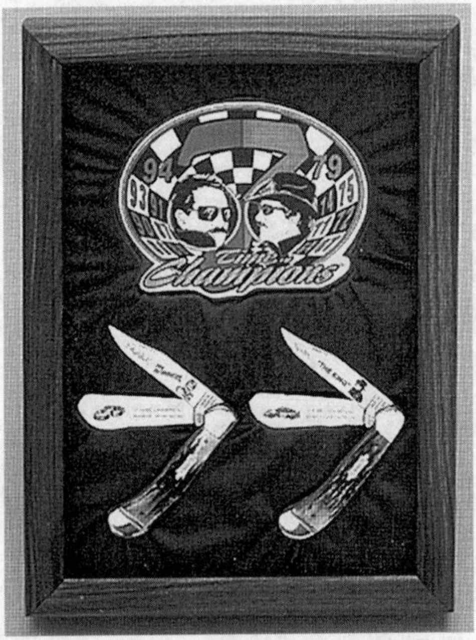

Petty/Earnhardt Bowie

Stag handled bowie with hand-painted, color-filled blade etching. Walnut display stand is laser etched. Limited issue of 1,000 pieces. Collector Value $400

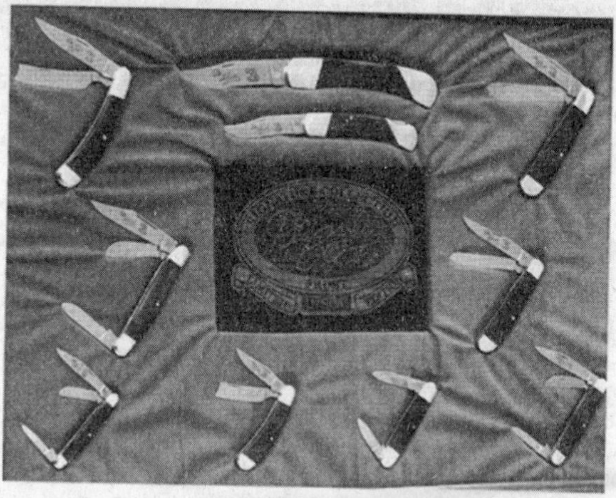

Petty/Earnhardt "Seven-Time Champions"

Limited issue of 1,000 sets, each consisting of two matching serial numbered Case 52100 trappers handled in stag and with deep color etched blades. Housed in a walnut display case, with special color printed logo and certificate of authenticity. Collector Value $350

The Petty Legend

A trio set of knives by Case that salutes the race-car driving Pettys of North Carolina. This 1990 issue is housed in a cherry presentation box and consists of large and small coke bottle patterns BWC61050SS, BW6125½ and BW6225½, each handled in burned bone. Collector Value $350

Rusty Wallace 1989 Winston Cup Champion

A 5⅜″ coke bottle pattern folder handled in brown jigged bone. The knife's single blade is color etched commemorating the driver's 1989 win, and the bolster is etched with serial number. Housed in laser-engraved walnut box. Value $175

Winston Motorsports 20th Anniversary Set

A twenty-one-knife collection housed in a special-made cherry wood display chest. Marketed by Little River Knives, the set features Case knives of several patterns. A variety of handle materials and colors are represented as well. Blades are etched with inscriptions saluting each year's Winston Cup winner and the display cover pictures and describes each year's winning car and driver. Value $2,000

ORIGINAL THIRTEEN COLONY SERIES

Set of fourteen knives issued beginning in March 1976, with a knife issued each month through the bicentennial. Thirteen of the knives were issued honoring the thirteen original colonies. These pewter, silver, brass and copper handled knives featured intricate artwork and a diamond-finished backspring. The fourteenth knife honored the United States and is a stag handled folding hunter with etched blade. Schrade Walden manufactured the 3,000 sets for Parker-Frost Cutlery. Collector Value $350

PARKER-FROST CUSTER'S LAST FIGHT

1,200 serially numbered knives made by Schrade for Parker-Frost Cutlery. This knife is a companion piece to the Trail of Tears and was issued at the same time. Some were sold in pairs with matching serial numbers. Deep blade etching commemorates Custer's last battle. Genuine stag handles. Collector Value $175

PARKER-FROST TENNESSEE WALKING HORSE AND KENTUCKY THOROUGHBRED

A two-knife set of stag handled lockback knives made by the Robert Klaas Co. (Kissing Crane) for Parker-Frost Cutlery. Three-color etching on the stainless steel blades designated them as the "Tennessee Walking Horse" or the "Kentucky Thoroughbred." 1,000 of each were made with matching serial numbers. Housed in satin-lined display case. A walnut plaque was available as an option. This is the last limited edition set to be marketed by Parker-Frost prior to the partnership dissolving in 1978. Collector Value $150

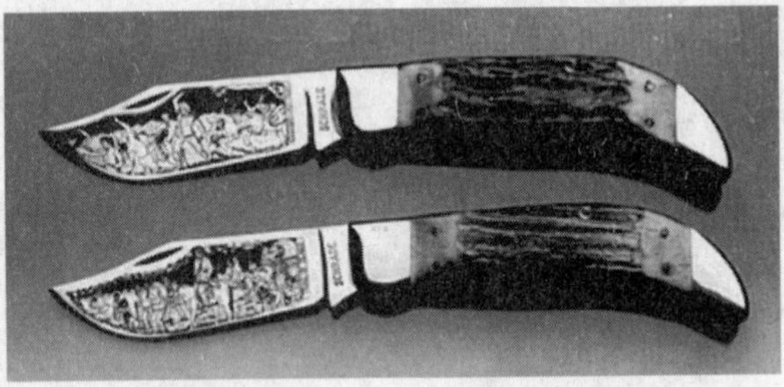

PARKER-FROST TRAIL OF TEARS SET

1,200 serially numbered sets made by Schrade for Parker-Frost, the blades are fully etched with an artistic representation of the Cherokee Indians' march on the Trail of Tears. Handles are thick genuine stag. Collector Value $225

PUMA 215TH ANNIVERSARY COMMEMORATIVE

Limited edition of 1,769 knives made in 1984 to commemorate the founding of PUMA-WERK in Solingen, Germany, in 1769. Ivory handle is hand engraved with a puma. Polished blade is etched in an attractive oak leaf design. Reverse side is gold-filled etched with serial number and "Puma Germany" and the dates "1769–1984." All etching is gold filled. Brass bolsters hand engraved. Rear bolsters engraved with the words "me fecit Solingen." Handle is European stag horn. Collector Value $350

PUMA—AFRICAN BIG FIVE COLLECTOR SET

In the early 1980s, Puma planned the production of 300 sets of five knives as a salute to Africa's big game animals. However, only 160 sets were made and sold. Each of the five lockback knives is a different model and decorative treatment differs. Each knife's blade, however, has "zebra striped" etching filled with gold on both sides and the wording "African Big Five." All handles are ivory micarta but individually scrimshawed by well-known artists—one side features the animal and the other side its name. Brass bolsters are elaborately hand engraved and the front bolster contains the Roman numeral V within an outline of Africa. Set is housed in wood presentation box. Collector Value $1500

PUMA CK-734 GRAF VON FRANKENBERG

Limited edition of 734 knives issued beginning in 1975 and continuing until 1979. Slightly less than half (330) were for U.S. distribution. This very high quality knife is handled in genuine ivory, hand engraved on the mark side with a wild boar and on the reverse side with a running red stag. Gold-filled bolsters are hand engraved with scroll work. Both sides of the blade are etched with an attractive gold-filled oak leaf design. The words "AD 734 Graf Von Frankenberg" are etched on the mark side and "Puma Germany"/serial number on the reverse side. Packaged in leather presentation box with parchment authentication insert. Collector Value $750

PUMA FOUR-STAR COLLECTOR SERIES

Four different Puma patterns: 16-156, 16-157, 16-158 and 16-159 in a unique offering for collectors. Each knife is hand carved and engraved on ivory micarta handles and brass bolsters by leading artists. Backspring and blade back feature hand-worked file designs. Knives are signed with artist's name and no two are alike. Certificate of authenticity with each knife. Collector Values (varies with knife pattern) $200–$600

RANDALL KNIVES 50TH ANNIVERSARY SPECIAL EDITION

300 knives produced in 1987 by Randall Knives to commemorate "Bo" Randall's fifty years in knife making. Crown stag handled Original cost was $375. Collector Value $2,600

REMINGTON SILVER BULLET

5,000 serial numbered knives produced in 1988 by Remington for Smoky Mountain Knifeworks. The R4466SB is a 3¾″ two-blade muskrat handled in bone with a sterling silver bullet shield inlay. Housed in display box. Collector Value $200

REMINGTON SILVER BULLET TRAPPER

5,000 serial numbered knives produced in 1989 by Remington for Smoky Mountain Knifeworks. A 4⅜″ pattern R1128SB, the knife is a two-blade trapper with bone handles and sterling silver bullet shield. With custom "bullet box." Collector Value $175

SCHRADE BEAR CULT

Folding hunter lockback knife with beaded suede leather sheath. Handled in scrimshaw decorated imitation ivory. Produced in 1985. Collector Value $85

SCHRADE BUFFALO BILL

A 4″ three-blade stockman knife packaged with a medallion in a satin-lined gift box. Collector Value $35

SCHRADE GRAND DAD'S OLD TIMER

A series of four different pattern knives produced by Schrade. Grand Dad's Old Timer No. 1 is a 4″, three-blade stock with a diamond-finish back spring. Collector Value $40

SCHRADE I*XL SERIES

Set consists of five knives honoring the combination of Schrade with I*XL. Consists of a stag handled canoe, a bone handled stockman, and three lockback knives handled in bone, stag and micarta. Housed in wood display. Collector Value $275 set

SCHRADE JIM BOWIE

18,000 serial numbered knives made by Schrade. 4″ stockman pattern handled in delrin with a bowie knife shield. Master blade tang is stamped "S. W. Cut. JBI, U.S.A." Serial number is stamped on the inside liner. Collector Value $40

SCHRADE KACHINA

10,000 knife and sheath sets produced by Schrade as a part of its American Indian Scrimshaw Series. Knife's scrimshaw honors the Hopi Indians and the Kachina. The Kachina sheath is genuine leather with a suede finish, covered with a hand-sewn layer of beads in the image of a Kachina doll. Collector Value $100

SCHRADE LIBERTY BELL, PAUL REVERE AND MINUTEMAN SERIES

24,000 each of three knives were made by Schrade in the early 1970s. Each is a 3⅝″ stockman pattern, Liberty Bell and Minuteman are handled in black composition and Paul Revere is in red composition. Serial numbers stamped on inside of liner. Collector Value $35

SCHRADE SILVER ANNIVERSARY OLD TIMER

5,000 produced in 1984. Knife is a bone handled pattern 34OT stockman. Bolsters and shield are sterling silver. Milled liners. Collector Value $55

SCHRADE SUNDANCE

Lockback folding hunter with scrimshaw decorated imitation ivory handle. Sheath is suede leather, hand beaded. Produced in 1986. Collector Value $85

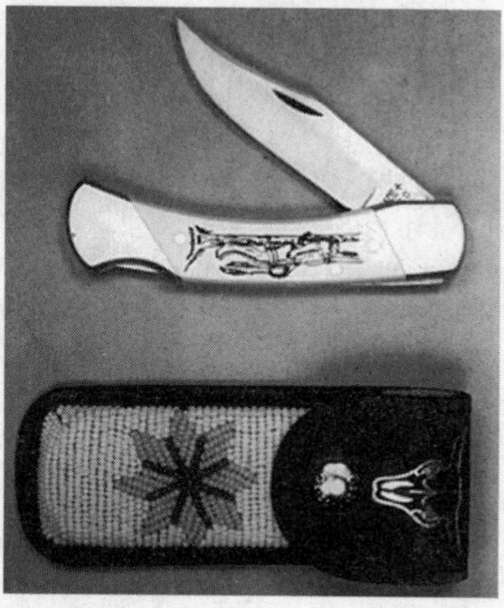

SCHRADE THUNDERBIRD

10,000 folding hunters made in 1981 as part of the scrimshaw series. Handled in imitation ivory decorated with an Indian scene. With a beaded sheath. Collector Value $100

SCHRADE VIETNAM MEMORIAL COMMEMORATIVE

Imperial-Schrade produced 2,000 serially numbered walnut handled lockback knives with "Vietnam Veterans Memorial" etched on the blade. Included in the oak display case are dog tags and a photograph of the memorial. Collector Value $50

SCHRADE-LOVELESS LIMITED EDITION HUNTER

Produced by Schrade to the specifications of its designer, Bob Loveless. Blade is of custom ground high-grade steel. Delrin handle with thumb groove. Collector Value $150

SEARS 100TH ANNIVERSARY KNIFE

A two-blade bullet pattern with bone stag handles inlaid with special Sears shield. Both blades etched. Housed in wood display box. Collector Value $135

75TH ANNIVERSARY OF AUTO AUTOMATION

Produced by Case for the Hastings Company commemorating the first auto assembly line. A pattern 41059L, the knife had never before been produced by Case. Tan composition handles engraved and filled in brown. Collector Value $40

SHAW-LEIBOWITZ BICENTENNIAL SERIES

A ten-knife set created in 1976 by the artist team of Sherrill Shaw and Leonard Leibowitz. Knives of several manufacturers were used as follows:

1. "The Boston Tea Party" etched on a Rigid knife
2. "The Ride of Paul Revere" etched on a Gerber knife
3. "The Shot Heard Round the World" etched on a No. P172 Case knife
4. "The Declaration of Independence" on a Westmark Western knife
5. "Washington Crossing the Delaware" etched on an Olsen Model 503 hunting knife
6. "John Paul Jones" etched on a No. 6250 Case sunfish knife
7. "Winter at Valley Forge" on a Gerber sheath knife
8. "Patrick Henry" on a Westmark knife
9. "The Victory at Yorktown" on a Case knife
10. "Washington's Triumphant Return to New York City" on a Rigid knife

Collector Value for the complete set $375–$1,000 (depending on serial number)

SHAW-LEIBOWITZ WILDLIFE SERIES

Shaw-Leibowitz produced a set of wildlife knives, beginning in 1974. 300 of each knife pattern was made. Numbers 1 to 15 were gold plated and retailed for $155; numbers 16 to 300 retailed for $105.

1. Grizzly on a Gerber lockback
2. Raccoon on a Schrade-Walden
3. Bobcat on a Case No. 62131
4. Moose on a Case No. 5275
5. Squirrel on a Case 6380
6. Deer on a Buck Esquire
7. Big horn sheep on a Case 6235½
8. Eagle on a Ka-Bar barlow
9. Elephant on a Case 6250
10. Buffalo on a Case P-172

Collector Value $800–$1,800 per set (depending on serial number)

SMITH & WESSON COLLECTORS SET

Limited edition of 1,000 sets released in 1975 by Smith & Wesson. Designed by Blackie Collins and made by Collins and his coworkers at Carolina Knife Co. Deep etched blades. All fixed blade knives with hardwood handles. Sterling silver guards and pommels. Hand-engraved estucheons inlaid into handles. Collector value $1,000

TENNESSEE HOMECOMING '86 CASE

Case trapper pattern with orange composition handle silk screened with outline of the state of Tennessee. "Tennessee Homecoming '86" etched on master blade. Collector Value $45

TENNESSEE HOMECOMING '86 CRIPPLE CREEK

100 knives produced in 1986. Trapper pattern with "Tennessee Homecoming '86" etched on master blade. Red, white and blue celluloid handles; the only Cripple Creek made with such handles. Collector Value $150

TENNESSEE HOMECOMING '86 UNITED BOKER

Trapper pattern made by United Boker. Red bone handles. Master blade etched "Tennessee Homecoming '86." Included in box is a commemorative .999 fine silver coin. Collector Value $50

TRIPLE CROWN SERIES

A special set of eleven knives made for Central Knife Exchange in 1980. Knives are built on the 1951 pattern Case with rosewood handles. A special etch was on each knife's blade and a knife was made for each winner of the Triple Crown, with the winner's name etched on the shield. Eleven sets were presented to the owners of the Triple Crown winning horses and a set was given to Churchill Downs racetrack. Collector Value $900

VIETNAM COMMEMORATIVE SECOND EDITION

1,000 produced by Case for Smoky Mountain Knifeworks. Trapper pattern with yellow composition handle and gun blued blades etched in gold. Collector Value $60

VIETNAM VETERANS SILVER EDITION

Commemorative knife and coin set with UNITED/Boker trapper and one-ounce silver coin honoring Vietnam veterans. Knife has smooth green bone handles and etched high-carbon steel blades. Gift boxed. Collector Value $45

WISS WHITTLER

24,000 three-blade whittlers made by Boker in 1973 to commemorate the 125th anniversary of Wiss Cutlery. Blade is etched "Wiss Commemorative 1848–1973." Serial number stamped on the master blade tang. White composition handles with special shield. Housed in plastic box. Collector Value $40

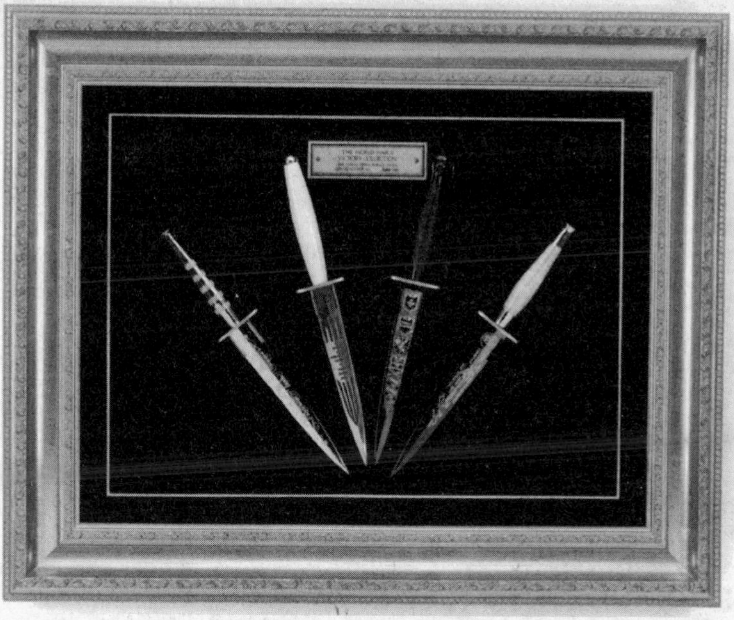

WORLD WAR II VICTORY COLLECTION

Two series of special commemorative fighting knives were produced for and marketed by the American Historical Foundation. Each knife in the two series was patterned after a variation of the famous Fairbairn-Sykes knife and is dedicated to a specific battle. The series are "War in Europe," with the knives made by Wilkinson Sword, and "War in the Pacific," with knives made by H. G. Long & Co. of Sheffield, England. Each series consists of six knives that were available either separately or, as most were sold, in matching serial numbered sets. Each of the knives is packaged in a velvet hard case with information about the battle it commemorates.

Collector Value (set of six knives) $900 (individual knives) $175

RESOURCES

The term "return on investment" is usually viewed from a dollar and cents point of view. While that factor certainly applies to collecting, a broader interpretation—one that costs very little money—deserves consideration. An investment of time and energy by getting more involved will surely pay dividends. One example is attendance at knife shows as discussed earlier in this book; other opportunities include knife club membership and knife swap meets. Further reading is a must, if one is to have the expertise that "gives an edge" to the astute collector. Today's knife collectors are exceptionally fortunate in the numbers of references available in print and on the Internet.

KNIFE COLLECTOR CLUBS

One of the more rewarding aspects of knife collecting is personal involvement with others who share the same or similar interest. It is likely that your own interest in knives as collectibles originated through association and friendship with another collector or would-be collector. Knife collecting clubs can and do provide excellent opportunities to further one's knowledge about knives, to enhance their own collection or to sell knives from a collection.

During the past quarter-century, there have been a large number of knife collecting clubs formed in most parts of the country. Many of these clubs, and especially the regional clubs, meet on a regular basis for fellowship, learning and the inevitable swapping—whether in the form of knives or information. Knife club meetings usually provide a forum and the facilities for a miniature knife show. Members bring knives for sale or trade, while others attend hoping to find that rare and illusive addition to their collection.

While active participating membership is always more desirable, membership and remote participation is not unusual. After all, there are thousands of collectors who may not be located close enough to attend a regular meeting but who wish to enjoy the privileges of club membership; there can be many. Most clubs publish a regular newsletter reporting items of interest to members. In addition, clubs usually have their own annual club knife that is available to members. The majority of club knives, especially those that have been carefully selected and are truly unique, have maintained a good reputation for value and collectibility within the knife world.

National or International Knife Collecting Clubs

Antique Bowie Knife Collectors Association: P.O. Box 674839, Marietta, GA 30006
Buck Collectors Club: 110 New Kent Rd., Goode, VA 24556
Camillus Collectors Club: 54 Main St., Camillus, NY 13031
Case Collectors Club: P.O. Box 4000, Bradford, PA 16701
Fight'n Rooster Cutlery Club: P.O. Box 936, Lebanon, TN 37087
Ka-Bar Collectors Club: P.O. Box 688, Olean, NY 14760
National Knife Collectors Association: P.O. Box 21070, Chattanooga, TN 37424
Queen Cutlery Collectors Inc.: P.O. Box 109, Titusville, PA 16354
Randall Knife Society of America: P.O. Box 539, Roseland, FL 32957
Robeson Collectors Club: P.O. Box 3483, Laurel, MD 20709

Knife Making Associations

American Bladesmith Society: P.O. Box 1481, Cypress, TX 77410
Knifemakers Guild: P.O. Box 5, Manti, UT 84642
Miniature Knifemakers' Society: Terry Wyeth, 1714 Park Place, Pocotella, ID 83204
Professional Knifemakers Association, Inc.: 319 N. 12th St., Salina, KS 67401

Regional Collecting Clubs

The addresses for regional clubs listed below are current as of the writing of this book. Since the officers of these nonprofit clubs periodically change, the contact address may also change. Should you be unsuccessful in contacting any club at the address listed below, current information may be received by contacting the regular knife publications listed elsewhere. *Knife World* publishes a listing of local clubs each month and response to your request for information may be received by writing *Knife World,* P.O. Box 3395, Knoxville, TN 37927.

Canada
Associated Blade Collectors
Bob Patrick
P.O. Box 18
Blaine, WA 98230

Arizona
Arizona Knife Collectors Association
7148 W Country Gables
Peoria, AZ 85381
E-Mail:
president@arizonaknifecollectors.com

Arkansas
Arkansas Knifemakers Association
Contact David Etchieson, Sec.
501-513-1019

California
Bay Area Knife Collectors Association
P.O. Box 135
Castro Valley, CA 94546
E-Mail: knfman@pacbell.net

California Knifemakers' Association
1261 Keats St.
Manhattan Beach, CA 90266

Southern California Blades
P.O. Box 1140
Lomita, CA 90717

Colorado
Rocky Mountain Blade Collectors
P.O. Box 324
Westminster, CO 80036

Florida
Florida Knife Collectors Association
P.O. 6405
Titusville, FL 32782

Fort Myers Knife Club
P.O. Box 706
St James City, FL 33956
E-Mail: rsmegal@earthlink.net

Gator Cutlery Club
Dan Piergallini, Sec.
813-967-1471

Gold Coast Knife Club
Alan Weinstein
954-747-1851
E-Mail: TLViking@aol.com

Georgia
Chattahoochee Cutlery Club
P.O. Box 568
Tucker, GA 30085

Ocmulgee Knife Collectors Club
263 Welker Circle
Macon, GA 31211

Three Rivers Knife Club
783 NE Jones Mill Road
Rome, GA 30165

Illinois
American Edge Collectors Association
24755 Hickory Ct.
Crete, IL 60417

Bunker Hill Knife Club
Dale Rice, Sec.
618-377-8050

Indiana
Indiana Knife Collectors
PO Box 101
Fountaintown, IN 46130

Iowa
Hawkeye Knife Collectors Club
515-266-0910
E-Mail: TCK0910@AOL.com

Kansas
Kansas Knife Collectors Association
PO Box 1125
Wichita, KS 67201

Kentucky
Central Kentucky Knife Club
P.O. Box 55049
Lexington, KY 40555

Kentucky Cutlery Association
6921 Woodrow Way
Louisville, KY 40228

Michigan
Wolverine Knife Collectors Club
P.O. Box 52
Belleville, MI 48112

Jackson Area Knife Collectors
P.O. Box 175
Hanover, MI 49241
Mid Michigan Knife Collectors
Contact: Greg Moe
517-642-5750

Missouri
Show Me Club
6 Linsdseu Dr.
Union, MO 63084
E-Mail: wipbrigg@msn.com

Gateway Area Knife Club
310 Andrews Tail
St. Peters, MO 63376
E-Mail: swirck@yahoo.com

Montana
Montana Knifemakers Association
P.O. Box 1374
Thompson Falls, MT 59873

New England Area
N. E. Cutlery Collectors Association
P.O. Box 624
Mansfield, MA 02048

North Carolina
Bechtler Mint Knife Club
P.O. Box 149
Rutherfordton, NC 28139

Tar Heel Cutlery Club
3682 Bowens Road
Tobaccoville, NC 27030

Ohio
Western Reserve Cutlery Association
P.O. Box 355
Dover, OH 44622

Johnny Appleseed Knife Collectors
2215 Haywood Dr.
Mansfield, OH 44903

Fort City Knife Club
8325 Star Rt. 128
Cleves, OH 45002

National Pike Knife Club
34841 Main St.
Barnesville, OH 43713

Oregon
Oregon Knife Collectors Association
P.O. Box 2091
Eugene, OR 97402

Pennsylvania
Allegheny Mountain Knife Collectors Association
P.O. Box 23
Hunker, PA 15639

Eastern Pennsylvania Knife Collectors Association
Phone: 610-965-9248

Keystone Blade Association
P.O. Box 92
Riverside, PA 17868

Mason-Dixon Knive Club
P.O. Box 66
Toms Brook, VA 22660

South Carolina
Palmetto Cutlery Club
P.O. Box 1356
Greer, SC 29652

Soddy Daisey Knife Collectors
P.O. Box 1224
Soddy Daisey, TN 37379
E-Mail: sdkca@wooden-box.com

Williamson County Knife Club
P.O. Box 681061
Franklin, TN 37068

Texas
Gulf Coast Knife Club
P.O. Box 265
Pasadena, TX 77501

Texas Knifemakers and Collectors Association
10649 Haddington, Ste. 180
Houston, TX 77043

Central Texas Knife Collectors Association
309 Highland Oaks Dr.
Harker Heights, TX 76548

Permian Basin Knife Club
4309 Roosevelt
Midland, TX 79703
E-Mail: wtnolley@clearsource.net

Virginia
Northern Virginia Knife Club
P.O. Box 501
Falls Church, VA 22046

Shenandoah Valley Knife Collectors
P.O. Box 843
Harrisonburg, VA 22801

Old Dominion Knife Collectors Association
224 Lakeridge Circle
Troutville, VA 24175.

Washington
North West Knife Collectors
1911 SW Campus Dr., Ste. 271
Federal Way, WA 98023
E-Mail: dhanham@earthlink.net

Wisconsin
Badger Knife Club
P.O. Box 511
Elm Grove, WI 53122
E-Mail: badgerknifeclub@aol.com

RECOMMENDED READING

Knife collecting has not only come of age with the increasing number of collectors involved, it has also matured a great deal within the past several years. The catalyst that perhaps deserves most credit for that increasing maturity has been the amount of reference materials available to the serious collector. Whereas only a dozen or so years ago the knife collector had few places to turn for education, there are today literally dozens of books available on most any subject within the world of knives.

Surely there is no lesson remembered quite so well as that learned in the "school of hard knocks," but there is no lesson so cheaply purchased as that learned from others. In spite of a rather limited market, there have been authors and publishers who were willing to share their knowledge through writing and publishing, although the pay was decidedly meager. Any collector who is at all serious about knives cannot afford to pass up the opportunities for learning offered in books and magazines.

Most books about knives and related materials are rather limited in numbers printed. Some achieve reasonably good success and are reprinted; others, although quite valuable as reference sources, are not available once the original printing is sold out. A number of the books listed below are out of print, but they may still be found from dealers or other collectors. Today's high-speed and readily available information search via the Internet will often find the source for whatever book you seek. In addition to an extensive listing of in-print books about knives, *Knife World* (P.O. Box 3395, Knoxville, TN 37927) actively buys and sells used books on knife subjects.

If you find an out-of-print book from one of these sources, buying it is highly recommended. If, once you've read it, you decide that the book is not one for your own bookshelf, there are surely other collectors who will be pleased to buy it from you.

Books

100 Legendary Knives, Pacella, Krause Publications, 2002
101 Patented Knife Designs; Portfolios #1 & #2, Will Hanna, published by the author, 1992
ABCA Price Guide to Antique Knives, Bruce Voyles, American Blade, 1990
Accouterments 1750–1850, Johnston, Golden Age Arms Co., 1993
Accouterments 1750–1850 II, Johnston, Golden Age Arms Co., 1995

Advertising Cutlery with Values, White, Shiffler, 1999
Advertising with a Sharp Edge, Ed Brady, published by the author, 1970
Allied Military Fighting Knives, Robert A. Buerlein, American Historical Foundation, 1984
Antler and Iron, Mountain Man Folding Knives, Chapman, published by the author, 1988
Antique American and European Arms & Militaria, auction catalog, Butterfields, August 1995
Antique Bowie Knife Book, The, Adams/Voyles/Moss, Museum Pub. Co., 1990
Antique Bowie Knife Collections of Berryman/Schreiner, The, auction catalog, Butterfields, March 1992
Antique Firearms, Swords, & Bowie Knives, Tannenbaum estate auction catalog, Butterfields, February 1993
American Bayonet, The, Hardin, Riling and Lentz, 1964, 3rd printing, 1987
American Handmade Knives of Today, B. R. Hughes, Pioneer Press, Union City TN, 1972
American Knives, Harold L. Peterson, Charles Scribner's Sons, New York, 1958
American Made Pocketknives, Union Cutlery Co., catalog reproduced by Cole National, Cleveland OH, 1972
American Pocketknives; History of Schatt & Morgan, Queen Cutlery, David A. Krauss, Krauss Pub., 2002
American Premium Guide to Pocketknives and Razors, 1st–5th eds., Jim Sargent, Books Americana, 1986–1999
American Primitive Knives: 1770–1870, Gordon B. Minnis, Museum Restoration Service, 1983
American Sword, The, Peterson, Petersen Publishing, 1954
American Swords and Sword Makers, Bezdek, Paladin Press, 1994
Battle Blades, Greg Walker, Paladin Press, 1993
Bayonets, From Janzen's Notebook, Janzen, Cedar Ridge Publications, 1987, 4th ed. 1995
Bayonets, Knives, & Scabbards, edited by Trzaska, published by Trzaska, 1998
Best of Knife World, Vol. 1, various, Knife World Books, 1979
Best of Knife World, Vol. 2, various, Knife World Books, 1982
Best of Knife World, Vol. 3, various, Knife World Books, 1993
Best of U.S. Military Knives, Bayonets, and Machetes, The, M. H. Cole, CJA Publications, Piqua OH, 2002
Big Book of Pocket Knives, Roy Ritchie and Ron Stewart, Collector Books, 2000
Book of Knives, The, Yvan A. de Riaz, Crown Publishers, Inc., 1981
Bowie Knife, Thorp, University New Mexico Press, 1948, reprint 1991
Bowie Knives, Robert Abels, published by the author, 1960
Bowie Knives (from the coll. of Robt. Abels & Ohio Historical Society), Keener, Ohio Historical Society, 1962, reprint 1988
Bowie Knives, Origin & Development, Eakin, Les Comm. des Avoyelles, 1979
Bowie Knives of the Ben Palmer Collection, Jim Phillips, William F. Moran and Ben Palmer, Phillips Publications, 1992
Bowie Knives of the Ben Palmer Collection, 2nd ed., Phillips, Moran and Palmer, Phillips Publications, 2001
Bowie Type Knives of American Interest, Robert Abels, published by the author, 1950s
British & Commonwealth Military Knives, Flook, Howell Press, 1999
Case Brothers Hand Forged Cutlery—1904, catalog reprint, Bob Cargill, 1977
Case Classics, Best in the Long Haul, Parker/Penley, James F. Parker, 1995
Case Factory Collection, The, knives from Case and Giles collections, Smoky Mountain Knifeworks, 1990
Case Factory Endorsed Pocket Price Guide, Sargent/Schleyer, Knife Nook, 1982
Case Factory Endorsed Pocket Price Guide, Sargent/Schleyer, Knife Nook, 1985
Case Knife Story, The, Allan Swayne, Knife World Books, 1987
Case Pocket Knives, Allan Swayne, published by the author, 1975
Case: The First 100 Years, James Giles, Smoky Mountain Knifeworks, 1989
Cattaraugus Cutlery Company, catalog reprint and values, Ritchie and Stewart, Collector Books, 1999
Cattaraugus Cutlery Co., reproduction by Dewey P. Ferguson, 1971
Chronology of Paul Knives 1975–1977, A, Paul Poehlmann, published by Melton Ferris, 1978
Civil War Knives, Newman, Paladin Press, 1998
Classic Bowie Knives, Robert Abels, Ft. Lauderdale FL, 1967

Classic Collectibles, Smoky Mountain Knifeworks, March 1989
Collection of U.S. Military Knives 1861–1968, A , M. H. Cole, published by the author, 1968
Collection of U.S. Military Knives 1861–1968, A, Book Two, M. H. Cole, published by the author, 1973
Collectors Illustrated Guide to Pocketknives, Schroeder, Collector Books, 1977
Collins Machetes and Bowies 1845–1965, D. E. Henry, Krause, 1995
Combat Fighting Knives, J. E. Smith Jr., EPJ&H Enterprises, 1987
Complete Book of Pocketknife Repair, The, Ben Kelley Jr., American Blade Book Service, 1983, revised 1987
Complete Gil Hibben Knife Throwing Guide, The, Hibben, United Cutlery Corp., 1994
Confederate Edged Weapons, Albaugh III, Harper & Bros., 1960, reprint 1993
Cooper Knives, Martin and Basch, Pioneer Publishing, 1991
Counterfeiting Antique Cutlery, Witcher, National Brokerage and Sales, 1997
Country Knives, Chapman, Oak and Iron Publishing, 1996
Custom Knife, The, Bates/Schippers, published by authors, 1973
Custom Knife II, The: The Book of Pocket Knives and Folding Hunters, Bates/Schippers, published by the authors, 1974
Custom Knifemaking: 10 Projects from a Master Craftsman, Tim McCreight, Stackpole Books, 1985
Damascus Steel: Myth, History, Technology, Applications, Sachse, Verlag Stahleisen, 1994
E. C. Simmons & Winchester, American Reprints, St. Louis MO, 1971
Edged Weapons: A Collector's Guide, Stephens, Spur Books, 1976
Edged Weapons of the American Revolution, 1775–1783, Neumann, American Defense Prep. Assn, 1975
Encyclopedia of Knives, An, Strung, J. P. Lippencott Co., 1976
Encyclopedia of Old Pocket Knives, Vols. 1–2, Roy Ehrhardt, Heart of America Press, 1974
Explanation or Key to the Various Manufactories of Sheffield, Smith, 1816, reprint 1975
Fight'n Rooster Knives, Yesterday-Today-Tomorrow, James F. Parker, published by the author, 1994
First Commando Knives, The, Yeaton/Applegate, published by Phillips Publications, 1996
For Knife Lovers Only, Harry K. McEvoy, Knife World Books, 1979
Fur Trade Cutlery Sketchbook, James A. Hanson, The Fur Press, Crawford NE, 1994
George Schrade: His Accomplishments to the Knife Industry, George M. Schrade, George Schrade Knife Co., 1982
Goins' Encyclopedia of Cutlery Markings, John E. Goins, Knife World Books, Knoxville TN, 1986
Goins' Encyclopedia of Cutlery Markings, 2nd ed., John and Charlotte Goins, published by the authors, 1998
Guide to Handmade Knives, A: Official Directory of Knifemakers Guild, Tappan, James Press, 1977
Guide to Pocket Knife Collecting, Sadler/Mayes, published by the authors, 1968
Gun Digest Book of Folding Knives, The, Hughes/Lewis, DBI Books, 1977
Gun Digest Book of Knives, The, B. R. Hughes and Jack Lewis, Digest Books Inc., 1973
Gun Digest Book of Knives, The, 2nd–5th eds., Jack Lewis and Roger Combs, DBI, Inc., 1982–1997
Hand Forged Knife, The; Karl Schroen, Knife World Books, 1984
Handbook for Pocket Knife Collectors, The, Hanby, D. H. Publications, 1971
Hear the Hammer: The Story of Montana's Ruana Knives, Mandell/Towsley, published by the authors, 1995
Hibberd Spencer Bartlett & Co., Chicago, 1933, catalog reprint, Ron Arteman, 1977
History & Collecting Case Pocket Knives, Ferguson, published by the author, 1969
History of Cutlery in the Connecticut Valley, A, Martha Van Hoesen Taber, Department of History, Smith College, Northampton MA, 1955
History of the John Russell Cutlery Co., Robert L. Merriam et. al., Bete Press, Greenfield MA, 1976
History of Knives, A, Harold Peterson, Scribner's, 1966
How Knives Are Made, Collins, Custom Knifemakers Supply, 1975, reprint 1982
How to Make Folding Knives, Frank Centofante, Ron Lake and Wayne Clay, Blade Books, 1988

How to Make Knives, Richard Barney and Robert Loveless, American Blade Book Service, 1982
How to Make Multiblade Folding Knives, Shadley and Davis, Krause Publications, 1997
IBCA Price Guide to Antique Knives, J. Bruce Voyles, Krause Publications, 1995
IBCA Price Guide to Commemorative Knives 1960–1990, J. Bruce Voyles, Krause Publications, 1995
Identification Guide to Remington Sheath Knives 1925–1940, D. Y. Grimm, published by the author, 1990
International Fight'n Rooster Knife Collector, 1977–1981, Buster, Frank Buster Cutlery Co, 1982
International Fight'n Rooster Knife Collector, 1977–1983, Buster, Frank Buster Cutlery Co, 1984
Introduction to Switchblade Knives, An, Ben and Lowell Meyers, American Eagle Publishing, Chicago IL, 1982
*I*XL Catalog—1885*, catalog reprinted by Atlanta Cutlery Corporation, Decatur GA, 1975
*I*XL Means I Excel*, William R. Williamson, published by the author, 1974
IXL Catalog—George Wostenholm & Sons, Sheffield, England 1885, Beinfeld Publishing, 1975
James Bowie and the Sandbar Fight, James L. Batson, Batson Engineering, Madison AL, 1992
John Nelson Cooper: Cooper Knives, William A. Martin and Paul Charles Basch, Pioneer Publishing Co., 1990
Joseph Rodgers & Sons: Exhibition Knives, Domenech, Samuel Setian, 1999
Joseph Rodgers & Sons, Cutlers, an antique catalog reprinted by Adrian Van Dyk, Marietta OH, 1974
Keen Kutter, 1930, American Reprints, 1971
Kentova Pocket Knife Guidebook, Spurlock, published by the author, 1968
Kentucky Knife Traders Manual, Roy Ritchie and Ron Stewart, published by the authors, 1980
Knife Album, The, Robert Mayes, published by the author, 1975
Knife Collection of Albert Blevins, The, Bernard Levine, Allon Schoener Associates, 1988
Knife Collection of Dr. Jack R. Holifield, The, auction catalog, Sotheby's, April 1978
Knife Collectors Handbook, The, Frazier/Ferguson, Revis C. Ferguson, 1966
Knife Digest, 1st ed., William L. Cassidy, Knife Digest Publishing Co., 1974
Knife Digest, 2nd ed., William L. Cassidy, Knife Digest Publishing Co., 1976
Knife Guide, The, Bernard Levine, Knife World Books, 1981
Knife in Homespun America, The, Madison Grant, Published by the author, 1984
Knife and Its History, The, Victorinox in celebration of its 100th anniversary, 1984
Knife Repair & Restoration, Adrian A. Harris, Tennessee Knifeworks, 1981
Knifecraft, Sid Latham, Stackpole Books, 1979
Knifemakers: An Official Directory of the Knifemakers Guild, Voyles, American Blade, 1984
Knifemakers Guild Directory of the Membership, The, Loveless, Guild Publishers, 1974
Knifemakers of Old San Francisco, Bernard R. Levine, Badger Books, San Francisco CA, 1977
Knifemakers Who Went West, The, Harvey Platts, Longs Peak Press, 1978
Knives 1981–2000, annual editions, Warner, DBI Books, 1981–1999
Knives 2001–2003, annual editions, Kertzman, Krause Publications, 2000–2002
Knives Can Talk: Story of the Robeson Cutlery Co., Tom Kalcevic, published by the author, 2000
Knives of Finland, The, Lester C. Ristinen, Suomi Shop, Wolfe Lake MN, 1991
Knives and Knifemakers, Latham, Winchester Press, 1973
Knives and the Law, James R. Nielsen, Knife World Books, 1980
Knives of Smith & Wesson, The, Rinke, published by the author, 1990
Knives of the U.S. Military in Vietnam, M. W. Silvey, published by the author, 1997
Knives of the U.S. Special Forces, Clinton, published by the author, c.1980s
Knives of the U.S. WWII, Silvey, published by the author, 1999
Knives: Points of Interest, Jim Weyer, Weyer International, 1984
Knives: Points of Interest II , Jim Weyer, Weyer International, 1987
Knives: Points of Interest III, Jim Weyer, Weyer International, 1990
Knives: Points of Interest IV by Jim Weyer, text by Shelley Berman, 1993

Levine's Guide to Knives and Their Values, Bernard Levine, DBI Books, 1986
Levine's Guide to Knives and Their Values, 2nd ed., Bernard Levine, DBI Books, Inc., 1989
Levine's Guide to Knives and Their Values, 3rd ed., Bernard Levine, DBI Books, Inc., 1993
Levine's Guide to Knives and Their Values, 4th ed., Bernard Levine, DBI Books, Inc., 1997
Levine's Guide to Knives and Their Values, 5th ed., edited by Bud Lang, Krause Publications, 2000
Light But Efficient, Albert N. Hardin Jr. and Robert W. Hedden, published by the authors, 1973
Living on the Edge: Logos of the Loveless Legend, Al Williams, Weyer International, Toledo OH, 1992
Marbles: Company History, Schmeling, published by the author, 1995
Marbles: Patents, Schmeling, published by the author, 1995
Marbles: Products, Schmeling, published by the author, 1994
Marbles Knives and Axes, Konrad F. Schreier Jr., Beinfield Publishing, 1978
Military Knife and Bayonet, The, Homer Brett, World Photo Press, 2001
Military Knives: A Reference Book, various, Knife World Books, 2001
Modern Handmade Knives, B. R. Hughes, Pioneer Press, Union City TN 1982
Moran: Fire & Steel, Wayne V. Holter, published by the author, 1982
Moran 50 Yrs. Anniversary Knives, Beaucant, 1997
Napanoch: White Man's Knife with a Red Man's Name, Rhett C. Stidham, Belpre OH, 1975
New England Cutlery, Philip R. Pankiewicz, Hollytree Publications, Gilman CT 1986
Official Guide to Collector Knives, The, 1st–8th eds., Parker/Voyles, House of Collectibles, 1976–1986
Official Guide to Collector Knives, The, 9th ed., James F. Parker, House of Collectibles, 1987
Official Guide to Collector Knives, The, 10th–13th eds., C. Houston Price, House of Collectibles, 1991–2000
Official Scout Blades, Holbrook, published by the author, 1999
Old Knife Book, The, Tracy Tudor, published by the author, 1978
On Damascus Steel, Leo S. Figiel, M.D., Atlantis Arts Press, Atlantis FL, 1991
Peacemakers, The: Arms and Adventure in the American West, Wilson, Random House, 1992
Penknives and Other Folding Knives, Moore, Shire Publications, 1988
Petersen's Complete Book of Knives, Hollis, Petersen Publishing, 1988
Pictorial Price Guide: Romance of Collecting Case Knives, 1st–4th eds., Dewey Ferguson, published by the author, 1972, 1974, 1976, 1978
Pictorial Price Guide to Romance of Collecting Catt., Robeson, Russell, and Queen, Ferguson, published by the author, 1978
Pocket Cutlery, U.S. Tariff Commission, 1939
Pocket Knife Traders Price Guide, Vols. 1–3, James F. Parker, published by the author, 1992, 1994, 1997
Pocket Knives of the U.S. Military, M. W. Silvey, published by the author, 2000
Pocket Price Guide: W. R. Case & Sons Cutlery, by Sargent/Schleyer, Knife Nook, 1981
Pocketknife Manual, The, Blackie Collins, Benchmark Division, Jenkins Metal, 1977
Pocketknives: A Collectors Guide, Bernard Levine, Quintet Pub. Ltd., 1993
Pocketknives: Markings, Manufacturers and Dealers, John E. Goins, published by the author, 1979
Pocketknives: Markings of Manufacturers and Dealers, 2nd ed., John E. Goins, Knife World Books, 1982
Practical Book of Knives, The, Ken Warner, Stoeger Sportsman's Library, 1976
*Price Guide to 2000 Winchester and Marbles Collectable*s, Larry and Roy Ehrhardt, Heart of America Press, 1973
Randall Made Knives, Robert L. Gaddis, Paladin Press, Boulder CO, 1993
Randall Saga, The, Beaucant, published by Blade Books, 1989
Randall Saga, The, Beaucant, published by the author, 1992
Razor Anthology, The, various, Knife World Books, 1995
Register of Trademarks of the Cutlers' Company of Sheffield, Whitham/Sykes, 1953
Remington Bullet Knives, Mel Brewster, Armory Publications, 1985
Remington Bullet Knives, 2nd ed., Brewster, Collector Knives Press, 1991

Remington Cutlery catalogs nos. 1, C4, C5, C30, reprints, various
Rodgers, Joseph and Sons, Cutlers, unknown, reprinted by Adrian Van Dyk, 1974
Romance of Collecting Case Knives, Dewey P. Ferguson, published by the author, 1972, 1974, 1976, 1978
Romance of Collecting Cattaraugas, Russell, Robeson & Queen, Mrs. Dewey P. Ferguson, Parker Cutlery, 1978
Romance of Knife Collecting, 1st–4th eds., Dewey Ferguson, published by the author, 1969, 1970, 1972, 1974
Russell Green River Cutlery 1884, Dewey Ferguson, published by the author, 1972
Scagel: The Man and His Knives, Harry McEvoy, Knife World Books, Knoxville TN, 1985
Schrade Pocketknives, Knife Collector's Publishing House, Fayetteville AR, 1971
Sharpening Made Easy, Steve Bottorff, Knife World Books, Knoxville TN, 2002
Sheffield Bowie and Pocket-knife Makers 1825–1925, Richard Washer, T. A. Vinall, 1974
Sheffield Exhibition Knives, Claussen, Watts and McMikle, Old World Publishing Corp. Ltd, 1999
Sheffield Knife Book, The: A History and Collectors' Guide, Tweedale, Hallamshire Press, 1996
Silver Folding Fruit Knives, W. C. Karsten, Knife World Books, 1986
Skinning Knife, The, M. H. Cole, published by the author, 1996
Spencers Guide to Australian Custom Knifemakers, Spencer, published by the author, c.1980s
Spencers Guide to Australasian Custom Knifemakers, Spencer, published by the author, 1990s
Standard Knife Collector's Guide, *The,* Ron Stewart and Roy Ritchie, Collector Books, Paducah KY, 1986
Standard Knife Collector's Guide, The, 2nd ed., by Roy Ritchie and Ron Stewart, Collector Books, 1993
Standard Knife Collectors Guide, The, 3rd ed., Ritchie/Stewart, Collector Books, 1997
Standard Knife Collectors Guide, The, 4th ed., Ritchie/Stewart, Collector Books, 2002
Steel Canvas: The Art of American Arms, Wilson, Random House, 1995
Step-by-Step Knifemaking, Boye, Rodale Press, 1977
Story of Buck Knives, The: A Family Business, Ables, Buck Knives, Inc., 1991
Story of Knives, The, Janes, G. P. Putnams Sons, 1967
Sunday Knives, John Roberts, published by the author, 1979
Sure Defence, A: The Bowie Knife Book, Kenneth J. Burton, W. R. Bright & Sons Pty. Ltd., Fairfield, N.S.W. Australia, 1988
Survival Knives and Survival, J. E. Smith Jr., EPJ Enterprises, Statesboro GA, 1984
Survival Knives and Survival, 2nd ed., J. E. Smith Jr., EPJ & H Enterprises, Inc., Statesboro GA, 1985
Swiss Army Knife Handbook, Kane, published by the author, 1988
Swords & Blades of the American Revolution, Neumann, Stackpole Books, 1973
Theater Made Military Knives of WW II, Bill and Debbie Wright, Shiffer, 2002
Union Cut. Co.: American Made Pocketknives—c.1912–23, reprinted by Cole National, 1977
United States Military Knives Collector's Guide, Michael W. Silvey and Gary D. Boyd, published by the authors, 1989
United States Military Knives 1941–1991, M. W. Silvey, published by the author, 1992
United States Military Knives Price Guide, M. W. Silvey, Gary Boyd and Houston Price, Knife World Books, 1993
United States Military Knives Price Guide, 2nd ed., Silvey, Boyd and Price, Knife World Books, 1994
U.S. M-3 Trench Knife of World War Two, The, Coniglio/Laden, published by the authors, 1996
U.S. Military Knives, Bayonets, and Machetes Book III, M. H. Cole, published by the author, 1979
U.S. Military Knives, Bayonets, and Machetes, Book IV, M. H. Cole, Birmingham AL, 1990
U.S. Military Knives & Bayonets Price Guide, Silvey, Boyd and Trzaska, Knife World Books, 1997
U.S. Military Knives & Bayonets Price Guide, 4th ed., Silvey, Boyd and Trzaska, Knife World Books, 2000
Will Hanna's Portfolio of Patents #1, Legend of the Knife 1878 to 1958, Hanna, published by the author, 1992

Will Hanna's Portfolio of Patents #2, Legend of the Knife 1862 to 1991, Hanna, published by the author, 1992
Winchester Product Catalog, C. H. Key Publishing, 1923, reprinted 1988
Working Folding Knife, The, Dick, Stoger Publishing, 1998

Magazines and Periodicals

The Blade Magazine
700 E. State St.
Iola, WI 54945
Phone: 715-445-2214

Knife World
P.O. Box 3395
Knoxville, TN 37927
Phone: 865-397-1955
Web site: www.knifeworld.com
E-Mail: knifepub@knifeworld.com

Knives Illustrated
2145 W. La Palma Ave.
Anaheim, CA 92801
Phone: 714-635-9040

Tactical Knives
1115 Broadway
New York, NY 10010
Phone: 212-807-7100

INDEX

ABOUT THE AUTHOR

Since 1979, C. Houston Price has been the publisher of *Knife World*, a monthly publication featuring articles of interest to cutlery collectors. He is a lifetime member and former director of the National Knife Collectors Association, and an honorary member of the Knifemakers' Guild, American Bladesmith Society, as well as numerous regional collecting clubs. Mr. Price has been the recipient of many awards in recognition of his contributions to the knife collecting hobby. In 1994, he joined other cutlery notables such as Bo Randall, Jim Bowie and "Uncle Henry" Baer as an inductee into the International Cutlery Hall of Fame and in 1997 he was inducted into the American Bladesmith Society's Hall of Fame.